GEORGIA I. HESSE, for 19 years Travel Editor of the *San Francisco Examiner and Chronicle,* is the author of guidebooks on France and Paris and has contributed articles on travel to almost every major North American magazine and newspaper. She was a Fulbright scholar at the University of Strasbourg, and in 1982 she was awarded the *Ordre National du Mérite* by the French government. She is the editorial consultant for this guidebook.

STEPHEN BREWER has edited several guidebooks in this series. He retreats to the south of France regularly, frequently on assignment for magazines and newspapers.

CHARLA CARTER is a freelance fashion editor and journalist in Paris. She has contributed articles on fashion and cultural affairs to American, British, and Australian *Vogue,* to *Elle,* and to *Vanity Fair, European Travel & Life,* and *Paris Passion.*

FRED HALLIDAY divides his time between Paris and Connecticut. He is a frequent contributor to *The New York Times* and to *Condé Nast Traveler, Travel & Leisure, Food & Wine,* and *Connoisseur* magazines.

EDWARD HERNSTADT is a freelance writer who lived in Paris for four years. He has contributed to publications in the United States, France, and Australia.

AMY HOLLOWELL is an editor at the *International Herald Tribune* in Paris, where she has lived since 1982. She also writes about French cultural and current affairs.

SALLY LEFEVRE, a native New Yorker, has lived in Turkey and England as well as Canada, where she produced a national radio program on tourism. She has now lived in France for more than 12 years and contributes to several U.S. and European publications and guidebooks.

STEPHEN O'SHEA is a writer and journalist who lived in Paris for many years. He currently lives in New York City.

JENNIFER QUALE, who contributes to many major publications, has written about France for *Food & Wine, The New York Times,* and *European Travel & Life*.

MIMI TOMPKINS, a journalist who has been based in Paris for the last seven years, writes about European culture, business, and politics for public radio networks, *U.S. News & World Report,* Toronto's *Globe & Mail,* and other publications.

JONATHAN WEBER is a business writer at the *Los Angeles Times*. He spent three years working as a reporter and editor in Paris and Geneva.

THE PENGUIN TRAVEL GUIDES

THE PENGUIN GUIDE TO FRANCE 1991

ALAN TUCKER

General Editor

PENGUIN BOOKS

PENGUIN BOOKS

Published by the Penguin Group
Viking Penguin, a division of Penguin Books USA Inc.,
375 Hudson Street, New York, New York 10014, U.S.A.
Penguin Books Ltd, 27 Wrights Lane,
London W8 5TZ, England
Penguin Books Australia Ltd, Ringwood,
Victoria, Australia
Penguin Books Canada Ltd, 2801 John Street,
Markham, Ontario, Canada L3R 1B4
Penguin Books (N.Z.) Ltd, 182-190 Wairau Road,
Auckland 10, New Zealand

Penguin Books Ltd, Registered Offices:
Harmondsworth, Middlesex, England

First published in Penguin Books 1989
First revised edition published 1990
This second revised edition published 1991

1　3　5　7　9　10　8　6　4　2

Copyright © Viking Penguin,
a division of Penguin Books USA Inc., 1989, 1990, 1991
All rights reserved

ISBN 0 14 019.929 2
ISSN 0897-683X

Printed in the United States of America

Set in ITC Garamond Light
Designed by Beth Tondreau Design
Maps by Vantage Art, Inc.
Illustrations by Bill Russell
Editorial Services by Carol Offen and Cindy Rosenthal
Edited by Lisa Leventer

THIS GUIDEBOOK

The Penguin Travel Guides are designed for people who are experienced travellers in search of exceptional information that will help them sharpen and deepen their enjoyment of the trips they take.

Where, for example, are the interesting, isolated, fun, charming, or romantic places within your budget to stay? The hotels described by our writers (each of whom is an experienced travel writer who either lives in or regularly tours the city or region of France he or she covers) are some of the special places, in all price ranges except for the lowest—not the run-of-the-mill, heavily marketed places on every travel agent's CRT display and in advertised airline and travel-agency packages. We indicate the approximate price level of each accommodation in our descriptions of it (no indication means it is moderate), and at the end of every chapter we supply contact information so that you can get precise, up-to-the-minute rates and make reservations.

The Penguin Guide to France 1991 highlights the more rewarding parts of the country so that you can quickly and efficiently home in on a good itinerary.

Of course, the guides do far more than just help you choose a hotel and plan your trip. *The Penguin Guide to France 1991* is designed for use *in* France. Our Penguin France writers tell you what you really need to know, what you can't find out so easily on your own. They identify and describe the truly out-of-the-ordinary restaurants, shops, activities, and sights, and tell you the best way to "do" your destination.

Our writers are highly selective. They bring out the significance of the places they cover, capturing the personality and the underlying cultural and historical resonances of a city or region—making clear its special appeal. For exhaustive detailed coverage of cultural attractions, we suggest that you also use a supplementary reference-type guidebook, such as a Blue Guide or a Michelin Green Guide, along with the Penguin Guide.

The Penguin Guide to France 1991 is full of reliable and timely information that is revised each year. We would like to know if you think we've left out some very special place.

ALAN TUCKER
General Editor
Penguin Travel Guides

375 Hudson Street
New York, New York 10014
or
27 Wrights Lane
London W8 5TZ

CONTENTS

MAPS

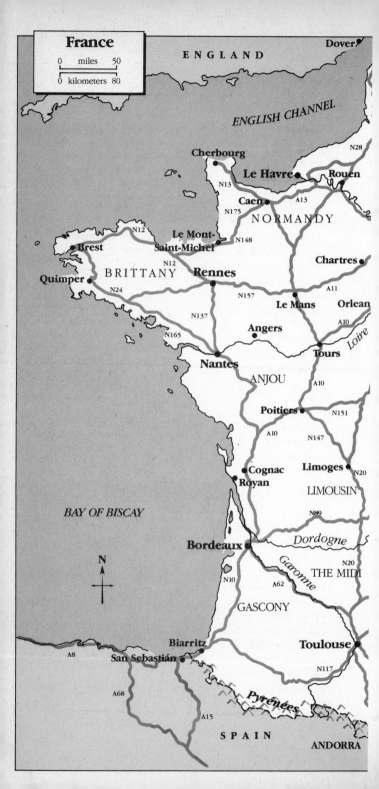

OVERVIEW

By Georgia I. Hesse

Georgia I. Hesse, for 19 years the Travel Editor of the San Francisco Sunday Examiner & Chronicle, *now contributes articles on travel and related subjects to many magazines and newspapers, including* Diversion, Endless Vacation, Travel & Leisure, *the* Chicago Tribune, *the* Los Angeles Times, *and the* San Francisco Examiner. *She is the author of a number of guidebooks, including one on France, and was a Fulbright scholar at the University of Strasbourg.*

"**A**sk the travelled inhabitant of any nation, In what country on earth would you rather live?—Certainly in my own, where are all my friends, my relations, and the earliest and sweetest affections and recollections of my life. Which would be your second choice? France."
—Thomas Jefferson, *Autobiography,* 1821

There are as many reasons to visit France as France has cheeses (265, according to Charles de Gaulle), among them:

- to live *la vie en rose* in Paris, or
- to potter through little villages lost in the snooze of yesteryear, or
- to appreciate art in all its various forms, including the art of living, or
- to transport yourself with haute cuisine (*mousseline de brochet, ragout de homard et morilles à la crème de Sauternes*) or with everyday cooking (*choucroute garnie*), or
- to sit in a shady square in Senlis, north of Paris, and think that "modern" France began there a thousand years ago.

To look at the map of France is to look at the head of a dog, a boxer, perhaps: The scruff of the neck is the Pas-de-Calais on the Belgian border, the head joins the body of Europe along the Alps and the Black Forest. The two ears are lower Normandy and Brittany, and the muzzle bites down on Andorra and Spain. It's a very square and handsome head, with Tours as an eyeball.

Ancient as it is in essence, France brought all its parts together only as recently as 1860, when Savoy became the final region to join that whole of which Hugues Capet was crowned king in 987. Of the regions known by their traditional names, such as Alsace or Burgundy, there are today 22, while a Revolutionary "reform" in 1790 established 96 *départements*. (Enthusiasts of France and of trivia will enjoy knowing that the number of each *département* is used for the last two figures of car registration numbers and the first two of postal codes.)

Fortunately, travel patterns have changed since the famous days of "If it's Tuesday, it must be Belgium." It's no longer smart to take in the well-known high points of all France (much less all Europe) at one sitting. The informed wanderer now considers the country region by region as suited to his or her own inclinations, choosing to see what he or she can at a comfortable pace and planning to return another time.

But few travellers call upon France without stopping to pay their respects to **Paris**, which, in the last several years, has sprinted forward like a runner from the blocks, leading even Parisians to wonder where all the energy (not to mention the money) is coming from. Jane Kramer (the worthy successor to the *New Yorker*'s Genêt) pinpoints De Gaulle as the last long-distance runner, who, she says "planned to leave himself to the French, and in a sense he did." Presidents since, however (Georges Pompidou, Valéry Giscard d'Estaing, François Mitterrand), have appeared to share the view, as expressed by Mitterrand, that France cannot have a *grande politique* without a *grande architecture*.

In the race, Parisians, their visitors, and *la culture* are the clear winners. (Culture is to the French what football is to Americans; Kramer wrote a few years ago that "One of the first duties of the French press is to distract the French from a fatal suspicion that France and civilization may not be entirely synonymous as concepts.")

No one knows today's Paris who does not know the Musée National d'Art Moderne (sometimes dubbed Chez

Pompidou); the Forum des Halles (born in 1979 but still overlooked by many foreigners—not without reason, some might say); the Musée Picasso in the reborn Marais; la Géode (with the world's largest projection screen) at the Cité des Sciences et de l'Industrie (in Parc de la Villette); the controversial and astonishingly successful Musée d'Orsay; the violently debated pyramidal glass entrance to the Louvre by I. M. Pei; the Musée des Arts Décoratifs in the Louvre; the Grande Arche de la Défense, a.k.a. the Tête Défense (also known irreverently as Mitterrand's square bagel); or the high-tech tapestry that is the Institut du Monde Arabe (with its fine rooftop restaurant), right on the Seine.

The latest *chantier* (construction site) is in Bercy, up-river from Notre-Dame, where the new headquarters of the Finance Ministry, the largest government building in Europe, stands. The Opéra de la Bastille opened (finally!) in late March 1990.

Paris so dominates its immediate region, the **Ile-de-France**, that many of the Ile's riches go unexploited by travellers. After all, the Ile-de-France once *was* France; its lures are as many and as diverse as the autumn leaves in the valley of the Chevreuse: Versailles, Fontainebleau, Chartres, Giverny, et cetera.

But France is not just Paris.

France generally is conceived of as a garden carefully tended and trimmed throughout generations and centuries, a rich, fat land where good things grow, nature made to order. Indeed it is.

France is also rugged, untamed, wild, and as mean as a sudden *mistral.* The hexagonal garden is walled in by hills, *massifs,* and mountains on several sides: the Vosges and Jura ranges to the northeast; the Alps (at almost 16,000 feet, Mont Blanc is Europe's highest peak) and Alpes-Maritimes to the east; the Pyrénées to the south; and the Massif Armoricain—windblown Brittany—in the northwest. The spine of the Massif Central has helped keep the Auvergne—the high country between Périgord and the Rhône valley, generally south of the town of Clermont-Ferrand—among the least trammeled regions of the country.

Following Paris, **Provence** and the Côte d'Azur (the Riviera) lure more non-European visitors than any other part of France, though surely no North American or Australian would go to France for the beaches alone, having more than a sufficiency of better ones at home. No, it's the essence of the region as a whole—the sun falling on old cultures and old stones, the air scented with roses and orange blossoms and basil and thyme and garlic, the welcoming inns with shaded gardens, the hillside picnics of salade Niçoise and a chilled rosé (perhaps Tavel) and a regional cheese (Pélardon or Bleu des Causses?), the countrysides that look like Impressionist paintings—and vice versa.

The **Côte d'Azur** is where the fashionable action is and has been since the mid-19th century, when Cannes was discovered and made chic by Baron Henry Peter Brougham and the Brits who followed him there. (Provence proper, on the other hand, is where most of the action isn't, and where almost no one wants it.)

Burgundy and the **Rhône Valley** fit neatly into a Provence–Côte d'Azur itinerary, whether you travel by *autoroute,* by back roads that twist like intestines, or by train. Burgundy is as rich in attractions as the wines that bear its name; a distinctive cuisine for one, more Romanesque churches than you can shake a sculpture at, Gallo-Roman art and archaeology, tiny towns and pine forests, and two major cities, Dijon and Lyon.

Another complete trip could (and should) be confined to the northeast alone, to **Champagne** and **Lorraine and Alsace**, with side trips into Picardie and Franche-Comté. These are the lands of the fatted calf and the stuffed goose, of storybook villages and refreshingly rural pastures and lanes, of a cocktail of cultures ("Let them speak German," Napoléon said of the Alsatians, "as long as they think in French"), the whole seen through a (wine) glass, lightly.

Along the Loire river (". . . mirroring from sea to source a hundred cities and five hundred towers," wrote Oscar Wilde), travellers wander in an oval path from Paris to Brittany, to Normandy, and back again. When the sun is out, they will move in a lazy, erratic pattern, one hopes, rather like butterflys in search of sweets on every side.

The **Loire Valley**, with its Renaissance châteaux and its white wines, is serene and civilized, the very essence of the notion of France. Like Alsace, **Brittany** is a land of its own, fiercely independent, unbendingly individual, a land of fishermen, saints, and puzzling standing stones. **Normandy**, on the other hand, is a dream of green, of soft and creamy cheeses (Camembert!), a tapestry of good things growing, torn to the west by the beaches of World War II.

Culinary as well as cultural adventures begin in **Bordeaux** in southwest France, leading devotees into the valleys of the **Dordogne**, the Isère, and the Lot; down into the Guienne and Gascony; to modish resorts and Medieval villages; to caves sheltering prehistoric art; and finally to Basque towns climbing the foothills of the **Pyrénées**.

In some respects, southwest France (with names on the map such as Landes, Gers, Tarn, Languedoc–Roussillon) is the largest and most complex of the regions, with an inheritance of linguistic confusions, religious upheavals, and economic and agricultural dislocations. It is also one of the most rewarding.

The queen city of the central south, **Toulouse** is France's fourth largest and one of the oldest; some scholars say it was founded before Rome. Its climate, its several architecturally remarkable structures, its emphasis on the arts, and its university-inspired liveliness make it a rewarding destination, while it also serves as a convenient jumping-off point for such smart, smaller cities as Auch and Albi to the west and east and Castelnaudary and Carcassonne to the southeast, in the direction of Languedoc's Mediterranean coast.

South of Toulouse, major routes and little roads as provocative as afterthoughts run through country unfamiliar to most foreigners; here still walk the ghosts of prehistoric peoples, of insurgents and heretics, of pilgrims and hermits and troubadours.

Phoenician fleets and Roman galleys called in **Languedoc–Roussillon**, where the landscape rises in theatrical tiers along the Golfe du Lion, from the Spanish border, the Côte Vermeille, and Perpignan in the south, eastward through beaches, marinas, and Montpellier to Nîmes and its Roman ruins. Here, too, are excitements often overlooked: the roads that wiggle inland from Collioure to Céret or through the forests and villages of the Parc National des Cévennes to the natural wonder that is the Gorges du Tarn.

Savoy and **Dauphiné** in winter are empires of ice and snow, of toney resorts such as Chamonix and Megève and Val d'Isère. The Winter Olympics will be staged around Albertville in 1992. In summer, these places constitute the promised land of mountaineers and lovers of lakes (including Lac du Bourget, France's largest) and Alpine scenery. Pretty spa cities such as Aix-les-Bains and Evian attract those who arrive "to take the waters"; beautifully sited old Grenoble is an attention-getter in its own right. Cooking in the French Alps tends to be just that—cooking rather than cuisine. The specialties are hearty and filling; *gratin,* for instance, a family of crusty potato-cheese dishes. Wines are light, dry, refreshing as the mountain air.

Franche-Comté fills the space from Alsace-Lorraine to the Rhône–Alpes region with thick woods, quiet lakes, and high pastures that back up against the **Jura** mountains and Switzerland. The "big city" is Besançon, where Victor Hugo was born and the door opens to the natural beauty of the countryside.

Clearly, France—with 55.8 million inhabitants occupying a space smaller than Texas—is inexhaustible. So it is that, in one volume, we have not attempted to exhaust, not even to completely cover, France. We are not encyclopedic; we have made choices.

Some roads remain undriven in these pages: the corkscrew of D 906 from Alès north of Nîmes to Le Puy. Some city streets also remain to be ambled through: those of Périgueux and Limoges, of La Rochelle and Lille, for example.

We leave those trips for another time.

USEFUL FACTS

When to Go

France, like other major European destinations, swarms with tourists in June, July, and August. The best weather and fewer crowds make September and October the finest months for general sightseeing, followed by late April to mid-June (although early spring can be rainy). The Christmas–New Year's week bring throngs to the ski slopes; plan a ski vacation for mid-January to early May (depending on resort altitudes), but *not* during school holidays.

Entry Documents

Holders of valid United States and Canadian passports are no longer required to have French visas for tourism visits of three months or less. Visas *are* required for diplomats, government officials, journalists on specific missions, and long-term students. In addition, visas are required for citizens of Australia, New Zealand, and many other countries. Citizens of Japan, Switzerland, Sweden, Norway, and other countries, as well as members of the European Community, *are not* required to have French visas. Anyone with doubts should check with the nearest French consulate *well in advance* of a trip.

Arrival at Major Gateways by Air

From North America and elsewhere outside Europe, most travellers to France arrive at Paris's international airports, **Roissy-Charles-de-Gaulle** (25 km/15.5 miles north via A 1 or RN 2) and **Orly** (16 km/10 miles south via A 6 or RN 7). The third international airport, old Le Bourget, is served by business aviation.

Note: There are two *aérogares* at De Gaulle, Aérogare 1 and Aérogare 2, and Aérogare 2 has three terminal buildings, A, B, and D (C is still up in the air). Before arrival and, especially, before departure, it's wise to check where, precisely, your plane will land or take off. That's particularly important when you are picking up a rental car at the airport or when instructing the taxi driver in Paris where to deliver you.

Aéroport de Paris (ADP) is building a huge business center with office towers, exhibitions, and new deluxe hotels at De Gaulle.

There are also two terminals at Orly: Orly-Ouest and Orly-Sud; again, check in advance of arrivals and departures. A new arrival-departure hall at Orly-Ouest will be finished by next year, and the new electronically-automated transport system (the VAL) will connect the two Orly terminals with the RER (Régional Express Métro) to Paris and De Gaulle airport.

Incoming and/or outgoing passengers at either Charles-de-Gaulle (hereafter CDG) or Orly should know there are restaurants and cafés of all persuasions at the airports: five at CDG 1 (including a branch of Maxim's proper and Grill Maxim's); three at CDG 2A (including the gastronomic hangout Le Cassiopée); and three at CDG 2B. At Orly-Ouest, the six outlets include a Maxim's and Jardin d'Orly, while Orly-Sud offers Le Grillardin for upscale meals as well as three other spots.

Free shuttles transfer passengers between airports and on-site hotels such as (at CDG): Sofitel (deluxe), Novotel (first class), and Arcade (standard); and (at Orly): Hilton (deluxe), Altéa (first class), and Arcade (standard).

Currently, more than 44 airlines serve CDG. The airlines of the Air France group (Air France, UTA, and Air Inter, France's domestic airline) serve Paris from the U.S. cities of Anchorage, Boston, Chicago, Houston, Los Angeles, Miami, New York, Newark, San Francisco, San Juan, and Washington, D.C. In addition, there are flights from New York and Newark to Bordeaux, Lille, Lyon, Marseille, Montpellier, Mulhouse, Nantes, Nice, Strasbourg, and Toulouse.

Among other major carriers, American Airlines flies to Orly from Dallas, Chicago, and New York; Continental to Orly from Newark; Delta to Orly from Atlanta; Northwest to Orly from Detroit; Pan Am to CDG and to Nice from New York; TWA to CDG from Los Angeles, New York, St. Louis, and Washington, D.C.; United Airlines to CDG from San Francisco via Chicago; Air Canada to CDG from Toronto; British Airways to CDG from London; KLM to CDG from Amsterdam; Lufthansa to CDG and Orly from Frankfurt; SAS to CDG and Orly from various Scandinavian cities; and Swissair to CDG from Zurich, Atlanta, Boston, Chicago, Cincinnati (seasonal), Montreal, New York, Orlando (seasonal), and Toronto.

British Air specializes in flights to airports in Brittany and Normandy out of London-Gatwick, and Air Vendée, a carrier in western France, has expanded to include London on its flights from Rouen.

Paris has two major in-town airport bus terminals: **Invalides** at 2, rue Esnault-Pelterie, on the Left Bank near the Pont (Bridge) Alexandre III, and **Porte Maillot/Palais de Congrès**, northwest of the Arc de Triomphe at the end of avenue de la Grande Armée. Invalides occupies a fairly small former railroad station, whereas Maillot sits within a skyscraping complex that's a veritable town in itself, with shops, a cinema, cafés, a parking lot, a disco, Métro station, etc. In contrast to the other two, the **Etoile** "terminal" is a streetside stop near the Arc de Triomphe on avenue Carnot, not recommended on rainy days or for passengers with bulky luggage. Two giant hotels serve the Porte Maillot/Palais de Congrès complex: the 1,027-room Méridien and, just across the street, the 974-room Concorde Lafayette.

Airports are linked to the terminals with frequent departures of Air France buses. These coaches leave from the sidewalks in front of baggage pick-up areas at Orly and from Porte (Gate) 36 at CDG's Aérogare 1 and Porte A5, Terminal A, and Porte B6 at Terminal B, both Aérogare 2. Directional signs are well placed.

The trip from CDG to Maillot takes about 30 minutes, departs every 12 minutes from 5:45 A.M. to 11:00 P.M., and costs about 40 francs. From Orly-Ouest/Orly-Sud to Gare

Montparnasse/Invalides, departures take place every 12 minutes from 5:50 A.M. to 11:00 P.M. for the 35-minute trip, which costs about 30 francs. New bus service links CDG with the Gare Montparnasse in the 14th *arrondissement;* the nine daily round trips are timed to connect passengers with new high-speed TGV Atlantique trains serving Brittany. The fare is 60 francs. Transportation between the two airports departs every 20 minutes, takes 75 minutes, and costs about 65 francs. Such connections are free of charge for connecting flight passengers who pick up vouchers at the Connections Desk when deplaning their first flight.

For travellers with considerable luggage, Air France coaches are preferable to the RATP buses discussed below. Both downtown air terminals are more conveniently located for travellers staying around the Champs-Elysées or place de la Concorde areas than for those going to the heart of the Left Bank or Ile-de-la-Cité.

To make transfers easier, a firm in the United States, **Marketing Challenges International**, sells tickets for the Air France coaches *before* passengers' departure from the U.S. Prices for Le Bus passes are $9 one way, $18 round trip as of this writing. Also available through MCI are the Paris Visite pass for use on the Métro or bus (one day, $5; three days, $15; five days, $25); La Carte pass, which covers admission to more than 60 Paris museums and attractions and allows the holder to go to the head of the entry line (one day, $10; three days, $20; five days, $30); and vouchers for sightseeing tours of Paris by day or night through Paris Vision ($20 per tour).

Marketing Challenges International's address is 10 East 21st Street, New York, NY 10010; Tel: (212) 529-8484; Fax: (212)-460-8287.

RATP (city) buses connect CDG to the Gare de l'Est and Gare du Nord train stations, CDG to place Nation, and Orly-Ouest/Orly-Sud—also called **Orlybus**—to place Denfert-Rochereau. (All fares range from 30 to 35 francs.)

Roissy-Rail links CDG by train to the Gare du Nord and such stops as Châtelet, Luxembourg, Port Royal, Denfert-Rochereau, and Cité Universitaire, leaving every 15 minutes from 5:30 A.M. to 11:30 P.M. (27 francs). **Orly-Rail** runs between Orly-Ouest/Orly-Sud and Gare d'Austerlitz with intermediate stops, leaving every 15 minutes from 5:30 A.M. to 8:45 P.M.; after that every 30 minutes until 10:45 P.M. (22 francs). Both rail systems are integrated with city-wide

Métro services. (De Gaulle airport is linked to the Gare du Nord via RER line B over the French Railways lines.)

Taxi fares between the airports and central Paris range from about 200 to 300 francs as of this writing, depending upon the airport (De Gaulle is slightly farther out), destination within the city, traffic conditions at the time, luggage surcharges, et cetera. A 10 percent tip is standard. Your hotel concierge will estimate the charge rather accurately.

Last year the duty-free boutiques at CDG's Aérogare 1 were upgraded to offer luxury goods at an average 31 percent below Paris prices; there's even an antiques shop at Aérogare 1.

Arrival by Train

Paris maintains six railroad stations, served by trains from some 6,000 communities in France as well as from all European countries. They are Gare d'Austerlitz (in the southeast of town), Gare de l'Est (east), Gare de Lyon (also southeast), Gare Montparnasse (west), Gare du Nord (north), and Gare St-Lazare (northwest). Passengers entering the country will have their passports and visas checked on the train before border crossings.

Major cities and regions served from the stations are as follows: from **Austerlitz**: Tours, Bordeaux, Toulouse, Madrid; from **Est**: Reims, Strasbourg, Frankfurt, Zurich; from **Lyon**: Dijon, Provence, Nice, Barcelona; from **Montparnasse**: Brittany, La Rochelle; from **Nord**: Lille, Brussels, Amsterdam, Hamburg, and also for boat-trains to Boulogne, Calais, Dunkirk; from **St-Lazare**: Normandy, boat-trains to Le Havre, Cherbourg.

Arrival by Sea from Britain

The construction of the railway Eurotunnel under the English Channel has been debated since the turn of the century. The problem-plagued project (the so-called Chunnel) now is underway and should be completed by 1993. When finished, as many as 15 million passengers annually will zoom through it at 186 miles per hour.

Several companies maintain ferry, hydrofoil, and Hovercraft services across the English Channel (*La Manche* in French). Crossings may be booked on the spot in Britain, but during the summer season it's wise to reserve well in advance. Travel agents in the U.S. and Canada can do that for you. Not all routes operate year-round.

Operators include Sealink (Tel: 0233-64-70-47, Ashford, Kent, and—through BritRail offices—212-575-2667 in New

York, 213-624-8787 in Los Angeles, 214-748-0860 in Dallas, 416-929-3334 in Toronto, 604-683-6896 in Vancouver); P & O European Ferries (Tel: 0304-20-33-88, Dover, and 516-747-8880 or 800-221-3254, International Cruise Center, Mineola, NY); Sally Line (Tel: 0843-59-55-22, Ramsgate, Kent, and 071-409-0536, London); Hoverspeed British Ferries (Tel: 0304-24-01-01, Dover, and 081-554-7061, London, or BritRail offices in the U.S., see above).

Other major lines are Brittany Ferries (Tel: 0705-82-77-01, Portsmouth, or International Cruise Center in the U.S., see above); Truckline Ferries (Tel: 0705-82-77-01, Poole, Dorset); and Sealink-Dieppe Ferries (Tel: 0273-51-22-66, East Sussex, or BritRail offices in the U.S., see above). Some of the companies mentioned above operate services to the Channel Islands as well.

Roscoff in Brittany is reached from Plymouth by Brittany Ferries; St-Malo from Portsmouth, Brittany Ferries; Cherbourg from Weymouth and Portsmouth, Sealink, and from Portsmouth only, P & O Ferries; Caen from Portsmouth, Brittany Ferries; Le Havre from Portsmouth, P & O Ferries; Dieppe from Newhaven, Sealink-Dieppe Ferries; Boulogne from Folkestone, Sealink, and from Dover, P & O Ferries and Hoverspeed; Calais from Dover, Sealink, P & O Ferries, and Hoverspeed; Dunkirk from Ramsgate, Sally Line.

Both day and night crossings are offered by the major lines, particularly P & O and Brittany Ferries. Typically, two- and four-berth cabins are offered and should be booked well in advance in high season. (Agents in the U.S. levy a service charge for reservations, usually about $25.) Hoverspeed Ferries makes the trip in as little as 35 minutes, carrying up to 424 passengers and 55 cars, with 29 round trips daily. For longer distance crossings, such as Plymouth to Roscoff or Portsmouth to Caen, the trip can take five, six, even up to nine hours (especially overnight).

River Tourism

France boasts the longest network of rivers and canals in Europe, 5,313 miles of them flowing through all regions of the country. Although barging on canals (especially in Burgundy) has been popular with overseas visitors for years, only recently have larger, more comfortable boats been constructed and put into service.

Vessels come in all shapes and sizes today, from floating homes called House Boats (even in French, due to their British origin) that accommodate from 2 to 12 people, to excursion boats carrying up to 500 passengers. About 30 hotel barges operate on rivers and canals, the oldest formula, while new boats with berths are being launched.

In 1989 the yacht-like, 100-passenger *Normandie* debuted seven-day sailings on the Seine between Paris and the historic art colony port of Honfleur, including shore excursions in the Norman countryside. Cruises are offered from June through October; for informational brochure, contact A.H.I. International, 701 Lee Street, Des Plaines, IL 60016; Tel: (800) 323-7373.

In 1990 the new French Cruise Lines (affiliated with A.H.I. International) put its 100-passenger sister ship, the *Arlene,* into service with seven-night Provence and Burgundy cruises on the Rhône and Saône rivers. For further details on these and other river-canal trips, check the Getting Around sections for individual regions.

Around France by Plane

Several airlines operate within the country, the largest of which is Air Inter, the domestic carrier within the Air France group. It serves some 30 major business and resort centers, and makes an average of 300 trips per day.

In the U.S., Air Inter offers the discount France Pass, while the Visite France Pass is offered to all visitors from abroad with purchase of a combined international ticket added to Air Inter flights. Ask for details from a travel agent or an Air France office.

The largest regional air carrier in France is TAT (Air France acts as its sales representative in Great Britain), which flies between many provincial cities. In 1988 Air Littoral was formed by the merger of two existing companies, and today operates mainly in the south and southwest. Air Vendée has served cities in western France for ten years and now joins those routes to a number of foreign cities, including Amsterdam, London, Brussels, and Barcelona.

Around France by Train

French Railways SNCF (*Société Nationale des Chemins de Fer Français*), whose American subsidiary is known as FrenchRail, Inc., operates the most advanced rail transportation system in the world with the fastest scheduled service—about 186 m.p.h. as of this writing on high-speed TGVs (*Trains à Grande Vitesse*). They were designed to run at 250 m.p.h. and could reach that speed in the near future.

As of this writing, the following schedules are maintained on TGVs: Paris–Lyon–St-Etienne (two hours to Lyon's Part-Dieu station, 10 minutes more to Lyon-Perrache); Paris–Avignon–Marseille–Toulon–Nice (Avignon, in four hours; even with multiple stops and trains not yet operating at TGV speeds the entire route, Nice is reached in just more than seven hours); Paris–Dijon (about one and a half hours); Paris–Le Mans–Angers–Nantes–La Baule (this is the new TGV Atlantique first stage; about two hours to Nantes without the intermediate stops, otherwise two and a half); Paris–Le Mans–Rennes–Brest; Paris–Nîmes–Montpellier–Béziers (about four and a half hours to Nîmes); Paris–Aix-les-Bains–either Chambéry or Annecy; Paris–Lyon–Grenoble (three hours and 20 minutes to Grenoble); Paris–Besançon or Paris–Beaune–Chalon-sur-Sâone; Lille–Douai–Arras–Lyon; Rouen–Lyon; and Lille–Grenoble.

TGVs also call in three Swiss cities on runs from Paris to Mâcon and Geneva (between three and a half and four hours, depending on intermediate stops) and Paris to either Lausanne or Bern.

On line are plans for TGV service to Strasbourg and beyond Lyon to Valence–Nice and Valence–Montpellier–Perpignan. It is hoped that by 1997 Paris will be linked to Avignon in two hours and 40 minutes, to Nice in four hours, and to Barcelona in four hours and 30 minutes. Beyond Strasbourg, the TGV-Est line will connect Paris to Munich in five hours.

The new generation of TGVs consists of three first-class cars per train (meals available at seats), one bar-snack car, and six second-class cars. When run in pairs, as on Paris–Lyon runs, capacity is almost 1,000 passengers. Some first-class cars are arranged for meetings or to accommodate groups; play spaces and nursery are available in second-class; the trains also offer telephone service en route; and access doors between cars have been removed to make moving about easier.

Not all trains, of course, are TGVs: Others include EuroCities, Corails, or Turbotrains, all air conditioned, soundproofed, and some with complete dining cars. On most night trains (such as the comfortable, traditional Nice–Paris Train Bleu), you may book a private sleeper or a berth in either first or second class. New EuroCity trains are put into service regularly; at the moment, 78 of them serve major cities across the Continent.

Franceshrinkers tours have been designed exclusively for the English-speaking traveller, combining the speed of the rail system with the convenience of motorcoach touring; five one-day tours and one two-day trip are available; fees are all-inclusive.

Information on all trains and tours as well as discounts described below can be supplied by your travel agent or by the office of FrenchRail, Inc.: 610 Fifth Avenue, New York, NY 10020; Tel: (212) 586-9276.

In Canada, contact FranceRail, 1500 Stanley Street, Suite 436, Montreal, Quebec HEA IR3; Tel: (514) 288-8255.

In the U.K., contact French Railways, Ltd., 179 Piccadilly, London W1 OBA; Tel: (071) 499-2153.

In Paris, SNCF's office is located at 10 place de Budapest; the English-speaking information number is 01-45-82-08-41.

In 1990, with the assumption of the Swiss Tourist Office's train activities and the signing of agreements with GermanRail, the Scandinavian Railroads, and Spanish Railroads, FrenchRail became a one-stop shopping center for rail travellers. There is not room here to detail all the passes and discount plans available in France, but they are worth inquiry and study: France Railpass, Rail 'N Drive Pass, Fly Rail & Drive Pass, in addition to the continent-wide Hertz Euraildrive Escape, Eurailpass, Eurail Youthpass, Eurail Saverpass, Eurail Flexipass. It's important to consider which fits your plans and to purchase your discount pass before leaving home.

Regular discounts on regular runs also are available for those who may plan to take just one point-to-point trip and who meet the requirements as members of couples, families, youth groups, et cetera. These are the so-called Bleu-Blanc-Rouge tariffs, which are available on certain days of each month; ask FrenchRail or travel agents for details.

New in North America is a Franco-British railpass known as the BritFrance Railpass that will provide five or 10 days of rail travel in both countries, usable over 15 consecutive days for the five-day pass or one month for the 10-day pass. It includes a round-trip ticket on the Hovercraft for Channel crossings and all supplements for the use of TGVs. All prices are guaranteed in U.S. dollars for the calendar year. For complete information, contact your travel agent or call FrenchRail at (212) 586-9276 or

Britrail in New York at (212) 575-2667; Chicago, (312)
427-8691; Dallas, (214) 748-0860; Los Angeles, (213) 274-
6934; San Francisco, (415) 982-1993; Toronto, (416) 929-
3334; or Vancouver, (604) 683-6896.

FrenchRail's brochure *See Europe by Train* provides
useful information about the various kinds of Eurailpasses.
Free copies may be obtained by writing: Eurailpass, P.O.
Box 300, Stamford, CT 06904-2383, or Eurailpass Distribution Centre, C.P. 300, Succursale R., Montreal, Canada H2S
3K9.

Renting a Car and Driving

A valid driver's license from the country of residence is
required; minimum age is 23 years, or 21 for credit card
holders. All vehicles must be insured; if you are renting a
car licensed in France, the rental company will take care
of the paperwork. The major rental car companies in
France are Avis, Budget-Milleville, Citer, Europcar (affiliated with National Car Rental), Hertz, InterRent, and
Mattei. International car rental credit cards are accepted
for payment, with no deposit required. Other cards accepted are American Express, Carte Blanche, Carte Bleue,
Visa, Air France, Air Inter, Diner's Club, and Eurocard
(MasterCard).

Normally, a good deal of money may be saved by
arranging for auto pick-ups well in advance of the trip
when discount plans may be booked. If you are planning
to spend a few days in Paris before driving into the
country, you may wish to pick up your car when leaving at
one of the airports, thus avoiding having to deal with
Paris traffic.

Avis has introduced the On Call Europe system, by
which renters of its autos can telephone a toll-free number in France that will automatically reach a data bank in
England which will give information on the nearest
English-speaking doctors and dentists, basic major city
information, museums and historical monuments, restaurants, and hotels. The number to dial in France is
19-05-90-83-85.

The most economical plan for rental periods of one
month or more is Renault's Financed Purchase-
Repurchase lease plan, by which the driver purchases a
new Renault, paying basic charges in advance and signing
a promissory note for the balance of the cost. The note is
discharged by return of the car in good condition to
Renault at an agreed time. The cost includes unlimited

mileage, government taxes, factory guarantee, registration, and insurance.

For information on Renault Purchase-Repurchase, inquire of: Auto Europe, Camden, Maine; Avis, Garden City, NY; Peugeot, New York City; Europe by Car, New York City; France Auto Vacances, New York City; Kemwell Group, Harrison, NY; Renault Overseas, New York City; A.M.C. Renault, Brampton (near Toronto), Canada; Inter-Car, Montreal; Renault U.K. Ltd., London; Renault Australia, Saint Leonards, N.S.W.

Local Time
Paris is one hour east of Greenwich Mean Time, which means by the clock it's one hour ahead of the U.K., six hours ahead of New York and the non-Maritime east coast of Canada, and nine hours ahead of California and western Canada. Sydney, Australia, is ten hours ahead of Paris. Because different countries go on and off it at different times, for short periods during Daylight Savings Time there will be an hour's variance in the differentials mentioned above.

Currency
The basic unit is the *franc,* which is divided into 100 centimes; there are banknotes for 10, 50, 100, and 500 francs and coins of 5, 10, and 20 centimes and ½, 1, 5, and 10 francs. When travelling in France, check listings at major banks or in the *International Herald Tribune* and other newspapers for current exchange rates.

Telephoning
The telephone area code for Paris is 01; for all other places in France, the area code is incorporated in the first two digits of the phone number. When phoning Paris from outside France, omit the zero from the area code. The international country code for France is 33.

Electric Current
Current in France is 220 V, 50 cycles AC. North American–made appliances require electric current converters and adapter plugs.

Business Hours and Holidays
Most banks in France are open from 9:00 A.M. to 4:30 P.M., every day of the week except Saturday, Sunday, and holidays. Banks usually close at noon the day before a holi-

day. Although banks may be closed, currency exchanges are open at Charles-de-Gaulle and Orly airports in Paris (from 6:00 or 6:30 A.M. to 11:30 P.M.) and from early morning until at least 9:00 P.M. at the Austerlitz, Est, Lyon, St-Lazare, and Nord railway stations. Crédit Commercial de France at 103, avenue des Champs-Elysées is open daily except Sunday from 8:30 A.M. to 8:00 P.M. (there is some Sunday service in summer), and Union de Banques à Paris at 154, avenue des Champs-Elysées is open on Sunday and holidays from 10:30 A.M. to 6:00 P.M.

Most department stores are open Monday through Saturday from 9:30 A.M. to 6:30 P.M., though some are closed on Monday mornings. They are usually open until 9:00 or 10:00 P.M. one or two evenings a week. Smaller shops close between noon and 2:00 P.M. or later.

Fashion boutiques, perfume stores, and the like are open Tuesday through Saturday from 10:00 A.M. to noon and 2:00 P.M. until 6:30 or 7:00 P.M.

Hairdressers close Monday and are usually open on Saturday from 9:00 A.M. to 6:00 or 7:00 P.M. Food shops are open Tuesday through Sunday from 7:00 A.M. until 1:30 P.M. and from 4:30 to 8:00 P.M. (except bakeries, often open from 2:00 to 8:00 P.M.). Food shops may close at noon on Sunday.

The French in general celebrate twelve national holidays: New Year's Day, Easter, Easter Monday, Labor Day (May 1), Ascension Day, May 8 (end of World War II), Whit Monday, Bastille Day (July 14), Assumption Day (August 15), All Saints Day (November 1), Armistice Day 1918 (November 11), and Christmas Day. Alsace also celebrates Good Friday and December 26.

In addition, some businesses in rural areas may close for some of the hundreds of local celebrations.

Credit Cards

Visa, paired with the French *Carte Bleue,* and MasterCard, affiliated with Eurocard, are the most widely accepted international cards in France in establishments small as well as large, rural as well as urban. American Express and Diner's Club are widely accepted in major shops, restaurants, and hotels. Gasoline credit cards are not accepted.

France in Chains

Experienced travellers who don't wish to make all hotel reservations in advance can make the going easier by studying the various groupings of accommodations available and then selecting a "chain" that is suitable in terms of cost, comfort, locations, et cetera. Unlike members of international companies, these "chains" are composed of individually owned and operated properties.

Most luxurious and prestigious are the inns of the **Relais & Châteaux**, many occupying castles and manors. They are also the most expensive. A catalog is available at some bookstores or by sending $5 to the group's newly opened office: Relais & Châteaux, North American Bureau, 2400 Lazy Hollow, Suite 152D, Houston, TX 77063.

On the other hand, the nearly 5,000 small and medium-size family-run inns of the **Logis et Auberges de France** provide warm welcomes, regional character, good comfort, and reasonable prices. Most *logis* are in villages of fewer than 5,000 people. The Logis guide, *Country Hotels & Inns of France,* is sold for about $11 in bookstores, from French Government Tourist Offices, or from Logis et Auberges de France, 25 rue Jean-Mermoz, 75008 Paris.

Newest of these groups is **Château**, which plays host in 91 privately-owned châteaux in four countries, 76 of them in France. The association was created in 1990 by Béraud and Diane de Vogüé; M. De Vogüé's parental home is one of them, La Verrerie in the Loire Valley. They offer the opportunity for a hospitable holiday in historic and beautiful homes with the owners as hosts. Rates are remarkably reasonable and are guaranteed in dollars at time of booking. Write or telephone B & D de Vogüé International, Inc., 1830 S. Mooney Boulevard, Suite 203, P.O. Box 1998, Visalia, CA 93279; Tel: (800) 727-4748 or (209) 733-7119; Fax: (209) 733-4094. In Paris contact: B & D de Vogüé Tours, 15 rue Mesnil, 75116 Paris; Tel: (toll-free) 05-00-57-47 or 01-45-53-56-00; Fax: 01-47-04-58-60. In Great Britain contact: Destination Marketing, Ltd., 2 Cinnamon Row, Plantation Wharf, York Place, London SW11 3TW; Tel: 071-978-5212; Fax: 071-924-3171. In Australia it's France-Bonjour, 13–15 Atchison Street, St. Leonards, N.S.W. 2065, Sydney; Tel: (02) 438-4733; Fax: (02) 439-8762, or France-Bonjour, 568 St. Kilda Road, Melbourne, Victoria 3004; Tel: (008) 226-014 (toll-free) or (03) 521-1915; Fax: (03) 529-5839.

B & D de Vogüé also arranges rentals in Paris from a selection of 300 apartments in the most fashionable areas. Rentals are for a one-week minimum, with rates ranging from about $110 per night for a studio to $650 for a four-bedroom suite. They will also arrange Paris tours and half-

and full-day excursions into the countryside in cooperation with Paris Vision.

For escapists from noise and wanderers of back roads,
the 139 members of **Relais du Silence** provide the kind of
calm that may make moving on impossible. A guide is
free (but enclose U.S.$3 for return postage) from: Relais
du Silence, 38640 Claix, Isère, France.

About 550 hotels in France and elsewhere in Europe
belong to the **France Accueil** group. (*Accueil* means
"welcome.") A Euro-Voucher is issued upon request,
allowing payment before the trip, making all rooms the
same price regardless of the hotel's rank. Some are slick
and motel-like, others are cozy country inns. Write
France Accueil, 85, rue de Dessous-des-Berges, 75013
Paris. Tel: 01-45-83-04-22.

From hotels without restaurants to private castles, the
182 members of **Châteaux-Hôtels Indépendents et Hos-
telleries d'Atmosphère** exude charm and style. They exist
in four classes: hotel-restaurant, hotel *sans* restaurant,
restaurant only, and private castle. For information, write
Châteaux-Hôtels Indépendents, Château de Pray, BP 146,
37401 Amboise, France.

Château Accueil includes about 60 private châteaux
that welcome paying guests. Reservations can be made
through Visafrance, 13, rue St-Louis, 78100 St-Germain-
en-Laye.

An old friend takes on a new name and manner in
Mapotel Best Western, now the largest lodging organization in the world. An advantage of Best Westerns is that
you may call a toll-free number in Phoenix, Arizona, (Tel:
800-528-1234) to make reservations at any member hotel
in France. In France, onward reservations may be made
by calling a Paris number; Tel: 01-46-28-05-50.

Travelling families may enjoy American comfort *à la
française* at **Campanile** hotels, usually located in the country near a city or village. Such modern amenities as built-
in alarm clocks, coffee makers, and radios are provided.
Rooms are rather large: *grils* on the premises resemble
country kitchens and are small and informal. Prices are
moderate for both rooms and meals; Tel: 01-64-62-46-46.

For Further Information

In 1990 the French Government Tourist Office (FGTO)
introduced a telephone information service to provide
North American travellers with information on travel to
continental France and the French West Indies. The France

On Call number, 1-900-420-2003, may be called from 9:00 A.M. to 7:00 P.M., Monday through Friday, for information on cultural and special events, hotels, transportation, restaurants, tour packages, airlines, car rentals, et cetera. Callers will pay 50 cents per minute and will receive additional information by mail. Within France, a new information number also has been created: Tel: 05-20-12-02; there is no fee for its use.

In 1987 FGTO around the world consolidated various activities under the umbrella of Maison de la France. Offices are located in New York (610 Fifth Avenue, Suite 222, NY 10020-2452; Tel: 212-757-1125); Chicago (645 N. Michigan Avenue, Suite 630, IL 60611-2836; Tel: 312-337-6301); Dallas (2305 Cedar Springs Boulevard, TX 75201; Tel: 214-720-4010); Los Angeles (9454 Wilshire Boulevard, Beverly Hills, CA 90212-2967; Tel: 213-272-2661); Montreal (1981 Avenue McGill College, Suite 490, Quebec H3A 2W9; Tel: 514-288-4264), Toronto (1 Dundas Street West, Suite 2405, Box 8, Ontario M5G 1Z3; Tel: 416-593-4723); London (178 Piccadilly, London W1V OAL; Tel: 071-629-1272); and Sydney (Kindersley House, 33 Bligh Street, N.S.W. 2000; Tel: 612-233-32-77).

BIBLIOGRAPHY

HENRY ADAMS, *Mont-St-Michel and Chartres* (1905 and 1913). This classic work goes far beyond its titular subjects into the art, philosophy, and culture of the period.

MICHAEL BAIGENT, RICHARD LEIGH, AND HENRY LINCOLN, *Holy Blood, Holy Grail*. This book has been called revolutionary, astonishing, bizarre, speculative, controversial. Whatever you've thought before about the Cathars, the Knights Templar—or Jesus—this will open your eyes and mind.

DEIRDRE BAIR, *Simone de Beauvoir*. Critics have called this a masterful portrait of one of the most admired and yet most controversial writers of the century; feminists in particular will find much to challenge their preconceptions.

SAMUEL CHAMBERLAIN, *Bouquet de France*. Whether he's supping in Strasbourg or climbing about Carcassonne, this epicurean is always entertaining.

RICHARD COBB AND COLIN JONES, *Voices of the French Revolution*. One of history's greatest and most fascinating convulsions is described in the words of its supporters, bystanders, and victims. The American influence upon events is interestingly treated; intriguing illustrations.

NICHOLAS DELBANCO, *Running in Place*. Provençal culture and history evoked in a personal manner by an English Francophile who returns to Provence with his family.

MARSHALL DILL, JR., *Paris in Time*. From the birth of Paris on the Ile de la Cité to its scrubbing at the hands of André Malraux, here is the great city and how it came to be.

MODRIS EKSTEINS, *Rites of Spring*. In a sense, the cataclysm that was the Great War began with the Paris premiere of Stravinsky's ballet, *Le Sacre du Printemps* . . . or so argues the author of this curious, fascinating study of the birth of the modern age.

DAVID HUGH FARMER, *The Oxford Dictionary of Saints*. Here are the stories of some of history's most interesting people (many of them French) by an English historian, once a monk.

M.F.K. FISHER, *Two Towns in Provence*. Memoirs of Aix-en-Provence and Marseille by this great food writer are as spicy and delicious as *ratatouille*.

NOEL RILEY FITCH, *Sylvia Beach and the Lost Generation*. Literary Paris of the 1920s and 1930s gathered at the book club of Shakespeare and Company. Here's what they did and said and thought: James Joyce, F. Scott Fitzgerald, et al.

JANET FLANNER (GENÊT), *Paris Journal 1944–1971*. Two volumes. No single writer has ever brought Paris's politics, art, and enchantment to life as did Genêt in her columns for *The New Yorker,* excerpted here.

————, *Paris Was Yesterday*. Selected from the journalist's *Letter From Paris* articles in *The New Yorker,* these well-chosen pieces bring to life the people and passions of Paris, from 1925 and the adored Josephine Baker to the *gaieté Parisienne* that preceded World War II.

FORD MADOX FORD, *Provence*. This is less a story of Provence than an evocation of it, a love letter to it; it is a literary *bouillabaisse*.

HUGH FORD, *Published in Paris*. The Lost Generation of American and British writers, printers, and publishers paints the glory years in Paris from 1920 to 1939.

MAVIS GALLANT, *Overhead in a Balloon*. The nuances of life in Paris are revealed in these 12 short stories characterized by finely textured prose.

HELEN GARDNER, *Art Through the Ages*. Published first in 1926, this is the amateur's best introduction to the arts, from cave paintings to Picasso.

FRANCES GIES, *Joan of Arc*. You thought you knew Joan of Arc; have you met Joan of Arc? Here, in a most unusually structured history, Gies makes the real Joan stand up.

————, *The Knight in History*. For six centuries the Medieval knight dominated the battlefields and stirred the imagination of the Western world. Here are the Crusaders, the Knights Templar, and individual heroes such as the Breton Bertrand du Guesclin, who changed the world that came after him.

FRANCES AND JOSEPH GIES, *Marriage and the Family in the Middle Ages*. A rewarding turn away from heroes and kings to daily life: What was the family, and how did it bring us to today?

ANTHONY GLYN, *The Seine*. Glyn is the best companion you could want on an amble: easygoing, anecdotal, curious, and thoughtful.

PIERRE GOUBERT, *The Course of French History*. Here's what you've been looking for for decades: the first general, readable, one-volume history of France available in English. It begins with the crowning of Hugues Capet in July 987 and ends with the uneasy *cohabitation* of Jacques Chirac and François Mitterrand in 1986.

ERNEST HEMINGWAY, *A Moveable Feast*. Here is the Paris for which the world is nostalgic, the days of wine and cafés.

DENIS HOLLIER (ED.), *A New History of French Literature*. Designed for the general reader, this is an extraordinary collection of essays covering the period A.D. 842 to 1985 by 164 American and European specialists.

JAMES A. HUSTON, *Across the Face of France*. The liberation and recovery of post–World War II France as seen by an American who served there.

PHILIP AND MARY HYMAN AND ROSEMARY GEORGE, *Webster's Wine Tours France*. Georges Bertrand is one of the talented new winemakers of Corbières, and Aloxe-Corton may be visited daily. This book is as helpful as a *tire-bouchon*.

MICHAEL JACOBS AND PAUL STIRTON, *The Knopf Traveler's Guides to Art*. The volume on France is an essential handbook for the traveller who doesn't want to miss a Gérôme in Vesoul or the tomb of a duke in Dreux.

HENRY JAMES, *A Little Tour in France*. The beautifully reissued "impressions" of the master, written in 1900, will amuse, delight, and sometimes irritate today's Francophile. They don't write books like this any more.

JOHN JAMES, *The Traveler's Key to Medieval France*. This guide and introduction to sacred architecture will be invaluable to anyone who knows that once you've seen one church you haven't seen 'em all.

AMY KELLY, *Eleanor of Aquitaine and the Four Kings*. Beautifully written, endlessly fascinating, this book is more difficult to put down than any murder mystery. The family that created half of 20th-century France still lives.

EMMANUEL LE ROY LADURIE, *Montaillou, the Promised Land of Error*. Peasants who lived more than 600 years ago live once again in the days of the Albigensian heresies; ethnography at its best.

ALEXIS LICHINE, *New Encyclopedia of Wines and Spirits*. This is the classic compendium for the discerning drinker.

A.J. LIEBLING. *Between Meals, An Appetite for Paris*. You may read this humorous tale at one sitting, sometimes laughing aloud; the author does nothing if not whet your appetite for more.

STANLEY LOOMIS, *Paris in the Terror*. A strikingly vivid—read gory—account of Revolutionary zeal gone wild.

PETER MAYLE, *A Year in Provence*. An Englishman's witty memoirs of life on the slopes of the lovely Mount Lubéron.

TED MORGAN, *An Uncertain Hour*. The disillusion and moral drift of the Vichy government, the Resistance, the persecution and deportation of Jews, and the Klaus Barbie trial will sadden most readers and intrigue them all.

BRIAN N. MORTON, *Americans in Paris*. Where did Henry Adams live and write? Where did Isadora Duncan dance in the gardens? Where did Elsa Maxwell entertain? See Paris in the company of dozens of Americans, from Louis Armstrong to Carnegie.

FRANCES MOSSIKER, *Madame de Sévigné*. No letter-writer has surpassed Madame de Sévigné's style or substance. Mossiker catches her in full literary flight.

JAMES POPE-HENNESSY, *Aspects of Provence*. A wanderer in the great tradition, educated and urbane, takes us by the hand from Lady Blessington's Nîmes to Merimée's St-Maximin.

JOHN REWALD, *The History of Impressionism*. Specialists will admire and amateurs enjoy this source-book on almost everybody's favorite painters. His *The History of Post-Impressionism* is of equal interest.

WAVERLEY ROOT, *The Food of France*. The late, great writer-gourmet at his hungry best.

MORT ROSENBLUM, *Mission to Civilize*. The French, they are a funny race; a senior foreign correspondent watches them ticking and tells us how they do it.

JOHN RUSSELL, *Paris*. The erudite art critic for *The New York Times* chooses Dufy, Cartier-Bresson, et al. to help him create the most beautiful and provocative coffee table book on the world's handsomest city.

GILES ST. AUBYN, *The Year of Three Kings, 1483*. During the dramatic year of 1483, three kings ruled over England— Edward IV, Edward V, and Richard III. Here is the intriguing blood feud of the War of the Roses, seen from across the Channel.

SIMON SCHAMA, *Citizens: A Chronicle of the French Revolution*. In a revolutionary look at the French Revolution, the author returns to life the men and women who created the movements that forever altered a continent's—and the world's—history. Studded with humor and anecdotes, this thick volume is almost too fascinating to put down.

KATHERINE SCHERMAN, *The Birth of France*. At once beautifully written, learned, and humorous, this book belongs in the library of everyone who cares about France.

JERROLD SEIGEL, *Bohemian Paris: Culture, Politics, and the Boundaries of Bourgeois Life, 1830–1930*. All the players are here—Verlaine, Baudelaire, Jarry, Satie, Apollinaire, Breton, and others—in this fascinating study of how the famous Bohemia of Paris came to be.

DESMOND SEWARD, *The Hundred Years War*. The endless, spaghetti-like tangles and twists of the French-English inheritance struggles from 1337 to 1453 are described in all their fascinating and intricate detail by a precise historian and excellent writer.

————, *Prince of the Renaissance*. No one who meets François I in these pages will ever look at the Loire's great châteaux in the same way again. Here in his finest moments and with flaws revealed lives the man who had more effect on France than any leader since Charlemagne.

————, *Napoléon's Family*. The gossip-mongering, backbiting, insatiably amorous Bonaparte clan portrayed in all their ambitious bitterness.

ANDRE L. SIMON, EDITOR, *Wines of the World*. As readable as it is authoritative, this volume belongs on every imbiber's bookshelf.

BARBARA TUCHMAN, *A Distant Mirror*. Here is the 14th century in all its glittering accomplishments and dreadful agonies; indispensible to an understanding of how modern France came to be.

PATRICIA WELLS, *The Food Lover's Guide to France*. Where to buy olive oil in a working mill, where to bite a *baguette* in Aix: It's all here.

THEODORE ZELDIN, *The French*. A witty writer spies on everyone from Montand to Mitterrand and tells how to deal with them.

We don't want to burden you with yet another essay on the greatness of French letters and philosophy. But to be fairly knowledgeable about the country and people of France—and, not coincidentally, to get more out of any visit to the country—there are some writers you should read or reread. We suggest them to you here as a reminder, a mouth-watering checklist presented in no particular order:

Colette, Marcel Aymé, Marcel Proust, Jean Anouilh, Jules Romains, Jean-Paul Sartre, Simone de Beauvoir, André Maurois, Paul Claudel, Françoise Sagan,

Antoine de Saint-Exupéry, Henry de Montherlant, Jean Giraudoux, Jean Giono, Romain Gary, Jacques Duhamel, François Rabelais, Joachim du Bellay, René Descartes, Pierre Corneille, Blaise Pascal, François–duc de La Rochefoucauld, Jean-Baptiste Poquelin (Molière), Jean de la Fontaine, Jean Racine, Jacques-Bénigne Bossuet, Jean de la Bruyère, Charles-Louis de Secondat (Baron de Montesquieu), Pierre Carlet de Chamblain de Marivaux, François-Marie Arouet (Voltaire), Denis Diderot, Jean-Jacques Rousseau (Swiss-French), Pierre-Augustin Caron de Beaumarchais, François-René (Vicomte de Châteaubriand), Alphonse-Marie-Louis de Lamartine, Alfred-Victor (Comte de Vigny), Honoré de Balzac, Victor-Marie Hugo, Louis-Charles-Alfred de Musset, Pierre-Jules-Théophile Gautier, Charles-Marie-René Leconte de Lisle, Gustave Flaubert, Charles-Pierre Baudelaire, Paul-Marie Verlaine, Emile-Edouard-Charles-Antoine Zola, Alphonse Daudet, Henri-René-Albert-Guy de Maupassant, Stephane Mallarmé, Jean-Nicolas-Arthur Rimbaud, Jacques-Anatole-François Thibault (Anatole France), Marie-Henri Bayle (Stendhal).

PARIS

By Stephen O'Shea

Stephen O'Shea, a writer and journalist who lived in Paris for many years, has written for British, American, Canadian, and French magazines on many aspects of Parisian and French life.

Paris has captivated the Western imagination for so long that even people who have never visited the city sometimes feel nostalgia for it. The mere mention of its river, the Seine, summons up thoughts of beauty, youthful heartbreak, and the creative dissipation that has lured foreigners to the city since Medieval times. With its superb restaurants, its districts devoted to high fashion, and its relentlessly romantic vistas, Paris is known throughout the world as Europe's pleasure dome. It is also a city marked by a turbulent past, its rich intellectual, artistic, and religious heritage surviving in museums, galleries, landmarks, churches, and the way Parisians speak and act in everyday life.

The modern metropolis has kept alive one Parisian tradition above all others—the city and its inhabitants remain fascinated by novelty. Anyone travelling to France, whether for the first or the fifteenth time, must have an exceptional excuse not to want to go to its capital.

MAJOR INTEREST

Museums
The Big Three: Louvre, Orsay, Pompidou
Noteworthy: Cluny, Picasso, Rodin

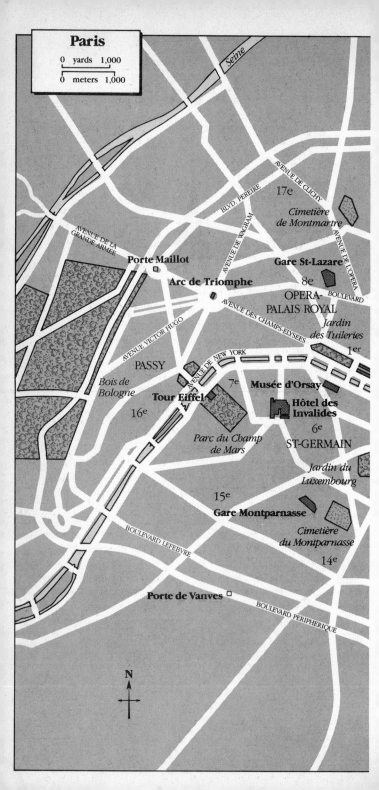

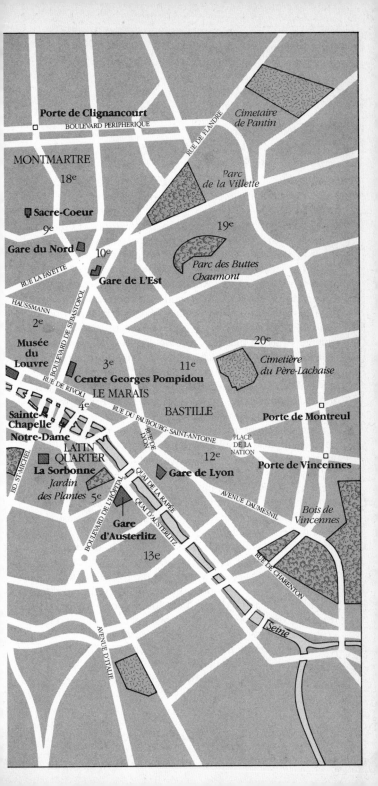

Sights
Notre-Dame, Sainte Chapelle, Champs-Elysées,
Eiffel Tower, Trocadéro, Invalides

Neighborhoods
Bastille, Latin Quarter/St-Germain, Marais, Opéra–
Palais Royal

Parks
Bois de Boulogne, Luxembourg, Tuileries

It is best to consider Paris as a performance. Certain
districts of the city hold center stage for a time, then step
back to let other neighborhoods reappear in the spotlight. The changing nature of this show is a source of both
pride and distress to lovers of Paris, fueling countless
café-counter arguments and public controversies. A familiar Parisian boast is that one lives or works in a *quartier
qui monte,* that is, an area where positive, usually trendy,
change is taking place. In present-day Paris, the Bastille
district is undergoing such change. Those opposed to the
trend point to dubious developments (the underground
Les Halles complex, for example) as an indication that
their contemporaries have absolutely no idea of what
they are doing.

Over the centuries a literary cottage industry has
sprung up, with distinguished authors bemoaning the
imminent destruction of the city's soul. Victor Hugo, in
Les Misérables, went into loving detail about the warren of
Medieval alleyways eliminated by the cutting of the boulevards in the middle of the 19th century. However, much
of Paris's later fame, and much of its charm, is associated
with these broad thoroughfares. In the same way, the
Eiffel Tower was almost universally loathed by the literary
upon its opening a hundred years ago. Guy de Maupassant said he enjoyed the view from the top of the tower
because it was the only place in the city where he wasn't
forced to look at the damn thing. Still, successive generations of artists came to use it as a symbol of the city, and it
is now almost impossible to imagine Paris without its iron
mast. At any given period of its history, Paris has been
described as a shadow of its former self or as a disfigured
beauty, yet the show still goes on, changing for each
generation and, as befits its quarrelsome audience, pro-
voking heated disagreements.

One of the principal reasons Parisians harbor such
strong emotions about their city is the accessible, human

scale on which it is built. Unlike greater London, which sprawls across miles of the Thames Valley, or even Manhattan, stretching out in a seemingly endless procession of linear neighborhoods, Paris is compact and easy to understand. The Seine, too, is not so much a physical barrier, like the Thames or the East River, as it is a beautiful boulevard for barge traffic. The metropolitan area, with its population of ten million, may be gigantic, but central Paris, its 20 *arrondissements* (districts) spiraling out from the Louvre district, can easily be crossed on foot in an afternoon.

Even more coherent is the city's growth. From an island settlement of Gauls huddled together in the midst of a watery plain to a 19th-century capital incorporating the hills that hem in the lowlands created by the Seine, Paris has grown outward in ever-widening rings. Roman Lutetia spilled over onto the Left Bank; the 12th-century battlements of King Philip II Augustus encompassed a bustling town extending from the drained marshes of the Right Bank to the monastery vineyards of the Left; and Louis XVI's Farmers-General Wall, a source of pre-Revolutionary irritation, formed a circuit of customs houses concentric to the present-day perimeter. The city's pie-shape would have a geometric elegance pleasing to all Cartesians, except that the crescent formed by the Seine bisects the circle so unequally that the true focal point of the city lies a little off center, like the human heart. After all, this is Paris.

THE ISLANDS
The Ile de la Cité

The birthplace of the city and the symbolic center of the nation, this small island in the Seine was first settled by the Parisii Gauls in the third century B.C. Long a miniature of French society, with the three Estates of clergy, nobility, and commoners crowded together, the Cité is now inhabited more by presences than by people. It is a place where the legendary and fictional have as great a right to exist—in French, *droit de cité*—as do the historical and factual. In the mind of the modern visitor, Quasimodo and Esmeralda loom larger than Abélard and Héloïse (who lived and loved at 9, quai aux Fleurs) as characters of Medieval Paris, and even Inspector Maigret, calmly puffing a pipe in his office at 24, quai des Orfèvres, seems far more believable than the fantastic relics once housed

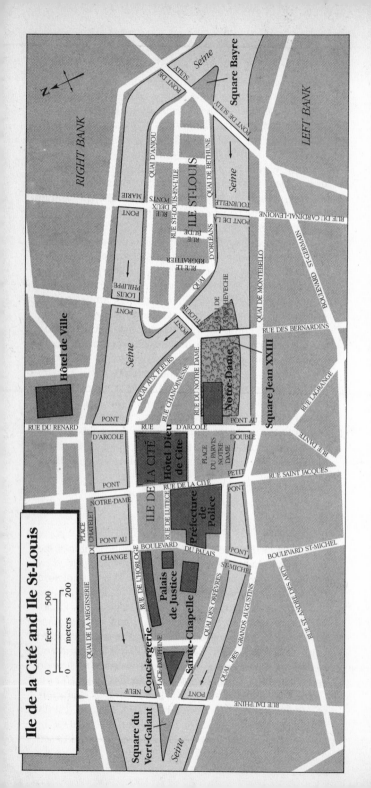

in the Sainte Chapelle. Romans, Norse, Knights Templar, and Jacobin revolutionaries have all passed this way, remembered not so much in stone as in the imaginative works they have inspired.

There are, however, two other forces that have left a lasting mark on the island. Church and State, wary partners throughout French history, have had dramatic clashes here. On the present-day Cité the standoff between the two is far more benign than it was in the past, but it remains striking nonetheless. Notre-Dame cathedral squares off opposite the sprawling central police station, and the Sainte Chapelle is dwarfed by a 19th-century courthouse. The Conciergerie, a vestige of the residence of Medieval kings, is less a symbol of State power than of its destructiveness: It was used as a prison during the Reign of Terror.

The colorful history of Church-State jostling on the island stretches as far back as Roman times. For more than four centuries the Ile de la Cité was the administrative and spiritual center of the bustling Roman provincial town of Lutetia. Foundations of houses from this period and the street plan of an ancient neighborhood are on view in an artfully designed archaeological crypt beneath the square in front of Notre-Dame. Fittingly, the Roman governor most closely associated with his "dear Lutetia" was Julian the Apostate, a troublemaker in both spiritual and temporal domains. As emperor from 361 to 363, Julian overthrew the Christian orthodoxy imposed on the empire by his uncle, Constantine the Great. When, from his balcony at the Prefect of Gaul's residence on the island, the 29-year-old devotee of the old gods first heard his legions acclaim him sole Augustus of the Roman world, the Cité's long tradition of rivalry between the sacred and the profane was born.

Certain events springing from this rivalry are the stuff of legend. On the western tip of the island, the **square du Vert-Galant** (now a favorite spot for lovers), King Philip the Fair brutally put an end to the crusading confraternity of Knights Templar on March 11, 1314, by first torturing its leaders, then burning them at the stake. Legend has it that Grand Master Jacques de Molay, before being consumed by the flames, invoked God to visit a curse on the malevolent king's family. Within a generation, the monarch and all his legitimate issue had met violent ends as France and England plunged into the Hundred Years War.

Above this park, on the **Pont Neuf**, stands an equestrian

statue of Henry IV, the king whose wedding celebrations were marred by the massacre of his fellow Huguenots and whose reign was marked by an uneasy truce between prelates and certain factions within the nobility. When Henry for dynastic reasons consented to convert to Catholicism (thereby ensuring the continuation of the royal Bourbon line he began), the famous impiety "Paris is worth a Mass" became the catchphrase to describe the depth of his religious conviction. The king was later murdered by Ravaillac, an ardent Catholic who did not share his cavalier attitude toward the faith. It is fitting that Henry's statue stands on the western, "secular" part of the island.

In 1804, an even more celebrated instance of clerical nose-tweaking occurred on the island, this time at the making of a modern emperor. In the midst of his solemn coronation ceremony at Notre-Dame, Napoléon snatched the crown out of the hands of Pope Pius VII and placed it on his own modest head. So that none of the assembled notables in the devastated church would miss the point about where true legitimacy and power lay, he then crowned Josephine de Beauharnais his empress. Jacques-Louis David's vivid rendering of the event now hangs in the Louvre.

Still, the two great works of religious architecture adorning the Cité attest to periods when Church and State coexisted peacefully. During the long reign of the pious King Louis IX (Saint Louis) in the 13th century, a nascent style of architecture, only later stigmatized as "Gothic"—thus, barbarian—by its Renaissance detractors, came to maturity in the Ile-de-France under the supervision of such master builders as Pierre de Montreuil. In 1246, Louis called on Montreuil to build a reliquary worthy of the objects he had obtained from the Holy Lands. A partial inventory: the Crown of Thorns, a piece of the True Cross, a vial of the Virgin's milk, and Jesus Christ's swaddling clothes. Montreuil's construction, the **Sainte Chapelle**, erected in 33 months of frantic activity, more than matched the extravagance of the monarch's faith. Even at a remove of seven centuries the chapel inspires awe, with its upper sanctuary seeming to be built entirely of brilliant stained glass. When the sun strikes the building in the late afternoon, especially in the spring and autumn, visitors studying the biblical scenes depicted in the 13th-century windows of this sanctuary will get the distinct impression that they are standing inside a large jewel. The light suffusing the upper chapel at this time of day has not grown any dimmer since the distant age of belief it first illuminated.

A more comprehensive example of the spirit of the age is **Notre-Dame**. Begun in 1163 and not completed until 170 years later, the cathedral is the collective work of generations of architects and craftsmen. At the time of its construction, the symbols of the power and the glory of the Church were being transferred from isolated monasteries in the countryside to the burgeoning cities and towns. Slowly, Romanesque architecture—with its massive pillars, rounded arches, and thick, almost windowless walls that suggested a fortress Church standing alone against a hostile world—gave way to the graceful lancets of the Gothic, with innovative flying buttresses strengthening walls that could now be pierced by huge stained-glass tableaux. As naves soared higher, and such embellishments as statuary and rose windows became ever more accomplished, the great cathedrals came to serve as spectacular illustrations of the teachings and ultimate message of the Medieval Church. The populace was both edified and awed by these sanctuaries, learning the lives of the saints and martyrs from the portals and windows as their eyes were inexorably drawn heavenward by the lines of the building. The large square cleared in front of Notre-Dame during the 19th century betrays an anachronism: The cathedral's façade was designed to be viewed at close quarters, its balanced composition sweeping the eye up the bell towers and beyond.

However solemn and instructive its purpose, Notre-Dame was never a museum. The church served as a refuge from civil authority in Medieval times, sheltering criminals and vagrants from the law. Markets were set up inside it and messy everyday life went on beneath the towering vault. Hence, the Notre-Dame of today, constantly filled with hundreds of people raising dust as they walk and talk their way around the ambulatory, is not so much a victim of mass tourism as its beneficiary, marked by the very human informality that reigned within it during the Middle Ages. The Sunday evening organ recital, jammed with listeners, chatterers, and worshipers, is a particularly good time to visit the church. So too is the *heure bleue,* when the morning sun strikes the north rose window and fills the transept with an otherworldly blue.

A commanding view of Paris is the reward for those

hardy enough to climb the 387 steps of the north tower of Notre-Dame. The famous gargoyles perched over the void (some of them 19th-century confections of Viollet-le-Duc, the architect who restored the church) look as if they can, indeed, frighten away demons. Viollet's renovation project was made possible after Victor Hugo's *The Hunchback of Notre-Dame* had raised public awareness of the cathedral's perilous state of dilapidation. The Revolution had taken its toll: Most of the statuary was destroyed, including the façade's 28 Kings of Judah, mistakenly thought to be the kings of France; much of the glasswork was smashed; the old bells, excluding the 17th-century Emmanuelle, which still sounds today, were melted down; and the Goddess of Reason cult, which put a pretty ballerina atop a pile of dirt in the transept, caused extensive structural damage. In fact, it was only the cathedral's transformation into a wine warehouse for military hospitals during the last phase of the Revolution that prevented it from being demolished altogether.

The spirit of Revolutionary excess is far more palpable at the **Conciergerie**. Although the building dates back to the 14th century (as does its remarkable outdoor clock), Parisians usually associate it with the early 1790s, when it held nobles and revolutionaries who had fallen from favor. Visitors can see the cells of Marie Antoinette, Danton, and Robespierre, as well as the courtyard where women and men prisoners were momentarily reunited before being led away to their deaths. A raised corridor at one end of the great Gothic room is known as the "rue de Paris," a reference to Monsieur de Paris, the name given to the city's executioner. From this vantage point the beauty of the large hall can be best appreciated—even if its historical associations are somewhat sinister. The Medieval kitchens, with their colossal hearths for roasting animals on spits, recall the earlier, more festive days of the Conciergerie.

Toward the western end of the Cité lies its most picturesque residential district, the **place Dauphine**. A triangular oasis of greenery, the spot is known throughout the city for its quiet charm. The houses lining two of the triangle's sides are a study in differing styles of architecture. Surrealist André Breton extravagantly proclaimed the square the "sex of Paris," which may be why Henry IV, the monarch famous for his dalliances, seems to be riding toward place Dauphine from his place of glory atop the Pont Neuf.

Ile St-Louis

After the surfeit of history on the neighboring island, it is a relief to visit Ile St-Louis, a fairly recent creation in a city as old as Paris. Developed by land speculators and parvenus of the 17th century, the island is characterized by houses that have what is called *du ventre,* the bellylike sag of old constructions. A provincial calm reigns on this small island, which is best viewed at dawn, when the different shades of gray (bridges, houses, and river) make it particularly beautiful. A walk around the island on the quais alongside the Seine is a romantic experience—and useful, if you are planning to sleep under a bridge. Of the six bridges leading from the Ile St-Louis, the most remarkable is the **Pont Marie**, with its elegant stone arches all of a different size.

Now a playground for weekenders in search of mellow but modern restaurants and shops, Ile St-Louis has always been outside of the mainstream of Paris life. As its rich occupants left for more-spacious accommodations elsewhere in the city, the island became a haven for artists. Its most famous resident was Charles Baudelaire, who used to frequent the Hôtel de Lauzun, where members of the Club des Haschischins ingested hashish in suitably exotic surroundings. Today things are considerably tamer, the consumption of Berthillon sherbet being the islanders' principal sensual indulgence. The resident creative community is consequently less lean than it was during the island's bohemian heyday, with such patrons of the arts as the Rothschilds and the widow of President Pompidou now living in the quaint neighborhood. The best reminder of the island's good old days of poetic self-destructiveness lies across the Pont de Sully on the Right Bank. At the first intersection there is a statue of Arthur Rimbaud in what can only be called a hallucinatory pose. His head and shoulders are dreamily separated from the rest of his body.

THE LEFT BANK
The Latin Quarter

For a long time simply called the Université (the other two districts of Paris were Cité, being the island, and Ville, being the Right Bank), the Latin Quarter embraces the area from the place Maubert on the east to the Odéon on

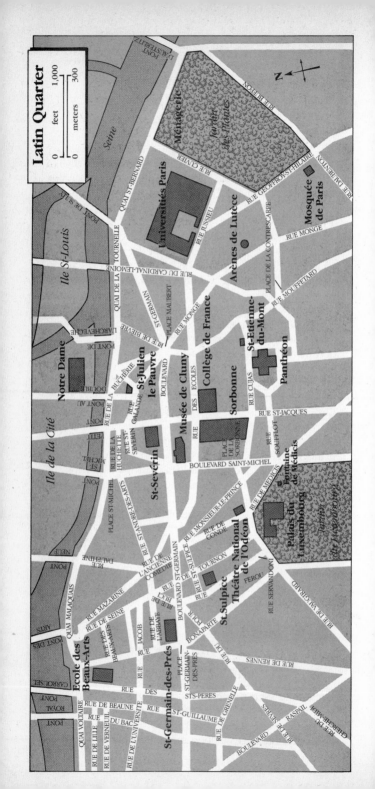

the west, with the Montagne Ste-Geneviève as its southern boundary. Immediately opposite the south flank of Notre-Dame is the **Maubert quarter**, a maze of old streets dotted with restaurants and exotic food shops. Once famed for the rats that infested the tanneries lining the Medieval confluence of the Seine and Bièvre (today an underground stream), the area is now the last word in left-wing gentility, housing successful academics, psychoanalysts, and politicians. The uniformed policemen on the narrow rue de Bièvre guard the house of the most successful of them all, François Mitterrand.

Of particular interest to lovers of Gothic architecture is the riverside square René Viviani. From this tranquil park the south flank of Notre-Dame cathedral can be seen in all its gracefully buttressed glory. Directly south of the park stands yet another Medieval gem, the tiny church of **St-Julien-le-Pauvre**. One of the first sanctuaries in the Ile de France region to have deserted Romanesque for Gothic, it has, since 1889, veered farther to the east in its vocation: St-Julien is the sole church in Paris where the mass of St. John Chrysostom, a Byzantine patriarch, is celebrated for Greek Catholics.

Farther downstream, across the old Roman road to Orléans, now called the rue St-Jacques, is another late-Medieval quarter that survived the great boulevard-building of the 19th century. Unlike its neighbor, the **St-Séverin quarter** has nothing genteel about it. It is the area of Paris that counts the most bouzouki players per square foot, and its tiny streets are crammed with Greek restaurants and take-out counters. Before deploring the current commercial state of the neighborhood, detractors should consult historian Robert Darnton's *Great Cat Massacre,* a study of the mock trial and execution of the area's cats that took place on the rue St-Séverin in the 1730s. It gives a fair idea of the grotesque entertainments enjoyed by the scribes, printers, and clerics who used to live and work in these streets. Fittingly, this peculiar neighborhood houses the minuscule theater (**Théâtre de la Huchette**) where nightly performances are given of Paris's longest-running show, two very absurd plays by Eugene Ionesco: *La Cantratrice Chauve* and *La Leçon.*

Despite the recent commercialization of the area, the St-Séverin quarter and the slightly more pleasant **St-André district** on the other side of the busy place St-Michel are still associated with eight centuries of student life. Even now, two decades after Paris's universities were dispersed throughout the city, this part of the Latin Quarter remains the symbolic home of student pranks—the hapless stroller or motorist who ventures into the area on Mardi Gras will be pelted with eggs and flour. This offense, however annoying, pales in comparison with the duels, cuckolding, and bawdy singing that once passed as normal behavior in the district. As early as the 12th century, students from the numerous religious colleges on the Cité found respite from their taskmasters in the alehouses of the area. Irreverence was the order of the day, with the inspirational choral singing known as the Ecole Notre-Dame finding its counterpoint in the licentious parodies belted out in Latin Quarter taverns. The best-known of these is the collection called "Carmina Burana." As Latin was the language of instruction and discourse in this quarter (hence its name), students of all nations were in on the earthy pleasantries.

Often tradition was flouted because it impeded knowledge. In Ian Littlewood's anecdotal *Paris: A Literary Companion,* a Medieval observer reports stumbling across a group of body snatchers at the St-Séverin cemetery—medical students, one hopes—intent on circumventing the Church's ban on the dissection of cadavers. Such applied skepticism has always been the hallmark of the area, ever since its earliest days when gifted rhetoricians drew crowds with their formal disputations. Pierre Abélard, in particular, was an idol of the neighborhood for his sheer genius in debate, handling contradictions and heckling with elegance and advancing novel ideas on the relation between Reason and Revelation, the central problem of Christian Medieval thought. His successors in the 13th and 14th centuries had a far more organized system of colleges at their disposal, and scholasticism found fertile ground for development in the scores of religious institutions then housed in the Latin Quarter. Thomas Aquinas, Albertus Magnus, and many other great thinkers spent stimulating years in the Université, as this collection of schools was called.

The only substantial physical relic of this period is the **Musée de Cluny**, a rich repository of art from the Middle Ages housed in a 15th-century mansion. (The entrance to this museum is on the tiny rue Sommerard, which leads into the boulevard St-Michel; for historical background, see the Burgundy and the Rhône Valley chapter, below.) The tapestry series on display in Room XI, "The Lady and the Unicorn," is in itself worth a visit. Illustrated with animals from the allegorical bestiary that inhabited the Medieval imagination, the subjects of the tapestries are the five senses. However, the meaning of the sixth and final tapestry in the series remains a beautiful mystery. Alongside the museum lie the extensive ruins of the splendid **Roman baths** that in the days of Lutetia occupied this part of the Left Bank. It should be noted that Cluny, like most state-run museums in the city, is closed on Tuesdays.

South of the Cluny are two competing giants of French thought, the Collège de France and the Sorbonne. Now undistinguished in appearance, they have been eminent rivals ever since King Francis I founded the Collège in 1530 as an intellectual counterweight to the dominant Sorbonne. Even today, the **Collège de France** prides itself on its anti-institutional slant, admitting anyone wishing to attend its public lectures. In recent years, Michel Foucault, Claude Lévi-Strauss, and Raymond Aron have given lecture series to halls packed with the studious, the curious, and just plain groupies. All you need to attend is an ability to decipher the arcane timetables posted outside the building.

Although most of its buildings date from the last century, the **Sorbonne** is one of the oldest universities in the world. Founded in 1253 by Robert de Sorbon, the confessor of Saint Louis, it quickly rose to preeminence among French universities, specializing in the study of theology and the defense of orthodoxy. A latter-day alumnus, Cardinal Richelieu, poured funds into restoring its facilities, and it is his impressive mausoleum, a 17th-century chapel, that overlooks the place de la Sorbonne. Paradoxically, this square, though it bears the name of an academy notorious for its ponderous resistance to change, has come to symbolize youthful revolt in France.

The most spectacular and far-reaching in effect of these outbursts occurred in May 1968, when a carnival spirit reigned in the quarter: The joyful anarchy and explosion of radical political thought almost toppled the central government. Chafing at the outdated formalism of university life and impatient with an older generation affected by its wartime experience, the *Soixante-huitards* (68ers) helped loosen the conservative bonds inhibiting French society. The revolt's climactic moment, both scorned and admired for its utter uselessness, was the occupation of the neighboring Odéon, the theater of an august state company that in the 1960s had been a showcase for contemporary drama under the direction of Jean-Louis Barrault. Although Barrault later lost his job for making clear where his sympathies lay, his Odéon will always be remembered for the spread of the movement's most dangerous idea: *L'imagination au pouvoir!* (Power to the imagination!). The legacy of this slogan and the revolt it inspired are still hotly debated in France today. For many Parisians now in early middle age, the acrid smell of tear gas that drifts over the capital from time to time is not so much a nuisance as it is a fragrant reminder of youth.

The Montagne Ste-Geneviève and the Contrescarpe

Two peculiar landmarks stand atop the Montagne Ste-Geneviève, a hill named after the fifth-century saint who convinced fleeing Parisians that Attila the Hun would bypass their town (which he did). The **Panthéon**, originally a pious project of Louis XV and Louis XVI, had the singular destiny of reaching completion just as the Revolution broke out. It passed the first century of its existence as an imposing question mark on the landscape, with successive regimes giving it to, then taking it from, the Church. Its definitive role as national mausoleum and temple of the Republic was established with the political stability of the late 19th century, when the body of Victor Hugo was installed with great pomp in its huge crypt. Other illustrious Frenchmen who now lie here are Voltaire and Rousseau (who poetically face each other for eternity), Emile Zola, Jean Jaurès, and Jean Moulin, the Resistance leader murdered by Klaus Barbie's men. The interior of the sanctuary is stridently nationalistic, and the enormous tableaux and other turn-of-the-century celebrations of the spirit of France are unsuited to modern tastes. At the same time that a reactionary Church was elevating its basilica of Sacré Coeur (yet another case of dubious aesthetics) on Montmartre, the progressive Third Republic was dressing up the Panthéon in the trappings of secular mysticism. The two domes still compete for attention on the Paris skyline.

The other striking monument on the hill is, indeed, a church, but it suffers from an earlier clash, relating almost entirely to taste. The interior of **St-Etienne-du-Mont** is Gothic—it is the only church in Paris to have kept its rood screen—yet the façade is a mishmash of Renaissance elements. Despite its confusing exterior, the church is of a rare beauty and provides a peaceful setting for a regular series of concerts (frequently featuring works by Vivaldi). Blaise Pascal, hedging his bet on salvation as in life, is buried here—not across the way in the Panthéon with the two giants of the Enlightenment.

Many of the streets winding down from the hilltop have considerable charm, particularly the **rue Mouffetard**, which follows the old Roman road from Paris to Lyon. Nothing from that distant Roman period exists here nowadays, although *la Mouffe* has kept the 20th century at bay much longer than have most Paris neighborhoods. Its upper stretch near the place de la Contrescarpe, despite a bewildering number of restaurants, is prized by sentimental Parisians fond of the local characters who are an enduring part of the human landscape of this quarter. On warm afternoons, an elderly bird lover known in the neighborhood as Madame Pigeon usually can be seen tending her flocks, always ready to share her encyclopedic knowledge of *la Mouffe* with passersby. Farther down the street toward its southern end the scene becomes unbearably picturesque, especially when the Mouffetard market opens for daily business. From behind the mounds of fruit and vegetables voluble merchants harangue shoppers in the flat accents of the native Parisian; in the cafés the clocks have stopped at the year 1900. The façade of the building at 134, rue Mouffetard, is easily Paris's most elaborately decorated storefront.

The other attractions of this *arrondissement* (the 5th) are notable for their diversity. Near the Seine, the **Jardin des Plantes** is a quiet haven of Enlightenment natural sciences, encompassing a small zoo (where the Sansculottes gaped in astonishment at the exotic animals that had been freed from royal menageries), rows of flowerbeds and herb gardens, mineralogical displays, musty old pavilions, and a cedar-of-Lebanon that was planted in 1734. In the summer of 1990, several important renovations were evident in Plantes: The Labyrinth had regained the aspect originally given it by naturalist Georges Leclerc, the Count de Buffon, in the 18th century. In addition, many tree-lined walks had been broadened, and the Alpine Garden, closed for years, had reopened. (In 1993 a gallery of evolution will open in the old zoological gallery.)

As is so often the case in this city, history has made strange bedfellows: The immediate neighbor of this Enlightenment garden is an enclave of non-Western values. The spiritual center of the hundreds of thousands of Muslims who have settled in France since the period of decolonization and subsequent North African immigration, the **Mosquée de Paris** is striking not only for its Hispano-Moorish beauty but also for its symbolic importance. As a new multiconfessional, multiracial France takes shape for the future (not without some bitter resistance from antediluvian nationalists), the cultures and customs of North Africa are more and more entering the French mainstream with the maturing of each successive generation. Although admittance to the mosque itself is reserved exclusively for the faithful, the adjoining gardens, tearoom, study center, and *hamam* (bathhouse) have become a meeting place for France and Islam, with Parisians of all backgrounds frequenting the facility. After a sybaritic evening spent in a Paris restaurant, many head to the mosque's soothing hamam for relief. Be sure to pick your night of excess carefully: The bath is open to women on Monday, Tuesday, Wednesday, Thursday, and Saturday, and to men on Friday and Sunday. Movie fans will be interested in knowing that Rita Hayworth married the son of the Aga Khan in this mosque.

The importance of Arabic cultures is emphasized further by a new presence along the Seine, a few yards west of the Jardin des Plantes along the Quai Saint Bernard: the **Institute of the Arab World**. It's open to the public afternoons except Monday and offers fine views and a restaurant.

Just a javelin's throw from the mosque and the Jardin des Plantes lies the Roman amphitheater of Paris. Much restored, the **Arènes de Lutèce** is an oasis of antiquity in the midst of a busy neighborhood, a perfect place to relax on a warm summer's day and watch the men play *boules* or the boys torture their younger brothers. For those with a taste for more organized carnage, the last week of June is particularly satisfying, for it is then that a professional stuntmen's association stages mock gladiator battles and other edifying spectacles in the arena.

St-Germain-des-Prés and the Jardin du Luxembourg

The **Pont des Arts**, an aptly named footbridge linking the galleries of the Louvre to the Left Bank, draws visitor and

Parisian alike to its unobstructed view of the Ile de la Cité to the east and the often brilliant sunsets over the Seine to the west. The Baroque edifice closing off the perspective to the south—the **Institut de France**—is notable for its dome, which, like Richelieu's Chapel of the Sorbonne, serves as a monument to a 17th-century cardinal with a flair for statecraft and intrigue. In this case the ostentatious prelate was Cardinal Mazarin, the gray eminence who ensured the transition from Louis XIII to Louis XIV.

The domed building is also home to the **Académie Française**, which is charged with removing, or at least recording, impurities that have crept into the French language. Admission to the Academy marks the official consecration of a French intellectual during his or her lifetime, although many intellectuals are quick to point out that truly great artists and thinkers have often been passed over in favor of inoffensive mediocrities. This may be a sour-grapes argument, or, more probably, the usual Parisian attitude of deference and derision toward the *académiciens*. The Academy's closest neighbors most clearly express these mixed feelings. Opposite the refined reading rooms beneath the dome stand the windswept bookstalls lining the Seine, which carry everything from faded photographs of James Dean to erotic novels and quirky monographs (as in a recent find, *Women Who Said No to Napoléon*). The *bouquinistes* (booksellers) are Paris's tribute to chaotic erudition, a tradition that is slightly older than the Academy itself: They first set up shop on the nearby Pont Neuf three decades before the founding of the Académie Française in 1635.

Through a short passageway in the Academy's west wing lies the rue de Seine, the main street of the **Beaux-Arts quarter**. Two small squares at its lower end contain statues that seem to have been placed here as a parting shot at the Academy: Voltaire, a true immortal, snickers at the *académiciens,* and Carolina, a naked girl, stares defiantly at the temple of official culture. The young nude is doubly appropriate, for she also stands at the entrance to an area given over almost entirely to the study and sale of art. Galleries, art bookstores, and art-supply shops crowd the narrow streets, which are often teeming with students from the nearby **Ecole Nationale des Beaux-Arts**. The cafés here are welcoming and informal, sometimes subjected to impromptu concerts by what may rank as the world's worst brass band, *le fanfare des Beaux-Arts*. This mix of art and frivolity has long made the neighborhood a

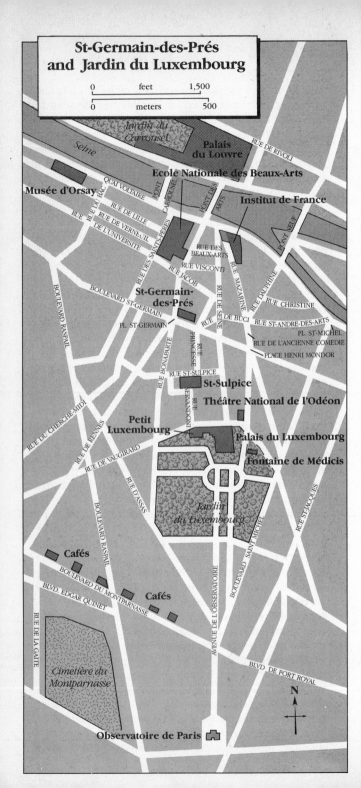

magnet for aesthetes of all nations. An ailing Oscar Wilde, who said of the rates at his hotel at 13, rue des Beaux Arts, "I'm dying beyond my means," is also reported to have looked at the wallpaper from his deathbed and sighed, "One of us will have to go." Parallel to Wilde's street is the tiny rue Visconti, one of the quarter's oldest. Formerly called rue des Marais-St-Germain, it was nicknamed "Little Geneva" for its Huguenot inhabitants in the mid-1500s, and in later periods it housed Racine, Molière, Balzac, Merimée, and Delacroix. Stendhal's masterpiece, *The Red and the Black,* was first printed here. A more recent fictional creation, the loathsome Grenouille of Patrick Süskind's *Perfume,* killed his first red-headed virgin in this street.

The most renowned spot of the Left Bank is the **place St-Germain-des-Prés**, from which the visitor can get a good idea of the radical changes Paris has undergone over the centuries. To the north is the Beaux-Arts district with its late Medieval façades; to the west, the 18th-century Faubourg St-Germain and the famous cafés of postwar Paris; to the south, the broad avenues of the 19th century and the tall Tour Montparnasse (a high-rise office tower) of the 20th; and to the east, the **abbey church of St-Germain** itself, a remnant of a time when this area was meadowland (*les prés*) cultivated by Benedictine monks. The Romanesque lines of the distinctive bell tower hint at the sanctuary's considerable age— Pope Alexander III consecrated the enlarged choir of this church only a few days before laying the cornerstone of Notre-Dame. Founded in the times of the Merovingian kings, the monastery recovered from the ravages of Viking raids in the ninth century and became prosperous around the year 1000, when the Cluniac reform of the Benedictines infused the order with renewed faith and vigor. Since then St-Germain has always figured prominently in the Parisian landscape, for many centuries as a rich country estate just beyond the city walls.

To the modern mind, St-Germain-des-Prés is associated with the Paris of the 1940s and 1950s, when prominent artists and intellectuals frequented the **Deux Magots** and **Flore** cafés. Simone Signoret, in her autobiography, *Nostalgia Isn't What It Used to Be,* gives a vivid description of the wartime Flore and its cast of artists, writers, and charlatans living a precarious existence in Nazi-occupied Paris. Just a few blocks away on the boulevard Raspail, the

Hôtel Lutetia served as Gestapo headquarters. After the war—perhaps because of it—existentialism and its message of hopelessness as a spur to action became the vogue in these literary cafés and in the nearby **Brasserie Lipp**, the upstairs dining room of which is still a favorite haunt of fast-talking intellectuals and hungry politicians. Thus, in the postwar period Jean-Paul Sartre and Simone de Beauvoir reigned as the undisputed sovereigns of daytime St-Germain. Night was the province of Boris Vian, a gifted writer and trumpeter who celebrated the cult of jazz in the many cellar clubs of the district. As France became embroiled in the Indo-Chinese War and memories of right-wing Vichy collaborators remained fresh, many of the intellectuals of St-Germain turned to Moscow for political inspiration—just as, at the same time, they were turning to New Orleans for enjoyment.

The contradictions are different now, as is the intellectual tenor of café life, but St-Germain has kept faith with some of its traditions. The center of France's publishing industry and, as such, the quarter of Paris with the greatest profusion of bookstores, it is also a popular area for nightlife. The **boulevard St-Germain** is lively well into the small hours of the morning, the crowds growing younger as you head eastward to the Latin Quarter. The two districts converge at the place Henri Mondor, a cinema-lined square dominated by a statue of Georges-Jacques Danton, a former resident of the area. Down the rue de l'Ancienne Comédie is the **Procope**, a café (now a restaurant) where revolutions—intellectual and political—have been hatched since the late 17th century. Behind the Procope runs an inconspicuous alleyway called the cour du Commerce-St-André, built alongside the Medieval ramparts erected by King Philip II Augustus (a vestige of a tower can be seen inside number 4). Nearby, at number 9, a certain Dr. J. I. Guillotin tested a machine that was to inspire terror in royalist and revolutionary alike. Danton, whose statue now stands proudly a few feet away in the square, was one of its many victims.

Slightly off the beaten track and, mercifully, much quieter than the boulevard, is the lovely square and fountain in front of the **church of St-Sulpice**. Slightly bombastic in appearance for a simple parish church built for the lay community that had grown up around the St-Germain monastery, St-Sulpice is best viewed at sunset, when the fading light softens the harsh stone and unforgiving classicism of its façade. Among the devotional works inside the church are three striking tableaux by Eugène Delacroix (whose studio on the nearby place Fürstemberg can be visited). The emptiness of the square outside of St-Sulpice is relieved only in June at successive antiques and poetry fairs that take place around the central fountain. As befits a literary neighborhood, the given name of this fountain, les Quatre Points Cardinaux (the Four Cardinal Points), is an elaborate pun: Depicting four churchmen facing the cardinal compass points, the fountain honors prelates whose defense of the Gallican church against Vatican interference guaranteed that they would not rise far in the Roman hierarchy—hence, they were *point* (which also means "not at all") cardinals.

By far the best way to escape the bustle of both the Latin Quarter and St-Germain-des-Prés is to enter the **Jardin du Luxembourg**, a large expanse of greenery to the south of these districts. It is arguably the city's most entertaining park. In its western reaches, near the Orangerie, old men play interminable games of chess, young couples afflicted with romantic melancholia stroll through the *jardins à l'anglaise,* which are dotted with statues of literary greats (and a miniature Statue of Liberty), and at the Grand Guignol, the French equivalent of Punch and Judy, the real stars of the show are the enthusiastic young spectators. A formal French garden flanked by terraces adorned with statues of great French women of the past makes up the central part of the park. A long prospect to the south opens onto the tree-lined avenue de l'Observatoire, so called for the domed observatory visible in the distance. Yet another institution inspired by the Enlightenment, the observatory fought to make its meridian the division between Eastern and Western hemispheres but lost this honor to Greenwich. As a result, the linear arbor leading from the Luxembourg is a rather prosaic 2° 20′ 14″ E.

The eastern edge of the Luxembourg encloses one of the most beautiful spots in the city, a rectangular pond surmounted by a three-tiered fountain on which the lovers Galatea and Acis are watched over by the giant Polyphemus. Overhanging plane trees cover the water with an uneven carpet of leaves, beneath which golden carp swim about languidly. Although the statuary dates from the Second Empire, the Italianate pond, called the **Fontaine de Médicis**, has remained unchanged since the early 17th century, when the widowed queen of Henry IV ordered the construction of the neighboring **Palais du**

Luxembourg. Marie de Médicis, who felt no compunction about raiding her late husband's treasury at the Bastille for funds, wanted to reproduce here the Pitti Palace of her beloved Florence. Though thwarted in this grand design, she managed to complete the palace and gardens even while plotting and counterplotting intrigues during the regency of her young son, Louis XIII. Rubens's 21 tableaux depicting her life, now hanging in the Louvre, do not represent Marie's final fate: death in exile, ultimately outfoxed by Richelieu. Her sumptuous palace is now occupied by the French Senate, a respected but powerless group of legislators. For readers of Dumas *père* uninterested in such contemporary niceties, the place to continue musing about Richelieu's perfidy is in the quiet neighborhood between the Luxembourg and St-Sulpice: At 12, rue Servandoni lived the thorn in the cardinal's side, the musketeer D'Artagnan.

In the 1920s the Jardin du Luxembourg served as the inexpensive alternative to the nearby cafés of **Montparnasse.** Although still a thriving boulevard dotted with restaurants, cafés, and movie houses, Montparnasse retains little of the flavor of its wild days when John Glassco, in his hilarious *Memoirs of Montparnasse,* could write about partying with Kiki (Man Ray's model), cajoling Emma Goldman out of a post-Bolshevik funk, and drinking heavily with French surrealists and American writers. Café society, especially at the **Coupole** and the **Select**, can still be slightly subversive, even if the spread of offices following the erection of the Tour Montparnasse has made the area more business-minded. Aside from its Lost Generation lore, which is still powerful enough to make you self-conscious about writing so much as a postcard in these cafés, the area has two further attractions: a Breton enclave near the boulevard Edgar Quinet, with crêperies and cider-fueled merriment, and a small theater district on the rue de la Gaîté. But Zelda and her friends have long gone, some of them to the nearby **Cimetière du Montparnasse.** An avant-garde pantheon from the 19th and 20th centuries, this burial ground shelters the graves of Baudelaire, Tsara, Zadkine, De Maupassant, and, of course, Sartre and De Beauvoir.

From Orsay to the Eiffel Tower

The Faubourg St-Germain, the area stretching from the rue des Saints-Pères to the Invalides, has remained frustratingly impenetrable to the commoner, its aristocratic 18th-century homes and gardens hidden behind massive stone gates. Developed when the nobility left the cramped streets of the old Marais district for the then wide-open spaces of the Grenelle Plain west of the St-Germain abbey, the Faubourg lost its ancien régime exclusiveness with the coming of the Revolution and the Bonapartes. The early 19th-century salons of the lovely Madame Récamier and the brilliant Madame de Staël restored some of the quarter's lost cachet, and even today a few fading dynasties match wits and offspring in the Proustian calm of their Faubourg drawing rooms. Still, most of these fine old homes are now occupied by government grandees, and the prospect of an elegant ministry here undoubtedly fuels the ambitions of provincial politicians. The Hôtel Matignon, its property encompassing Paris's largest private park, is reserved for the prime minister, the public figure who is expected to thrive best in the miasma of French party politics. Fittingly, Matignon's fashionable rue de Varenne address was on the calling card of French history's most formidable political survivor, Charles-Maurice de Talleyrand.

If the houses of the Faubourg remain closed to the curious, at least some elements of their decor are on view—and on sale—to the public in the **Carré Rive Gauche,** a grid of streets bordered on the north by the quai Voltaire. Its concentration of antiques and furniture shops makes window shopping here a rewarding pastime, particularly in May, when the *carré*'s Days of the Extraordinary Object give pride of place to some truly weird creations foisted on old and new money alike. An entertaining appraisal of the carré appears in "Old Paris," a sardonic essay by Saul Bellow: "Who would have thought that Europe contained so much old junk? Or that, the servant class having disappeared, hearts nostalgic for the bourgeois epoch would hunt so eagerly for Empire breakfronts, Récamier sofas, and curule chairs?"

Nostalgia for the 19th century runs even deeper at the nearby **Musée d'Orsay,** a refurbished Belle Epoque railway terminal that houses the city's rich artistic legacy from the period 1848 to 1914. The creation of this mammoth new way station in the art lover's tour of Paris brought about the removal here of the collection of French Impressionists from its quaint isolation in the Jeu de Paume pavilion of the Tuileries. In many ways, its transfer to a train station is appropriate, given the Impressionists' conviction that

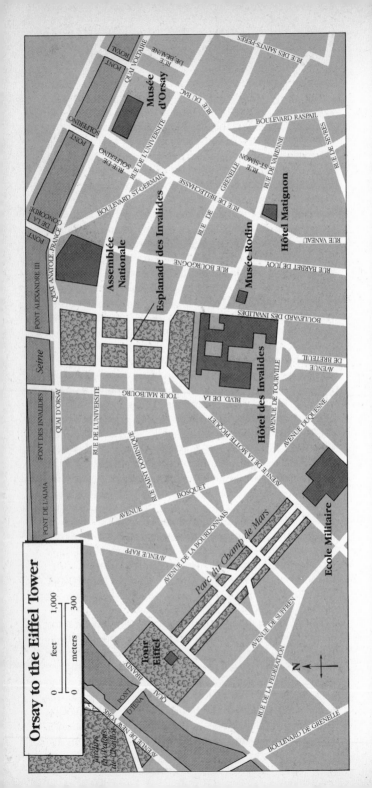

Orsay to the Eiffel Tower

feet 1,000
0
meters 300
0

Musée d'Orsay

QUAI VOLTAIRE
RUE DE BEAUNE
RUE DES SAINTS-PÈRES
RUE DU BAC

BOULEVARD RASPAIL

PONT SOLFÉRINO

RUE DE SOLFÉRINO
RUE DE L'UNIVERSITÉ

BOULEVARD ST-GERMAIN
RUE DE GRENELLE
RUE DE VARENNE
RUE DE SÈVRES
RUE DE BELLECHASSE
RUE-ST-SIMON

Hôtel Matignon

PONT DE LA CONCORDE
QUAI ANATOLE FRANCE

Assemblée Nationale
Esplanade des Invalides
RUE DE
Musée Rodin
RUE BOURGOGNE
RUE VANEAU

PONT ALEXANDRE III

Seine

RUE BARBET DE JOUY

BOULEVARD DES INVALIDES

PONT DES INVALIDES
QUAI D'ORSAY

RUE DE L'UNIVERSITÉ
TOUR MAUBOURG

Hôtel des Invalides
BLVD. DE LA
AVENUE DE TOURVILLE
AVENUE DE BRETEUIL

PONT DE L'ALMA
RUE SAINT DOMINIQUE

AVENUE
BOSQUET

AVENUE DE LA MOTTE PICQUET
AVENUE DE LA BOURDONNAIS
AVENUE RAPP

AVENUE DUQUESNE

Parc du Champ de Mars

Ecole Militaire

QUAI BRANLY
Tour Eiffel

AVENUE DE SUFFREN
AVENUE DE LA FÉDÉRATION

PONT D'IÉNA
AVENUE DE NEW YORK

BOULEVARD DE GRENELLE

Jardins du Palais de Chaillot

N

scenes from everyday life, whether in the country or in the city (indeed, the Gare St-Lazare served Claude Monet as inspiration), were worthy subjects for the painter. Some critics have faulted the Orsay for being indiscriminate in its all-embracing sweep of the 19th century and for giving *pompier* excesses as much exposure as recognized masterpieces. Whatever its contradictions in presentation and contents, Orsay stands as a striking testament to France's continued expertise in converting old buildings to new uses. Whether the result is philistine is a question that visitors must answer for themselves. Those with a taste for coherence can play with the interactive video monitors designed to explain how the social context of France's tempestuous 19th century influenced the bewildering variety of artistic expression housed in the museum. A less intellectual but far more heady pleasure is to visit the museum's top-floor coffee shop and walk out onto the balcony—between the train station's mammoth outdoor clocks—for a commanding view of the Right Bank to the north.

The Hôtel Biron, an older example of a successfully converted building and the only 18th-century home in the area that is open to the public, stands at the opposite corner of the Faubourg St-Germain. In 1910 the French government reserved this property for the use of artists, among them Isadora Duncan, Henri Matisse, Rainer Maria Rilke, and Auguste Rodin. Rodin later signed an agreement bequeathing his work to the State in exchange for freedom to work and live in the Hôtel Biron at public expense. The result of this ideal arrangement is the **Musée Rodin**, a quiet, sensual place where such sculptures as *The Kiss, The Thinker,* and *The Burghers of Calais* blend in surprisingly well with their Neoclassical surroundings. Recently, the work of the gifted Camille Claudel, the mistress of the sculptor—her high-strung genius brought her to a tragic end in an asylum for the insane—has belatedly emerged from her lover's shadow and received public recognition in its own right. Her life story is often cited by French feminists as a cautionary tale of great talent frustrated by misogynist times.

The Rodin museum's low-key celebration of the arts of love is in contrast to the full-blown cult of martial glory displayed by the neighboring **Invalides**. An imposing Parisian landmark since its completion in 1706, the Invalides is Louis XIV's legacy to the capital he shunned for Versailles. The king's numerous wars of conquest, although successful in expanding the borders of France and ensuring his reputation as Europe's most powerful monarch, brought about great human misery, some of which this veterans' hospital tried to alleviate. The humanitarian impulse was gradually supplanted by the desire to make the building a showplace for French arms: Indeed, the Revolution, hardly sympathetic to past royal initiatives, made the place a Temple of Mars, and the Invalides became a museum honoring French soldiery. Thus it is appropriate, if anachronistic, that Jules Hardouin-Mansart's superb domed church is principally known as the mausoleum of Napoléon Bonaparte, the greatest soldier France has ever produced. In the eyes of French nationalists, the stature of the two historical figures connected with the Invalides, the Emperor and the Sun King, augments its prestige, making the place a symbol of the grandeur of their country. For those of other political persuasions, the evocation of grandeur is a defense of absolutism and should, like the Invalides itself, be avoided.

These two strong opposing viewpoints, the desire for a strong central authority and the egalitarian impulse, have been at war in the French mind since 1789, and the struggle is still evident in the contemporary Fifth Republic, in which a multitude of elective offices are dwarfed by the tremendous power of the president. The bridge linking the Esplanade des Invalides to the Right Bank is a more striking illustration of this long-standing ambiguity. Built for the World's Fair of 1900, when many politicians of the Third Republic were fighting the antidemocratic forces of Church and Army (on such issues as public education and the Dreyfus Affair, respectively), the **Pont Alexandre III** honors the most absolutist regime of its time, the Russia of the tsars. True, anti-Prussian motives had made France and Tsar Nicholas II unlikely allies, yet the mere fact that Paris, the reputedly godless, regicidal capital of a progressive republic, could build such an exuberant monument to an autocrat is still something of a wonder today. It is also our good fortune: The bridge's ornamentation and statuary (the central groups depict the Seine and Neva rivers) make it an overdone Belle Epoque gem and, as such, very photogenic.

Farther downstream, the river is spanned by the **Pont de l'Alma**, famous for the Zouave (French-Algerian soldier) standing at its base and acting as the city's unofficial marker of high and low waters. It may come as a relief to know that the bridge's neighboring attractions have nothing to do with art or politics. On the Left Bank is the public entrance to the sewers of Paris, a 19th-century engineering achievement that can be visited—whenever the Seine is well below the Zouave's feet—on Monday and Wednesday as well as the last Saturday of every month. Across the river on the Right Bank lies the main embarkation point for the **bateaux-mouches**, the monstrously large glass tour boats that ply the Seine year-round. Contrary to the prejudices of seasoned travellers, these boats are not tourist traps. A quick tour of Paris's riverfront is beautiful day or night, provided you can put up with a tiresome recorded spiel in every major European language (it's best to sit outside). The dinner boat, however, takes too long to make the circuit but not long enough to allow for a leisurely Parisian feast; far better to take the regular cruise and dine at a good restaurant on shore. For those with a lot of time to kill, there is the newly inaugurated Batobus (bus-boat) that plies the Seine. Not quite vaporetti, the Batobus fleet—old bateaux-mouches bought by the city—dallies maddeningly at each stop, making a full circuit of the Seine an afternoon proposition. At 30 francs a ticket, it might be better to wait until the transit authority irons the bugs out of this service.

In addition to the bateaux-mouches and Batobus, five other companies operate various craft on the Seine and its canals. Of particular interest to those who've already "done" the Seine are the three-hour Canal St-Martin cruises of Canauxrama, and the cruises of Paris-Canal boats (also three hours) between the Musée d'Orsay and Parc de la Villette.

The westernmost part of this large swath of the Left Bank is taken up by the **Champs de Mars**, the elegant park that once served as a parade ground for the Ecole Militaire. When Napoléon was graduated from this academy in 1785, his instructor's prescient evaluation of Bonaparte read, "Will go far, if circumstances permit." Aside from its military past and its rare status as a Parisian park where you are allowed to sit on the grass (a little beyond the midway point to the river, off the side alleys), the Champs de Mars is most famous for its riverside monument, the **Eiffel Tower**. Built for the World's Fair of 1889, the tower was intended to be the iron icon of France's industrial and engineering might—and to be a temporary structure. Civic pride over having the world's tallest structure at that time forestalled demolition, and the invention of the wireless gave Gustav Eiffel's implausible creation a new lease on life as a radio mast. Its ironwork seems surprisingly light and delicate to 20th-century eyes, particularly when viewed from directly beneath the structure, and recent renovations have been hailed by all Parisians as a success. The nighttime illumination creates the illusion that the tower is covered in cheap gold-colored paint, making it the world's largest souvenir of itself. Long a symbol of the industrial age, the Eiffel Tower is now entering its second century as Paris's most unexpected tribute to Postmodernism.

The Champs de Mars is only one of Paris's popular outbursts of greenery, and may become a hallmark of the 1990s. It will be completely reworked and replanted from the foot of the Eiffel Tower to its opposite end at place Joffre. The project began in August 1990 and should be finished by March 1991.

THE RIGHT BANK
The 16th *Arrondissement* and the Bois de Boulogne

There are few places where the performance aspect of Paris is more in evidence than on the Right Bank across the Seine from the Eiffel Tower. The hilltop **Palais de Chaillot**, built for the 1937 World's Fair at the place du Trocadéro, forms a large Art Deco backdrop to the play of fountains in the gardens sloping down toward the Seine. Monumental statues adorn these fountains, which send their powerful jets of water spraying out over a long reflecting pool. This area and the terrace above, a striking lookout over the Left Bank, are the playgrounds of roller skaters, skateboarders, and members of other strenuous urban subcultures who suspend their year-round cavorting at Chaillot only for such special occasions as Bastille Day, when the palace is brilliantly illuminated by fireworks.

The two wings of the palace make up an impressive cultural complex containing a major national theater and three large museums: the **Musée de la Marine** (begun by Louis XIV's minister, Jean-Baptiste Colbert), the **Musée de l'Homme** (the showcase of French anthropology), and the **Musée des Monuments Français** (featuring reproductions of the finest works of art to be found in the French provinces). Down the avenue Président-Wilson are three other museums of note. The **Musée Guimet** houses a

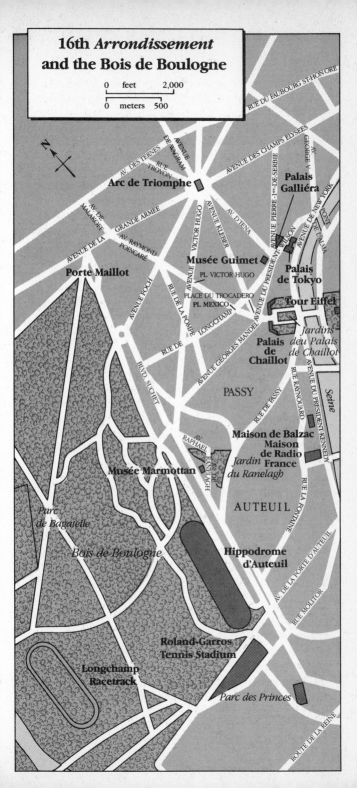

16th *Arrondissement*
and the Bois de Boulogne

| 0 | feet | 2,000 |
| 0 | meters | 500 |

Arc de Triomphe

Palais Galliéra

AVENUE DES CHAMPS ELYSÉES

RUE DU FAUBOURG ST-HONORE

AV. DES TERNES

AVENUE DE WAGRAM

RUE TROYON

AV. GEORGE V

AVENUE PIERRE 1er-DE-SERBIE

AV. DE MALAKOFF

AVENUE DE LA GRANDE ARMÉE

AV. RAYMOND POINCARÉ

AVENUE DE NEW YORK

AVENUE FOCH

AVENUE KLEBER

AVENUE D'IENA

AVENUE VICTOR HUGO

AVENUE DE L'ALMA

Porte Maillot

Musée Guimet

PL. VICTOR HUGO

PLACE DU TROCADERO

PL. MEXICO

Palais de Tokyo

Tour Eiffel

RUE DE LA POMPE

RUE DE LONGCHAMP

RUE DE LA POMPE

AVENUE GEORGES MANDEL

AVENUE DU PRÉSIDENT-WILSON

Jardins deu Palais de Chaillot

Palais de Chaillot

BLVD. SUCHET

AVENUE GEORGES MANDEL

PASSY

RUE DE PASSY

AVENUE DU PRÉSIDENT-KENNEDY

RUE RAYNOUARD

Seine

AV. RAPHAEL

AV. DU RANELAGH

Maison de Balzac

Maison de Radio France

Musée Marmottan

Jardin du Ranelagh

AUTEUIL

RUE LA FONTAINE

Parc de Bagatelle

Bois de Boulogne

Hippodrome d'Auteuil

AV. DE LA PORTE D'AUTEUIL

RUE MOLITOR

Roland-Garros Tennis Stadium

Longchamp Racetrack

Parc des Princes

ROUTE DE LA REINE

world-famous collection of art from the Far East, while two neighboring palaces, **Galliéra** and **Tokyo**, respectively, exhibit clothing fashions dating back to the 18th century and the municipality's modern art holdings. The Tokyo Palace was built for the 1937 World's Fair and, like its larger contemporary atop the Chaillot hill, serves several purposes. The gallery's photographic exhibits are extremely popular with Parisians, especially during the biennial Mois de la Photo, a citywide celebration of the camera held in November. It also houses France's *cinémathèque,* which contains the celluloid archives of the nation and has several screening rooms open to the public.

On the southern slope of the Chaillot hill stretches the quiet neighborhood of **Passy**. Literary pilgrims can visit the house at 47, rue Raynouard, where Balzac lived from 1840 to 1847. Constantly beset by creditors, the author of the *Comédie Humaine* became one of its most colorful characters by residing in this suburban hideout expressly to evade bill collectors (an exit at a lower level made it easy for him to disappear at the sound of a door knocker). Balzac's coffeepot, in which he brewed the stuff that kept him awake and writing through the long nights, now sits idly on display.

Passy and its environs have since been swallowed up by the 16th *arrondissement,* the district of Paris known for its splendid isolation. Long a bucolic retreat for aristocrats, artists, and diplomats (Benjamin Franklin spent many years in Passy), the area developed into a fashionable residential quarter at the close of the last century, when most of its stately apartments were built. Today the 16th is home to the Parisians satirically known as the BCBG (*bon chic, bon genre*), the well-scrubbed, well-off, well-dressed conservatives who can be seen, their dogs at their feet, sipping drinks in the fashionable cafés of the place du Trocadéro and place Victor Hugo. At night this residential district is dead, especially in the summer months when its inhabitants answer the call of the civilized and move out to their country homes. Passy's Jardin du Ranelagh serves as a nursery for their impeccably turned-out toddlers and as an elegant antechamber for visiting lovers of Monet—nearby on rue L. Broilly is the **Musée Marmottan**, where many of the painter's greatest works are on exhibit.

Although the 16th is deserted at night, the same cannot be said of the neighboring **Bois de Boulogne**, which as soon as the sun sets becomes the hunting ground of peculiar human fauna. In the daytime, however, the 2,200-plus-acre park is populated with more innocent pleasure seekers who stroll, jog, cycle (bikes can be rented near the Jardin d'Acclimatation), or ride horses through its maze of forest pathways. On the urging of Napoléon III (in perhaps the only of his many town-planning initiatives to be universally applauded by Parisians), the designers of the Bois set about creating a Hyde Park for Paris, their Anglophilia driving them so far as to plant a Shakespeare Garden at its heart. This enclosure features all of the flora the Bard ever mentioned in his works. Of the park's many attractions (restaurants, artificial lakes, country clubs, children's playgrounds), the oldest is Bagatelle, a country pavilion that the count of Artois constructed in the record time of seven weeks to win a bet with his sister-in-law, Marie Antoinette. However charming this *folie* may be, it is Bagatelle's floral gardens that more truly merit a visit. The azaleas (April) and roses (June and July) draw crowds of admirers whom the resident·peacocks assume to be well-wishers. The combination of colorful flowerbeds and proud peacocks can be quite spectacular.

Peacocks of the human variety are on display at the Bois de Boulogne's most famous attraction, the **Long-champ racetrack**. On the first Sunday in October, the plumage becomes extravagant at the main event of the season, the Prix de l'Arc de Triomphe, Europe's richest horse race. The Longchamp tradition stretches back to Second Empire days of ostentatious social jockeying and still retains a certain cachet. Auteuil, the other track of the Bois, is definitely the poor cousin, although its immediate neighbor, the **Roland-Garros** tennis stadium, has lately risen in social standing, and tickets to the French Open in May are now very difficult to obtain. South of the Bois is another sports venue, the Parc des Princes, where French soccer and rugby matches are played.

From the Arc de Triomphe
to the Tuileries

From atop the **Arc de Triomphe**, Napoléon's monument to his military invincibility (completed 21 years after Waterloo), the visitor has a good view of imperial Paris and the 12 avenues radiating from the Etoile, the star. Far to

the west are the towers of La Défense, a suburban business district where striking skyscrapers and wind-tunnel
esplanades successfully suggest the might of corporate
France. A massive new arch, glorifying communications
and media, was splashily opened during France's bicentennial summer at La Défense. It is the final monument in
the prospect that runs from the Louvre's place du
Carrousel, up the Champs-Elysées, and out of the city. All
told, this triumphal way counts three arches (Napoléon is
celebrated by another Arc de Triomphe, smaller and
more graceful, at the eastern end of the Tuileries), an
Egyptian obelisk (in the place de la Concorde), and an
equestrian statue by Bernini (in the place du Carrousel).
It should hardly come as a surprise that Bernini's horseman is Louis XIV, Napoléon's ancien régime counterpart
in the grandeur stakes.

In fact, the whole failed point of the Champs-Elysées is
grandeur. From its beginnings, when Louis XIV's landscap-
ing genius, André Le Nôtre, first laid it out as a tree-lined
prospect stretching from the Jardin des Tuileries to a
distant, elevated horizon, the avenue was intended to
represent the sublime and the permanent. Instead, it has
been the theater of the temporary, largely because its
development took place during France's stormy 19th century. When the avenue was saddled with a name evocative
of the gods walking the Elysian Fields, its fate as colossal
irony was sealed. From the Palais de l'Elysée, Louis-
Napoléon (the emperor's nephew) engineered the over-
throw of the Second Republic in order to set himself up
as a mid-century Augustus, leading Karl Marx to remark of
this Bonapartist replay on the avenue, "History occurs
first as tragedy, then repeats itself as farce." As Emperor
Napoléon III, Louis lived in absolutist style in the 16th-
century Tuileries palace, only to be run out of the country
in 1870 after being utterly humiliated in the war against
Bismarck's Prussians. A year later, embittered Parisians
put the palace to the torch during the Communard uprising, thereby giving notice that they had had enough of
imperial pretensions from their rulers. The avenue's opulent mansions, built by 19th-century capitalists who were
as ostentatious as Faubourg-St-Germain aristocrats were
discreet, gradually fell under the wrecker's ball, to be
replaced by office buildings and apartments. (A remarkable survivor stands at number 25.)

Today the Champs-Elysées serves as a stage for Republican spectacles. The French president resides in the

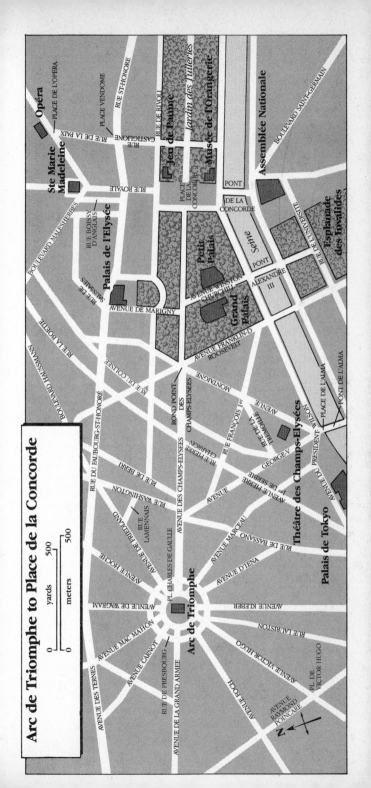

Arc de Triomphe to Place de la Concorde

Opéra
PLACE DE L'OPÉRA
RUE DE LA PAIX
Ste Marie Madeleine
RUE ROYALE
BOULEVARD MALESHERBES
RUE BOISSY D'ANGLAIS
Palais de l'Elysée
RUE DE SAUSSAIES
RUE LA BOËTIE
BOULEVARD HAUSSMANN
AVENUE DE MARIGNY
RUE DU COLISÉE
ROND POINT DES CHAMPS-ELYSÉES
RUE DU FAUBOURG-ST-HONORÉ
RUE DE BERRI
RUE WASHINGTON
RUE LAMENNAIS
AVENUE DE FRIEDLAND
AVENUE HOCHE
AVENUE DES TERNES
AVENUE MAC MAHON
AVENUE CARNOT
RUE DE PRESBOURG
AVENUE DE LA GRANDE ARMÉE
PL. CHARLES DE GAULLE
Arc de Triomphe
AVENUE DE WAGRAM
AVENUE DES CHAMPS-ELYSÉES
AVENUE KLÉBER
RUE LAURISTON
AVENUE VICTOR HUGO
AVENUE D'IENA
AVENUE MARCEAU
AVENUE RAYMOND POINCARÉ
AVENUE FOCH
PL. DE VICTOR HUGO
AVENUE DE BASSANO
RUE DE BELLOY
RUE PIERRE 1er DE SERBIE
GEORGE-V
AVENUE MONTAIGNE
RUE PIERRE CHARRON
RUE FRANÇOIS 1er
RUE MARBEUF
Théâtre des Champs-Elysées
Palais de Tokyo
AVENUE DU PRÉSIDENT-WILSON
PLACE DE L'ALMA
PONT DE L'ALMA
AVENUE FRANKLIN-D. ROOSEVELT
Grand Palais
Petit Palais
AVENUE WINSTON CHURCHILL
ALEXANDRE III
PONT
Seine
PONT DE LA CONCORDE
Place de la Concorde
Jeu de Paume
Jardin des Tuileries
Musée de l'Orangerie
RUE DE RIVOLI
RUE ST-HONORÉ
RUE DE PAIME
RUE CASTIGLIONE
PLACE VENDÔME
Assemblée Nationale
BOULEVARD SAINT-GERMAIN
RUE DE L'UNIVERSITÉ
Esplanade des Invalides

yards 500
meters 500

N

Palais de l'Elysée, receiving dignitaries in a style that the building's best-known tenant, Madame de Pompadour, would find congenial. On July 14, Bastille Day, the avenue becomes a parade ground for the army, the latest in French weaponry passing in review of the president and thousands of patriotic Parisians. As on other anniversaries of martial significance, a giant tricolor hangs from the Arc de Triomphe, giving rise in many hearts to what is sardonically called *"cocorico"* ("cock-a-doodle-do," or chauvinistic nationalism). Whatever misfortunes have befallen the French army in the past one hundred years, the grandiose—and to many Frenchmen, moving—sight of the flag billowing above the tomb of the unknown soldier is a reminder of past sacrifices and victories.

Fortunately, the avenue's aspirations to grandeur are overshadowed by its pursuit of the frivolous. Despite its historical significance, the **Etoile** (officially place Charles-de-Gaulle), for many Parisians, is simply the most exhilarating place in the city to drive, especially at night at a fast clip. (Do not even consider walking across the Etoile to get to the Arc; take the lifesaving underground passageway instead.) The best way to visit the **Champs-Elysées** is on foot, with occasional stops to watch everybody watching everybody else. Here is where the urban myth of the extortionate price of coffee in Paris actually has some grounding in fact, so be prepared to nurse a demitasse of espresso for as long as you care to sit and stare. The walker should also cross the street at least once, pausing in the middle of the roadway to get the full effect of the monumental symmetry and the blinking lights of the long lines of traffic. The speed at which this traffic whizzes past accounts for the absence of cyclists: The only time they appear in any number is at the end of July, when the month-long Tour de France bicycle race concludes here in a blaze of publicity.

For all its bright lights, the modern-day showiness of the Champs-Elysées is fairly empty and need only be taken in once. Cinemas, airline offices, car dealerships, and chain restaurants line the street, with a few shopping arcades scattered about for the benefit of luxury souvenir hounds. At number 127, the Paris tourist office provides a mine of information about festivals, concerts, and special events taking place in the city. Near the Franklin Roosevelt Metro stop stands the newly opened **Virgin Megastore**, one of the best cassette and CD emporiums in the world. On the nearby avenue George-V is one of the city's most popular permanent shows, the daring girlie revue of the **Crazy Horse Saloon**, a perennial favorite of visiting Middle Eastern potentates. The area stretching to the east of George-V contains a large number of restaurants and fashionable boutiques, especially in the quarter around the elegant **avenue Montaigne**, which is vying with the rue du Faubourg-St-Honoré (to the north and parallel to the Champs-Elysées) for the title of the city's most exclusive thoroughfare. **Faubourg-St-Honoré** is longer, older, and more established, but the scents wafting from passersby are just as expensive on Montaigne, and the avenue itself is broad, tree-lined, and uncongested. The street can also lay claim to the new fine-art auctioneering facility of Paris, **Drouot-Montaigne**; the theater (**Théâtre des Champs-Elysées**) in which Nijinsky was booed at the premiere of Stravinsky's *Rite of Spring;* and a fashionable mix of diplomats, TV people, and haute couturiers.

The avenue Montaigne meets the triumphal way at the fountains and flowerbeds of the Rond-Point des Champs-Elysées. At this midway mark of the Champs, shaded pedestrian alleyways take over from the lively business district. The northern side of the avenue, near the avenue de Marigny, holds a stamp, coin, and old postcard market on Thursday, Saturday, and Sunday, a charming outdoor affair that draws a good number of the city's eccentrics. This green belt, now sedate and often deserted, is forever linked with the most extravagant of Parisian vogues, the *Incroyables* and the *Merveilleux* (the Incredible and the Marvelous) of the post-Revolutionary period. Fashion for strollers through this area at that time dictated outlandish, immodest dress, and a relaxing of morals encouraged the type of libertine behavior that previously had been the preserve of the nobility. Revolutionary fervor even demanded new diction: The rolling French of the aristocracy was so detested and the accent of the Caribbean so admired that the letter "r" was abolished from speech altogether. Couples tempted to be incwedible and mawvelous in the area's secluded shrubbery should remember that times have changed.

The sole intersection breaking up the greenery is impressive for its double vista: the long view up the Champs-Elysées to the west and the broad avenue Winston Churchill leading south to the distant dome of the Invalides. Flanking this avenue are the **Grand** and **Petit Palais**, pavilions built for the World's Fair of 1900 and now used for the more important temporary art exhibitions and trade shows that come to the city. (The Petit Palais also houses the **Musée des Beaux-Arts de la Ville de Paris**, which includes a permanent collection.) A pleasant, inexpensive way to enjoy this imposing urbanism entails catching the **number 83 bus** at the Rond-Point des Champs-Elysées. As this is one of the two routes in the city on which every bus has a rear balcony, the passenger can stand in the open air and watch the show go by. At sunset this ride down the Champs-Elysées, across the Pont Alexandre III, briefly along the quais of the Left Bank, then on to the Jardin du Luxembourg and beyond makes even the most blasé Parisians lift their noses out of their newspapers.

The other major landmark of the Champs-Elysées is the **place de la Concorde**, an impressive combination of rushing traffic, beautiful streetlamps, imposing statues of women representing the major cities of France, allegorical fountains, and, of course, the obelisk. The view from the Concorde is special as well. The two buildings on the northern side of the square, occupied by the Hôtel Crillon and the ministry of the Navy, are colonnaded palaces designed by Jacques-Ange Gabriel for Louis XVI. The rue Royale, separating the two buildings, gives onto the Corinthian excess of the **church of the Madeleine** (Mary Magdalene). Impossible as it may seem, even more pillars are evident to the south, where the Napoleonic façade of the Assemblée Nationale, France's fractious parliament, stands facing the square from the Left Bank. On the east and west sides equestrian groups by Coustou (the *Horses of Marly*) and Coysevox (the *Winged Horses*) guard the entrances to the Champs-Elysées and Tuileries, respectively.

Like the Champs-Elysées, the Concorde does not live up to its name, for the simple reason that the square has traditionally been associated with discord. During the 1770 wedding celebrations of Louis XVI and Marie Antoinette, 133 people died in a stampede caused by panic over exploding stores of fireworks. In 1793–1794, the square was the Revolution's most prestigious execution site, and 1,119 prisoners rode the tumbrils the length of the rue St-Honoré to their final appointment here. Among those whose heads rolled were Danton, Charlotte Corday (Marat's assassin), Robespierre, Marie Antoinette, and Louis XVI. Two decades later the Bourbons were returned to power and decided to adorn the square with a distinctly apolitical obelisk that Mohammed Ali, Viceroy of Egypt, offered to them. However, by the time the 3,000-year-old gift arrived in Paris, the Bourbons had once again been shown the door and the Orléanist usurper of their throne, King Louis-Philippe, had the pleasure of welcoming the exotic monument to Paris. In later Republican days, the Concorde became the theater of the white-hot *revanchard* sentiment over the loss of Alsace and Lorraine to the Prussians in 1873. The statue of Strasbourg was smothered in flowers for more than 50 years, and the timorous few to oppose the cult of the lost provinces were soon punished. A fashionable ice-cream merchant on the rue Royale had his shop destroyed for daring to put a German flag in his window (his property was quickly snapped up by an enterprising waiter named Maxim Gaillard, and thus Maxim's was born). In 1934 the most violent riot of modern times in France took place at the Concorde, with members of extreme-right groups rushing the Assemblée Nationale to throw parliamentarians into the river. Fifteen died and 300 were wounded, many of them on the **Pont de la Concorde**, the one Paris bridge to have been constructed with building material freed in another memorable riot. Much of its stone comes from the Bastille, demolished in 1789.

By contrast, the **Jardin des Tuileries** is almost always associated with the gentler pastime of doing absolutely nothing, although it too was the scene of memorable incidents in the Revolution. A formal French garden designed by Le Nôtre, the Tuileries has been a favorite Parisian promenade since the 17th century, its pools, terraces, and statuary unerringly lined up by landscape geometers. The sole exception is modern: a series of sensual female nudes sculpted by Maillol and scattered about the park's eastern extremity. During the past few years, the upkeep of the gardens has been less than careful. Thus, in the fall of 1990, they were made subject (under the auspices of President Mitterand himself) to an extensive program of restoration and recreation, which will result in the old Tuileries forming an architectural continuity from the pyramid du Louvre to the place de la Concorde. The debut of the almost-new park is planned for September 1992.

For those uneasy about idling away too much time on a vacation, however lovely the surroundings, the arcades of the commercial rue de Rivoli that run the length of the Tuileries's northern edge are always ready for shoppers. A more edifying antidote to lazing about the Tuileries can be found at the two galleries near the place de la Concorde.

The **Jeu de Paume**, now bereft of Impressionist glory, holds temporary exhibits, while the **Orangerie**, containing the superb Manet, Cézanne, Renoir, and Douanier Rousseau canvases of the Walter-Guillaume collection, remains one of the city's most surprising—and least visited—small galleries.

The Louvre and Châtelet

When King Philip Augustus decided to construct the Louvre in order to protect Paris while he was off gallivanting with Richard the Lion-Hearted on the Third Crusade, he unwittingly created the architectural hobbyhorse of the French nation. Few buildings in the country have been so assiduously rebuilt, extended, and modified. The result is a glorious monster, glaringly imperfect yet miraculously possessing three fine expressions of the builder's art: the Cour Carré, a courtyard built over the course of several reigns that shows the shift from Renaissance to Baroque to Neoclassical in French architecture; the Galerie du Bord de l'Eau, the center section of the riverside wing built for Henri IV; and the Colonnade de Perrault, the imposing easternmost façade constructed for Louis XIV. The latest expression of the 700-year-old tradition of tinkering with the Louvre—an underground concourse of shops, conference rooms, and restaurants designed by I. M. Pei—was inaugurated in 1988.

The newcomer departs from its underground discretion only once, in a tall, pyramid-shaped skylight that rises from the middle of the Cour Napoléon. However you feel about this daring addition to the Louvre, there can be no doubt that the modern facility meets several needs. It provides a glimpse of the formerly inaccessible Medieval palace (visitors can now walk underground through the moats), cleans up the confusion that once reigned in the Cour Napoléon, and, in rationalizing the Louvre's entranceway, gives some order to a museum that has long been notorious among art lovers for playing hide-and-seek with its cultural treasures. The reorganization of the Louvre's collections, some of which are gathering dust out of view, is expected to continue until the year 2000—that is, if obstacles such as the one encountered in the mid-1980s, when a French finance minister pettishly refused to move his offices from the building's northern wing, can be successfully circumvented. A compromise allowing the minister in question to hang on to his fancy address was eventually struck, but not before Parisians had enjoyed an unseemly fight between private vanity and public interest.

Once inside the Louvre it is easy to forget these recent squabbles and to thank the Revolution for finally opening the building to the public, in 1793. Louis XVI had considered, but never adopted, the idea. The first sight for many visitors, the monumental Daru staircase, crowned by the *Winged Victory* of Samothrace, is a foretaste of the masterpieces to follow and of the enjoyment to be derived from them, provided, of course, the temptation to sprint through the entire building at one go can be resisted. As many of the paintings come from the private collections of Bourbon and Valois monarchs, it is hardly surprising that the Louvre is particularly rich in art from Italy, the country long synonymous with civilization for France's rulers. As is only natural, French painting is also well represented, particularly in the giant tableaux from the early 19th century. Other famous collections include a priceless selection of Flemish and Dutch masters and, for classicists, extensive Greek and Roman holdings. France's enduring fascination with the pharaohs, spurred by Napoléon's adventures on the Nile, is evident in the museum's large Egyptology department. In the northwestern wing of the building, along the rue de Rivoli, is the refurbished **Musée des Arts Décoratifs**. Given over to the traditional arts from Medieval times to the present (with an annex devoted to haute couture), this museum forms a practical counterpart to the more famous collection of art for art's sake to be found elsewhere in the palace.

Associated in the modern mind with two women, the *Venus de Milo* and the *Mona Lisa,* the Louvre must often have seemed to its royal occupants more aptly represented by another artwork now in the museum, Hieronymus Bosch's *Ship of Fools.* The history of the Louvre, for seven centuries home to the French court, is rich in incident and intrigue. In the **Petite Galerie** visitors can still see the apartments of the Renaissance Valois monarchs. Their turbulent reign during France's religious wars made the Louvre a nest of plotting noblemen, minions, mistresses, and royal bastards. The 16th-century Louvre was a place of vicious rumor (about sexual and religious practices), suspect foreign connections (the Protestants with England, the Catholics with Spain), and frequent poisonings. Paris, a Catholic fief—it is often forgotten that Saint Ignatius Loyola founded the Society of Jesus on Montmartre—showed little tolerance for the winds of reform reaching France from Geneva, while the Huguenots, disciples of John Calvin, viewed the capital as a sink of corruption under the baleful Italian influence of Catherine de Médicis, the Queen Mother. As the number of Huguenots steadily grew among nobles and common-ers alike, many powerful French Catholic clans, led by the Guise family of Lorraine, saw a threat to the secular and ecclesiastical connections that were the sources of their great wealth and power. In 1572, at the wedding of Cather-ine's daughter, Margaret of Valois, to a Huguenot prince, Henry of Navarre (later Henry IV), the Catholic faction hit upon an expedient solution to the problem posed by French Protestants: Kill them all.

Accordingly, early in the morning of August 23, the eve of the feast of Saint Bartholomew, bells in the rear belfry of **St-Germain l'Auxerrois**, the church opposite the Louvre's eastern façade, chimed the signal for the slaughter to begin. Daggers and swords drawn, the king's men raced through the Louvre killing Huguenot wedding guests in their beds, while armed bands of thugs were dispatched to roam the city and murder at will. News of this bloodbath sent both Catholic and Protestant Europe reeling in shock and disgust, no group more so than the Huguenots them-selves, whose aristocratic spokesmen had suddenly disap-peared. Today a statue of the leader of the movement, Gaspard de Coligny, the Admiral of France murdered by his king on St. Bartholomew's Day, looks reproachfully at the Louvre's northern façade, his monument discreetly—perhaps a bit too discreetly—placed behind the grillwork separating the rue de Rivoli from a Protestant oratory. The Huguenots gained a respite from persecution two decades later when the bridegroom of that memorable wedding party became King Henry IV, converted to Catholicism, and promptly decreed religious toleration in the Edict of Nantes. Unfortunately, his grandson, Louis XIV, set the clock—and France's development—back by revoking the edict and driving the Huguenots into exile.

The neighborhood east of the Louvre has lost all trace of its colorful past, commerce and theater being its princi-pal modern occupations. The quai de la Mégisserie is the capital's shop for pets and edible animals, with ducks, rabbits, geese, hamsters, kittens, and white mice compet-ing for attention. The relative scarcity of dogs at this market is puzzling, for the incautious pedestrian in Paris quickly realizes that the city's canine population is large and uninhibited. At the corner of the quai and the Pont Neuf stands the Samaritaine department store, much like its competitors in all respects but one: Its circular rooftop observation deck offers, for free, a superb view of Paris and the Seine.

Performing Arts

The next major intersection to the east is **Châtelet**, formerly the dungeon, torture chamber, and slaughterhouse of the city. Since the 19th century the square has had a far gentler vocation: music at the **Théâtre Musical de Paris**; dance and drama at the **Théâtre de la Ville**. The latter, the stage on which Sarah Bernhardt reigned as queen of Paris theater, is the municipality's riposte to the national companies scattered throughout the city: Odéon, Comédie-Française, and Chaillot. Other such state-subsidized theaters as the Bouffes du Nord (home to Peter Brook productions) and Ariane Mnouchkine's Cartoucherie, where her imaginative troupe works out of an old ammunition factory in the eastern Bois de Vincennes, have received international acclaim for their treatments of exotic epics and Shakespeare (the Bard is ever popular in France), while the enduring *cocu* (cuckold) plot device is alive and well in the farces staged in the district of the Grands Boulevards. Paris has scores of theaters, café-theaters (cabarets where gatling-gun French punning is the rule), and performing-art venues. To make sense of it all, pick up an inexpensive weekly entertainment guide (*Pariscope* or *Officiel des Spectacles*) at a newsstand.

Palais-Royal, Place Vendôme, and Opéra

These neighborhoods constitute the "Right Bank," an expression synonymous with Parisian elegance, luxury, and liveliness. This is the Paris of fashion magnates and advertisers, of models with slinky legs sliding out of limousines, tripping into stylish shops along the rue du Faubourg-St-Honoré, and strolling down glittering boulevards with a suitably perfect man in tow. Glamor long ago replaced grandeur as Paris's trademark, which is why the triangle formed by the place Vendôme, Palais-Royal, and Opéra

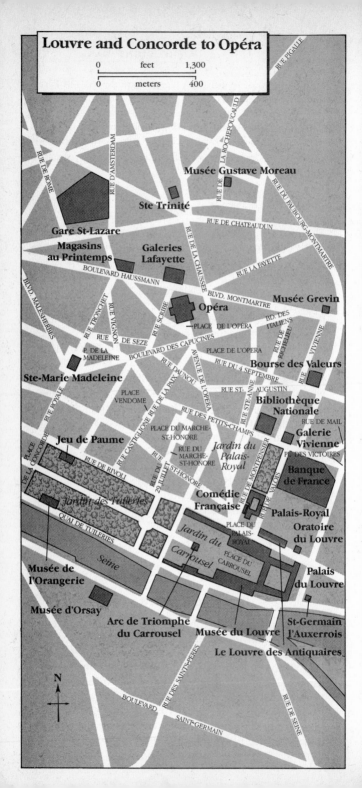

Louvre and Concorde to Opéra

0   feet   1,300

0   meters   400

RUE PIGALLE

RUE DE ROME

RUE D'AMSTERDAM

RUE DE LA ROCHEFOUCAULD

Musée Gustave Moreau

RUE DE

RUE DU FAUBOURG-MONTMARTRE

Ste Trinité

RUE DE CHATEAUDUN

Gare St-Lazare

RUE DE LA CHAUSSÉE

Magasins au Printemps

Galeries Lafayette

BOULEVARD HAUSSMANN

RUE LA FAYETTE

BLVD. MALESHERBES

BLVD. MONTMARTRE

Musée Grevin

Opéra

RUE TRONCHET

RUE VIGNON

RUE SCRIBE

PLACE DE L'OPÉRA

BD. DES ITALIENS

RUE DE SEZE

BOULEVARD DES CAPUCINES

PLACE DE L'OPÉRA

RUE DE RICHELIEU

RUE VIVIENNE

P. DE LA MADELEINE

AVENUE DE L'OPÉRA

RUE DAUNOU

RUE DU 4 SEPTEMBRE

Bourse des Valeurs

Ste-Marie Madeleine

RUE ROYALE

PLACE VENDOME

RUE DE LA PAIX

RUE ST-ANNE

RUE ST- AUGUSTIN

Bibliothèque Nationale

RUE DE MAIL

RUE DES PETITS-CHAMPS

Galerie Vivienne

Jeu de Paume

PLACE DE LA CONCORDE

RUE CASTIGLIONE

PLACE DU MARCHÉ-ST-HONORÉ

Jardin du Palais-Royal

P. DES VICTOIRES

Banque de France

RUE DE RIVOLI

RUE DU MARCHÉ-ST-HONORÉ

RUE DU 29 JUILLET

RUE ST-HONORÉ

RUE DE MONTPENSIER

RUE DE VALOIS

Comédie Française

Palais-Royal

QUAI DE TUILERIES

Jardin des Tuileries

PLACE DU PALAIS-ROYAL

Oratoire du Louvre

Seine

Jardin du Carrousel

PLACE DU CARROUSEL

Musée de l'Orangerie

Palais du Louvre

Musée d'Orsay

Arc de Triomphe du Carrousel

Musée du Louvre

St-Germain l'Auxerrois

Le Louvre des Antiquaires

N

BOULEVARD

RUE DES SAINTS-PÈRES

SAINT-GERMAIN

RUE DE SEINE

districts is now far more emblematic of the city than the Champs-Elysées. First developed when the Parisian bourgeoisie was shaking free of feudal bonds to King and Bishop, this area has significantly few ministries and churches—the presence of two major financial institutions, the Bank of France and the Stock Exchange, indicating its role as the cradle of French capitalism.

North of the Louvre on the rue de Rivoli is the Right Bank's equivalent of the Carré Rive Gauche, the **Louvre des Antiquaires**, today a rich man's flea market, with dozens of shops selling objets d'art and antique curios to collectors. To people of more modest means, the building is perfect for wistful window shopping, especially on those rare muggy days when the facility's most un-Parisian feature, air-conditioning, makes it particularly attractive. There is a far quieter place to loiter across the street at the **Palais-Royal**, where a garden enclosed on three sides by graceful if neglected apartments has been open to the public since 1784. The present peacefulness of the spot belies its noisy past, for the musty arcades now lined with booksellers and military-memorabilia shops once housed the Continent's most raucous cafés. The site served first as Cardinal Richelieu's town house, then as a second home to the monarchs (hence its name), before falling, in 1780, into the hands of Louis-Philippe d'Orléans, a high-living, hard-up nobleman who rebuilt the place and opened it to private businesses. His cousin at Versailles, Louis XVI, is reported to have sniffed, "Now that you're a shopkeeper, we'll no doubt see you only on Sundays."

The Palais-Royal was an overnight success, instantly becoming the city's intellectual center, amusement park, and fleshpot. This last unsavory facet of the place lives on in a skipping rhyme still sung, in all innocence, by French schoolgirls, *"Le Palais-Royal est un beau quartier/Toutes les jeunes filles sont à marier"* ("The Palais-Royal is a fine neighborhood/All the girls there are ready to wed"). As for the other attractions, the garden's mountebanks, card-sharps, palm readers, and freak shows competed with the strange cafés of the Palais, each of which had its own peculiar novelty. Outside the Café des Mille Colonnes (formerly at 36, galerie de Valois), Madame Rollain, the "most beautiful woman in the world," sat on a raised platform to beguile customers, while at the Café Mécanique (formerly at 121, galerie de Valois) a clever system of dumbwaiters in the center of every table served and took away drinks without the need for human intervention. The cafés of the Palais-Royal also provided a political forum for encyclopedists, democrats, republicans, and rabble-rousers to discuss the ideas and problems of their day with great freedom.

In the summer of 1789, the air rife with rumors about imminent measures to be taken against the city of Paris and the Estates-General, Camille Desmoulins stood up in the Café de Foy at 46, galerie de Montpensier and incited his listeners to arm themselves against the government. That evening, July 13, they raided the Invalides for guns and later the next day stormed the Bastille, a symbol, if not a true representative (as it then held only seven prisoners) of absolutist repression. Few people thronging the Palais-Royal that evening realized that their revolt would turn into a revolution of unprecedented proportions, bringing down not only a dynasty but also the entire monarchical principle. It is hard to think of the present-day Palais-Royal as a crucible of modern Europe or a place of great social ferment (tellingly, the French Ministry of Culture now snoozes above the galerie de Valois), yet this is where the ancien régime collapsed, the educated yet unenfranchised classes who came here having had enough of the web of privilege woven by aristocracy and clergy. Louis-Philippe d'Orléans, who unwittingly lit the fuse by making his palace a safe-house for sedition, was not spared the guillotine, despite the caution he showed by renaming himself Philippe-Egalité.

He might find the spot more to his tastes today, for, curiously enough, France's ultraconservative streak is nowhere more in evidence than it is here. The 300-year-old **Comédie Française** performs at the Palais-Royal—and is excoriated by its public whenever it experiments. The installation in 1986 of *Les Trois Plateaux,* a photogenic artwork consisting of truncated black-and-white columns placed in what had been used as the Palais's parking lot, earned its creator, Daniel Buren, a frightening amount of mail marked by pure hatred. Still, the neighborhood has always been a place of controversy: In the Régence Café that once stood across from the Comédie-Française, Marx and Engels first decided to form a working partnership. It should be noted that both men were initially drawn to the area by the presence of the **Bibliothèque Nationale**. Located just north of the Palais-Royal on the rue de Richelieu, France's national library was first placed here in 1724 by a prescient Louis XV. A complex of 18th-century mansions and Second Empire reading rooms, the "BN"—as it is known to its thousands of scholarly regulars—often puts on temporary exhibits of its most precious holdings.

The **place Vendôme** has never had the questionable connections of the Palais-Royal; its serenity has been troubled only by the toppling, re-erecting, melting down, and statue-switching effected on the Napoleonic replica of Trajan's column that stands in its center. Playing musical chairs with monuments, however, was something of a national sport in France during the 19th century, so the fate of the Vendôme column was not exceptional. The fame of the square lies more in its ordered Louis XIV elegance (another example is the place des Victoires, north of the Palais-Royal) and in its prestige. The Ritz, recently refurbished by an Egyptian businessman who also picked up Harrod's on a London shopping spree, gives onto the square, as do several of the world's most exclusive jewelers. At sundown, when the streetlamps blink on and the display windows sparkle, place Vendôme can be captivating, a sensation appropriate to a spot that once housed Dr. Friedrich Anton Mesmer, an 18th-century physician who treated patients simply by staring at them. Many people, however, are spellbound by the square's suggestion of limitless wealth. As every player of the French version of Monopoly knows, the adjoining rue de la Paix is the city's most valuable piece of property.

The rue de la Paix runs north into the **place de l'Opéra**, the centerpiece of Napoléon III's scheme to make Paris the "most beautiful capital in the universe." His town planner, Baron Georges Eugène Haussmann, cut swaths through the historic fabric of Paris by driving wide boulevards into the heart of old neighborhoods, much to the dismay of residents. The police were delighted, for the new layout allowed them to isolate disturbances by deploying on the boulevards, putting an end to the age-old insurgent tradition of erecting barricades and scampering to further adventure through the city-wide labyrinth of tiny streets and alleyways. The outbreaks of 1830 (portrayed in *Les Misérables*) and 1848 (which ignited the rest of Europe) haunted the emerging ruling classes of capitalist France, who, although at first sympathetic to the risings, did not want to see things get out of hand. The "arsonist-turned-fireman" syndrome, by which each generation of Parisian bourgeois would begin adulthood as constitutional hotheads and finish it as crotchety reactionaries, was commonplace in 19th-century France, as the newly ascendant elites faced a sustained salvo from a wide range of antagonists. Aside from suffering the indignity of Honoré Daumier's withering caricatures (which are beautifully displayed at the Musée d'Orsay), the bourgeoisie of post-Napoleonic times was shaken in its Gallic complacency by the Anglophilia of the French Romantics, and, on another front, attacked in its religious faiths by the writings of such Positivist visionaries as Claude de Saint-Simon and Auguste Comte. The more the business of France became the making of money, the fiercer became the critique of commerce as a sign of moral depravity— a notion that lurks in the back of the French mind even today. Fueling the bourgeois-bashing impulse was class hatred born of economic injustice. The misery of the urban working class, the subject of much of Emile Zola's work, stood in stark contrast to the opulent homes on the Champs-Elysées and to the upper classes' most grandiose riposte to their critics, the **Paris Opéra**.

Completed in 1875 after 13 years of construction (and five years after its sponsor, Napoléon III, had been deposed), Charles Garnier's Opéra remains Europe's largest theater and still impresses by its sheer excess. Its colorful monumental staircase, tailor-made for gawking at gowns and tiaras, is a riot of marble and statuary. The same holds true for the reception rooms and the great hall itself, dominated by a six-ton chandelier—which has come crashing down on operagoers only once, in 1896— and a ceiling decorated by Marc Chagall in 1964. Tickets to the Opéra are difficult both to obtain and to afford, although guides rattling off impressive figures about kilometers of upholstery and square meters of stage surface conduct tours daily. It is always a challenge to catch a glimpse of the real phantom of this Opéra: good taste. Still, the building has acquired the cachet of underdog since the opening of the very expensive new opera at the Bastille. Garnier's massive stage, once the arbiter of French operatic taste, is now reserved solely for ballet performances.

The Opéra district was the setting for the 19th-century naughtiness associated with the notion of "gay Paree." To the east stretches the long strip known as the Grands Boulevards (ironically, one of the few broad thoroughfares not created by Baron Haussmann), where the bourgeois, boulevardiers, and soubrettes once came together in a mix worthy of an Offenbach operetta or Feydeau farce.

Today the district is lively but progressively shabbier as you head east, its only real links to the past being its numerous theaters and its **Musée Grévin** (10, boulevard Montmartre), a typical 19th-century entertainment consisting of wax figures, trompe l'oeil devices, and sound and light shows. To the west of the Opéra, the boulevard des Capucines leads prosperously down to the **Madeleine**, a rectangular church built to look like a Roman temple. Perhaps not surprisingly, French military families have long chosen the Madeleine to mix Mars and Venus at elaborate formal weddings.

To the north of the Opéra, the successors to the Second Empire boulevards and the turn-of-the-century Belle Epoque restaurants now pull in the crowds: Such *grands magasins* as Au Printemps and Galeries Lafayette, each a triumph of the 20th-century mass market, line up on the **boulevard Haussmann**. It is difficult to say whether the Baron would be flattered or appalled.

Just beyond this bustling commercial neighborhood, hidden in the rue La Rochefoucauld, one of the oddest expressions of France's 19th-century artistic development can be visited. The three floors of the **Musée Gustave Moreau** house most of the prodigious output of this Symbolist painter, whose work inspired the art-and-artifice worshipers associated with fin-de-siècle decadence. A quiet, peculiar place, where every inch of wall space is covered in darkly sensual paintings, the museum seems out of time, awash in a sensibility that could not have had any bearing on the real-life struggles of Moreau's contemporaries. The warmest praise for the painter's works appeared in J. K. Huysmans's *A Rebours* (*Against the Grain*), a grotesque tale hailed as "the breviary of decadence." It was this book, infused with the esoteric aesthetics of Huysmans and Moreau, that was supposed to have corrupted the youthful Dorian Gray. Thus, the pictures in the museum deserve careful study.

Les Halles, Beaubourg, and Le Marais

What Zola called the "belly of Paris" is now its hole. The **Halles** district, for eight centuries the central food market of the city, is an undistinguished pedestrian zone with an underground shopping mall, the Forum des Halles. It also marks the point where the trendy part of the city begins,

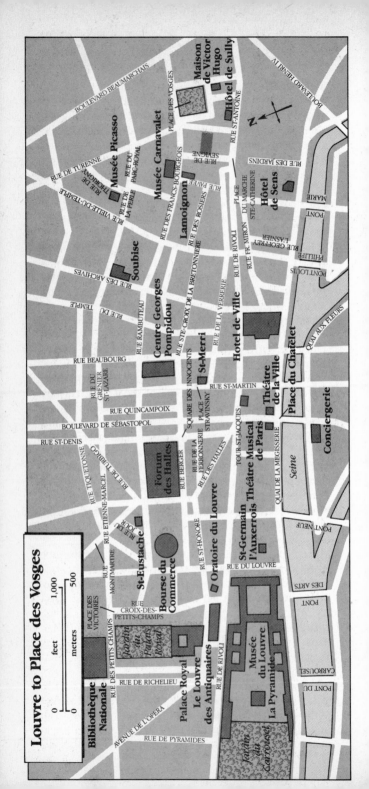

Louvre to Place des Vosges

feet 0 — 1,000
meters 0 — 500

- Bibliothèque Nationale
- PLACE DES VICTOIRES
- Jardin du Palais Royal
- Palace Royal
- Le Louvre des Antiquaires
- RUE DE RICHELIEU
- RUE DES PETITS CHAMPS
- RUE CROIX-DES-PETITS-CHAMPS
- AVENUE DE L'OPERA
- RUE DE PYRAMIDES
- Musée du Louvre
- La Pyramide
- RUE DE RIVOLI
- Jardin du Carrousel
- PONT DU CARROUSEL
- PONT DES ARTS
- St-Eustache
- Bourse du Commerce
- Forum des Halles
- RUE MONTMARTRE
- RUE ETIENNE-MARCEL
- RUE TIQUETONNE
- RUE ST-DENIS
- RUE DU JOUR
- RUE TURBIGO
- BOULEVARD DE SÉBASTOPOL
- RUE QUINCAMPOIX
- RUE BEAUBOURG
- RUE DU GRENIER ST-LAZARE
- RUE RAMBUTEAU
- RUE DU TEMPLE
- RUE DES ARCHIVES
- RUE VIEILLE-DU-TEMPLE
- RUE DE LA PERLE
- RUE DE THORIGNY
- RUE DE TURENNE
- BOULEVARD BEAUMARCHAIS
- RUE DU PARC-ROYAL
- Musée Picasso
- Soubise
- Centre Georges Pompidou
- St-Merri
- Lamoignon
- Musée Carnavalet
- PLACE DES VOSGES
- Maison de Victor Hugo
- Hôtel de Sully
- RUE ST-ANTOINE
- RUE DE SÉVIGNÉ
- RUE DES FRANCS-BOURGEOIS
- RUE PAVÉE
- RUE DES ROSIERS
- RUE STE-CROIX DE LA BRETONNERIE
- RUE DE RIVOLI
- RUE DE LA VERRERIE
- RUE FR. MIRON
- Hôtel de Ville
- PLACE DU MARCHÉ STE-CATHERINE
- RUE GEOFFROY L'ASNIER
- Hôtel de Sens
- RUE DES JARDINS
- MARIE
- PONT MARIE
- PONT LOUIS PHILIPPE
- QUAI AUX FLEURS
- BOULEVARD HENRI IV
- RUE ST-MARTIN
- Théâtre de la Ville
- Place du Châtelet
- Conciergerie
- PLACE STRAVINSKY
- SQUARE DES INNOCENTS
- RUE BERGER
- RUE DE LA FERRONNERIE
- RUE DES HALLES
- TOUR ST-JACQUES
- RUE ST-JACQUES
- QUAI DE LA MÉGISSERIE
- Seine
- PONT NEUF
- St-Germain l'Auxerrois
- Théâtre Musical de Paris
- Oratoire du Louvre
- RUE ST-HONORE
- RUE DU LOUVRE
- N

the blues and greens of the western Parisian wardrobe giving way to the blacks and grays of the east. In ten years—the time it took the government to decide what to do with the yawning crater left by the demolition of the 19th-century market buildings—the area changed from a charming anachronism in the heart of a traffic nightmare to a shining example of gimcrack urbanism. This is in keeping with a long tradition, for Les Halles has never been a genteel or refined neighborhood.

The peep-show area around the rue St-Denis was once the center of cutthroat Paris, the names of such alleyways as Petite and Grande Truanderie (Little and Big Thuggery) giving a fair idea of the locals' profession. However, the former seaminess of the Grande Truanderie's *Cour des Miracles,* where mutilated beggars by day became whole and hearty by night (simply by taking off their contrived handicaps), pales in comparison to the past squalor of the square des Innocents. Currently known for the never-ending parade of urban fauna filing past its central Renaissance fountain (built by Pierre Lescot, architect for much of the Valois Louvre), the square long had the dubious honor of being the city's largest cemetery and charnel house and the source of horrific anecdotes. An example: One evening in 1780 the southern retaining wall of the overcrowded Innocents cemetery gave way under the weight of the bodies piled high against it. Tenants sleeping peacefully on the lower floors of the adjacent building (the long, 17th-century construction that still borders the square's south side) were rudely awakened—and almost smothered—by the horde of uninvited and very dead guests crashing into the bedrooms of the living. This disaster spurred efforts to remove the remains from city cemeteries to the catacombs of Denfert-Rochereau—now a ghoulish tourist attraction.

This public-health nightmare, an undisciplined graveyard alongside the city's central food market, has now totally vanished, together with almost everything else. The square des Innocents gives out onto an artlessly landscaped expanse whose saving grace lies in the unobstructed view it provides of the **church of St-Eustache**. A 16th-century Gothic behemoth on the outside, St-Eustache impresses even more inside. Its towering nave often resounds with choral singing, and one of its radiating chapels is touchingly dedicated to the butchers, fishwives, and other food merchants who once made up the sanctuary's colorful congregation. Where their stalls once stood, on the sanctuary's southern flank, is a small hemicycle, dominated by Henri DeMiller's 50-ton sculpture of a head lying on its side, staring off into space. Little imagination is needed to see that the eyes are turned toward the solitary pillar at the Halles's western end, an astrological column used by Catherine de Médicis's court seer, Nostradamus.

Across the boulevard Sebastopol lies the **Beaubourg quarter**, yet another pedestrian zone. Whereas the neighboring Halles is entirely given over to commerce, Beaubourg's vocation is modern art. Galleries line its narrow rue Quincampoix, and its ever-popular **Centre Georges Pompidou** has become Paris's biggest tourist attraction, outdrawing the Eiffel Tower and Louvre combined. Opened in 1977 to groans from Parisians dismayed at seeing a mammoth, multicolored, glass-and-steel structure erected in a picturesque old quarter, the facility, known locally as "Beaubourg," is now a familiar landmark. Its upper-floor permanent collection, the **Musée National d'Art Moderne**, encompasses an exhaustive range of 20th-century art, although only 1,000 of Beaubourg's 8,000 artworks are on display at any one time, because of space limitations. The museum is unquestionably one of the "musts" of a Paris visit, partly because its outstanding collection—including wonderful Picassos, Klees, Modiglianis, and such—also has considerable depth in artists not all that well represented outside of France, such as Rouault. Sharing the center building with permanent collections are a library and *vidéothèque*—chaotically organized victims of their own success—and the occasional mega-show that draws hordes of art lovers and ensures excruciatingly long lines. The large plaza that has been cleared in front of the museum serves as a stage for street musicians, fire-eaters, contortionists, and crackpots who compete for the attention of the crowds with the neighboring mechanical show, Jacques Monestier's ingenious "Defender of Time" clock (affixed to a wall in the adjacent Quartier de l'Horloge). Overlooking the plaza stands yet another clock, the Nemo design group's Genitron, a digital scoreboard that, since its installation in 1987, has been neurotically counting down the seconds left in our millennium.

Immediately south of the Pompidou center is the Beaubourg quarter's photogenic showstopper, the **Stravinsky fountain**. The fountain's silly reflecting pool, containing Jean Tinguely's idiosyncratic machines and Nikki de St-Phalle's mobile sculptures, forms an irreverent roof to the underground IRCAM complex, noted for its research into experimental music. The unlikely backdrop to the place Stravinsky is the 16th-century **church of St-Merri**. Some critics think its grace is disfigured by the proximity of such an odd neighbor, but the charge betrays ignorance of the history of the church. Its long association with bizarre practices and secretive sects is indicated by the little figure atop the central portal: Baphomet, a grinning hermaphroditic devil. Nearby, the Tour St-Jacques, the lone vestige of a church that was once the starting point of the pilgrimage to Santiago de Compostela in northwest Spain, was a favorite haunt of the mysterious Nicolas Flamel, the alchemist who inspired both fear and respect in 14th-century Parisians. The weird Stravinsky fountain is obviously in good company.

From Beaubourg east to the Bastille stretches an area known as **Le Marais** (the swamp), a reference to its once-marshy soil. A district totally distinct from the rest of Paris, it has retained a late-Medieval flavor, escaping the great changes of the 19th century and narrowly avoiding large-scale demolition in the 20th, thanks to the efforts of culture minister André Malraux in the 1960s. The Marais is studded with magnificent *hôtels particuliers,* aristocratic mansions built when the area was the most elegant urban quarter of France. This was particularly true of the late 17th century, a time of great intellectual ferment in the Marais, the aristocratic *précieuses* holding their salons for the great men of the day: Molière, La Fontaine, Boileau, and La Rochefoucauld. The greatest woman of her time, Madame de Sévigné, lived, wrote, and received in the Hôtel Carnavalet, bequeathing a lively depiction of that glittering milieu in her letters.

The physical evidence of the past is everywhere present in the Marais. Along the rue des Jardins stands a 225-foot-long stretch of the 12th-century city rampart, its original crenellation intact. Bordering a playground, the wall is taken for granted in a neighborhood where stunning courtyards and mansions are commonplace. (If you see an open gate in the Marais, take advantage of the situation to go in and snoop around.) Four great *hôtels* permanently open for public inspection are grouped around the rues des Francs-Bourgeois and Archives: **Lamoignon** (the historical library of Paris); **Carnavalet** (the very rewarding history museum of Paris, a logical follow-up to a visit to the

Medieval Cluny museum); **Le Peletier de Saint-Fargeau** (which was renovated in 1989 to absorb some of the Carnavalet's collections, especially the art and artifacts of the Revolution in Paris); and **Soubise** (the national archives, with a permanent exhibition of important French documents from Merovingian times to the present). On the rue St-Antoine, the **Hôtel de Sully** (named for Henry IV's shrewd finance minister) holds temporary exhibits about other French monuments, although its real interest is intrinsic. Like the interior of the other *hôtels,* the decor of Sully gives the visitor a taste of Baroque splendor. Slightly older than Sully and converted to use as an extraordinary public library is the riverside **Hôtel de Sens**, a half-Medieval, half-Renaissance mansion that once served the fanatical Guise family as a Parisian pied-à-terre for hatching their murderous plots. At nightfall especially, this building looks the part.

A popular *hôtel* among modern visitors is Salé, since 1986 home of the **Musée Picasso**. Created from duties imposed by the French government on the artist's heirs, the collection includes more than 200 paintings and sculptures, handsomely displayed in the 17th-century mansion on rue de Thorigny. The aristocratic neighborhood—the tranquil **Parc Royal** is just around the corner—seems to suit the master. The only other artist thus honored in the Marais is Victor Hugo, whose former residence at the **place des Vosges** has been converted into a quirky museum (the **Musée Victor Hugo**) concentrating on the great man's private life. His fame, however, is secondary to that of the square, a graceful 17th-century fund-raising project that Henry IV and Sully dreamed up. In the place of the rustic horse-trading market that occupied this spot, a regal square was envisioned, its identical pavilions to be sold off to the highest bidders. The promise of occasional royal occupancy (the queen's apartment in the center of the north side, the king's in the south) was dangled as prestigious bait, which nobles and rich merchants were quick to snap at. The enterprise was a resounding success, proof that business and beauty can coexist. Even the square's name is tied up with cold hard cash: In 1800 the Vosges was the first region to pay its taxes.

Aside from its relative antiquity in the Parisian landscape, the contemporary Marais is also known for the variety of its human geography. Affluent professionals clever enough to have picked up apartments when the prices were right (in the 1970s) displaced many of the area's artisans, although quaint businesses still exist alongside dance studios and graphic arts wonderlands. The rues Ste-Croix de la Bretonnerie and Vieille du Temple form the meeting place of the old and new Marais populaces, with gays, trendy designers, and old-time residents strolling past kosher food stores, café-theaters, and antiques shops. Nearby, the square du Marché Ste-Catherine, a restaurant-dotted expanse in the maze of narrow streets, fills pleasantly on summer evenings, while the Bastille Day Bal des Sapeurs-Pompiers (Fireman's Ball) in the firehall on the rue de Sévigné is by far the most entertaining in the city, with its mix of the comfortably fashion-conscious and the casually fashion-oblivious.

Completing this mosaic is the age-old **Jewish quarter** centered on the rue des Rosiers. French Jewry has long maintained a welcoming place for immigrants in the area, once known as the *pletzl* (square) to its Yiddish-speaking newcomers. Today the accents heard here are more likely to be North African, as many Sephardic Jews have moved to France in the wake of decolonization. The rue des Rosiers, although an anachronistic representative of the French Jewish community, is nonetheless a powerful symbol in a country where a current of anti-Semitism runs deep. Long denied civil rights and subject to sporadic persecutions, the community met its greatest trials in the past hundred years. The turn-of-the-century Dreyfus Affair, which shocked the visiting Viennese journalist Theodor Herzl and strengthened his belief in the need for a Jewish homeland, sullied the French Republic's reputation for tolerance and added further ugliness to the rabid nationalism espoused by such figures as Maurice Barrès. French Jews suffered terribly during World War II, tens of thousands being sent to their deaths by the Nazi occupiers or their French underlings. A monument to the Unknown Jewish Martyr stands on the rue Geoffroy l'Asnier, and an underground memorial to victims of the Holocaust can be visited at the easternmost tip of Ile de la Cité. However, the rue des Rosiers, its three blocks teeming with life in an otherwise quiet Medieval quarter, remains the most vivid reminder of a hard-won victory over bigotry.

Eastern Paris and Montmartre

The cutting edge of Paris these days is the **Bastille district**, a neighborhood no longer living paradoxically in the

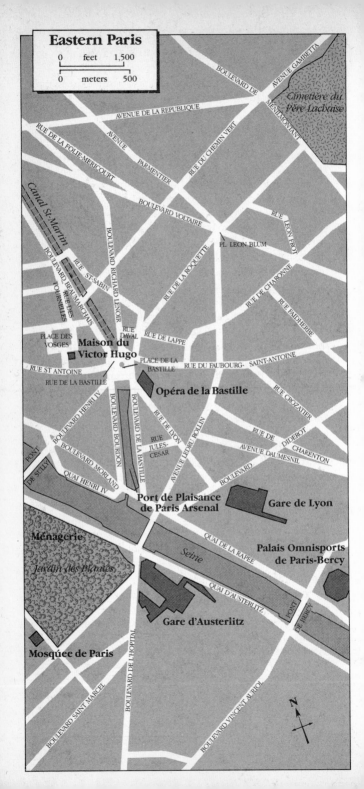

shadow of a demolished building. The Bastille was torn down in the heady days of 1789, and for many years thereafter the area, called the Faubourg St-Antoine, was known for furniture manufacture and working-class militancy. Those days are over, too, the old-time *musette* (the Auvergnat accordion music associated with romantic Paris) halls giving way to—or alternating nights with—New Age trend setters, while the district's warehouses are being converted into lofts, studios, and galleries. Gentrification here, however, is in a far less advanced phase than in the neighboring Marais, and the "hot" street of the Bastille, the rue de Lappe, is still a bit daunting to faint-hearted explorers of the night. The Bastille's new **Opéra de la Bastille**—officially inaugurated 200 years less one day after the storming of the Bastille—is a facility that architect Carlos Ott designed to make opera more accessible to a larger public, and points to the future of the area as the cultural laboratory of Paris. For the moment, the Bastille is Paris's *quartier qui monte,* possessing a mix of the shabby and the genteel that many young Parisians find compelling.

The improvements in the Bastille area go along with a general redevelopment scheme for the whole of eastern Paris. Long considered the poor cousin of the more historic neighborhoods of central Paris and the wealthy *beaux quartiers* of the west, this large, densely populated section of the city is now experiencing a boom. Slum clearance and renovation here are high on city hall's list of priorities. The canal linking the Bastille to the Seine has been transformed into the Arsenal Marina for pleasure boats, and the rough area behind the Gare de Lyon, Bercy, was chosen as the site for the Palais Omnisports, an all-purpose indoor stadium, a daring new American Center, and a spectacular French Finance Ministry. The **Canal St-Martin**, stretching from the Arsenal at the Seine, continues underground for a mile or so north of the Bastille and reemerges as a picturesque waterway threading through a series of locks and pedestrian bridges; it is now lined with artists' studios and new housing projects. A long, lazy barge tour of the canal leaves daily in the summertime from the Arsenal Marina, allowing visitors to take an unorthodox trip that ends close to the most peculiar of Paris's new attractions, the science center at **La Villette**. A textbook example of centralized planning gone awry (the Villette was built as a giant slaughterhouse at about the same time that the central food market was being moved to

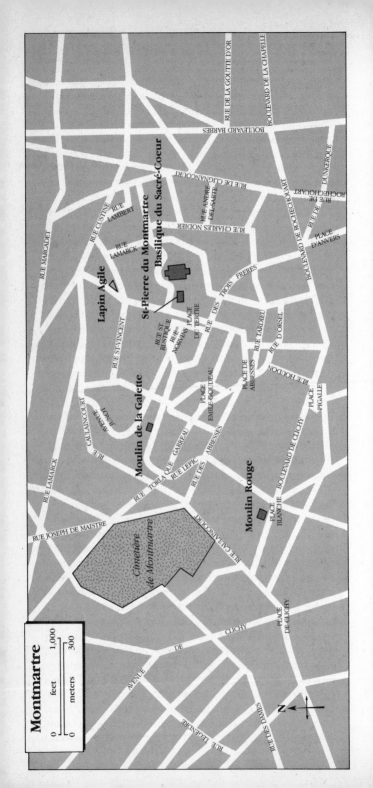

Montmartre

feet 0 — 1,000
meters 0 — 300

N

- Lapin Agile
- St-Pierre du Montmartre
- Basilique du Sacré-Coeur
- Moulin de la Galette
- Moulin Rouge
- Cimetière de Montmartre

RUE MARCADET
RUE CUSTINE
RUE LAMBERT
RUE LAMARCK
RUE DE LA GOUTTE D'OR
BOULEVARD DE LA CHAPELLE
BOULEVARD BARBÈS
RUE DE CLIGNANCOURT
RUE ANDRÉ-DEL-SARTE
RUE DE DUNKERQUE
RUE DE ROCHECHOUART
RUE CHARLES NODIER
PLACE D'ANVERS
BOULEVARD DE ROCHECHOUART
RUE DES TROIS FRÈRES
RUE ST-RUSTIQUE
RUE NORVINS
PLACE DU TERTRE
RUE DES SAULES
RUE TARDIEU
RUE D'ORSEL
RUE ST-VINCENT
PLACE EMILE-GOUDEAU
PLACE DE ABBESSES
RUE HOUDON
RUE CALLAINCOURT
RUE JUNOT
RUE D'ORCHAMPT
RUE TOURLAQUE
RUE GARREAU
RUE DES ABBESSES
RUE LEPIC
PIGALLE
RUE LAMARCK
RUE JOSEPH DE MAISTRE
BOULEVARD DE CLICHY
RUE CAULAINCOURT
PLACE BLANCHE
AVENUE DE CLICHY
PLACE DE CLICHY
RUE LEGENDRE
RUE DES DAMES

the southern suburb of Rungis), the complex ended its career as the city's most conspicuous white elephant when billions of francs were poured in during the 1980s to convert it into a showcase for French and European technology. Its most striking feature is the Géode, a spherical cinema that shows stomach-wrenching documentaries. A faster way to reach this far northeastern corner of Paris is to take the Métro (direction La Courneuve–8 Mai 1945) and get off at the Porte de la Villette station.

The best-known of eastern Paris sights is the **Père-Lachaise cemetery**, a hilltop city of the dead noted for the celebrity of its occupants and the fantasy of its funerary art. A Napoleonic scheme designed to put an end to such horrors as the Innocents cemetery by moving the capital's burial ground outside of the city, the graveyard quickly became the fashionable place for interment—once its caretakers had hit on the publicity stunt of transferring whichever illustrious remains they could get their hands on (e.g., Molière, Abélard, and Héloïse) to the then-suburban hillside. Its reputation grew as wealthy Parisian families erected extravagant monuments to their dead and as its roll call of the famous grew longer with the passing of each generation. It is advisable to tip the gatekeeper in exchange for a map that will help you locate the graves of Marcel Proust, Oscar Wilde, Edith Piaf, Frédéric Chopin, Honoré de Balzac, Sarah Bernhardt, Jim Morrison, Georges Bizet, Gertrude Stein, and scores of others. The strangest tomb of the lot is that of spiritualist Allan Kardec, always covered with flowers and often surrounded by séance holders intent on finding a way of communicating with deceased relatives. In the cemetery's northeastern corner is another pilgrimage site: the wall where, on the night of May 27, 1871, the last of the Communard insurgents were summarily executed after an eerie battle amidst the graves. The Paris Commune, a revolutionary city government that lasted three months and ended in savage repression by the army and wholesale arson by the Communards, was the most spectacular uprising of the 19th century, its legacy a continuing bitter division between Right and Left in French society.

The other redoubt of the Communards is associated more with life and art than with death and politics. **Montmartre**, the northernmost of the city's perimeter hills, was originally a religious refuge, its 12th-century

church of St-Pierre showing its antiquity in a vaulted ceiling that looks ready to topple over at any moment. Monasteries were gradually displaced as the city grew out to meet and engulf this village of wine makers and stone-cutters. By the last half of the 19th century, its windmills had been converted into dance halls (the 20th would change some of them into condominiums), where absinthe fueled much of the merrymaking and where such painters as Renoir (who frequented and painted the Moulin de la Galette) and Toulouse-Lautrec (the Moulin Rouge) found inspiration. Montmartre became the center of cabarets and bohemia, which, thanks to the new boulevards, more staid Parisians could easily visit for an evening out.

The hill might have stayed a purely local phenomenon had not artists of genius worked a revolution here. At such studios as the Bateau-Lavoir, Picasso, Modigliani, Utrillo, and many others used Montmartre as a subject for experimentation with figurative art, their radical departures defended by writer Guillaume Apollinaire and often accompanied, musically, by Erik Satie. The **Lapin Agile**, a cabaret where the avant-garde mixed with the criminal element, still exists, though it is now peopled by the nostalgic rather than the creative. The same might be said of Montmartre itself, a victim of its own fame. The **place du Tertre** in the warm months is crammed with people looking at the airport art for sale, and the **basilica of Sacré Coeur**, a blemish inflicted on the hillside by a vengeful French episcopacy in the wake of the Commune, has become an obligatory stop for every oversized tour bus in Europe. It's best to visit Montmartre in the winter or not at all.

If you do go to Montmartre, by all means visit the narrow strip on the southern slope, between the crush on the summit and the unrelieved sleaze of Pigalle and Clichy at the foot of the hill. The streets leading up from the **place des Abbesses** are picturesque and quiet, offering lovely, unexpected views over Paris. The rue Lepic, winding up the hill from place Blanche and the Moulin Rouge, is the site of a charming outdoor market. Here even the most seasoned travellers feel tempted to become maudlin over this extraordinary city, so don't worry if your eyes start misting over. In the springtime bring a handkerchief or, better still, someone you love. This is Paris, after all.

GETTING AROUND

As Paris is a major world capital, there is no mystery to getting there. Charles-de-Gaulle airport in Roissy to the north handles regular international flights, while Orly to the south takes charters, domestic flights, and a number of overseas carriers (American Airlines, Continental, and a few others). Both facilities are served by **Air France buses** that go to the central city terminals at Invalides and Porte Maillot (the latter being a modern hotel and convention center complex to the east of the city). In addition, **Orlybus**, a regular city transit line, provides an efficient service to Denfert-Rochereau. From Roissy, take the **RER** suburban railway line (look for the sign *Paris par le train*) that follows the B route directly and quickly to the Gare du Nord, Châtelet–Les Halles, St-Michel–Notre-Dame, Luxembourg, and Denfert-Rochereau. The cost for all the above is in the 30 to 40 francs range, whereas taxi fare from either airport to the center of Paris runs from 150 to 200 francs.

Paris is well serviced by France's efficient SNCF railway system. The city's six major train stations (St-Lazare, Nord, Est, Lyon, Austerlitz, and Montparnasse) are all served by the Métro, city buses, and taxis. Driving into Paris on the major expressways should present no problem except on Sunday nights or the last evening of holiday weekends, when long traffic jams are a certainty. The ring road (called the boulevard Périphérique) can sometimes involve drivers in a challenging game of chicken, especially when merging cars exercise their right, unique to this expressway, to zip into the right-hand lane without a moment's hesitation or notice.

When in Paris, walk; it is the best way to see and enjoy the city. Pedestrians usually ignore traffic signals. Avoid the busier streets between 5:00 and 7:00 in the evening— the pollution can be overwhelming. If you like cycling, this is not the city for you.

The public transit system is excellent. The **Métro** (subway) is open from 5:30 A.M. to 1:00 A.M. every day. The different lines are indicated by their termini; thus, you should know the direction in which you are going—*the name of the terminus*—rather than the number or color of the line. A Métro station is usually exited by way of glass doors (a natural mistake is to push the metal frame of these doors—which will not open them—instead of the green glass marked *Poussez*). A book of ten Métro tickets (a *carnet*) costs about 30 francs. Each ticket is good for one ride regardless of the number of transfers made. There are first-class cars in the middle of each train, although this curious class system is only in effect from 9:00 A.M. to 5:00 P.M. If confronted by a ticket inspector—a rare occurrence, except at the Louvre stop in the summer—you must have a valid ticket or a 100-franc banknote to pay the fine. If you are staying in Paris for an extended period, weekly and monthly passes are available.

The **RER** system provides even faster transit within the city, the four lines (A, B, C, D) having far fewer stops in Paris than the Métro. Thus, to go from the easternmost Bois de Vincennes to the central Châtelet–Les Halles transfer station on RER entails only two stops. If you stay within Paris on the RER system, regular Métro tickets can be used, the only novelty being the need to insert them in turnstiles on leaving RER stations. (Never throw away your ticket in the Paris underground.) Leaving Paris on the system (on a day trip to Versailles, Malmaison, or St-Germain-en-Laye, for example) requires purchasing a ticket whose price varies according to the length of your journey. As with the Métro, you must know the terminus of the line you wish to take in order to find the correct platform. Once there, make sure to check the electric signboard: Although RER trains do not skip stops within Paris, once out in the suburbs they may become super-expresses.

You should closely examine the easy-to-read Metro maps posted at each station to determine which Metro lines connect with the RER (which are marked on the map with wider lines and bolder colors). Also, to save time when taking the RER out of town, it's fairly easy to use an automatic ticket dispenser. Look for one that has an illuminated green "Je rends la monnaie" ("I make change") sign. Then press a destination button (all stops outside Paris are listed alphabetically), followed by the button for first or second class ("2ᵉ classe place entière" is the normal adult fare), and finally the button for a one-way ("aller simple") or return ("aller retour") ticket. The machine displays the sum required. Deposit your money, and a ticket, as well as change, will be issued. Despite the length of this explanation, it is an effortless, fast way to avoid RER ticket agents, who are known, even among irascible Parisians, for their less than rosy view of the world.

RER trains are identified both by destination and by a

letter. To add to the confusion, trains on line C—which serves Versailles—also have *names* (CORA, for example). Ignore the names; it is enough to follow the destination and letter, making sure, of course, that your desired station is on the platform sign that lists the stops for the incoming train.

The **buses** use the same yellow tickets as the Métro, although there are no transfers between the two systems or even between different bus routes. According to the length of your bus trip, you have to punch one, two, or three tickets in the little box located directly behind the driver. This number is determined by the number of zones you will pass through, as shown on the route map affixed to your bus stop. Information about times, frequency, and last bus runs should also be there. You can always ask fellow bus passengers: They tend to be more civil than the Métro riders (although Britons should not expect to see an orderly queue at a bus stop).

Contrary to Francophobe legend, Paris **taxi** drivers are not swindlers. It is true, however, that they drive like maniacs and that they sometimes have to be persuaded to take a customer who is not going their way. At cab stands the driver cannot refuse you—even if you're just going around the corner. You should know that hailing a cab in the central business districts between 6:00 P.M. and 7:00 P.M. is an enterprise only for the extremely patient or the irresistibly beautiful. Parisian cabbies are few in number—complaints from tourists and locals alike flow into City Hall every year—and when the demand for cabs is high (at rush hour and at 1:00 A.M., just after the Métro closes), the customer is most definitely not the king.

If you insist on driving in Paris, forget your manners and behave like a spoiled child. For all their admirable qualities, Parisians tend to become arrogant and impatient behind a steering wheel. Avoid driving on weekend evenings, and in central Paris be prepared to spend a good deal of time looking for a parking space. Cars are parked illegally everywhere, but at the high risk of being towed away. A very pleasant experience is to drive around Paris after eleven or so on a weeknight, past all the floodlit monuments. Cruising down the boulevards and around the Concorde and Etoile is pure, unadulterated fun.

ACCOMMODATIONS

Like any world capital, Paris brims with hotels that range from the exquisite to the execrable. The top end offers incomparable luxury and impeccable service; the bottom end is not worth talking about. Unfortunately, prices fit the same pattern. The hotels listed below are divided into two groups: the palace hotels, as they are called, where willing patrons pay at least 2,000 francs per night for a double room and far more for a suite or apartment (the most deluxe of which can reach 50,000 francs); and the rest, which cost between 100 and 2,000 francs per night. The latter are listed here as "upper range," 900 francs and up; "middle range," 450 to 900 francs; and "lower range," 100 to 450 francs. The hotels also fall into three geographic regions: the area around the Arc de Triomphe; the center, stretching from the Opéra to the Marais; and the Left Bank from the place Maubert to the Invalides.

The telephone country code for France is 33; the city code for Paris is 1.

THE PALACES

The Ritz. The Ritz is so classy that its name has come to mean sophistication. Owned now by an Egyptian businessman, the hotel has lost none of the charm, elegance, and snob appeal that made it famous—its neighbors on the exclusive place Vendôme include several of the world's most exclusive jewelers. In fact, the new owner created the Ritz-Hemingway literary award (winners so far include Marguerite Duras and Peter Taylor), a real-life paean to the man who claimed to have "liberated" the Ritz bar in 1944 and then decimated its cellars. The first hotel with a bathroom in the room, the Ritz now offers such comforts as window awnings that can be worked while you are still in bed, Jacuzzi bathtubs, and all business necessities. An excellent restaurant, too.

15, place Vendôme, 75001. Tel: 42-60-38-30; in U.S., (212) 838-3110 or (800) 223-6800; Telex: 670112; Fax: 42-86-00-91.

Meurice. Whenever he came to Paris, Salvador Dalí would swagger through the Meurice lobby, a cape swirling from his shoulders and brandishing a silver-headed cane, which says a lot about both the hotel's service—to keep such a demanding patron—and its personality—to attract such a commanding one. A block from the Ritz, the Meurice has a long and distinguished tradition; in the 19th century Edmund Rostand and Talleyrand favored it, and today such people as Liza Minnelli and Shirley Temple Black like to visit. Recent renovations include air-conditioning and remarkably elegant and modern bathrooms. The personal service inspires great loyalty in the customers.

228, rue de Rivoli, 75001. Tel: 42-60-38-60; in U.S., (212) 935-9540 or (800) 221-2340; Telex: 230673; Fax: 40-15-92-31.

Inter-Continental. Designed by Garnier of Paris Opéra fame, this is the largest of the palace hotels, though its size takes away nothing from its level of comfort. Seven courtyards break up the massive building (one of them is a delightful garden café), and the industrious staff negotiates miles of corridors to ensure that everything is just so. The very advanced business center—with fax, computer, and secretarial facilities—and a central location bordering the Tuileries gardens make it popular with the international business set, and VCRs are available for those unwilling to leave the luxury of their rooms.

3, rue Castiglione, 75001. Tel: 42-60-37-80; in U.S., (800) 327-0200; Telex: 220114; Fax: 42-61-14-03.

Crillon. The Taittinger Champagne family runs the Crillon, and the hotel is suffused with a vivaciousness that recalls the days when men refused to step out-of-doors without a top hat and women felt naked without a triple strand of pearls. The stunning setting—bounded on one side by the place de la Concorde, with views of the Assemblée Nationale and the Eiffel Tower across the river—is matched by a sumptuous decor: Glowing 18th-century wood paneling and marble bathrooms are standard. The personalized service draws such patrons from the diplomatic and political ranks as Edward Kennedy and Richard Nixon. Try to get a room with a balcony overlooking the place de la Concorde.

10, place de la Concorde, 75008. Tel: 42-65-24-24; in U.S., (212) 696-1323; Telex: 290204; Fax: 47-42-72-10.

Bristol. The softly lit white façade a block from the Champs-Elysées seems to promise exactly the sort of transcendent service this hotel in fact supplies. From the sixth-floor swimming pool to bathrooms brightened by Lalique windows and shower doors to the vivid bouquets of flowers everywhere, this hotel is particularly strong at what the Bristol management considers the basics—for almost anyone else the height of comfort. There are several fine dining rooms and a very pretty garden behind, which contribute to the calm, assured atmosphere. The Bristol is popular with the idle rich and well-heeled business people, as well as Bruce Springsteen. Lovely Art Deco decor.

112, rue du Faubourg-St-Honoré, 75008. Tel: 42-66-91-45; Telex: 280961; Fax: 42-66-68-68.

George V. Like the Ritz, the George V has become synonymous with luxury. The building, situated between the Champs-Elysées and the Seine, was constructed when Art Deco was at its most popular; its architecture is majestic yet completely un–Art Deco. Antiques fill the rooms, and an art gallery is necessary to supply paintings grand enough for the dining room. Recent management changes have restored the hotel to the top rank; today the front entrance is always lined with expensive foreign cars, and a mink-farm worth of coats swings through the main revolving door every night. Large extended suites can be created on certain floors, so this hotel is a favorite for big parties or for people with retinues, and the basement conference rooms draw major meetings and fancy balls.

31, avenue George-V, 75008. Tel: 47-23-54-00; in U.S., (800) 225-5843; Telex: 650082; Fax: 47-20-40-00.

Plaza-Athénée. The discreet entrance a few doors from the place d'Alma modestly guards what is probably the most beautiful of the palace hotels. In the spring, red geraniums blanket the building's façade, and the public rooms on the inside are alive with extravagant floral arrangements. The rooms are large and perfectly appointed, and not a whisper of traffic from the street below is allowed to reach them. During the fall and spring Paris fashion shows, the Plaza Athenée is packed with the most haute of the haute couture crowd (the hotel is reserved for two years in advance), and the Art Deco grillroom supplies top designers from the *quartier* with their daily nourishment. Sour notes and missed cues are illegal at the Plaza Athenée, which has satisfied such guests as Mata Hari and Katharine Hepburn as well as just about everyone else who ever stayed there.

25, avenue Montaigne, 75008. Tel: 47-23-78-33; in U.S., (800) 225-5843; Telex: 650092; Fax: 47-20-20-70.

THE RIGHT BANK

Arc de Triomphe and Trocadéro

Named after a great 15th-century general, Louis II de la Trémoille, **La Trémoille** is anything but warlike. Situated in a lovely, late 19th-century building, this lavishly and taste-fully decorated hotel provides clients with a private, ele-gant retreat from the city (Orson Welles once stayed sev-eral months and almost never left his room), complete with balconies alive with flower boxes. An intimate, wood-paneled bar leads to an even more intimate dining room with a crackling fire.

14, rue de la Trémoille, 75008. Tel: 47-23-34-20; in U.S., (212) 838-3110 or (800) 223-6800; Telex: 640344; Fax: 40-70-01-08. Upper range.

The **Raphaël** is like a slightly smaller, slightly clubbier version of the Trémoille. The wood paneling is dark rather than light, the plaster moldings are a bit more elaborate, and thick Oriental rugs cover the marble floors. The very large rooms are favored by high-flying business people and those needing personalized service. A very pretty, very distinguished hotel.

17, avenue Kléber, 75116. Tel: 45-02-16-00; in U.S., (212) 477-1600 or (800) 366-1510; Telex: 610356; Fax: 45-01-21-50. Upper range.

The **Lancaster** is another smaller but no less luxurious option to the palace hotels. Just off the Champs-Elysées, in a gracefully designed building with a stained-glass ceiling in the entry and a tranquil garden courtyard com-plete with fountains and statues, the Lancaster offers afflu-ent travellers a graceful home away from home—if you happen to live as Santiago Drake del Castillo did when he built the house in 1899. Run by the Savoy group.

7, rue de Berri, 75008. Tel: 43-59-90-43; in U.S., (800) 223-5581; Telex: 640991; Fax: 42-89-22-71. Upper range.

Up the block from the Elysée palace, home to the French president, the **Hôtel de l'Elysée** is a very reason-ably priced possibility in an expensive neighborhood. The rooms are lovely; some have terrific balcony views, and the ones on the top floor have cozy dormer windows and wood beams. Restoration decor with lots of trompe l'oeil murals.

12, rue des Saussaies, 75008. Tel: 42-65-29-25; Telex: 281665; Fax: 42-65-64-28. Lower-to-middle range.

The Center

With its marble floors, gilded chandeliers, and extraordi-narily well preserved Belle Epoque woodwork framing graceful beveled-glass windows, the elegant entrance of the **Hotel Regina** belies the slightly faded splendor of its very spacious rooms. Built in the waning days of the

Second Empire, the Regina's convenient location just opposite the Tuileries (a two-minute walk from the Louvre's glass pyramid) and airy rooms are its best features. Every room is well equipped with modern comforts, including double-paned windows to muffle the traffic sounds below, and a cozy bar and pretty little courtyard garden round out the charming amenities.

2, place des Pyramides/192, rue de Rivoli, 75001. Tel: 42-60-31-10; Telex: 670834; Fax: 40-15-95-16. Upper range.

Wedged between the Louvre and the Comédie-Française, facing the famed shopping street rue du Faubourg-St-Honoré and peering up the avenue de l'Opéra, the **Louvre-Concorde** could hardly be more central. A severely formal two-story lobby shimmers under the huge crystal chandelier, and, beyond, a formal staircase leads up to the high-ceilinged, comfortable, and fairly expensive rooms. The mirrored dining room can be confusing, but a good outdoor café looks out onto the busy square and Palais-Royal.

Place André-Malraux, 75001. Tel: 42-61-56-01; in U.S., (800) THE-OMNI; Telex: 220412; Fax: 42-60-45-81. Upper range.

Smack in the heart of Les Halles, the **Prince Hôtel Forum** provides character and service at moderate cost in a lively neighborhood. Rooms are sound-proofed so that proximity to the action won't interfere with your sleep at night. With pleasant, recently remodeled rooms in a very old building, the hotel has a full range of services.

83, rue Rambuteau, 75001. Tel: 42-36-15-90. Middle range.

The **Henri IV** is a tiny, ancient hotel on a tiny, ancient square, the place Dauphine on the Ile de la Cité. The management is very nice and the rooms are clean, if not particularly tasteful. Be sure to ask for one on the *place,* though, since the airshaft rooms are rather bleak. It's cheap, central, fun, and always packed with younger travellers. Write for a reservation.

25, place Dauphine, 75001. Tel: 43-54-44-53. No credit cards. Lower range.

Maybe it isn't as opulent as its MGM namesake, but **Le Grand Hôtel** on the place de l'Opéra is pretty grand indeed. The recently renovated rooms are nicely done up and on the whole tasteful (especially the suites), and the columned and gilded dining room and garden restaurant are spectacular examples of Second Empire excess. The

Grand is very large, on the expensive side, and at times a little impersonal, but the service is generally quite good.

2, rue Scribe, 75009. Tel: 40-07-32-32; in U.S., (800) 327-0200; Telex: 220875; Fax: 42-66-12-51. Upper range.

A former 18th-century convent named after its most famous resident, the **Baudelaire Opéra** is a much more reasonably priced option in the Opéra area than the Grand. The rooms are plain, with an occasional touch of splendor. The sparkling lobby is dominated by a somewhat Roman fresco, a theme that is halfheartedly repeated throughout the hotel. Conveniently located between the Opéra and the Palais-Royal.

61, rue Ste-Anne, 75002. Tel: 42-97-50-62; Telex: 216116. Lower-to-middle range.

The hotel **Bretonnerie** in the heart of the Marais is the perfect headquarters for people who love wandering the *quartier*'s ancient, charming streets. The moderately priced rooms are neat and pleasant, though decorated with less than effective attention to matching colors and patterns, and each has a comfortable bathroom. The rooms on the airshaft are a bit dim, so it's best to avoid them. Redolent of a somewhat dated Paris bourgeois life. The management is quite cheerful.

22, rue Ste-Croix-de-la-Bretonnerie, 75004. Tel: 48-87-77-63; Fax: 42-77-26-78. Lower-to-middle range.

Mere minutes from the place des Vosges, a 1682 structure has been transformed into the **Hôtel Saint-Paul le Marais**. Two partners diligently oversee this small (there are only 27 equally small rooms) but spotless and comfortable family hotel. The bathrooms are modern, if cramped, and the breakfast room in the restored *cave* is contained within comfortable stone arches.

8, rue de Sévigné, 75004. Tel: 48-04-97-27; Fax: 48-87-37-04. Lower-to-middle range.

The historic place des Vosges houses only one hotel, an honor reserved for the **Pavillon de la Reine**. This quiet, attractive, and luxurious hotel with a garden courtyard and interestingly decorated rooms and suites (a mix of modern and antique that can be fairly oppressive) is a favorite of those looking for high style and privacy. There is a nice fireplace in the wood-paneled lounge, but no restaurant.

28, place des Vosges, 75003. Tel: 42-77-96-40; in U.S., (212) 477-1600 or (800) 366-1510; Telex: 216160; Fax: 42-77-63-06. Upper range.

Within sight of the place de la Bastille and surrounded by worthwhile restaurants, the **Hôtel Bastille Spéria** is an inexpensive option in a very hip part of town. There's no Old World charm, as it's quite new, nor any real views, but the small rooms are spotless and crammed with features such as minibars and televisions that come as a surprise considering its inexpensive rates. The location cannot be beat and the mattresses are firm.

1, rue de la Bastille, 75004. Tel: 42-72-04-01; Fax: 42-72-56-38. Lower range.

Just behind the St-Merri church, which bounds the Stravinsky fountain next to the Centre Georges Pompidou (yes, it is central), the small, cozy **Saint Merry** hotel offers an eccentric decor that seems to draw a very attractive clientele. Everything—bedspreads, wallpaper, curtains, even the wastebaskets—bears the same pattern. Several of the church's flying buttresses launch themselves through rooms, which poses a danger for sleepwalkers or sudden wakers. Fun and very reasonably priced.

78, rue de la Verrerie, 75004. Tel: 42-78-14-15. No credit cards. Lower-to-middle range.

The **Hôtel du Jeu de Paume** is a welcome and comfortable addition to the charming Ile St-Louis. The dramatic cathedral lobby, framed by the same 17th-century wood beams that once housed a royal *jeu de paume* (an indoors court for an old game similar to tennis), gives patrons a delightful sense of old Paris. The rooms, while on the small side, are graciously decorated and packed with all the modern comforts. The marble-filled bathrooms are especially luxurious. Room 109 has a nice view of the pretty little Italian garden, but wherever you stay, take the glass elevator to the top floor for a panorama of the ancient game hall.

54, rue St-Louis-en-l'Ile, 75004. Tel: 43-26-14-18. Rooms, middle range; suites, upper range.

The 17th-century hotel **Deux-Iles**, old fashioned and quaint, features a very welcoming lobby with flowered couches and white-painted beams. Ask for the biggest room in the house, because they are all very small. The **Saint Louis** specializes in long stays and is charmingly and tastefully decorated.

Deux-Iles: 59, rue St-Louis-en-l'Ile, 75004. Tel: 43-26-13-35. Saint Louis: 75, rue St-Louis-en-l'Ile, 75004. Tel: 46-34-04-80; in U.S. for both, (212) 477-1600 or (800) 366-1510. No credit cards at either hotel. Lower-to-middle range.

Montmartre offers the modern **Timhôtel**, a very conveniently located member of a medium-priced chain. Bordering the picturesque and quiet place Emile-Goudeau, the hotel has tasteful rooms, with those on the fourth and fifth floors offering extraordinary views of Paris. On Saturday mornings a talented accordion player cranks out old French love songs. Picasso's and Braque's one-time studio, the Bateau-Lavoir, is next door (not open).

11, place Emile-Goudeau, 75018. Tel: 42-55-74-79. Lower range.

The 18th-*arrondissement* charm almost entirely absent from Sacré Coeur and the place de Tertes blossoms in full on the pretty place des Abbesses and the little market streets bordering it. **Regyn's Montmartre**, overlooking the *place,* benefits from both its location and the lovely garden courtyard within the hotel (request rooms on the courtyard away from the incessantly ringing church bells). The rooms are pleasantly priced and renovated, and the breakfast room is as bright and cheerful as the staff.

18, place des Abbesses, 75018. Tel: 42-54-45-21. Lower range.

Two things particularly recommend the **Hôtel Le Laumière**: its proximity to both France's Communist Party headquarters—an odd building that looks like a giant unearthed bomb shelter—and what is perhaps the most touching of Paris parks, the Parc aux Buttes Chaumont; and its very low prices. One of the few hotels in the isolated 19th *arrondissement,* Le Laumière offers neither views nor antique furniture but is nonetheless a well-run little outpost in a neighborhood too little explored.

4, rue Petit, 75019. Tel: 42-06-10-77. Lower range.

THE LEFT BANK

Left Bank hotels tend to be smaller and more intimate than those across the Seine, and, other than the following trio of high-class options, they are usually more affordable.

L'Hôtel is the grandest accommodation on the Left Bank, a sliver of a building on a street crammed with art galleries and character, near the place de l'Odéon. Each of the 27 luxuriously appointed rooms has a different decor, and the superb service is as straightforward as the name. There is an excellent piano bar in the hotel. It was here that Oscar Wilde spent his last days dying beyond his means.

13, rue des Beaux-Arts, 75006. Tel: 43-25-27-22; in U.S., (212) 477-1600 or (800) 366-1510. Upper range.

The **Relais Christine**, opposite a repertory movie house

a block from the Seine, is only a half-step behind L'Hôtel in terms of luxury. An abbey in the 16th century, the building features a handsome courtyard and a lovely garden. Breakfast is served in an ancient vaulted cave, and cocktail hour takes place in a clubby, wood-paneled lounge. Medieval artifacts—including beams that still bear the trace of their original paint job, tapestries, and suits of armor—set the tone. Most of the bathrooms have been redone in marble, but ask especially for a finished one if only stone will do.

3, rue Christine, 75006. Tel: 43-26-71-80; in U.S., (212) 477-1600 or (800) 366-1510; Telex: 202606; Fax: 43-26-89-38. Upper range.

The **Lutétia** was refurbished and rejuvenated a few years ago to recapture much of the Art Deco glory that made it famous (especially the stunning paneling in the excellent **Le Paris** restaurant). Some of the rooms are very large (a luxury for which you will pay) and have pretty views of the tree-filled place Boulicaut at Sèvres-Babylone across the street. There are imposing yet comfortable sitting rooms off the lobby, and its **Brasserie Lutétia** is a pretty, if predictable, restaurant.

45, boulevard Raspail, 75006. Tel: 45-44-38-10; in U.S., (212) 593-2988 or (800) 223-5652; Telex: 270424; Fax: 45-44-50-50. Upper range.

Esmeralda, named after Quasimodo's bohemian flame, has the slightly eccentric, slightly funky character you might expect from such an inspiration. A block from both the Shakespeare and Co. bookshop and the Seine, the structure was built in 1640. The tiny lobby, with its stone walls and huge wood beams, leads to a handful of uniquely decorated rooms—and a sauna. Such actors as Julie Christie and Jane Birkin, who obviously appreciate a good bargain, have come here for the pleasantly odd atmosphere.

4, rue St-Julien-le-Pauvre, 75005. Tel: 43-54-19-20; in U.S., (212) 477-1600 or (800) 366-1510. No credit cards. Lower range.

The **Hôtel de Nesle** is one of the most colorful places to stay in Paris. The expansive, friendly proprietress takes a personal interest in the young, decidedly Anglophone crowd that populates this small hotel on a short side street near the Seine. The office is more like a lounge or library, with a very Oriental feel. The rooms are adequate and quite cheap, and any shortcomings are overcome by the Nesle's vivacious personality.

7, rue de Nesle, 75006. Tel: 43-54-62-41. No credit cards. Lower range.

A true writer's hotel should be slightly seedy and on a bustling egalitarian street, and it should charge egalitarian prices. **Louisiane** qualifies. It housed Sartre and Jacques Prévert in the old days, and it is home to a few real-life writers today. Overlooking the rue de Buci market, Louisiane is perhaps not the quietest of hotels, but the lively rows of fruit stands, green-grocers, butchers, and more are worth the bustle. Ask for the round rooms; they embody the absence of sharp edges one finds here.

60, rue de Seine, 75006. Tel: 43-29-59-30. No American Express; lower range.

In the heart of the Latin Quarter, the hotel **St-André-des-Arts** offers rooms ranging from tiny and cheap on the top floor to spacious and inexpensive on the lower floors. The inner rooms are somewhat shielded from the rollicking street outside, and the clientele runs to artists, dancers, and models.

66, rue St-André-des-Arts, 75006. Tel: 43-26-96-16. No credit cards; lower range.

One of Louis XIV's architects designed the **Hôtel des Saints-Pères** in 1658, and the structure reflects the period's fondness for rich decor—including some terrific frescoes and painted panels and a very pretty little garden courtyard. In warm months, breakfast and tea are served outside; there is a small, comfortable bar off the foyer. Friendly in a faintly formal way and relatively inexpensive.

65, rue des Saints-Pères, 75006. Tel: 45-44-50-00; in U.S., (212) 477-1600 or (800) 366-1510; Telex: 205424; Fax: 45-44-90-83. No American Express; middle range.

Between the graceful church of St-Germain-des-Prés and the massive St-Sulpice church, the medium-priced **Hôtel de l'Odéon** features a wood-beamed lobby, a warm reception, and some outstanding four-poster beds. Even the smaller rooms have an old-fashioned charm. The location is excellent. Half the rooms overlook the street, which is generally quiet at night, and half overlook the courtyard.

13, rue St-Sulpice, 75006. Tel: 43-25-70-11; Telex: 206731. Middle range.

Nestled between the Ecole des Beaux-Arts and the Faculté de Médecine, the rue Jacob boasts the **Marronniers** ("the chestnut trees"), a lovely little hotel complete with a garden patio for breakfast. Ask for a room on the top floor, amid the mansards and cornices, for a view of the bell tower of the church of St-Germain-des-Prés, or for a room just above the garden. Quiet, reasonably priced, personable, and charming, the Marronniers is just right for a few romantic days in the Latin Quarter.

21, rue Jacob, 75006. Tel: 43-25-30-60. No credit cards. Lower-to-middle range.

A St-Germain-des-Prés option that is best for the traveller who doesn't plan to live in the room is the early 19th-century **Hotel Danube**. The location is great, the price reasonable, and the bathrooms all new, but the "modern-ugly" decor and small rooms detract somewhat from the overall effect. Breakfast is served, when the weather permits, on a prettily flowered terrace.

58, rue Jacob, 75006. Tel: 42-60-34-70. Lower-to-middle range (for 3-person rooms and suites).

An ancient façade cloaks Paris's most modern hotel interior at **La Villa**. The relentlessly designed rooms, with their quirky stools, built-in beds, and glamorous chrome-and-glass bathrooms, clash with the spirit of the *quartier,* but not with anyone interested in contemporary French design. Though not overly spacious, the rooms are well-equipped, and no one can fail to appreciate the numbers beamed onto the carpet in front of each door. The ground floor bar is a good place to meet for a drink.

29, rue Jacob, 75006. Tel: 43-26-60-00; Fax: 46-34-63-63. Middle-to-upper range.

The **Récamier** is a simple hotel with a dated French decor (flowered wallpaper, pseudo-antique furniture) right on the place St-Sulpice and a three-minute walk from the Luxembourg gardens. Nothing special, except that it is solid, dependable, moderately priced, and superbly located. Ask for one of the five rooms with windows on both the square and the courtyard—the light is great.

3 bis, place St-Sulpice, 75006. Tel: 43-26-04-89. No credit cards; lower range.

Also near the Luxembourg gardens, the **Bonaparte**, like Napoléon's parceling out of Europe, is a family affair (the same family has kept patrons happy for several generations). Pleasant rooms and a homey salon have exposed beams and a dash of oddness to give them character. The Bonaparte is a good, less-expensive option, although prices have risen somewhat after recent renovations.

61, rue Bonaparte, 75006. Tel: 43-26-97-37. Lower range.

Called the **Angleterre** because it once housed the English embassy—Benjamin Franklin refused to enter its doors to sign a treaty because it was British territory—this affordable hotel retains many touches of its former splendor. Canopy beds adorn the deluxe suites, and ancient wood beams stretch across their ceilings. Rooms 40, 42, 47, and 49 are huge and worth the slight surcharge, so reserve well ahead. The lobby sports a bar and piano lounge, and there is a lovely flower-filled patio. Hemingway once lived here.

44, rue Jacob, 75006. Tel: 42-60-34-72; Fax: 42-60-16-93. Middle range.

Old France retains some vigor in the pretty little **Université**, a 17th-century *hôtel particulier* with exposed wood beams and a general air of charm and discretion. The rooms are small but well appointed, and the comfortable bathrooms feature marble tubs. Try for the room with the fireplace that overlooks the pretty courtyard or one of the two top-floor rooms with a terrace. Breakfast at the long table off the lobby is communal.

22, rue de l'Université, 75007. Tel: 42-61-09-39. No credit cards; middle range.

The **Ferrandi** offers 19th-century charm in a period house, which means that some of the rooms tread a delicate balance between pretty and kitschy. Others, though, are truly beautiful, such as rooms 33 and 43, which are large and sport canopy beds, and rooms 40 and 49, done in a neat Baroque style. Well-kept and well-run in a quiet neighborhood in the southwest corner of the 6th *arrondissement*.

92, rue du Cherche-Midi, 75006. Tel: 42-22-97-40; Telex: 205201; Fax: 45-44-89-97. Lower-to-middle range.

The **Quai Voltaire** hotel is nestled on the quay from which it takes its name, square between the Bibliothèque Mazarin and the Musée d'Orsay. Most rooms have superb views of the Seine and unfortunately good acoustics: The traffic from the street below can get loud. The building is old and not all the rooms are in tiptop shape, but it still has the charm—and the rates—that drew composers Wagner and Sibelius.

19, quai Voltaire, 75007. Tel: 42-61-50-91. Lower-to-middle range.

Faux marbre walls in the corridors and trompe l'oeil murals in the breakfast room may give you the impression that the **Duc de St-Simon** is not for real. It is, being a very tasteful hotel in a late 17th-century *maison particulier*. The rooms, some with a small terrace, are quite pretty, and the suites are very comfortable. There is a garden on the first floor, and the street is particularly picturesque.

14, rue St-Simon, 75007. Tel: 45-48-35-66; Telex: 203277; Fax: 45-48-68-25. No credit cards; middle-to-upper range.

Sixty years ago the **Lenox** was a *pension* favored by such folks as James Joyce and Ezra Pound. Later the Lost Generation prowled its halls. Today the small, welcoming lobby is still welcoming, and the rooms are very nice (especially 22, 32, and 42) and nicely priced. For a splurge ask for the duplex suite. The cozy Art Deco bar is a quiet place for a late drink.

9, rue de l'Université, 75007. Tel: 42-96-10-95; in U.S., (201) 235-1990; Telex: 260745; Fax: 42-61-52-83. Lower-to-middle range.

—*Edward Hernstadt*

DINING

Paris has long had a justly earned reputation for its superb cuisine. But in a city of some 20,000 restaurants and cafés, eating well is a surprisingly difficult challenge. Guidebooks are a must: The seemingly similar cafés and small brasseries that line almost every street are too often similar in their mediocrity as well, and many visitors leave Paris sadly dissatisfied. With a little care, though, you can dine as beautifully as the city's fame promises.

Paris *haute cuisine,* though more expensive than ever, still sets the world standard for sublime and inventive meals served with an emphasis on extreme comfort. The resulting pool of talented chefs means that there is also a reasonably broad range of restaurants that are distinctly less costly (250 to 500 francs per person, rather than 550 francs and up), yet offer innovative and tasty dishes.

Bistros and brasseries still form the solid middle level of Paris restaurants, in terms of price (100 to 300 francs), originality, and tastiness of the food. If you want to eat after the witching hour (for most restaurants and cafés, 10:30 P.M.), these old-time eateries are the best and often only bet.

Wine bars take two forms: the modern, which offer *nouvelle* dishes along with a selection of wines, and the traditional, where it is customary to munch on cheese or sausages and Poilane bread. In both, a satisfying repast for less than 130 francs is standard.

Cafés and tea-rooms fall more or less into the same price range as wine bars: The former feature such traditional snacks as *croques monsieur* and baguette sandwiches, while the latter emphasize tarts (both sweet and with vegetables) and quiches.

HAUTE CUISINE

Gloriously refined meals in sumptuously appointed rooms; attentive waiters hovering discreetly just out of sight; magnificent wines glowing in balloon glasses as one astoundingly subtle and elegant dish succeeds another: the stuff of dreams, perhaps, but in Paris not an impossibility. In fact, the *haute gamme* food business is raging on vigorously, ignoring the death of *nouvelle cuisine* and such sub-species as *cuisine de terroir* (almost unrecognizably refined "country" food) and "light" dishes for dieters.

Today the world of fine dining is ruled by chefs rather than by restaurant owners or the great "names," the Maxims, of yore. Some chefs, like Joël Robuchon, are very low key, content to remain sequestered in the kitchen, rarely even showing themselves at the end of a service. Others, like Alain Senderens, have cultivated a reputation away from the cutting board (Senderens enjoys his role of "philosopher/chef," making weighty declarations on the state of cooking and frequently sporting ties and eyeglasses of a matching color). But the best chefs, in any guise, are worth the 550- to 1,000-franc bill that is standard at their restaurants, as well as the straining waistline and general aura of peace on earth and good will toward men that suffuses your amble home. For all of these, reserve at least five days in advance, if not far earlier.

Right Bank

Jamin (Joël Robuchon), at 32, rue de Longchamp in the 16th *arrondissement,* is unquestionably the best mix of the mysterious ingredients that signal greatness in a restaurant. The small main room is intimate and elegant. Huge bouquets of flowers and folding screens of vaguely ancient origin isolate the tables; Roman busts, dated engravings, and tasteful red-velvet banquettes contribute to the refined and harmonious ambience. The food is truly sublime: roast duck with spices for two, cooked in an enormous copper casserole with a ring of pastry baked around the rim to seal in every molecule of flavor; *purée de pommes de terre* (the world's best mashed potatoes, with a hint of garlic); boned leg of lamb baked in a salt and thyme crust; *langoustines,* either in ravioli or with cabbage. The wine list is extensive and excellent, and everyone, from the wine steward to the maître d'hôtel, is remarkably courteous and down-to-earth. The bad news? Reserve at least a month in advance. Tel: 47-27-12-27.

Henri Faugeron redid his restaurant's strange, dark decor with a more restrained and harmonious feel—soft blues and yellows and gilded Deco touches—without changing in the least the consistently notable caliber of his cooking. His creations are less gaudy and thus perhaps less outstanding than those of some of his compatriots, but dishes like the house-smoked salmon, shrimp and cabbage salad, the several versions of heartfelt roast duck, and *ris de veau* with lentil-stuffed ravioli are delectable. The solid cooking (though in these circles, that means eye-opening) and more relaxed atmosphere make Faugeron a popular spot. The service, as is usual for any of these restaurants, is dedicated. Faugeron and three other chefs, Les Toques Gourmands, banded together to buy wine in bulk and rented a huge underground warehouse to store their now vast communal cellar, which means that the wine list is quite good, though better on the more recent vintages. 52, rue de Longchamp. Tel: 47-04-24-53.

On the other side of the Arc de Triomphe, at 18, rue Troyon in the 17th *arrondissement,* **Guy Savoy** continues to minister to the hungry in what was once Le Bernardin (now in New York). This is wonderful, because his former headquarters in the rue Duret was just too cramped to contain the faithful who flocked to experience the monk-like Savoy's marvelous mixture of country, traditional, and completely inventive cooking. This young chef is constantly experimenting and growing in the kitchen. The best and most adventurous move: Order *le menu dégustation* and try Savoy's latest original and beautifully presented dishes. He has a sure touch with *langoustine* and lobster, and his variations on duck are all winners. The cheeses are particularly good, and for dessert have his *mille-feuilles* (what in the United States and often in the United Kingdom is served in a heavy-handed and limited version as "Napoleon")—they are always works of art. Avoid lunch, which is made almost drab by the multitudes of somber-suited businessmen. His two new bistros are also top-notch (see Bistro de l'Etoile, below). Tel: 43-80-40-61.

Michel Rostang has side-by-side restaurants in the 17th

arrondissement (see Bistro d'à Côté, below) and comes to the trade by blood: His father and younger brother run the wonderful La Bonne Auberge in Antibes. Rostang's first-string restaurant, with its formal, fancy, and, to the delicate, perhaps oppressive decor, is a mighty work indeed. The cuisine is varied and moves from the classic bourgeois—his ambrosial ravioli stuffed with goat's cheese in a chicken broth—to the otherworldly—quails' eggs poached inside sea urchins. The delicate, rosy lamb, redolent with herbs, is exactly what you dream lamb should be. One possible drawback to a quiet, intimate, oh-so-French dinner is the quantity of Anglophones, though the dollar's current weakness has alleviated this problem in all of Paris's great restaurants. Order the Pantagruelian menu if only a seven-course feast will suffice. The cheeses and desserts are delicious, the wine list ample, and the refined atmosphere conducive to those who take their pleasure at the table. 20, rue Rennequin. Tel: 47-63-40-77.

When Philippe Groult left the large, stone-walled Manoir de Paris to open his own restaurant, he changed everything but the excellence of his cooking, which has only improved with his move to independence. **Amphyclès** is a tiny, very pretty room overflowing with flowers and friendly, spirited service at 78, avenue des Ternes in the 17th *arrondissement*. Groult sticks to the basics in his cuisine, with the superb *raviolis de pigeon* a good example of his craft: chunks of pungent, earthy pigeon folded into a giant, melting ravioli with creamy morsels of foie gras and hints of truffles. Each ingredient enhances the particular delicacy and character of the other, the whole exceeding its parts. Order the most interesting and exotic dishes on the menu, as the more standard items tend to be just that: extremely well executed standards. The cheese tray is fabulous and desserts are worth saving room for, especially the *pot de crème*. The wine list is both a bit pricey and a bit limited, though there are some good bargains, and the sommelier is a real pro. Very good value for the money. Reserve; Tel: 40-68-01-01.

Rounding out the sedate 17th *arrondissement* is **Apicius**, at 122, avenue de Villiers, one of the more casual of the pantheon of exquisite restaurants. The cool, rather small room, the young and attractive Madame Vigato, and the lively atmosphere make Apicius a place for you and friends to eat extremely well and make some noise doing it. Jean-Pierre Vigato is another one of those young and creative chefs who has moved well past the strictures of *nouvelle cuisine* and simply cooks what he thinks is tasty. Grilled pig's trotters and exquisite sautéed foie gras sit side by side on the menu. Other winners include the frog's legs, succulent *coquilles St-Jacques* reminiscent of those at the old Ambroisie, and a lovely, meaty rabbit that is so good you will forever after think of "bunny" as a consumable dish. Desserts are fine though unspectacular, and the varied wine list includes some fairly reasonably priced bottles. Vigato has also opened a second, less expensive, restaurant just outside the city gates (see Manufacture, below). Tel: 43-80-19-66.

Champs-Elysées

There is probably a greater concentration of immodestly expensive restaurants in the 8th *arrondissement* than anywhere else in Paris, though unfortunately that does not mean an equal concentration of culinary wonders. Still, three stops in particular are worth the weighty checks: Taillevent, Les Ambassadeurs, and Lucas-Carton. Alain Rayé, a fourth, far more reasonably priced alternative, has rapidly climbed the ranks of "good" restaurants and is today one of the best bargains—and finest kitchens—in the *quartier*.

If style, class, and a dignified atmosphere are as important as cooking, **Taillevent** is the best restaurant in Paris. Set in a well-preserved Second Empire *hôtel particulier* at 15, rue Lamennais, Taillevent better defines the art of dining out than that of eating well. The tasteful woodpaneled walls and crystal chandeliers in the main room, or the ornate yet unimposing grandeur of the smaller room; the perfect, understated service (you rarely see a waiter until, alerted by some imperceptible gesture or stray thought, one sweeps up to the table an instant before being signaled); the gracious welcome of Jean-Claude Vrinat, the restaurateur who should be a template for all restaurant owners (Vrinat is so gracious, and confident, that he insists the food at Robuchon is the best in Paris); the vast, varied, and surprisingly affordable wine list—these embody the Taillevent dining experience.

Unfortunately, magical, inventive cuisine was left off the list. The food, by Claude Deligne, is awfully good but cannot live up to the experience of eating it. The ingredients are always fresh, the dishes of a modified classicism, and the menu changes frequently (upon request, the house will give diners an outdated one). Order according to what rings true or ask M. Vrinat for his recommendations—everything is tasty, especially the desserts. The bill will be appropriately serious, but you need no longer fear for your safety carrying an immense sheaf of 500-franc bills: They finally accept Visa. Reserve at least two months in advance for dinner, less for lunch. Tel: 45-61-12-90.

A different kind of style typifies **Les Ambassadeurs**, the majestic dining room of the Hôtel Crillon at 10, place de la Concorde, a stone's throw from both the U.S. and British embassies. The hotel itself was built in 1758 by the architect Jacques-Ange Gabriel and was used as a residence until 1920. Entrance to the restaurant is through the hotel's opulent front hall, past the piano bar and courtyard—which in the summer is itself a delightful spot to lunch—and into a room that looks exactly like what it once was: the imposing grand salon of a fabulous *hôtel particulier*. Red, beige, and white Sienese marble walls and floors greet the eye, and the vast 30-foot windows look out onto the place de la Concorde and the illuminated Egyptian obelisk that sits placidly on the same spot where during the revolution of 1793–1794 thousands died, their heads sliced from their bodies as neatly as Les Ambassadeurs's chef now dices zucchini.

The atmosphere is formal (famed food critic Henri Gault advises that "if you don't wear a tie you will be shot, with a look, anyway, and someone will bring you one") but not at all oppressive. It's as if the staff assumes that if one dines at Les Ambassadeurs, one is a member of an elite club and due all privileges granted thereby, which is a far cry from the haughtiness of the staffs of some top Parisian restaurants. The food has slipped somewhat from excellent to merely very good, but this is surely just a phase, and the room itself is so marvelous that a meal here is only a small gamble. Go to the Crillon for a romantic and anachronistic meal; the surroundings give you a sense of the extreme luxury that defined the ancien régime. Tel: 42-65-24-24.

Lucas-Carton is perhaps the most controversial great restaurant in Paris; master chef Alain Senderens does his best to ensure that. The reservation list is long (at least a month for dinner), the portions can be minute, the dishes can miss the mark, and the prices are monumental (a group of eight Americans are alleged to have spent 55,000 francs on a meal—most of it on rare wines). Nonetheless, Senderens prepares some of the best food in the world;

order well and a successful meal at Lucas-Carton is as memorable as a feast hosted by Tolstoy's Count Ilya Rostov.

The magnificent Belle Epoque decor announces that something special is at hand: rich, burnished, wood-paneled walls by Louis Majorelle; comfortable, dark-brown banquettes separated into individual dining spaces by carved wood and glass dividers; tall, beveled mirrors; and huge floral arrangements. Senderens, who perhaps considers himself the best-dressed chef in Paris, has outfit-ted his many waiters, stewards, and captains in sober tuxedos, the different pastel shades of the requisite bow tie alone distinguishing each staff member's station.

Senderens is no stranger to the long-renowned restau-rant at 9, place de la Madeleine: He worked in the kitchen there more than 30 years ago. In a sense, his return to his beginnings in the mid-1980s mirrors his philosophy at the stove, where he constantly revives and updates ancient recipes (like the famous honey-and-spice-covered *canard Apicius*, which dates back at least 2,000 years). Today Senderens continues to innovate—he was perhaps the first to impose Oriental combinations and ideas on French cuisine—and his masterpieces are extraordinary indeed. Anything with *langoustine,* foie gras (such as the warm foie gras salad latticed with sheafs of truffles), lobster (such as the miraculous lobster in vanilla sauce), or game is bound to be impeccable and original. The service has gotten better (that is, less pretentious and pressured), and the wine list is extensive. Senderens's latest obsession is the "marriage of food and wine," so it behooves you to try a *menu dégustation* with selected wines included, or the cheese dish consisting of five cheeses and five (usually unexpected) wines. And be prepared to cash in your Christmas Club fund before you go. Tel: 42-65-22-90.

Underrated, intimate, comfortable, elegant, "reason-ably" priced. These careful words describe **Alain Rayé**'s very pretty little second-floor restaurant without really giving a sense of the satisfaction you feel after a meal under his precisely appointed roof. Everything, from the cordial welcome downstairs to the dignified yet warm service to the quietly imaginative dishes, exudes class without pretension. Perhaps it is the room's somewhat isolated location at 49, rue du Colisée—on the edge of the heart of the *quartier*—or its relative newness that has kept Alain Rayé's name off the list of Paris's top chefs, but this is an oversight to be exploited while it lasts. The menu changes daily according to the reticent chef's morning grocery haul, but always features dishes that subtly complement one another. The lamb is remarkable, the cheese selection ravishing, and dessert reserved for those strong-willed enough not to devour the prodigious platter of treats—madeleines, tarts, chocolates, sorbets, and more—that precedes it. The checks are, of course, serious, but relatively petite for the quality and service. Tel: 42-25-66-76.

Center

Alain Dutournier has settled beautifully in his polished, eccentric place Vendôme restaurant, the **Carré des Feuillants** at 14, rue de Castiglione. Moreover, Dutournier has continued to grow in the kitchen, daily showing himself to be one of the most consistently brilliant and imaginative chefs in Paris. The new restaurant cost a fortune to build, with its odd, half-majestic, half-absurd stone entrance hall—featuring an ice-filled sarcophagus that is used to cool Champagne, and plastic bunches of grapes housing light fixtures—striking blond wood walls, and sober, surreal paintings of monstrous fruits and vegetables being carried to market. At first this lavish expense—a far cry from his more modest 12th *arrondissement* gem Au Trou Gascon—put a heavy financial burden on Dutournier, which may explain the occasionally hurried service or dishes that didn't live up to the very high expectations his cooking had raised.

Today *chez* Dutournier is a marvel, and it is perhaps the only great restaurant in Paris that exhibits its owner's sense of humor in addition to his commitment to the highest cooking standards. The cuisine is a fascinating mix of southwest traditional and innovation. All the duck dishes are wonderful, as are the foie gras creations (especially the sublime *risotto au foie gras*). Dutournier is especially good at using rustic foods in a sophisticated way, perhaps evidenced most remarkably by his appetizer of cold lentils mixed with fresh raw oysters under a layer of wafer-thin slices of raw sea scallop. The extremely pleasant sommelier, Jean-Guy Loustau, sports one of the most distinguished mustaches in Paris and makes a point of recommending lesser known (and less expensive) wines. Despite its growing pains, the Carré des Feuillants is an extremely enjoyable place to dine. Tel: 42-86-82-82.

When Bernard Pacaud moved **l'Ambroisie** from its cramped home down the block from the Tour d'Argent, he locked the door and threw away the key. And why not? The old Ambroisie, with only 12 tables, was intimate. It had to be. Because the kitchen was so tiny, it also featured a limited menu. Perhaps now in his refined and sumptuous new restaurant at number 9 on the venerable place des Vosges, in the 4th *arrondissement,* the resoundingly imaginative Pacaud will get the recognition his wonderful and quintessentially tasteful (you can detect the full flavor of any ingredient Pacaud chooses to use) cooking deserves.

The restaurant itself is particularly inviting: The high ceilings, massive chandelier, stone walls, and floral displays transform its two rooms into a sanctuary of fine dining. But the fare is the feature here. Pacaud, like Dutournier, revels in renovating and adapting traditional recipes and ingredients in dynamic ways. For years his red-pepper mousse dominated discussion of his cooking. Pacaud uses the now-trademark dish as an *amuse-bouche* (literally "amuse your mouth"—an appetizer before the appetizer to get the salivary glands flowing), but try the huge, succulent sea scallops or the meaty, complex wild duck and foie gras "cake." The wine list is pricey but good. Tel: 42-78-51-45.

Left Bank

Strangely, there are only two truly great restaurants on the Left Bank: Olympe and L'Arpège. Michelin still gives the Tour d'Argent its mythic three-star rating, but that must be on the basis of price rather than quality. Certainly the view—of Notre-Dame's spotlit flying buttresses—is unparalleled. And the history is undeniable: Relics include the preserved, glass-domed table where three emperors—Alexander II, the Czar of Russia; his son, Alexander III; and Wilhelm I of Prussia—and Chancellor Bismarck of Prussia once dined; and the signatures of famous customers, including Richard Nixon, that paper the foyer and elevator. But even a postcard recording forever the serial number of the particular duck—rather boringly prepared—that you consumed, or a phone booth that was once a *palanquin* can't make up for the uninspired food and unbelievable prices (such as a truffle salad for $140, a lobster appetizer—last seen being fed to one diner's hound—for $110, or a dish of clear soup for $45). Perhaps after an enormously costly meal the unwary diner won't, as did Jean-Baptiste Grenouille's first master in *Perfume,* fall into the Seine and drown, but he will feel as if his bank account had.

Dominique Nahmias is the only woman ever discussed under the rubric "great chef," a result not only of the scarcity of "great chefs" but also of the fiercely male bias that dominates the top end of French cuisine. Whatever the case, Nahmias, or **Olympe**, as she and her restaurant are called, is an extremely talented chef. Of the top restaurants, Olympe is the youngest at heart and its clientele the most chic. Accordingly, the decor—a 1930s look dominated by maroon, with genuine carved panels from the Orient Express, and many mirrors—and the hours (dinner is served until midnight) are funky. The cuisine and, unfortunately, service, can be spotty, but on the whole the former, at least, is magnificent. Game dishes, ravioli (stuffed with lobster), foie gras, and kidneys (especially the *rognon* suffused with lemon) are the best bets, though Nahmias shows the same sure touch with fish and her ambrosial lamb with rosemary. Desserts are also great (her *mille-feuille* is one of the few in Paris that can rate with that of Guy Savoy), and the wine list is good if expensive. 8, rue Nicolas Charlet, 75015. Tel: 47-34-86-08.

Former Alain Senderens student Alain Passard has mimicked his teacher in two ways only: in his inventiveness and in setting up a restaurant in the former quarters of his old master at 84, rue de Varenne in the 7th *arrondissement*. **L'Arpège** and Passard's own particular and innovative style of cooking now reign in what was once Senderens's Archestrate. The room is no larger, and certainly no quieter, but the tone and prices are different. While it is true that L'Arpège is one of the best restaurants for the price in Paris, especially the bargain lunch menu, it would be worth visiting at twice the price. The menu is full of wonderful-sounding and delicious-tasting dishes, including a remarkable rosemary lobster in leek leaves, a sauté of mixed shellfish, and a duck cooked "according to my mother's recipe." Also delectable are the hare and the pigeon. High chairbacks break the tiny space into clearly defined areas, and the service, while a bit slow, is quite friendly. The wine list is somewhat limited, but who cares? Tel: 45-51-20-02.

EXPENSIVE AND MODERATE

Unfortunately, *les crèmes de la crème* are often completely booked up or just too expensive. But there is a second tier of restaurants in Paris that are almost as good as the finest, definitely more accessible, and often far less costly (200–500 francs). Some, like the Jules Verne in the Eiffel Tower, are exceptional for their location or view, while others, like Le Divellec, feature cuisine of a very high standard.

Right Bank

Pile ou Face takes its name—"heads or tails"—from its proximity to the Paris stock exchange, the Bourse. But a meal here is no gamble: The fresh ingredients and careful, frequently original preparation guarantee a toothsome repast. It is also one of the pleasantest restaurants in Paris, situated at 52 bis, rue Notre-Dame des Victoires, in the 2nd *arrondissement,* on two tiny floors in three tinier rooms—none of which has more than five tables. Lunchtime crowds are dominated by huddled stockbrokers plotting their afternoon trades, but at dinner Pile ou Face's true charm comes into play. The lighting is muted, and soft classical music wafts gently through the charming rooms. The comfortable 1930s decor adds to the romantic atmosphere. The service is attentive enough, and the rabbit with rosemary is especially tasty. Tel: 42-33-64-33.

The sign outside **Pharamond** promises a "true" tripe from Normandy, and a genuine *tripe à la mode de Caen* you get—one of the best in Paris. But even if you don't favor that particular specialty, this little restaurant in the heart of the changing Les Halles neighborhood in the 1st *arrondissement* is still worth a visit. The turn-of-the-century decor (mirrored windows, bright ceramic tiles portraying our favorite fruits and flowers, a delicate restored steel staircase leading up to the second floor) and the immaculate table settings and formal service are a joy. So too is the food, with delicious duck and many typical Normandy dishes. The apple cider, also from Normandy, is outstanding. 24, rue de la Grande-Truanderie. Tel: 42-33-06-72.

The **Ambassade d'Auvergne** in the 3rd *arrondissement* also specializes in a regional cuisine—so successfully that it could actually be the Auvergnat embassy in Paris. The comfortable restaurant at 22, rue du Grenier St-Lazare, spread over two floors under low, wood-beamed ceilings, features such specialties as a silky *aligot* (potatoes and Cantal cheese), delicious stuffed cabbage, and lentil cassoulet (usually this hearty mix of sausage, duck or goose, and meats is served with white beans). Two appetizers are also noteworthy: the lentil salad and the warm chopped cabbage, bacon, and vinegar salad. Everything is good here, though, and there are daily specials to accommodate regular patrons. The restaurant has recently been renovated, with no loss of either atmosphere or quality. Tel: 42-72-31-22.

Though the food at **Le Dômarais** is very good, its remarkable decor, unique in Paris, is also a compelling reason to try this small restaurant near the National Archives in the Marais district. Passing through a rather nondescript courtyard, you enter what was once the first auction hall in Paris, built during the reign of Louis XVI. The small room is dominated from above by a magnificent glass dome, and intimacy results more from the vertical spaciousness than from the distance between tables. A circular staircase on one side leads up to a catwalk overlooking the opulent salon where jewels and precious objets d'art were once displayed. The cuisine is a fine, slightly *nouvelle* rendering of such standard dishes as veal with foie gras, roast duck with fruit or *au poivre,* and an excellent puff pastry with wild mushrooms. The classical music completes the sensation of dining in long-gone splendor. 53 bis, rue des Francs-Bourgeois, 75004. Tel: 42-74-54-17.

A new and very successful restaurant in a colorful part of town (at 2, place d'Anvers, 75009, a block from Pigalle, one of Paris's more notorious red-light districts), **La Table d'Anvers** features inventive cooking in a funky, slightly tacky room dominated by lacquered oranges and grays and leafy plants. The cook and staff are young and tend to be slow, but they are full of charm and have a will to please. The food is very pleasing indeed, with a delectable oyster salad, plump roast fish, and a very tasty roast shoulder of lamb. The prices are reasonably low, so it's a good place to go with friends to eat in style without paying a fortune. Tel: 48-78-35-21.

That Michel Derbane started his professional life as a couturier is obvious. The decor at his **Les Chants du Piano**, 10, rue Lambert, just behind Sacré Coeur in the 18th *arrondissement,* is too artfully conceived to be the result of any but a trained eye: Harmonious peach-and-green walls, cover-plates bordered with rows of piano keys, and a precious fireplace make the small space cozy as well as elegant. Derbane's menu, which changes with the season, is varied and interesting, featuring a flavorful duck in the fall and a marvelous *crêpe de petits gris*—tiny, chewy snails sautéed in garlic and butter and enrobed in a wafer-thin pancake. And no less a source than the *Institut National de la Propriété Industrielle* attests to his inventiveness: Patent No. 84-03389 certifies that Derbane alone can take credit for his *sorbet de foie gras*—a sherbet of fattened duck liver topped with caramel. This odd concoction is infinitely better than it sounds, and it typifies the quirky imagination behind the stove and the restaurant's very pleasant atmosphere. Tel: 42-62-02-14.

There are some restaurants you know are not long for this world, most because they are terrible, but a certain resplendent few because they are so comfortable and so good that it is only a matter of time before the chef can no longer withstand the glowing reviews and the sad duty of turning away dozens of hopeful customers each night. We can only hope that Marcel and Marie-Noëlle Baudis resolutely resist these forces and barricade themselves in **L'Oulette** for as long as possible. A tiny, pretty room at 38, rue des Tournelles in the 3rd *arrondissement,* just minutes from the Bastille, L'Oulette is one of the better things to happen to Paris dining in years. Young master Baudis and his wife have created a restaurant that is intimate, homey, fun, genuinely cheap, and blessed with food that is extraordinarily good and screaming with character. To start, the *escabèche,* carpaccio, or escargots are exquisite, yet soulful, and the *pintade* and stuffed chicken leg make your palate ache with pleasure. The service, proffered in large part by Madame Baudis (who recommends the restaurant's small, very reasonable, southwest-dominated wines) is perfect. Call a week in advance for a reservation or write ahead. L'Oulette is a must. Tel: 42-71-43-33.

Deep in the heart of the 11th *arrondissement,* a vast and, for most tourists, untravelled region, lies **A Sousceyrac**, a restaurant redolent of an old-time dedication to solid, grand bourgeois cooking and a neighborly atmosphere. The bright interior, divided neatly into smaller areas by the ancient oak wainscoting, is as welcoming as the chef, Gabriel Asfaux, who regularly wanders out from the kitchen to gossip with the regulars and make sure newcomers are happy. The food is traditional and leans heavily to game—especially the restaurant's renowned, and today hard-to-find, *lièvre à la royale,* a heady mix of hare, shallots, onion, and cinnamon wrapped around foie gras and truffles. The menu also features such dishes as a particularly rich cassoulet, sausage, foie gras, and a handful of newer creations. To dine in this honest and pleasant restaurant at 35, rue Faidherbe is to enjoy the special character of an idyllic French eating experience. Tel: 43-71-65-30.

Despite Alain Dutournier's defection to posher quarters near the place Vendôme (see Haute Cuisine), **Au Trou Gascon**, with his wife, Nicole, at the helm, is still a wonderful place to eat. The bustling bistro, with now-decorative brass coatracks behind the banquettes and lovely plaster half-columns, is as lively as ever, and the food is almost as good as when the Gascon master himself patrolled the kitchen. It is difficult to imagine a more exquisite duck breast: rich, succulent, graced with a fatal half-inch of crackling skin and fat so precisely cooked that it's like a single heavy wafer of manna. The same care and quality mark all the other dishes, from the delectable salmon to the exquisite foie gras and truffle ravioli in a consommé to the escargot and cèpe pancake. The cheeses, both of them, are perfectly ripe, and the wine list is excellent. The collection of Armagnacs is one of the best in Paris. 40, rue Taine, 75012. Tel: 43-44-34-26.

Left Bank

The rough, wood-paneled walls and bright quai-side location opposite Notre-Dame make the tiny **La Timonerie** seem more like a welcoming country kitchen in chef Philippe de Givenchy's (yes, that fashion family) native Brittany than a very fine little restaurant. But the precisely cooked fresh pastas and fish creations soon clear up any misapprehensions. Excellent desserts, a very satisfactory wine list, and friendly waiters sensitive to dieters and those on a tight budget alike (they will split dishes without a murmur) round out a pleasant and reasonably priced dining experience. 35, quai de la Tournelle, 75005. Tel: 43-25-44-42.

Le Divellec is far more expensive than most of the places mentioned here—but rightfully so, since it almost matches the ethereal standards of the "greats." The bright blue-and-white decor promises the sea, which chef Jacques Le Divellec delivers as he knows best: in the form of interesting and stunningly fresh fish dishes—sautéed, poached, steamed, or raw. The oysters with seaweed are particularly good, and Le Divellec never destroys the flavor of a fish with too heavy a sauce. Rather formal service and a lengthy wine list complete the experience. 107, rue de l'Université, 75007. Tel: 45-51-91-96.

La Cagouille, 10, place Constantin Brancusi in the 14th *arrondissement,* is another, though far less formal, haven for fish-lovers. Chef Gérard Allemandou does the shopping himself at the fish markets near Orly airport south of Paris, and this care shows in the impeccable freshness of his creations. Allemandou cooks like a man whose heart is pure: Simple, straightforward dishes—like his two-inch tuna steaks seared on the outside and sushi-raw at the center—are prepared with grace and devotion, untainted by any sauce that might diminish the natural glory of the fish. The somewhat iconoclastic restaurant has a good, if limited, selection of wines and old-fashioned desserts. Tel: 43-22-09-01.

Jules Verne is for the romantic who doesn't let the possibility of doing something "touristy" get in the way of having a good time (the kind of soul who can appreciate kitschy but great *bateaux-mouches* rides on the Seine). On the second "floor" of the Eiffel Tower, this darkly elegant restaurant features all the touches such a hybrid—half monument, half deluxe eatery—ought to. What's missing is outstanding cuisine. The food is actually better than might be expected, but it doesn't live up to the impossible standards set by the truly remarkable views (especially at night, when the shimmering plain of Paris is broken only by spotlit church towers). How could it? But the comfortable black leather chairs and banquettes, somehow more appropriate to the first-class section of an airplane than to a restaurant; the odd paper orchids and designer lamps that grace each table; and the pianist in the bar all add up to a seductive atmosphere. Jules Verne is first and foremost a spot from which to drink in the heady wine of Paris from a truly romantic perspective. Tel: 45-55-61-44.

If the food at the **Maison Blanche** weren't so good, this completely out-of-the-way restaurant (82, boulevard Lefèbvre in the 15th *arrondissement*) would have vanished in a few weeks. Instead, chef José Lampréia's consistently excellent creations have attracted one of the most chic crowds in Paris to a lovely, rather American room on the outskirts of town. Polished parquet floors, muted off-white walls, vast urns of flowers, and the most confusing bathroom in town—all mirrors, even, it seems, the fixtures—set the tone for such intelligent Lampréia dishes as the tuna with beef marrow or the sweet-and-sour duck. The service can be lackadaisical, but it's fun to people-watch, and the quality of the food and relatively low (though increasingly less so) prices (especially the bargain lunch menu) make a meal in the "white house" worthwhile. Tel: 48-28-38-83.

Unlike their fellow 17th *arrondissement* master chefs Guy Savoy and Michel Rostang, Jean-Pierre and Madeleine Vigato followed up the success of their *haute gamme* flagship restaurant (Apicius, see above) not with a bistro, but with the very chic and young **Manufacture** just south of the city gates. The high-ceilinged, white-washed room once housed a tobacco plant and is now home to giant, colorful paintings, sharp Art Deco chairs and plates, and a collection of odd paintings crowned by the enormous Egyptian palm that centers the room. The menu is plain but interesting, with an emphasis on imaginative dishes at moderate prices. The very fine yet simple renditions of market-fresh fish and dangerous mashed potatoes are convincing. The wine list is small but carefully selected and excellently priced. Skip the boring cheeses. Well worth the trip one mile past the Porte de Versailles south of the 15th *arrondissement*. 30 rue Ernest Renan, 92130 Issy-les-Moulineaux. Tel: 40-93-08-98.

Go to the restaurant atop the **Institut du Monde Arabe** for the following: the glorious view of the Seine and Notre-Dame, especially while having an appertif on the open terrace; a chance to visit the beautiful Institut building itself or to wander through one of the cultural exhibits; and the *pastilla,* an excellent version of the sole Arab dish on the menu. Do not go for the following: the rather tedious French cuisine that, unfortunately, is the mainstay of the menu. Lunch is a wiser choice than dinner because at lunch the rest of the building is open, and because the building's maintenance contract inexplicably requires that the bathroom lights be doused at 8:00 P.M. Institut du Monde Arabe, 1, rue des Fossés-St-Bernard, 75005. Tel: 40-51-38-38.

FOREIGN DINING

Like any city with a large population of immigrants and refugees, Paris enjoys an abundance of foreign restaurants. Some are the fruit of France's traditional ties, either colonial—Vietnamese, North African, and West African—or cultural. Others are the inevitable beachheads established by immigrant communities digging in far from home. A good rule of thumb when considering a foreign restaurant: The more exotic, or chic, the better (outstanding Italian food, for example, just doesn't exist in Paris).

The better ventures, though, can be both cultural and culinary adventures.

North African and Middle Eastern

When in 1954 a guerrilla war for independence erupted in Algeria, a French colonial possession since 1830, France was thrown into sometimes violent confusion. It took Charles de Gaulle, the only statesman whose clout was as great with the public sector as with the military, to end the political turmoil, suppress a revolt by a handful of renegade generals, and give Gallic blessings to an independent Algeria. In the aftermath of the war, a wave of pro-French Algerians emigrated to France, many of them settling in Paris. Moroccans, too, have moved in by the thousands (Morocco was a French protectorate from 1912 to 1956), as have Lebanese, leaving a troubled land for the city many already considered their spiritual home. Paris's profusion of North African and Middle Eastern restaurants reflects these demographics, and there are now some particularly worthwhile dining stops among them.

The **Timgad** is Paris Central for authentic North African dishes in a classy and romantic North African setting. Rough stones, a fountain, and carefully dimmed lighting provide the background for excellent couscous, *tagine,* and *pastilla.* 21, rue Brunel, in the 17th; Tel: 45-74-23-70. **Le Baalbeck,** an authentic Lebanese restaurant at 10, rue Mazagran, tucked away in the heart of Paris's small Turkish quarter in the 10th *arrondissement,* is a must for fans of true exotica. The standard Middle Eastern fare such as shish kebabs and *houmous* is accompanied by a spectacular show: Belly dancers writhe around the room, vendors come to the tables with jasmine, and everyone laughs loudly and cavorts to his heart's content. Reserve; Tel: 47-70-70-02.

Vietnamese

Vietnamese settlers came to Paris in two waves: after France's humiliation at Dien Bien Phu and subsequent withdrawal from Indochina in 1954; and then in the 1970s after the American withdrawal from the country. As a result, there are many Vietnamese restaurants in Paris, including some with Cambodian or Thai accents.

Le Palanquin is all Vietnamese. Delicate Oriental screens and a gracious welcome set the atmosphere, and the food is well presented and delicious. The Tran sisters run the comfortable wood-beamed room, at 12, rue Princesse in the 6th *arrondissement,* with quiet charm and complete efficiency. Pleasure awaits in the form of crab claws in lemon sauce or the other specialties of the house. Tel: 43-29-77-66. **Tan Dinh,** at 60, rue de Verneuil in the neighboring 7th *arrondissement,* features high-quality products imported directly from Vietnam. The dishes that result from these links to the homeland are among the most honest and successful in Paris. The soothing red-and-black lacquered decor is both traditional Eastern and obliquely French. Reserve; Tel: 45-44-04-84.

Afriques-Antilles

France's former colonial ties with West Africa (Ivory Coast, Benin, Senegal) and the Antilles (Martinique and Guadeloupe) account for most of Paris's black population. And though the cultures and histories of these two areas are completely different—the Antilles have been very French for centuries—in restaurants and nightclubs they are often hyphenated: Afriques-Antilles.

Unquestionably, the *boîtes de nuit* (nightclubs) are the most exciting representatives of African culture in Paris. The restaurant **Babylone,** however, is an exception to the rule. The walls and ceiling are covered with leopard and other animal skins, and an enormous wood carving completely fills one wall. Plants add to the veld atmosphere, as does the hot young crowd. Babylone is open until 8:00 A.M. for those who prefer to dine late. 34, rue Tiquetonne, 75002. Reserve; Tel: 42-33-48-35.

The **Plantation'**s modern façade fronts an equally modern interior made tropical by the glorious island-blue that dominates the room. The menu is as exotic as the Antilles themselves, featuring a cuisine that mixes Caribbean accents and ingredients with French style at the stove. A well-heeled crowd is drawn by the restaurant's combination of colorful food and dignified atmosphere. The desserts are great. 5, rue Jules-César, 75012. Tel: 43-07-64-15.

American

Though there are many "American" joints in Paris, all serving the requisite burgers and barbecued ribs and chicken, most are either mediocre or simply uninteresting to Anglophone travellers. One, though, might titillate the sociologically inclined.

The **Rival Coffee Shop,** at 59, rue de la Roquette in the 11th *arrondissement,* is a bizarre combination: Two

Frenchmen imported an entire diner from New Jersey—plastic squeeze mustard containers, swivel stools, "juice-o-mat," and all. It's almost a 1950s museum of Americana, complete with French chefs who serve up recognizable renditions of U.S. standbys: breakfast specials with salad instead of potatoes, roast beef sandwiches with an avocado puree, and the like. Just show up.

Chinese

Though the Chinese community in the 13th *arrondissement* includes several fine restaurants and is quite fascinating to explore, and the Bellevue *quartier* in the 18th is home to many ethnically fascinating spots, no one restaurant stands out in either neighborhood. For highbrow Chinese cuisine, though, **Chez Vong** in Les Halles—one of an international chain—takes the prize. The deluxe comfort of the small private rooms, Oriental pottery, lacquer finishes, and subtle lighting is matched by sophisticated, carefully prepared Chinese cuisine. The dim sum is especially good. 10, rue de la Grande-Truanderie, 75001. Reserve; Tel: 40-39-99-89.

Jewish and Middle Eastern

For centuries before World War II, the Marais area was home to the majority of Parisian Jews. Nazi raids (aided by the collaborationist government and French police) nearly decimated the community, which has slowly regained some of its former vigor through the influx of Sephardic Jews from North Africa and the Middle East. The rue des Rosiers in the 4th *arrondissement* is the gastronomic center of this community, featuring a row of kosher restaurants, butchers, fish-sellers, and a pizzeria.

Jo Goldenberg at number 7 is probably the best-known restaurateur in the Marais. The plate-glass window, bulging with pastramis and smoked fish, also bears scars from a 1982 machine-gun and grenade attack that killed six. The food is tasty and honest—though not really of New York caliber—the matzoh ball soup is nurturing, and Goldenberg's has the best deli department in the neighborhood. **Chez Marianne** has more of a Middle Eastern menu: *tarama, falafel,* stuffed grape leaves, et cetera. There's also a barrel of pungent, homemade pickles that the sensitive of nose should try to sit far from. Service is very warm. For takeout as well. 2, rue des Hospitalières-St-Gervais, 75004.

Tucked onto a narrow street in the Marais, **Esther**

Street is a comfortable, well-lit place that serves up motherly portions of lovingly prepared Eastern European and Sephardic food. From the rich stuffed cabbage to the marvelous meat-filled kreplach to the tangy garlic pickles, every dish is tasty, satisfying, and heartwarming. A great spot for a zesty, well-cooked meal. 6, rue de Jarente, 75004. Tel: 40-29-03-03.

Japanese

Isse is widely considered the best culinary representative of a culture whose mounting popularity matches its homeland's increasing presence in Paris. While the Japanese business profile here has been steadily on the rise for years, the proliferation of clothing designers from the Far East has had at least as important an impact, with the latter adding more than the former to fashion-conscious France's estimation of the Japanese. Two factors serve notice that Isse, 56, rue Ste-Anne in the 1st *arrondissement,* is the top sushi and sashimi outlet in Paris: the lines outside and the predominantly Japanese crowd. The decor is pleasant, though nothing special, and the fish is fresh and of very high quality. No credit cards. Reserve; Tel: 42-96-67-76.

The cult film *Tampopo* introduced Western audiences to a different breed of Japanese restaurant: the noodle shop frequented by working and commuting classes in Japan. **Higuma**, at 32 bis, rue Ste-Anne, is a bustling example of this eating experience. Free of cute Oriental ornaments, save the racks of Japanese comic-book literature in the middle of the three rooms, Higuma is devoted to the art of the noodle. They are freshly made each day in the huge steaming cauldrons that dominate the front room and are served in a soup or stir-fried, with pork, vegetables, or calamari. Dumpling fans won't be disappointed, and the toothpicks are . . . special. No need to reserve; just come and wait.

Eastern European

Eastern Europe has probably the most romantic history of involvement with Paris. Artists such as Frédéric Chopin and Franz Liszt left Warsaw and Budapest for the French capital; Czarist Russia (Napoléon's invasion notwithstanding) had strong ties with France; and such writers as Ivan Turgenev, Eugène Ionesco, and Milan Kundera have made their homes here. Little wonder, then, that a host of restaurants representing the region's several cuisines sprinkle the streets of Paris.

Of the many Russian choices, which range from inexpensive restaurants serving blinis, tarama, and brochettes to very elegant caviar emporiums, one of the nicest is **Le Coin du Caviar**. Just off the place de la Bastille at 2, rue de la Bastille, this refined and tastefully decorated restaurant features hot and cold Russian specialties, including delicious blinis, smoked-fish plates, and caviar worth the not insignificant price tag. The atmosphere is quiet and pre-Revolutionary, and vodka is served in carafes frozen in a block of ice. Reservations may be necessary; Tel: 48-04-82-93.

The **Mazurka** is quite a different enterprise. Two charming little rooms in a slightly seedy part of town in the 18th *arrondissement,* this Polish restaurant serves healthy portions of hearty country dishes, including great stews and stuffed cabbage. Everyone, from the waiters to the cooks (who look like stereotypes of heavy Polish housewives waiting in line outside a shoe store) to the musicians who sing at the tables, is either a Pole or a near neighbor, so there's an unrestrained Eastern European air to the place. No credit cards. 3, rue André-del-Sarte.

FASHIONABLE RESTAURANTS

In a city as committed to eating and as populated with restaurants as Paris, it is inevitable that every year a generation of slick new restaurants springs up in the dining-out marketplace. But it is important to note that in Paris high-tech, chic restaurants make up only a fraction of the new additions. As opposed to New York, say, where the city's frenetic, revolving-door culture compels new ventures to be as up-to-date and as instantly popular as possible, new Paris restaurateurs have long gastronomic traditions to guide them. Thus hundreds of restaurants imitating existing genres open their doors yearly, leaving the culinary avant-garde open to a brave few.

It should come as no surprise, then, that having no working model of their own, fast-track entrepreneurs have coopted ideas found in New York or elsewhere, transplanting them more or less Frenchified, more or less successfully to Paris. Nor should it come as a surprise that the majority of these ventures have a decidedly American edge—either overtly, as in popular "American" restaurants like Joe Allen's or Marshal's—or stylistically. This second type of eatery, and other more original attempts, are most worth visiting.

Right Bank

The **African Queen** is a restaurant you might find in New York. It is set on three floors (at 34–36, rue Montorgueil in the 1st *arrondissement*) and designed down to the last spoon: The china, chair backs, and door all bear the restaurant's symbol, and everything else, from the muted beige and brown decor to the Christian Duc furniture, has been carefully integrated into a soothing, harmonious whole. The food will be a pleasant surprise for those used to an inverse relationship between the quality of the decor and cuisine. The inventive mix of West African and French *nouvelle* is prepared with care, using fresh and exotic ingredients (such as manioc, coconut, and kiwi). Owner Mai Ollivier is half-tribal North African (Peul), worked for years in West Africa, and brings both a solid restaurant background and her very warm and open personality to the venture. Reserve; Tel: 40-26-36-46.

Le Comptoir, an offshoot of Dominique Nahmias's Olympe, is a very chic French version of a *tapas* bar that gets more chic every time it expands. The young, exceedingly well-dressed-and-coiffed habitués of this rather groovy spot nibble on plates of grilled chicken, fried calamari and *merlan* (whiting), and fresh, tiny anchovies. The selection of wines is more than adequate, and the music as trendy and compelling as the crowd. 37, rue Berger, 75001.

Were it not for its setting, **Cargo** could easily be the latest rage in New York's SoHo instead of in Paris. But the Canal St-Martin, a favored background for *policiers* (detective stories in the James Cain mold), where Cargo occupies the ground floor of an 1850s warehouse perched above a worn but still working lock, is all French. The converted warehouse, with its high ceilings, thick white-painted support beams, and stellar view of the placid yet somehow menacing canal, makes for an airy and pleasant space. Owner Patrice Taravella has filled it with Mallet-Stevens re-editions—very fancy designer furniture indeed. But the bar is great, and the food, a very New Yorkish quasi-*nouvelle,* is light and tasty. 41 bis, quai de la Loire, 75019. Reserve; Tel: 42-41-34-34.

The creator of **The Studio** is very French, but his perfect southern accent carries over to the impeccable

Tex-Mex decor and country & western music. The Studio exemplifies the restaurant *à l'Américain* in Paris; it was opened by a Frenchman homesick for the U.S. who intuited that transplanted Americana would be a magnet for young Parisians. He was right, and this actually quite good Mexican restaurant, tucked away in an ancient courtyard at 41, rue du Temple in the 4th *arrondissement,* one of Paris's most ancient neighborhoods, is packed nightly with a predominantly French—and chic—crowd. One of the city's great summer courtyards, and a fun place to watch people, or, when feeling nostalgic, to sup on tacos and nachos while listening to the Flying Burrito Brothers. Reserve; Tel: 42-74-10-38; or wait in the courtyard with a margarita.

Go to **La Perla** to drink as much as to eat; the atmosphere is equally conducive to both. The menu is straightforward Mexican, but the owners are civilized enough to place a shaker-full of cayenne pepper on every table; the drinks menu is quite pretty and meant to be taken seriously. There is a rack of tequilas on the wall and frozen margaritas for the homesick. The best thing about the place is its atmosphere: La Perla manages to retain its neighborhood-y atmosphere and be terribly chic at the same time. 26, rue François Miron, 75004.

The Bastille area is the center of gentrification in Paris. No street shows this more than the 11th *arrondissement*'s rue de Lappe, and no dining spot exemplifies it better than **Tapas Nocturne** at number 17. A sliver of a restaurant just down the block from the very chic dance spot **Balajo**, it specializes in the dainty and tasty appetizers called *tapas.* It can be quite entertaining, but go early, because after 9:00 P.M. even the chic wait in line. No credit cards.

Orève used to be one of the most exclusive florists in the rarefied 16th *arrondissement;* then it was one of the hottest restaurants in Paris. Now it is a very pretty place, with its seven architecturally isolated spaces and lovely steel beams forming the hothouse sections, which dishes out serviceable Swedish-French food. No longer trendy, it is still an eyeful. Tel: 45-04-80-52. 25, rue de la Pompe.

Avoid the Sweet World Café on the rue Montmartre, even if it was created by the owners of the relentlessly "in" discos Les Bains and Le Palace. Avoid with even more vigor any attempt anyone makes to take you to La Poste, a seriously trendy spot in a gorgeous Rococo former post office. The downstairs bar is cozy, and the decor, with its profusion of cherubs, columns, statues, moldings, and mirrors, rather awesome. But the spiritless food, rude service, and absurd checks destroy even the falsetto versions of Shubert lieder and English-language sing-alongs of American show tunes.

Left Bank

Le Télégraphe is chic in the Orève mode. A gorgeous, high-ceilinged, wood-paneled space with a bar-lover's bar, it occupies what was the dining room of the *foyer* (dormitory) that once housed the young women who operated the massive banks of telegraphs at the neighboring Gare d'Orsay (now the museum of 19th-century art). Between the foyer's close after the abandonment of the station and its resuscitation as a restaurant, the space housed an embassy and was a German commissariat during the war. Today discreet spotlighting illumines the carved-wood trim and formal mirrors, and painfully cool young waiters in loose, casually expensive outfits attend. While carefully avoiding true excellence, and burdened by a traditional and limited menu, the restaurant serves food that is actually quite good. Stick to the basics, like the salad with confit or butterfly of leeks; the marinated sea trout is also tasty. Desserts range from indifferent to good, but the coffee is terrible. The delightful little terrace out back is used in the summer. Go for the ambience alone and you will be pleasantly surprised by the caliber of the food. 41, rue de Lille, 75007. Tel: 40-15-06-65.

The **Café Pacifico** is to Amsterdam, Paris, and London what the Hard Rock Café is to London, New York, and wherever, only better. Created by Tom Estes, a former high-school teacher and wrestling coach and one of the nicest guys ever to pull on a clean white tee-shirt, the Paris branch serves the best Mexican food in town and more brands of tequila and mezcal than you can shake some salt at (17, at last count). Though the happy hour and atmosphere are American, the crowd (and that word is not used lightly here) is mostly French, young, good-looking, and excited. Rowdy and rambunctious, Café Pacifico is not for the fainthearted. 50, boulevard du Montparnasse, 75014. Reserve; Tel: 45-48-63-87.

BISTROS AND BRASSERIES

Bistros and brasseries are perhaps the most typical French restaurants, offering the most traditional dishes and liveliest atmosphere. With some few exceptions (Hemingway eating potato salad and drinking beer at the Brasserie Lipp, or Jean-Paul Sartre dining at his customary table at La Coupole), there is no great literary tradition associated with these kinds of restaurant—they were too crowded with well-fed bourgeoisie and more expensive than the lower-rent cafés favored by the ink-stained for several centuries. Today meals will cost between 100 and 350 francs, depending on the quality of the food or grandeur of the decor.

Contemporary bistro and brasserie menus share many of the same dishes. Generally, bistros serve the rustic dishes Mom and Dad used to cook up, with a devoted emphasis on stews (*pot-au-feu*, cassoulet, *daube*), duck (*confit de canard, magret de canard*, foie gras), internal organs, all the varied and wondrous parts of pigs (including knuckles, feet, ears, sausages, hams—cooked, smoked, or aged—and kidneys), lamb (including the rack, shoulder, saddle, feet, and head), and veal (the standard cuts, liver, kidney, pancreas, feet, and head; one critic, in fact, warns readers away from a restaurant because the owner "insists on buying the head ready-rolled, so you miss out on the brains and tongue"). This hearty and sometimes heavy fare goes down best in fall and winter months, though of course poultry, rabbit, fish, and many of the lighter meats are delicious year-round, especially when washed down with plenty of good wine.

Brasseries take their name from the word for "brewery" and are predominantly Alsatian, or advertise themselves as such, so beer and Riesling wine are plentiful. They tend to stay open later than bistros and often feature fresh seafood and shellfish, *choucroute* (sauerkraut and sausage), chicory salad with bacon and a poached egg, and the like.

Understandably, the area surrounding the old Les Halles food market, until 1968 Zola's "belly of Paris," features a number of excellent bistros and brasseries. Some are still open all night, as they were when hungry farmers and butchers refreshed their weary bodies with liters of beer and wine and huge plates of rich country cooking at 5:00 A.M. Unfortunate victims of the market's move to Rungis, near Orly airport, include the row of colorful brasseries on the rue Coquillière, such as the Pied de Cochon, once a magnet for top-hatted society seeking a plebeian meal after a night's revels, all now renovated, refurbished, and reduced beyond all recognition (though the Pied de Cochon *is* still quite fun in the wee hours, glitter and all). Most of the other good spots are spread around the Right Bank, from the Porte Maillot to Nation, with only a cluster of restaurants representing the Left Bank.

Les Halles

Chez Denise (or A la Tour de Montlhéry, to the uninitiated) is a good example of a bistro. The woman behind the cash register is as formidable as her longtime partner's luxuriant mustache, but the food is great and the portions enormous. The salt pork with lentils could feed a nuclear family or a starving merrymaker wandering in for a dawn feast. The (three) wines offered are fine, and the decor—hams swinging from the rafters, signed posters, and sketches of the mustachioed man out front—is eclectic and warm. 5, rue des Prouvaires, 75001. Reservations are a must and are given out only for every odd hour; Tel: 42-36-21-82.

On the other side of the rue du Louvre, at 25, rue Jean-Jacques Rousseau, is the **Epi d'Or**, one of the most typical bistros in Paris. From the mimeographed menu to the checked tablecloth to the knickknacks placed around the room to the gracious hosts, everything bespeaks the warmth and care that is at the heart of bistros. Portions are particularly healthy, and everything is hot and hearty. Desserts are worthwhile, and little touches like the peach wine evidence the restaurant's conscious effort to keep up with new developments while maintaining its traditional form.

Five minutes away, the **Fermette du Sud-Ouest** would be cloyingly rustic if the dishes pork butcher–turned-chef Christian Naulet turned out weren't so authentic and soul-warming. The very high quality of this bistro makes it without question one of the finest in town. Set on two floors at 31, rue Coquillière, with enough wooden beams and rough stone to build a real farm, the Fermette has, as you might expect, exceptionally good sausages of all types, including *boudin* and *andouillette* (a rough tripe sausage that is exquisite when made well and inedible when not). Naulet also sports a particularly fine mustache. It's best to reserve; Tel: 42-36-73-55.

At 1, rue de Mail, near the fashionable place des Victoires (home to several high-toned clothing shops) in the 2nd *arrondissement*, **Chez Georges** continues a tradition as well: that of the utterly dependable neighborhood bistro. The long, somewhat stark, mirrored room with its white tile floor and bright lights is made welcoming by the sweet, motherly waitresses in black dresses and white aprons. The menu is standard and the food quite tasty—in season, the garlicky sautéed cèpes are delicious. During the day patrons are a mixed crowd of stockbrokers, bankers from the nearby Banque de France, and fashion people. The homier evening crowd is made up mostly of locals. Chez Georges serves an impressive collection of Bordeaux wines. The checks have grown somewhat out of proportion, and no credit cards are accepted. Tel: 42-60-07-11.

Chez Pauline, a block from the Palais-Royal, one-time home to Cardinal Richelieu, D'Artagnan's bane, is understandably pretty swank. The charm of the classic decor, complete with stern, avuncular waiters and plenty of flowers, compensates somewhat for the fact that it's a bit overpriced, as do the excellent boeuf bourguignon and rice pudding. More modern dishes, anathema to many bistro chefs, are also available. Chez Pauline is popular with just about everyone. It's best to reserve. 5, rue Villedo, 75001; Tel: 42-96-20-70.

Bordering Les Halles to the north, **Aux Crus de Bourgogne** is one bistro that has never seen the need to inflate its prices; what the French lovingly call the *rapport qualité-prix* (quality-cost ratio) is very high here. Just off the rue Montorgueil, one of Paris's finest market streets, at 3, rue Bachaumont in the 2nd *arrondissement,* this lovely old room with long communal tables and private booths brightened by red-checked tablecloths and boisterous waiters would cheer even Lear, with good stews, dishes with luscious wild mushrooms (cèpes and morels), and, in season, wild game (from duck to boar). The *langoustines* are great, and are easily the most affordable in town. Very reasonable wines are served. No credit cards.

A short stroll down the block at 50, rue Montorgueil, those wacky Bretons who oversee the rambunctious beverage consumption at Le Baragouin (see Bars) have opened a diminutive and marvelously spirited restaurant. **Le Brin de Zinc**, which refers to the beautiful old zinc bar, is populated by waiters whose exuberant personalities are rivaled by the hearty, artery-clogging bistro fare. And while the waiters make you feel like old friends, the beautifully restored decor makes you wish they were. Nothing spectacular, just rich, tasty dishes prepared with love and served with heartfelt care. Very good little wine list. Tel: 42-21-10-80.

If middle-aged restaurateurs prone to flirtation amuse you, **Chez Pierrot**, 18 rue Etienne-Marcel, in the 2nd *arrondissement,* is the place. Monsieur Losson's ministerings are meant to add to the lighthearted atmosphere of this bright, bustling bistro, not to offend. And he ministers to the stomach as well, with vast portions of everything: an entire plate of sausages to cut from at will; a vat of chocolate mousse from which to scoop spoonfuls to your heart's content. The crowd is unified only in its good humor, with businessmen and fashion mavens such as Jean-Paul Gaultier rubbing elbows over their leeks in vinaigrette sauce, *daubes,* and chicken fricassees. No credit cards. Tel: 45-08-05-48.

Benoit is an extremely elegant version of the bistro, and prices are constructed accordingly. From the shrubs outside that protect diners from inquiring eyes to the fresh, white foyer and gracious welcome, to the impeccable decor (unchanged since the restaurant opened in 1912), to the heaping portions of perfectly prepared dishes like the *salade de boeuf,* braised-beef stew, and roast red mullet, everything is of the highest quality. Benoit is so pretty and the food so good that it's quite popular despite the prices. Reservations are a necessity. No credit cards. 20, rue St-Martin, 75004. Tel: 42-72-25-76.

Right Bank

Like the remnant of a richer past, **Chez Georges**—this one at 273, boulevard Péreire in the 17th *arrondissement*—maintains its 60-year-old bistro traditions in the face of the poured-concrete modernity of the Palais de Congrès hotel/shopping mall/theater center that has transfigured the Porte Maillot across the street. The dining room, created and redone by Art Deco design king Slavik, is run with care by Roger Mazarguil, who has carried on the appetite-enhancing policy of carving succulent slabs of roast beef and leg of lamb right at the table. It's easy to enjoy the high quality, careful preparation, and atmosphere suggestive of successful people congregating, though the prices are a little steep. Tel: 45-74-31-00.

If Michel Rostang has taken a gorgeous old *épicerie fine* (gourmet grocery store for Proust's crowd) and transformed it into one of the best bistros in town, it is because his talent wouldn't let him do otherwise. At 10, rue Gustave-Flaubert in the 17th *arrondissement,* a few doors down from his eponymous temple of haute cuisine (see Haute Cuisine, above), **Le Bistrot d'à Côté Flaubert** is a small tile-and-wood room filled with old-fashioned candy jars, ceramic plates, mismatched tables and chairs, and a variety of other antiques (most are for sale). This attention to detail is mirrored in the service and the food, which is rigorously of the bistro genre—in itself an act of imagination for such an inventive chef. There's a pleasant terrace, and an excellent repast is guaranteed. Best to reserve; Tel: 42-67-05-81.

Guy Savoy, like Michel Rostang, reached out from his marvelous, eponymous restaurant to create a bistro (and then another) that specialized in perfecting the art of this unpretentious cuisine. The **Bistro de l'Etoile**, a cramped, lively room, serves up fairly modest portions of superbly prepared traditional bistro dishes with occasional modern touches. Everything comes hot from the oven, and the ingredients are particularly fresh. The newer branch, on avenue Niel, is larger and features a terrace. 13, rue Troyon, 75017, Tel: 42-67-25-95; and 75, avenue Niel, 75017, Tel: 42-27-88-44.

The **Cochon d'Or** is a small, gorgeous hideaway in the bowels of the 19th *arrondissement* at 192, avenue Jean-Jaurès. The deep-red banquettes, richly paneled walls, stained-glass lamp shades, long mirrored wall opposite a perfect zinc bar, and starched white linens all fill one with a confidence easily confirmed by the meal to come. The restaurant is a near neighbor of La Villette, the slaughteryards-turned–science center, and meat has been the name of the game since the Ayral family opened the Cochon's doors in 1924. The gorgeous slabs of beef, heady kidneys that are flavorful without being astringent, and the rich sauces are enough to make anyone feel that the trip to the hinterlands was worthwhile. Reserve; Tel: 42-45-46-46.

Jean-Paul Bucher has succeeded in creating a chain of restaurants that share almost identical menus, wine lists, and style of service without making them dreary and repetitious. How? By taking old brasseries, each with its own unique history and decor, carefully renovating them, and limiting the cuisine to the foie gras, Riesling, fresh shellfish, and good grilled meats God intended brasseries to serve. His abysmal and horrifying "renovation" of La Coupole is the sole exception.

One warning: Make reservations, and better early or late (all the chain's restaurants are open until 2:00 A.M.), since even patrons with reservations join the hordes waiting for tables at the bars of each of these restaurants.

The **Flo**, two long, low rooms with dark, polished wood walls, stained-glass beer-hall windows, and a pretty zinc bar, was the first to open. Overtly Alsatian, it's the most traditionally brasserie-esque of the five and emphasizes its sometimes mediocre *choucroute*. There is often a Rolls-Royce parked out front, watched over by the trays of fresh oysters, clams, crabs, and other shellfish. 7, cour des Petites-Ecuries, 75010. Tel: 47-70-13-59.

Julien, whose fabulous 1889 Belle Epoque decor was created only three years after the more somber rooms of the Flo, is a loud, bright restaurant looking out of place amid the surrounding markets and exotic fast-food shops. The two rooms are separated by a marble bar; the smaller front space is all crisp white linens and crushed velvet banquettes, whereas the main dining area is capped by a magnificent stained-glass dome and made larger by the vast mirrors bracketed by ornate period hats. 16, rue du Faubourg-St-Denis, 75010. Tel: 47-70-12-06.

Across the street from the Gare du Nord, the penultimate stop for battalions of young men on their way to the trenches of the Somme, the **Terminus Nord**'s lovely design suggests not the slaughter of World War I but Art Deco's calm postwar precision. Large, airy, sprawling rooms with numerous bouquets of flowers and a huge bar in the center play host to the featured seafood platters, light fish dishes in butter sauces, and other standards. 23, rue de Dunkerque, 75010. Tel: 42-85-05-15.

Probably the most civilized of Bucher's eateries, the **Vaudeville** does not suffer from its nearness (20 yards) to the business of the Bourse. The very pretty 1925 marble-and-mirror walls reflect the chatter of a rather chic crowd, all tucking into trays of fresh oysters (and their shellfish brethren) and thick steaks. In the summer the terrace, which looks out onto the stock exchange's imposing columned façade, is especially fun. 29, rue Vivienne, 75002. Tel: 42-33-39-31.

The **Boeuf sur la Toit**, an Art Deco masterpiece, is the most historic of the bunch. In its heyday, artists, writers, and musicians (such as Jean Cocteau and Pablo Picasso) were drawn to this gorgeous restaurant, with its innumerable mirrors, symmetrical staircases, and little hidden nooks. Because of its beauty and location (not far from the Champs-Elysées), it is probably the most popular as well. 34, rue du Colisée, 75008. Tel: 43-59-83-80.

La Coupole once defined Montparnasse dining, but we include it here to emphasize the sacrilege and destruction

Jean-Paul Bucher has wreaked in its once-hallowed confines. After buying La Coupole—the monument that was once home to the most special ambience in Paris—in 1988, Bucher and his butchers proceeded to "improve" the restaurant. Modifications include: destroying the perfect bar by ripping away the partitions that hid it from the restaurant proper and allowed you to eat with your mate and have cocktails with your lover in the same evening; "upgrading" the familiar, worn, maroon banquettes by recovering them with material of an unfortunate shade of brown; and entirely replacing, it seems, the professional troupe of colorful, avuncular waiters and captains with inferior, witless "Flo" clones (that is, the "Flo" design that was successful in reviving dead restaurants, imposed on the still vibrant Coupole). Other "improvements" are just as grating: the tedious "Flo" menu, smaller and far less personable than the old Coupole one; the same "Flo" glasses and tableware; the patented "Flo" crush of patrons; and worst, a bustle that vaguely recalls the Coupole, but without that establishment's humor and grace. To be fair, the food is just as good if not better than before, and the restaurant is still packed. And even the harshest critic must admit that Bucher did a good job cleaning the splendid Deco pillars that punctuate the restaurant—though they are invisible through the tears that cloud the eyes of anyone yearning for what was once the essence of Parisian dining. Try it out if you are strong of spirit. 102, boulevard du Montparnasse, 75014. Tel: 43-20-14-20.

Though the mythic Antoine Magnin no longer minds the stove in the cramped kitchen at l'Ami Louis, little has changed. The splendidly decrepit decor (which looks as if paintbrushes were banned from the premises before the war) is as shabby as ever, and the slabs of foie gras remain as monstrous. The service is haphazard and the renowned game dishes (pheasant, wild duck) are sometimes disappointing. But the new management has maintained the cuisine at about the same level, and the snails, foie gras, and sometimes surreal atmosphere are still addicting. The only real change, in fact, is that the insanely high prices have risen to an even more mind-numbing level. L'Ami Louis today is a place where you can pay more than you ever thought possible for a fun meal. 32, rue de Vertbois, 75003. Reserve; Tel: 48-87-77-48.

Better just to call it Chez Philippe, like everyone else: Auberge Pyrénées-Cévennes might be too difficult to remember, and this very fine bistro is not one to forget.

Stone walls the color of spicy mustard and red-tiled floors make a comfortable setting for the locals and well-to-do business people who depend on Philippe Serbource to provide them with regular doses of his excellent foie gras and cassoulet. It is easy to make a pig of yourself over the delicious *cochonnailles* (sausages)—customers are free to serve themselves—but it's best to save room for the tasty stews and southwest specialties. No credit cards. 106, rue de la Folie-Mericourt, 75011.

In the 3rd *arrondissement,* five minutes from Chez Philippe and bordering the place de la République at 39, boulevard du Temple, **Chez Jenny** offers a different kind of fare but with a similar honesty and enthusiasm. A monument to traditional Alsatian garb and cuisine, Jenny features one of Paris's most authentic *choucroutes*—succulent sausage and sharp sauerkraut—rather than the tasteless, stringy affair many brasseries pawn off on unwary diners. The huge, wood-paneled dining area is well staffed with buxom, costumed waitresses eager to plunk a liter of Alsatian beer on the table. There's also fresh shellfish, a little out of place amid the cabbage, and a fine roast lamb. While the atmosphere may be a little too fairy-tale, the very reasonable prices are not.

Most demonstrations in Paris gather at the place de la République and march to the place de la Bastille, the Saint Peter's Square of French revolutionary spirit since 1789, when enraged Sans-culottes destroyed the ominous Bastille prison, a symbol of monarchal arbitrariness, and joyously marched the handful of mostly insane prisoners through the streets of Paris. Today an occasional tourist still asks directions to the long-gone prison; he or she would do better to ask the way to **Bofinger,** a block from the *place,* at 5, rue de la Bastille in the 4th *arrondissement.* Most of Paris regularly visits the restaurant's two delightfully restored rooms (the larger graced by a stunning glass dome put up in 1919), paying homage to the long zinc bar where in 1864 Paris's first draft beer was served. Tel: 42-72-87-82.

The decor of the **Train Bleu** at the Gare de Lyon train station epitomizes the grandeur of the high Belle Epoque: comfortable banquettes with plenty of space between them for luggage; seriously romantic blue-dominated murals on all the walls; molded plaster on the ceiling that encloses even more intricate murals; and sometimes infrequent, avuncular waiters (a special 45-minute menu is available if you have a train to catch). The food and wine

ty good as well, but it is really the eye-boggling
that makes this grand restaurant worth visiting.
e de Lyon, 20, boulevard Diderot, 75012. Tel: 43-43-
J9-06.

Left Bank

Twenty years ago Allard reigned as one of the great
bistros in Paris. Since then M. Allard has died and Fer-
nande, his wife and longtime chef, has retired. But the
spirit and high-quality food that had made this deluxe
bistro a watchword among gastronomes since 1903 remain; **Allard** is still a culinary force to be reckoned with.
The two dining rooms are separated by the kitchen and
shimmering zinc bar and are much brighter when you
are looking past a floral arrangement out the lovely
etched windows than when gazing in through the dreary
cast-iron bars that protect the windows from high-spirited
passersby. People come here to feast on the generous
portions of the very well prepared stews (such as the
delicious *navarin d'agneau* or *coq au vin*), escargots, or
specials (such as the dozen grilled pig kidneys a table of
serious diners has been known to consume). It's on the
expensive side, but it's a pretty place with high standards.
41, rue St-André-des Arts, 75006. Tel: 43-26-48-23.

A few blocks away from Allard, the **Petit Zinc**, also in
the 6th, serves up a tasty mix of standard bistro dishes,
fresh shellfish, and hearty country specials in a truly
republican atmosphere: The waiters treat everyone with
the same familiarity, as if each diner were a friend of a
friend. The two cramped upper rooms could use a
fresher look, perhaps, and downstairs bustles more than
above. The terrace tables are one of summer dining's
most popular stops. The grand old zinc bar that gives the
restaurant its name is barely used, but it looks special. 25,
rue de Buci.

Perhaps it's not as cheap as it used to be, but the
Restaurant des Beaux-Arts is still one of the best deals
in town: respectable, sometimes excellent cuisine at bargain prices and an atmosphere that immediately recalls
the student days you might imagine after reading too
much Baudelaire at the nearby Ecole des Beaux-Arts,
when hungry artists would throw down the brushes and
quit the turpentined haven of the studio for a big boeuf
bourguignon and many bottles of rough red wine, argu-
ing endlessly whether that Delacroix fellow was a genius
or a charlatan. The good old days are gone, but the

mood still remains, fueled by an energetic young crowd and a warm decor (enormous canvases cover the walls). At 11, rue Bonaparte, in the 6th *arrondissement,* this bistro is a good time. No credit cards.

WINE BARS AND WINE BISTROS

For all the hoopla in France about wine, wine *bars* are a fairly recent innovation. Wine *bistros*—and there is a difference—have been a Paris institution since a Russian soldier allegedly shouted *"bistro!"* ("hurry!") in an attempt to speed up a laggard barman (circa the Napoleonic wars). The latter, honest *bistrots à vin,* are usually grimier and more personable than what the high-tech 1980s termed a wine bar. Modern, cloned mini-chains can be worth visiting—like the six l'Ecluses, which serve only Bordeaux; the three le Pain et le Vin, created by four chefs who joined together to buy wine (including Henri Faugeron and Alain Dutournier, both mentioned above), which feature some interesting wines and understandably excellent snacks; and Les Domaines, where the Philippe Starck design is so modern it hurts. But these new drinking spots simply lack the character and comfort of Paris's original wine bars and some other newcomers.

The **Taverne Henri IV** is a good place to sample an old-style *bistrot à vin.* On the western end of the Ile de la Cité facing the large equestrian statue of Henri IV, the well-liked king whose assassination in 1610 probably caused many mourners to visit wine bars, the Taverne specializes in crisp whites from the Loire valley, a selection of fine Beaujolais, and the rare Jura region wines. Add to this farm-fresh cheeses, hams, and sausages, mix in a boisterous owner and a clientele devoted to all of the above, and the result is a terrific place to lunch or taste wines of an afternoon. 13, place du Pont-Neuf, 75001.

People flock to **Jacques Mélac** for four reasons: the moderately priced wines, the lively crowds, Mélac's luxuriant mustache, and the annual harvest of the house grapevine, for many locals a festive occasion inspiring the consumption of vast quantities of wine. Luckily, they are in the right place. The bar is tucked away in the 11th *arrondissement* at 42, rue Léon-Frot, but it is worth the trip: There are fine Côtes-du-Rhône and tempting platters of *charcuterie* and cheese. Hearty lunch specials and dinner are available on Tuesdays and Thursdays, and many of the wines can be bought to take out.

On a small side street in the gritty 11th *arrondissement,*

L'Ange Vin (get the pun?) embodies all that is wonderful about neighborhood wine bars. Host Jean-Pierre Robinot's jovial exuberance is matched only by the care with which he selects the delicate, sweet white wines from lesser-known regions and vineyards that are the bar's specialty. A former wine critic, he employs the same attention when choosing red wines, but *vins molleux,* he claims, leave him helpless, and are the glasses he presses on his willing patrons. Lunch is either a plate of vibrant mountain ham and some of the great cheeses or a toothsome daily special. The bread is great and the atmosphere designed for those who love wine. Open for dinner on Tuesdays and Thursdays (and until 2:00 A.M. for an after-dinner tasting). 24, rue Richard Lenoir, 75011. Tel: 43-48-20-20.

La Tartine would be hard-pressed to have a more interesting history: it kept the leaders of the Russian Revolution fed and oiled. Trotsky lived right around the corner, and Lenin and Tito were also frequent hangers-out. But La Tartine today is the same modest café/*bar à vin* it was then, and its past speaks for itself. Such contemporary luminaries as Gérard Depardieu and Nathalie Baye frequent the bar these days, as do fans of the large wine list (drawn from the nearly 30,000 bottles in the cellar below) and the peasant-bread sandwiches. The atmosphere is warm yet anonymous, made up in equal parts of locals, workers, business people, and foreign students. The common ground they share—wine—is a good enough reason to be friendly. 24, rue de Rivoli, 75004.

Two upstart establishments have earned the label "true wine bar" by dint of hard work, a deep knowledge of the Côtes-du-Rhône, and sharp, dry English wit. **Willi's Wine Bar**, named not after acerbic English owner Mark Williamson but after one of Colette's husbands, broke new ground in the Paris wine world. Williamson has created a bar/restaurant with great charm, excellent food, and a weekly choice of often little-known wines by the glass. The rough stone walls and wood beams play host to an international crowd, fans of both the very large selection of fine wines (especially from the Côtes-du-Rhône) and the atmosphere. 13, rue de Petits-Champs, 75001.

Williamson, with partner Tim Johnston, went on and opened **Juvenile's** (named, oddly enough, after another of Colette's husbands) just around the corner from Willi's, at 47, rue de Richelieu. The wines are less rarefied, though no less carefully selected, with an eclectic mix of French, Spanish, Italian, Californian, and even Australian. The bar's faintly Spanish (though quite Anglicized) air is evident in the *tapas* and the selection of sherries, which is one of the best in town. Juvenile's is basically a lower-key, lower-priced alternative to Willi's. (Despite having English owners, neither bar is an expatriate haven.)

The **Duc de Richelieu** may share the same street as Juvenile's (at number 110), but in terms of wine bars it's a world away. Owner Paul George serves only Beaujolais (even bottling his own in the basement) and features some of the best vintage wine in Paris from that abused region. With extraordinarily civilized hours (it's closed only between 5:00 A.M. and 7:00 A.M.), good, reasonably priced food all night, and a rambunctious crowd, the Duc might not be the classiest wine bar around, but it's one of the most fun.

Despite its neighborhood—the chic Marché-St-Honoré—**Le Rubis** is as honest and old-fashioned as wine bars get. From the emptied half-barrels that serve as tables outside the always crowded bar to the broad choice of affordable Côtes-du-Rhône to the very high quality cheeses and *charcuterie* to the wise and wisecracking waitresses, Le Rubis is like the movie set of some imagined 1950s *bistrot à vin*. As you might expect, it is easy to have a good time here. 10, rue du Marché-St-Honoré, 75001.

After a glowing meal at the Brin de Zinc, the wise troop to the cellar below to allow their dinners to settle in the company of seemingly endless glasses of wine. **Le Père Boutgras** shares with its sibling restaurant (and bar, the Baragouin) a rambunctious Breton spirit and infectiously fun atmosphere. The 17th-century cellar, with its arching stone walls and low, cozy ceiling, is brightened by flags, plants, and Japanese lanterns. The wine selection is fine, but marked more by a love for than a reverence of the beverage. Below the Brin de Zinc at 50, rue Montorgueil.

Tucked away in the far reaches of the 20th *arrondissement,* the **Bistrot–Cave des Envièrges** exemplifies what a radical with a passion for wine can do when the Socialists have been elected and prove no better than the Gaullists. A former *Soixante-huitard* (member of the revolutionary 1968 movement) has translated his commitment to political struggle to more genteel turf—the grape—in this exceptionally friendly and personable *bistrot.* The large selection of wines leans to the Loire valley and includes many rare and fascinating bottles, all at very good prices. Lunchtime platters are invariably of the freshest ingredients and built to satisfy the deepest hunger. The atmosphere is as special as the wines; political discussion leaning to the left is standard, and social awareness extends even to deliveries of wine, when the bar empties out on the street and everyone pitches in to help unload the truck. 11, rue des Envièrges; Tel: 46-36-47-84.

La Micro Brasserie is no wine bar. It is, however, the only beer bar in Paris with a brewery on the premises. The extremely tasty house brew—Morgane by name—ages in the huge steel vats visible behind the bar, mellowing even as you sip. Special seasonal varieties are offered at Christmas (Noël beer) and on the bar's birthday. The menu contains only dishes cooked with beer, such as *coq à la Kriek* or *tarte chaude Morgane*. Fascinating. 106, rue de Richelieu, 75002.

SALONS DE THÉ

Tearooms are the romantic, warm, and welcoming hideaways for those looking for a light lunch or a cozy spot to dawdle. Calmer than restaurants, quieter than cafés, usually graced with classical music and a relaxing atmosphere, tearooms are for foul weather—or for any day when only a spot of comfort will cure what ails.

Right Bank

There are tearooms and there are tearooms. The **Plaza Athénée** falls in the latter category. Which is to say that tea is taken quite seriously at the Plaza, thank you, either in the Relais, a quiet room washed with gentle harp music, or in the hall, where the famous and the wealthy come to refresh themselves after a long day of being famous and wealthy. 25, avenue Montaigne, 75008.

A. J. Liebling remembers growing up at **Angelina** when it was called Rumplemeyer's (until 1948). Thousands of French haute-preppies (*bon chic, bon genre;* i.e., the right people with the right stuff) spend their lives here at number 226, down the street from the W. H. Smith bookshop on the rue de Rivoli, as does a broad segment of "beautiful" Paris. History and habitués apart, the famous old room with its green marble tables and mirrored walls is quite pretty, and the hot chocolate should be picketed by the staff of the heart-disease center.

The Ritz offers the classiest and most classic tea in town; it is served in a lovely, high-ceilinged room just off the main lobby, complete with formal waiters and table settings, soft music wafting from a grand piano, and a fireplace. And, ah, the scones and cakes, the tiny smoked salmon or cucumber sandwiches. Dress for the part, both for the hotel, which takes ties as seriously as teas, and for yourself. 15, place Vendôme, 75001.

On a lighter note, **Tea Follies**, on a tree-filled square in the not-too-chic 9th *arrondissement,* typifies the kind of tearoom that is visited for many reasons. Go for lunch and the tasty *tartes salées* or chicken pie, for Sunday brunch and raisin and bran scones and spinach quiche, or on any afternoon to read the stack of papers that builds up over the course of the day and to look over the month's art show, with works accepted only from customers. A welcoming place, at 6, place Gustave-Toudouze.

A Priori Thé is the best place in town to sit outside on a rainy summer day. It's in Paris's most beautifully restored covered passageway, the Galerie Vivienne, off the rue des Petits-Champs in the 2nd *arrondissement* (sharing space with the likes of fashion designer Jean-Paul Gaultier), so all you suffer is the relaxing sound of rain pattering on the gallery's glass roof. There are comfortable white wicker chairs and rough wood tables, daily lunch specials, and an inviting, equally comfortable atmosphere.

At the unfashionable end of the rue St-Honoré (number 91), **Rose-Thé** is hidden in a courtyard complex of antiques shops. The one small room looks like an antiques shop itself: None of the tables or chairs, which range from deep, overstuffed armchairs to spindly Louis-XVI imitations, matches. Because tables are given out on a first-come-first-served basis, some amusing seating arrangements have ensued, with over-stuffed patrons perched precariously on thin-legged chairs. Rose-Thé has terrific tarts (especially the meat), salads, and desserts. Very pleasant.

Down the block from the Centre Pompidou, but on a street so tiny and aged it appears a world away, **Quincambosse** features some of the best and most intricate salads and tarts in town. The raw stone walls have character, though occasional art exhibits take away from their natural beauty. Great for lunch, less great for sitting around. 13, rue Quincampoix, 75004.

The **Loir dans la Théière** (Lewis Carroll's dormouse in a teapot), on the other hand, is a great place for hanging around. At one end of the rue de Rosiers—number 3—in the 4th *arrondissement,* a few doors down from a public steam bath for men and women, this rumpled, comfortable tearoom looks like the common room of some ideal social club. Mismatched tables and chairs, including huge, gratifyingly form-fitting ones near the door, set the tone, and a fairly young crowd that seems to have time on its hands makes for a pleasantly lackadaisical air. Good lunches and cakes.

A pair of tea rooms in the Marais reaffirm that neighborhood as one of the best in which to wander in all of Paris. The truly serious tea connoissuer should absolutely not miss a stop in **Mariage Frèges**, perhaps the most serious maison de thé in town. Its sober wood-paneled exterior and handsome front room—bulging with hundreds of jars of tea, a vast array of tea services, and every other tea-related machine known to civilization—promise exactly the sort of comfortable, skylit room you find in the back. Delectable cakes and sandwiches round out the experience. The 1930s delivery van you occasionally spy rumbling about Paris is a joy. Open every day until 7:30 P.M., at 30–32, rue du Bourg-Tibourg, 75004.

The **British Colonies** recalls a different era, with its Raj decor of tall, leafy plants, dark wood walls, and general air of gentility. They do a high tea of sorts, and serve tasty sandwiches, tarts, soups, and salads all afternoon. The room is for nonsmokers only, and features a Sunday brunch. 40, rue Vielle-du-Temple, 75004.

The plate-glass windows at the **Flore-en-l'Ile** afford a magnificent view of Notre-Dame's flying buttresses, summertime sunbathers, and the organ grinders, storytellers, and mimes who inhabit the pedestrian bridge leading from the Ile St-Louis to the Ile de la Cité. The food is pretty good, and the Flore stocks the famed Berthillon ice cream, which is handy, since lines at the store stretch for blocks during the summer. 42, quai d'Orléans, 75004.

The place Dauphine is a bit odd anyway: a pretty little park dwarfed on one side by the Palais de Justice and guarded on the other by the large statue of a mounted Henri IV. It's no wonder that **Fanny Tea**, at 20, place Dauphine, is odd too. It looks like the library that time forgot, with books and candles all over the place, tea instruments someone's great-aunt left behind back in 1907, and an intense owner. But it does give new meaning to the word "interesting," and the cakes and pies are awfully good. Yves Montand is a neighbor.

Left Bank

Hidden away at 59–61, rue St-André-des-Arts in the 6th *arrondissement,* not far from the place de l'Odéon, **La**

Cour de Rohan is a pretty little tearoom in greens and whites with good furniture. Soothing classical music and fine tarts and pastries make it a nice spot for those rendez-vous you hope will linger on. Quite English and yet romantic.

The first mosque built in Paris (**Mosquée de Paris**) contains a restaurant, a steam bath, and, of course, a tearoom. And what a tearoom! If it weren't so crowded with students from the nearby university, it would be easy to dally all day, sipping small glasses of sweet, fresh mint tea, staring at tiled floors and romantic Eastern architecture. 1, rue Daubenton and 39, rue Geoffroy-St-Hilaire, 75005.

CAFÉS

Cafés are the traditional Paris spots for a quick lunch, a rendezvous, or just to while away a few hours with a book or a diary. And rightly so. The city is rich with these half-bar, half-restaurants: They come in a variety of guises, offering a wide range of settings, atmospheres, and pleasures. The best are graced with a fascinating history and aspects of the character that originally made them historical.

Right Bank

Fouquet's (pronounced, in the English fashion so popular during the Belle Epoque, foo-KETS) is technically a café, though of the rarefied sort. Snacks do not come cheap here, but Fouquet's is one of the last remnants, and certainly the classiest one, of the glory that was once the Champs-Elysées before fast-food emporiums, automobile showrooms, and movie theaters overran the avenue. James Joyce was a regular back when dinner was affordable, and today artists of a different sort (journalists and actors) still pack the lively terrace and dining room. The coffee is pretty good, and it is an excellent vantage point for people-watching, as well as a fun place. 99, avenue des Champs-Elysées, 75008. Tel: 47-23-70-60.

Another relic, though with less of its former grandeur, the **Café de la Paix** still dominates the large square in front of the Opéra. Like Fouquet's, it is now a national monument, so it is likely neither to disappear nor to improve. But most of the civilized world at one point or another passes by, so a good afternoon's examination of what Parisians look like this year can be had.

The **Bon Pêcheur**, at 14, rue Pierre-Lescot, was the first café brave enough to open after the unfortunately ugly Les Halles shopping mall debuted in the late 1970s. Today it is one of the pleasantest in the *quartier:* small, cool (the waiters sport Hawaiian shirts and sunglasses that are at least as chic as the customers'), and personable. The *bouffe* ("chow") is good as far as café fare goes, and the location is ideal for a sunny afternoon's reading of the paper. A mime who is somewhat less annoying than the norm often provides entertainment, following and imitating innocent passersby.

When the **Café Costes** opened its doors at 4, rue Berger, on the square des Innocents in the 1st *arrondissement* in early 1985, it set off a citywide design revolution. Philippe Starck's hard-edged neo–Art Deco interior was an instant success, and suddenly everyone opening a bar or restaurant either wanted Starck to design it or mimicked his approach (Costes's tables and chairs, logo, coffee cups, and more were created by Starck). Today the design still stands up—a little cold, perhaps, but coherent and attractive. As you might expect, Costes is one of the most chic cafés in Paris (and charges accordingly). In warmer months the well-dressed crowd packing the terrace tables present the facing square des Innocents (once an overcrowded cemetery) with a sea of designer sunglasses and men with ponytails. All the same, Costes can be a fun place to hang out.

A few hundred yards away, at 100, rue St-Martin, on the place Beaubourg, another Costes has set up shop in another very trendy café. The **Café Beaubourg**, opened by Gilbert Costes and his brother Jean-Louis, takes up where the Café Costes leaves off. Total design is, again, the emphasis, but here comfort seems to have been taken into account. There are different areas with different chair designs to suit the needs of a range of customers. Upstairs, private nooks shield the romantic from inquiring eyes; opposite the bar downstairs, a pile of the week's papers in several languages (French, German, Italian, and English) awaits those settling into the most comfortable chairs for a long stay. The food is particularly good here, especially the breakfast egg dishes and the *café crème*. The crowd, on the other hand, is not as chic as at Costes; some bloods are put off, perhaps, by the portly gents breathing fire, eating glass, and lying on beds of nails across the way.

Of the many cafés in the Marais, two stand out: **Ma Bourgogne** and the Fer à Cheval. The former is nestled under the red-brick arches that make up the arcade of perimeter of the place des Vosges, once the home Henri IV. The old-time rattan chairs afford a view of a beautiful little park, where the very fashionable neighborhood's young mothers bring their children to play and where other locals, young and old, come to sunbathe and read in the summer. Inspector Maigret would wander over here from his Ile de la Cité office to drink coffee and ponder his surprisingly light caseload. The **Fer à Cheval**, which was a wine shop in the 1800s and for nearly a century one of the most popular cafés in the *quartier,* takes its name from the lovely horseshoe-shaped marble bar that dominates the small room. A center for troublemakers during the May 1968 student uprising, it's still an excellent hangout. 30, rue Vieille-du-Temple.

One of Paris's odder cafés, the **Clown Bar** is a fairly seedy spot next to the Cirque d'Hiver (Winter Circus), and the bar's name, decor, and patrons take their cue from this location. Photos of circus stars share wall space with decrepit murals of clowns and bareback riders. Although the food and coffee aren't great, the Clown Bar is worth visiting for its warm, run-down atmosphere. 114, rue Amelot, 75011.

Left Bank

A grand old café with dark-wood walls and a long, classic zinc bar, **La Palette** is still a favorite with art and other students. And well it should be. Good, cheap sandwiches; an open, bustling atmosphere; and plenty of history ("what famous painter, then as unknown as myself, could have sat right here?")—all make for a café that seems to define the genre. 43, rue de Seine, 75006.

The Café Deux Magots and Café de Flore are the kings of St-Germain-des-Prés café life. They've been homes away from home to more artists, writers, and thinkers than the Académie Française, and today they remain beacons for the intellectually prominent.

The **Deux Magots**, opposite the church of St-Germain-des-Prés, is the more boisterous, and touristy, of the two. (It was behind the church monastery that D'Artagnan, about to duel Athos, Porthos, and Artemis, joined the Musketeers against the cardinal's men who suddenly appeared.) A favorite hangout of Cubists and other arty types, Deux Magots became after World War II the second office of Jean-Paul Sartre. Today the prices keep starving artists away, but many glitterati still frequent its hallowed red banquettes. Many street musicians serenade the café during summer months.

The nearby **Flore** (the two cafés are always thought of together) has a more literary tradition, though Picasso did move here after the war. Sartre, Camus, and de Beauvoir made the café the headquarters of existentialism, though today few of the literary set go there to ponder questions of being and nothingness, unless it's to ponder their status as cultural icons. A fine place for a coffee or beer, a breakfast of soft-boiled eggs, or the best Welsh rarebit in town.

The **Select** is the only member of the Montparnasse pantheon of cheap cafés still living and breathing as it once did. The Dôme has been renovated so hideously it should be closed to preserve the memory of its former greatness, and the Coupole has been thoroughly disfigured. But the Select (with the two other cafés just mentioned, the 6th *arrondissement* epicenter of all that life had to offer for the Lost Generation) has retained some of its former glory. The grand terrace, at number 99, lets onto the ravaged boulevard Montparnasse, now housing a procession of movie theaters and overshadowed by the drab Montparnasse tower, and is filled with a young crowd reading books and soaking up the sun.

—*Edward Hernstadt*

BARS

In France drinking is considered an integral part of the process of eating and talking. Thus, the French bounty of alcohol is usually consumed in a restaurant or a café, although neither institution truly does justice to the drinker's art. Fortunately, cosmopolitan influences on Paris have tempered the Gallic prejudice against going out to any place where chewing and digesting are not the principal activities, as is evident in the foreign origin of many of the city's best watering holes. Because drinking for the sake of drinking is an exotic proposition for many Parisians, prices in pubs and bars can be quite steep. Be prepared to pay 30 francs and up for a cocktail or a humble glass of beer. So much for the bad news. The good news is that tipping is not required, or even expected, to keep drinks flowing to your table.

The best example of an outpost of the bar culture is **Harry's New York Bar**, an American fixture of the Opéra

district since 1911. Its wood-paneled walls are hung with
pennants from every notable U.S. college, which contrast
with the more discreet Oxbridge coats of arms also on
view. A favorite of expatriates and French people who
enjoy feeling like expatriates, Harry's is known for the
famed straw poll of Americans on the eve of presidential
elections, which has been wrong only once (1976, when
barflies picked Ford over Carter). The bar is the birthplace of the Bloody Mary (1927) and of the city's most
corny Franglais joke: Harry's prints its address as "Sank
roo doe noo" (5, rue Daunou).

At the nearby place Vendôme, Americans have yet another home away from home. The bars at the Ritz are still
proud of their Lost Generation connections, none more
so than the **Bar Hemingway**, a shrinelike affair dominated
by a bust of Papa. He is supposed to have liberated this
bar in 1944, when, presumably, the dress code was not as
strict. Men must now wear a tie. Around the corner from
the Ritz, on the rue des Capucines, is a Dublin newcomer
to the district, **Kitty O'Shea's**. Named for the woman
whose adulterous affair with Parnell caused such a fuss in
the late 19th century, the bar is the headquarters for Irish
Eurocrats and well-heeled Bretons desperately seeking
Celtic camaraderie. And yes, the Guinness is good.

The area near the Etoile is noted for two elaborately
ersatz British pubs, the **Lady Hamilton** at 82, avenue
Marceau and the **Winston Churchill**, 5, rue Presbourg.
The latter is grander and possesses a greater variety of
Scotch whisky. It also has two cellar bars, one done up in
the French conception of a London local, the other in
dark Neolithic modern.

The Champs-Elysées district has discos and piano bars
by the dozen, many of them far too distracting for serious
drinkers. Exceptions are the **Bar des Anglais** (what else?)
in the Plaza-Athénée Hotel (25, avenue Montaigne) and the
bar at **Le Doyen** restaurant. The latter is the neglected gem
of the entire district, set amid the greenery behind the Petit
Palais. Summer calls for long, cool drinks on the terrace;
winter, for grogs and "medicinal" coffees in the unpretentious elegance of the barroom. Le Doyen is, surprisingly,
medium-priced, uncrowded, and 100 percent French.

For haute-couture barflies, the best place to wet your
whistle after a hard day's splurge is in the bar of the
Bristol Hôtel, at 112, rue du Faubourg-St-Honoré. Gobelins tapestries and huge bouquets of flowers make up the
decor.

The Halles district, for all its devotion to play, is not well endowed with decent drinking spots that are not cafés. Its development in the late 1970s, which coincided with a great gush of Americanophilia, has left a legacy of New World barrooms. The best of these is **Conway's** (73, rue St-Denis), a crowded restaurant anteroom cluttered with boxing photos and American sports exotica. Its location, where Les Halles turns sleazy, makes it a point of departure for adventures in respectability or vice, depending on whether you head south or north, respectively. Southward, at Châtelet, the ground-floor room above the **Petit Opportun** cellar jazz club (15, rue Lavandières-Ste-Opportune) exudes mellow, early middle-aged funkiness until four or five in the morning. Northward, on the tiny rue Tiquetonne, **Le Baragouin** gives an idea of what it is to be young, rowdy, and broke in Paris.

The Marais is more of a restaurant- than a bar district, except to the city's gay population. Two gay bars in particular should be noted: **Le Piano Zinc**, 49, rue des Blancs Manteaux, which has a cabaret in its cellar, and **Le Swing**, 42, rue Vieille-du-Temple, a relaxed 1950s study in gray. Around the corner, the deliberately shabby **Au Rendez-Vous des Amis**, 10, rue Ste-Croix-de-la-Bretonnerie, is precisely that: a place for friends—of all persuasions—to get together for a drink in the early evening. A nearby café, the **Fer à Cheval** on the rue Vieille du Temple, is what every aperitif joint should be: intimate and cheap. At the point where the Marais meets the Bastille lies one of the city's handsomest bars. **La Mousson**, 9, rue de la Bastille, prides itself on its imperial connections: not, as you might expect, with Paris's ubiquitous Napoléon, but with the days of the Raj. Mock-rattan furniture, lazy overhead fans, and a few posters of posh ocean liners evoke the world of Kipling and Maugham for well-dressed clients in their twenties and thirties. French is the lingua franca of this corner of the empire.

The Bastille district is, according to *The New York Times,* "thug chic." The area near the rue de Lappe, now the nesting ground of the city's night owls, looks mildly threatening and thus is of great interest for barroom adventurers. Of the many drinking spots, the **Cactus Bleu** (on the rue de Lappe) is the most garish, overdesigned in accordance with the current tenets of Parisian taste. For lovers of *rai* music (Algerian rock 'n' roll) and honky-tonk rowdiness, the tiny **Bastide** bar a few doors down is a far more congenial place. Not for the faint-hearted. Where rue de Lappe runs into rue de Charonne, the **Entre Pots** celebrates old advertising campaigns and displays halogen lights for a quietly trendy crowd. A spacious place on the rue de Charenton called the **China Club** is currently the favorite with mellow hipsters and fans of piped-in Ella Fitzgerald and Billie Holiday. If you are uncomfortable with comfort, less genteel places are very easy to find around here. On rue de la Roquette, just a block or two north of rue de Lappe, stands the least genteel of all: **Phify's**, the gathering place for Parisian bikers and their gum-chewing dates. On Saturday nights in this bar, prepare to see suburban kids dressed for an evening out—in 1955.

In the great stretches of the Right Bank off the beaten track, several bars are worth visiting. In the 11th *arrondissement,* the area that promises one day to supplant the Bastille as an up-and-coming neighborhood (Paris is an ever-changing city), the **H₂O** at the place Léon Blum (rue Godefroy Cavaignac) is building a reputation for creative cocktail-mixing, one of the few refinements neglected by French civilization. Farther into the central business district, near the Folies Bergère, **Au Général La Fayette** stands as proof of the constant surprises Paris has to offer. Located on the otherwise unremarkable rue La Fayette, this lively bar is one of the most agreeable spots to quaff ale in the city.

At Montmartre, pseudo-cafés serving a full range of expensive drinks (including pastis, which, after all, is pseudo-absinthe) are the norm. For good downmarket fun, a cramped crêperie-café-piano bar called **Le Tire Bouchon** (on the tiny rue Norvins) should be tried.

The Left Bank is usually associated with café life, and for good reason: Decent bars are hard to come by. One very worthwhile exception is the **Caveau de la Bolée**, a charming hole in the wall hidden away in the rue de l'Hirondelle, a deserted alleyway close to the crowded place St-Michel. Named for the bowls (*bolées*) of cider that poor Sorbonne students favored in Medieval times, this quiet all-night spot is now the haunt of chess fiends, who are sent to the back of the cave to indulge in their sleepless passion. The good old days—or rather, nights— of jazz on the Left Bank are kept alive at such places as **La Paillote**, 45, rue Monsieur Le Prince, a place done up to look like an African hut, and **Birdland**, at the corner of the rues Princesse and Guisarde, a minuscule bar in the heart of St-Germain-des-Prés. Both bars have admirable collections of jazz records.

At Montparnasse, once famous for the cafés and bars where French surrealists rubbed shoulders and lifted elbows with the young and talented from all over the world, chain restaurants and high rents—fallout from the giant office complex built here in the 1970s—have moved in. The sole bar of the area that is worth a visit nowadays is the **Rosebud** (11 bis, rue Delambre), a tranquil spot where young professionals and failed artists converge over cocktails, chile con carne, and recorded jazz. A friendly place.

—*Stephen O'Shea*

NIGHTLIFE AND ENTERTAINMENT

For the Victorians, Paris was where you came for "culture" and to sow your oats, which together usually meant the opera, fancy-dress balls, carriage rides in the Tuileries, and perhaps a mistress. For North Americans, Paris symbolized the cynical worldliness that gathered itself under the rubric "Europe" and tempted young men to stray from the straight and narrow. Henry James recognized the compelling character of Paris quite well: Even Lambert Strether in *The Ambassadors,* old and wise enough to know better, was seduced by the city's subtle beauty. Today the world has shrunk, and so too have many of the illusions that served to enliven it. Paris, however, is a city in which illusions are still respected and nostalgia revered. It is also a city that loves the night and considers it to be as much a territory of the imagination as of the senses.

Today's Parisian "night" can be broken into four categories: *music, spectacles* (revues), *dancing,* and *classical culture* (concerts, opera, dance, and theater). Visitors should consult the weekly *Pariscope* or the *Officiel des Spectacles,* on sale at any kiosk, to see what's playing at the theaters or clubs. Movies are also listed in these publications; *v.o.* means that the film is shown in its original form with subtitles in French; *v.f.* means that it is dubbed. The Paris Extra section of *Paris Passion* magazine has more limited listings in English of events around town.

MUSIC

The French have long been mad about jazz, and Paris has long been a haven for American jazz musicians unable to find an audience, or work, in the United States. A cult sprang up around Josephine Baker in the 1920s, and in the 1940s and 1950s as much good jazz could be heard in Paris as anywhere else in the world. Bernard Tavernier's 1986 film 'Round Midnight is a touching tribute to the reverence many French people have for jazz musicians and clubs. Today there is a wealth of clubs and piano bars that still feature top American musicians, as well as the leading homegrown practitioners. Venues for contemporary non-jazz genres are far rarer, as are quality French bands for them, but Paris is an important stop on the international circuit and there are always a few rock concerts in town.

Piano Bars

The **Ascot** and the **Ritz** are probably the most elegant piano bars in Paris. The former offers reasonable prices and the subdued horsey interior you imagine exists only in English men's clubs, while the latter offers luxury and refinement in a relaxed, slightly snobby atmosphere. Ascot: 66, rue Pierre-Charron, 75008, until 4:00 A.M. Ritz: 15, place Vendôme, 75001, until 1:00 A.M.

The hotel-auditorium-mall complex at the Porte Maillot has two piano bars: the **Lafayette**, in the hotel of the same name, and the **Lionel Hampton**, in the Hôtel Méridien. They share a common element: Despite the built-in disadvantage of being hotel bars, they are both surprisingly nice. Both have "modern" decor and frequent guest performers. Lafayette: Hôtel Concorde-Lafayette, 3, place Géneral-Koenig, 75017, until 2:00 A.M. Lionel Hampton: Hôtel Méridien, 81, boulevard Gouvion-St-Cyr, 75017, until 10:00 P.M.

The late Joe Turner, one of the transplanted kings of jazz, stayed in Paris, he used to say, "Because I haven't been out of work for 30 years." He would park himself behind a piano and a cigar every night from midnight till dawn at the intimate **Calavados**, pounding out classics in his warm and inimitable style. 40, avenue Pierre-1er-de-Serbie, 75008.

Les Trois Maillets occupies an ancient building in the heart of the Latin Quarter and offers jazz on two floors. The homey, crowded piano bar above has become a second home for very lower bourgeois France—a sight in itself. Downstairs in the cramped *cave,* groups and combos ranging from jazz to the blues to gospel play every night. 56, rue Galande, 75005.

Clubs

Club action doesn't start until after dinner—10:00 at the earliest—and generally continues until the wee hours. The better clubs impose a cover charge. Expect fairly costly cocktails in all of these.

Four *boîtes* dominate Les Halles, offering a variety of musical options:

The **Baiser Salé** presents an international mix of styles, from blues to Brazilian, in a comfortable though somewhat expensive club. 58, rue des Lombards, 75001.

The **Slow Club** has one of the best neon signs in Paris and quality swing jazz in a lively setting. Be careful: When no concert is scheduled, and often after 1:00 A.M., it turns into a dreadful disco. 130, rue de Rivoli, 75001.

The **Petit Opportun**, a stone's throw away, is a more traditional club: The bartender in the cramped upstairs room plays rare recordings, while top musicians reign in the charming old *cave* below. 15, rue des Lavandières-Ste-Opportune, 75001.

Distrito, a restaurant-cum-jazz-and-rock-club, is a newer addition to the district. The crowd is young and verges on tough, in a chic sort of way, and some of Paris's best local bands play here from midnight till the wee hours. 49, rue Berger, 75001.

Five other Right Bank clubs feature an eclectic choice of genres:

The **Cambridge**, a few blocks from the Arc de Triomphe, is one of the only places in town to hear Dixieland jazz. 17, avenue Wagram, 75017.

The **New Morning** attracts the best foreign artists who come to Paris, and they play everything from jazz to blues to rock. It's a cavernous club in what was once a newspaper printing plant. 5–7, rue des Petites-Ecuries, 75010.

Le Gibus is the only real rock-and-roll club in Paris doing well today, after an unhealthy punk period in the early 1980s. It occasionally features some very raw, exciting bands. 18, rue du Faubourg-du-Temple, 75011.

The **Cigale**, a former 1890s music hall, has been redesigned by the ubiquitous Philippe Starck and is, as would be expected, exceedingly cool. Plays, special screenings, and music production take place here, as do rock concerts. 120, boulevard de Rochechouart, 75018.

La Chapelle des Lombards, in the hot Bastille area, features salsa and samba music. 19, rue de Lappe, 75011.

Four dependable Latin Quarter clubs present topnotch jazz every night:

Caveau de la Huchette, a center for swing and big-band music. 5, rue de la Huchette, 75005.

Le Petit Journal St-Michel, on three cramped floors, presents leading French acts such as Claude Bolling and such big-name Americans as Benny Waters. 71, boulevard St-Michel, 75005.

Le Furstemberg, a lively bar below a busy brasserie. A standard band plays standard tunes, but the atmosphere is pleasant. 28, rue de Buci, 75006.

Montana, a tiny bar where Champagne is the house drink and combos squeeze onto the stage. 28, rue St-Benoît, 75006.

Three clubs dominate the music scene in the Montparnasse area:

Le Petit Journal Montparnasse, which is as good as its mate in the Latin Quarter. 13, rue du Commandant-R. Mouchotte, 75014.

Utopia-Jazz Club, an odd bar that is headquarters for blues, bluegrass, and country *à la Française* (just think about it). 79, rue de l'Ouest, 75014.

Dunois, which specializes in the cutting edge of jazz and hosts the most innovative groups. 28, rue Dunois, 75013.

SPECTACLES

The Las Vegas "girlie revue" took its inspiration from Paris's *grands spectacles*. But, built on schlock as Vegas is, the Nevada versions cannot compare with the sheer exuberance and grandeur of the originals. While there are dozens of supper clubs and small revues in Paris, the rule of thumb is simple: The most famous are, quite simply, the best. Shows typically feature troupes of women dancing gamely without the benefit of tops and balancing enormous, gaudy headpieces or dragging long, glittering capes; men, usually in supporting roles, traipsing onto the stage in a variety of outlandish outfits; archetypic nightclub singers crooning; and a slew of vaudeville acts performing outside the curtain while teams change the vast and complicated sets.

One more common feature: song and dance numbers

that cannot be described without an army of exclamation marks. The world's most beautiful women! Spectacular story lines! Lavish scenery! Unbelievable special effects! Drama! Excitement! These shows are probably the world's finest Grade-B entertainment, and that alone elevates them to a form of art. They are also terrific fun. The ticket price includes entry, a drink—usually a half-bottle of Champagne—and your meal at the dinner shows.

The **Lido** is the most Las Vegas–like of the shows, and probably the most spectacular. An intricate hydraulic system means that finales often include swimming pools or ice-skating rinks and that a real pit is available for the disposal of "virgins" being sacrificed to the gods. 116, Champs-Elysées, 75008. Tel: 45-63-11-61. Dinner at 8:00, 510 francs; shows at 10:15 and 12:15, 395 francs.

The **Folies Bergère** is undoubtedly the best-known show in Paris; it turned 100 in 1987. Charlie Chaplin, Colette, Maurice Chevalier, and Josephine Baker are just some of the entertainers who have graced the boards here, and Manet painted a waitress behind the bar. The opulent sets still include many designed by Erté. The Folies always features a truly talented singer, who shares the spotlight with the dance numbers, something the other shows can't claim. 32, rue Richer, 75009. Tel: 42-46-77-11. Show at 9:00. 93–378 francs, depending on seating and eating.

The **Moulin Rouge** puts on the most stereotypically French spectacle, in keeping with its history. The place is nothing like the dance hall Toulouse-Lautrec created posters for, but still the Moulin has retained its *musette* character, with plush red banquettes and lights on lampposts. The shows still feature the can-can, a number that over the years has lost none of its stunning athleticism and drama. Place Blanche, 75018. Tel: 46-06-00-19. Dinner at 8:00, 510 francs; shows at 10:00 and 12:00, 395 francs, including a half-bottle of Champagne.

The **Paradis Latin**, on the other hand, is a more genuinely French show. Set in a comfortable theater with three long rows of closely packed tables, the spectacle includes old-time singers and lively vaudeville acts, and encourages audience participation. The Paradis has a homier, more intimate feeling than the giants do. 28, rue du Cardinal-Lemoine, 75005. Tel: 43-25-28-28. Dinner at 8:30, 510 francs; show at 10:00, 395 francs.

The **Crazy Horse Saloon** stages the most exotic show in town, featuring nude dancers sporting bits of ribbon and lace and names like Polly Underground, Tiny Semaphore, and Funny Cumulus. Favorites with businessmen from Japan, the dances are actually a pretty amazing sight: The Western-theme bar is small, so the performers loom enormously on the tiny stage, and the choreographer occasionally manages to be interesting. An experience. 12, avenue George-V, 75008. Tel: 47-23-32-32. Shows at 9:30 and 11:30; weekends at 8:15, 10:35, and 12:50. 195 francs at the bar; 360 francs in the wings; 440 francs in the mezzanine; 490 francs in the orchestra.

DANCING

Three types of dancing spots exist in Paris: old-fashioned tango palaces, where serious practitioners of the art congregate; rich, glitzy discos around the Arc de Triomphe; and high-fashion clubs favored by the young, artistic, and cool. Discos tend to be extremely expensive and to be geared to middle-aged jet setters, Greek shipping czars, and starlets who haven't quite made it. (If interested, check out Atmosphère, 5th Avenue, Régine's, Olivia Valère, or Castel's at your own risk.) Clubs are generally open until at least 5:00 A.M., and the most popular often have ugly-tempered bouncers and long lines outside. Dress up to speed your way in, but be reassured: New York–style fascist entry rules are not yet in effect. Drinks start at 50 francs, entrance 70 francs and up.

La Coupole is more than a historic restaurant—it is also one of the best dance clubs in town. Downstairs, conservatively dressed middle-aged men and women gather to tango the evenings away. Not for those unfamiliar with the precise, erotic dance. 102, boulevard du Montparnasse, 75014.

Chez Gégène opened just after World War I broke out and features both tango and *musette* (typically French accordion songs). A wonderfully folksy and traditional place to dance close, the way men and women were meant to do. 126 bis, quai de Polangis, Joinville-le-Pont.

The **Balajo** has a split personality. Weekday afternoons it is a great dance hall packed with couples swinging around the floor. Monday evenings it is also packed, but with trendy young Parisians twisting to thumping disco and rock songs. Quite fun. 9, rue de Lappe, 75011.

Keur-Samba is the one 8th-*arrondissement* club that everyone loves. Terribly private (one of the hardest to get into) and done up in what Abercrombie and Fitch might consider correct disco decor, the Keur features African music and is popular with the rich and famous. 79, rue de la Boétie. From 11:00.

The Locomotive is one of the newer clubs but is already very popular. When not used for rock concerts or art exhibits, its three levels—including a large dance floor and the basement, which winds through the boilers of the Moulin Rouge next door—are full of trendy young people. 90, boulevard Clichy, 75018. From 11:00.

Le Palace is the old standby of the younger-spirited clubs. That the trio who own Les Bains (below) bought Le Palace in late 1988 and brought their very trendy decorator in to redo the huge onetime theater has helped keep it popular. It tends to have fairly good music, playing less disco and more "dance" tracks (long versions with heavy bass lines) of popular songs. A brief closing by the police after a patron in poor shape was put out of the club and subsequently died has not hurt the club's popularity. 8, rue du Faubourg-Montmartre, 75009. From 11:00.

Les Bains has dominated the club scene in recent years, though that may mean nothing tomorrow. The highly stylized decor and many, many dressed-to-kill artsy types remain, though. The place gets unbelievably crowded on weekends. 7, rue Bourg-l'Abbé, 75003. From 11:30.

Le Tango is an intimate, friendly club where young Africans, South Americans, and Parisians squeeze together to dance to the latest hits from two continents. This was an early rap center, too. 14, rue au Maire, 75003. From 11:00.

Over the past few years, the Paris night scene has seen the emergence of the one-night stands, clubs open for one night of the week only. The **Balajo**, at 9, rue de Lappe in the 11th, on Mondays from 11:30, 100 francs entry, was the first. Others include **The Acid House at Studio A**, at 49, rue de Ponthieu, 75008, on Thursdays; and, on Fridays, **La Nouvelle Eve**, to view rich French trendies and yuppies, from 10:00, 100 francs, entry at 25, rue Fontaine, 75009.

CLASSICAL MUSIC, DANCE, AND THEATER

Of course, the joys of Paris nights are not limited to jazz and the jitterbug. As a world capital and traditional center of the arts, Paris has long been home to a wealth of talented and innovative musicians, conductors, dancers, directors, and playwrights.

Though Paris today is not the preeminent music center it once was, and the Orchestre de Paris has been called second tier, its concert halls still draw many of the world's greatest artists.

Ballet was invented in France during the reign of Louis XIV, with the Sun King himself often performing in the first dances. Today Paris is home to several world-caliber companies (including the Paris Opera Ballet, directed by Rudolf Nureyev), and every year the world's finest companies, including the Kirov, the Bolshoi, Maurice Béjart's Ballet of the 20th Century, and the New York City Ballet, grace Paris stages.

The French theater tradition is old, glorious, and alive, as attested to by ongoing productions of Molière and Racine, both of whose plays still crackle with wit and verve. Avant-garde theater was in part developed in Paris, and two of Ionesco's plays, *La Leçon* and *La Cantatrice Chauve,* are still running (though in seriously fatigued stagings) after more than 30 years. Though a 1987 "culture crisis" deprived French theaters and theater companies of a portion of their supporting funds, there are always dozens of reasonably priced plays to be seen, and they run the gamut from Sam Shepard (in bilingual versions) to archaic avant-garde to cutting edge. For most cultural events in Paris, you should reserve tickets well in advance of performances.

The most notable concert halls and theaters in Paris are:

- Les Bouffes du Nord. 37 bis, boulevard de la Chapelle. Tel: 42-39-34-50. Major center for modern theater.
- Centre Georges Pompidou. Place Beaubourg. Tel: 42-74-42-19. Avant-garde music.
- La Comédie Française. 2, rue de Richelieu. Tel: 40-15-00-15. The classic French repertory in a beautiful theater.
- Opéra Comique (Salle Favart). 5, rue Favart. Tel: 42-96-06-11. Opera, dance, and shows.
- Paris Opéra. Place de l'Opéra. Tel: 47-42-53-71. Opera and dance in opulent surroundings. Chagall painted the ceiling. Home of the Paris Opéra Ballet, directed by Rudolf Nureyev.
- Opéra de la Bastille. Place de la Bastille. Tel: 43-

42-92-92. Opera and concerts, directed by Myung Whun-chung.

- Salle Cortot. 78, rue Cardinet. Tel: 43-96-48-48. Concerts.
- Salle Gaveau. 45, rue de la Boétie. Tel: 45-63-20-30. Concerts.
- Salle Pleyel. 252, rue du Faubourg St-Honoré. Tel: 45-63-88-73. Concerts. Home of the Orchestre de Paris.
- Théâtre de la Bastille. 76, rue de la Roquette. Tel: 43-57-42-14. A leading forum for avant-garde theater, dance, and music.
- Théâtre de la Ville. 2, place du Châtelet. Tel: 42-74-22-77. Concerts and dance.
- Théâtre des Champs-Elysées. 15, avenue Montaigne. Tel: 47-20-36-37. Plays and touring shows (such as Marcel Marceau).
- Théâtre Musical de Paris. Place du Châtelet. Tel: 40-28-28-40. Concerts, dance, and touring shows.
- Théâtre National de Chaillot. Place du Trocadéro. Tel: 47-27-81-15. Plays and dance.
- Théâtre National de l'Odéon, place Paul-Claudel. Tel: 47-27-81-15. Bold and innovative theater productions.

Many churches feature organ recitals and choral pieces—among them, a regular Sunday concert at Notre-Dame.

Many sporting events are held at the Palais des Sports, porte des Versailles (Tel: 48-28-40-90), and the main convention center is the Palais des Congrès, 2, place de la Porte Maillot (Tel: 47-58-22-22). There are three racetracks in Paris or its suburbs: Auteuil in the Bois de Boulogne; Vincennes in the Bois de Vincennes for trotters; and Longchamp just outside the Bois de Boulogne for flat racing.

—*Edward Hernstadt*

SHOPS AND SHOPPING

In Paris shopping transcends self-indulgence, for here shopping is not so much an exercise in consumerism as an education in style and taste. For the French, choosing the perfect Brie from an open-air market stall is imbued with the same sense of ritual as selecting a Louis XV commode from a quai Voltaire *antiquaire,* and wrapping a box of candied fruits becomes an art. The French traditions of quality, craftsmanship, and attention to detail can be appreciated painlessly—and with a minimum of pedagogy—by the shopper alerted to Paris's mercantile possibilities and their nuances.

This is a city of serendipitous discovery. Although Paris's well-defined *quartiers* do attract certain habitués—and boutiques and restaurants are often geared toward them—wonderful shops sometimes appear where you would least expect to find them. Explore on foot and, given Paris's cobblestone streets and unpredictable weather, wear good, sturdy shoes. Shopping hours tend to be somewhat *fantaisiste.* Department stores reliably open at 10:00 A.M. and close at 7:00 P.M., but Paris's smaller boutiques sometimes don't open before 10:30 A.M., close at lunchtime, and, if they deign to open for business on Saturdays, sometimes close on Mondays to compensate. Visa and MasterCard are the most universally accepted credit cards in Parisian stores. Traveller's checks often cause confusion due to fluctuating exchange rates; French francs are consistently welcome.

The city's shopping terrain can be roughly divided into three geographic areas. The Right Bank—traditionally Paris's chic side of the river Seine—now reveals a split personality. Southwest of the Opéra, on the place Vendôme, the rue Royale, the rue du Faubourg-St-Honoré, and the avenue Montaigne, luxury reigns. Eastward, at the Palais-Royal, the place des Victoires, the recently renovated Les Halles, and the newly rediscovered Marais and Bastille areas, trendy takes over. The Left Bank's St-Germain-des-Prés area remains a bastion of "typically Parisian" fashion as well as an art-and-antiques-lover's mecca.

Place de la Concorde

Where to start? First decide on your priorities, or determine the target area you'd like to explore. For a crash course in French *art de vivre,* a good jumping-off point is the grandiose place de la Concorde, which many Parisians consider the hub of the city. Certain Parisian luxury shops demand token homage, and many of these legendary institutions are found on or around the streets radiating from here: **Lalique** crystal, a few doors down from Maxim's restaurant at 11, rue Royale; **Christofle** silver, which supplies much of the world's remaining royalty with its flatware, at number 12; and the city's most

glorious—and costly—florist, **Lachaume**, next door. Farther up the rue Royale are a number of chic fashion
boutiques: **Façonnable** and **Cerruti 1881** for classically
inclined men (with a small Cerruti women's boutique in
between), **Gucci** and **Mario Valentino** for flashy Italian
shoes and leather goods, and the American new kid on
the block, **Ralph Lauren**, at 2, place de la Madeleine.
Tucked off the rue Royale in the cité Berryer (a passageway lifted straight from the pages of Zola) is **The Blue Fox**
bar, which offers quiche, salad, and a glass of Bordeaux to
an attractive lunchtime crowd of well-dressed shoppers,
fashion-press attachés, and stockbrokers from the nearby
place Vendôme.

The prestigious saddlers-turned-leather-goods house
of **Hermès** is a two-minute walk away, at 24, rue du
Faubourg-St-Honoré. Hardened indeed is the heart that
doesn't leap at the sight of a brown-ribboned orange box
from Hermès containing one of the house staples: a silk
scarf, a "Kelly" handbag (made famous by its most celebrated advocate, Princess Grace), or the ultimate status
accessory, Hermès's pigskin Métro ticket holder.

Sitting smugly in the midst of all this *luxe* is the magnificent Hôtel de Crillon, at 10, place de la Concorde. Its
Obélisque Bar, reached by the hotel's rue Boissy-d'Anglas
side entrance, used to be a watering hole for journalists
in the prewar Paris of Janet Flanner and is still an irresistibly romantic rendezvous spot.

Just beside it is the kind of shop that collectors of the
rare, the wonderful, and even the slightly kitschy come to
Paris for: **Au Bain Marie**, at 12, rue Boissy-d'Anglas. Specializing in *l'art de la table,* Au Bain Marie's huge interior
is chockablock with antique and re-edited items for the
kitchen and dining room: turn-of-the-century silverware
purchased from defunct hotels, antique Daum and St.
Louis crystal glasses, Memphis dishes and 1930s Bakelite
tableware, and exquisite vintage and modern table and
bed linens.

Place de la Madeleine: Food

In a country where food has been elevated to the status of
religion, it seems only fitting that Paris's highest concentration of luxury food shops be found in the shadow of
one of its most illustrious temples, La Madeleine. Here,
clustered around the place de la Madeleine, are some of
the world's most dazzling names in gastronomy. The
windows alone of **Fauchon**, at 26, place de la Madeleine,

are an ode to gluttony. Inside, myriad culinary delights await: fresh foie gras and Beluga caviar, scented oils and out-of-season tropical fruits, as well as a stock of more humble imported goods catering to homesick Americans. Across the street at Fauchon's stand-up lunchroom you can wash down a frothy *pâtisserie* with a cup of some of the best coffee in Paris. On the other side of the *place,* at number 21, is **Hédiard**, *épicier par excellence,* specializing in exotic fruits and vegetables, its own selection of teas, honeys, spice blends, and fresh-fruit jellied candies known to every Parisian hostess as *les pâtes de fruits de chez Hédiard.* **Caviar Kaspia**, at 17, place de la Madeleine, offers caviar, smoked salmon, and blinis to go (an upstairs restaurant serves the same thing), and next door's **La Maison de la Truffe** supplies fresh truffles from November to March (out of season they are available dried or preserved for less rarefied palates).

The adjacent rue Vignon boasts the quintessential *fromagerie,* **La Ferme St-Hubert**, at number 21, which in addition to its vast selection of cheeses also serves cheese dishes at its tiny adjoining restaurant. While on the rue Vignon don't miss **Pulcinella**, a small shop with a persimmon awning at 10, rue Vignon that sells wonderful antique jewelry and other collectibles, and at number 11, **Jean Lafont**, one of Paris's oldest and most renowned optometrists, specializing in Clark Kent–style, mock-tortoiseshell spectacles. On the corner of the rue Vignon and the rue de Sèze is the French equivalent of the old corner drugstore, **Pharmacie Leclerc**, whose fine face powders, alcohol-free tonic lotions, and grandmother's-recipe face creams are favorites with Paris-based models and other fashion fauna.

Rue Tronchet and the Grands Magasins

The rue Tronchet is a bustling commercial artery leading north from the place de la Madeleine to the Parisian *grands magasins,* Au Printemps and Galeries Lafayette. On the second floor of number 13 (the third floor, to Americans), celebrated hatmaker **Jean Barthet** concocts fanciful headgear for Paris couturiers as well as provincial mothers-of-the-bride. At the intersection of the rue Tronchet and the boulevard Haussmann is another throwback to a more genteel era, **Aux Tortues** (at 55, boulevard Haussmann), whose caramel-colored marble façade decorated with bronze elephants has stood since 1864. Although its once-standard stock of tortoiseshell-backed boar-bristle brushes, ivory pocket combs, and eyelash brushes is dwindling (there is, apparently, no longer a clientele for tortoiseshell hand mirrors at 8,500 francs), Aux Tortues still has the best selection of polished Baltic amber necklaces and ivory and coral chokers in town.

Paris's two major department stores, **Au Printemps** and **Galeries Lafayette**, at numbers 64 and 40, boulevard Haussmann, are wonders of Belle Epoque architecture: Galeries Lafayette's stained-glass dome bathes the entire store in pastel light, and Printemps's top-floor terrace restaurant is known for its elaborate 19th-century decor. They are Paris's answer to New York's Bloomingdale's (at least the Bloomingdale's of ten years ago) and London's Harrod's. Both *magasins* have been recently renovated, and a shopper short on time can find at them Paris's best names in beauty, fashion, and interior design. Both stores accept most major credit cards and are open Monday through Saturday, Au Printemps from 9:30 A.M. to 6:30 P.M. and Galeries Lafayette from 9:30 A.M. to 7:00 P.M. Note: Possibly the world's most exhaustive selection of hardware and household bits and pieces—from hinges, locks, and doorknobs to wooden shoe trees and typically Parisian mailboxes—can be found at Paris's **BHV** (Bazar de l'Hôtel de Ville) department store, at 52–64, rue de Rivoli. Open Monday through Saturday from 9:00 A.M. to 6:30 P.M.

A distinct advantage for foreigners shopping at one of Paris's department stores is the ease in garnering the *détaxe*—the refund of the French excise tax to which visitors from abroad are entitled on purchases of up to 2,200 francs or more if they live within the European Community, or on purchases of up to 1,200 francs if they live outside the EC. Shoppers from outside the EC must fill out a special *détaxe* form—with receipts of purchases made within a period of six months—which they surrender to customs for stamped approval when they leave France. Paris's *grands magasins* all have special *détaxe* departments that help to demystify this all-too-often bewildering process.

Check out the labels on a Parisian dandy and chances are that at least one thing he's wearing comes from **Charvet**, *the* Paris men's haberdashery, located a few minutes' walk from *les grands magasins,* down the rue de la Paix at 28, place Vendôme. A seven-floor sanctuary on the majestic, 17th-century place Vendôme, Charvet has offered everything for the impeccable man—and for such women enamored of masculine classics as the novelist George Sand, who used to have her shirts made here—since 1838.

Place Vendôme

Clustered around the place Vendôme are France's most prestigious names in *haute joaillerie,* the centuries-old family jewelers **Chaumet**, **Boucheron**, **Mauboussin**, **Van Cleef et Arpels**—and **Cartier**, just up the street on the rue de la Paix. With the graceful, curved awnings of the Hôtel Ritz rimming one side, the glittering storefronts of these distinguished jewelers the other, the place Vendôme on a spring afternoon is the closest approximation of Proust's Paris that the city can offer today.

A visitor can prolong the remembrance of Paris past at two neighboring boutiques: **Annick Goutal**'s glorious, gilded scent shop at 14, rue de Castiglione, and **Cassegrain**, 422, rue St-Honoré, stationers and engravers to Paris since Proust's times. Those nostalgic for the more genteel days of steamship and rail travel should stop by **Morabito**, at 1, place Vendôme, whose windows are perennially, defiantly piled high with gleaming black crocodile luggage (which some countries prohibit under customs laws).

Place du Marché St-Honoré

A *place* no less charming, but of an entirely different nature, is the place du Marché St-Honoré, which you can reach by making a left onto the rue St-Honoré from the place Vendôme's southern end and turning left again on the narrow rue du Marché St-Honoré. A fire station occupies the place of honor here, and around it are a jumble of colorful restaurants and boutiques. **Jean-Charles Castelbajac**, at 31, place du Marché St-Honoré, is a designer-clothing store where fashion often blends couture and cartoon; and wacky accessory designer **Philippe Model**, at number 33, supplies rose-trimmed toques, tasseled suede gloves, and fuchsia silk pumps to Parisiennes with the wit—and the self-assurance—to wear them. A note of austerity recently added to the *place* is the **Comme des Garçons** furniture boutique at 23, place du Marché St-Honoré, whose minimalist steel creations are the interior-design equivalent of Japanese fashion label Comme des Garçons' purist fashions. **Corinne Cobson** sells sleek, sexy, and affordable fashion separates at number 28.

Rue de Rivoli

Do an about-face on the rue du Marché St-Honoré and it becomes—in yet another one of Paris's inexplicable street-name changes—the rue du 29 Juillet, which leads onto the colonnaded rue de Rivoli. If you're looking for gilt Eiffel Towers, Mona Lisa sweatshirts, and Paris-monument-printed acetate scarves to take home, any one of the closet-sized souvenir shops on the rue de Rivoli will be able to provide them.

Exceptions to the general tourist-trap ambience of the rue de Rivoli are the English bookshops **W. H. Smith** at number 248 and **Galignani**, said to be the oldest English language bookshop in Paris, at number 224. Visitors hoping to take home with them more than just a memory of Paris streets should check out **Galerie d'Architecture Miniature**'s tiny, handmade faïence reproductions of Paris buildings (206, rue de Rivoli). And **Angelina's**, at number 226, Paris's tearoom *par excellence,* is the gilt-and-mirrored meeting place for chic Parisians, a must for anyone seeking to understand French *belles manières.* Sipping a cup of Angelina's sinfully rich hot chocolate—poured in dollops from tiny porcelain pitchers—over an equally rich chestnut-and-cream Mont Blanc *pâtisserie* is many a Parisian's way of whiling away a long winter afternoon. For wonderful, offbeat mementos, **Destination Paris**, at 9, rue du 29 Juillet, offers artisan-made and generally wacky souvenirs of the City of Light.

If big-game antiques are your bag, **Le Louvre des Antiquaires**, left off the rue de Rivoli, at 2, place du Palais-Royal, is a well-stocked hunting ground. In this highly civilized three-story gallery are 250 shops devoted to fine French furniture, rich leather-bound books, and heavy bronzes. Unlike the tiny *brocanteurs* you find along the Left Bank's rue du Bac or rue Jacob, whose wares are reminiscent of *grandmère's* attic treasures, Le Louvre des Antiquaires's offerings are of a decidedly grander sort—and carry price tags to match. Most of Le Louvre des Antiquaires' shops accept major credit cards, but note that although they are open on Sundays, stores here traditionally close Mondays.

Men for whom the traditional pleasures of smoking and hunting remain as compelling as they were in earlier centuries will find two boutiques here to their liking: **A La Civette**, 157, rue St-Honoré, a *tabac* that has been providing smokers with the tools of their vice—fine Havana cigars, aromatic tobaccos, handmade pipes—since the 17th century, and **Faure le Page**, 8, rue de Richelieu, which sells arms and munitions and other hunting and shooting accessories. This shop, located on the same corner as the Comédie Française since 1716, holds no charm for those who don't share its passion, but it carries a noteworthy distinction: It was here, in 1789, that the Paris mob stole the gunpowder with which they blew up the Bastille.

Palais-Royal

Off the place du Palais-Royal are the tree-lined gardens of the Palais-Royal, whose graceful stone arcades have stood since 1780, when Louis-Philippe of Orléans built this ground-level shopping mall in Paris's first recorded get-rich-quick building scheme. Colette lived and died in one of the sumptuous apartments overlooking the gardens; the **Grand Véfour** restaurant, which began life here as a café in 1760, boasts a menu with a Jean Cocteau sketch on the cover and a small brass plaque indicating Victor Hugo's habitual dining place. Old mosaic floor tiles outside still proclaim long-gone shopowners' names, their places now occupied by a mixed bag of unusual boutiques.

Here are cloistered shops selling old stamps, antique jewels, beribboned medals and orders. **Didier Ludot**, 22–24, rue de Montpensier, sells one-of-a-kind antique leather accessories: Hermès bags and belts, crocodile wallets, and shoes. Next door at 19–20 is Ludot's vintage couture clothing annex. **Costea**, 63–64, galerie Montpensier, offers geometrically shaped *objets d'art* for home and office in stark ebony wood and ivory, tortoiseshell, and shiny nickeled bronze.

On the northern end of the gardens at 9, rue de Beaujolais is **Anna Joliet**, a delightful boutique that sells music boxes both old and new. Just behind it are the turn-of-the-century glass-roofed shopping "malls," galeries **Colbert** and **Vivienne**. The Galerie Vivienne, in addition to an assortment of tearooms, clothing boutiques, and interior-design shops and the oldest bookstore in Paris—the **Librairie Petit Siroux**—counts **Jean-Paul Gaultier's** post-high-tech Baroque boutique among its tenants. Childhood nostalgics shouldn't miss **Si Tu Veux**, at 62, galerie Vivienne, which sells charming traditional toys and games—wooden alphabet blocks, farm animal cardboard cutouts, and "real" teddy bears for parents and children weary of computerized fun. The newly renovated Galerie Colbert's **Bibliothèque Nationale Gift Shop**—France's national library is right next door—offers distinctive souvenirs, all adapted from the library's archives.

Place des Victoires

Where the rue des Petits-Champs meets the rue Etienne-Marcel sits the place des Victoires, an elegant 17th-century *place* with an equestrian statue of Louis XIV in its center. Circling it are some of Paris's best fashion storefronts: Kenzo, Thierry Mugler, Stéphane Kélian, Enrico Coveri, Charles Chevignon, Victoire, and recent American import Esprit. Its overflow has spilled onto the high-tech rue Etienne-Marcel, which has become the Paris address for the Japanese designers **Comme des Garçons** and **Yohji Yamamoto**, active-wear designers **Marithé and François Girbaud**, the British knitwear house **Joseph Tricot**, and the French ready-to-wear house **Cacharel**. At number 50, rue Etienne-Marcel, is **La Galerie en Attendant les Barberes**, a showcase for naturalistic furnishings from the "New Barbarians," the group of young designers who are currently redefining avant-garde Paris interiors. The small streets radiating from the place des Victoires—the rue Croix-des-Petits-Champs, the rue du Mail, the rue Hérold, and the nearby rue de la Coquillière—are full of interesting, affordable fashion boutiques for both men and women.

Les Halles

Next stop on the Right Bank shopping tour is the neighborhood known as Les Halles, which has been the subject of much controversy in the past decade. Out of the rubble of what Zola once called the "belly of Paris" and in the place of the sprawling market that for more than 800 years supplied the housewives, restaurateurs, and market stalls of Paris with fresh produce has risen an ultra-modern shopping complex, Le Forum des Halles. Though totally lacking in charm, this chrome-and-glass monument to modern consumerism does have something for everybody: bookshops, sporting-goods stores, fashionable clothing boutiques, cinemas—if you can find your way around the elaborate labyrinth of escalators.

The surrounding *quartier* is an eclectic mix of chic boutiques and sex shops, trendy bars, and fast-food establishments that draws a particular species of Parisian whose characteristic dress often includes black leather, combat boots, and tin can lid–sized hoop earrings. Les Halles's other shopping options are only a stone's throw

from the Pompidou Center, whose entrance, with its mot-
ley congregation of fire-swallowers, African drum bands,
and mimes, resembles a Medieval fairground. The place
Ste-Opportune and the rue de la Ferronnerie are pedestrian areas bustling with enterprising boutiques; the rue
du Cygne and the rue Pierre-Lescot are the streets to
comb for 1950s and 1960s *fripes,* or secondhand clothes.
The **Papeterie Moderne**, at 12, rue de la Ferronnerie, is
the place to find life-size copies of Paris's green-trimmed,
blue-metal street signs as well as the bona fide plastic
pâté de campagne and *terrine de lièvre* signs of French
charcuteries. Next door, **Opox Rapax**, also at 12, rue de la
Ferronnerie, is *the* Paris address for big, bulky, hand-knit
sweaters.

The rue du Jour, in the shadow of the imposing St-
Eustache church, where Louis XIV celebrated his first communion and Molière was baptized, is the bastion of Paris's
wildly successful ready-to-wear designer **Agnès B.** The
designer makes simple, relatively inexpensive clothes for
men, women, and children, and each category has its own
boutique here. Also worth checking out on the rue du Jour:
La Droguerie, at number 9, a treasure trove of yarns,
ribbons, buttons, and beads where teenage Parisians come
to find parts for their first pair of funky earrings; **Pom
d'Api**, at number 13, for amusing sneakers and other original shoe styles for tots (the "grown-up" store, **Free Lance**,
is nearby, at 22, rue Mondétour); at number 7, Jean-Paul
Gaultier's **Junior Gaultier** boutique; **Claudie Pierlot** and
Oblique, at numbers 4 and 19, for reasonably priced fashion separates. For those tin can lid–hoop earrings, check
out **Scooter**, at 10, rue de Turbigo, which also sells ethnic-
inspired, funky sportswear for men and women.

Gourmet Equipment

A five-minute walk away are two establishments for aspir-
ing Cordon Bleu chefs: **A. Simon**, 36, rue Etienne-Marcel,
and **E. Dehillerin**, 18–20, rue Coquillière (off rue du
Louvre), both vestiges of the days when Les Halles was the
city's wholesale market. A. Simon is a family-run business
that has been providing restaurateurs and hoteliers with
kitchen and dining equipment since 1884. A vast selection
of traditional French table items can be purchased here at
almost wholesale prices, from the utilitarian stainless-
steel-and-glass salt, pepper, and mustard-pot sets found on
any Paris bistro table to a select choice of Baccarat crystal at
a 10 percent saving; also available are Villeroy and Boch

porcelain dinner services at 25 to 30 percent less than in Paris department stores. Across the street, at 48, rue Montmartre, is A. Simon's kitchenware annex, where a stock of Sabatier and Tour Eiffel knives and Cousances and Le Creuset enameled cast-iron cookware await the would-be kitchen wizard. Pots and pans are E. Dehillerin's specialty: shallow cast-iron crêpe pans, weighty steel frying pans, and the shiny copper pots of French country kitchens.

Le Marais

East of Les Halles, tucked in among the jumble of crooked streets, kosher delicatessens, and splendid, half-hidden 17th-century town houses that make up Paris's historic Marais quarter, are several unusual boutiques that reflect the *quartier*'s unique character. Stroll along the rue Vieille-du-Temple, a street that has retained much of its old flavor. At number 26 is a delightful shop, **A La Bonne Renommée**, which sells spools of embroidered ribbons, reams of calico, and everything that could be concocted from a combination of the two. At number 47 the smell of fresh-ground coffee wafts from **La Maison des Colonies**, a gleaming emporium of imported coffees and exotic teas. At number 58 **Jean Lapierre** offers 18th-century carved-stone mantelpieces and blackened 17th-century iron coats of arms ferreted out from demolished buildings. **Casta Diva**, next door, is an opera and ballet lover's nirvana: a red-carpeted, red-walled boutique specializing in records, books, magazines, and photographs on opera and dance.

On the adjoining rue des Francs-Bourgeois (which got its name, "the men who pay no tax," in 1332 from the almshouses built there for the poor) is **Janine Kaganski**, at number 41, a mother-and-daughter shop selling 18th- and 19th-century wood furniture from Bavaria and Alsace painted in polychrome patterns of flowers and fruit. At number 45, **A l'Image du Grenier sur l'Eau** has over a million vintage postcards for sale—from kitsch to classic 1950s film stills—lovingly amassed by the shop's owner over ten years. Artga's charming orange paper–wrapped map of the Marais can be purchased at **Marais Plus**, a bookstore-cum-tearoom at 20, rue des Francs-Bourgeois. **S.M.A.R.T.**, at 22, rue des Francs-Bourgeois, offers artisan-made, hand-painted ceramic tiles for bathrooms, kitchens, or floors—including *tommettes*, the clay-colored floor tiles so popular in Provençal homes. S.M.A.R.T. will also produce tiles of your own design and ship them. At number 17, the idiosyncratic **Jean-Pierre** de Castro sells silver-plated cutlery by the kilo, as well as unusual jewelry fashioned from old knives, forks, and spoons. You'll find a dazzling display of beautiful antique glassware on l'Harlequin's dusty, floor-to-ceiling shelves at number 13. Carnavalette, at number 2, is the place to find the ideal Marais souvenir: an old bound copy of Madame de Sévigné's *Lettres,* which chronicles the day-to-day events of aristocratic 17th-century Paris, or an 18th-century *gravure* of the nearby place des Vosges. And catering to idle Sunday shoppers (the Marais is one of the rare shopping areas in Paris open on Sundays) are two shops drawing Paris's crop of "cocooners": Autour du Monde, at number 12, and Chevignon Trading Post, at number 6, selling Southwest-style Navajo rugs, hand-hewn furniture, and other Santa Fe–inspired bits and pieces.

Place des Vosges, the oldest square in Paris, awaits you at the end of the rue des Francs-Bourgeois. Once the scene of elegant courtly parades, raucous festivities, and duels at dawn, the place des Vosges—known in the days of Henri IV as the place Royale—is today a quiet park where children play and old men reminisce on sun-warmed benches. Rows of antiques shops, restaurants, and boutiques have sprung up under its stone arcades; don't miss Franco-Italian fashion designer Popy Moreni's clean, geometric, three-floor shopping space at number 13; Les Deux Orphelins, a *brocanteur* filled with amusing bric-a-brac at number 21; Japanese designer boutiques Issey Miyake and Paco Funada at numbers 5 and 17; Jardin de Flore's limited re-editions of antique illuminated manuscripts and exquisite copies of 17th-century Venetian globes at number 24; and Librairie Sylvie's jumble of books and handmade marionettes at number 26, place des Vosges. Music lovers and those who admire fine workmanship no matter what the craft should stop by André Bissonet, just off the north end of the place des Vosges, at 6, rue du Pas-de-la-Mule. Here, in an erstwhile butcher's shop (decor intact), the erstwhile butcher himself, André Bissonet, restores and sells an intriguing array of antique musical instruments: an 18th-century viola, a 17th-century harp, even carnival hurdy-gurdies that have seen better days. For players of string instruments, François Perrin's Lutherie, at 4, rue Elzévir, also in the Marais near the Picasso Museum, buys, restores, and sells violins, violas, harps, and other old string instruments.

Just off the serene garden of the Hôtel Le Peletier de

Saint-Fargeau at 4, rue du Parc-Royal, is **Delisle**, a centuries-old lighting manufacturer whose lamps adorn Versailles and which today sells convincing reproductions of a variety of period lighting fixtures. **Christian Gibeaux**, at number 6, is a master at making *faux* marble lamps, tables, and other objects from wood and resin. Down the street at numbers 14–16 is **La Maison des Dinandiers**, an intriguing shop offering objects of hand-beaten pewter, copper, aluminum, silver, and gold for the home and table.

In the past few years the Marais area has become the domain of many of Paris's young, trendy designers. **Azzedine Alaia's** body-hugging fashions can be found behind a discreet, dark-green lacquered door at 17, rue du Parc-Royal; **Lolita Lempicka**, who dresses many fashionable Parisians in witty, feminine dresses and suits, is at 15, rue Pavée (her "younger," better-priced line, **Lolita Bis**, is sold at a shop of that name just across the street); and **Alain Mikli**'s avant-garde eyewear at 1, rue des Rosiers.

The rue des Rosiers, once the heart of Paris's traditional Jewish quarter, has become a shopper's mecca. **Jo Goldenberg**, the capital's best Jewish deli, still stands at number 7, and **Sacha Finkelsztain** has been supplying bona fide bagels, pirozhki, and cheesecake "*de père en fils, depuis 1946*," but both are now flanked by trendy fashion boutiques. There's **Autre Chose**, at number 2; **Label's**, selling a hodge-podge of saucy young labels, at number 3 *bis;* **Tehen** at number 5 *bis,* with **Charles Kammer** shoes and **Olivier Chanas** hats just across the street. On the nearby rue Malher are more amusing hats at **Anna Kaszer**, number 7, and **Paule Ka**'s Audrey Hepburn–style black cocktail dresses at number 20. One street over, at 46, rue de Sévigné, is Italian designer **Romeo Gigli**'s Paris boutique, across the street from Paris's most enchanting history museum, the Musée Carnavalet.

La Bastille

A ten-minute walk eastward from the Marais is La Bastille, an area that has emerged in recent years as the latest candidate for the title of "the insider's Paris." The controversial Bastille Opera House was inaugurated in July 1989 for the Bicentennial of the French Revolution, and the *quartier*— once a humble working-class neighborhood—has really spruced itself up for the occasion. La Bastille now offers a lively selection of offbeat restaurants and gutsy P.M. fare for those in search of alternative forms of entertainment. It's no wonder, then, that **Pom Pin Disques**, a record shop specializing in hard-to-find collector's records from reggae to funk, New Wave to Edith Piaf, at 17, rue de Lappe, stays open sometimes until 2:00 A.M. By day this area rife with artists' ateliers and galleries welcomes art amateurs and collectors in search of contemporary alternatives to Picasso and Gauguin. **Galerie Bastille**, at 28, rue de Lappe, which opened in 1979 when La Bastille was still primarily a furniture wholesalers' district, now includes John Cage, Ruffin Cooper, and Michel Faublée among its stable of artists. **Franka Berndt Bastille** devotes its high-ceilinged, cool white-and-gray gallery at 11, rue St-Sabin to constructivist works; and **Lavigne Bastille**, 27, rue de Charonne, to new painters and sculptors.

In a space the size of a walk-in closet, **Duelle** (21, rue Daval) displays another kind of art, avant-garde jewelry: papier-mâché bangles in paintbox colors, resin earrings translucent as uncut stones. "I'm on the lookout for pieces with humor," says the lavender-locked owner, Claude Deilhes. Farther down, where the rue Daval becomes the rue de Lappe, at number 26, is a shop devoted to the gentleman's game of billiards, **Le Maître Billiardier**, supplying the well-equipped game room with everything from cushioned bistro stools and antique mechanical pianos to the ubiquitous billiard table—from a run-of-the-mill 45,000-franc model to a claw-footed 450,000-franc Charles X antique.

Rue du Pont Louis-Philippe

Double back from the place des Vosges (south on rue de Birague off the *place,* then a right turn) on the rue St-Antoine and trace the rue François-Miron to where the rue du Pont Louis-Philippe leads to the Seine. Number 68, rue François-Miron, is the 17th-century mansion built for Anne of Austria's first woman of the bedchamber in return for her having initiated the 16-year-old Louis XIV in the delights of love. Although fallen into disrepair, the Hôtel de Beauvais is still majestic; its curving, carved-stone staircase is magnificent.

Facing each other on the rue du Pont Louis-Philippe are two boutiques for lovers of beautiful stationery: **Papier +**, at number 9, which sells heavy handmade papers, fabric-covered notebooks, and photo albums; and **Mélodies Graphiques**, at number 10, which carries Florence's famous "Il Papiro" stationery items made from marbleized endpapers.

The Left Bank

Just across the bridge lies the Latin Quarter. Although this Medieval *quartier* retains its status as the intellectual heart of Paris—the Sorbonne, the Beaux-Arts, and the *grandes écoles* are all located here—Sartre's table at Aux Deux Magots is likely to have been usurped by a weary shopper, so dense is the concentration of boutiques in the area. The maze of streets nearest the river—the rues des Sts-Pères, de Lille, du Bac, de Verneuil, Bonaparte, and Jacob—are a paradise for the antiques and art gallery aficionado.

On the river itself, not far from the Ecole des Beaux-Arts, at 3, quai Voltaire, is **Sennelier**, an art-supply shop smelling of chalk and linseed oil that Paris painters have known and loved since 1887. Just behind it, **Robert Montagut** (15, rue de Lille) is a perfectly reconstructed antique Provençal *pharmacie,* whose gleaming niches hold antique apothecary jars of all shapes and sizes on sale for 1,500 to 150,000 francs! Lovers of ballet will find their spiritual home at 14, rue de Beaune, where **La Danse** offers books, magazines, prints, and watercolors on dance, even Degas-esque bronze statuettes of graceful ballerinas. **La Rose des Vents**, at 25, rue de Beaune, sells old ship's wheels, antique brass compasses, and other ancient nautical treasures. **Le Temps Libre**, down the adjacent rue de Verneuil at number 9, offers children's playthings rescued from attic trunks: odd bits and pieces of porcelain dolls and their houses, long-forgotten board games, and other juvenile oddities. Next door at number 7 is **Parsua**, where Parisian housewives bring their heirloom carpets to be restored and where you can pick up a length of 18th-century Lyonnaise silk for an appropriately princely sum. On the other side of the rue du Bac, at 47, rue de Verneuil, is the quirky **Galerie Jacques Fischer-Chantal Kiener**, an almost-secret source for affordable 19th-century drawings, paintings, and sculpture.

The rue Bonaparte leads to the place St-Germain-des-Prés and its surrounding cluster of bookshops. At 31, rue Bonaparte, the **Librairie Bonaparte**'s window is lined with books in many languages on *le spectacle*—ballet, theater, modern dance. The imposing **Librairie F. De Nobele**, next door at number 35, specializes in old tomes and literature related to *les beaux-arts:* fashion, art, design. On the corner of the rue de l'Abbaye and the rue Bonaparte is **Le Divan**, whose name (the kind of tongue-in-cheek reference French wags delight in) means "the couch," indicating this bookseller's bent for psychology and philosophy titles. And sandwiched between the celebrated Parisian cafés Aux Deux Magots and Café de Flore is the no less celebrated **La Hune** bookstore, at 170, boulevard St-Germain, with its wealth of "humanist" books—on poetry, photography, architecture, literature, music, theater, cinema, and fashion. **Elbé**, the best place in Paris for old prints, is up the boulevard at 213 *bis*. And those on the trail of Hemingway's Paris shouldn't miss **Shakespeare and Company**, near St-Germain's place Maubert at 37, rue de la Bûcherie. Although today's bookshop is not the Sylvia Beach original, American expatriate owner George Whitman has faithfully reproduced its namesake's bohemian literary atmosphere, offering poetry readings, upstairs beds for itinerant writers, and a mixed bag of English, American, German, and other European-language books.

On the other side of the boulevard St-Germain are hundreds of boutiques. The rues Bonaparte, du Four, St-Sulpice, de Rennes, du Cherche-Midi, des Sts-Pères, and de Sèvres are all showcases for the latest Paris fashions and accessories. A determined shopper short on time can start at the rue du Four and, following the rue de Grenelle westward, encounter an inexhaustible lineup of clothing and shoe shops: Sonia Rykiel, Prada, Boutique d'Emilia, Charles Kammer, Chacok, Christian Aujard, Stéphane Kélian, Miss Maud, Odile Lancon, Claude Montana, Tokio Kumagai, Cerruti 1881, Kenzo, and more. **Casse-grain**, suppliers and engravers of fine writing paper since 1919, has its Left Bank branch at number 81, rue des Sts-Pères, the place to order those oh-so French outsize *cartes de visite*. Another St-Germain street attracting a concentration of interesting, affordable fashions is the tiny rue du Pré-aux-Clercs, which begins life just off the boulevard St-Germain as the rue St-Guillaume. Boutiques that sell inexpensive ready-to-wear clothes are Irié, Michel Klein, Corinne Sarrut (an ex-Cacharel designer), and Peggy Roche.

Art and antique buffs should not miss the quaint rue de Seine and the parallel rue Mazarine. Both are lined with galleries selling some of Paris's finest 1920s and '30s antiques, old prints, and contemporary art. The side-by-side **Vallois** galleries specializing in Art Deco at number 41, rue de Seine, are a must. (And when you've tired of tramping the cobblestones, stop for a glass of Beaujolais at **La Palette**, one of Paris's oldest and most picturesque cafés, at the corner of rue Jacques-Callot.)

Other unique boutiques in the area are **Soleiado**, at 78, rue de Seine, which carries reams of colorful Provençalprint cotton fabrics and a selection of household and fashion accessories made from them, and **Beauté Divine**, 40, rue St-Sulpice, a reconstructed 19th-century store specializing in beauty and bathroom items from bygone eras: Baccarat crystal perfume flacons, ivory nail buffers, antique porcelain pitchers. Another plush turn-of-the-century replica, **Diners en Ville**, at 89, rue du Bac, focuses once again on that popular French preoccupation—dining—but with an emphasis on originality and color. Here are the amusing trompe l'oeil plates the French call *barbotines,* vintage glass and crystal carafes, and refurbished antique paisley tablecloths. Candles to decorate a dining table can be found at **Point à la Ligne** (177, boulevard St-Germain), which sells imaginative fantasy candles: silvery oysters to pile up, as the French do with the real thing, on holiday tables, wax raspberry tarts, and watermelon slices. For the kind of lingerie trousseaux are made of, visit **Sabbia Rosa**, 71–73, rue des Sts-Pères, where sumptuous, lace-trimmed satin nightgowns, camisoles, and sexy tap pants hang in languid pastel rows against lacquered gray walls. For sheer delight, visit **Madeleine Gély**, 218, boulevard St-Germain, a doll-size boutique—crammed full of umbrellas, parasols, and canes both old and new—that has been in existence since 1834. Gély will still custom-make umbrellas for too-short or too-tall clients in their choice of fabric, and with wood, ivory, or horn handles. For a crash course in traditional Parisian pint-sized elegance, there's **Bon Point** (67, rue de l'Université; furniture at 7, rue de Solférino), which sells the same navy blue coats, gray flannel shorts, and smocked dresses French children have been wearing for decades. For sleek suede and kid gloves and, especially, unique scents sold in a gilded 18th-century style setting, don't miss **Maître Parfumeur et Gantier** at 84 *bis,* rue de Grenelle.

Avenue Montaigne

Coming full circle, you will return to the Right Bank by the Pont de l'Alma near the Eiffel Tower and, via the avenue Montaigne, enter a world of unbridled luxury. If your stay in Paris has still not converted you to the gilded life, a stroll down the tree-lined avenue Montaigne will. This is home to much of the haute couture—Dior, Emanuel Ungaro, Guy Laroche, Hanae Mori, with Yves St-Laurent and Givenchy nearby. The crimson-awninged, geranium-banked Hôtel Plaza Athénée presides over the avenue like a serene princess. Its Relais Plaza grill room, with a 1930s ocean-liner decor, is the lunchtime spot for Paris's *beau monde,* and postprandial shoppers need only turn left outside the door to check out Italian jeweler **Bulgari**'s latest creations (27, avenue Montaigne). **Valentino** is just next door, at 17–19, avenue Montaigne; **Chanel**, at 42, avenue Montaigne. **Louis Vuitton**'s newest boutique is at number 54. At number 16 is an extraordinary accessory shop, **Isabel Canovas**, a cobalt-blue, mirrored Ali Baba's cave filled with artisan-made jewel-studded cuffs and earrings, brilliant silk-velour shawls, and embroidered bags. **D. Porthault**, at 18, avenue Montaigne, is where house-proud Parisians buy their bed, bath, and table linens; the store's fresh, floral-print cotton percale bedsheets are world famous. **Parfums Caron**, at 34, avenue Montaigne, dispenses Caron perfume classics from gold-etched Baccarat crystal urns. **Puiforcat**, next door to **Fouquet**'s 65-year-old sweet shop at 22, rue François-Ier, sells re-edited versions of the streamlined sterling silver table settings and tea and coffee services that made them so popular in Paris in the 1930s. A few streets up from the Plaza Athénée at 45, rue Pierre-Charron, is **Hobbs**, a shop specializing in quality Scottish cashmere sweaters in a rainbow of 50 colors and a variety of amusing patterns. Just around the corner at number 33, rue François-Ier, is the perfume and fashion house of **Rochas**, with its Riccardo Bofill–designed Neoclassical façade, offering a wealth of 18th century–style fashion accessories, *objets* for the home, and, as of October 1990, a complete women's ready-to-wear clothing line. (A Rochas boutique for men opened last summer at 29, avenue George-V.) And for the best classic men's fedora, there is the 1887-vintage **Motsch Fils**, a five-minute walk away at 42, avenue George-V, a hat shop that also sells Panamas, Homburgs, and hunting caps, in addition to boasting one of the most beautiful wood-paneled storefronts in town.

Although the nearby avenue des Champs-Elysées still inspires awe, the recent profusion of pinball halls, flashy cinemas, and fast-food establishments has robbed it of its past standing as Paris's ultimate chic shopping avenue. The fragrance house **Guerlain**, at 68, avenue des Champs-Elysées, is a staunch exception: Its marble walls and atmosphere of hallowed *luxe* make it an obligatory stop for those on the trail of typically Parisian, Old World luxury. A recent addition to "the Champs" is the monumental **Virgin Records**, a bank-turned-music-emporium at 52, avenue des Champs-Elysées.

Flea Markets

No shopping devotee could leave Paris without a pilgrimage to one of Paris's *marchés aux puces,* or flea markets: the **Porte de Montreuil** for antique clothing and odd bits of furniture; the **Porte de Vanves** for bric-a-brac; and especially the **Porte de Clignancourt** for more than 3,000 stands selling everything from used clothing to gilded Regency furniture. All the flea markets are located in the northern, southern, or eastern outskirts of Paris, "Porte" referring to one of the gateways to the Périphérique (the highway circling the city). For serious antiques hunters, the Porte de Clignancourt's 200-stand Marché Biron sells what is generally considered to be the *crème de la crème* of the *puces:* old silver- and bronze-framed mirrors, Limoges porcelain, and other treasures. The Marché St-Paul is a scavenger's dream, offering a mixed bag of chipped crockery, old dentist's mirrors, brass candlesticks; and for fabulous vintage Louis Vuitton steamer trunks (complete with old hotel stickers) don't miss Stand 232, Allée 6, of the Port de Clignancourt's Marché Paul-Bert. Be warned: Although most flea market shopkeepers will arrange shipping of these sometimes unwieldy souvenirs back home, depending on weight and choice of air mail or slow boat, transport could almost double the price of your Paris "bargain."

—*Charla Carter*

ILE-DE-FRANCE
DAY TRIPS FROM PARIS

By Edward Hernstadt and Amy Hollowell

Edward Hernstadt is a freelance writer who lived in Paris for four years. He has contributed to publications in the United States, France, and Australia. Amy Hollowell is an editor at the International Herald Tribune *in Paris. She also writes about various aspects of life in France, where she has lived for eight years.*

Paris is a city of marvels: old and new, secular and religious, vulgar and exquisite. It is also a modern city and can be as congested and wearying as any other urban center. However, Paris need not be limited by the bounds of the Périphérique: Its 23 centuries of continuous occupation have left a mark on the surrounding countryside. Today the Ile-de-France, as the region is called, encompasses Paris as well as the towns and castles around it: the Medieval villages that traded with or provided a refuge from the city; the religious centers that spread the word of God among peasants; the hunting lodges and country houses of France's kings; and the grand châteaux of the French nobility.

A day in the country can provide both an enriching perspective on the history of Paris as well as the opportunity to spend some time in beautiful valleys and forests. Many destinations are accessible by train; others are best reached by car. Most are on the tourist-bus circuit, but this option could prove constricting, as organized tours

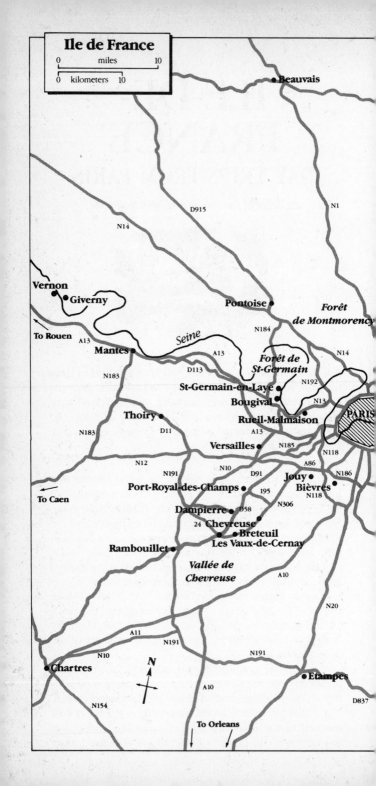

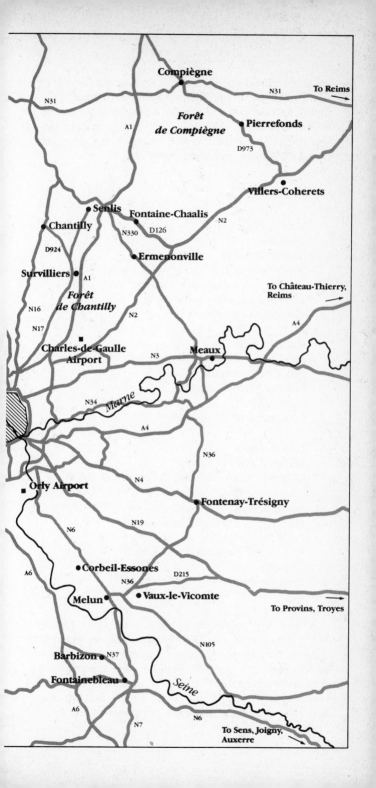

are often crowded and don't allow time for dawdling. Finally, all these destinations are within 90 minutes of the capital, and any one will provide a pleasant day's outing. With the exception of Versailles, which is open every day year-round, the museums and châteaux are generally closed on Tuesday, unless otherwise stated.

MAJOR INTEREST

West of Paris
Versailles
Rueil-Malmaison
St-Germain-en-Laye castle and gardens
Monet's home and garden at Giverny
Thoiry château and game park
Chartres cathedral

South of Paris
Fondation Cartier in Jouy-en-Josas
Vallée de Chevreuse
Château Vaux-le-Vicomte
Barbizon
Fontainebleau

East of Paris
Medieval town of Provins
Château-Thierry and Bois Belleau battle sites

North of Paris
Pierrefonds and Compiègne châteaux
Forêt de Compiègne armistice site
Roman and Medieval town of Senlis
Chantilly
Beauvais cathedral

A brief note on the chief players in the Ile-de-France: François I, the Ramses II of France, built or added to many of the châteaux mentioned, as did Louis XIV. Louis Le Vau and Jules Hardouin-Mansart were the predominant architects of the 17th century; Charles Le Brun, the preeminent decorator; and André Le Nôtre is arguably the most important landscape artist in the history of France.

WEST
Versailles

Versailles is as much a conviction as a château—the conviction that "bigger *is* better" and that "moral ostentatiousness *is* more tasteful." The château is enormous, imposing, imperial, and rock solid, and still conveys Louis XIV's message of French omnipotence and his own glory. This is not an unpopular message with the French, who have long struggled to reconcile their longings for monarchal pomp with their pride in the egalitarianism that led to the Revolution. Not surprisingly, the Revolution struck especially hard at Versailles, symbol of the crown's arrogance, and the château has not been a royal residence since Louis XVI was beheaded in 1793.

Versailles is one of the few châteaux in France without a long history of renovations; it was built in two phases, which together turned a sleepy farm town into the apogee of 17th-century luxury. Louis XIII enjoyed hunting and built a small lodge here in 1624. Seven years later he bought the entire town and had the architect Philibert Le Roy construct a small château. When his son Louis XIV assumed power in 1661, his first step was to outdo mere mortals like Nicolas Fouquet, whose château at Vaux-le-Vicomte he envied. Louis instructed the architect Louis Le Vau, the decorator and painter Charles Le Brun, and the landscape artist André Le Nôtre to build the grandest, most opulent, most expensive château in France. Louis had another motive: He sought to distance himself and his courtiers from the dangerous political intrigues of Paris.

Work began slowly. Le Vau extended the existing château while Le Brun commanded an army of artisans and Le Nôtre planned and laid out the gardens. In 1678 the architect Jules Hardouin-Mansart took over the design of the château, which occupied him for the next 30 years; during this time he added the two monumental wings and the Galerie des Glaces (Hall of Mirrors). The artists faced enormous logistical problems: The palace and grounds had to be large enough for the entire court—which then comprised some 6,000 people—yet everything had to be decorated and landscaped down to the last cornice and begonia. The numbers that resulted from these requirements are almost too vast to have parallels in everyday life: 36,000 workers were involved; some 3,000 trees were moved in and out of hothouses every season; 1,400 fountains were constructed; and a vast reservoir was built to store water diverted from the river Seine. Although work continued until the end of Louis XIV's reign, the château was in use by 1663.

A heavy cast-iron gate opens onto a large courtyard flanked by two buildings that once housed government ministers. A monumental statue of Louis XIV stands in the Cour Royale (Royal Courtyard), and behind it the Cour de Marbre (Marble Courtyard), constructed from squares of white and black marble, is surrounded by the original château, whose façade is by Hardouin-Mansart. The ministerial wings break up the building's nearly half-mile-long façade. From behind, however, the perspective is striking, with the center of the château set forward to add relief. Statues and vases break the line of the balustrade, and statues of Apollo and Diana cap the central, royal, section.

The apartments are relentlessly luxurious. Marble, gilt, moldings, and frescoes are everywhere. It is difficult to understand how any business requiring concentration could have been accomplished in the palace—the sheer mass and ostentation of the decor is distracting. It is also superbly crafted: Le Brun's team of talented artisans executed his designs with precision and grace. The château may be pretentious, but its decor is the most completely realized of the period.

The chapel, a sumptuous study in white and gold with intricately carved pillars, is one of Hardouin-Mansart's masterpieces. On the second floor, the Grands Appartements, where Louis XIV and his court ate, played pool, and listened to concerts, consists of a series of thematic rooms: of Mars, Venus, Mercury, and Diana; the throne room belongs to Apollo. The staggering **Galerie des Glaces** was in its heyday a ballroom. The mirrored walls reflect Le Brun's ceiling frescoes, which describe Louis XIV's early years, and were designed to show off the wildly expensive costumes of the ladies and courtiers.

Two events that determined the contours of Europe took place in the Galerie des Glaces. In 1871, after soundly defeating France in a war engineered by Otto von Bismarck to unify the various states of Germany under the leadership of Prussia, Germany announced the German Empire to the world from Versailles. This new Germany also seized the disputed territories of Alsace-Lorraine at the war's end, thus augmenting the tensions that resulted in World War I. And it was here in 1919 that the defeated Germany signed the Treaty of Versailles, the unbalanced document that led indirectly to World War II.

After the showy luxury of the apartments, which were designed primarily to celebrate the importance and majesty of Louis XIV, the planned beauty of the gardens is a delight. Directly behind the château, steps lead down to two large basins. To the right a parterre wends through flower beds to the Neptune fountain, the largest at Versailles. To the left more gardens lead to the Orangerie, where hundreds of orange and palm trees bloom every summer. Paths lined with statues thread through the garden, which is divided into areas where different geometric patterns dominate. A long central path, the Tapis Vert (Green Carpet), runs from the center of the château perpendicular to the Grand Canal. It, too, is bounded with statues, and the view of the château façade over gardens and fountains is stunning. The Grand Canal extends to the horizon from the perspective of the château and, as it is laid out on an east/west axis, the setting sun is reflected in it. The gardens behind the Trianons are more rustic; designed in the country style favored in the 18th century, the winding paths are almost emblematically pastoral and lovely to walk along.

Other buildings occupy the grounds, notably the Grand Trianon, the Petit Trianon, and the Hameau. Louis XIV first constructed the Trianon de Porcelain, where he escaped the court with his first mistress, Madame de Montespan. By the time he replaced her with Madame de Maintenon (whom he secretly married after the death of his wife), the porcelain had decayed. So Louis built the **Grand Trianon**. It was used principally for receptions by succeeding kings, and in 1962 Charles de Gaulle restored it as a residence for visiting dignitaries. Among those who have enjoyed the royal lodgings are Queen Elizabeth II of England and Leonid Brezhnev. Today it is furnished in the 19th-century style of the Restoration kings. Highlights include the malachite room, which takes its name from the malachite vases and candelabra Czar Alexander gave Napoléon at Tilsit, and the *galerie,* filled with crystal and paintings of the gardens as they looked in the 17th century.

Louis XV commissioned the **Petit Trianon**, and it was a favorite retreat of Louis XVI and Marie-Antoinette. This frivolous queen also built the **Hameau**, a charming, idealized reproduction of what the wealthy imagined farms to be, and she loved to pretend to herd sheep there. Ironically, she was near the Hameau when a messenger brought word that rebellious Parisians were marching on Versailles. Marie-Antoinette fled and never saw the Hameau again. Napoléon III's empress, Eugénie, who sympathized with her, collected many of the late queen's possessions in a little museum there.

Other important sites are spread throughout Versailles, including the **Menus-Plaisirs** at 22, avenue de Paris, and the **Salle du Jeu de Paume**, just off the rue Satory (restored and open to the public several days a week; check at the local tourist office). When the Estates-General (the three estates of the clergy, the nobility, and the bourgeoisie) convened in 1789, they met in a makeshift structure erected in the courtyard of the building housing the King's entertainers, the *menus-plaisirs*. Many of the dramatic events that led to the first stage of the French Revolution took place here, including the drafting of the constitution and the Declaration of the Rights of Man. And the Estates-General took the famous "Tennis Court Oath," vowing not to disband until a constitution was accepted by the crown, during the three days they met at the Salle du Jeu de Paume.

Travellers who would like to make themselves at home almost within the royal purlieu should consider the stately **Trianon-Palace** on the edge of the gardens. The 110 rooms have been renovated and a swimming pool and fitness club added to the premises.

Versailles is also home to **Les Trois Marches**, one of the Ile-de-France's most respected restaurants; a luxurious meal in this very refined house may be a perfect conclusion to a day spent drinking in the opulence of the château. (3, rue Colbert; Tel: 39-50-13-21.) Many other cafés and small restaurants in Versailles offer fine meals. Or you might bring a picnic; it would be hard to find a more inviting picnic spot than the gardens at Versailles. You can reach Versailles, less than an hour from Paris, by car via A 13, N 185, or N 10, or by RER, line C, direction Versailles-RG (the château is visible from the station).

Rueil-Malmaison

For Napoléon and Joséphine, Malmaison was first a house and then a place of refuge. Joséphine bought the pretty brownstone château in 1799 when Napoléon was still first consul, and in it he escaped the pressures of the capital in the frivolous, completely unpolitical atmosphere Joséphine created. The house and extensive, beautiful grounds, which are threaded with peaceful paths and rose gardens, remained Joséphine's favorite retreat after Napoléon proclaimed himself emperor in 1804. After their divorce in 1809 she retired to a life of relative calm at Malmaison, living out her days where she had been most content.

Napoléon, too, returned to Malmaison: first in triumph after his escape from Elba in 1814, and then during the darkness that followed his defeat at Waterloo and final exile on the island of Saint Helena. Napoléon III also owned the château, and it was his wife, the Empress Eugénie, who conceived the idea of the museum, devoted to Napoléon and Joséphine, that eventually opened here in 1906.

The château itself, built in a lovely, symmetrical style, is fairly modest as châteaux go. Because it is small, a satisfying tour can be completed in 45 minutes, allowing ample time to wander through the now-reduced, but still appealing, park and gardens. The most interesting rooms are the council chamber, which is dressed up to look like a campaign tent and is where Napoléon plotted some of his early victories; the library, a heavy, serious room packed with tomes on the art of war; and Joséphine's bedroom, an over-decorated boudoir that reveals both her vanity—it's full of mirrors, toiletries, and jewels—and her extravagance—receipts for some of her luxurious gowns are on display. Occasionally, international horse shows are held on the grounds.

Cafés are well hidden in the town of Rueil-Malmaison, but a fine lunch can be had on the lovely terrace at **El Chiquito**, a rather expensive restaurant specializing in seafood. Reservations are recommended; Tel: 47-51-00-53. (126, avenue Paul-Doumer.) You can reach Malmaison in about 20 minutes on the RER line A; go in the direction of St-Germain-en-Laye and get off at Rueil-Malmaison. By car, leave Paris on the N 13.

St-Germain-en-Laye

St-Germain-en-Laye's long and involved history is reflected in the château itself. Originally constructed in the 12th century by Louis VI, who thought the commanding hillside site would be ideal for repelling unwelcome guests, the castle was destroyed, rebuilt, and added to for the next five centuries. England's Black Prince, Edward, eradicated the original structure (except for the chapel erected by pious Saint Louis in 1230) during the Hundred Years War, and Charles V rebuilt it in 1368. François I redesigned the castle in 1539, retaining only Charles's dungeon and the chapel. In addition to the kings of France, inhabitants have included Mary Queen of Scots, before her brief marriage to François II, and James II, after England's 1688 Glorious Revolution. Louis XIII died here, and Henri II, Charles IX, and Louis XIV were born here.

In its current (and probably final) form, the castle is shaped like an unbalanced pentagon. None of the rooms is open to the public; most are storerooms and offices for the château's **Musée des Antiquités Nationales**, which is open to the public. The museum was created by Napoléon III to house prehistoric, Celtic, and Gallo-Roman artifacts. Saint Louis's chapel, almost certainly built for the king by Pierre of Montreuil, who later constructed the Sainte Chapelle in Paris, is open to the public; the bare stone church offers only the beauty of its solemn architecture. The castle's plain stone façade is enlivened by red brick windows and chimneys, and massive stone urns punctuate the balustrade that runs along the roof.

The gardens are the main reason to visit St-Germain. Enter through the gate to the left of the château's main door. A large graveled space opens to lawns, flower beds, and what was once a fountain. To the right, carefully laid-out paths wind through chestnut trees to the more dramatic English garden, where curving paths swing through well-tended lawns (lawns that you actually can sit on, something of a rarity in France) and more flowers. Le Nôtre's masterful **Grande Terrasse** (about a mile and a half long) borders the ridge. It is one of the most famous promenades in the Paris area and overlooks a steep hill and the Seine. In 1547 a duel was fought on the parterre that splits the two gardens and leads to the terrace, one of the last of those contests appealing to God's judgment. The formidable La Chataigneraie, one of Europe's great swordsmen, fell to a certain Monsieur Jarnac, who employed a devious Italian ruse and switched his sword to his left hand to administer the killing blow. La Chataigneraie might have survived, but he was so infuriated by defeat that he refused all help and perished on the spot.

The town of St-Germain-en-Laye is quite pretty and

merits a stroll. The square facing the château (where the RER exits, and over a convenient underground parking lot) shows signs of the 1980s with its videocassette outlet, a "western" shop, and an American restaurant. Some of the town's other restaurants, however, offer a more sophisticated cuisine. The **Pavillon Henri IV**, at 21, rue Thiers (Tel: 34-51-62-62), set within the smart confines of the 45-room hotel of the same name, is the most historic of these: Louis XIV was anointed here, and Alexandre Dumas wrote both *The Three Musketeers* and *The Count of Monte Cristo* while he was a guest. Unfortunately, because of the terrace's fantastic view, the restaurant is overpriced. Instead, you might want to try the classic **Cazaudehore**, with its pretty garden (1, avenue du Président-Kennedy; Tel: 34-51-93-80) or the more modern **Le 7 Rue des Coches**, on the street of the same name (Tel: 39-73-66-40). Reservations are recommended at all three restaurants.

To the north, virtually bordering on the château grounds, lies the vast and beautiful **Forêt de St-Germain**, which is a superb setting for afternoon hikes and picnics. Several interesting buildings are in the forest, including a former hunting lodge rebuilt by Jules Hardouin-Mansart that now serves as a retreat for members of the Legion of Honor. You can reach St-Germain-en-Laye in half an hour via the RER, line A; by car, take N 13 from Paris.

Giverny

Everybody comes here. In the last weeks of autumn, just before the house and gardens close for the winter and after most of the flowers have died, the parking lot at Giverny is still full of tour buses. Even if you shy away from tourists and prefer to discover sites in relative solitude, Giverny is worth visiting.

Claude Monet made Giverny his home from 1883 until his death in 1926. Monet's son left the house to the Académie des Beaux-Arts, which opened the restored property in 1980 as a museum. An enormous amount of work went into replanting the gardens to re-create the palette of colors Monet himself created and then depicted in hundreds of paintings.

His studio—called the Nymphéas—and house have also been renovated; the former is filled with reproductions of his most famous works as well as period photographs that show him in the studio during the 1910s, when the originals of those same works hung on the walls. The house is a more typical museum. The artist's collection of Japanese prints as well as additional reproductions of his works are hung as the originals were when he lived here, and the rooms look as if Monet had just stepped out to go to the bakery. This exactitude is almost spooky, but the house is actually quite lovely and the kitchen looks, today, like something out of a "do-your-own-rustic-look" catalog.

The raison d'être of the place, though, is the garden: a glorious, floral candy shop in shades of blue, pink, yellow, red, white, and purple. Monet moved through it like a bearded Druid, addressing the flowers by name and coaxing ever more brilliant colors from them. Across the road is the water garden, complete with the Japanese footbridge, weeping willows, and water lilies that inspired so many canvases (including the huge works in New York's Museum of Modern Art and Paris's Orangerie).

Because of the number of tourists, picnics are not allowed, although plenty of suitable spots can be found in the Vernon woods behind Giverny. A tearoom and flower shop share the museum's parking lot, and there are several cafés in Vernon. For a traditional regional lunch, try **Les Fleurs**, an old-style bistro in Vernon between the train station and Giverny that features good fish and a wonderful apple tarte (71, rue Carnot). You can reach Giverny in about 90 minutes via SNCF from Paris St-Lazare to Vernon; from the station it's a brisk walk of about 4 km (2.5 miles) along the Seine to the house. Taxis or buses are available, and bicycles can be rented at the station. By car, take A 13 from Paris. The museum and gardens are open from April 1 through October 31.

Thoiry

The vicomtesse de la Panouse (information director for the Château Thoiry and wife of the comte de la Panouse, whose family has owned and lived in the house since 1564) is quick to call Thoiry a marvel, and she is right. The Château Thoiry is an astounding mixture of history, kitsch, aggressive marketing, physical beauty, and unrestrained imagination.

Where to start? In the African game park, where camels, zebras, bears, lions, and other creatures cavort on the château's ancestral grounds? Or perhaps in the museum of gastronomy, where those whose eyes are bigger than their stomachs can view replicas of extraordinary desserts? Or maybe in the reptile house, where snakes and alligators slither in the dark cellars beneath the parterre designed by Le Nôtre? The park also has a pond filled with swans and flamingos, a "city of apes," a children's zoo, and assorted tigers, wolves, and hyenas.

There are tours of the house and its treasures, which include a Sèvres pitcher and basin once used by Marie Antoinette, and a small, fascinating archives museum, filled with four centuries of correspondence between the comtes de la Panouse and various prominent international figures. The whole place is actually quite amazing, and the spectacle of the visitors, many of whom are children, is as interesting as the château. The stables have been converted into a restaurant, tearoom, and conference facility. Classical concerts (with dinner) are offered year-round, most frequently during the summer. The game park and museums are open year-round. You can reach Château Thoiry from Paris in an hour by car via A 13, then D 11.

Chartres

Today's visitors to Chartres see the same awesome vista that has greeted pilgrims for centuries: a towering cathedral rising from rough fields, emerging slowly as you near the town and gradually dominating the horizon and countryside. The area has remained as proportionally rural as it was when Edward III laid siege to the town during the Hundred Years War, or when the prince of Condé attacked it as a center of Catholicism. It is something of a mystery why so magnificent a cathedral, one that set the standard for Gothic cathedrals all over Europe, sprang up so far from any major commercial center.

Chartres has always been a place of worship and a place of pilgrimage. Churches have stood on the same spot as the cathedral for more than two millennia. Before the birth of Christ, Chartres was a center of Druid rites. When the Romans conquered the Gauls, they built a temple to the Earth Mother here. With the rise of Christianity, the icon of this goddess was interpreted as a prefigure of the Virgin Mary, renamed Notre-Dame-sous-Terre, and consigned to a special chapel. Today the ninth-century **chapel of Notre-Dame-sous-Terre** is still devoted to this pagan idol. Worship of her successor, the Virgin, has long been strong at Chartres: Charles the Bald saw fit to give the church the sacred Tunic of the Virgin in 876. The first Christian church on the site dates from the fourth century, and successive buildings have been erected and subsequently destroyed by raiders. The present **cathedral of Chartres** was initiated by the bishop of Chartres, Saint Fulbert, after a fire destroyed an earlier structure in 1020. The upper church, crypt, and ambulatory were completed by 1134, when another fire damaged the façade and bell tower. Work then began on the north tower, the impressively Gothic one on the left. It is known as the "new bell tower," although it is actually older than the Romanesque south tower, because its spire wasn't erected until 1506. In 1194 yet another fire destroyed the entire church except for the façade, towers, and crypt. This tragedy rocked the international Christian community, because by then the pilgrimage to the Virgin of Chartres was one of Europe's most popular pastimes.

An appeal was made, and local church authorities pledged their tithes for three years, while the area's burghers responded in kind. A spirit approaching frenzy fueled the reconstruction of the cathedral, and most of the work was finished by 1220 in a record 26 years; the outside towers were completed 40 years after that. The relative speed with which it was built gives the church a rare coherence of style: It was rebuilt from a single set of plans, and construction was directed by a single, unknown master builder.

If you regard the cathedral from the place Jean Moulin (named after the World War II French resistance leader who was murdered by Klaus Barbie), the striking main towers will draw your eye first. The towers were begun and completed within ten years of each other (north: 1134–1150; south: 1144–1160), yet the architectural styles are startlingly dissimilar. The north tower is a superb example of early Gothic techniques; it is built in two stories and has an intricately carved tower. The south tower is unique; its pious severity and balanced proportions contrast dramatically with the sweeping lines of its mate. It is considered one of the world's great examples of the Romanesque style.

The cathedral is famous for its sensitively carved figures. The main, or "royal," portal dates from the mid-12th century, and it is another masterpiece of Romanesque art. Originally designed as the narthex of an 11th-century structure, it later became the main entrance to the cathedral. In hundreds of naïve sculpted figures, the three doors depict Christ's birth, ascension, and second coming. To the right is the story of Mary, culminating in the birth of Christ; to the left is the story of his betrayal and ascension; the central door is devoted to the Day of Judgment. The figures are carved with an unusual intensity of expression and a wealth of charm.

The south portal, on the right side of the cathedral, is a fascinating mix of sobriety and gore. At the center of the central bay, a peaceful Christ oversees acts of charity, with the 12 Apostles ranged behind him, each bearing the instrument of his martyrdom (or, in the case of Saint Peter, his symbol). The left bay depicts a host of martyrs in the act of being slaughtered; note particularly John the Baptist being beheaded and Saint Blaise being flayed alive. In the right bay saints performing acts of charity and miracles are depicted.

Inside the cathedral two features are particularly outstanding: the beautiful choir screen, consisting of sculptures depicting the lives of Mary and Christ; and the sublime stained-glass windows. These windows, built in the 12th and 13th centuries (with some later additions), are among the finest in France. Their astounding "Chartres blue" is an intense, luminous shade that has never been reproduced.

While the town surrounding the cathedral has grown greatly over the centuries, it is still quite charming. The stained-glass museum (just behind the cathedral), the **Centre International du Vitrail,** is worth visiting, as are several of the smaller churches in town. A stroll through the *quartier*'s streets is also very pleasant. A number of cafés and tearooms surround the cathedral. A nearby restaurant of note is **La Vielle Maison,** at 5, rue au Lait. The menu of simple local fare changes regularly according to what the chef finds at the market. You can reach Chartres by car via A 10, A 11, and then N 10, or by train from the Gare Montparnasse, in a little more than an hour. You'll be able to see the cathedral from the train station.

SOUTH
Fondation Cartier

In the mid-18th century Baron C. P. Oberkampf opened a cloth factory that eventually employed 1,200 Indian workers and manufactured an instantly popular fabric that put both the baron and **Jouy-en-Josas** on the map. Louis XVI gave him a title; Napoléon approved of his methods; and all of France clamored for his *toile de Jouy*. Today the Fondation Cartier, opened in 1984, has taken over Oberkampf's estate and shows works of very contemporary art in an imaginative way on grounds that the baron's wife landscaped in the English fashion.

You can make your way around the park in less than an hour, which gives you time to gawk at such permanent works as Arman's monumental *Long Term Parking,* a gigantic upright rectangle of wrecked cars and poured concrete at least 200 feet tall. On summer days the wide lawns are perfect for lolling and tanning or reading a book. There's a bookstore, a library, and a very high-tech café, furnished by Pascal Mourgue, that's open on weekends for lunch. The Fondation is 6 km (3.5 miles) from Versailles. You can reach it from Paris via train from the Gare d'Austerlitz to Jouy-en-Josas; on the RER, take direction Sceaux to Massy-Palaiseau; change there for direction Versailles-Chantiers and get off at Jouy, where signs point toward the park. By car follow N 118 to Bièvres, then drive west to Jouy.

Vallée de Chevreuse

The Vallée de Chevreuse is actually a series of valleys in 25,000 acres of forest, with the quaint town of Chevreuse at its center, all of it less than an hour from Paris. The only way to see the valley properly is by car or bicycle (and those who favor the latter should be warned that the terrain is extremely hilly). The region is justly famous for its great beauty: narrow roads lined with cypress trees winding through lush forests, streams, and small farms; solemn ruins of Medieval castles and abbeys; and several very lovely châteaux. Bicycles can be rented on weekends and holidays by the hour or the day at the Courcelle-sur-Yvette RER station, line B, direction St-Rémy-les-Chevreuse.

By car follow D 91 from Versailles to **Port-Royal-des-Champs**, where you can wander through the ruins of the once-famous abbey. Port-Royal reached its peak under the leadership of Mother Angelica, an austere nun who became mother superior in 1602 at the age of 11 and subsequently reformed the practices of the abbey. Later that century the abbey became the center of Jansenism in France and as such was notorious in Catholic circles. A doctrinal system that denied free will, Jansenism maintained that human nature is corrupt and that Christ died for the elect and not for all people. Blaise Pascal's sister Jacqueline entered the convent here in 1651; Pascal himself was a defender of Jansenism (especially in his masterful *Lettres Provinciales*). Louis XIV decided to close the troublesome abbey in the late 17th century, and a crew of king's musketeers evicted the remaining nuns (who were denounced by the sisters at the Paris Port-Royal Abbey) in a final expulsion some 30 years later.

From Port-Royal follow D 195 east to D 95 and turn off onto N 306 east to Chevreuse. After a walk around Chevreuse and a visit to the beautiful little Hôtel de Ville, continue west on D 58 to Dampierre.

The château at **Dampierre** is one of the most charming in the region. Designed by Hardouin-Mansart in 1683 for the duc de Luynes, it is smaller than most châteaux and set at the lowest point of a gentle valley so that the wooded hills behind dominate and frame the house. The Luynes family still lives here and has opened one of the two wings to tourists. The 45-minute tour (with no chance of escape) provides some insight into how the nobility actually lived. The rooms still exhibit the exquisite workmanship (especially of the wood panels and parquet floors) and classic design of the era. Part of the house was redecorated in the desperately overdone Third Empire style—all trompe l'oeil murals and gilt.

Le Nôtre designed the gardens and park, which are lovely to walk in; stroll through the formal parterre, feed the ducks and swans in the pond or the carp in the moat, and then hike in the woods behind the opulent château, so comfortably placed in this tranquil setting. The stables have been transformed into a fine restaurant (oddly decorated with hundreds of mounted animal trophies, many from Africa). The tiny village offers a few unexceptional restaurants, all within a five-minute walk. The house is open from April to mid-October.

One kilometer (about half a mile) to the south is the **Parc Floral**. Its extensive gardens were created to feature the seasonal brilliance of hundreds of flowers, especially summer roses—there are 150 varieties, including some very old strains.

From Dampierre continue south on D 91 to **Les Vaux de Cernay**, a beautiful valley in which you can walk beneath ancient oaks along the Vau stream, past a small waterfall, and perhaps have a picnic beside the Cernay pond. From here, N 306 north leads to **Breteuil**, another very pretty château.

The Breteuil family is one of the oldest in France and has occupied the château since its construction in 1550. An early Norman ancestor, Raoul, possessed a voice so powerful that he once set the entire French army to flight with it. His son William was a compatriot of William the Conqueror, who gave the family its title after the Battle of Hastings. The château was constructed in the simple but imposing architectural style favored by Henri IV. Set on a small promontory in the middle of a park, it presents a formal grandeur to motorists driving up the tree-lined avenue. The building, of tan stone and red brick, houses an excellent collection of period furniture and china, as well as the family's own wax museum, which depicts famous visitors and momentous events in the life of the Breteuils.

From Les Vaux de Cernay continue straight up D 24 to N 10, or take any one of the tiny, badly marked roads and explore the countryside more thoroughly. This beautiful drive makes for a pleasant day's outing.

Vaux-le-Vicomte

Vaux-le-Vicomte is arguably the most perfectly realized château in France. Nicolas Fouquet, minister of finance under Louis XIV, built the first completely planned château and gardens in the country as a monument to his exalted position in France. When Cardinal Jules Mazarin, then first minister, appointed Fouquet finance minister in 1653, the royal treasury had just declared bankruptcy and defaulted on its enormous debts. Fouquet was given the daunting task of reestablishing the crown as a viable credit risk. He proved himself to be one of the most brilliant, able, and loyal ministers ever to work for the crown, yet ambition (his own and that of others), naïveté, and carelessness led him to disaster.

Fouquet's fall came in 1661 after years of conspicuous spending and a period of courting a woman Louis XIV wanted for himself. He held a ball for the king that gave the word ostentation new meaning: His guests ate off 6,000 silver plates, served themselves from 432 large silver platters, and wiped their mouths with 1,440 linen napkins. Louis was so enraged and envious—he'd just been forced to sell his own silver to pay for one of his many wars—that he wanted to arrest Fouquet on the spot. Remembering his obligations as a guest, though, he graciously refrained and 19 days later sent a musketeer to haul the unfortunate minister off to jail.

Five years earlier, however, Fouquet had given Le Vau, Le Brun, and Le Nôtre—the architect, decorator, and landscaper whom Louis XIV, intending to surpass Vaux-le-Vicomte's splendor, later enlisted to create Versailles—the rare opportunity to design a landscape from scratch. He bought a 1,500-acre expanse on which he changed the course of one river and razed three small towns to make the land "virgin" again. The three artists, the greatest of the era, responded by fashioning a house of matchless grace, with an interior that was exquisitely Baroque yet not disturbingly flamboyant, and a park that was the first and is still the finest example of the "French" garden.

Le Vau's design is ornate yet harmonious. The Grand Salon, which was unfinished at the time of Fouquet's arrest and remains so today, gives the clearest evidence of his plan's clarity and coherence. Le Brun's paintings, frescoes, trompe l'oeil murals, and cameos are better than anything he did at Versailles. They fill the house's magnificent rooms, as do period furnishings, tapestries, and rush mats (which were widely used in the 17th century, when carpets were still rare). The château is so impeccably preserved that it warrants the one- to two-hour tour, and you can easily spend an entire day in the incomparable gardens. That the estate still exists is due to some quick thinking by the comtesse during the Revolution—she convinced the arts commission to declare it a national monument. In 1875 Alfred Sommier, a sugar magnate and patron of the arts, purchased and restored Vaux after it had been abandoned.

You can reach the château, an hour southeast of Paris, via N 6 to Melun, following N 105 to N 36, and then D 215 east. At the sign, turn down a long, elegant, tree-lined avenue and prepare yourself for the sight of this stunning château on the right. There is a café in the refurbished stables. Candlelight tours are available Saturday evenings at 8:30, June through September, and elaborate fountain shows are held on the second and last Saturdays of each month. Vaux-le-Vicomte is closed in December and January, and in November, February, and March is open only on weekend and holiday afternoons.

Barbizon

Barbizon is a small, quaint town between Vaux-le-Vicomte and Fontainebleau that is best known as the home of most of France's great mid-18th-century artists. Painters such as Théodore Rousseau, Jean-François Millet, and Jean-Baptiste-Camille Corot would pack palettes and canvases and head into the idyllic countryside around the town to paint. Charles Baudelaire attacked the Barbizon School, as this group of painters was called, for merely reproducing landscapes; he wrote, "In this silly cult of nature unpurified, unexplained by imagination, I see the evident signs of a general decline."

The surrounding country is still quiet and very lovely, as is the Fontainebleau forest, which bounds one side of the town and offers marvelous walks. On Barbizon's single main street, the rue Grande, are the former studios, now museums, of Millet and Rousseau; both artists are buried in the local cemetery. The Auberge de Ganne, where the artists used to congregate to eat, drink coffee, and chat with neighbors George Sand and the Goncourt brothers, is also a museum. If you want to stay the night, the **Bas-Bréau**, right in town, is a beautifully restored farmhouse with rustic, comfortable, well-appointed, and expensive rooms and an excellent restaurant (see also the chapter on the Loire Valley). Leaders of the Seven Nations Economic Group stayed at the inn during their 1984 summit. Just down the street, at 26, rue Grande, is **La Flambée**, a country auberge featuring simple, hearty fare such as grilled meat and baked potatoes. For a fine meal overlooking the Fontainebleau forest, try **Au Grand Veneur**, a rustic hunting lodge–like restaurant about a mile outside of Barbizon via N 7. Reservations are recommended; Tel: 60-66-40-44. (63, rue Gabriel-Séailles.) You can reach Barbizon via A 6 or by train from the Gare de Lyon to Melun and then by taxi.

Fontainebleau

Fontainebleau has been a royal residence since the 12th century and was originally a hunting lodge. Louis VI and Saint Louis came here to hunt stag and boar in the magnificent forests, and Philippe le Bel died here after a fall from his horse. While the town center is a bit run-down in places, there are many beautiful houses, and France's most prestigious business school, INSEAD, is located here as well. The main post office and town hall are quite pretty, and there are some noteworthy buildings along the rue Grande as well as a variety of bakers and *traiteurs* (gussied-up delis, basically).

The main entrance to Fontainebleau proper is from the place du Général de Gaulle, where a gilded cast-iron gate leads to the Cour de Cheval Blanc, or the Cour des Adieux, so named because it was from this courtyard that Napoléon left for exile on Elba. The courtyard is divided into four squares of perfectly manicured lawn bounded by sculpted pine trees. The minister's wing on the left is one of a pair constructed by Gilles Le Breton, whom François I commissioned to rebuild the palace after he pulled down most of an earlier Medieval castle. Its mate was destroyed by Louis XV, who had Jacques-Ange Gabriel build the existing wing. The opposing styles make for a good comparison between 16th- and 18th-century architecture.

The central building, which was expanded by every king from François I to Louis XV, is dominated by the handsome Fer-à-Cheval staircase (a Louis XIII production); it was from this majestic podium that Napoléon, the general who decimated two generations of French youth, bade farewell to his beloved guards, asking them always to look after France: "Her happiness," he said, "is my only thought." While emperor, Napoléon lived at Fontainebleau and not Versailles, where the ghost of the Sun King challenged his position in the pantheon of great Frenchmen. The Louis XV wing now houses the **Napoléon Museum**, which displays uniforms and mementos from the reigns of both Napoléons (closed Tuesdays).

The palace itself is a remarkable monument to the incredible luxury with which the kings of France surrounded themselves. The sheer richness of the decor, which covers every imaginable surface in three centuries' worth of decorative styles, stirs even the most jaded. It is less coherent than Versailles because it is the work of master artists from several centuries, but its variety gives a sense of the wastefulness of French rulers who destroyed superbly crafted rooms and buildings not because they were in need of repair (though this was sometimes the case) but merely because they were unfashionable.

Highlights of the *grands appartements,* which you can visit without a guide, include the fantastically decorated **Chapelle de la Ste-Trinité**, every surface of which is covered with gilt, paint, or carved wood, and the gorgeous **Galerie de François I**. This long hall is made entirely of carved wood, stucco, and painted panels—a style that was created by the Italian decorator Francesco Primaticcio (known in France as Le Primatice), who belonged to the Fontainebleau School. The enormous **Salle de Bal**, with its 40-foot ceiling and wood panels and its exquisite view of the Cour de la Fontaine and pond and park behind, is undoubtedly the most spectacular room in the palace. Built by François I and completed by Henri II, the room is bathed in light and inspires visions of gowned women swinging on the arms of bewigged men in a space awash with music, splendor, and an indomitable belief in the future. The less fascinating *petits appartements* and those of Pope Pius VII are open only to guided tours.

The large, pretty park and English garden are well tended and perfect for an afternoon's stroll. Together, they offer a choice of atmospheres: wild (the garden, with its sweeping paths and inviting lawns) or ordered (the carefully geometric park). The Etang des Carpes is filled with large carp; feeding them and watching them splash for the food is a favorite Fontainebleau sport. Pony rides around the parterre are popular among younger visitors to the palace. The place du Général de Gaulle is ringed with generally reliable cafés and restaurants.

For devotees of sublime cooking, **A la Côte St-Jacques**, a luxurious and expensive hotel and restaurant in **Joigny** about 80 km (50 miles) southeast via A 6, has one of the finest, most innovative kitchens in France; Tel: 86-62-09-70.

You can reach Fontainebleau in an hour by train from the Gare d'Austerlitz. By car, go via A 6. If you drive do not, at any cost, miss a ride through the magnificent woods. There is also horseback riding along paths once reserved for kings, as well as mushroom picking (in season) and beautiful walks. Picnic spots abound. The forest is also home to the world's premier "boulder garden"—groups of rocks that climbers use to train or improve their technique. Horseback riding can be arranged at **Les Ecuries de la Dame Jehanne** (Tel: 64-28-35-47) in Larchant, on the southern edge of the forest about 6 miles from Fontainebleau via N 7 and D 16.

EAST

Provins

The Medieval city of Provins, southeast of Paris, rises from the surrounding fields like a quiet acknowledgment of the earth's long memory. The first records of the village date from the ninth century. In 1120 it provided refuge for Pierre Abélard, one of history's best-known and most unfortunate lovers. His audacious philosophical positions were unpopular with the authorities, and he was forced to flee Paris, leaving the heartbroken Héloïse behind. By the end of the 12th century, Henri le Libéral had solidi-fied the commercial importance of the town, and for 200 years the annual fair of Provins was a major marketplace for merchants from Italy, Germany, Holland, Marseille, and Spain. In the mid-13th century, Edmund of Lancaster, whose coat of arms included the then-rare red rose, was sovereign of Provins, and today the town is famous for the radiant rose gardens below the old ramparts. (It was the red rose of Lancaster that battled the white rose of York in the Wars of the Roses, 1455–1485.)

Enter the Ville Haute, the Medieval town, through the Porte St-Jean, a 12th-century gate in the 30-foot-thick ram-parts. The reinforcements, archers' slits, and walkways along the top of the wall are visible from the gate. Follow the road to the central square, the place du Châtel, where an ancient well is covered by an iron gate. The **Tour de César**, a 12th-century dungeon, still dominates Provins; climb the stairs for a terrific view of the entire region. The **church of St-Quiriace**, behind the tower, dates from 1140, but it wasn't completed until the 17th century. It is in use today, and the sound of hymns on a Sunday does much to emphasize the tangible Medieval quality of this town. Beautiful restored houses, barely visible over their protec-tive walls, share the rest of the hill. The French filmmaker Louis Malle thought the town so unspoiled he used it for the setting of his award-winning 1987 film, *Au Revoir les Enfants*.

Several cafés bound the place du Châtel, the best of which is **Au Vieux Grandpère**. You can reach Provins by train from the Gare de l'Est or in a little over an hour by car on N 19 from Paris; exit at the Porte de Bercy.

Château-Thierry and Bois Belleau

The château that gave the small town of Château-Thierry its name once commanded the plain of the river Marne from the hill that rises steeply behind the town. The original castle was built in the early eighth century and gradually fell into ruin. Château-Thierry is most interest-ing for its involvement in the Napoleonic Wars and both world wars. One major battle was fought below its walls, and the town was invaded and liberated three times.

The English came first, conquering the city during the Hundred Years War. Joan of Arc then liberated it in 1429. In 1814 Napoléon fought off the Russo-Prussian army commanded by Marshal Gebhard von Blücher. Then, in 1914, the German army held Château-Thierry for a week before they were forced to retreat. During the last great offensive of the war, the Germans took it once again and this time held it for almost two months. American troops helped push back the "pocket" of German forces that had penetrated deep into the Marne valley. Both times the attacking army sacked the town.

Château-Thierry has another, more pacific, claim to fame: Jean de la Fontaine, the poet and writer of fairy tales and fables, was born here in 1621. His house is open to the public, and some mementos are on display.

A few kilometers to the north, three monuments commemorate the battles that raged during World War I in the expanse of the **Bois Belleau**. The Aisne-Marne memorial rests on a knoll overlooking the river Marne. A small road winds through placid fields to the massive structure, a symbol of "friendship and cooperation between French and American armies." Families now picnic on the lawns that sweep down from the memorial to the hill's edge, and men play *boules* on the gravel paths. French youths play Frisbee or, more appropriately, baseball instead of their fathers' traditional game. The only impediments to the view of the valley are the chemical plants along the river.

The American cemetery is about a thousand feet away at the end of a tree-lined avenue. Impeccably tended lawns and rosebushes guard the footpath to the memorial chapel, on whose walls are inscribed the names of every American who fell in the vicious battle for the wooded hill behind the cemetery. The neat rows of crosses and stars extend far into the distance, marking the graves of the 2,288 men who died here. The graveyard's beautiful situation, flush against a hill and under towering trees, is a tranquil and powerful reminder of the war that was supposed to end all wars, the war that so many Americans have forgotten.

Within eyesight a second, almost unmarked cemetery honors the dead of the army that lost. The 8,625 Germans who fell in the battle are buried here. Only a small plaque on one of the two stone buildings that front it marks their presence. The ironies of World War I, which abounded during the conflict, are clearly still with us.

Château-Thierry features the usual assortment of local cafés and restaurants. Of note, however, is the **Auberge Jean de la Fontaine**, across the river from the château at 10, rue Filoirs, which serves fine cuisine and wines from the nearby Champagne region. Reservations are recommended; Tel: 23-83-63-89.

You can reach Château-Thierry, a little over an hour from Paris, by train from the Gare de l'Est, or by car via A 4, and south on D 1. For a more leisurely drive you might follow N 3 from Paris. The drives throughout the Marne valley area are often very pretty.

NORTH
Pierrefonds and Compiègne

Set on a commanding hilltop on the southeastern edge of the vast and beautiful Forêt de Compiègne, Pierrefonds is one of the most striking châteaux in France. If you drive here from the north or west you'll wind through small valleys until, quite suddenly, you'll see the majestic towers and battlements of this restored Medieval fortress rising before you. The château was first erected in the 12th century, then was rebuilt by Louis d'Orléans, brother of King Charles VI and regent of France during the Hundred Years War until his assassination by Jean the Fearless in 1407. Eventually the château became the property of François d'Estrées. When he imprudently and unsuccessfully rebelled against the crown, Pierrefonds was partially pulled down and fell into a state of such disrepair that Napoléon was able to buy it in 1813 for only 3,000 francs.

In 1857 Napoléon III, taken with the feudal magnificence of the setting, decided to rebuild the house at great expense, a move that was criticized by those who felt the fortress's ancien régime roots should remain buried. Eugène-Emmanuel Viollet-le-Duc, who directed the restoration, based his design on the walls that remained, and re-created the massive Medieval structure.

And an overwhelming edifice it is. Huge, compelling, secure, and self-contained, the castle controls the entire valley by virtue of its strategic location and its imposing appearance. In design, it is true to 14th-century principles: Only a handful of windows open to the outside, and the eight towers and many archers' slits determine the fortress's interaction with the world. The towers are crowned by (and named after) massive sculptures of King Arthur, Charlemagne, Alexander the Great, and Caesar, among others. The castle entrance crosses a drawbridge and passes through 15-foot-thick walls into a central courtyard. The chapel and the Escalier d'Honneur in the courtyard are both Second Empire; the rest of the buildings and interior, however, are reasonably accurate reproductions of the original castle. The tour is well worthwhile.

The town itself is rather small; a pretty lake with rowboats for rent is at its center. A pleasant café/restaurant, **Le Chalet du Lac**, offers lakeside lunches. You can reach Pierrefonds by car in a quarter of an hour via D 973 from Compiègne, or from Paris by SNCF to Compiègne and then by taxi or bus.

Compiègne has been a favorite residence of French kings since Charles the Bald established a palace here in 873. By the 13th century a bustling town had grown around the castle, and in 1374 Charles V built a château on the site of the current palace. It was at Compiègne, in 1430, that Joan of Arc's inspired military career came to an end when a risky sortie across the river to scout English positions resulted in her capture. Louis XIV, dissatisfied with the accommodations at Compiègne, made additions to the château, claiming that "At Versailles I live like a king, at Fontainebleau like a prince, and at Compiègne like a peasant." His great-grandson, Louis XV (Louis XIV reigned for 72 years, outliving both his son and his grandson), completely rebuilt and enlarged the palace so that his entire court could live here in comfort. Jacques-Ange Gabriel, who built the *hôtels particuliers* facing the place de la Concorde in Paris, oversaw the work and is responsible for the château's classical lines. Wars and revolutions repeatedly interrupted construction—Louis XVI made only one visit to the partially renovated château before the exigencies of the incipient revolution called him back to Paris—and it wasn't until Napoléon chose it as his imperial residence that the building was finally finished.

Today Gabriel's imposing façade, which resembles, not coincidentally, many government offices in Paris, faces the pretty place du Palais. The north wing has been given over to an automobile museum, and the rooms at the end of the courtyard, including the Salle des Gardes and the striking Escalier d'Honneur, now house changing art exhibits. Entrance to the château's most beautiful apartments, those of Napoléon and Marie-Antoinette, is just to the right. Guided tours only are offered, but the history of the château is so convoluted that this is a welcome requirement. As you might expect, the rooms are luxuriously decorated in a grand mix of royal styles. The Salon des Cartes contains a fascinating collection of maps of the forest, which Louis XV used to consult for his hunts. The apartments have a stellar view of the well-tended, flower-filled gardens and the park, which extends to the forest.

The **church of St-Jacques**, where Joan of Arc took communion on the day of her capture, dates from the 13th century and has a very pretty bell tower. The **Hôtel de Ville**, a good example of Gothic architecture, boasts one of the country's oldest clocks. The town itself is lovely, and a brief stroll through its older sections, with their Tudor buildings and ancient walls, is in order. Many small restaurants and cafés, as well as expensive shops, dot the streets; a good omelette *paysan* is available at the charming **Café des Lombards**, on the street of the same name.

The **Forêt de Compiègne** is another example of the wild beauty of the terrain around Paris. Nobles once hunted game in the forest, and today it's a beautiful area through which to drive or bicycle (bicycles can be rented at the Compiègne train station). Ruins of abbeys, stands of ancient oak trees, and hills offering spectacular views of the forest abound. One particularly fascinating stop is the **Clairière de l'Armistice**, a clearing where on November 10, 1918, Marshal Foch and representatives of the Allied armies and Germany met in the marshal's train car to sign the armistice ending World War I. The site of the rolling battle headquarters has been preserved as a monument to the French military, and a giant statue of Foch, the savior of France, stands here. The display makes no mention of a second armistice signed on this spot: In 1940 Adolf Hitler ordered that occupied France capitulate here in the original train car in which Germany surrendered at the end of World War I. The train car was destroyed in 1945 near Berlin, perhaps to prevent yet another surrender in the Compiègne forest; the car on display now is a reproduction.

You can reach Compiègne by car via A 1 from the Porte de la Villette in Paris, or by SNCF from the Gare du Nord. From the station, cross the bridge into town, turn left at the church of St-Jacques, and continue to the château. A tourist office is located in the Hôtel de Ville.

Senlis

Senlis was a major town in Gallo-Roman times—a first-century amphitheater and the old walls still mark the Roman presence—and, for centuries, was the religious center of France, a bishop's seat until 1901. Today it is a well-preserved little hilltop village with cobblestone streets that echo with history. It was at a gathering of feudal lords in Senlis castle in 987 that the archbishop of Reims proposed Hugues Capet as the first king of France.

What makes Senlis special and worth visiting is the palpable sense of antiquity and continuity the town exudes. It's very small, and often crowded, so a few hours are enough to explore the entire village. Wandering through the ancient streets, under Roman gates and past Tudor houses, you might share the sharp and certain feeling that centuries ago people traversed the same stone paths past the same buildings.

The cathedral of Notre-Dame here was begun ten years before Paris's Notre-Dame and is an excellent example of both early Gothic architecture and the evolution of the style through succeeding centuries. The cathedral is built on a smaller scale than its more famous namesake. Another church in Senlis, the St-Pierre, exhibits both Roman and Gothic design. The town's château is rather modest (perhaps that explains why kings preferred the comforts of Compiègne; Henri IV was the last to stay here), as is the park behind it. The grounds also include a hunting museum.

Jean-Jacques Rousseau lived in **Ermenonville**, 13 km (8 miles) southeast. A pilgrimage to his memorial on the Ile des Peuples remains *de rigueur,* although his body now rests in Paris's Panthéon. You can take beautiful walks through the woods the philosopher loved (once the grounds of the château in which he died) and across the odd Mer de Sable—a vast expanse of sand. In a geologic fluke, the climatic warming that ended the glacial era also opened holes in the vegetation here, baring the underlying layer of sand, which dates from the Tertiary period—approximately 70 million years ago.

A nice lunch can be had on the edge of the woods between Senlis and Ermenonville, via N 330 and then D

126 north, at the **Auberge de Fontaine** in Fontaine-Chaalis. (22, Grande Rue; Tel: 44-54-20-22.)

You can reach Senlis by car, an hour from Paris, via A 1 (the N 17 is a slower, more scenic option), or by SNCF from the Gare du Nord. From the station, walk up the hill to the old town. Ermenonville can be reached by car via N 330 from Senlis.

Chantilly

Chantilly has one of the prettiest settings of any château in France: It rises almost ethereally from the tranquil lagoon that encircles it. Built and rebuilt in fits and starts over seven centuries, the château has seen more than its share of sieges and sacks, and the history of its occupying families is particularly interesting. In the 14th century, Pierre d'Orgemont, then chancellor of France, purchased the property and erected a fortified castle on the ruins of a 10th-century château that had been destroyed in the Jacquerie (the peasant uprising of 1358).

The Montmorency family bought the estate in 1450, and Anne (a man) demolished the fortress and built what is now called the Petit Château—then separated from the main structure by a moat. As high constable of France, Anne was a man of tremendous wealth, energy, and influence—he was a friend and adviser to every king from Louis XII to Charles IX. At home, he was responsible for enlarging the grounds of the estate, as well as building the elegant square that fronts the château. He died at 70 in a battle with Protestants at St-Denis, and it took five stab wounds, two slashes to the head, and a bullet to the spine to kill him.

Henri II was the last Montmorency to rule at Chantilly; he was beheaded at Toulouse for leading a revolt against Cardinal Richelieu. In the tradition of his ancestor, it took 18 wounds, including five bullets, to convince Henri to surrender. In his will, Henri left the cardinal the two Michelangelo *Slaves* that now stand in the Louvre. Henri II de Bourbon-Condé, who married Montmorency's daughter, inherited the estate, thus initiating the era of the Condés, the longest-lasting and best-known residents of Chantilly. The Grand Condé, Louis II, hired André Le Nôtre to design the renowned gardens and began yet another renovation of the château according to plans by Hardouin-Mansart. The vain Sun King, Louis XIV, was said to be envious of Henri's fountains, which were deemed the most beautiful in France. Henri made Chantilly a center of the arts in France by attracting such writers as Jean-Baptiste Molière, Jean de la Fontaine, and Jean Racine. Henri's chef, Vatel, also elevated cooking to the highest levels, at least in terms of artistic temperament: Distraught that a batch of fish hadn't arrived in time to feed Louis XIV and the 5,000 courtiers who accompanied him everywhere, Vatel fell on his sword. Later it was discovered that the fish had, in fact, come. The Château d'Enghien, the last main addition to the house, was built in 1767 for the presumptive heir, the duc d'Enghien.

The estate was pillaged during the Revolution; the family fled and later died off. Today the castle owes its excellent condition to the duc d'Aumale, fourth son of King Louis-Philippe. A Bourbon like the Condé family, he devoted himself to completing the restoration begun by his predecessor and repairing the ravages of both time and revolution. Aumale died without an heir and left both the castle and his collections to the Institut de France.

The château, now the **Musée Condé**, houses little of the art that belonged to the family; the bulk of the collection was scattered during the Revolution. The interior is extraordinarily rich, with marble staircases, glowing parquet floors, and ornate tapestries. The museum's collections include a gorgeous 15th-century illuminated manuscript (the Limbourg brothers' famous *Très Riches Heures du Duc de Berry*) and works by Botticelli and Raphael. In the Petit Château a long gallery is lined with canvases depicting the military victories of the Grand Condé. The grounds are also outstanding; their manicured lawns and immaculate paths invite leisurely strolls through the relaxed English garden, the wooded park, or along the great canal.

The monumental **Grandes Ecuries** (stables) across the road from the château constitute one of the best examples of 18th-century architecture in the country and are also open to visitors. The stables are still in use and house a horse museum, complete with dressage demonstrations and Shetland ponies. Race horses that train on the track are also stabled here. The stables and tracks have made Chantilly one of France's equestrian centers, and every June the **Prix de Diane**, the most important race in the world for three-year-old fillies, attracts the most beautiful of beautiful people to the track, their antique Rolls-Royces, colorful summer suits, and formal top hats filling the infield.

The attractive old château village, which is entered through a large gate connected to the stables, has many restaurants and cafés; one of the best is the **Relais Condé** opposite the racetrack at 42, avenue du Maréchal-Joffre. The **Captainerie du Château** in the castle's courtyard is a pleasant tearoom. You can reach Chantilly by car in less than an hour from Paris via A 1 to Survilliers, and then D 924A, or via N 16 for a more pleasant drive, or by SNCF from the Gare du Nord. From the station, you can take a bus or walk up the avenue du Maréchal-Joffre, turn right on the rue du Connétable, and continue on to the château. The walk takes about 30 minutes.

Beauvais

Much of Beauvais was destroyed by savage bombing during World War II, but the mammoth cathedral—the world's tallest—survived. Actually the town has an appealingly stormy history. The Romans dismantled it first after defeating the army of Gaul. In 1429 the bishop of Beauvais was run out of town by honest burghers for supporting England in the Hundred Years War; one year later he condemned Joan of Arc to the stake. In 1472 Beauvais got its own heroine, when Joan of the Hatchet rallied the town to repulse an invasion by the duke of Burgundy. While her townspeople ran along the city walls, panicked by the huge army facing them, Joan took a hatchet to an enemy soldier carrying a banner and hacked him off the wall. The townspeople, inspired by her courage, regrouped and resisted the attack.

The **cathedral of St-Pierre**, which dominates the town (and is in fact the only real reason to visit Beauvais, now a modern provincial outpost laden with neon and roadwork), is a marvel. Some call it a miracle that defies the law of gravity; others call it an act of extreme hubris. The plans were so grandiose and costly that when construction was abandoned four centuries after work began in 1225, the building still had no towers. As it turned out, the structure could not support the weight of the stonework, and by 1284 the cathedral had begun to collapse. Only constant patchwork and jerry-rigging kept it—and keep it—standing.

Inside, however, the audaciousness of the design seems justified. Majestic, sweeping columns support a ceiling that seems to be miles away, reaching perhaps to heaven. The stained-glass windows are sublime, especially the southern rose window, depicting the creation, and the windows along the north transept, showing ten Sybils, who face ten prophets on the south wall.

From Paris you can reach Beauvais, about 90 minutes away, by car via N 1 from the Porte de la Villette, or by SNCF from the Gare du Nord. From the station, take a bus or taxi. Or, make the half-mile walk up the avenue de la République, then right onto the rue Malherbe; the cathedral will become visible on your left.

GETTING AROUND

Although it intersects with the Métro at some stations, the RER is an entirely separate network and has its own platforms. RER trains are identified both by destination and by a letter. To add to the confusion, trains on line C— which serves Versailles—also have *names* (CORA, for example). Ignore the names; it is enough to follow the destination and letter, making sure, of course, that your desired station is on the platform sign that lists the stops for the incoming train.

Maps can be acquired at any Métro or RER station; tickets can be purchased at the ticket window in RER stations or from a machine at the stations. To use the machines, which give change, punch the button corresponding to your destination (Versailles RG, for example) and the type of ticket that you want (1st or 2nd class). After the price appears on the screen, insert your money. The ticket and your change will then follow.

ACCOMMODATIONS REFERENCE

▶ **A la Côte St-Jacques**. 14, faubourg de Paris, 89300 **Joigny**. Tel: 86-62-09-70; Telex: 801458; in U.S., (212) 696-1323.

▶ **Bas-Bréau**. 22, rue Grande, 77630 **Barbizon**. Tel: 60-66-40-05; Telex: 690953; in U.S., (212) 696-1323.

▶ **Pavillon Henri IV**. 21, rue Thiers, 78100 **St-Germain-en-Laye**. Tel: 34-51-62-62; Fax: 39-73-93-73.

▶ **Trianon Palace**. 1, boulevard de la Reine, 78000 **Versailles**. Tel: 39-50-34-12; Fax: 39-49-00-77.

CHAMPAGNE

By Fred Halliday with Georgia I. Hesse

In the beginning, before it sparkled in the eyes of the world, Champagne was already an important wine region. But it produced only what could be called "amusing little wines," country wines. People would come up to the region from Paris and go from village to village tasting the *crus,* each with its certain nonexportable charm. Seeing these local villages is how any visit to Champagne should properly begin.

From down the streets of Hautvillers, halfway up the mountain of Reims, anyone can see the fortunes of Champagne flowing toward the Marne. Here are the golden vineyards, in neat rows, tilting toward the river. Downward run the villages that wine built. To name just a few, there are Hautvillers, with its Benedictine abbey; Bouzy, of the now-fashionable red Champagne; Cumières, with one just as good but less known and less expensive; and, down on the floor of the valley, Ay, the little stone town with the stone steeple that rings out the Angelus. Finally there is Epernay, a larger town with a village feel and a main street that rings of worldly wealth, the avenue de Champagne.

The region is bounded by the Ile-de-France in the west and Lorraine in the east, the Ardennes and Belgium in the north and Burgundy in the south. The larger cities around which the country radiates are Reims, of the justly famous cathedral, and Troyes, a bit out of the way to the south, but well worth a visit.

Many of Champagne's superb churches and cathedrals are covered in this chapter. To them enthusiasts of architecture can add the towns of Laon (Notre-Dame) and Soissons (abbey of St-Jean-des-Vignes and the cathedral of

St-Gervais-et-St-Protais, of which only the transept and choir survived the battles of World War I). Both towns are northwest of Champagne proper.

MAJOR INTEREST

The "country" villages of Champagne, especially Hautvillers

Epernay
The Champagne *caves*
Avenue de Champagne

Reims
Cathedral of Notre-Dame
Basilica of St-Remi
The Champagne *caves*
Musée St-Denis
Musée et Hôtel Le Vergeur
Palais du Tau

Troyes
Cathedral of St-Pierre-et-St-Paul
Musée d'Art Moderne
The ancient St-Jean quarter

Elsewhere in Champagne
Cathedral of St-Etienne in Châlons-sur-Marne
Basilica of Notre-Dame in L'Epine

The Wine Country

If you are coming from Paris, it is best to take the train to Epernay and there rent a car. From Epernay three main roads form a triangle that may define the perimeter of your visit to the region, allowing for the occasional foray outside the immediate area. The first and most important road, N 51, goes up the Montagne de Reims from Epernay to Reims; the next, N 3, runs along the Marne river and anchors Epernay to Châlons-sur-Marne; and the third, N 44, makes a picturesque hypotenuse of the ridges going past Verzenay from Châlons-sur-Marne to Reims. Feel free to drop in on anything so circumscribed.

Just north of Epernay, across the Marne on D 1 and D 9, respectively, are Ay and Avenay-Val-d'Or. **Ay** is the home of Bollinger, James Bond's Champagne, and of Deutz; **Avenay** is a luscious sort of wine town surrounded by vineyards. An American GI who arrived here with Gen-

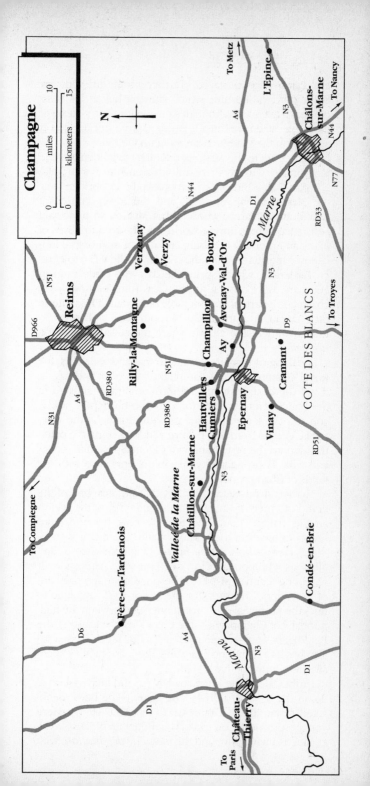

eral Patton's forces stayed to marry a local girl and now bottles Ricciuti-Revolte, which you can buy at his *chais* (winery). Avenay is a good destination for the first taste of morning, when the mist is on the Marne but the sun is already on the vineyards stepping up the hill.

Farther out to the west, abandoning the golden triangle temporarily, a lovely drive unfolds along the Marne. Take N 3 past Port-à-Binson, which boasts the last bridge over the Marne to fall in 1940, and the lovely church at Châtillon-sur-Marne, whose abbot Michot, an important resistance fighter during World War II, saved the lives of many an American bombing crew. For a memorable luncheon experience, cross the river and follow D 6 to **Fère-en-Tardenois**, where springlike days can come even in February. Here among the timeless ruins of a Medieval château is a park of considerable beauty and **l'Hostellerie du Château**, an impeccable 14-room hotel with a restaurant of undeniable charm where the cuisine is not too *nouvelle*.

Speaking of restaurants, and to that add wine lists, the **Royal Champagne**, in Champillon back near Epernay, is, if not the best, certainly the most admirably situated in the region. Here, in a restored 18th-century post house, you can drink a red Cumières while gazing at the vineyards. The surrounding picture windows bring the countryside into the restaurant with CinemaScope-like reality, and what is brought to your table seems alive with the fields of Champagne.

The Royal was started by David Desvignes, one of the grand old men of Champagne, a true lover of the region and its fruits. Though he is gone now, his firm hand seems to hover in the restaurant still. The menu is traditional *champenois: truite bleue,* Chaource cheese, and glorious Philipponat Clos des Goisses Champagne. It would be a grave mistake, in responding to the pressure of more modish urges, for the visitor to Champagne to miss the Royal. Savor it on a sunny Sunday when the high poobahs of Champagne—the Chandons, the Lansons, the Pol Rogers, et al—come parading in for lunch. The Royal also has 24 rooms and one suite; these are rather expensive, and only one has a view.

Farther along the same road, N 51, and then east on D 26, in the town of **Rilly-la-Montagne**, is the newly renovated restaurant **le Grand Cerf** (Tel: 26-97-60-07). Here you are practically on top of the mountain of Reims. The cuisine is imaginative and the *menu de dégustation,* with its tempting tiny tidbits, is completely satisfying. Ask to be seated at the tables at the back of the restaurant, which give a view of the vineyards.

If you want to soak up the atmosphere of life in a small, traditional wine-making community, you have only to poke your nose along the road out of Rilly (still D 26) as it leads into Verzenay. The distances are small, the rewards are great. On Verzenay's main drag (in the direction of Verzy) is the **Restaurant-Bar le Verzenay**. Run by an unflappable chef named Claudette, it's crowded at noon with bikers, vineyard workers, and the pinging sounds of pinball, but Claudette's luncheon specials (highlighted with herbs and potatoes flecked with parsley), are always tasty and hover at around 65 francs.

For a longer stay in the lap of Saint Vincent (the patron saint of wine growers), try the **Auberge Saint Vincent**. Try it as a hotel, a restaurant, or a bar, for it's all three. It's only 11 km (7 miles) south of Verzy in the village with the onomatopoetic name of **Ambonnay** (farther down the bountiful D 26), a town that flaunts its charm. Its streets are lined with old wrought-iron signs that creak over the cobbler's shop, the grocer's, the baker's. The 10-room Auberge Saint Vincent, newly renovated in 19th-century period style, is the *in* inn in Champagne for those with a taste for the reasonably authentic at reasonable prices. The rooms are neatly done for country living, with little-print curtains framing shining windows. The public rooms harbor antiques, and everywhere is the smell of wood wax. The welcome is warm, for the management is new, but it is in the restaurant that the auberge earns its spurs. The menu revolves around a cuisine neither modish nor classical, but regionally Champagne. And regional cuisine means fresh cuisine, for the produce is local.

What's local in Champagne? Try all manner of *crudités*, as well as ham, turkey, smoked wild boar, and thrush pâté. There's haunch of venison, quail in embers, filet of sole in Champagne, chicken in Champagne, *petits-gris* (very small snails) in herb butter, pig's feet in a mustard to drive you wild, and, of course, icy flutes of Champagne. Two cheeses to try, here and in the North, are Boulette d'Avesnes and Maroilles.

With all this under your belt, what better awaits than **Bouzy**? The town that gives its name to the most famous still wine to come from Champagne lies just 2.5 km (1.5 miles) west of Ambonnay on D 19. Elsewhere the wine is overpriced, so the town is undersold. But Bouzy offers

Bouzy at prices that are guaranteed to put cases in your car. Three wineries to try here: **Champagne Paul Bara** (Tel: 26-57-00-50), **George Vesselle** (Tel: 26-57-00-15), and **Champagne Barancourt** (Tel: 26-57-00-67). In France it's always best to phone ahead, even if it's from a booth on the corner; most wineries offer free visits from April to October.

Finally, those who want a restaurant over on the Côte des Blancs should try **Le Mesnil** in le Mesnil-sur-Oger (Tel: 26-57-95-57), south of the Marne (via Avenay-Val-d'Or) on D 9. They have most everybody's Champagne, and the prices are low and the quality high.

Before leaving the mountain of Reims, there's one vineyard town on its eastern flank that no lover of Champagne and its history should miss. Turn off N 51 at the Royal Champagne and go down the lane that leads from the side of the restaurant and runs around the rim of the vineyards to the singular village of **Hautvillers**.

Here the intimate relationship between the vine and the people can be explored close up. From its steep side streets Hautvillers affords stunning views of the plantings, with the looping course of the misty Marne far below. The streets are quiet, but precipitous and narrow—no place for a car—so it's a good idea to park, stroll around, and get in touch with what a successful wine village is. Little backyard gardens, which anywhere else in the world— even in France—would boast clematis or tomatoes, or maybe a clothesline, are here strung for vines. There is at least one known widow and many a pensioner who scan the newspaper for hints of what their investment will bring in the fall. This is a cottage enterprise not lightly entered into, for these are the most expensive grapes in the world. So, should you pass by the widow's house— and she will yell at you from the window if you do— please, do not squeeze the grapes.

It was in Hautvillers during the 17th century that the sightless Dom Pérignon worked as a cellarmaster, and the Benedictine abbey where he labored still stands, transformed by Möet & Chandon into a museum. Here the traditional story of the step-by-step development of Champagne is told on the very spot where much of it first happened. Like many happy accidents, the discovery of Champagne resulted partly from effort and partly from blind luck. Pérignon had long been immersed in the dark arts of vinification and double fermentation, and it was here that the old monk first announced his immortal words, which rank with Marconi's and Alexander Graham Bell's: "Come quickly; I'm drinking stars!"

So here, with scores of others, are the picturesque villages of Champagne. It is in the wine capitals of Epernay and Reims, however, that the various flows from the vineyards of these small villages are put into the marketable stream now known as Champagne.

Epernay

Why is it that even though Reims is the literal capital of the province of Champagne, and bottles roughly the same amount of wine annually as the much smaller Epernay down on the Marne, that the latter is thought of as the capital of Champagne? It must be because of the **avenue de Champagne**.

On this single street, which leads from the place de la République in Epernay up to the fertile plain of Seran about 10 km (6 miles) away, is assembled the greatest concentration of Champagne wealth in the world: the houses of Möet & Chandon, Pol Roger, Perrier-Jouët, Charbaut, Mercier. The municipal museum on the north side of the avenue opposite Caves Mercier is really three museums; those of wine (with a great collection of labels) and regional archaeology (pottery, glassware, arms, and the finds from tombs) are the most interesting. And, if your legs hold out, you can follow the avenue all the way up to the plain of Seran and the glass-bottle plant of St-Gobins on top, where you'll find all the steam and clatter of bottles being made from sand to finish.

The story of Champagne and how it is made (with a free tasting at the end) is told at many of the great houses in the course of a visit to their *caves*. It is a hospitality enormously appreciated. Moët alone has 12 permanent guides conducting free tours of their miles of underground galleries all day long, seven days a week from April to October (Monday to Friday the rest of the year), and in all major languages. Last year they guided almost 200,000 visitors, who consumed roughly 30,000 bottles.

The **Restaurant Chapon Fin** on place Mendès-France is a reasonable and lusty place to sample local wines, while for accommodations a good choice is **La Briqueterie** in Vinay, just south of Epernay on D 11. Its 42 rooms go for around 600 francs a night, the food sometimes approaches the memorable, and the *carte des vins* ranks with that of the Royal.

Reims

Reims is the official capital of Champagne. It has as many *grande marques*—Veuve Clicquot, Taittinger, Mumm, Krug, Pommery, Roederer, Lanson, and Piper Heidsieck among the better known—and all receive visitors. It is also the only place where *les crayères*—chalk quarries—the most spectacular *caves* of Champagne, are found. *Les crayères* were created by the Romans, who built Reims, and therein lies the tale of the roots of Champagne. The whole region sits on a vast cake of pure chalk—not limestone or a chalky substance: chalk. Break off a piece and you can write with it. This mammoth monolith, one of the largest single chalk deposits in the world, lies just under the surface, a matter sometimes of feet, sometimes of inches, and serves as a filtering agent for the aquifer still farther down (300 yards). It is this composition that gives Champagne its dry, austere quality and that made the fortune of the region. The Romans used this chalk as a building material and inadvertently contributed to the development of wine one thousand years later. As Reims grew, Roman cave work became more extensive; serving as cutting grottoes and quarries, *crayères* became connected by tunnels and pushed farther and farther under Reims and out into the countryside. Today there are more than 120 miles of *caves* beneath the hills and dales of the Champagne region.

After the Romans left, the French discovered that the cool and constant temperature of the *caves* provided excellent conditions for storing things. Wine. The most impressive *crayères* existing today can be visited at the Champagne houses of Taittinger, Veuve Clicquot, Piper Heidsieck, and Pommery.

But quite apart from the vine, and unlike Epernay, Reims has another life. It is also a university city, full of busy sidewalk cafés, pedestrian zones, and interesting shops. It has a great metropolitan newspaper, *l'Union,* which grew out of the resistance and serves the north of France. Most of the street life swirls along the rue de Vesles and the elongated place Drouet-d'Erlon. Geographically, the cathedral of Notre-Dame is the heart of the city; from it, most notable attractions are within walking distance, with the exception of the Basilique St-Remi to the south and the Champagne *caves* to the north and the southeast.

Surrounded by cafés and stores ranging from chic to utilitarian, the **Hôtel de la Paix** is the best headquarters for in-town meandering. A classic, old structure that has been renovated, it offers pleasant and comfortable rooms, a locally respected restaurant, and a bar that is a meeting place for local business people as well as visitors.

Reims was capital of Gallic Belgium when Paris was a mere village, and its wines were so renowned that in A.D. 92 the Roman Emperor Domitian ordered that the vines be destroyed because they were unfair competition to those of Italy. Reims owes its name to a Gallic tribe, the Rèmes, but its Roman conquerors dubbed it Durocortorum and made it capital of Lower Belgium. From the third to the eighth century Reims served as a veritable cradle of saints, producing at least 13, including Remi (properly, Remigius; A.D. 440–533). On Christmas Day 496, Remi (of the propitious Champagne name) baptized Clovis, the Merovingian king of the Franks, on the site where the cathedral of Notre-Dame stands today. Later kings wished to be consecrated in the same place and with the same oil as was Clovis, and according to history 37 of them were, down to Charles X in 1825. The coronation that has received the most press was that of Charles VII in 1429—thanks largely to Joan of Arc.

Notre-Dame, smack in the center of Reims and reached via rue Libergier if you are coming from the direction of Paris, is one of the three or four great cathedrals of the world, the supreme work of a time and place, the focus of all earthly talents. It is justly renowned for its 13th-century stained-glass windows and its superbly sculpted façade, which is best seen and photographed just before twilight, when a dying sun enlivens its tympanum, gables, pinnacles, and statue-filled portals. First admire the entry portals; then take a turn to the left to view the colossal angel sculptures. The harmony of the cathedral's interior is striking. Here was where the kings of France chose to be crowned; what they drank afterward to toast such an exhilarating experience is a foregone conclusion.

Just to the right as you face the cathedral is the **Palais du Tau**, originally a residence of the king and later the archbishopric. Within are admirable statues from the Champagne school, among them a fine *Coronation of the Virgin* and a *Goliath*. Among the many worthwhile tapestries, that honoring the life and times of King Clovis stands out. The two rooms that constitute the treasury of the Palais du Tau are rich in holy ornaments, talismans, chalices, reliquaries, and objects used in the ceremony of Holy Communion.

Across the *place* and east of Notre-Dame, the **Musée St-Denis** houses in several huge rooms statues, tapestries, grisaille paintings, and French canvases from the 17th to the 20th centuries, including several notable Impressionist works.

Amble up rue de Vesle, turn left at place Royale (a harmonious Louis XVI square), then right at place du Forum and you will reach the **Musée et Hôtel Le Vergeur**, home of artworks, furniture, engravings, and the like dating from the days of Old Reims. One room is devoted to some splendid Dürer engravings.

On the southern edge of town, in a quarter called Fléchambault, stands the **basilica of St-Remi**, built in the 11th and 12th centuries atop the saint's tomb. It has endured several reconstructions necessitated by war and remains the repository of many early archbishops and kings of France; the tomb of Remi is behind the altar, which was reworked in 1847.

It should be noted that Reims is the home of one of those restaurants that guidebooks like to call elegant, which is a concept often difficult to swallow. **Boyer "Les Crayères"** has *petit point* chairs, Villeroy & Boch china, and a cuisine that can be described as early Kandinsky on rice paper. (Some think it's a long way to come—and a stiff price to pay—for something that resembles Japanese food.) In an impressive, refined mansion, Boyer also offers 16 very expensive bedrooms and three suites to diners who may wish to collapse in style after their marc de Champagne.

Châlons-sur-Marne
and L'Epine

Châlons, southeast of Reims just off the A 4, is a proper town with memories of Attila the Hun, Napoléon, and Nazi bombings. Today Châlons (the name means "shallows in the river") is the administrative capital of the region, its narrow streets filled with traffic (there's one road in and one out), a bishopric, a prison, and bureaucrats. L'Epine remains a Medieval outpost on today's highway, a spot renowned in the Middle Ages for pilgrimages to its basilica.

Châlons does, however, offer the **cathedral of St-Etienne**, with windows and artworks of a very high order, and the **church of Notre-Dame-en-Vaux**, which is interesting for the meeting of Roman capitals and Gothic arches.

L'Epine's **basilica of Notre-Dame** occupies a site a bit to the east of Châlons where in the Middle Ages shepherds came upon a statue of the Virgin in a burning thornbush. Resulting pilgrimages attracted such of the eminent faithful as Charles VII, Louis XI, and René of Anjou. Nicolas Froment was moved to create the famous *Buisson Ardent* (burning bush) triptych now in the cathedral of Aix-en-Provence.

Constructed in Flamboyant Gothic style in the 15th century, the basilica is the size of a major cathedral. Its façade presents a fantasy, almost a riot, of architectural details, in particular gargoyles, which in wonderfully varied shapes symbolize the faces of evil and of wicked spirits.

The liveliness of the basilica's exterior is belied by its somber interior, the choir enclosed by a beautiful 16th-century rood screen. If you arrive during services, you will be struck by the spine-tingling sounds from the Renaissance organ bank.

Somewhat surprisingly, this hamlet is home to a pleasantly decorated 40-room hotel, reasonable in price, that prizes quiet and prides itself on its kitchen: **Aux Armes de Champagne**. This is a triumph in kitchen architecture, what the French call *restauration*. The dining room is formal but cozy, with fruitwood tables that are at once heavy (in weight) and light (in color); some of them overlook the recently sandblasted basilica. Try to dine while the light is still fading, for the basilica faces west. In the dying light the sky goes from azure to indigo, the church façade and spire from blanched white to pink. Then it comes to light in white again as the façade is electrically lit, the night around it black. It is an experience that warrants a memorable Champagne; try a 1985 Pol Roger. After a stop here it's over the Marne and down route N 77 to the unsullied delights of Troyes.

Troyes

Troyes is a market town, its streets aswarm with shoppers, sightseers, and diners. Its antique riches are evident in museums, churches, and handsome old houses. Yet many visitors to the region overlook this town, perhaps because it sits beside the Seine at the southern fringes of the Champagne region just off the direct Sens-to-Burgundy route.

In the 12th and 13th centuries, things were different. Along with Lagny-sur-Marne, Provins (both now considered within the greater environs of Paris), and Bar-sur-Aube, about 52 km (32 miles) to the east, Troyes staged an annual Champagne fair that attracted merchants from all over civilized Europe and established standards for Continent-wide commerce. (Troyes gave its name to our system of troy-weight measurements.) In the 12th century Saint Bernard established one of Christianity's most illustrious monasteries at Clairvaux, 14 km (9 miles) southeast of Bar-sur-Aube by N 19-N 36. The Cistercian abbey is today a prison.

Until recently, the cathedral was Troyes's top attraction. Today the **Musée d'Art Moderne** (Musée Levy) has taken its place. In 1976 Pierre and Denise Levy presented a part of their enormous art collection to Troyes, their home town. After arduous restoration, the museum opened in the renovated bishops' palace near the cathedral. Of most significance are the paintings dating to the late 19th and 20th centuries, representing almost every major French artist of the period. Also on display are prints, drawings, bronze and African sculptures, ceramics, and glassware.

The façade of the **cathedral of St-Pierre-et-St-Paul** (in the northeast quarter of town, off the place St-Pierre) was ornately sculpted by Martin Chambiges, who also worked on the cathedrals of Beauvais and Sens. The beautiful Flamboyant rose window remains (Flamboyant style features window tracery with a flamelike rhythm), while the statues of the portals were destroyed during the Revolution. Joan of Arc visited the cathedral in 1429 on her way to the crowning of Charles VII.

Among the fine stained glass from the 13th to 16th centuries is a curious window that portrays Christ stretched out across the planks of a wine press as the blood pours out of the wound in his side into a handy chalice. Meanwhile, a vine stalk grows out of his chest, and the 12 Apostles sit on its branches.

Of the other half-dozen major churches in town, visit **St-Pantaléon** for its Renaissance altar screens and statues (in the southwest quarter, off rue Emile Zola) and the **basilica of St-Urbain** (in the center of town, off the place de la Libération) for its superb Gothic choir. The oldest church,

Ste-Madeleine (on rue du Général-de-Gaulle not far from the railway station), owns a remarkable 16th-century rood screen in Flamboyant style and a statue of Sainte Marthe dressed as a common woman, the best example of the Champagne school of that century.

Very near the cathedral, the 17th-century **Abbaye St-Loup** (named for the fifth-century bishop whose virtues persuaded Attila the Hun not to sack the town), now houses two museums, one devoted to natural history and the other (**Musée des Beaux-Arts**) mainly to regional archaeology. The **Musée Historique de Troyes et de la Champagne**, in the superb Renaissance Hôtel de Vauluisant, near St-Pantaléon, illustrates the city's history and possesses the only hosiery museum in France. (Stockings, gloves, and hats were even more important to Medieval Troyes than were *andouillettes*.)

Remarkable preservation work is ongoing in the **St-Jean quarter**, where the Medieval fairs were staged. It's the 16th century revisited, from the smartly turned turrets atop the Maison de l'Orfèvre to the recobbled, archaic-looking ruelle des Chats.

An original Troyes foodstuff is the *andouillette* (tripe sausage), which was extremely popular in the 16th century. Royalist troops who were supposed to be attacking the city sat down to gorge in the *andouillette* quarter (St-Denis) and were set upon and massacred by Troyes's defenders. Even Louis the Stammerer dined on this delicacy when he was crowned in 878; it may have been responsible for his epithet.

Troyes's best restaurant is generally considered to be **Le Bourgogne**, at 40, rue du Général-de-Gaulle near the church of St-Remy. Le Bourgogne's pike mousseline and duck slivers in Bouzy are featured, as is game in season (Tel: 25-73-02-67). A pleasant choice, and more modest, is **Le Valentino** on cour de la Rencontre near the Hôtel de Ville (Tel: 25-73-14-14).

As is often the case in provincial French towns, a good hotel is right near the railway station—the **Grand** on avenue Maréchal-Joffre. It is quite reasonably priced and boasts three restaurants, each good in its category: **Le Champagne**, a formal dining room; a grill called **Jardin de la Louisiane**; and the **Pizzéria Grill Aquarius** (be warned that the pizza here may seem inexpensive at 30 francs, but the portions are quite small).

Travellers in search of really off-the-beaten-track towns and villages for overnight stops might take N 19 east for 43 km (27 miles) toward Bar-sur-Aube (itself a tranquil, stream-wreathed gem) and stop just 9 km (6 miles) northwest of the latter at the hamlet of Dolancourt and the unpretentious but comfortable, modestly priced, 16-room **Moulin du Landion**, with its own small park, mill-wheel, and cozy dining room.

There's one last piece of Champagne to visit: **Colombeyles-Deux-Eglises**, the resting place of France's greatest 20th-century soldier-statesman. Here, in his country house, La Boisserie, Charles de Gaulle died on November 9, 1970. From his study you can gaze across a rolling green landscape and read the words of the general and president: "This part of Champagne is impregnated with calm, vast, worn, and sad horizons; melancholy woods, pastures, crops, and lands lying fallow; tranquil and rather poor villages of which nothing, for a millennium, has changed the soul. . . . "

Outside town, on a rise simply called "The Mountain," a Cross of Lorraine (the general's double-barred symbol) dominates—as did the general himself—the landscape. A celebration of his memory should properly be made here. What the toast should consist of is obvious.

GETTING AROUND

The fastest way from Paris to Champagne is by train from the Gare de l'Est to Epernay; there are several a day. Those who prefer to drive a more scenic route can begin by cutting off A 4 at about Ferté-sous-Jouarre, then taking Route 3-380 via Château-Thierry.

The Champagne Road (brochures are available in English at tourist offices) is divided into three routes designated by colors: blue (the mountain of Reims), red (the Marne valley), and green (the Côte des Blancs). The blue route, about 50 miles long, departs Reims on N 31 in the direction of Epernay and passes through such villages as Rilly, Verzy, and Bouzy. The route ends in Ay (visits to Bollinger by appointment only).

The red route, 41 miles along the Marne valley, starts in Tours-sur-Marne on D 1 and winds through Hautvillers (via N 386), then past Châtillon-sur-Marne to Dormans and back to Epernay.

The green route winds for 31 miles along the Côte des Blancs from Epernay on N 51 in the direction of Troyes, then to Monthelon and Bergères-les-Vertus (via D 240 and D 9) and back to Epernay. Most of the small producers are open only by appointment, which may be arranged through tourist offices in Reims or Epernay.

The **Champagne Air Show** offers ballooning trips of one, two, or three days, with accommodations in a château hotel (15 bis, place St-Nicaise, 51100 Reims). At the same address, you can make arrangements for custom-tailored canal cruising. A two-day, one-night Spirit of Champagne bus tour for those without time to drive on their own is available from travel agents in Paris.

ACCOMMODATIONS REFERENCE

▶ **Aux Armes de Champagne.** 51460 L'Epine. Tel: 26-66-96-79; Fax: 26-66-92-31.

▶ **Auberge Saint Vincent.** 51150 **Ambonnay.** Tel: 26-57-01-98.

▶ **Boyer "Les Crayères."** 64, boulevard Vasnier, 51100 **Reims.** Tel: 26-82-80-80; Telex: 830959; Fax: 26-82-65-52; in U.S., (212) 696-1323.

▶ **La Briqueterie.** route de Sézanne, 51200 **Vinay.** Tel: 26-59-99-99; Telex: 842007; Fax: 26-59-92-10.

▶ **Grand Hôtel.** 4, avenue Maréchal Joffre, 10000 **Troyes.** Tel: 25-79-90-90; Fax: 25-78-48-93.

▶ **L'Hostellerie du Château.** 02130 **Fère-en-Tardenois.** Tel: 23-82-21-13; Telex: 145526; Fax: 23-82-37-81.

▶ **Hôtel de la Paix.** 9, rue Buirette, 51100 **Reims.** Tel: 26-40-04-08; Telex: 830974; Fax: 26-47-75-04.

▶ **Moulin du Landion.** Dolancourt, 10200 **Bar-sur-Aube.** Tel: 25-27-92-17.

▶ **Royal Champagne.** 51160 **Champillon-Bellevue.** Tel: 26-52-87-11; Telex: 830111; Fax: 26-52-89-69; in U.S., (212) 696-1323.

ALSACE-LORRAINE

By Georgia I. Hesse

The hyphen that forever binds these two distinct provinces is also what divides them: the Vosges range, a granite and sandstone spine that slices the land north to south from Wissembourg and the West German border to Belfort. The Vosges are old, comfortable mountains suited more to rambling than rappeling, to *piques-niques* than pitons. In the thick, dark forests, you would not be surprised to stumble upon Hansel and Gretel. The highest point, the Grand Ballon, rises less than 1,000 feet. More French than foreigners take time to divert themselves in this pleasant land of lakes (the largest is Gérardmer; the deepest, Blanc) by fishing, camping, swimming, boating and, in season, casual, unchallenging skiing.

The best excursion center for visitors in search of an idle idyll is Gérardmer, where you might settle down in **La Réserve** (just off the lakeside esplanade), with its one-star kitchen (try the mountain ham in a cream-Alsatian wine sauce), or the cozy 18-room **Hostellerie Bas-Rupts** in that nearby hamlet, also offering fine cooking.

West of these mountains lies the plateau of Lorraine, an expanse rich in forests, lakes, and croplands that reaches toward Champagne and the Paris basin. To the east of the Vosges is the narrow plain of Alsace, a region thick with grapevines and half-timbered villages bordered by the river Rhine and facing the homeland of those ancient antagonists the Alemanni, a tribe whose name became synonymous with *Allemagne,* the French name for Germany.

226

The late food writer Waverley Root lumped the two lands together in his so-called Domain of Fat, a happy description for today's traveller, who will find here a wealth not only of hearty cooking but also of history, natural beauty, art and architecture, local traditions and cultures, and important industries (glassmaking in the village of Baccarat in particular).

Both Celtic countries, Lorraine and Alsace have shared a lineage of conquest and liberation almost two thousand years long, from their occupation by Roman legions in 58 and 52 B.C. to the devastating battles of 1914–1918 and 1939–1945. These frequent struggles have resulted in today's resolute pride in being French, although in both cases that nationality is a surprisingly recent phenomenon. France acquired Alsace in 1648 by the Treaty of Münster (except for Strasbourg, which remained independent until 1681) and annexed Lorraine in 1766 upon the death of Stanislas Leszczyński, the former king of Poland, duke of Lorraine, and, not incidentally, father-in-law of Louis XV.

This intertwining of Germanic and Frankish inheritances gives Lorraine and, especially, Alsace much of their contemporary fascination: the village architecture, imported from beyond the Rhine, of half-timbered houses and wood-sculpted oriels (encorbelled windows) projecting over the street; the substantial Germanic peasant fare of wine-cured sausages and sauerkraut; the Rhenish art created by German masters; the folkloric costumes, songs, and pilgrimages unlike any others in France; even the traditional arts and crafts that are more closely related to those of Germany's Black Forest than to those of the Ile-de-France.

MAJOR INTEREST IN LORRAINE

Nancy
Place Stanislas
The ducal palace (Musée Historique Lorrain)
Musée des Beaux-Arts

Near Nancy
St-Nicolas-de-Port (basilica)
Toul (cathedral of St-Etienne)
Bar-le-Duc (15th-century church with macabre tomb sculpture known as *Le Squelette;* Sacred Way)
Domrémy-la-Pucelle (birthplace of Joan of Arc)

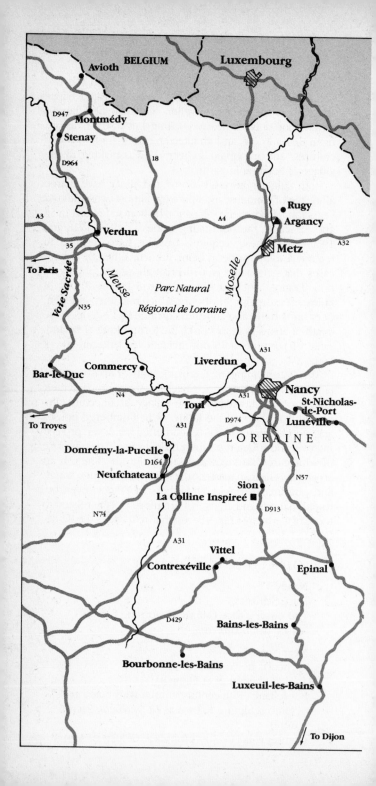

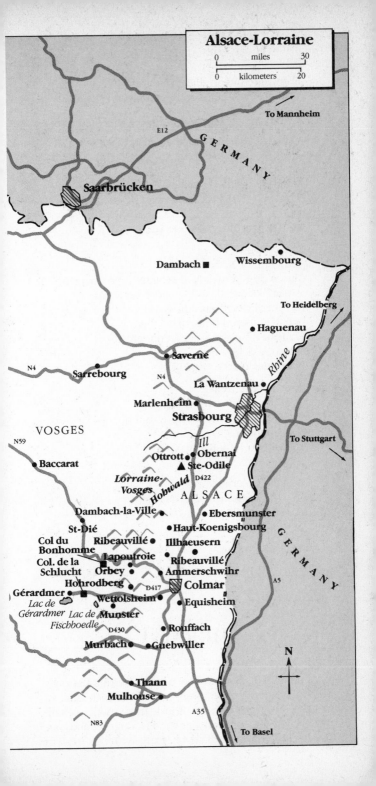

Elsewhere in Lorraine

Verdun (battlefields and monuments)

Avioth (basilica)

Metz (cathedral of St-Etienne, notable for its stained-glass windows; museums in former Carmelite convent)

Vittel area spas

Lunéville ("Little Versailles")

Baccarat (crystal museum, workshops, and sales)

MAJOR INTEREST IN ALSACE

Strasbourg

Cathedral of Notre-Dame

Musée de l'Oeuvre Notre-Dame (pre-Roman, Roman, Medieval, and Renaissance artworks)

La Petite France (ancient quarter of town, featuring half-timbered houses)

Château des Rohan and its museums

Musée Alsacien

Boat rides on the river Ill

Elsewhere in Alsace

La Route du Vin and its villages

Mont-Ste-Odile and the Hohwald region

Ebersmunster

Château du Haut-Koenigsbourg

Colmar

Musée d'Unterlinden

La Petite Venise (the old quarter)

Musée Bartholdi

Munster valley

Murbach

LORRAINE

Lorraine owes its name to the Treaty of Verdun (843), by which Charlemagne's empire—all the Christian lands of Western Europe except the British Isles, southern Italy, and Sicily—was divided among his three grandsons. Charles II (Charles the Bald, or le Chauve) took western

France, Louis II (Louis the German) the eastern territories, and Lothair I the lands in between, as well as the capitals at Rome and Aix-la-Chapelle and the title of Emperor of the West. Lothair's turf, named Lotharingia after his son and successor, has metamorphosed into modern-day Lorraine.

Lorraine boasts two major cities, Nancy and Metz. In addition to their historical, artistic, and culinary attractions, the interest of most North American and British visitors will center on the reminders of World Wars I and II: battlefields, cemeteries, memorials, and monuments.

In general, English-speaking travellers are only beginning to savor the delights and benefits of *thermalisme,* or the spa vacation, an activity enjoyed for the most part by the French and Germans.

The **Parc Naturel Régional de Lorraine**, established in 1974, caters to the health-and-fitness-conscious visitor with hiking trails, horseback riding, bicycling, picnicking, and bird-watching. Rich in lakes, ponds, and resultant bird life, the park extends between the Meuse and Moselle rivers and from about Metz in the north to Nancy and route N 4 in the south. Visitors' centers (Maisons du Parc) have been arranged to explain some important characteristics of life in Lorraine: artisan and craft activities, community arts and rural traditions, and even the production of salt, a valuable regional product.

Food is another area of interest, and excellent restaurants abound; at least three in the metropolitan area of Nancy alone rate one Michelin star, 11 in the region as a whole. Here you may sample such delicacies as *quiche Lorraine;* a hearty pork stew named *potée Lorraine* that immortalizes the great, floppy-eared Celtic breed of hog; *tourte à la Lorraine,* a fine marinated meat dish cooked in a crusty cloak; and *boudin,* or blood pudding, which the food writer Waverley Root said may be the oldest on the French menu, since it seems to have been invented in Tyre by the Assyrians.

Other regional specialties include géromé, Lorraine's most famous cheese, and Marcel Proust's muse, the *madeleine,* born in Commercy (buy some there at **Maison Grojean** on place Charles-de-Gaulle). Bar-le-Duc is renowned for its jams and jellies, particularly those made of currants.

The *vins gris* native to Lorraine are rosés, and the best come from Toul, due west of Nancy. They don't compare with the wines of Alsace but get along well with regional fare, as do the beers. Lorraine also produces several fruity *eaux-de-vie,* the finest of which is probably Mirabelle de Lorraine, distilled from plums.

Nancy is the center of Lorraine. Most excursions throughout the area can be staged from there.

NANCY

Nancy is a pretty, informal town, its people much given to ambling and café-sitting; in conversation they appear to accept—but with some resentment—the greater fame of Strasbourg. Much attention attaches to jazz, and concerts of recorded classical music are given near the ducal palace at La Pépinière.

In style, in appearance, and in essence, Nancy, the seat of the dukes of Lorraine, lives in the 18th century, the era of its master-builder, Stanislas Leszczyński. This former king of Poland was the father of Marie Leszczyńska, who wed Louis XV and became queen of France. Upon this marriage Louis installed his father-in-law as the duke of Lorraine and Bar, with the understanding that upon Stanislas's death, those lands were to pass to Marie and thus to France. And so it was.

Most of the elegant provincial city Leszczyński created remains. Forming the heart of the town is the aptly named **place Stanislas**, a rectangular public space between the Old Town and the commercial area. Originally called place Royale out of loyalty to the crown, it was once the site of a statue of Louis XV that was pulled down during the Revolution. Place Stanislas sits right on the southern edge of the **old town**, generally that area between the Arc de Triomphe (18th century, a copy of that of Septimius Severus in Rome), at the southern end of the elongated place de la Carrière, and Porte de la Craffe, to the north of the church of the Cordeliers. This old town was sheltered in the 14th century by a substantial wall, of which only the **Porte de la Craffe** remains. Until after the Revolution, the gate served as a prison; today it displays Medieval sculptures.

The harmony, the superb detailing, and the majesty of place Stanislas is the work of two talents: the architect Emmanuel Héré and Jean Lamour, the creator of the gilded wrought-iron grills that distinguish this square from any other in the country. The best and most atmospheric accommodations in town are found in the 18th-century palace right on the square, the **Grand Hôtel de la Reine**, with its **Restaurant Stanislas**. Those travellers who prefer to soothe their souls in country settings might want to try the **Hostellerie les Vannes** in the village of Liverdun, just 16 km (10 miles) north of Nancy. Poised above the languidly curving Moselle, it's an excellent restaurant with 11 rooms.

Of the superb palaces around place Stanislas, the largest is the **Hôtel de Ville**, or town hall, worth visiting for its grand architectural details, its salons, and the wide-angle view it offers over the square. The whole area is particularly evocative on summer nights, when it is outlined by floodlighting.

Beyond the Arc de Triomphe stretches the **place de la Carrière**, with its 18th-century houses flanked by handsome rows of trees and, in the background, the Palais du Gouvernement. To the right in this remarkable composition is **La Pépinière**, a garden in the style the French call English, offering promenades, a zoo, and a statue by Rodin of the painter Claude Gellée, who was better known as Claude Lorrain.

Neighboring the government palace on the east is the former ducal palace, first constructed in the late 13th century and much reworked (intelligently); it houses the **Musée Historique Lorrain,** a dusty gathering of archaeological and ethnographic items, Medieval sculptures (the most interesting displays), tapestries, furniture, and enough likenesses of the various dukes to make them seem like personal acquaintances.

Across a narrow way from the museum is the **church of the Cordeliers**, in whose crypt lie the remains of the dukes of Lorraine (and a duchess or so) in beautifully worked stone tombs; for this reason it has been likened to St-Denis, the Ile-de-France's repository of crowned heads.

The **Musée des Beaux-Arts**, right on place Stanislas, devotes itself to European paintings from the 14th century to the present, showing off such familiars as Manet, Courbet, Delacroix, Dufy, Utrillo, Perugino, Tintoretto, and Rubens. Particularly interesting in this setting is Delacroix's *Death of Charles the Bold at the Battle of Nancy;* ironically, though, native Lorraine artists such as Claude Lorrain and Georges de La Tour are well represented nowhere in town.

Just off place Stanislas, the quite modern **Capucin Gourmand** on rue Gambetta is as popular today for its Lorraine specialties as it was back in the 1950s with the wandering gourmet-writer Samuel Chamberlain. Reserve; Tel: 83-35-26-98. Now joining it as tops right in town, **Le Goéland** on rue des Ponts near the Musée Historique specializes in seafood. Reserve; Tel: 83-35-17-25.

An alternative to the Grand Hôtel de la Reine, the **Altéa Thiers** on the rue Poincaré is close to the railway station and offers a good restaurant, **La Toison d'Or**. Another recommended dining spot is **La Gentilhommière**, not far from place Stanislas on rue des Maréchaux. Tradition says Victor Hugo's ancestors dwelt upon the spot where today *filet de sole* is a specialty. (Tel: 83-32-26-44.)

Between 1871 and 1918, the city welcomed so many refugees as a result of various regional upheavals that a new Nancy grew up to the west, where you'll find (with some difficulty) the **Musée de l'Ecole de Nancy**, whose collections embody the indigenous style that became a precursor of the so-called modern French style. The museum houses an exciting collection of late 19th- and early 20th-century furniture, glassware, and faïence and other ceramics by refreshingly unfamiliar artists.

To reach this worthwhile museum, drive south on boulevard de Scarpone until it becomes rue Victor-Hugo, turn west at the church of St-Joseph and the parc Ste-Marie, and continue a short distance to rue Sergent-Blandan. The museum is a jog to the south at 38–46, rue Sergent-Blandan. On the same street as the museum, farther along at number 107, the city auction house occasionally offers interesting buys in antique furniture.

South of town proper in the small, resolutely industrial suburb of **St-Nicolas-de-Port** is—unexpectedly—a superb **basilica** in Flamboyant Gothic style, built on the site of an earlier sanctuary that once possessed a most precious ancient relic, a finger bone of Saint Nicholas. Joan of Arc knelt here to ask help on her expedition, as have faithful travellers ever since.

NEAR NANCY

Rewarding excursions of a few hours each can be made to the west and southwest of Nancy in one long day; the only practical, and the most pleasant, way to do it is by car.

Toul and Bar-le-Duc

Toul, a little city of almost 18,000 Toulois, is a short drive west of Nancy on A 31. Three centuries were devoted to the construction of its former **cathedral of St-Etienne**, which has not been returned to its former status since being severely damaged during the battles of 1940. Its façade—on the place du Parvis—and its Gothic nave are still admirable, however. It's a little east of the center of town, just inside the old ramparts.

A pleasant walk west of St-Etienne, the **church of St-Gengoult** near the place du Marché is a proud example of the Gothic school of Champagne, raised from the 13th into the 15th centuries. Most appealing is the 16th-century Flamboyant-style cloister.

Just to the east of the church on rue Michâtel, a lovely Renaissance house replete with gargoyles was the home of the 17th-century prelate Jacques Bossuet, while several other treasured Renaissance houses stand on rue de Général-Gengoult, a couple of streets west of the church.

If the luncheon hour should toll during your sojourn in Toul, consider the small but comfortable **La Belle Epoque**, on the west edge of town on avenue Victor Hugo near the Marne canal (reserve; Tel: 83-43-23-71). Try the Côtes de Toul wines, among the best in Lorraine; they are rosés, locally called *gris,* or gray. For finer fare seek out **Le Dauphin**, to the north of town in the direction of Verdun. A specialty is a *mille-feuille* of potatoes and foie gras. Reserve; Tel: 83-43-13-46.

Bar-le-Duc, west of Toul and about 75 km (45 miles) from Nancy, is only slightly larger than Toul but plays a much greater commercial role, as befits its status as a county capital more than a thousand years ago. The town boasts a fairly interesting art and archaeological museum (**Musée Barrois**) on the west side of town, but almost everybody stops only to visit the **church of St-Etienne**.

For some reason Anne de Lorraine, widow of René de Châlon, prince of Orange, commissioned one Ligier Richier to depict her husband's body in stone as the decomposed corpse it would look three years after his death (he was killed in 1544 during the siege of St-Dizier). The macabre, not to say repellent, *Le Squelette* may be seen in St-Etienne.

Equally macabre in its way is the **Voie Sacrée** (Sacred Way), that dangerous stretch of road between Bar-le-Duc and Verdun along which supply convoys rolled night and

day during the Battle of Verdun in 1916, supplying French
defenders in spite of the constant threat (and reality) of
death and destruction. To pick it up, take N 35 east from
Bar-le-Duc across the Marne canal.

Regional specialties recognized nationwide are the
seedless red currant preserves produced in Bar-le-Duc,
which are good to pack along for picnics and are available almost everywhere you look. Across the street from
the clock tower is a small, pleasant café in a former
monastery on rue François-de-Guise, **La Meuse Gour-
mande** (reserve; Tel: 29-79-28-40).

Should you wish to stay over, try the pleasant 26-room
Hôtel du Duc across the street from parc Bradfer.

Domrémy-La-Pucelle

The pilgrimage to Domrémy is made easily in a one-day
excursion southwest from Nancy via D 974 to N 74 to
Neufchâteau, then north on D 164. (The Colombey just
down the road is not De Gaulle's town; Colombey-les-
Deux-Eglises is quite a bit farther on.)

With fewer than 300 inhabitants, this village is as sleepy
today as it was in 1412 when Isabelle Romée and her
husband, Jacques d'Arc, gave birth to Joan (Jeanne in
French), the humble peasant girl who was to lead an army,
give France a king, and burn at the stake in one of history's
most famous martyrdoms. According to the historian
Frances Gies, Joan was called Jeanette in the village, and
was sometimes given her mother's surname of Romée, as
was the country custom. During her military career and for
a century afterward, however, she was known as Jeanne *la
Pucelle,* or "the Maid."

Although a peasant, Jacques d'Arc was prosperous: His
thick-walled house was built of stone in a time when most
were of timber. Restored in the 19th century to eliminate
side structures that had been added throughout the years,
it is simple, solid, unpretentious, and firm—very much
like Joan herself.

The village church has been much reworked since
Joan's day, but several vestiges the Maid would recognize
remain, the basin for holy water and the baptismal font
among them.

About a mile away, the **basilica of Bois-Chenu**, consecrated in 1926, rises rather pretentiously above the spot
where Joan heard the voices that inspired her mission,
those of saints Catherine, Marguerite, and Michael.

Joan's story has inspired the French for half a millennium; Charles de Gaulle adopted the Cross of Lorraine as the emblem of a Free France besieged.

Domrémy really has no dining spot to recommend; best to return to Neufchâteau to try the restaurant of the **St-Christophe** hotel on the avenue de la Grande-Fontaine or the unpretentious **L'Amie Lune** on rue Neuve.

Travellers interested in Roman antiquities should inquire at the local Syndicat d'Initiative near the post office in Neufchâteau for directions to **Grand**, despite its name a minute village not located on maps, about 23 km (14 miles) west of Neufchâteau. Here there are many ruins and excavations, including the largest mosaic in France, in the town's basilica.

VERDUN

In 1916 Verdun, about 110 km (67 miles) northwest of Nancy, was, along with Toul, the most stubborn French stronghold. Its strategic position had commanded battle lines since the days of the Gauls and then the Romans, under whom it was called Virodunum Castrum.

To visit today the sites where hundreds of thousands of soldiers from both sides died in the epic struggle of World War I is to look back in sadness. That may be why, as years pass and fewer of the dead remain living in memory, fewer foreign visitors make this particular pilgrimage.

The **Citadelle**, in the heart of town near the cathedral of Notre-Dame, was the work of perhaps the most renowned military architect in Europe since the days of the Romans, Sébastien le Prestre de Vauban (1633–1707). In his characteristic star-within-star design (the best example of which is in Lille), the Citadelle sits atop the remains of a tenth-century abbey, houses a **war museum**, and gives access to the famous tunnels that once sheltered the defensive army.

For anyone who wishes to survey the theater of combat from the air, Verdun's Aero-Club de Rozelier organizes flights over the battlefields; inquire at the Office de Tourisme on place Nation.

Just beyond town on the right bank of the Meuse—the "Red Zone" of the battle—drive first to the military cemetery of Faubourg-Pavé (from which the body of one Unknown Soldier was taken to lie beneath the Arc de Triomphe in Paris), then to the monument of the **Maginot Line** and to the Fort de Vaux, a fortification that held out for almost three months against the German onslaughts of 1916. More interesting than Vaux itself are the nearby **Museum of the Battle of Verdun** and the sparse ruins of the village of Fleury, which was captured and recaptured 26 times.

Housing the bones of men killed here, the **Ossuaire de Douaumont**, near the Fort de Douaumont (about 21 km/ 13 miles northeast of Verdun), is the most important World War I memorial in France and is dedicated to the 400,000 French soldiers who died in this one battle. On the left bank of the Meuse is the **American Cemetery of Romagne-sous-Montfaucon**, which contains more than 14,000 tombs in an eerily peaceful setting.

Verdun may well be explored in one long day out of Metz; otherwise, a good hotel choice is the **Hostellerie Coq Hardi**, well regarded for decades, with its excellent restaurant featuring regional specialties. Reserve; Tel: 29-86-36-36.

Avioth

North of Verdun about 40 km (25 miles) via country roads, near the Belgian border, you come upon the hamlet (108 inhabitants) of Avioth. More truthfully, you don't come upon it without some effort, since its name rarely appears except on large-scale regional maps. From Verdun, follow D 964 north to Stenay, angle east on D 947 to Montmédy, and pick up directional signs to Avioth, 8 km (5 miles) to the north of Montmédy.

Those who persist in search of hidden treasures will be rewarded by a magnificent **basilica** founded in the 13th century, some 200 years after the discovery of a miraculous statue of the Virgin Mary at the site. Construction continued for another 200 years or so. Were the stones then as warm and golden in hue as they appear today? Who knows? Gilded in soft late-afternoon light, the 70 figures of the Passion seem harmonious and real, as if they had been frozen alive and preserved throughout time, the little angels sounding their trumpets down the centuries.

METZ

Metz, a city of about 118,000 citizens (known as Messins), has been important almost forever—or at least since the sixth-century days of the Merovingian ruler Theodoric I, the son of Clovis I and king of Metz. Under Sigibert I and his famous wife, Brunhild, Metz became the capital of Austrasia, one of the two major Merovingian kingdoms, the other being Neustria (with Soissons as its capital).

Today this port on the Moselle river north of Nancy is an industrial town, but a less grim one than most of its northern neighbors. Metz's major attractions are churches, of which it boasts an inordinate number for its size, and museums. In mid-November it plays host to an international festival of contemporary music that leans toward New Age.

The treasures of Metz can be appreciated during a one-day round trip from Nancy. If you prefer to spend the night, try one of two major hotels in town—**Novotel** and **Altéa St-Thiébault**—or the very pleasant 40-room **La Bergerie**, in a 16th-century house 12 km (7.5 miles) to the north in Rugy.

The nave of Metz's Gothic **cathedral of St-Etienne** soars highest in France after those of St-Pierre in Beauvais and Notre-Dame in Amiens. While the exterior is very richly detailed, it is the interior, with its stunning ensemble of stained glass ranging from the 13th and 14th centuries up to the 20th, including the creations of Marc Chagall, that makes the church remarkable. Because of the glass, the cathedral has been nicknamed the Lantern of God. The building's curious design results from the 12th-century linking together of two churches, Notre-Dame-la-Ronde and St-Etienne, across a tiny road. Most of old Metz lies east of a spur of the Moselle river, arranging itself (as is so often the case) around the cathedral. If you feel faint after exploring the cathedral, drop into the very traditional **La Ville de Lyon** nearby at 7, rue des Piques. (Try the *crêpes Suzette*.) Also nearby, on place d'Armes, is the Regional Tourism Office.

Four museums are housed in a 17th-century Carmelite convent and its adjoining grain storage shed and several outbuildings. Premier among them, the **Musée d'Art et d'Histoire** is a treasure trove of relics from archaeological digs in the region that have revealed the importance of this Gallo-Roman crossroads town, which became a center of culture under the Carolingians. Exhibits include evidence of the Romans' skill in engineering baths and sewers.

The three other museums are Beaux-Arts (paintings, engravings, polychrome wood statues); a military collection; and a natural history and zoological collection. The convent is located behind St-Etienne off the rue du Chèvremont.

In good weather, stroll around the **Esplanade**, the adjoining place de la République, and the banks of an offshoot of the Moselle river called **Lac des Cygnes** (Swan Lake), where, on Friday, Saturday, and Sunday evenings in summer a *son-et-lumière* performance is staged.

Near the Esplanade is **St-Pierre-aux-Nonnains**; thought to be the oldest church in France, it was founded by a Benedictine abbey in the seventh century on the site of a fourth-century Roman edifice. Visiting the church usually requires the permission of the Regional Tourism Office.

Toward the end of August and beginning of September, singers and dancers in folk costumes and decorated carts march in the Fête de Mirabelle to celebrate the little plum from which the fiery liqueur is made.

A very pleasant place for dining in Metz is **La Dinanderie**, 2, rue de Paris, on an island between the Moselle and one of its canals. Reserve; Tel: 87-30-14-40.

VITTEL AND OTHER SPAS

"Taking the waters," or *thermalisme,* in the European sense remains a pastime little known to most North Americans and Australians in their own countries but is slightly more familiar to the British. The current dieting fad favoring fancy bottled waters has made the name Vittel popular with outsiders who know their waters if not their spas. Wanderers have come here to cure various ills since the days of the Romans; when those bath-happy occupiers departed the springs were forgotten, to be rediscovered only as recently as 1845.

The plains and uplands of the Vosges south of Nancy are rich in healing springs both cold and hot, and the waters emerge both with and without natural carbonation.

Of the spa towns—Vittel, nearby Contrexéville, Bains-les-Bains, Bourbonne-les-Bains, and Luxeuil-les-Bains—Vittel is the largest (with 6,500 or so permanent residents) and the best known, and offers the possibility of tours and tastings at the bottling factory. The Foire aux Grenouilles (Frog Fair) in Vittel takes place the last weekend in April.

The best hotels, however, are in **Contrexéville**, a favorite retreat of Stanislas Leszczyński. Tops are the 29-room **Grand Hôtel Etablissement** next to the baths, with its good **Grill Relais Stanislas**, and the 81-room **Cosmos** near the park. There is something quaint, turn-of-the-

century, self-consciously healthful, and studiously manicured about spa villages like Contrexéville. They offer a
slightly skewed version of French life that is overlooked
by many foreigners.

La Colline Inspirée

About halfway along the Nancy–Vittel route that begins as
D 913, a detour of a few miles to the west brings you to
Sion and La Colline Inspirée, or Hill of Inspiration, a
lonely place sacred to the gods of war and peace where
prayers have been offered up for more than two thousand years.

Celts worshiped here first in what must have been all
but total seclusion. Since then the hill has been a pilgrimage site for followers of the Crusades, those liberated
from German domination, the faithful freed of the Prus-
sian yoke, the French writer Maurice Barrès (who gave
the spot its name), enthusiasts of French unity, and, in
1973's Peace Festival, thousands of former prisoners of
Nazi concentration camps.

Atop the hill (actually a crescent-shaped limestone
mesa), three sites are worth a short visit: the archaeological museum in the hamlet of Sion, where the history of
the spot is outlined; the Signal de Vaudémont, an overlook above the Lorraine plateau with an orientation chart;
and the ruins of the 11th-century Château de Vaudémont,
cradle of the family of the dukes of Lorraine. There is
even an unpretentious hotel, the 15-room **Notre Dame** in
Sion, where you can have a modest meal.

Epinal

East of Vittel en route to Alsace is Epinal, home to the
**Musée Départemental des Vosges et Musée International
de l'Imagerie**, which houses local Roman and Gallo-
Roman works, including a very fine mosaic, Medieval
sculptures, and exhibitions of daily private life in the
Vosges region. There are also a few outstanding paintings,
many drawings, and a display of the history of printmaking from the Middle Ages to the present.

On the Wednesday before Easter the children of Epinal
draw lighted boats along a large pond near the Hôtel de
Ville for the Fête des Champs-Golots; during June there is
an international printmaking festival.

EN ROUTE TO ALSACE

The great Stanislas died in 1766 at **Lunéville** in the château that became known as "Little Versailles," which now contains a museum of faïence. The château presents a *son-et-lumière* show in its chapel for large groups only (30 or more) with advance reservations.

Baccarat's crystal factory was established in 1764 and has been making news and quality glassware ever since. A visit to the Musée du Cristal makes the most nonacquisitive traveller acquisitive. Old and new pieces are on display, their production is extremely well documented, and a sales shop lies conveniently at hand.

St-Dié in its little valley at the feet of pine-studded hills grew up around a seventh-century Benedictine monastery and today calls itself, with some pride, the "birthplace of America." U.S. citizens aware of the association usually make their way on arrival in town to the Bibliothèque Municipale near the cathedral and its Gothic cloister and ask to be directed to the rare 16th-century book, *Cosmographiae Introductio,* a kind of early atlas.

In the *Cosmographiae,* a work of Vosgian academics, credit is given to Amerigo Vespucci for the discovery of a new continent and the word "America" is inscribed upon a map of it for the first time.

From St-Dié, southeast of Baccarat on N 59, the most direct route to Alsace winds over the Col du Bonhomme and through the villages of Lapoutroie and Kaysersberg to Colmar. An alternate route to Colmar via the summer resort of **Gérardmer** and its lake is more scenic, winding over the Col de la Schlucht through some of the prettiest Vosges countryside. On the Sunday nearest April 20, Gérardmer stages its Jonquil Festival, with various musical groups parading through the beflowered town. A giant fireworks display lights up the night and the lake in mid-August.

ALSACE

France's most distinctive and, to some eyes, most picturesque province is a green corridor 120 miles long and

32 miles wide wedged between Lorraine to the west, Germany to the north and east, and Switzerland to the southeast.

A long history of independent kingdoms, duchies, and other regional entities constitutes one of France's greatest attractions: her deep and lasting variety. Within that diversity Alsace seems still foreign, a land unto itself, with its own culture, cooking, architecture, tradition, even language.

Even more than Lorraine's, Alsace's history is one of turmoil and tempest between Germanic and Frankish peoples. Though Alsatians today are proudly French, their inheritance is strongly Germanic; witness the Alsatian dialect, which sounds something like Swiss-German and offends or amuses the ears of almost everyone who doesn't speak it. The name Alsace itself derives from *Illsass,* the dialect word meaning "country of the Ill river."

Alsatian Food and Drink

There is an earthiness, a naturalness, a refreshing absence of vanity to eating and drinking in Alsace. That is not to say there is no *haute cuisine* to be found, however. One of France's 19 Michelin-ranked three-star restaurants, **L'Auberge de l'Ill**, in Illhaeusern (reserve well in advance; Tel: 89-71-83-23), is considered by many epicures the finest in the country. In 1989 Strasbourg's Le Crocodile was elevated to equal stardom (see below). There are four places with two-star ratings, and single stars are scattered about like storks' nests.

The province's specialties are soul- as well as stomach-satisfying: the irresistible *choucroute,* wine-cured sauerkraut buried under ham hocks, sausages, smoked bacon, pork slabs, and potatoes; the fatted goose that yields up its liver as foie gras, giving gastronomy *pâté de foie gras en croute;* roasted suckling pig; fried carp and game; *tarte à l'oignon; kugelhopf,* a large, breadlike cake resembling a Teuton prince's crown; *tuiles,* thin, delicate pastry sheets shaped like roof tiles; *tartes mirabelles,* employing a small, rosy plum; fir-tree honey; and creamy Munster cheese.

Vines have been cultivated in Alsace since A.D. 222. Unlike the standard procedure in Bordeaux, Burgundy, and elsewhere, wines here are labeled after the grape: Sylvaner, Pinot (*blanc* and *noir* and even *gris*), Riesling, Muscat, Traminer, Chasselas. Gewürztraminer means simply a spicy (*gewürz*) Traminer; Tokay d'Alsace is a Pinot

Gris; a table wine of blended grapes is called Zwicker, and a Zwicker of blended fine grapes is Edelzwicker. The sparkling Crémant d'Alsace is made by the *méthode champenoise* from the Pinot Blanc or Riesling grape. Rosé d'Alsace is rather well known, but Alsatian reds from Ottrott and Marlenheim are rare.

In 1975 legislation created the *Grand Cru* appellation in Alsace, and it has been awarded to 25 vineyards. In 1984 late-harvest wines—*Vendanges Tardives*—were recognized. Deep and rich in flavor, they are reminiscent of heavy Sauternes. Even more rare is the sweet *Sélection des Grains Nobles,* produced only in great years from individually selected grapes affected by "noble rot," the fungus mold *Botrytis cinerea,* which enhances their flavor. The *eaux-de-vie* (brandy-like liqueurs) are forceful but refined. Best known are *framboise* (raspberry), *mirabelle* (plum), *kirsch* (cherry), and *myrtille* (blueberry). The Gilbert Miclo Distillery in Lapoutroie, on the route from St-Dié to Colmar, makes the best.

France is much less renowned for its beers than its wines, but Kronenbourg, an Alsatian brew, is widely known and one of the best commercial brands.

Every day of the week except Sunday it's market day somewhere in Alsace. Patricia Wells, the author of *The Food Lover's Guide to France,* reports that the liveliest take place on Wednesdays in Gérardmer; Fridays in Haguenau and Strasbourg; and Saturdays in Colmar, Mulhouse, Munster, Strasbourg, and Wissembourg.

In late April to early May the Foire de Printemps (Spring Fair) is held in Strasbourg, and in Wissembourg an international folkfest is staged in June. In June Ribeauvillé puts on its Fête du Kugelhopf, while Saverne holds its Festival de la Rose. Orbey's Fête de la Tarte au Fromage (cheese tart) takes place from late June to early July. Hoff's Fête du Fromage Blanc et des Traditions Rurales (white cheese and folklore) is held in August; Ribeauvillé's Foire aux Vins et Fête Folklorique in July; Thann's Fête de la Poitrine Farcie (stuffed veal breast) in July; Haguenau's Fête du Houblon et Semaine Gastronomique (hops festival and food week) in August; Colmar's Foire aux Vins et Représentations Folkloriques in August; and Obernai's Fête des Vendanges (grape harvest) in October.

The city of Strasbourg is the principal gateway for trips in the Alsace region. The Route du Vin runs south from near

Strasbourg past Obernai, Colmar, then the Munster Valley and on down to Thann, near Mulhouse and the Swiss border.

STRASBOURG

Strataburgum, as its Roman name suggests, has been a European crossroads since its founding.

The capital of Alsace, seat of the Council of Europe since its foundation in 1949, and one of the three capitals of the European Parliament (the other two are Luxembourg and Brussels), Strasbourg is resolutely international and business-minded in outlook and focus. Yet as former mayor Marcel Rudloff put it, "We *Strasbourgeois* are sometimes accused of being too attached to the past ... if you pass by our cathedral you will understand why we cannot help feeling attached to such a glorious background."

Doubtless it is evidence of that "glorious background" that the foreign traveller seeks out, but the sense of vitality and contemporary busyness comes as a dividend.

Born in 10 B.C. as Argentoratum, the Roman stronghold that is now Strasbourg was renamed Strataburgum under Clovis, king of the Franks, and developed into a major crossroads of commerce, warfare, and Christianity. In the sixth century Scottish monks began to worship on the site of today's church of St-Thomas, where Albert Schweitzer once served as an organist.

In the 11th century Strasbourg came under the rule of the Hapsburgs, and during the Crusades Frederick Barbarossa had many fortresses and convents built in the region; in 1201 Strasbourg was sanctioned as a free city of the Holy Roman Empire.

From 1336 onward the privilege of staging an annual European fair was granted to Strasbourg, and it is still held here, during the first half of September. The 14th century also saw the city become a center of Rhenish mysticism and then, in the 15th and 16th centuries, a capital of humanism and Protestantism.

Johann Gutenberg perfected the printing press in Strasbourg between 1434 and 1444. A statue of him commands today's **place Gutenberg**; the American Declaration of Independence is for some reason engraved on its pedestal.

In 1681 Louis XIV brought Strasbourg under French

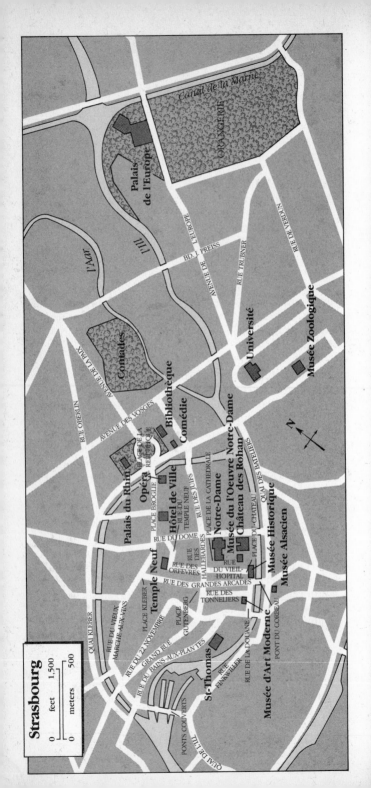

rule; in 1871 it was ceded to Germany, but in 1919 it again became French; in 1940 the Germans claimed it, and held it until 1944, when it was once again declared part of France.

Strasbourg is the sixth-largest city in the country and the second-largest port on the Rhine (Rotterdam being the largest). It's also the seat of several international institutions: the European Court of Human Rights, the European Youth Center, the European Foundation of Science, the International Institute of Human Rights, the Central Committee for Rhine Navigation, and the International Faculty of Comparative Law.

Strasbourg accords great importance to music, staging the **International Music Festival**, Europe's oldest, in June. In addition to enjoying concerts by the Strasbourg Philharmonic and the Percussions of Strasbourg, travellers may be seduced by performances by the Opera of the Rhine, Strasbourg National Theater, Rhine Ballet, Alsatian Theater, and the satirical cabaret Barabli.

A flea market is held Wednesdays and Saturdays on the rue du Vieil-Hôpital.

The heart of old Strasbourg is an egg-shaped parcel of land cradled within the arms of the River Ill and its canals. At its western end, the quays, canals, and half-timbered houses of La Petite France doze in a picturesque haze of nostalgia, while on the east, beyond the place Broglie, the Théâtre Municipal, and the Hôtel de Ville, bridges link the old city to the Germanic 19th century across the river.

Beginning in about 1870, the Germans erected grand public buildings in an attempt to create a new city center. Here is the large, beautifully gardened place de la République, with its two wings of the Palace of the Rhine on one side and the Théâtre Nationale and Bibliothèque Nationale on the other. The same area includes the place de l'Université and the university buildings, the gardens of the Orangerie, the Palais de Congrès and Palais de l'Europe, and the great port of the Rhine (known as Le Port Autonome; excursions available).

Inside the oval, most major attractions are within ambling distance of one another: place Kléber, somewhat off-center; the cathedral of Notre-Dame and a cluster of museums to the southwest, right off the river; and several worthwhile churches in the western half of the city.

In Strasbourg, regularly scheduled boat sailings on the Ill depart the Château des Rohan every half hour in summer, both day and night. Less frequent but longer sailings on the Rhine depart from the promenade Dauphine. Except in midwinter, minitrains take visitors on a 45-minute-tour that begins near the cathedral, with commentary in English, French, or German.

The Cathedral Quarter

Notre-Dame will stop zealous cathedral visitors in their tracks. Begun in the Romanesque style in 1015 on the site of a temple to Hercules, it was not declared finished until 1439, by which time it had become mostly—and superbly—Gothic.

Strasbourg's life has been intimately entwined with that of its cathedral. Martin Luther's 95 theses were posted here as well as on the church door in Wittenberg, Germany, and during the ensuing Reformation (1520–1689), Strasbourg became a center of the Protestant movement; Protestants and Catholics battled beneath the 14th-century Wise and Foolish Virgins sculpted on the church's right-hand portal. Only in 1681, when the city was seized by Louis XIV, was its cathedral returned to Catholicism.

It was here, in 1725, that Louis XV married Marie Leszczyńska, and here, too, in 1770, that Marie Antoinette arrived from Vienna en route to her marriage to the future Louis XVI. At the same time, a university student named Johann Wolfgang von Goethe was climbing to the top of the tower and looking woozily into space in an attempt to cure his dizzy spells.

In addition to its famous spire and façade, Notre-Dame's treasures include 12th- to 14th-century stained-glass windows (the finest were removed, piece by piece, during World War II, and found afterward buried in salt mines in Wurtemberg), the pulpit in Flamboyant Gothic style, the 17th-century tapestries, and the **astronomical clock**. The clock runs slow by half an hour and now goes through its daily noon celebrations at 12:30 P.M. Crowds assemble to watch at least half an hour in advance.

A *son-et-lumière* production in the cathedral illustrates Strasbourg's two thousand years of history every night except certain annual holidays; the program is given in German at 8:15 P.M. and in French at 9:15 P.M.

Across the leafy place du Château is the **Musée de l'Oeuvre Notre-Dame**, which is devoted to Alsatian arts from the Middle Ages and Renaissance, original sculptures from the cathedral (because of weather damage, many of the pink sandstone figures have had to be replaced), Roman and pre-Roman sculptures, and paintings of the Alsatian School. The most celebrated item is a head of Christ, the oldest figure known in stained glass (1070).

Also across the place du Château is the **Château des Rohan**, constructed in 1704 for Cardinal Armand de Rohan-Soubise, bishop of Strasbourg. It now houses the Musée des Beaux-Arts, the Musée Archéologique, and the Musée des Arts Décoratifs.

Renaissance painters and primitives of the Italian school are particularly well represented in the **Beaux-Arts**, with less emphasis on the Spanish (aside from a wonderful El Greco Virgin) and the Dutch-Flemish (but one superb Pieter de Hooch). The collection of still lifes is highly touted.

The **Musée Archéologique** devotes itself largely to prehistoric discoveries made in Alsace but also has fine displays of Roman and Merovingian relics. The finest grouping of ceramics in France is on show at **Arts Décoratifs**, including fine faïence from 18th-century Strasbourg, the best of which comes from the famous "blue" period. In addition to the museums, the château houses a stamp and art library.

Just off the place de la Cathédrale, the **Hôtel des Rohan** offers 36 stylish rooms furnished in Louis XV fashion or regional rustic decor, but with up-to-date conveniences and even minibars. The clientele is one that appreciates quiet and restrained surroundings and scorns both the prices and the activity of the town's top-rated hotels. Nonetheless, Rohan is surrounded by cathedral and bistro noise and bustle; guests who are bothered by such things should inquire about rooms away from the street.

Good restaurants in varying degrees of informality cluster near the cathedral, of which **Maison Kammerzell** (built between 1467 and 1589) is the best known, largely because of its stunning woodwork. It is a fine place in which to sample regional specialties (reserve; Tel: 88-32-42-14). Old Alsatian decor and quiet characterize **Zimmer**, a perennial favorite with the Strasbourgeois that is located at 8, rue du Temple Neuf.

Winstubs, historic, informal places suited to settling the world's problems over long lunches of traditional fare, abound in the cathedral quarter. The best are **Strissel**, 5, place de la Grande-Boucherie; **Tire-Bouchon**, 5, rue des Tailleurs-de-Pierres; and **Au Pigeon**, 23, rue des Tonneliers, an amiably rustic spot that has been in business since the Middle Ages.

Three top *winstubs* that cater more to tourists are the

brasserie-like **Le Dauphin**, right across from Notre-Dame; **Aux Armes de Strasbourg**, 9, place Gutenberg, with the best French fries in town; and **L'Ancienne Douane**, 6, rue de la Douane, which has a terrace overlooking the Ill. (*Winstubs* and brasseries are alike in their informality, simplicity of traditional fare served, and coziness in cold weather. Originally, as their names imply, *winstubs* were directly in or connected to individual wineries, while brasseries bore the same relationship to breweries. Today they usually have no physical relationship to a production site but may serve chiefly one brand of drink.)

Of the many *bierstubs,* currently the best is **Les Douze Apôtres** on rue Mercière, where special brews from around the world are served. The same street also boasts the city's most elegant *salon de thé* (tearoom), **Christian**.

The winding streets to the northwest of Notre-Dame are chic shopping country; Strasbourg is one of the smartest of French cities as far as style is concerned. Particularly attractive are the rue des Hallebardes, rue du Dôme, and rue des Orfèvres, this last gaily decorated with banners representing the cities and regions of Alsace. Gastronomic souvenirs, specially packaged—foie gras, sausages, *choucroute,* cheeses, mustards, honey, chocolates, wines, and liqueurs—are found in rich plenty at places on the rue des Orfèvres.

On the north bank of the Ill, the **Musée Historique** (in the 16th-century slaughterhouse) and the **Musée d'Art Moderne** (in the reconstructed custom house) face each other across the bustling rue des Grandes Arcades. The former is fascinating to visitors interested in arms, armory, uniforms, and other trappings of war; the latter to enthusiasts of modern French painting, including works by Jean Arp, a Strasbourgeois, and stained glass by such makers as Jean Lurçat.

Across the Ill via the Pont du Corbeau, a pleasant bridge from which child murderers and parricides were suspended in iron cages until they drowned, is the **Musée Alsacien**. Occupying three adjoining 16th- and 17th-century houses, it displays to perfection the Alsatian past in costumes, bedchambers, and kitchens—all the essentials of everyday life.

La Petite France

Once upon a time tanners, fishermen, and millers made this quarter in the western part of the old town their own.

Now, with its narrow streets that wind along the Ill and its canals lined by beautiful 16th- and 17th-century half-timbered houses, La Petite France is the most picturesque part of Strasbourg. The excellent restaurants and small art and gift shops of the district attract a sizable permanent population as well as a touristic one.

The "main" street of this quarter is the rue du Bain-aux-Plantes, but all are worth strolling before taking a little nourishment at **La Maison des Tanneurs**, a restaurant in perhaps the prettiest of the old houses that offers a warm welcome and excellent regional cooking, including *choucroute au Champagne* (reserve; Tel: 88-32-79-70).

Spanning the Ill and what remains of the ancient ramparts are the **Ponts Couverts**, three bridges each topped with a 14th-century tower. Convenient to this point of architectural and historical interest is a good, informal *bierstub-winstub* called **L'Ami Schutz**. Of the several other welcoming retreats in the neighborhood, the most attractive, because of its curious *orgue de Barbarie* (an antique player-piano), is **Lohkäs**. Students in winter and tourists in summer pack the four-story restaurant **Au Pont St-Martin** to enjoy the large terrace and panoramic view.

Behind the Ponts Couverts, a *péniche* (moored barge) serves as a floating disco known as **La Péniche-Le Fantasc**, which draws an older crowd than the Club des Moulins.

Place Kléber

Although it is the commercial heart of the city, place Kléber is nonetheless quite handsome. In the square's center is a statue of a local boy who made good, Général Jean-Baptiste Kléber, born here in 1753 and assassinated in Cairo in 1800. On the statue's base are carved the words with which he replied to an English admiral's suggestion of surrender: "Soldiers, one responds to such insolence only with victories."

A giant parking garage underneath place Kléber is the best place to park while you explore the city. On the north side of the square the enormous 18th-century **Aubette** supplies a cafeteria, a travel agency, a tourist shop, and an American Express office.

An easy amble to the east and west are two of the town's top epicurean retreats, **Le Crocodile**, where owner-chef Emile Jung was awarded his third Michelin star in 1989 (sure to be more heavily booked than ever; reserve well in advance; Tel: 88-32-13-02), and **Valentin Sorg**, which offers classic cuisine and a superb view from the 14th floor of a rather off-putting skyscraper.

Just off the *place,* the **Nouvel Hôtel Maison Rouge** is comfortably old-fashioned in appearance and atmosphere, though guest rooms were renovated not long ago. In the middle of the local price range, it is very handily located for people who like to walk.

Strasbourg's **Hilton Hotel** is just as modern and well outfitted as you might imagine, though rather more than a stroll from the center of town. It offers all the comforts of home and some particular amenities for business people and small meetings, and its dining room, **La Maison du Boeuf** (reserve; Tel: 88-37-10-10), ranks highly even in this city full of good restaurants; rates are as up-to-date as the design.

The **Hôtel Terminus-Gruber**, right across the place de la Gare from the railway station, is the choice of travellers who like their inns elegantly turned out in the Old World manner yet unpretentious and welcoming. The **Cour de Rosemont** dining room is also quite good.

Strasbourg University and l'Orangerie

Strasbourg's vitality stems in great part from its university, since its founding in the 17th century one of the foremost in France. Perhaps among its 35,000 students today there is another Goethe, a Napoléon, or a Metternich. A drive around the university and its handsome gardens—and perhaps a stop at its Musée Zoologique—is a pleasant detour en route to the **Palais de l'Europe**.

The palais is home to both the Council of Europe (21 member states) and the European Parliament (434 members representing more than 270 million people). Guided tours are offered to the public.

Neighboring the Palais is the **Orangerie**, a park laid out by the famous garden architect André le Nôtre in 1692. A walk through its handsome gardens is preparation for a meal at the beautifully sited and two-starred **Buerehiesel** (reserve; Tel: 88-61-62-24), where chef Antoine Westermann serves highly rated cuisine in a rustic, traditional Alsatian house. He ranks among the Maîtres Cuisiniers de France (master chefs), as does his colleague Jung at the aforementioned Le Crocodile.

LA ROUTE DU VIN

A drive down the 100-mile so-called wine road from **Marlenheim** in the north (due west of Strasbourg) to **Thann** in the south ranks among the most intriguing excursions in Europe. People have been known to do it in one day, but they can't have been satisfied with that. Three days should be the minimum.

En route, wine tasting and/or tours are offered at many vineyards. Stops are recommended in Barr at **Maison Willm** (Klevner de Heiligenstein from the rare Sauvignan rosé grape would be an interesting buy); in Eguisheim at **Léon Beyer** (family-owned vineyards since 1580—standouts are the Cuvée des Comtes Gewürtzminer and Cuvée des Ecaillers Riesling); in Kaysersberg at **Mme. Theo Faller et Ses Filles** (consider the Tokey-Pinot Gris); in Ribeauvillé at **F.-E. Trimbach** (try the Reislings); and in Riquewihr at **Dopff Au Moulin** (try the late harvest wines) and **Hugel et Fils** (try the late harvest and Grains Nobles vintages).

Every twist and turn of the road seems to demand a stop for photographing hill-climbing vineyards, Renaissance town halls and oriels, busy markets, Medieval walls, châteaux in ruins and various states of disrepair, Romanesque clock towers, Gothic churches, streets dressed in brilliant flowers, folk festivals, and shop windows full of good things to eat and drink. **Riquewihr** would be the most provocative village along the route—were it not for the horrendous crowds that throng through the tiny, irresistibly picturesque streets. Try to arrive out of season and lunch at **Au Petit Gourmet**.

Ribeauvillé, generally considered among the most picturesque of the villages, is the home of the prestigious, 150-year-old **Manufacture d'Impression sur Etoffes**, a textile firm that has printed fabrics for the Galeries Lafayette department store chain and specialized boutiques in France, as well as for Neiman-Marcus, Bergdorf Goodman, and Bullocks Wilshire. Their tablecloths and napkins, extremely well priced on the site, are available at the factory outlet store; walk down Grand'Rue past the 13th-century Tour des Bouchers and go a few hundred feet toward Ste-Marie-aux-Mines.

Only 30 km (19 miles) southeast of Strasbourg, the picturesque town of **Obernai** is becoming a headquarters for growing numbers of travellers who eschew the big city by night, preferring the atmospheric quiet of the countryside. It boasts as many handsome half-timbered houses as do the smaller villages and, in the seventh century, was the birthplace of Saint Odile, patron saint of Alsace. Among the several recommended hotels, best are the tranquil, 30-room, moderately-expensive **A la Cour d'Alsace**, or, in a less expensive but still-comfortable category, the **Diligence, Résidence Exquisit et Bel Air**, with a total of 46 rooms and four apartments.

Look for the traditional pottery, glassware, and wooden handicrafts of Alsace at **Dietrich's** on the attractive place du Marché.

Tradition lives in **Turckheim**, outside Colmar, where at 10:00 on summer evenings the last night watchman extant in Alsace passes through quiet streets in his greatcoat, carrying halberd, lamp, and trumpet and calling out the hour and "All's well."

Dining throughout the region is universally good; especially recommended are:

- **Hostellerie du Cerf** (Marlenheim)
- **Beau Site** (Ottrott-le-Haut)
- **Le Clos St-Vincent** (Ribeauvillé)
- **Résidence Chambard** (Kaysersberg, hometown of Albert Schweitzer)
- **Aux Armes de France** (Ammerschwihr)
- **Auberge du Père Floranc** (Wettolsheim, where winegrowing began in Roman times)
- **Le Caveau** (Eguisheim)
- **Château d'Isenbourg** (Rouffach)
- **Résidence les Violettes** (Guebwiller–Jungholtz)

All but Le Caveau are also inns, for those wanting to sleep off a surfeit of *terrine de foie gras au vieux Gewürztraminer.*

At least nine routes in addition to the Route du Vin have been designed for travellers with special interests: Route des Crêtes (mountaintop road); Route Fleurie (for those interested in gardens, parks, decorated homes); Route de la Plaine et des Forêts (North Vosges regional park, local color and folklore); a l'Assaut des Vieux Châteaux (Assault on Old Castles—for enthusiasts of Medieval ruins); and others devoted to open spaces, tobacco, cheese, liqueurs, and even fried carp. (See Getting Around at the end of this chapter.)

There are other places and items of interest in Alsace

besides the Route du Vin, of course; we cover them parallel to this route, from Strasbourg, at the northern end of Alsace, running southward through Colmar toward Thann and Mulhouse.

MONT STE-ODILE

Something about the deep green, worn old Vosges inspires brooding, and a good place to indulge in that lonesome mood is this mount, southwest of Strasbourg, dedicated to the patron saint of Alsace.

Away to the south of the **convent of Ste-Odile**, the so-called **pagan wall** curves through the forests. This wall of immense stone blocks once must have belted a camp, a fortification of some sort, in the days before French memory. Was it Gallic? Was it Celtic? Nobody knows, but it makes the Roman road nearby look positively new.

The setting is a fine one for the telling of the tale of Odile, a blind and weak child born in the seventh century in the village of Obernai just down the hill. She was the daughter of the sullen and loathsome Duke Adalric, a.k.a. Etichon, who, because of Odile's miserable condition and because she was, in any case, a girl, ordered her put to death.

The story twists and turns like today's road up the mountain. Suffice it to say the wicked Etichon lost in the war of life; Odile won and founded a convent in her father's château, Hohenbourg. She also established the abbey of Niedermunster, which served after her death and throughout the Middle Ages as a great pilgrimage site. In the 16th century a fire destroyed most of the antique structures; these were replaced in the 17th century, but an 11th-century chapel survived, and there the ashes of Etichon remain; those of Odile repose nearby in an eighth-century stone sarcophagus.

A day may be spent happily driving south of Mont Ste-Odile in the **Hohwald** (the name means "high woods") glimpsing old châteaux and monasteries in the forests, coming upon neat villages, and slowing down for the views that on clear days stretch to Switzerland's Bernese Alps.

When night comes on, you might stay at the small, quiet **Beau Site** in nearby Ottrott-le-Haut, which also offers a fine restaurant (wild duck with cassis is a specialty there in autumn).

EBERSMUNSTER

Only in the Swiss Vorarlberg will you find Baroque abbeys comparable to Ebersmunster's. This burst of Baroque exuberance was associated with the Counter-Reformation and the desire of Catholic crusaders to move the Church away from the Gothic style, which had begun to seem barbaric. Here is richness that stops short of excess, embodied in a magnificence of gold leaf, stucco ornamentation, a sumptuous high altar, frescoes and paintings in glowing pastels, floral abstractions, garlands and sculptures, and angels as plump as Italian *putti*. The woodwork is remarkable as well, particularly in the choir stalls and in a pulpit supported by Samson, his brow wrinkled with effort. The superb organ is the 18th-century creation of André Silbermann; concerts in May show it off.

The history of Ebersmunster, which today has fewer than 500 inhabitants, is as old as that of Christianity in Alsace and edges back into legend. Etichon, the father of Saint Odile, is said to have constructed an abbey here, perhaps to atone for his meanness.

Ebersmunster tends to appear only on large-scale regional maps. To find it (via a highly recommended detour off the Route du Vin), wind due east of Dambach-la-Ville on back roads. More easily, take N 83 northeast of Sélestat for about 20 km (12 miles).

HAUT-KOENIGSBOURG

The reworked feudal castle in Haut-Koenigsbourg (north of Colmar), considered to be the most important in the Vosges, was the seat of Swiss counts before it was burned down by Swedish invaders in 1633 during the Thirty Years' War. Today it provides some observers with grounds for the argument that ruins can be more satisfying than restorations.

COLMAR

In the days when Charlemagne kept a regal residence on the banks of the river Lauch, a hamlet of workers and farmers grew up around the villa's tower and its dovecote. The Villa Columbaria, or house of *colombes* (doves), was to give its name to the growing town.

Today Colmar's popularity with some travellers surpasses even that of Strasbourg's, in part because it is comfortably smaller (population about 64,000) and less an industrial and business center than a vital repository of art and Alsatian architecture.

In Colmar there is a strong sense of connection with the United States. In 1986 many Americans celebrating the centennial of the Statue of Liberty made pilgrimages here to visit the home of the statue's sculptor, Frédéric Auguste Bartholdi. Since that time Colmariens have been even more conscious of their American ties, as the city's newspapers remind readers that Americans as diverse as Henry Firestone and the film director William Wyler were Alsatian. Colmariens also believe that everybody in the States is familiar with Castroville, a community established in Texas in 1844 that is known as "Little Alsace." Also, it was during the dreadful winter of 1944–45 that the Third and Seventh American Armies, joined by the First French Army, fought in the famous Pocket of Colmar, driving the Germans back across the Rhine in February 1945.

Colmar centers on the 13th- to 14th-century **church of St-Martin**, worth seeing particularly for the sculptures on its façade; from the square all the most important sites in town may be investigated in one long day's stroll. The area is also good sidewalk-café country.

Near the church, at 30, rue des Marchands, is the **Musée Bartholdi**, installed in the family home where the sculptor was born. Examples of his sculpture abound in the museum, but even more interesting are his paintings and the porcelain, furniture, family portraits, project models, and other personal effects. All over town the walker will encounter Bartholdi: the statue of Général Rapp in the place of the same name; the Roesselmann fountain, dedicated to local heroes; the winegrowers' fountain; and other monuments. A statue of Bartholdi himself—chisel in hand, his elbow resting on his workstool near a tiny Statue of Liberty—sculpted in 1907 by the Parisian Louis Noël, stands in a pretty garden near the court of appeals.

An extraordinary **Bartholdi grave monument** in the cemetery shows a brave soldier trying, in death, to struggle out from under the cracked lid of his tomb. It is unsettling, and worth a detour.

By far the most important site in Colmar is the **Musée**

d'Unterlinden at place d'Unterlinden. Installed in the former convent of the Unterlinden Dominicans, and comprising its chapel and 13th-century cloisters as well as the museum's greatest treasure, the 16th-century **Issenheim Altarpiece** of Mathias Grünewald, Musée d'Unterlinden alone is worth the trip to northeastern France. The museum also houses paintings by local artists, items of historical and folkloric interest, winepresses, stone engravings and sculptures, and some superb stained glass.

Narrow cobbled and beflowered streets flanked by 16th- and 17th-century half-timbered houses curve prettily through **La Petite Venise**, the old town, and the **Krutenau quarter**, once a fortified suburb, near the canals of the Lauch. A good, typical, informal luncheon may be had in the **Caveau St-Pierre**, just off the canal on rue Herse.

Not far away cluster many of the area's handsomest old houses: the old customhouse, **Ancienne Douane; Maison Pfister**, ornamented with frescoes and medallions; and **Maison des Têtes**, a Renaissance house occupied by a fine and popular restaurant.

The best hotel in Colmar is the handsome, cozy **Terminus-Bristol**, near the railway station, with its popular restaurant, l'**Auberge**, and its formal, award-winning one, **Rendez-vous de Chasse**. Reserve well in advance (Tel: 89-41-10-10) and, from July to December, order the saddle of venison with *airelles* (European blueberries).

For its size, Colmar boasts a remarkable number of truly outstanding restaurants. Best in town usually is acclaimed to be the elegant **Schillinger** on rue Stanislas (reserve; Tel: 89-41-43-17). Two other standouts are **Au Fer Rouge** in a beautiful old Alsatian house—try the *choucroute* made with *sandre,* a regional fish (reserve; Tel: 89-41-37-24)—and **Da Alberto**, offering Italian dining in a lovely outdoor garden, weather permitting (reserve; Tel: 89-23-37-89).

On Saturdays the Colmar market is particularly interesting. In early August the Foire aux Vins et Représentations Folkloriques lures people from all over eastern France, while the first three Saturdays in September, an ideal season for visiting, bring Les Journées de la Choucroute (Sauerkraut Days). During June the Colmar festival features concerts of classical music.

THE MUNSTER VALLEY

In the seventh century Irish monks retreated into the rich and quiet valleys west of Colmar, establishing there a monastery, or *munster,* that has been famous since the 15th century for its production of the cheese that bears its name. The village of Munster is a modest holiday spot with a handful of small, unpretentious inns, as is Hohrodberg, which is substantially higher in altitude. The best time to visit Munster is in June during the **Albert Schweitzer Music Festival**, when concerts are held in the Romanesque Munster church. The gem of the whole region is the small, circular lake called **Fischboedle**.

MURBACH

"Proud as the dog of Murbach" was a saying understood for the thousand years that the **abbey of Murbach**, bearing upon its coat of arms a silver greyhound, reigned over the region of Guebwiller and enjoyed the protection of Charlemagne and the Holy Roman Empire.

Proud indeed. Founded, according to legend, by Saint Pirmin in 727, it was the repository of the riches of one of the great lords of the day, Count Eberhard of Eguisheim. Murbach's monks were knights; its armies looted and raided and exacted tribute in good feudal tradition, and only ranking nobility could enter its doors. The abbey even minted its own money.

Great imagination is required today to summon up the lost might of Murbach, and imagination is aided only by the serenity of the site, a remote and wooded valley in the foothills of the Vosges. What remains of the abbey are the choir and the transept, with its twin 12th-century towers; the nave has vanished. To find Murbach, take D 430 west up the Vallée de Guebwiller from Guebwiller itself (south of Colmar on the Route du Vin) or, if following the Route des Crêtes, turn east on D 430 from Le Markstein, a winter-sports center.

Mulhouse (moo-LOSE) is of no particular interest to the visitor, who will probably pass through it en route to the Jura, Burgundy, or Switzerland. Enthusiasts of automobiles, however, may wish to detour to the **Musée de l'Automobile** just north of the city center at 192, avenue de

Colmar. Two other museums that may be of interest are the **Musée du Chemin de Fer** (Railroad Museum) and the **Musée de l'Impression sur Etoffes** (Museum of Printed Fabrics), the latter illustrating the history of that branch of textile production.

GETTING AROUND

Lorraine

The major autoroute from Paris to Nancy passes through Reims and cuts south through Metz. A more direct route, though probably no faster, follows E 17 through Vitry-le-François. For horseback riding and other outdoor touring, see A.R.T.E. Lorraine, Dombrot-le-Sec, 88140 Contrexéville.

Lorraine's canal network is extensive, encompassing 438 miles of waterways including the Marne-Rhine Canal and the Moselle river. Self-drive boats can be rented through Lorraine Fluvial in Pagny-sur-Moselle; Tel: 87-81-52-48. For barge cruises, see below.

Alsace

The fastest route from Paris to Strasbourg is Autoroute 4 via Reims. Drivers coming from Nancy and other points in Lorraine may choose from among several routes of varying persuasions; the two major ones are via Sarrebourg to the north and via St-Dié to the south.

Air France now flies to Strasbourg from New York, with an intermediate stop in Lyon. Air Inter (France's major internal airline) maintains several daily flights to Strasbourg from both Orly-Ouest and Charles-de-Gaulle in Paris as well as from other cities in France and Europe (including London); there are daily flights between Orly-Ouest and Colmar. TAT, a regional airline, serves Colmar, Nancy, and Metz from Paris Orly. Several trains leave Paris's Gare de l'Est daily for Strasbourg and for Colmar.

A car is essential for exploring Alsace. Five rental companies maintain offices in Strasbourg; Avis is right on the railroad square, and Hertz, Budget, Europcar, and Citer are available as well. Autos may also be rented in Colmar and Mulhouse.

Maps of the **Route du Vin** and other itineraries are available from the tourism offices in Strasbourg and Colmar.

Alsace-Lorraine is one of the most popular areas of France for luxury **barge cruising**. Abercrombie & Kent operates the *Fleur de Lys* (up to seven passengers, crew of six) on charters for nine nights from Boofzheim (near Strasbourg) to Nancy; check Abercrombie & Kent, 212 Kensington Road, Oak Brook, IL 60521-2106; Tel: (708) 954-2944; also their London office at Sloan Square House, Holbein Place, London SW1 W8NS. French Country Waterways carries 18 guests along the canals in Alsace aboard the air-conditioned *Esprit;* seven-day itineraries between Nancy and Strasbourg and between Strasbourg and Dole in the Jura. For further information and/or reservations, write French Country Waterways, P.O. Box 2195, Duxbury, MA 02331; Tel: (800) 222-1236 or, in Massachusetts, (617) 934-2454; Fax: (617) 934-9048. B & D de Vogüé cruises the hotel-barge *Stella Maris* along the Canal de la Marne in Alsace-Lorraine. Write B & D de Vogüé, P.O. Box 1998, Visalia, CA 93279; Tel: (800) 444-1188 or, in California, (209) 733-7119; Fax: (209) 733-4094.

Rhine cruises of from three to six days may be booked through Alsace Croisières, 12 rue de la Division Leclerc, 67000 Strasbourg; Tel: 88-32-44-55; Fax: 88-32-49-96. For sailings of from one to four hours or a day-long cruise on the Rhine, the Marne-Rhine Canal, or the Ill river, inquire at Alligator, 11 boulevard d'Anvers (Tel: 88-61-10-00); La Vie sur l'Eau, Poste Restante (Tel: 88-36-71-31); or Port Autonome de Strasbourg, 15 rue de Nantes (Tel: 88-84-13-13), all in Strasbourg.

Self-drive boats on the Marne-Rhine Canal can be rented through Blue Line Alsace/Lorraine, Port du Canal, Hesse, 57400 Sarrebourg (Tel: 87-03-61-74); Canal Evasion, 58, rue des Jardiniers, 67000 Strasbourg (Tel: 88-31-53-64); or Locaboat Plaisance, Quai du Port au Bois, 89300 Joigny (Tel: 86-91-72-72).

Other trips are available from Floating Through Europe, New York, NY (Tel: 212-685-5600 or 800-221-3140).

Sightseeing flights over Strasbourg and the Alsatian plain are available. Tourist offices can provide information but not bookings.

ACCOMMODATIONS REFERENCE

▶ **Altéa St-Thiébault.** 29, place St-Thiébault, 57000 **Metz.** Tel: 87-36-17-69; Fax: 87-75-48-18; in U.S., Tel: (800) 223-9862 or (212) 719-9363.

▶ **Altéa Thiers.** 11, rue Poincaré, 54000 **Nancy.** Tel: 83-35-61-01; Fax: 83-32-78-17; in U.S., Tel: (800) 223-9862 or (212) 719-9363.

▶ **Aux Armes de France.** 68770 **Ammerschwihr.** Tel: 89-

47-10-12. Ten rooms are available in this inn with a two-star restaurant; reservations are essential.

▶ **Auberge du Père Floranc.** 9 rue Herzog, Wettolsheim 68000 **Colmar.** Tel: 89-80-79-14; Fax: 89-79-77-00.

▶ **Beau Site.** 67530 **Ottrott-le-Haut.** Tel: 88-95-80-61.

▶ **La Bergerie.** Rugy 57640 **Argancy.** Tel: 87-77-82-27; Fax: 87-77-87-07.

▶ **Château d'Isenbourg.** 68250 **Rouffach.** Tel: 89-49-63-53; in U.S., Tel: (713) 783-8033; Fax: (713) 783-0951; in Australia, Tel: (02) 957-4511; Fax: (02) 929-6326.

▶ **Le Clos St-Vincent.** Route de Bergheim, 68150 **Ribeauvillé.** Tel: 89-73-67-65; Fax: 89-73-32-20; in U.S., Tel: (800) 372-1323 or (212) 696-1323; Fax: (212) 757-0313.

▶ **Cosmos.** Rue Metz, 88140 **Contrexéville.** Tel: 29-08-15-90; Fax: 29-08-24-19.

▶ **A la Cour d'Alsace.** 3 rue Gail, 67210 **Obernai.** Tel: 88-95-07-00.

▶ **Diligence, Résidence Exquisit et Bel Air.** 23 place de la Mairie, 67210 **Obernai.** Tel: 88-95-55-69.

▶ **Aux Ducs de Lorraine.** 16, Route de Vin, 68590 **St-Hippolyte.** Tel: 89-73-00-09; Fax: 89-73-05-46. Good headquarters along the Route du Vin; new wing with especially comfortable rooms.

▶ **Grand Hôtel.** 68410 **Les Trois Epis.** Tel: 89-49-80-65. Beautifully sited 50-room Vosges resort with pool, sauna, solarium, massage, and other amenities.

▶ **Grand Hôtel Etablissement.** 88140 **Contrexéville.** Tel: 29-08-17-30; Fax: 29-08-24-19.

▶ **Grand Hôtel de la Reine.** 2, place Stanislas, 54000 **Nancy.** Tel: 83-35-03-01; Fax: 83-32-86-04; in U.S., Tel: (800) THE-OMNI or (713) 783-8033; Fax: (713) 783-0951; in Australia, Tel: (02) 957-4511; Fax: (02) 929-6326.

▶ **Hilton Hotel.** Avenue Herrenschmidt, 67000 **Strasbourg.** Tel: 88-37-10-10; Fax: 88-36-83-27; in U.S., Tel: (212) 697-9370, (800) 223-1146, or (800) 445-8667.

▶ **Hostellerie Bas-Rupts.** 88400 **Gérardmer.** Tel: 29-63-09-25; Fax: 29-63-00-40.

▶ **Hostellerie du Cerf.** 67520. **Marlenheim.** Tel: 88-87-73-73; Fax: 88-87-73-73. Seventeen quiet rooms enhance the pleasure of this two-star restaurant; reserve.

▶ **Hostellerie La Cheneaudière.** 67420 **Colroy-La-Roche.** Tel: 88-97-61-64; Fax: 88-47-21-73; in U.S., Tel: (713) 783-8033; Fax: (713) 783-0951; in Australia, Tel: (02) 957-4511; Fax: (02) 929-6326. Only 23 rooms in this elegant, gardened retreat in a village of 431 people; two-star restaurant.

► **Hostellerie Coq Hardi**. 8, avenue Victoire, 55100 **Verdun**. Tel: 29-86-36-36.

► **Hostellerie les Vannes**. 6, rue de la Porte-Haute, 54460 **Liverdun**. Tel: 83-24-46-01.

► **Hôtel du Duc**. 55000 **Bar-le-Duc**. Tel: 29-79-32-66.

► **Hôtel au Moulin**. 27, route de Strasbourg, 67610 **Wantzenau**. Tel: 88-96-27-83; Fax: 88-96-68-32. Unpretentious inn with a good restaurant in a former mill on the river in a small Strasbourg suburb.

► **Hôtel des Rohan**. 17, rue du Maroquin, 67000 **Strasbourg**. Tel: 88-32-85-11; Fax: 88-75-65-37; in U.S., Tel: (212) 686-9213, (212) 477-1600, (800) 233-1356, or (800) 366-1510.

► **Hôtel St-Barnabé**. Murbach 68530 **Guebwiller**. Tel: 89-76-92-15; Fax: 89-76-67-80. Small, modestly-priced valley retreat.

► **Hôtel Terminus-Gruber**. 10, place de la Gare, 67000 **Strasbourg**. Tel: 88-32-87-00; in U.S., Tel: (800) 528-1234; Fax: (602) 957-5695.

► **Notre Dame**. Sion 54330 **Vézelise**. Tel: 88-25-13-31.

► **Nouvel Hôtel Maison Rouge**. 4, rue des Francs-Bourgeois, 67000 **Strasbourg**. Tel: 88-32-08-60; Fax: 88-22-43-73.

► **Novotel**. Place Paraiges, 57000 **Metz**. Tel: 87-37-38-39; Fax: 87-36-10-00; in U.S., Tel: (800) 221-4542 or (914) 472-0370.

► **La Réserve**. Esplanade du Lac, 88400 **Gérardmer**. Tel: 29-63-21-60.

► **Résidence Chambard**. Rue Général-de-Gaulle, 68240 **Kaysersberg**. Tel: 89-47-10-17; Fax: 89-47-35-03.

► **Résidence les Violettes**. Jungholtz-Thierenbach 68500 **Guebwiller**. Tel: 89-76-91-19.

► **Terminus-Bristol**. 7, place de la Gare, 68000 **Colmar**. Tel: 89-23-59-50; Fax: 89-23-92-26; in U.S., Tel: (800) 528-1234; Fax: (602) 957-5695.

NORMANDY

By Fred Halliday

Fred Halliday, a frequent contributor to Food & Wine, Connoisseur, *and* Condé Nast Traveler, *divides his time between his residences in Connecticut and Paris.*

Everyone talks about Normandy's pungent flavors. There is the flavor of its cheeses—Camembert, Livarot, Pont-l'Evêque—strong and unlike anything else in the world. There is the character of its drinks—Calvados and Benedictine—spirited and flowery. There is the personality of its people, known even among the French for boundless stubbornness. William the Conqueror was Norman; so was Claude Monet.

The Norman landscape, too, has its dichotomy. In the main the division is between the gaming spas of its coast and the terrain of its interior, liberally sprinkled with apple orchards and dairy cows.

History has made a continual march through Normandy, invading its beaches and passing through crossroads hamlets to its landlocked capital, Rouen. Tracing those footprints is perhaps the visitor's most rewarding objective.

MAJOR INTEREST

Verdant rural landscape, especially in the Pays d'Auge

Calvados and Benedictine

Camembert and other cheeses

Seacoast, especially the ports of Fécamp and Honfleur, the resort of Deauville, and the D-Day landing beaches

Rouen
Cathedral
Antiques shops
Museums, especially the Musée de la Céramique
    and Musée des Beaux-Arts
Medieval quarter around the rue du Gros Horloge
Palais de Justice

Musée des Beaux-Arts André Malraux in Le Havre

Abbaye aux Hommes in Caen

Bayeux Tapestry

ROUEN

If there is only one city in France the traveller will pass through other than Paris, let it be Rouen. It should be seen well, for it is a crown studded with the gems of France's history and character. Here is the passion of Joan of Arc, the very square where she was burned at the stake; here is the cathedral Monet found so irresistible that he painted it so many times in so many different shades of light. Here is a maze of Medieval streets and buildings to explore on foot—car traffic is banned. (The railroad station is a good place to leave your car.) There are excellent cafés, with the best Bordeaux lists outside the Médoc; the Norman loves to dine. Parisian antiques dealers come to Rouen to buy; go into the shops where you see their station wagons—the ones whose license plate numbers end in 75—illegally parked outside. And here you can find the best pressed duck (*canard au sang,* a local specialty) in the world. When strolling down the rue du Gros Horloge, remember that Rouen has wonderful chocolates and caramels, and any of the sweet shops you find along here will be happy to send packages home. (There are no emulsifiers, so be sure to specify air mail lest your chocolate arrive white.) Deviate long enough from the stroll to take in the **Palais de Justice** (adjacent to the rue du Gros Horloge). Linger in the courtyard and savor the 15th-century Late Gothic façade, the most impressive part of the palace. Blown apart in World War II, unlike Humpty Dumpty it was successfully put back together again.

The place du Vieux-Marché, west across rue Jeanne d'Arc, is a wide, bustling square; either the **Couronne**, in a 14th-century building, or **l'Auberge l'Ecu de France** is a

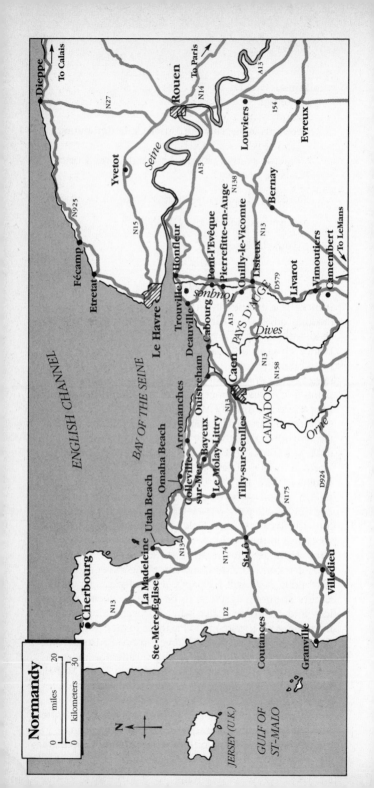

good place for lunch here. Try hot prawns and Normandy sole, a special treat for North Americans, who have probably tasted only the flounder their restaurants *call* sole; it isn't. *Demoiselles à la crème* (small lobsters in cream sauce) are also a good choice. You can wash everything down with the excellent local cider, but remember, there's a lot of walking to do in the afternoon, and you'll want to save some room for dinner.

In the center of the city is the **old town**, which partly escaped the war and was partly reconstructed in its aftermath. Except for a few modern refurbishments, mostly of glass and Lucite, appearances would make the average person think that nothing had changed here for 500 years.

In the old town the visitor enters the Middle Ages down the quarter-mile amble of old cobblestones that is the rue du Gros Horloge, lined with overhung stucco-and-beam houses (work called *colombage*). Because buildings were originally taxed according to the street space they took up, they were generally constructed with a small ground floor and upper floors—which were not taxed at all—that jutted out over the street. Originally a commercial thoroughfare, the rue du Gros Horloge has retained its hustle-and-bustle character with cafés, the aforementioned sweet shops, and little boutiques that make it worth a trip just for window shopping. Halfway down the street is its namesake, the **Gros Horloge** itself, a big clock spanning the street like a bridge, the pedestrians all walking underneath it and knowing the time.

Catercorner to the clock is a bell tower. If it's open, according to a complex schedule, you can visit a collection of clocks and clockworks inside. From the top of the tower a sparkling view gives out over the whole museumlike village. At your feet there's the quiet Medieval neighborhood of the rue Martainville, lined with half-timbered houses and cloisters. An amble down this narrow street leads past 15th-century wooden houses, notably number 184–186, one of the last charnel houses of the host of Middle Ages plagues. Its courtyard posts are covered with a frieze of figures, skulls, and skeletal parts in a danse macabre.

Just ahead of the Gros Horloge looms the **cathedral of Notre-Dame de Rouen**, whose splendid Gothic logic Monet never tired of painting in all its sunlit variations. It presented to the painter, as it does to visitors today, one of the most immense façades in all of Gothicdom, bristling with design detail and flanked by two towers of dissimilar style and appeal—the tower of St. Romain on the left and the "spire of Butter" on the right. This dissimilarity served the Impressionists, with their techniques of fragmentation of color, particularly well. The St. Romain tower, at nearly 900 years of age, is older and represents a more primitive Gothic style. The Butter spire, so called because those who contributed to its construction were permitted to eat dairy products otherwise taboo during a certain religious observance, was finished 400 years later. Instead of a cross a crown of 56 bells lies on top.

Among the many other sights, churches, and museums in Rouen is the **Musée de la Céramique** (near the Musée des Beaux-Arts on square Verdrel); the city was long an important originator of painted stoneware, and the museum's collection of ceramics dating from the 16th to early 19th centuries is particularly fine, rivaling any ceramic collection in Europe. The porcelain and stoneware (faïence) of Rouen has a fine reputation in France and is one of the bargains to be shopped for. Particularly attractive are the large serving pieces. The **Musée des Beaux-Arts** galleries house works by several name-brand Impressionists as well as art of other periods. The Musée Corneille, on rue de la Pie, and the Musée Flaubert, at 51, rue de Lecat (both writers were natives of Rouen; Flaubert's father was a surgeon, so the family mansion is a surgical history museum as well as one of writing), are worth visiting, but the *grand musée* in Rouen is really its streets. What awaits indoors are primarily the pleasures of the Norman table.

About half the fermented soft cheese—the high-quality cheese—of France is produced in Normandy. It is no wonder, then, that dairy products are the basis of Norman cuisine. The velvety white *sauce normande* is used with everything from eggs to vegetables and chicken and is particularly fine on seafood, as the world well knows. However, there is another specialty of Rouen the visitor ought to sample.

The hotel **Dieppe**, just across from the railroad station on Rouen's main square, is a good place to go. It's a pre-chain hotel of average size (42 rooms), but its rooms are unique, shaped by the outline of their particular cranny or hall. All in all, staying here is like having your own cozy apartment in France. But the real draw of the hotel is its restaurant, **Le Quatre Saisons**. This is the place to order the famous *canard au sang* (pressed duck). As the menu at the Quatre Saisons will explain, their duck is a special variety. The animal is taken from a nearby backwater of the Seine where the local wild breed, the *col vert*—a type that resembles the mallard—crosses quite naturally with the domestic duck and then remains sedentary. The results are happy, as in delicious.

The Quatre Saisons is one of those places that awakens us to the truth: how good the top *centre ville* restaurant can be anywhere in the provinces, especially in the north of France. In an era often submerged by fad and bluff, the table of such an establishment is one of the best reasons for visiting the countryside—no less viable a reason than any art museum or barge tour down a river.

The duck is served at Quatre Saisons with an evident love of theater. You can observe the birds turning in their own juices in a spitarium. At just the right moment the thighs are carved off and taken to the kitchen for extra cooking and special preparation. Then the cart, with its towering duck press, is wheeled beside your table; it is your turn. The carcass is carved, two knives, no hands touching the flesh. Bones, neck, and giblets are pushed, cracked, and pressed in the gleaming machine; the blood is drawn off, the sauce made, poured, flambéed. And *voila!*—served.

Before a three-hour dinner like this, it might be wise to book a room at the hotel.

The bar here, as good a place as any to educate your palate, possesses a splendid array of that heady Norman passion, Calvados. Calva, as its lovers call it, is to the apple what Cognac is to the grape. This distillate of cider is aged in wood and bottled in grades. The least expensive is plain Calvados; then comes Calvados Pays d'Auge Réglémentée. Aging is a factor in grading, and within each grade there are the usual variations of quality according to bottler. One of the finest is Vieux Calvados from the house of Jean-Louis Favennec. To compare it to Cognac would be to belittle it.

You may see people around you quaffing Calvados during the meal; in fact, it is quite correct to do so. This is the *trou normand* (Norman hole) of which you may have heard tell, the idea behind the vivid phrase being that because the Norman meal is very heavy, you have to punch a hole in it—with some Calvados—and then proceed to fill it.

There is likewise a reason to drink Calva at the end of the meal, and a phrase to go along with it. The coffee is *coiffé,* the Normans say, and *recoiffé,* or spiked, with the brandy.

One final note: Many people who say they cannot drink brandy because it keeps them awake at night report that drinking Calva induces sound sleep—with wild dreams. At any rate, after a Rouen dinner of *canard au sang,* fortified with a *trou normand* and a café *recoiffé,* sound sleep is a safe presumption.

The Pays d'Auge

This sun-dappled *bocage,* a 30-mile-long and 15-mile-wide valley of brooks, hills, and farms southwest of Rouen, with cows grazing on slopes that are as green as parsley, is what most people imagine when they think of Normandy. It is best to enter the Pays d'Auge from the south, through the little town with the big name in cheese, **Camembert**. This town could be the start of the Route du Fromage, if such a thing existed, for it is marked with a suitable shrine—in the town square of Camembert is a statue to Marie Harel, a local farm woman. Other communities put up statues of soldiers and conquerors, but this Norman town chooses to honor the woman who invented a cheese. In an age when Caesar is a salad, Napoléon a pastry, and Bismarck a herring, who can say the villagers are wrong?

Camembert tastes best, of course, in the land of its birth. In a local bistro or café, the Camembert to ask for is *camembert fermier,* which is made on the farm and has little to do with the perfumed and pasteurized dandies the big cheese factories concoct. The one consumed in the village is rich with the creamy kick that Marie Harel invented and is worth the trip.

The farms of the Pays d'Auge are built like enclosed compounds, with silo, granary, coops, and living quarters all cemented together within a continuous wall, as if to withstand a siege—which they might have had to do in the time when the Vikings ranged these coasts. Country homes and manors—architecturally unique in the Western world—are built along the same lines and are often rectangular, with turrets on the corners, watchtowers, high walls, and moats. This may give you some idea that the average Norman farm is hardly territory for the travelling salesman or, for that matter, the casual tourist.

The farmers won't mind your looking at their manors and farms from a distance. As for approaching the doorway, be forewarned that the local attitude toward the uninvited is perhaps best summed up by this sign observed over one bell: "Useless to ring. The château admits no one."

Homes that you can visit, however, may be found just after **Livarot**, which is an obligatory stop on our Route du Fromage about 10 km (6 miles) north of Camembert; it is also one of the very few places where you can taste a 600-year-old cheese. A left turn onto D 47 just beyond the town will take you to the incomparable manor of Coupesarte, with its moat and fortified wall. Just a bit farther on is the Château Grandchamp, a 16th-century example of Norman privacy ringed by earthen levees meant to protect livestock and granaries against invaders and wind. From a distance the manors look like verdant oases, hedged with oak or elms and floating on a sea of grass. However, you can enter neither place. At Coupesarte they'll give you a tour around the outside—a satisfactory visit, really—for a donation. At Grandchamp you are expected to keep your distance.

About 7 km (4 miles) south of Lisieux is **St-Germain-de-Livet**, a château that puts out a real welcome mat. Besides its display of frescoes and lithography, the château offers an approximation of the sort of home atmosphere you might have expected there during the 16th century. Judging by the pitched Norman roofs and massive fireplaces, winters were much more snowy then than they are now.

Lisieux, for centuries a commercial hub (all Pays d'Auge roads lead there), was, with the exception of its cathedral, almost completely razed by the bombardments of World War II. Although the rebuilt town retains little of its former charm, it nonetheless remains a busy center of the region's produce and agricultural industry.

The road leaving Lisieux for Pont-l'Evêque to the north (D 579) is particularly picturesque, passing by **Ouilly-le-Vicomte**, where one of the oldest churches in Normandy—parts from the tenth century still survive—can be seen on its lovely islet in the river Touques. Farther downstream is Pierrefitte-en-Auge and, looking like any old house of the hamlet, the **Auberge des Deux Tonneaux**. Here is a good place to stop for refreshments or a bed, and the innkeeper can provide you with the key that unlocks the local church. Everything is close together along this route; quaint towns come swiftly one after the other, each with a church that possesses its individual treasures—a rare statuette, a carving, an especially beautiful Virgin.

Pont-l'Evêque, just a few miles beyond, is the last stop on our Route du Fromage. Aside from cheeses, the town is curiously loaded with lawyers. Everybody in the surrounding countryside seems to have a lawyer whose *cabinet* is here. With so much litigation in the air, you'd be wise not to hit anything. Bombed during World War II, the Pont-l'Evêque of today is far from a Medieval experience. Yet there are a few buildings left that give an authentic taste of what was old Norman town style, with a courtyard for animals and food stocks attached.

On the rue St-Michel a nest of old buildings huddles around such a court bordering a stream, which made for easy provisioning. Also, at 68, rue de Vaucelles, the 16th-century inn l'Aigle d'Or has a classic courtyard for a coach and six.

And who can know France without knowing her classic cheeses? Pont-l'Evêque's special variety was being eaten well before America was discovered. Modern marketing techniques, however, have made overseas connoisseurship difficult if not altogether impossible. Nowadays many cheeses are produced at factories, and those earmarked for overseas sale are made to pass various regulations, including (horrors!) taste tests to ensure that they will satisfy differing overseas markets. Particularly hard hit by all this are the fermenting cheeses such as Camembert, Livarot, and Pont-l'Evêque, which are tamed for the trip to faraway markets and for "international" tastes. Even the milk for this kind of production is standardized, coming in the main from high-yield, low-butterfat producers—Holstein cows that feed on grain. But in the Pays d'Auge the visitor can taste the genuine item made from the milk of the original *race normande* breed, which graze purely on grass, not in feedlots. These cheeses will surprise you with their renowned richness, only the barest hint of which exists in the mass-produced products that bear their names.

The D 579 out of Pont-l'Evêque leads north to one of the most charming ports on the whole Norman coast: Honfleur.

Honfleur and the
Painters of Normandy

There are those who say that Impressionism began in Honfleur. Certainly this claim is supported by the fact that its leading practitioner, Claude Monet, began to paint here, and that his mentor, the outstanding pre-Impressionist painter Eugène Boudin, was a native son. Honfleur has all the basic ingredients for Impressionistic painting: water, sky, and flowers. It also has a port that is as pretty as any ever pictured on a postcard, a spot that has long been an attraction for painters. Corot came here; so did Courbet. Honfleur offered yet another important ingredient, a typically Norman one: something the artists called white light, a quality in the sunlight that seemed to let the colors of things stand out in their own essentials. When Monet later set up shop in Giverny, it was this light that would keep him coming back to Honfleur. Something else about this region that suited French painters was its proximity to Paris, the major art market. And again, something more: the Norman character, affording neighbors who minded their own business.

For these reasons, then, Normandy became a cradle of modern art. And not only French art: England's Richard Bonington transferred the blues of Honfleur's beaches to his canvases in the early 19th century, and the Dutch Fauvist Kees van Dongen captured the social elegance of Deauville.

After the darkness of the Barbizon School the palette of modern painting escaped the studio completely and headed for the liberating outdoors, and that outdoors was Normandy. And the movement didn't stop with Impressionism; here Seurat and Signac broke down the white Norman light into seven colors, painting only with these and giving birth to Pointillism. The bold colors of Fauvism followed these Impressionist and post-Impressionist palettes. Contemporary painters continued to live and work in Normandy: Félix Vallotton, Albert Marquet, and Raoul Dufy.

The interesting **Musée Eugène-Boudin** here features works by Boudin himself, his friends, and his artistic offspring. The prophet who helped chart a course for contemporary art is indeed honored in his hometown and throughout his native province. The Musée des Beaux-Arts André Malraux in Le Havre contains a more comprehensive collection (see below).

And Honfleur itself? The little harbor and fishing fleet here remain painterly subjects as compelling now as they were then for Boudin and his friends. For some people this is the essence of Honfleur. To walk around the port, especially when the light is emphasizing a different aspect of some scene—a green door here, a yellow boat there—and to sit over a Belgian beer in a café, contemplating a sunset, are experiences no trip to Normandy should be without.

For an especially bucolic setting in which to enjoy lunch, visit **La Ferme St-Siméon** nearby. It will make you want to stay; the accommodations are superb. The drive up the cliffside to the inn gives a seagull's view of Honfleur and arouses the appetite. Swathed in wisteria and rhododendrons, this is *the* picturebook inn of the region. It is also the place that was home away from home for the budding Impressionists, the farm where they came for their meals and, perhaps, to spend a weekend. Now you can, too, though the price is certainly steeper and the service a little more professional than when Old Mother Toutain set a table for the starving types Boudin always seemed to be attracting.

Le Havre and Environs

Today Le Havre, on the north side of the Seine, across from Honfleur, is the second port of France, with two car ferry lines serving tourists bound for England and Ireland. It's difficult to give the visitor wandering about the sometimes institutional-looking city and seeking the 16th century an idea of how much Le Havre suffered during World War II. Perhaps figures will tell the story.

Le Havre was not a place to be in the 1940s. It was bombed 146 times by the Americans and English alone, making it the most heavily damaged port in Europe. Nearly 10,000 buildings were flattened, another 10,000 damaged. More than 4,000 people were killed. For their part, the Germans were extra tenacious in Le Havre. After the Battle of Normandy was over—even after Paris was liberated—the Wehrmacht held onto the port. During the first weeks of September 1944 Allied raids reached a crescendo, which the Germans topped with a farewell Götterdämmerung of dynamite that destroyed what was left. Hitler didn't have to ask; Le Havre was burning. Excavating its rubble after the war took two years.

Yet it was in this port that, almost a hundred and seventy years earlier, the United States got started, for the revolutionaries drew their supplies from the "forest of masts" of Le Havre's Porte Océane. Later, it was in Le Havre that the French Line began, launched on the prow of the steamship *Washington* in 1864, toward the end of the U.S. Civil War. So America and Le Havre always have been linked, curiously, by war.

Porte Océane today is at the end of avenue Foch, a majestic if thoroughly modern promenade designed by an architect known as the "magician of concrete."

In its concrete maze, Le Havre is vast and confining, with arms of the sea blocking this street and that. The way to see it is by boat. Tours leave frequently but irregularly (depending on how many people show up) all day long from the quai de la Marine at Porte Océane; they are detailed and fascinating, so park the car. For those over-nighting for the ferry, the hotel **France et Bourgogne**, 21, cours République, has a reasonable restaurant; the **Astoria** hotel, on the same street at number 13, is even more reasonable. The restaurant in the same building has gone Oriental, a trend sweeping much of France.

Though there are museums everywhere in Normandy, the Norman contribution to art is most gratifyingly worked out and illuminated at the **Musée des Beaux-Arts André Malraux** in Le Havre. There is a stunning collection of works by Raoul Dufy, who was a native of Normandy and depicted its themes: regattas, horse races, outdoor dances, beaches, movement, and explosive color. The André Malraux collection defines Normandy's unique influence on painting with works by Boudin and Monet, Marquet and Van Dongen; ever present in these paintings is the Norman landscape—the sea cliffs of Etretat, the beaches at Deauville and Trouville, and the port of Honfleur.

The cliffs of **Etretat** themselves are a short distance (28 km/ 17 miles) from Le Havre and are a recommended side trip from the port after you've seen the paintings. The white cliffs, reflecting the sea, have been tunneled and carved to form limbs and bridges of themselves. In a coastline filled with wonders, they are particularly worth seeing for the variations in texture and shades of the color white, which change with the reflections of the sea and sky.

There are many paths to choose from running the length of these limestone cliffs. Most can be ambled in the course of an afternoon, and a picnic in the wind is a fine idea here. Provision in the marketplace in town on the place Maréchal-Foch.

Should the study of spirits prove fascinating, travellers can set their sights on **Fécamp**, a delicious slip of a fishing village cradled in a cleft of white, chalky cliffs 17 km (11 miles) northeast of Etretat. Here, the ruined abbey where the cordial Benedictine was discovered in 1510 has been rebuilt as a distillery and as the **Musée de la Bénédictine**, entered through massive wrought-iron gates and Gothic arcades. The spacious Salle des Abbés is presided over by stone (or stoned) statues of 16 past abbots. The monk who rediscovered the formula for Bénédictine (it was once lost) is depicted, with a trumpeting angel and a bottle of the elixir, in a stained-glass window.

Fécamp was also the home of Guy de Maupassant, and many of his short stories are imbued with the atmosphere of its streets. Cod fishing is no longer a local industry, but the marina is still interesting and the quai de la Marne receives massive quantities of other fish, as well as cargoes of raw chemicals and timber bound for French sawmills. Along the wharves are canneries, fish-dressing plants, and drydocks for boat repairs. On the place du General Leclerc is the **Eglise de la Trinité**. In its length it rivals the longest churches in France, being less than ten feet short of Notre-Dame de Paris, and its spire is the quintessence of Norman towers. Any of the cafés on the *place* is suitable for lunch or a snack.

The Coast and Casinos

After Honfleur—unless you first cross over to Le Havre, Etretat, and Fécamp—the Corniche Normande to the west, with its beaches at Trouville and Deauville, will be your next destination.

Trouville, just 15 km (9 miles) southwest of Honfleur, has a wide, sandy beach, the north end of which harbors reasonably priced family hotels, the type the French call "correct," and a casino and swimming pool—which may tell you something about the temperature of the sea. There is also a commercial fishing fleet docked along the river Touques, giving the spa a nice waterfront animation off-season. The shopping streets are clean and well ordered, the buildings still low enough to allow sunlight to reach the pedestrians. The stroller gets the feeling that Trouville is a town that has kept up to date but has not let progress run rampant.

Deauville, the grande dame of the seacoast, just to the west of Trouville, still bespeaks the elegant life. Most representative is the **Normandy**, one of the plushest restaurant/hotel-cum-casinos in the world. The players still dress in black tie and look exactly like Zachary Scott and Jean Harlow. There is a well-protected yacht basin for pleasure craft, two race tracks—steeplechase and the flats—a yearling sale, shows of Norman livestock, and finally, an American film festival that closes the season in September.

But hideous new high-rises are crowding in, cutting off once-open spaces and sea perspectives. A heavy population of ex-colonialists from Algeria and elsewhere in North Africa now compete with Parisians for sun space. Although the side streets and main streets of Deauville still host a pleasing variety of boutiques, cute cafés, swimming clubs for children (**Club des Canards**, for example), and restaurants, elbow room is at a premium and you'll feel as if you are paying a high price for the privilege.

Not far from here to the west is **Cabourg**, a smaller, family-oriented Deauville that has remained *toujours élégant,* implacably French, and structured for the longer stay. Families from Neuilly and Paris's 16th *arrondissement* still come here and plant themselves for the summer—or at least for August. Papa may run back to the City of Light weekdays, but he returns for the bright lights of the casino on weekends, when the hanky-panky—from Monday to Friday—usually ends. Not to worry; it picks up again on Sunday nights when he's gone. Bookings here should be for at least a week. The **Pullman Grand Hôtel** is on the beach, *centre plage* of everything. On the other side of the river Orne from Cabourg, and to the south, is Caen.

Caen and Bayeux

Caen, the capital of lower Normandy and county seat of Calvados, was much fought over, in, and around, with the result that three-quarters of it was destroyed in the last war. It is still, however, a place with its own particular style of Gothic architecture, a city adding up to more than its façades, where a visitor can go into and experience its public buildings. Start with the 16th-century **Hôtel d'Escoville** in the center of town. It's hard to believe this magnificent ensemble of separate wings, adjoining courtyards, and domed space was completely destroyed in World War II. Today it bears not a scratch of conflict and is all that it ever was: Flamboyant Gothic, a mid-16th-century version of what may be called Caen Renaissance. Decidedly Italian, it sends the spirit soaring over the vault of its mammoth proportions. The tourist office is located inside this opulent structure, so it's the ideal spot to collect maps and brochures and to get your bearings. This tourist office is one of France's favorites.

There are statues of Apollo and his harp, Marsyas with his flute, Judith carrying the head of Holofernes, and David with Goliath's.

The **church of St-Pierre**, just across the place St-Pierre from the Hôtel d'Escoville, is another fine example of this joyful Gothic style. The **Musée des Beaux-Arts** in the nearby castle is full of the works of well-known painters from the 15th to 20th centuries. It is a comprehensive and rich collection—as befitting Caen's longstanding position on the coast—including primitive Italians and Flemish from the 15th century, 16th-century Venetians, Rubens and Van Dyck (17th century), 17th- and 18th-century portrait painters (Rigaud, Lefèvre), and 19th- and 20th-century masters such as Delacroix, Courbet, Corot, Monet, and Bonnard. Add to that Limoges enamel, French porcelain, furniture, gold and silver work, tapestries, and, in the basement, some 50,000 etchings by Corot, Durer, and Rembrandt.

With all this, however, critics and tourists alike agree that it is the **Abbaye aux Hommes** (founded by William the Conqueror) and its church, **St-Etienne**, across town, that is Caen's true masterpiece. There is hardly a façade more imposing in all Romanesque architecture, a French garden more pleasing, or a church more harmoniously wedded to an abbey. Caen's **castle**, also built by William the Conqueror, houses, in addition to the aforementioned Musée des Beaux-Arts, the **Musée de Normandie**, filled with popular art and implements of home and farm essential to an understanding of the Normans. A good hotel—the **Relais des Gourmets**—overlooks the walls of the citadel.

There are more churches to be seen—St-Sauveur and Trinité—and another abbey, Trinité's 11th-century **Abbaye aux Dames** (founded by Queen Matilda, William's wife, as a sister house to the Abbaye aux Hommes), to give equality, if not equal architectural distinction, to the sexes.

Beside all of this the people of Caen have a genuine affinity for their Anglo-Saxon brothers-in-arms. Their welcome is as warm as their Calva, and the *trou normand* is a common practice here.

On the road between Caen and Bayeux, and within easy distance of both at Audrieu, is the **Relais Château d'Audrieu**. The hotel is an 18th-century building within its own park and provides deluxe accommodations, a swimming pool, and an intriguing restaurant. Try the snail and lobster soup.

Bayeux, 28 km (17.5 miles) northwest of Caen, was the first French town to be liberated during World War II (on June 8, 1944), and so, happily, suffered no damage. Everything remains intact on the old streets of St-Martin and St-Malo; their buildings remain precious treasures of this Medieval crossroads town. The 11th-century **cathedral of Notre-Dame**, with its three-story choir, is another treasure. But housed in the Centre Guillaume le Conquérant, a short walk east of the cathedral at the bottom of rue de Nesmond, is the town's most prized possession, Queen Matilda's **Bayeux Tapestry**, embroidered with hieroglyphs of Anglo-Norman history.

Almost as long as a football field but not two feet high, the Bayeux Tapestry occupies a building all its own, with slides, films, and a museum devoted to it. To read the story of the Norman invasion of England in 1066 from beginning to end, the visitor can follow the tapestry's length around the four walls of the main viewing room, where the wool-embroidered linen cloth stretches in a continuous band. More than a traditional Gobelins or Aubusson tapestry, it resembles a flowing pictograph, an illuminated comic strip charmingly complete with naïve characters in roles that play themselves out across its length, as in a film or morality play. There are William the Conqueror and Harold of Hastings, plus a cast of hundreds: oarsmen and archers, friars and knights. The English are depicted with mustaches, the Normans with shaved napes. The principals are all labeled and easily recognizable in a sequence of more than 50 subtitled scenes (Latin and Saxon only, sorry; a pamphlet provides an English translation). The tapestry is more a storyteller's success than the triumph of an art form. Those coming to view the Bayeux Tapestry with *La Dame à la Licorne* (at the Musée de Cluny in Paris) in mind as an ideal will find that their notions of textile art must be redefined.

In one of those ironies that history seems ever fond of, it is barely five miles from this depiction of the last Norman invasion of Britain to the site where a more recent invasion occurred on Normandy's own shores.

The Landing Beaches
of Normandy

The Allied action that took place on D-Day, June 6, 1944, is well documented and needs no repetition here. The

beaches—and the war museums—form a line west from
Ouistreham. To visit them, but more specifically to stand at
the headlands above the beaches and just look out, will
give an idea of the difficulties encountered that day that no
amount of reading or film viewing can offer. The roll call of
coast towns rings out with names of beaches that were
assaulted: Ste-Mère-Eglise; Omaha Beach (at Colleville);
Utah Beach (at La Madeleine); Sword, Juno, and Gold
beaches (from Arromanches to Ouistreham). There are
markers where the actions took place; here and there
broken blockhouses loom. There's a film show at Arromanches and white crosses dotting the green carpets that
roll down toward the sea at Omaha Beach.

After the landings the fighting continued. The Battle of
Normandy, as it was called, quickly became a desperate
struggle. The British, Americans, and Canadians fought so
as not to be thrown back into the sea; the Germans fought
to keep the Allies from advancing. More than 200,000
homes were destroyed in the onslaught; ports and crossroads like Le Havre, Rouen, Caen, and Lisieux were virtually flattened. After ten weeks of attack and counterattack,
the Battle of Normandy ended on August 19. The Germans had lost about half a million men, the route to Paris
was open, and the world was about to be reordered into
the one we know today.

GETTING AROUND

Rouen, in the center of Normandy, is just 139 km (85
miles) northwest of Paris on A 13 (Autoroute de Normandie), which continues for another 125 km (75 miles)
past Rouen west to Caen. Along the Autoroute from
Rouen to Caen are exits for Le Havre, Honfleur, Deauville,
and many other points on the Normandy coast. Route N
15 leads north and west from Rouen toward Fécamp and
Etretat.

Trains run regularly from the Gare St-Lazare in Paris to
Rouen, Caen, Le Havre, and all other major cities in
Normandy. TGVs run to Caen and Rouen. It's best to
check schedules at time of ticket purchase, as fare supple-
ments and changes are no strangers to the SNCF. Travel-
ling by boat from the U.K., the major points of entry in
Normandy are: Caen, from Portsmouth; Cherbourg, from
Portsmouth and Weymouth; and Dieppe, from Newhaven.
There is limited air service from London to Normandy
cities on Brit Air, which flies from Gatwick Airport to
Caen, and Air Vendée, which flies from Gatwick to Rouen.

ACCOMMODATIONS REFERENCE

▶ **Astoria.** 13, cours République, 76600 **Le Havre**. Tel: 35-25-00-03; Telex: 190075; Fax: 35-26-48-34.

▶ **Auberge des Deux Tonneaux.** Pierrefitte-en-Auge 14130 **Pont-l'Evêque**. Tel: 31-64-09-31.

▶ **Dieppe.** Place Bernard-Tissot, 76000 **Rouen**. Tel: 35-71-96-00; Telex: 180413; Fax: 35-89-65-21.

▶ **La Ferme St-Siméon.** Route Adolphe-Marais, 14600 **Honfleur**. Tel: 31-89-23-61; Telex: 171031; Fax: 31-89-48-48.

▶ **France et Bourgogne.** 21, cours République, 76600 **Le Havre**. Tel: 35-25-40-34.

▶ **Normandy.** 38, rue Jean-Mermoz, 14800 **Deauville**. Tel: 31-88-09-21; Telex: 170617; Fax: 31-98-66-23; in U.S., Tel: (212) 477-1600 or (800) 366-1510.

▶ **Pullman Grand Hôtel.** Promenade Marcel Proust, 14390 **Cabourg**. Tel: 31-91-01-79; Telex: 171364; Fax: 31-24-03-20.

▶ **Relais Château d'Audrieu.** Tilly-sur-Seulles 14250 **Audrieu** (13 km/9 miles south of Bayeux on Route D 158). Tel: 31-80-21-52; Fax: 31-80-24-73; in U.S., Tel: (212) 696-1323.

▶ **Relais des Gourmets.** 15, rue Geôle, 14300 **Caen**. Tel: 31-86-06-01; Telex: 171657; Fax: 31-39-06-00.

BRITTANY

By Fred Halliday

Brittany, of the wild, glorious coastline, of oysters, of crêpes and a spirited people, is often described by the French from Gascony to the Loire Valley as "the part of France with the most character. You should go."

But how? Seeing Brittany is not like seeing other parts of France. For one thing, it's hard to get to, even from Paris. Air Inter flies there, but space is so limited that reservations must be made far in advance, and then if you don't stick to your schedule it's quite probable you won't get a seat when you want to return—so it's back to the reservations line.

Also, the roads to Quimper (cam-PEAR) that cover the 553 km (346 miles) from Paris are a mixed bag. There is no direct autoroute, but it's no bargain for shunpikers either; some of the towns along the way are more obstructions than delights.

For the tourist determined to see Brittany there is one good answer: the train. If you're travelling from Paris, get up early, because the 7:07 A.M. for Quimper, which leaves from the Gare Montparnasse, is the one you want to catch. Why? Because it's the only train that will get you to Quimper before its crêperies close their doors at 1:00 P.M. sharp.

MAJOR INTEREST

Quimper
Old city
Shops selling local stoneware

Seacoast, especially the dramatic scenery at Pointe du Raz

Medieval architecture, especially the towns of
Concarneau, Dinan, and Paimpol
Prehistoric megaliths, especially those at Carnac
and Locmariaquer
Calvaires, granite monuments in parish closes illus-
trating Christ's Passion
Oysters, crêpes, and *galettes*

Le Mont-Saint-Michel

St-Malo
Ramparts
Houses from the 15th to 17th centuries

Côtes d'Emeraude et du Granit Rose

Tréguier's cathedral

THE SOUTH COAST
To Quimper

If you've got just two weeks in the country that leads the
world in gastronomic pleasure, every meal should be an
important event. Forget the airline food on the world's
fastest trains and save your taste buds for Old Quimper.
The 7:07 A.M. Paris train pulls into the Quimper station at
12:56 P.M. This means you've got only four minutes to
get from the station to the crêperies, so you'd better take
a cab from the stand at the entrance to the station.
Crêperie du Vieux Quimper will not shut the door on
any Anglo-Saxons who call ahead (Tel: 98-95-31-34) from
Paris the day before to say they are going to be a few
minutes late. French trains are usually on time and the
Vieux Quimper is only five minutes from the station, at
20, rue Verdelait, so you should just make it. Dawdle,
however, and you will find out why Bretons are the
French with the most character.

Entering the Crêperie du Vieux Quimper, you will see
that getting up for the 7:07 gets you not only lunch but
into the Breton swing of things right away. The dining
room is full of old beams, antique Quimper dishes (more
about that later) on the walls, and the sizzle of batter
hitting the pan. You just know the crêpes you eat here will
somehow be thinner, hotter, crisper, and more delicious
than any to be found in Paris or on almost any other table,
even in Brittany. Aside from luncheon and dessert types,
there are two things you should know about crêpes: They

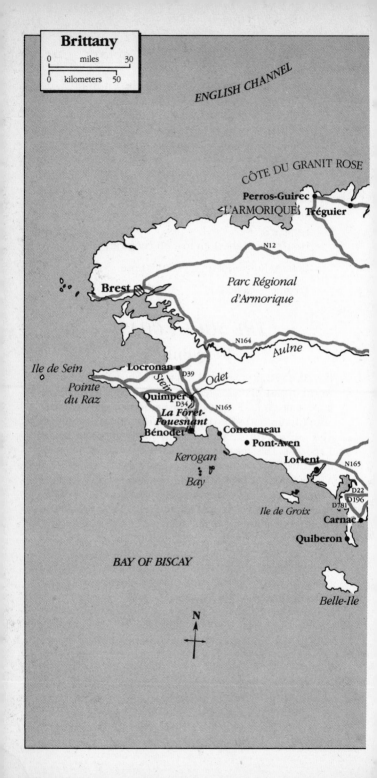

are made with either *froment* (white flour) or *sarrasin* (buckwheat flour). For main-course lunch crêpes take the buckwheat. It will come sizzling and slightly crunchy. What it is filled with is your choice. Very good as a base is Gruyère (a Swiss cheese), to which you can have ham or lettuce added, or you can have all three. From the more than 20 combinations you might also try mushrooms and seafood. Forget wine, as do the Bretons, and wash your crêpes down with cider. They serve the very best at Vieux Quimper; it's fairly mild, about 6 percent alcohol. If you eat a lot (most diners down two to three crêpes each) and drink a lot (a half to a full bottle is the rule), it would be wise to walk around and see Quimper before taking the wheel of your rental car. Another tip: Before leaving the table, order dessert. Especially recommended is a chocolate crêpe.

Seeing Quimper

Perched way out in Finistère (land's end), where the land smells of the sea, Quimper is one of the larger cities in Brittany where the traditional Breton atmosphere exists in abundance. It can be seen in the many streets closed to cars; in the cathedral, especially its windows, the pride of the town; and in the shops, filled with things Breton. (The name Quimper is the French spelling of the Breton *Kemper,* meaning "place of the confluence of two rivers.")

What is it to be a Breton? The Breton people and their language are Celtic in origin, their roots extending across the sea to the Cornish coast of England, Ireland, Wales, and Scotland, and to wherever the Celts put a *currah* (bark) in the water. Bretons go so far as to claim that the legend of King Arthur and the Round Table originated in Brittany, not in England, and some "scholars" substantiate the theory.

These Celtic origins are quite apparent in the faces of the people you encounter on the streets. Pick up a walking map at the chamber of commerce (Syndicat d'Initiative, place de la Résistance) and join in the flow of blue eyes, fair faces, freckles, and red hair.

Located on the cathedral square, the most Breton shop in town is **L'Art du Cornouaille** (Tel: 98-95-39-24), perhaps the best place to buy the city's famous stoneware dishes, which are known throughout the world simply as Quimper. The Henriot factory, just outside the old town and another good place to shop, sells only its own seconds, however, while L'Art du Cornouaille sells stoneware (called faïence in France) from many Breton manufacturers at perhaps one-third of North American prices—and it also has a huge selection you won't find outside Quimper. The shop will dispatch a messenger up the hill to the factory to get what you want if they're out, do all the packing, put everything on a credit card, put on the stamps, add in any duty, and ship to your home. L'Art du Cornouaille is also a very good source for grandfather clocks, armoires, and Brittany lace.

For more things Breton, the annual Festival of Breton Folklore takes place here on the fourth Sunday (and the preceding week) of July; the **Musée Breton**, on the quai de l'Odet, has interesting exhibits that highlight the region's heritage.

Quimper is full of architectural surprises. To experience these, follow the pretty Odet and Steir rivers along banks that meander around homes and under buildings. You can also take a boat down the river Odet to the sea, a trip of 16 km (10 miles). A cruise from Kerogan Bay to the seaside resort of Bénodet, an hour and a half of meandering through forested cliffs and rocky heights, is highly recommended. Consult the Syndicat for details.

As the Celts were seafarers, so are the Bretons, and as you would expect, a seafaring people takes its menu live from the sea. In choosing a Breton dinner, there is only one admonition: Keep it simple. Beware "cuisine." Steer clear of sauces—turbot in Béarnaise (nice for Paris but not here), sole meunière—any sauce except *sauce armoricaine* (more about that specialty later). In Brittany the taste is freshness: good staples, simply presented and pure.

A nice hotel in Quimper is the 25-room **Gradlon**, at 30, rue Brest. It's near the train station, the elevator works, and the rooms are as neat as a pin.

Locronan

For the Breton taste you could not do better than at the **Fer à Cheval** in Locronan. Fer à Cheval is a completely captivating inn—two stories of ancient stone, the top floor hanging over the town square—located in a completely captivating village 17 km (11 miles) northwest of Quimper. Since you must rent a car to see the rest of Brittany properly, Quimper is as good a place as any to do that. From there to Locronan it is an easy drive on Route D 39 and D 63. Arrive while there is still enough light to see the Brittany of times past. You will want two hours to walk around the central square and the streets radiating from it.

The village's buildings are made entirely of stone, some dating from the 15th century, and are heavily covered with moss because of their proximity to the sea. Unless you have been to western Ireland, you have never seen a village like this. Of course you must also see the musty 15th-century church right on the square. And sign the book inside; the youngsters in Locronan love to see from how far away their many visitors come. The churchyard is also a must, the markers being so many Celtic crosses. These are similar to the *calvaires,* the many-figured granite sculptures to be seen in Breton churchyards. (A good place to see them is near the church at Bénodet, south of Quimper on Route D 34.)

On the Locronan square itself is possibly the best sweet shop in all of Brittany, **Guillou-Nicholas Jean.** Without fail try the *kouign-aman,* the Breton specialty of puff pastry and sugar. Here it's a succulent delicacy, while in places such as Paris you would gag on it. This is also a good place to buy tins of Breton *galettes* (butter cookies) for your friends, and *crêpes dentelles* (fluted fruit-filled wafers)— raspberry's the best. These are all things to pack as gifts or to open later for a taste of Breton goodness back home; for your night in Locronan, it's *plateau des fruits de mer* at the Fer à Cheval.

The platter of seafood known as *cotriade,* which you should not leave Brittany without tasting (somewhere, anywhere, if not at the Fer à Cheval—but is there any other place that does it so well?), comes on a bed of hot French fries, which makes us remember how good the simple potato tastes in this country. On this steaming bed, their briny shells brimming with juices, are an assortment of oysters—*belons, fines de claire,* and *cancales*—an overlapping layer of clams and *palourdes* (in succulence, to clams what the capon is to chicken), stray shrimp, crayfish, a spiny *langouste,* a spidery crab, and, best of all, sea snails, periwinkles, and other creatures you'll be delighted to discover. Wash all this down with an icy glass of Muscadet from vineyards near Nantes.

First, of course, make sure there's a room at the inn. Before turning in for the evening, or else in the morning, take a stroll around the square, where you will find some artisans' boutiques, including a woolens shop that carries authentic Breton fishermen's sweaters (people will try to buy yours off your back when you get home), and a woodcarver's shop, where a husband-and-wife team makes functioning puppets (not inexpensive).

To the End of Land's End

This whole part of Brittany, with its gentle green hills rolling down to the sea, ends not far (57 km/35 miles) from Locronan at a place called **Pointe du Raz**.

Pointe du Raz is the westernmost point of continental France and one of the world's most dramatic seascapes. It is a 300-foot drop at the end of a long escarpment stuck out like a finger and carved by the furious wind and sea.

The visit down the cliffs can be dangerous, so it is organized. The *tour de la pointe* (July and August only), which leaves from the parking lot, starts whenever the guide has five people willing to go, and takes an hour. It is wise to wear nonskid shoes and to be in reasonably good shape. Those who stay up top will nonetheless enjoy the spectacular panorama of the Atlantic and the Ile de Sein, and can watch from that safe perch the terrible *raz,* the riptide "before which nothing passes without fear or pain" as it races between the island and the point.

Concarneau and the Morbihan Coast

Concarneau, 24 km (15 miles) southeast of Quimper, is a great attraction, a walled island-city attached to the mainland by two very small bridges. In summer you will encounter within its perfect ramparts happy crowds of the sort that charmed Pinocchio on Stromboli, artistic residents in the midst of their muse, tour-bus passengers looking for restrooms, seafood bistros (try the *friture*), antiques shops, pottery sheds, and card and curio shops. Seeing Concarneau in summertime is like visiting a town during the World Cup or the World Series. In winter, though, the people are gone, many of the shops are closed, and the place seems to lose something. **Auberge Les Grandes Roches** in Trégunc (6.5 km/4 miles to the southeast) is the place to stay, if not pronounce. The auberge is a restored farm and has a restaurant, a park, and parking.

But a mere hop and a skip farther down the road there are even older sites.

Pont-Aven and Carnac

Fifteen kilometers (9 miles) east of Concarneau is Pont-Aven, an artists' colony with a difference: cookies. Pont-Aven was a home to Gauguin and many other painters; see the art museum—the **Musée Municipal**—and galleries here. If you don't have the money to buy art and want something that will fit in your suitcase, you might instead buy a tin of Breton *galettes* in Pont-Aven, since it is home to one of the great cookie companies of the world, Trou Mad. Their tins of delicious butter cookies are relatively cheap and have paintings by Gauguin and various Breton motifs on the lid. They make wonderful gifts and are available in many card and curio shops on the main route through town.

Carnac, southeast along the coast (near Quiberon), preserves the rubble of antiquity and is sort of a mini-Stonehenge along the road. These are Stone Age dolmens, monuments, possibly tombs, dug out of their original sites—which you can also visit. A field of white sabertooth megaliths, a hundred yards wide, half a mile long, and numbering 1,099 rocks, runs next to the roadside less than a mile from Carnac along route D 196. No one knows why or how prehistoric man put the stones there; suffice it to say he did. The largest megalith in the region is at **Locmariaquer**. This broken giant, measuring some 60 feet in length and weighing nearly 350 tons, is 13 km (8 miles) east of Carnac on Route D 781.

Within Carnac, the **Tumulus de St-Michel** provides an intimate look, by candlelight, into a tomb of the prehistoric race that erected these giants in stone and then disappeared so completely.

On a peninsula just west of Carnac is **Quiberon**, a jumping-off point should you wish to visit the bucolic **Belle-Ile-en-Mer**, the largest island of Brittany. Here are wild coasts lined with grottoes and seabirds, as well as Sarah Bernhardt's summer retreat. Boats to the isle leave from Quiberon every day, and the ride, always cool and bracing, takes under an hour; for information Tel: 97-31-80-01. Try the charming **Le Cardinal** in the port of Sauzon on Belle-Ile for an overnight stay in the area.

Farther east along the coast is La Baule, with its big hotels, casinos, and five-mile-long beach. **Hermitage** in La Baule is among the most stylish retreats along France's entire west coast—with prices to match.) After that there remains only Nantes near the mouth of the Loire—if the nearby Muscadet vineyards interest you.

THE NORTH COAST
Rennes

Most visitors would do best to reboard the train at Vannes, on the Golfe du Morbihan northeast of Carnac, or at Quimper, and head back toward Paris as far as Rennes, the principal entry point for the north Breton coast.

Rennes is the capital of Brittany. Almost any Breton (except a bureaucrat, who probably comes from Paris) will tell you it's "not really Brittany." It certainly is a railhead, though, and Rennes is as close as you can comfortably come (primarily for scheduling reasons) to the great group of north coast attractions: Le Mont-Saint-Michel (it's actually in Normandy but makes most sense approached from Rennes), St-Malo (often overlooked, which you shouldn't do), and Brittany's Côte d'Emeraude (Emerald Coast), plus splendid oyster-eating places all along the way.

There's really not much to hold you in Rennes. The rental car agencies are handy to the train station—just follow the signs marked SNCF, the French National Railroad. It's just as well to get an early start toward Mont-Saint-Michel to the north. Though the distance is not great (65 km/40 miles), the turns in the road (N 175) are numerous and you'll probably see some things worth a short stop along the way—most likely in the form of a crêperie—so figure a morning or an afternoon to get there comfortably.

Le Mont-Saint-Michel

According to how the sands at the mouth of the estuary have shifted, this wonder of the Medieval world, built over a span of three centuries, is either in Normandy or in Brittany. Right now it's in Normandy.

Plan your itinerary to arrive during daylight. The outline of the island and its spindle-shaped spire visible from afar form one of the most memorable sights in all of France and must not be missed. Watch how it changes as you approach leisurely, the island getting larger, the road descending, the country flattening out into salt marshes, where sheep graze on grass on the fringes of the sea. They are your dinner, the famous *pré-salé*—salt-meadow—sheep of Mont-Saint-Michel. The salt in the marsh grass gives the sheep a delectable taste, and for that reason lamb is the regional specialty.

If you lodge in the Mont-Saint-Michel area it should be at **La Mère Poulard**. Write, phone, or telegram ahead. There are not many times this effort is required, but it would be madness to leave the area without experiencing it. Should management claim that a room is not available, try tears. Should they still not yield, you can overnight at St-Malo (52 km/32 miles—about a half hour—to the west), where one hotel is as good as another and prices are softer, but remember to reserve for dinner at La Mère Poulard. The pleasure of its table is the great evening joy of Mont-Saint-Michel.

First there's the aforementioned *pré-salé,* done to a turn here. You sit at a long table under wooden beams and the whole room rings with the work of men in leather aprons standing in the fireplace. What are they doing there? Making your dessert.

The sound comes from wire whisks in great copper bowls, the perfect implements for whipping egg whites into mountains of creamy foam to create the frothiest, softest of soufflés that ever emerged from a hearth. Naturally you'll have one.

After dinner, with the whole Mont under lights and (maybe) under stars, is the time to take a stroll—but go before dessert, before you lose the lights. La Mère will hold the soufflé for you if you're still at table. Walk outside the walls and down the causeway to take in the entire island lit up, from the sheer ramparts growing out of the gray rock to the spire etched against the night sky.

Both fortress and religious shrine, during the Middle Ages the Mont was especially rich in pilgrims' gifts. It was protected against sack and invasion by the ferocious tide, which comes roaring in with the speed of a racehorse and with enough power to splatter besieging armies against the seawall. This fact of nature, along with a hearty band of monks, was the only defense the pyramiding spires of Mont-Saint-Michel—collectively called, as they are, "the miracle"—ever needed. Miraculous is the word that best describes the superb Gothic ensemble of the uppermost north façade of the islet.

(One marauding despot did devise a subtle ploy to rob Mont-Saint-Michel of its treasures on a night the tide was out. He thought to bribe the monks to pull his army up a dumbwaiter to the heights of the Mont, from which the invaders would take the keep from within. All night long the monks labored, but at dawn the drawbridge did not come crashing down—for all night long the monks had drawn the soldiers up the shaft and, one by one, beheaded them.)

The structures are built in a heavenly ascent from earth to sky. They begin, above the rampart wall, with the Aumonerie, the great residence of chaplains and monks, on one side. On the other is the great hall of knights. The next tier is the cloister with arcades and galleries that seem to hover in the sky. What a miracle this must have seemed to the ancients—to walk 200 feet above the water. (Could heaven be much higher?) There are wonderfully worked sculptures to see in these walks—busts and whole human shapes, and animals, too, amid the decor of surrounding leaves. The arcades overhead are suspended by the lightest and airiest of spindle columns. The water font at the entry was for the washing of feet.

But above this colonnade is still another step on the stairway to heaven: the great refectory. This large, luminous building has long, narrow windows, and everything that enters is bathed in a sanctifying light. Here the whole host of knights (on pilgrimage) and monks assembled. Eating here, a borderline sin, must have seemed celestial.

And above all this was the final step on the way to the final reward, as it is the final statement in Mont-Saint-Michel's architecture. There, atop an esplanade of terraces and buttresses, soars the church, its spire thrusting 500 feet into the sky, the final achivement in the architectural ensemble and in the ascent of Western Medieval man.

St-Malo

After Mont-Saint-Michel at night and the sight of the galloping tide that once ran down invading armies as it rushed in, what more can the coast hold? St-Malo, a Renaissance city surrounded by a wall and the sea.

Here is the Breton port to see, a virtual fort. The Breton corsairs, the men of St-Malo, declared themselves "neither French nor Breton, but Malouïn." If there was ever a Venice of the north of France, a place where seafaring commerce was king (with a little piracy thrown in), this is it. The wall was the Malouïns' attempt to protect themselves against their competition and against raids by the English.

The best way to experience this old port is to enter through the ramparts, find a bakery, buy a bag of glazed chestnuts (those of St-Malo are easily the best in France), climb atop the ramparts, and, munching and marching, walk the entire circumference of the wall. Here is an opportunity to take a tour of some of the loveliest Renaissance architecture in France at its second-story level. The height advantage exposes rooflines and other details—extravagant chimney pots, for example—seldom seen in homes of the upper bourgeoisie, as well as a view of the maritime life below. All the while you will be refreshed by the sea, which almost completely rings the city. The spectacle is best when the tide reaches its 30-foot height, for then the sea is at its wildest, but at any time you will get a close-up view of the many old buildings, now successfully restored after their almost total destruction during World War II.

A sort of second resurrection of St-Malo is currently visible in the many mansions marked by recent gentrification; wealthy landowners from the surrounding countryside are now flocking to buy vacation homes here, precipitating a flight *to* the city instead of the usual other way around. Those who want to stay *intra muros* (within the walls) of this fascinating town could do no better than the **Hotel Central**, a fine downtown hotel, with its restaurant **La Frégate** serving Breton seafood. And the restaurant **La Duchesse Anne** (5, place Guy La Chambre; Tel: 99-40-85-33) offers Breton grilled lobster, *fruits de mer,* and fresh *foie gras,* which has nothing to do with Brittany but everything to do with gastronomy. At any hotel in town, pick a room on an upper floor; with building elevations regulated your room will be filled with sunshine.

Any great city, especially a port, has its own special mystique. Along the wall thrust out into the harbor is St-Malo's statue to Jacques Cartier, the first native son to cross the Atlantic, braving the wild seas that begin at the foot of the wall. On his second such voyage Cartier was amazed to find a Breton fishing fleet already in Canadian waters; news of a good fishing spot travelled far even then. The Breton fleet still puts in appearances on the Grand Banks in quest of the singular salmon and cod.

Cancale and Oysters

Along this bay- and inlet-riddled coast, the monstrous tides often leave beaches so naked that it is possible to wade a quarter of a mile out to sea with the water remaining at your ankles. Here in its most productive beds is that most celebrated of Breton shellfish, the oyster. It couldn't be better met than in one of the region's famous oyster towns, Cancale, 14 km (9 miles) east of St-Malo.

The key to good eating in Brittany, in place after place along the coast and inland, is to order fresh produce, simply prepared. To keep an oyster feast simple, all you want is oysters, bread—pumpernickel—and wine (some people also nibble *pommes frites*). The place to go for these is any one of Cancale's bars or cafés facing the port. The wine to order is Muscadet.

A short course on ordering: Oysters in France are sized and priced according to a ubiquitous grading system. The largest size is described on a menu as "000." These are seldom seen. The next are "00"; most menus begin with this size, and these are the costliest. Six will usually do. The next size, the "0," is about a third again as small. Note that the price of the oyster will decline with size, but only within its type; oyster variety is the other price consideration. *Cancales* and *belons*—the flat (*plat*) oysters—are usually the most expensive types, followed by *fines de claire* and *papillons*. (*Cancale* oysters are so called because all of those taken from its waters—between Mont-Saint-Michel and St-Malo—have such a strong "personality." An oyster expert, of which there are of course many in France, can taste the difference between a *cancale* and a *belon* (a South Coast oyster) as surely as a wine expert discerns the difference between a Bordeaux and a Burgundy.) All are ordered by the dozen in "0" size. A real Breton oyster tasting is one of the musts when you are in Brittany; it is part of the culture, and in no other place in the world can you do it as well.

The French don't wash oysters in fresh water, nor do they soak them in barley water to purge them as it is done in foreign oyster bars and restaurants. The French have a horror of such practices. "Why do you want to wash an oyster?" they ask. Why should you want to purge them? An oyster should taste of the sea! That's the idea. Indeed, it is this sea taste—those of Cancale, for example, are marked with the particularly rich flavor of the plankton in the bay of Mont-Saint-Michel—that makes each oyster a fingerprint of the area it comes from. Also, in France oysters are opened by oyster openers. Even in Paris this man is usually Breton. His fingers are as fat and red as his nose and scarred by occasional slips of the knife on the shell. This is all he does in life; as he opens an oyster, in the bat of an eye he knows if it is one to discard or one to add to the pile for your table.

So if this is your first feast on the Breton oyster, watch out. Your tongue is about to be aggressed. No lemon-squirted, watery-eyed candidate for cocktail sauce is this oyster, but something of the sauce primeval—the sea.

Côte d'Emeraude

Westward from St-Malo lies the Côte d'Emeraude (Emerald Coast), a progression of dramatic seascapes, cathedrals, colorful fishing fleets, and quaint villages.

The first stop is **St-Servan**, just south of St-Malo, with a good sandy bathing beach, a lively spit of forest, and elegant buildings. The town offers lovely views of St-Malo and the Ile du Grand-Bé, with its fortified tower and the tomb of Chateaubriand. Across the Rance estuary and almost facing St-Malo is **Dinard**, the gem of the Côte d'Emeraude. Where St-Malo is walled in and fortified, Dinard is open and social. Where in St-Malo there are history and rocks, in Dinard there is sand. Where in St-Malo there are statues to Jacques Cartier and the mansions of burghers, in Dinard there are casinos, swimming pools, and tennis. Dinard's Grande Plage is an astonishing beach filled with astonishing bathers. The bikini may be a French invention, but there are plenty of American and English accents here. On the other side of the little peninsula is another beach with a serpentine walk called the Promenade du Clair de Lune (Moonlight Promenade). The **Reine Hortense** hotel is convenient to both beaches. It has no restaurant but its rooms are luxurious.

Save morning daylight for Dinard, too. There are villas niched into its coves and green hills enveloped by the balmy breezes of a mild microclimate. The Gulf Stream ends around here and, having ended, flirts. The climate of Brittany is in general much warmer than you might expect; there is never winter. Finistère exports spring vegetables, shallots, new potatoes, and tomatoes to much of the world year-round. Exuberant bursts of tropical flora—aloe plants, palm trees, mimosa—may surprise you. If you climb the fingerlike green hills that splay out into the Atlantic you will attain the simultaneous pleasures of watching a tempestuous sea and being in a tropical paradise.

An excursion not to be missed is a trip down the Rance. Boats leave from Dinard at the river's mouth and go to where the estuary, gulf size at first, narrows to barge-canal width. This hour-and-a-half journey will show you what the North Breton coast is all about: the river and the sea, and in between, the steep forested folds that rise to mountainous heights. Back near Dinard at the mouth of the Rance is a technological wonder to behold: French engineers have harnessed the dramatic tides that run upriver and converted their power to electricity at the Marémotrice de la Rance, the world's first tidal-energy station.

Dinan, down where the canal begins and not to be confused with Dinard, is a village filled with so much Medieval charm that, were it indoors, it could pass for a museum. In fact, it *is* almost small enough to qualify, which makes it all the easier to see. The town's crooked old streets (see especially the rue du Jerzual) and antique houses, timbered and overhanging the street, are interspersed with gardens and trees. There are ramparts, a massive château, a great clock tower, and a good crêperie. Dinan is an excellent place to rest and watch the hands of its 15th-century clock turn. The hotel **D'Avaugour** is central, in step with the town's spirit, and a good place to stay.

The West Beaches

Farther west, the beaches of the Côte d'Emeraude open up at every turn. The town of **St-Lunaire**, just 4.5 km (3 miles) west of Dinard, has two elegant beaches, tennis courts, a long promenade out to sea, and the **Grotte de la Goule-aux-Fées** (Grotto of the Sirens), a hole in a rock through which the wind howls mournfully.

Just around the bend is **St-Briac**, cheek by jowl with **Lancieux**; both are quiet, with less casino action and more family feeling. Farther on comes **St-Cast**: seven beaches and two superb lookout points—a popular place with the locals. After several more twists in the road, you'll come to the remarkable, brooding Fort de la Latte (an hour away); then the corniche road arrives on what is arguably the most splendid lookout on a whole coast of splendid lookouts: **Cap Fréhel**. From here, a panorama of sky and sea with plumes of spray shooting off the end of the point, you can look north to England, whence the Bretons came; westward to America, where many went; or back to St-Malo. It is one of the great natural wonders of Brittany, and one that gives some understanding of this region's hazards.

After Cap Fréhel the Côte d'Emeraude peters out. There's a charming beach at **Le Val-André** and a family beach at **St-Brieuc**, which also has a fortified church, but it is at Paimpol where the sun creates a coast of a different color.

Côte du Granit Rose

The landscape now changes to outcroppings of rocks marching seaward, where the surf boils into ribbons of foam. This is not a place to go bathing. Everywhere the rocks are blushed with rose, as if in an eternal sunset. And although they are made of the same stuff, the villages here are more accommodating than the beaches.

Paimpol was celebrated in song and in literature as the most typically Breton town of all. The hero of Pierre Loti's novel *Pêcheur d'Islande* (*An Iceland Fisherman*) comes from here (Breton fishermen make the storm-tossed voyage to Iceland routinely, even in winter); Loti did for Paimpol what Marcel Pagnol did for Marseille. Yet Paimpol is pleasingly sleepy and isolated among its rocks. The wild pinks and *bleuets* that bloom here are not trampled under tourists' soles; the stone pier that juts into the sea to welcome the fishing fleet—and a well-sheltered cove it creates, too—does not groan under the crush of humanity. You can find your place in the sun here. Under the pretty parasols that line the beach you can sip a cider, watch the boats, or read a book peacefully.

The town, like the rocks, is in eternal sunset, or sunrise, being entirely built of pink granite—right down to the quaint church.

But as the song goes, when in Paimpol follow *la Paimpolaise*. And where does she go? Why, to the **Ile de Bréhat**. The island, less than two miles long, is very near—ten minutes from Arcouest—and automobiles are forbidden there. You can spend several hours climbing the slopes and drinking in a surprising variety of wild Breton flora: cedars, fig trees, palm trees. There are great rock crevices down by the sea that in low tide can be used for swimming holes—an ideal way to recharge the spirit for the wear and tear of the road. A little town, Port Clos, and citadel are huddled around its lovely enclosed harbor, where cafés offer light refreshment to those visitors without picnics.

Tréguier

The town of Tréguier, 15 km (9 miles) west of Paimpol, is complemented by a host of attractive beaches, the beach at the nearby resort of **Perros-Guirec** having the most to offer. But it is Tréguier itself that is the most interesting.

If you've come this far, you will have begun to know Brittany and so must see Tréguier, for it contains the major elements of the region's mystique: a saint, the sea, and the products of the sea. All three are centered around the cathedral.

The cathedral of Tréguier is one of the most beautiful in Brittany, in both its scale and its rapport with the town. The **cathedral of St-Tugdual** and its attached cloister rise from the center of the great place du Martray in the middle of the town, where none of the surrounding buildings is close enough to hem them in. The visitor thus gets an upsweeping view of the cathedral and its spire, which soars like a ship's mast above the marketplace.

All towns in Brittany have their churches, but this cathedral is one you should definitely enter—not only for the windows, sculpture, and architecture, or out of devotion, but for the story it tells of the region.

Erected from the 13th to the 15th centuries, the cathedral has three towers that mark three points of the cross, one with a spire and one containing a magnificent rose window. Everywhere the granite is worked with a lightness and finesse that is now a lost art. The two Christs, in wood, are particularly fine, but the statue of Saint Yves is especially noteworthy here.

This may be Saint Tugdual's cathedral, but it is Saint Yves who is the more popular here. Indeed, he is the most popular saint in Brittany, where he is known as "Monsieur Saint-Yves." Yves was born in nearby Minihy-Tréguier in the middle of the 13th century. After becoming a priest and finishing his studies in Paris, he returned to Tréguier as the bishop's assistant and did legal work for the poor. Yves argued their cases so well and so purely that he was canonized a hundred years later as the patron saint of lawyers. Along with a page from his prayer book the cathedral possesses Saint Yves's skull, a relic whose closely spaced eye sockets still convey the bony stare of a lawyer.

Outside in the square, the sights and sounds of market morning will reanimate you. A good time to catch all French markets at their liveliest is an hour before mealtime—just the time it takes the locals to go to the market, see what's fresh, and take it home and cook it. Because this is Brittany, the market on Tréguier's place du Martray offers primarily fish. To visitors the produce and its plenty is astonishing.

Everything is raw, cold, and fresh, and heaped in baskets and barrels: sole, mullet, turbot, rays, sea bass, and mackerel; oysters, mussels, clams, lobster, *langouste,* and more sea creatures. If you have a camper or a boat with a freezer, Tréguier is a good place to fill more than your eyes.

L'Armorique

This is the word that causes so much confusion for writers of menus and cookbooks. After Perros-Guirec it appears on road signs—the Corniche d'Armorique begins just a few miles away, then come the l'Armorique mountains, then the Pays Armorique . . . l'Armorique . . . l'Amérique. A slip of the tongue or pen can cause a jump of 3,000 miles.

Is it correct to call the well-known recipe for lobster in tomato sauce *homard à l'américaine?* Or should it be *homard à l'armoricaine?* There is a story that goes with the untangling tale.

It seems there was a young man from Armorique—the ancient name for Brittany—who went to make his mark in Amérique—to "chercher l'Amérique" as many other French had done. This young Breton opened a restaurant there and was astonished at the high quality of the lobsters. "I know what to do with these," he supposedly said, and he prepared them according to an old recipe of his maiden aunt's, an Armoricaine. As he worked hard and became famous for the recipe, his restaurant was visited by travelling French chefs (definitely not Breton) who sampled the lobsters and, astonished that so fine a dish could be found in a country with so rude a culinary background, brought it back home to Paris, where it was christened *"homard à l'américaine."* It was quite natural that Parisians might make this mistake, for most of them had never heard of l'Armorique (the name derives from a Breton word meaning "by the sea").

This in fact is the Breton lament: Stuck out on their peninsula, they are the forgotten French. No matter what they do, they hardly ever get recognition, and even when they do someone else gets the credit.

So you will pardon them if they seem a little standoffish. You will not take offense if they speak their Breton tongue when a tourist—Parisian included—is within earshot. It's not that they're rude or suspicious of strangers; it's because they choose not to change the essentials of who they are to suit anyone else. That's why Brittany is "the part of France with the most character." No matter how French it gets it will always be France with a difference.

GETTING AROUND

The gateway to Brittany is Rennes, 350 km (210 miles) from Paris on Autoroute A 11 (Autoroute de l'Oceanne), which becomes A 81 at Le Mans, and now only two hours from Paris by the TGV, which goes on to Brest, on one trunk, and to Nantes and Le Croisic on the other. There are frequent flights on Air Inter from all Paris airports to Rennes, Lorient, Quimper, and Brest. (Seats are hard to come by, so reserve far in advance.) Brit Air flies from London's Gatwick Airport to Quimper and Rennes, but most travellers cross the Channel to St-Malo on the ferries from Plymouth and Portsmouth.

Buses of the French National Railway Network connect Rennes with the major seaside resorts. The best way to see the countryside, though, is by car. Hertz, Avis, Europcar, and other major car-rental firms have offices in Rennes.

Nantes, in Brittany's southwest corner, is served directly from Newark International Airport in New Jersey by Air France and by the new TGV Atlantique (two to two and a half hours) from Paris.

ACCOMMODATIONS REFERENCE

▶ **Auberge Les Grandes Roches**. 29910 **Trégunc** Tel: 98-97-62-97.

▶ **D'Avaugour**. 1, place du Champ Clos, 22100 **Dinan**. Tel: 96-39-07-49.

▶ **Le Cardinal**. Sauzon 56360 **Belle-Ile-en-Mer**. Tel: 97-31-61-60.

▶ **Le Central et restaurant La Frégate**. 6, Grande Rue, 35400 **St-Malo**. Tel: 99-40-87-70.

▶ **Gradlon**. 30, rue Brest, 29000 **Quimper**. Tel: 98-95-04-39; Fax: 98-95-61-25.

▶ **Hermitage**. Esplanade François André, 44500 **La Baule**. Tel: 40-60-37-00; Fax: 40-24-33-65.

▶ **Hôtel Au Fer à Cheval**. Route du Bois-de-Nevet, 29180 **Locronan**. Tel: 98-91-70-67.

▶ **La Mère Poulard**. 50116 **Le Mont-Saint-Michel**. Tel: 33-60-14-01; Telex: 170197; Fax: 33-60-14-01.

▶ **Reine Hortense**. 19, rue Malouine, 35800 **Dinard**. Tel: 99-46-54-31.

THE LOIRE VALLEY

By *Georgia I. Hesse, Jennifer Quale,*
and Sally Lefèvre

Georgia I. Hesse is the editorial consultant for this guide-
book. Jennifer Quale has written about France for Food
& Wine, The New York Times, *and* European Travel &
Life. *She lives in New York City. Sally Lefèvre has lived in*
Turkey and England as well as Canada, where she pro-
duced a national radio program on tourism. She now
lives in France, where she has lived more than 12 years,
and contributes to several U.S. and European publica-
tions and guidebooks.

The Loire river, which seems to have few raisons d'être
other than enchantment, flows through land that by any
name—the garden of France, château country, the erstwhile playground of kings—is infused with spring and
summer richness. (Meteorologists call it a microclimate.)
The Loire Valley suggests idling, an afternoon picnic under leafy trees, back roads scented by lilacs and "glycines"
(wisteria), light wines, and perhaps a nap. This is not
country to be hurried through, though one-day tours out
of Paris exist for that very purpose.

The traveller's Loire includes 15 *départements,* but historical regional names more truly reflect the cultures,
habits, and allegiances of the people: Orléanais, Touraine,
Anjou (the old capital of which was Angers), Maine, and
maybe, by pushing things slightly, Berry.

Following strictly the curving river's course, you could
begin in Sancerre (home of the brisk white wine, a lovely

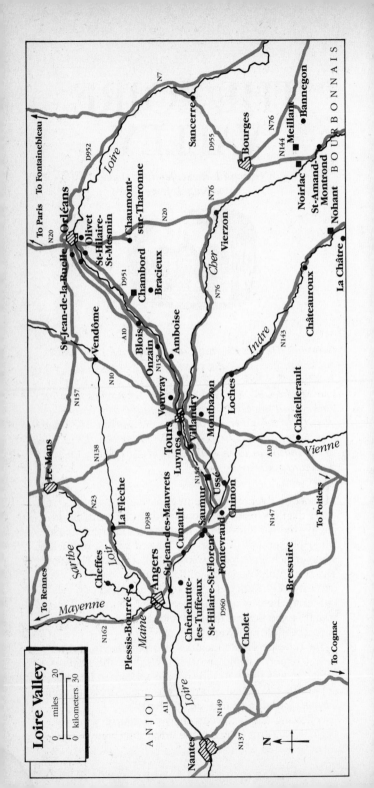

Loire Valley

0 miles 20
0 kilometers 30

rosé, and a lesser-known light red) in the east and wander via Tours and Angers to about Nantes (home of the seafood-lover's Muscadet wines) in the west. But driving from Paris you meet the Loire at Orléans; with such a route, Sancerre would be relegated to a Burgundian itinerary and Nantes to a Breton tour.

Starting at Orléans and working west along the river Loire through Tours to Angers in the west, the tour described here then backtracks to Bourges toward the southeast as a side trip and ends at Sancerre as a jumping-off point for Burgundy.

MAJOR INTEREST

The six most remarkable châteaux: Chambord, Blois, Amboise, Chenonceaux, Loches, and Azay-le-Rideau

Other important châteaux: Villandry, Langeais, Chinon, Chaumont, Cheverny, Ussé

Church of Cunault

Abbey of Fontevraud (Plantagenêt tombs)

Châteaux to stay in

Regional wines (Vouvray, Chinon, Sancerre, Bourgueil, Montlouis, etc.)

River fish (notably perchlike *sandre*) with *beurre blanc,* local *chèvres,* and produce

Tours
Cathedral of St-Gatien
Musée des Beaux-Arts

Angers
The château (Apocalypse tapestries)
Cathedral of St-Maurice
Musée Turpin de Crissé

Bourges
Cathedral of St-Etienne
Palais Jacques-Coeur
Cistercian abbey of Noirlac

Sancerre

Orléans

A trade and business center since its very beginnings, Orléans, despite being the largest city on the route from Paris to the Loire Valley, is of little tourist interest today, possibly because its center was severely damaged by fire during World War II. Were it not for Joan of Arc, the "Maid of Orléans," who came to town to relieve it from the English siege in May 1429, probably even fewer Loire-bound travellers would now stop here.

Orléans's one star shines everywhere: on the rue Jeanne d'Arc, in the Maison de Jeanne d'Arc, the Joan of Arc school, the statue of Joan of Arc in the place du Martroi, the chapel and stained-glass windows of Joan of Arc in the cathedral of Ste-Croix. Then, of course, there are also the stores that do a brisk business in Joan of Arc memorabilia (including Joan of Arc key chains) and the inevitable Café Jeanne d'Arc. The festival of Joan of Arc is held each year during the first week in May.

There is an Orléans beyond Joan of Arc, however. The **Musée des Beaux-Arts**, in the same square as the cathedral, makes up in modern functionalism for what it lacks in style. Among the early paintings a Velázquez, a Louis Le Nain, and a Georges de La Tour are standouts, but there are also fine 18th- and 19th-century French paintings, particularly portraits. The **cathedral of Ste-Croix**, almost the size of Paris's Notre-Dame, is notable chiefly for the 18th-century woodwork in its chancel.

Orléans's top hotel is the modern, 109-room link in the **Sofitel** hotel chain right off the river on quai Barentin, in the lower-expensive category. Its poolside dining room, **La Vénerie**, is of a high standard. Otherwise, local hotels are rather ordinary. About 7 km (4 miles) to the southwest in St-Hilaire-St-Mesmin, the peaceful, 20-room **Escale du Port Arthur** offers a pretty location and franc-wise rates. Another reasonable find is the small **Le Rivage** on rue de la Reine Blanche in Olivet, about 5 km (3 miles) south of Orléans. Here, at this grand old house on the banks of the Loiret, you can expect good meals as well.

The restaurant scene in Orléans is smarter. Vying for the top spot are **La Crémaillère** (34, rue Notre-Dame-de-Recouvrance; Tel: 38-53-49-17) and **La Poutrière** (8, rue de la Brèche; Tel: 38-66-02-30). What the setting at La Crémaillère lacks in pizzazz, the respected Breton chef more than compensates for with such seafood specialties as *saucisson de homard*. The cozier La Poutrière (*poutre* means "beam") offers classic cuisine with original touches in its mirrored dining room or outside on a lovely garden terrace. **Les Antiquaires** at 2, rue au Lin (Tel: 38-53-52-35) draws a loyal clientele for its caring service, comfortable surroundings, and affordable prices—as well as fish fresh from the Loire.

The Era of the Great Châteaux

In the 15th and 16th centuries everybody who was anybody had to have a château, from Hurault de Cheverny (whose classic castle still belongs to the family) to François I (who needed at least a dozen and employed Cellini as his jeweler, Raphael as his portraitist, and Andrea del Sarto and Leonardo da Vinci as his court painters).

The Italian Renaissance in architecture, which began in Florence around 1420, had by the end of the century been exported to France. The reign of François I (1515–1547) was, in the words of his biographer, Desmond Seward, "the most radiant, the most creative in French history, a reign in which two brilliant cultures came together, those of Gothic France and Renaissance Italy... no ruler since Charlemagne has had a more direct influence upon the civilization of France."

The newer châteaux were quite distinct from the *châteaux forts,* or strongholds, of the 10th and 11th centuries, which were dark, dank, dirty, and cold. Over the centuries the *châteaux forts,* some of them veritable fortified towns, metamorphosed from fortresses into palaces. Arrow slits grew into proper windows, naked stone was covered with panels in a fan of colors and complex designs, genuine military-defense structures were translated into architectural caprices, and castles moved from protected heights down onto great greenswards. The châteaux built in the 17th and 18th centuries, on the other hand, are less proper châteaux than country seats (though far more elaborate than country homes or manor houses of today). Like their Renaissance forebears, a handful of hoteliers today collect châteaux to parlay them into the most sumptuous hotels outside of Paris. Other chatelains, with more modest budgets but equal entrepreneurial gusto, are turning their centuries-old family homes into bed-and-breakfasts nonpareil—thus beating the high property taxes.

Nobody knows exactly how many châteaux exist in the forests and parklands along the Loire and its tributaries. Of the more than 1,000, there may be about 300 major ones; the following covers the most significant and attractive. Typically many châteaux open to the public offer cultural or sound-and-light programs as well as guided tours.

Château de Chambord

En route from Paris or Sancerre (from the northeast or the east), you come first to Chambord, the valley's biggest and perhaps most incredible château, with 218 rooms, 365 chimneys, and a fantasy of turrets, dormers, and gables (Seward likens the roof to "an overcrowded chessboard"). Chambord has a renowned octagonal staircase, a double helix in stone that allows people (or, in its time, horses) ascending to see but never meet those descending.

Some say Leonardo may have been the architect of Chambord, but because he died before serious construction began and because his sketchbooks give no details, odds go to Domenico da Cortona, who may well have shown his model to Leonardo as well as François.

François was passionate about Chambord, continuing to build through good times and bad (at one point the king ordered work to continue even though he hadn't the cash to ransom his son from Spain). Once he even considered diverting the Loire to have it run by the château.

If it is true that Chambord was intended mainly as a hunting lodge, it continues to function as planned, for it commands a giant 13,000-acre reserve, **le Parc de Chambord**, which has been set aside for hunting but also has platforms for viewing deer and wild boar at feeding times.

In 1670 Molière's *Le Bourgeois Gentilhomme* premiered at Chambord. Nowadays a sound-and-light performance on the life of François I is held at the château in summer.

Château de Cheverny

This classic château south of Chambord via D 112 and D 102, constructed in a single, continuous stroke, is more elegant, better dressed, and altogether more warming and welcoming as a residence than any of its castle colleagues. For one thing, it retains almost entirely the 17th-century furnishings and decorations from the days of its builder, Hurault de Cheverny. For another, it is still kept within the family, the possession of a descendant of the builder, the marquis de Vibraye.

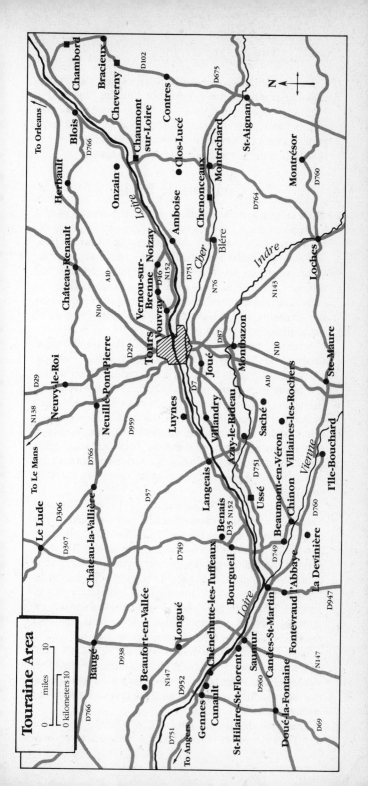

The home boasts five Gobelins tapestries and several valuable paintings; the kennels for hunting dogs and a hunting museum are open to the public. More than 2,500 sets of deer antlers testify to the good aim of several generations of Chevernois. A sound-and-light show on Louis XII is performed here in July and August.

Château de Blois

Originally, a fort designed to thwart the attacks of the Vikings stood upon this defensive site west of Chambord on the river. Of that, only the 13th-century **Tour du Foix** and **Salle des Etats** remain. To circle the courtyard with your eyes is to see the history of French architecture through the Gothic and early Renaissance periods of Louis XII, past the pure Renaissance style of François I, to the severely classical **Gaston d'Orléans wing**, the work of François Mansart for Louis XIII.

Louis XII took over from Charles VIII in 1498 when Charles, on his way to a tennis match at his castle at Amboise, struck his head upon a door lintel and died a few hours later. Louis married Charles's widow, Anne de Bretagne (Brittany), moved the court to Blois, and began building. His contributions are the brick and stone **Galerie Charles-d'Orléans**, the **Chapelle-St-Calais** (of which only the chancel remains), and the **Louis XII wing**. Each has a delightful, airy, informal quality, even though they were too heavily restored—to some tastes—in the 19th century.

Soon after Louis XII's death in 1515, his daughter, Claude de France, married François I, who ascended to the throne. Claude died at Blois in 1524, having borne François seven children in eight years. She was 25. The best parts of Blois date from this period, especially the carved, white stone spiral **Grand Escalier** (Grand Staircase) in an octagonal well. On a platform at each level, according to Seward, "François' guard paraded in tiers in their striped uniforms of blue, red, and white, holding halberds—and torches at night—to salute him when he rode in."

Blois Château's fairly dull interior, the result of a 19th-century restoration by a pupil of Eugène-Emmanuel Viollet-le-Duc, pales by comparison with the exciting exterior, save for the fact that so much drama was played out within the walls.

This was the home, after all, of Charles d'Orléans (1391–1465), son of Louis d'Orléans, who was taken prisoner by the English at the Battle of Agincourt and remained a prisoner for 25 years, during which time he polished his great gift for poetry. On his return to France in 1440 Charles married Marie de Clèves; he was 50 years old, she 14. Charles had a part of the old fortress torn down and more livable quarters raised, in which he created a kind of *beaux-arts* court. He was 71 when his son—the future Louis XII—was born.

In 1588 the sniveling Henri III saw to the murder of his rival, the duc de Guise, on the second floor of the château, and the following year his remarkable mother, Catherine de Médicis (Catherine of the Bad Press, it could be said now), died there. Visitors are dutifully shown the cabinets on the first floor in which Catherine is supposed to have secreted her poisons.

The château includes a *beaux-arts* museum and the Robert Houdin gallery; the magician Henry Houdini named himself after this master illusionist, who was a native of Blois. In June the stunning historical drama "Once Upon a Time, Louis XII" is performed with more than 300 characters in period costume. Between mid-March and mid-September the *son-et-lumière* "Spirits Prefer the Night" is shown (in English and French).

Blois the Town

Serene and hospitable, Blois makes for easy strolling and absorbing the unhurried pace of the region. Take a café au lait or pink beer (flavored with grenadine syrup) at the outdoor **Bar Louis XII** across from the château and watch the youngsters zip along the ramparts' edge on skateboards.

The old quarter around the cathedral of St-Louis is worth exploring for its picturesque houses, the beautiful gardens of the **Bishops' Palace**, and the statue of the Huguenot Denis Papin, the inventor of the pressure cooker. The **church of St-Nicolas**, near the château, is the most interesting in Blois; the capitals in the chancel should especially be noted.

The aroma of chocolate permeates much of the area: Almost every chocoholic visitor stops by **Chocolaterie Poulain**, not far from the château on the avenue Gambetta, if not for a factory tour at least for a sample of the famed candies made here since 1848.

Wednesdays and Saturdays are the best market days, especially when strawberries and asparagus are in season. Although the local restaurant scene has apparently always been bleak, now **Le Bocca d'Or**, in a delightful 14th-century vaulted cellar on rue Haute, gives reason to feast on something other than chocolate in Blois; Tel: 54-78-04-74. Patricia Wells, in *The Food Lover's Guide to France,* recommends driving 18 km (12 miles) east to Bracieux, where Bernard and Christine Robin prepare regional specialties in an old coaching inn at 1, avenue Chambord. Indeed, **Bernard Robin** (reserve; Tel: 54-46-41-22), formerly Le Relais, ranks among the best restaurants in the Loire Valley. Hats off to its fish and game dishes.

The top hostelry in the vicinity (Blois proper, of almost 50,000 people, offers little) is the **Domaine des Hauts de Loire**, reflected in the swan pond of its own park just 17 km (11.5 miles) southwest along the river in Onzain. A genteel air pervades the ivy-covered manoir, known for understated elegance in both its decor and its cuisine. There are tennis courts are on the property, and the Bonnigal family, who own the hotel, will gladly make arrangements for fishing, golf, and horseback riding. Nearby, the small **Château des Tertres**, a bed-and-breakfast on a leafy knoll, is a pleasant, less expensive alternative, though it is modest by château standards.

Château de Chaumont

About 40 km (27 miles) upriver from Tours and just downriver from Blois, this is the fortresslike château, complete with drawbridge and cylindrical dungeon, that Catherine de Médicis gave to Diane de Poitiers when she herself took Chenonceaux. Chaumont isn't undesirable, but Diane was spoiled, and she sulked and betook herself to more gracious Anet, near Paris. Students of symbols and inscriptions will immediately take note of the intertwined *C*s of Charles d'Amboise (one of the 16th-century owners) and of his wife, Catherine; the emblem of *chaud mont* (a volcano or, literally, "hot mountain"); and the intertwined *D*s of Diane de Poitiers that, with the hunting horn here and there, suggest Diane as the classical Diana the Huntress.

Then there are the coat of arms of France, the initials of Louis XII and Anne de Bretagne, the hat of Cardinal d'Amboise, and the coat of arms of Charles d'Amboise. Students of classical carvings have a veritable field day at Chaumont.

Chaumont has an American connection: In the 18th century it was owned by a financier named Le Ray, who supported American independence. Benjamin Franklin, when he was minister to the French court, was frequently entertained at the château. Franklin was able to persuade Le Ray to support freebooter John Paul Jones and thus to become instrumental in the creation of the American navy.

Château d'Amboise

There is something irresistible about this castle, a bit downriver from Chaumont, although what remains is only a part of the dominant fortress that stood here in the 16th century. Perhaps it's the handsome setting above the town, or the glittering artistic history, or the fact that Leonardo da Vinci worked and died here.

Charles VIII was born to Louis XI and Charlotte of Savoy at Amboise. Only 13 years old when he assumed the throne, Charles began rebuilding and new construction in 1492, eventually creating one of the finest royal residences on the Loire. The masterpiece from this period is the Gothic **Chapelle St-Hubert**, dedicated to the patron saint of the hunt. The chapel, at one time a portion of the apartments of Queen Anne de Bretagne, is rich in decoration; the stained-glass windows that were destroyed in 1940 have been suitably replaced by Max Ingrand. From an expedition to Italy (which was undertaken to conquer Naples for the House of Valois), Charles returned with an exuberance of artworks, furniture, fabrics, and people: decorators, gardeners, artists, even a chicken breeder.

When Charles died in 1498 (see Bourges), the boy who would become King François I moved to Amboise at the age of six with his mother, Louise of Savoy, and his sister, who would one day become the learned Margaret of Navarre.

As a child, François loved action, shows, tournaments, and display; his enthusiasm for such excesses never left him. In 1518 a particularly diverting mock battle was staged at the château, during which the king and company of 600 men defended a wooden model town against a like force led by the dukes of Bourbon and Vendôme.

"It was the finest mock battle that had ever been seen," Florange wrote, "but it did not please everyone, for some were killed and others terrified."

François enlarged Amboise and made it more magnifi-

cent, but his greatest accomplishment was the importa-
tion of Leonardo da Vinci, who brought with him his
Mona Lisa and *Virgin of the Rocks,* both now in the
Louvre. This one-man Renaissance spent the last three
years of his life in a manor house a cobble's toss from the
château and died there on May 2, 1519 (see below).

War, however, has always been insensitive to artistic
greatness: That August, Leonardo's bones were buried in
the cloister of the church of St-Florentin, as he had asked,
but during the Wars of Religion his remains and those of
hundreds of others were dug up and tossed away. A
plaque in the north transept of the Chapelle St-Hubert
claims Leonardo's bones are there with others, but nobody knows.

A 100-minute *son-et-lumière,* "At the Court of King
François," featuring 420 regional citizens in period dress,
plays during June, July, and August.

Amboise the Town

Before visiting the château (it's a crowded mess in the
afternoons), stop at **Le Clos-Lucé**, the Renaissance manor
where Leonardo spent the last years of his life. The *Mona
Lisa* sojourned here during that time, keeping her smile
despite the long journey from Rome with her master over
the Alps by mules. Le Clos-Lucé is now a museum furnished with 15th- and 16th-century antiques. No originals
are displayed, but models from Leonardo's drawings
show the extraordinary talents he had as an engineer.
There are also small-scale displays, an armored tank, a
helicopter, and a drawbridge among them.

Stop by to see Armand and Janine Langlois (who've
moved their shop from Montpoupon) at **Galerie Atelier
Langlois**, just across the street at 5, rue du Clos-Lucé.
Experts in refined French folk arts, they combine their
talents to produce wooden creatures of the forest mas-
querading in Renaissance finery—at prices far less than
boutiques abroad command. Not far from Clos-Lucé
(everything is easily accessible in Amboise), **Le Manoir St-
Thomas** at place Richelieu (Tel: 47-57-22-52) serves elegant meals in a pretty garden. If you want to stay in
Amboise overnight, a good (but pricey) choice is **Le
Choiseul**. Its 25 rooms, pool, and lovely dining room
overlooking the Loire (and, unfortunately, a campground
across the river) draw a slightly older crowd.

Château de Pray, to the northeast of the village, is

charming. Each of its 16 rooms (many of which overlook the expansive park) is named after a dignitary who has graced the château with his presence since 1244. A particularly nice room is the Duc de Choiseul's, with its large canopy bed. The château also boasts a commendable restaurant. Prices, which are reasonable at present, may well escalate with renovations (such as a pool) in the works.

Château de Chenonceaux

At one time, Chenonceaux (south of Amboise), like most other great châteaux along the Loire, came under the sign of the salamander (the symbol of François I). François was not its builder, though; the structure that is admired today is the 16th-century creation of his tax collector, Thomas Bohier. If you were to explore but a single castle in the Loire, a good choice would be Chenonceaux.

The story of Bohier himself reads somewhat like a Balzac novel, but it is the women who star in the story of the Château of Six Women: Catherine Briçonnet, Bohier's wife; Diane de Poitiers, Henri II's famously beautiful mistress; Catherine de Médicis; Louise of Lorraine, wife and widow of Henri III, who after the king's murder lived out her life in black and white; Madame Dupin, who employed Rousseau as tutor to her son—his *Emile* was written at Chenonceaux—and whose kindness to the local peasantry saved Chenonceaux from destruction during the Revolution; and Madame Pelouze, who restored the whole to its original state.

No castle is more stunning on first glimpse (if you can overlook the rows of parked tour buses). Up a superb avenue flanked by plane trees, you approach (no trumpet fanfare, alas) the great keep, the 15th-century *donjon* of the original structure. To the left blooms the **formal garden of Diane**. Diane was the rival of Henri II's wife, Catherine, whose garden to the right is somewhat smaller. Behind the keep, Diane's marvelous **Grande Galerie** (topped off by the image of Catherine, as it happens) spans the river Cher in five bounds. After Henri's death in a jousting tournament, Catherine took spiteful pleasure in tossing Diane out of Chenonceaux and into Medieval Chaumont. (Diane never liked Chaumont, and she retired to her own, prettier, Anet.)

Unlike some others, this château is extremely well furnished; its rooms and artworks are of great interest. An unfortunate corollary is that Chenonceaux is almost always thronged, so it's best seen out of season.

Chenonceaux's *son-et-lumière*, "In the Times of the Women of Chenonceaux," is presented from mid-June to mid-September.

About 5 km (3 miles) east of Chenonceaux in the Cher valley, the **Château de Chissay** offers perhaps the most tastefully (and often whimsically) furnished accommodations in the Loire Valley. This is one château with a soul. In addition to the trendy staff and clientele and large pool (only Eskimos would agree it's heated), the guest quarters bedazzle even the most jaded of travellers. Stop by the 13th-century chapel on your way up to the dungeon suite—if you can stand the stone-wedge staircase to the topmost tower—the most unusual digs around, with its transparent bathroom floor looming over the luxurious bedroom. Only the French could pull this off with good taste.

A great spot for lunching in this area is the **Maison du Passeur**, in Montrichard, 4 km (2.5 miles) east of Chissay. Once a toll house (circa 1500), this tiny, rustic restaurant perched on the river's bridge exudes an old-time air of conviviality (never mind the growling resident spaniel) and simple cooking. Order *andouillettes* or *boudin* from the grill and savor the old photographs in the leather album–cum-wine list.

Loches

If Chenonceaux seduces with grace, Loches, south of Chenonceaux and southeast of Tours on N 143, strikes right between the eyes with its dungeons, turrets, keep, torture chambers, round towers, and ramparts: all the discomforts of home in the Middle Ages.

The town of Loches (about 7,000 people) lies at the foot of what was really a Medieval entrenched camp on the banks of the river Indre.

Loches is a prominent part of the history of the great feudal families of Anjou and Plantagenêt. Henri (England's Henry II) created fortifications here; his son, Jean-sans-Terre, had it wrested away from him by King Philippe-Auguste; Jean's brother, Richard the Lion-Hearted, returning from prison in Austria, was so angry he took it back in a three-hour battle; when Richard died, Philippe-Auguste took it back again.

Joan of Arc was here in 1459, but the real *dame du château* is Agnès Sorel, mistress of Charles VII and benefactor of a very good pun: She was known as *la Dame de Beauté* not entirely because of her good looks but more because Charles gave her an estate known as Beauté-sur-Marne. Respects may be paid at the tomb of Agnès Recumbent in the château, where angels support her head and her feet rest on lambs.

Everything in the Medieval enclosure of Loches is worth seeing; some of its dungeons and cells are open to visitors. Louis XI liked to put his prisoners into wooden and ironwork cages here and then suspend them from the ceiling of the **Tour Ronde**. One prisoner-cardinal is said to have dangled there for 11 years. Ludovico Sforza, the duke of Milan, spent eight years in the dungeons of **Martelet** (the most oppressive in the complex); Sforza wrote and painted on its walls and fell dead the moment he observed the sunlight of freedom.

TOURS

In the days of the Pax Romana, under the name of Caesarodunum (Caesar's Hill), Tours became a prosperous free city with an administrative center, baths, arenas, and other Roman necessities near the site of the cathedral of St-Gatien.

By the fourth century, Tours (named for a Celtic tribe, the Turones) was the bustling center of Roman Gaul in the west. Five roads, reaching from Spain to Roman settlements in the far north, met in Tours, which allowed for important land commerce in addition to that provided by the river. Saint Martin, today the patron saint of France, was born in what was then called Pannonia (Hungary). Despite his wishes, he was sent off to military duty in northern Gaul, where, near Amiens, he performed the kindness that was to start him down his long religious road.

The story varies in its details. Historian Katherine Scherman, in *The Birth of France,* tells that in a wintry Amiens, Martin came upon a nearly naked beggar at the city gates asking passersby for pity. Martin whipped off his heavy cloak, rent it in two with his sword, and gave half to the beggar. That night he dreamed of Christ, the beggar in the cloak.

In 360 Martin founded a monastery, the first in Gaul, at

Ligugé, near Poitiers, and in 372 he was named bishop of Tours. He was particularly beloved because of his homely miracles, but he is invoked frequently because of the expression he gave the French language. He died at Candes in November 397, and as his body was being transported by boat to Tours trees in the region suddenly leaped into leaf, flowers bloomed, and birds began to sing. The warmth that comes after the first frosts of autumn has been known in France ever since as Saint Martin's Summer. It was at this very site that a basilica was erected over his tomb, and where St. Martin's abbey was created.

Candes-St-Martin (about halfway between Tours and Angers at the impressive confluence of the Vienne and Loire rivers) is important today mainly because of the church that sits atop the place where Martin died. Built in the 12th and 13th centuries, it mixes a quasi-military appearance with lavish decoration on the façade.

As the cult of Saint Martin grew, his constituency prospered. His abbey spread branches to almost all the provinces of France and to other great countries of Europe.

The first French historian, Gregory of Tours, became bishop of the see in 573. In the eighth century the Anglo-Saxon monk and scholar Alcuin, brought out of England by Charlemagne, created an intellectual and artistic school in Tours that produced such notable illuminated manuscripts as the Bible of Charles le Chauve (the Bald). Alcuin was named abbot of St. Martin's abbey in A.D. 796, and played a significant role in the development of Charlemagne's Carolingian Empire. Following Alcuin's death on Whitsunday in 804, Tours remained an important religious and cultural center until the Norman invasions of 853. It experienced further troubled times during the struggles of the Reformation, and was extensively damaged during World Wars I and II.

There are more than 136,000 (250,000 including suburban areas) Tourangeaux today, working mostly in various medium and heavy industries. An industrial zone between the north bank of the river and the airport has permitted important construction for electronic and metallurgic industries. So far, however, the vital industrial element of the city has been prevented from impinging on the traditional cultural attractions that lure travellers.

Tours is also a college town, and thus about the only place in the Loire with any degree of nightlife (a good spot to get a drink at midnight is the **Relais de Cigognes** on a corner of the place Plumereau). As throughout its long history, the university of Tours remains a significant institution, and Tourangeaux continue to boast and believe that the French spoken here is the purest in France.

Music is important to the life of Tours: A summer's schedule will include jazz, rock, and classical concerts, drawing names such as Jango Edwards or Sviatoslav Richter. The Grand Théâtre devotes itself, in the main, to symphonic and choral productions; recitals are held in several churches and in the Salle des Tanneurs; chamber orchestras frequently perform in the Salle des Fêtes of the Hôtel de Ville.

For ticket and other information, inquire at the Comité Départemental de Tourisme, 16, rue Buffon, near the railroad station.

The Old City

Vieux Tours has been tastefully restored. It centers on **place Plumereau**, originally a marketplace for hatters. Most of the area is off-limits to vehicles, resulting in pleasurably winding streets lined with a variety of chic boutiques that offer everything from traditional arts and crafts to *au courant* toys and fashions.

The 15th-century half-timbered houses and gabled façades of the old city shelter seductive sidewalk cafés and restaurants as well as pizzerias. Various styles of town houses cluster on rue Briçonnet near the **Musée de Gemmail**. The relatively modern art of *gemmail,* colored glass pieces assembled and artificially lighted from the back or inside to create a contemporary version of stained glass, was invented by the painter John Crotti (1878–1958). Works of *gemmail* may be original or they may re-create frescoes, mosaics, and the like.

This tangle of streets also shows off the **Hôtel Gouin,** an ornate Renaissance mansion that somehow survived the battering the area underwent in World War II. Here visitors can view the collections of the Touraine archaeological society, including prehistoric and Gallo-Roman treasures, as well as late Medieval sculptures and other items.

Next to the Hôtel Gouin, **La Rôtisserie Tourangelle,** aside from its rather bourgeois decor, is a friendly, fairly moderate restaurant offering *sandre au sabayon de Vouvray* (a perchlike Loire fish in creamy Vouvray wine sauce) and *aiguillette de canard au fumet de Bourgueil* (sliced duck breast in Bourgueil stock).

Just off the rue des Halles at rue Descartes and near the central marketplace are the ruins of the **basilica of St-Martin**, dating from the fifth century, when a sanctuary was built to shelter the saint's remains. That was destroyed by the Normans but replaced in the 13th century by a magnificent basilica. That in turn was sacked by the Huguenots in 1562 during the Wars of Religion. What's left of *that* are two towers, the Tour Charlemagne and Tour de l'Horloge, both heavily restored. The new basilica of St-Martin, finished in 1924, comprises a corner of the former structure and claims to preserve the tomb of the saint in its crypt, the exact spot where it lay in antiquity.

Elsewhere in the City

From Old Tours it's a pleasant walk east on rue Colbert toward the cathedral and less-touristy quarter of St-Gatien. The **Musée du Compagnonnage**, on rue Nationale next to the church of St-Julien, is installed in a 16th-century monks' dormitory. It traces the history, techniques, tools, and accomplished works of artisans in the region. (Its name is a happy one: It joins derivatives of the Latin *com-* and *panis,* meaning one with whom bread is shared; the French slang for buddy is *copain,* and the English *companion* clearly shares the same root.)

The 13th-century **church of St-Julien** glows with light shining through the 20th-century stained-glass windows of Max Ingrand; there's a museum of the wines of Touraine in its cloister cellar.

Enthusiasts and collectors of antiquities will not be able to pass by the cluster of antiques shops, particularly **Bruneau** (for its paintings) on rue Colbert, and those on the rue de la Scellerie, parallel to rue Colbert.

Begun in the 13th century and not completed until the 16th, the **cathedral of St-Gatien** shows off the entire extensive genius of the Gothic style, most of the evolution being visible on the recently restored façade. Romanesque sits in the form of towers upon a Gallo-Roman wall; Flamboyant dances on the façade; Renaissance triumphs in the turret towers. Inside, the premier attractions are the 13th- to 15th-century stained-glass windows. The top of the south tower is a good position for photography.

In the immediate vicinity of the cathedral, the **Cloître de la Psalette** (where one sings psalms) has fine 15th- and

16th-century frescoes. The **Musée des Beaux-Arts**, located in a 17th- to 18th-century palace of the archbishops, has attempted to bring alive, in several completely outfitted rooms, the styles of the 18th century: Regency, Louis XV, Louis XVI. This is one of the most comprehensive art museums in the Loire Valley, with French paintings from the 15th to 19th centuries displayed chronologically; the early Italian works are particularly interesting.

Right near the river, off quai d'Orléans, the 12th-century **Tour de Guise** is all that remains of the Château de Tours, in which the young duc de Guise was imprisoned after the murder of his father by Henri III; here Joan of Arc was received by Charles VII. Within the château the **Historial de Touraine**, a wax museum, is worth a short stop, as is the small aquarium also on the premises.

Markets are held daily in Tours, either at the Marché des Halles or place Velpeau, said to be best on weekends. Porcelain, pottery, and wickerwork may be good finds at the flea market on place des Victoires on Wednesdays and Sundays.

A garlic and basil fair puts Tours in good odor near the end of July; 10 km (6 miles) north via A 10, the Touraine music festival is staged in late June at the **Grange de Meslay**, a 13th-century ensemble of farm buildings.

Dining is most expensively done in Tours at **Jean Bardet** (Tel: 47-41-41-11), a bright and airy restaurant that consistently wins rave reviews for exemplary up-to-the-minute cuisine. Sequestered in a tiny park on the north bank of the river, Bardet also offers 15 rooms and suites in its early-19th-century villa—as well as a heated pool. Cooking courses in English are offered here off season. Within walking distance, at 101, avenue de la Tranchée, the venerable **Barrier** (Tel: 47-54-20-39) continues to serve impeccable classical dishes in its hush-hush formal dining room. New on the restaurant scene and in this same neighborhood of gastronomical delights is the **Jardin du Castel** (part of the Hôtel de Groison), at 10, rue Groison. Try the "menu surprise" created by master chef Guy Tricon in his most attractive dining room (Tel: 47-41-94-40). If you've spent too many francs on such glorious meals, stay at the nearby hotel **Italia** at 19, rue Devilde. What it lacks in aesthetics it makes up for with the friendliness of its kind hosts and rock-bottom prices.

Near the Tour de Guise less extravagant local fare is offered by the rustic **Les Tuffeaux**, including *blanc de turbot au vin de Layon et melon* (turbot with sweet white

wine and melon). Master chef Jean Sabat turns out irresistible pastries here at 19, rue Lavoisier (Tel: 47-47-19-89).

Centrally located, the old-fashioned **Univers** on the
wide boulevard Heurteloup is perhaps Tours's best choice
in a city with many good hotels. Travellers in search of
serenity (and who don't mind then having to drive into
town to sightsee) would prefer the **Domaine de Beauvois**,
and its fine restaurant, 13 km (8 miles) west in Luynes.
Beauvois, with its knowledgeable staff (particularly the
good-natured British concierge, Brian Byron), draws lots
of American and English guests. Done up in comparatively
bright colors, this is one manor house where you can wear
jeans and not worry about offending history. Tennis, fishing, swimming, and ballooning are offered on the immense estate, along with a library and TV (in the rooms)
for rainy days. Especially appetizing on the restaurant's
menu is the *mille-feuille croquant de saumon au raifort*
(salmon in pastry with horseradish) and the *suprême de
faisane farçie au foie gras* (foie gras–stuffed pheasant).
After dinner, classical music quartets lull satisfied guests
before they retire to their tastefully appointed rooms.

Another good summer choice because of its access to
public tennis courts and swimming pool next door is the
Château de Beaulieu, 5 km (3 miles) southwest of Tours.
The rooms are small and simple, but manager and master
chef Jean-Pierre Lozay and his lovely Scottish wife couldn't
make you feel more at home. Their noted restaurant specializes in such culinary treats as hot oysters in white leek
sauce and wild duck in truffle butter.

Vouvray

Oenophiles and would-be cave dwellers will head to
Vouvray, a popped-cork east of Tours on the north bank of
the Loire. Renowned for its *pétillant*—bubbly—and
tranquille—still—wines, the village itself lacks character,
but its landscapes still possess the charm often described
by Balzac. Plan to stay at **Les Hautes Roches**, along the
way in Rochecorbon. Not as gimmicky as it may seem, this
hotel turns old troglodyte quarters into luxurious—
though not for the claustrophobic—guest rooms and a
commendable restaurant specializing in seafood to draw
more than curiosity seekers. A good quick-stop lunch in
Vouvray can be had at the little roadside café **B. Loré** on
route N 152 (look for the ten-foot-high green wine bottle
stuck in the driveway). The proprietors sell their own

wine, but the place to sample and buy Vouvray is at **Daniel Jarry**, off route N 152 at 99, rue La Vallée Coquette, or **Daniel Allias** just up the road at Le Petit Mont.

Just a few minutes east of Vouvray via D 46 and D 1 in Vernou-sur-Brenne is the modest, ivy-covered **Hostellerie des Perce-Neige** (meaning snowdrops). Although the rooms and bathrooms are in need of a face-lift, the welcome here by manager Monsieur Allain and the low prices more than compensate. The restaurant is cozy and offers excellent local fare, also at a good price.

If you feel more in the mood for castle dwelling, by all means stay at the **Château de Noizay**, just five minutes farther to the east. Like many chatelains wishing to maintain their homes, Monsieur Hubert André has transformed his family château of generations into a full-fledged hotel this year, and a superb one it is. The reception rooms are gracious and personalized with many family heirlooms, and each of the 14 bedrooms is graced with period furniture. The château also offers a fine restaurant, a pool, tennis, and a putting green.

Villandry

The remarkable element of the fortress here, some 20 km (12.5 miles) west of Tours, is not the interior (though that also is worthwhile, especially for 18th-century woodwork), but the gardens. Nothing like them exists elsewhere. Perfectly manicured, set on three rising terraces, these are ornamental gardens you would consider eating. Flowers are plentiful, but there are also geometrical, color-coordinated growths of chard, cabbage, fruit trees—all the good-looking vegetables except the potato, which had yet to arrive in France in the 16th century.

A decent restaurant exists in this village of about 750 inhabitants: **Cheval Rouge**, in an old house with an odd modern façade and a pretty garden terrace in the rear. Although the cuisine is classic Loire fare, the chef has a flair for creating attractive dishes from fresh seasonal vegetables and fruits (Tel: 47-50-02-07).

Azay-le-Rideau

On an autumn afternoon when the air is as golden as the leaves, the pretty promenade to the **Château d'Azay**, in its island setting of woods and water southwest of Tours, seems an invitation to a dream. You will feel you must have lived here in another, more serene life—an elegant escape that was translated from Gothic to Renaissance perfection.

Constructed by financier Gilles Berthelot between 1518 and 1529, Azay is a superb example of Medieval defenses become less useful than graceful, not deadly but decorative.

The château today is a fine Renaissance museum with beautiful furnishings and tapestries. From late May to late September, a nightly *son-et-lumière,* "Since We Have No Other Image of You," features a walk around the château with the disembodied voices of five actors.

The lazy river Indre winding through Azay renders the village one of the loveliest in the Loire Valley. A morning market is held on Wednesdays, and there's an apple fair in late October. If it's lunchtime head for a table on the terrace at **Le Grand Monarque**, an unpretentious vine-covered hotel with a kitchen specializing in fine local fare, such as green salad in walnut-oil vinaigrette, grilled *sandre,* goat cheese (from nearby Ste-Maure), and crunchy *baguettes.* The owners of the 18th-century hotel make the most of its rustic charms and have christened each of the 30 rooms after a different château.

Only 5 km (3 miles) south at Villaines-les-Rochers, the basket weavers of **La Vannerie** have been turning out beautiful wicker goods for generations (even Balzac fancied them) and are happy to ship them overseas.

At the château in **Saché**, 7 km (4 miles) east of Azay-le-Rideau by a back road (off of D 17), you may pay respects to Honoré de Balzac, who wrote all or part of *Le Père Goriot, La Recherche de l'Absolu,* and other works there. Balzac's bedroom-workroom remains as it was in the mid-19th century; the whole is a small museum. (In July a *son-et-lumière* on the writer may interest you.) Alexander Calder (1898–1976) lived and worked on his mobiles and stabiles near Saché from 1953 until his death. Keep an eye out for homegrown kiwis and *noix* (walnuts) sold on the side of the smaller roads.

Among the most regal hostelries in France is the **Château d'Artigny**, between Azay-le-Rideau and Tours just outside the village of **Montbazon** (population 3,000-plus). It's smart, stylish, and feels like a big-city hotel, if not a stage set for a period costume drama (*musicales* are in order come weekends). D'Artigny reeks of opulence and draws an appropriately international clientele that revels in its meticulously landscaped park along with the heated pool, putting green, and tennis courts. The kitchen is excellent, the dining room festooned with gilt, and the regional wine list among the area's most comprehensive (and pricey).

About 2 km (little more than a mile) north of Montbazon, the family-run **Domaine de la Tortinière** presents a less formidable, more soothing château in a private park overlooking the river Indre and a ruined tenth-century tower on the opposite bank; there are 21 quiet rooms (including 7 suites) and an outstanding kitchen, where cooking courses are available off season. Just to the west, nestled on the banks of the Indre, **Moulin Fleuri** is small (12 rooms) and intimate. Travellers who don't mind the flimsy mattresses love this spot for its winsome setting and no-frills cooking at extremely reasonable prices.

If you're in the mood to drop a bundle (even the artistic furniture is for sale), head to the elegant ivy-covered **La Chancelière** (Tel: 47-26-00-67) on place des Marronniers in Montbazon. No other restaurant in the Loire Valley has risen so high or fast in the estimate of French "foodies," who carry indelible memories of its oyster-stuffed ravioli and warm foie gras.

Langeais

The harmony of this Medieval residence (its appearance from the outside bespeaks more a feudal fortress) results from its having been built in the relatively short time of five years or so. Fortunately, also, it has never undergone substantial restoration. It lies on the Loire west of Tours and near Azay-le-Rideau. The ruins of a tenth-century keep stand in the gardens. Within, the *appartements* are unusually well furnished and precisely descriptive of life in the 15th century; Gothic furniture and Flemish tapestries abound. Charles VIII married Anne de Bretagne in the Grand Salon.

Langeais is the idyllic town you've been looking for, with its narrow streets that wind around the château and fetching shops, flower boxes bedecking every window and balcony. If your visit here coincides with lunchtime, try **Le Langeais** in the modest hotel Hosten on rue Gambetta. It's known for grilled Loire baby eels and the *blanquette de sole et turbot* (Tel: 47-96-82-12).

A few minutes' drive west along the Loire brings you to St-Patrice and the **Hostellerie du Château de Rochecotte**, once Talleyrand's country estate and now a family-run hotel with what are surely the valley's only 18th-century interiors ablaze with uplights. Further, Rochecotte's cuisine comes off with unexpected dash and finesse. Even dogs are welcome in the palmy dining salon, as long as they don't attempt to sing along with Pavarotti and other operatic greats on tape.

One of the region's best wineries, producing the currant-scented, tannic Bourgueil wine, is located about 10 km (6 miles) west of Rochecotte, just north of D 35 in the wee village of **Benais**. Look for **La Croix Rouge**, the house and bottling plant of the amiable vintner Pierre-Jacques Druet; Tel: 47-97-37-34. Well-fed locals take lunch at **Auberge Campagnarde**, a charming discovery in the heart of the village; Tel: 47-97-30-08.

Château d'Ussé

For some reason this massive, fortified, rather grim château, southwest of Langeais along the Loire, does not play the feature role it should within its company. It always catches photographers with their lenses down (the best shots are from the small bridge on D 113), yet it is the very model of fairy-tale writer Perrault's *Sleeping Beauty* keep (waxwork tableaux in the attic illustrate the story). The château bristles like a brush with turrets, clock towers, chimneys, dormers, roof trapdoors (the better for pouring boiling oil), and so forth. In comparison with the fairly fierce exterior, the interior rooms are comfortable, even gracious. A small tearoom opposite the château serves light lunches and snacks.

Château de Chinon

While the château in Chinon southwest of Tours is what most travellers come to see—a fortress that played major roles in the nearly endless Anglo-French fights, where Charles VII retreated when the power of Paris really belonged to England's Henry IV, where Joan of Arc came to announce the mission her "voices" had commanded—the old town here, built on a rise flanking the river embankment, is at least as alluring.

The château is really three adjoining ruins south of Ussé above the river Vienne: **Fort St-Georges**, of which little remains but memories of the death of Henri II; **Château du Milieu**, entered through the still impressive

Tour de l'Horloge and housing the Musée Jeanne-d'Arc; and the **Château de Coudray**, where the Maid resided. Opposite the château a walled vineyard of Chinon grapes flourishes on a sloping plateau, producing one of the finest wines in the Loire Valley—Clos de L'Echo—which can be tasted and purchased at the **Maison Couly-Dutheil**, 12, rue Diderot.

The Middle Ages still can be sensed in the old town, particularly along rue Voltaire (where the Office de Tourisme is) and at the crossroads known as **Grand Carroi**, heart of the Medieval action and today the center of ambience. (The old days are restaged on the first weekend in August at the annual "Medieval Market" festival.)

A good restaurant choice in Chinon is the **Hostellerie Gargantua**, named after Rabelais's famous character. This 500-year-old stone mansion is said to be where the writer's father practiced law. Be sure to order the famous house omelette; the recipe has remained a secret for more than 200 years. Spend a few minutes with the gregarious owner, who has many tales to tell (and who also may have rooms available).

It is believed that *Gargantua and Pantagruel* is actually the autobiography of François Rabelais, written in his modest manor home, **La Devinière**, about 5 km (3 miles) southwest of Chinon. La Devinière is now a museum devoted to his life and work.

Just 7 km (4 miles) south, across the river, the **Château de Marçay** is surrounded by its own vineyards on a wide, open plain. Everything about the handsome 15th-century fortress bespeaks good taste. Marçay, with 38 guest rooms, abounds with terraces for dining, sunning, and reading, and the swimming pool, bicycling, hot-air ballooning, and tennis courts attract a young, zippy clientele. Its restaurant, actually a pair of dining salons, is decorated with exquisite taste and serves commendable fare such as sliced *sandre* with oysters in Chinon wine butter, *feuilleté* of farm pigeon from Druye, and bread baked on the premises. The real *tatin* apple tart is a must here, as is a visit to Marçay's impressive wine cellar.

Two hotels in Beaumont-en-Véron, a few kilometers northwest of Chinon, are also worth considering. The privileged few might like the opulence of the **Château de Danzay**, dating from 1461. It's recently become a full-fledged hotel (with a grand total of seven rooms) and a restaurant. Antiques collectors and history buffs will relish the valuable paintings, artifacts, and period furniture carefully chosen over the years by the owners, the Sarfatis.

Much less austere and right down the road in a beautiful rural setting is **La Giraudière**. Here the proprietor, an outgoing ex-philosophy professor, will tell you amazing tales of the region, and if you're lucky he'll play the organ for you and perhaps take you to a veritable haunted house. Rooms and suites with kitchenettes are very simple, and so the prices are extremely low. This is a popular choice for the young and hearty (bicycle groups often stay overnight).

The Abbey of Fontevraud

Richard the Lion-Hearted is so familiar he seems almost fanciful, the overstated hero, the Superman of antiquity. Paying a pilgrimage to his tomb (or perhaps to that of his parents, Henry II Plantagenêt, king of England, and Queen Eleanor of Aquitaine) involves a drive to Fontevraud from Saumur in the west or from Chinon or Ussé in the east. The tiny town of Fontevraud (or Fontevrault, in the old spelling) grew up to support the royal abbey, one of the finest examples of monastic architecture.

In 1099 (when Jerusalem was captured during the First Crusade), a hermit named Robert d'Arbrissel settled in the forested valley of Fontevraud near a formidable spring. Eventually convents were built at the site: St-Lazarus for lepers and Ste-Magdalene's for women. An abbess was put in charge and given absolute power. From the 12th century into the 18th century, 36 abbesses, all of princely descent, ruled over Fontevraud.

Today the traveller marches single-mindedly through the Romanesque church, past the high altar—which survived the Revolution and is now enduring extensive archaeological digs at its base (they're searching for old tombs and will continue to do so well into the next century)—and into the transept room, where, recumbent upon their tombs, lie Richard, Eleanor, Henry, and their daughter-in-law, Isabelle d'Angoulême, third wife of Bad King John Lackland. Behind a protective glass wall they are splendid in peeling polychrome limestone (Isabelle is in wood); Eleanor in death, as in life, is reading a book.

Other elements of the abbey—the chapter house, the cloisters, the refectory—are excellent, but the most curious is the old **kitchen**, the only one extant from the Romanesque period in France. It is octagonal, with semicircular attached towers topped by witches' hats in upside-down tiles. Inside, a staff of cooks worked over six hellishly hot wood-fire hearths; smoke soared 89 feet and exited through 20 flues.

Leaving at evening, you may hear church bells in the distance and look back 700 years. History enthusiasts may want to bed down for the night at the **Abbaye**—in one of the restored old nun's cells. (Priority is given to groups.)

Saumur

To see the château is to feel a sense of déjà vu, its 14th-century silhouette familiar from Christmas cards bearing a likeness of the Limbourg brothers' illumination for *Les Très Riches Heures du Duc de Berry,* now in the Condé museum in Chantilly. Two fine and distinct museums can be found in the château: the **Musée du Cheval** (Museum of the Horse) and the **Musée des Arts Décoratifs**. In the first, the horse rides through all ages and countries, bareback, saddled, bridled, spurred, and stirruped. The Musée des Arts Décoratifs is notable for its collection of fine ceramics.

Saumur, a stately town of 18th-century houses with wrought-iron balconies overlooking the river, has always been renowned for its wines (especially the *mousseux*—sparkling—ones, such as Crémant de Loire), its mushrooms, and its cavalry school. It is also Europe's foremost maker of masks for Carnival.

Sherman and Patton tanks, the British Conqueror, German Panzers, and landing craft from D-Day are among the items in the **Musée des Blindés** (armored vehicles), near the river and the northern corner of the large place du Chardonnet. The **Cavalry Museum** shows off historic swords, sabers, uniforms, and other military memorabilia. Guided tours are available in the afternoons; ask for written authority to enter at the office of the cavalry school in the same building (entrance off avenue Foch).

Most unusual is the **Musée du Champignon** (Museum of the Mushroom) in neighboring St-Hilaire-St-Florent, where Louis Bouchard grows the fragrant fungus in the darkness of underground caves. Local mushrooms account for 70 percent of the national production.

Sharp-eyed drivers who travel around the riverside cliffs near Saumur—and in other venues on the north bank of the Loire—will spot dozens of centuries-old cave dwellings of present-day troglodytes; some are carpeted and outfitted with electricity, heating, and running water.

A suit of armor in the tiny lobby reached by a narrow, spiral stone staircase greets guests at **Le Prieuré**, a restored Renaissance manor (with a motel-style wing) in nearby Chênehutte-les-Tuffeaux. Set on a wooded hillside high above the river, the 37-room hotel offers staggering views of the terrain (especially from the rooms with private terraces). The rather large dining room provides, along with exquisite cuisine, an additional panorama. Try the *gigotin du lotte* and the foie gras medallions, served with a glass of sweetish wine from nearby Layon.

Cunault

The Loire's collection of castles, churches, museums, and country inns could not be exhausted in a lifetime. Still, time should be taken for a traipse to the Benedictine monastery's **church of Cunault**, about 12 km (7.5 miles) northwest of Saumur. The church is thought to embody the finest elements of Romanesque architecture in the Loire Valley. Sculpted figures on the 200 column capitals demand a close look with a long camera lens or binoculars. Some Medieval painted decoration remains.

ANGERS

The old capital of the counts and dukes of Anjou, at the western end of the traditional Loire Valley sightseeing region, occupies a splendid (and easily defensible) site above the banks of the river Maine, about 8 km (5 miles) from its confluence with the Loire. During Roman times it was called Juliomagus, and Tacitus mentioned the existence of an ancient people on a local site called Andes or Andecavi, but very little is otherwise known of this prehistoric culture. By Roman times the town served as crossroads for routes from Rennes, Nantes, and Tours. Some second-century baths remain from Gallo-Roman days, as do some portions of the third-century ramparts.

The first House of Anjou (10th to 12th centuries) and the second (13th to 15th centuries) were separated by the dynasties of the Plantagenêts and Capéts. The first of the Plantagenêts was Geoffrey, who plucked a sprig of broom (*plante de genêt*) to put upon his hat, thereby naming a vital line of French and British rulers. Geoffrey's son Henry II (of England) died at Chinon in 1189, as did his

son, Richard the Lion-Hearted, ten years later. Anjou became part of the French domain in 1204, though England
and France battled over it until the Hundred Years War
(1337 to 1453) had come to an end.

First of the dukes of Anjou was Charles, who received
the dukedom as a gift from his brother, Saint Louis (Louis
IX), in 1246; he added to it Sicily and the kingdom of
Naples by conquest. Good King René (linguist, musician,
poet, painter, stage manager of grand entertainments,
writer of chivalric sagas) reigned as the last duke before
the lands were annexed by King Louis XI in 1474. During
the 1789 revolution, the cathedral became a Temple of
Reason.

The small city (about 142,000 Angevins) and its surroundings deserve an exploration of at least three days;
Angers is less known but more inviting than either Tours
or Orléans. An *entrepôt* for wines, liqueurs (Cointreau),
flowers, and agricultural products, Angers hosts an annual wine fair in late September. Known as an arts center
since the Renaissance, Angers also stages the cultural
festival of Anjou in July.

The **Château d'Angers** looms high above the Maine—a
formidable feudal retreat that looks as if it might even
today defeat any conventional-weapons attack. Still standing are the 17 mighty towers, between 130 and 195 feet
high, that were once capped by what were called pepper-
pot roofs (*poivrières*). Formal Medieval gardens bloom in
the impressive moat.

Inside, magnificent tapestries from the 14th to the 17th
centuries are displayed, including the remarkable **Tenture
de l'Apocalypse**, the oldest and largest tapestry known, a
14th-century marvel 551 feet long and more than 16 feet
high, woven in seven sections. It is displayed in a room
constructed especially for that purpose.

On nearby place Freppel, the **cathedral of St-Maurice**,
dating to the 12th and 13th centuries, epitomizes
Plantagenêt-Angevin style; the 12th-century tympanum
above the porch is particularly fine. Close observers will
note that the Gothic vaulting of the nave—the earliest in
Anjou—is rather unusual. The stained-glass windows provide a review of the history of the art in France from the
12th to the 18th centuries. (No stained glass from before
the 12th century is known.)

Collections of Greek and Etruscan vases, amphora, Renaissance art and furnishings, engravings, Chinese and

Japanese objets d'art, and enamels are shown in the **Musée Turpin de Crissé** in the Renaissance mansion known as l'Hôtel Pincé, just a few blocks from the cathedral up rue Chaperonnière on rue Lenepveu.

In the former 13th-century abbey **Toussaint** (All Saints), a block from the cathedral down rue Toussaint, the David d'Angers (1788–1856) gallery displays the works of this native son and sculptor, including statuary and some 500 medallions (round bronze wall plaques) of his contemporaries from the Romantic period (Hugo, Goethe, Châteaubriand, Balzac, and others).

On the other side of the Maine, near the Pont de la Haute Chaine, the **Ancien Hôpital St-Jean** (12th century) is the oldest hospital in France. It houses the **Musée Lurçat**, with ten tapestries by the artist Jean Lurçat (1892–1966), known collectively as *Song of the World*.

Angers is a pleasant place to idle away a day by café sitting, ambling along the river, or even indulging in nine holes of golf at nearby **St-Jean-des-Mauvrets**. The town is also convenient to such sites in the Mayenne Valley as the seignorial **Château de Plessis-Bourré**, with its exquisite 18th-century furniture and fascinating ceiling in the guard room (painted with outrageous depictions of fables and proverbs).

Markets are held in Angers daily except Mondays. Fish from the Loire is particularly well cooked and served at **Le Toussaint**, 7, place Kennedy (Tel: 41-87-46-20). Of local hotels, the best is the **Anjou**, with its restaurant **La Salamandre**, on the boulevard du Maréchal-Foch. But it might be nicer to try a country retreat such as that 24 km (15 miles) away in Cheffes-sur-Sarthe: The lushly set **Château de Teildras**, overlooking its own pond, boasts 11 rooms in a 16th-century country house that's intimate and more livable than many château hotels. Some complain about the curt service while others revel in the company of the young, spirited châtelaine and her American writer husband. Regardless, the tiny dining room serves tantalizing cuisine, especially the *tarte aux pommes*.

Head about 15 miles east of Angers to the **Château de Montgeoffroy**, which has remained in the family since it was built in the 18th century. Its signed pieces of furniture by Gourdin, Garnier, and Durand, and paintings by Van Loo, Rigaud, and others, haven't budged a centimeter since their arrival two centuries ago. The kitchen is also beautifully preserved.

BOURGES OF BERRY

Bourges and its nearby attractions make a rewarding side trip (out of the Loire Valley), roughly south of Orléans or roughly east of Tours. Even today, Bourges, capital of the old region of Grand Berry–Limousin, is a stranger to most foreigners and to many French. The little city of about 80,000 Berruyers sits somewhat off the tourist trails of Burgundy to the east, the Loire to the north, and Brittany–Normandy to the west.

In truth, Bourges is the heart of the matter, only 36 km (22 miles) north of the measured center of this measured land, the hamlet of Bruère. That fact did not interest Stendhal at all; he saw Bourges as "surrounded by plains of a bitter ugliness." Only someone born near the up-thrust magnificence of the Alps around Grenoble could feel that way.

Between 80 and 60 B.C., a Celtic people called the Bituriges occupied the site of the future Bourges and called it Avarich (in Latin, Avaricum, "a well-watered place"). Because they believed the town to be an easily defensible site, the Bituriges persuaded their ally, Vercingétorix, not to burn it (as was his custom) in the face of the advancing Roman armies. *Hélas,* Vercingétorix gave in, the Romans attacked, and in 52 B.C. they massacred some 40,000 citizens of what Caesar had called one of the "most beautiful cities in Gaul."

Bourges prospered under the Romans (though the slaughter remains unforgotten), becoming a major city of Aquitaine, a vital marketplace, and the site of a great amphitheater (at today's place de la Nation). By the third century, Avaricum was hemmed in by a wall crowned with almost 50 towers; remnants of the wall may be seen along rue Bourbonnoux.

Euric, king of the Visigoths, took control of the area in 476. After Pépin the Short (Charlemagne's father) conquered the territory in 762, Bourges became the southern base of the Capétian kingdom.

Lucky cities have their protectors, their enhancers, and their patrons; Bourges had all three in the persons of two men: Jean, duc de Berry, third son of King Jean II the Good and brother of Charles V; and the creative business-man and enthusiast of architecture Jacques Coeur.

In 1360 Berry was still numb from the raids of England's Black Prince (Edward, Prince of Wales) in 1356 and from the general ravages of the Hundred Years War. Jean, returned from captivity in England, was awarded Berry and Auvergne and, through various family inheritances, eventually came also into control of Poitou and Languedoc.

A man of great taste and even greater extravagance, Jean decorated his "empire" with palaces, princely residences, collections of manuscripts, tapestries, rare animals and birds, and jewels. It was he who hired the Flemish artist Pol de Limbourg and his brothers to create *Les Très Riches Heures du Duc de Berry,* perhaps the most exquisite illuminated manuscript known.

When Jean died at age 76, Charles VII took over. Disinherited from the throne, with half the lands of France in English and Burgundian hands, he endured with fairly good grace the nickname king of Bourges. Luckily, he had as treasurer, minister of finances, whatever, the nimble-minded Jacques Coeur.

Coeur was a canny merchant whose fleet of trading ships, which carried to France the wares of the Levant, made him the most illustrious financier of his age. Because of Coeur, France began to contend successfully with the great trading republics of Italy, and in 1436 he was summoned by Charles VII to become master of the mint, to reform the coinage and royal expenditure systems. His brilliance resulted in France's increasing supremacy among trading nations in the East, and he went on to represent his country in three embassies.

Jacques, son of a furrier, was born in Bourges in about 1400. Many travellers pay their respects at a handsome half-timbered *pâtisserie* at the corner of rue d'Auron and rue des Armuriers that some guidebooks—and an inscription on the place—cite as his natal home. However, it's more likely that the present building dates from only the early 16th century, and the house it replaced came to Coeur only after his marriage.

Nonetheless, it is intriguing to think of the few yards and many achievements separating this unpretentious corner bakery from the sumptuous Gothic manse, the Palais Jacques-Coeur (see below), just up the sloping street.

Bourges the Town

The town will come as a happy surprise to anyone who has planned to see only "the reds of Bourges" in the cathedral and the rich decorations of the Palais Jacques-Coeur and then skip away. It is a town not to pass through quickly but to be meandered through and then used as a base for exploration of a countryside as yet unplundered by mass tourism.

In 1963 the first of several Maisons de la Culture was inaugurated in Bourges by André Malraux and Charles de Gaulle, charged with devotion to and promotion of theater, cinema, music, dance, arts and crafts, expositions, and scientific and cultural conferences.

Today the maison is a home for such happenings as Le Printemps de Bourges, which in late April brings French and foreign singers and songs to the public, putting special emphasis on the discovery of new talent. It houses as well the festival of electro-acoustical music near the end of May and beginning of June.

Other annual goings-on include the Fête de la Vieille Ville (Old Town Festival) near the end of May, featuring concerts, plays, and folkloric events; a national fair and exposition during the last half of June; and the Foires Jacques Coeur, with travelling shows and entertainment, held in place Séraucourt, near the Maison de la Culture, from mid-June to mid-July.

In addition, Bourges maintains a national school of music, several experimental music and theater groups, and a national *beaux-arts* academy. In summer, nearby Val d'Auron is the site of water sports.

The Old City

Almost the entire heart of the old city has been preserved or artfully restored. Hosts of half-timbered houses still stand to the north of the cathedral in the vicinity of the **Gallo-Roman wall**. Rue Bourbonnoux (where you can have a pleasant sidewalk luncheon at the **Bar Remparts**) debouches into place Gordaine with its bustling little park, sidewalk cafés, and the magnificent Renaissance **Hôtel Lallement**, now a museum of decorative arts. The house itself is a major attraction, heightened by collections of 16th- and 17th-century furnishings, tapestries, paintings, and marquetry, in addition to ivories, enamels, and the like.

Smart and trendy shops line the **rue Mirabeau**, veering off place Gordaine, interspersed with fast-food places such as Lucky Burger Luke.

"One must see the reds of Bourges and the blues of

Chartres," a student of stained glass once said. Well, the blues of Bourges aren't so shabby either.

In fact, the 13th- to 16th-century windows of the **cathedral of St-Etienne** will cause the stiffest of necks to swivel: This is one of the most astonishing collections in France. Here the impious of the Middle Ages could see moral misbehavior writ large, as in the window depicting the bad rich man, who turns aside from a beggar named Lazarus dying with ulcers and then dies himself. In agony, he begs Father Abraham for pity, only to be told, "Look, you got yours in life and so did Lazarus. Now your roles are reversed." Or words to that effect.

If the windows are the initial lure of St-Etienne, the Gothic interior—with four side aisles in the place of transepts—is of almost equal interest. Jean de Berry lies entombed in the 12th-century **crypt**.

Circling up the steps of the **north tower** is recommended to enthusiasts of city overviews, photographers who enjoy taking shots of double-winged buttresses through pseudo arrow-slits, and others stout of heart. (This is also called the butter tower, because it was built with funds donated by citizens in return for dispensations allowing them to consume butter and milk during Lent.)

Also within the old city is one of the handsomest, richest, and most elegant and precisely turned private structures of the Gothic period in France, the **Palais Jacques-Coeur**, begun in 1443 and completed in fewer than ten years. Seen from its entrance on the place Jacques-Coeur, it seems a fortress that's taken a fanciful turn, with two sculpted false windows on either side of the entrance, from which stony heads spy out—servants, or perhaps Jacques and his wife, Mace. (Place Jacques-Coeur features a small restaurant named, not incidentally, **Jacques Coeur**, called "estimable" by Samuel Chamberlain in the 1960s but now, alas, only pleasant.)

Whatever was beautiful, practical, or inventive was what Coeur wanted and what he got. The Palais Jacques-Coeur contains 43 rooms, of which visitors are permitted to visit 15 or 16. The most impressive elements are the monumental ornamental fireplace in the banquet room; the storage-loft ceiling in the shape of a wooden upside-down ship's keel; the several painted ceilings and secret chapels; and—far from least—an engineering system that provided water for hot baths.

One of the mottoes of the man of the house is inscribed on the central tower: "*Dire, Faire, Taire*" (loosely translated, "Say it, do it, shut up"). Having inherited no great coat of arms, the master merchant invented one and had it placed on the palatial façade: a cockleshell for Jacques (reminiscent of the pilgrimages to Santiago—*Jacques*—de Compostela in Spain), a heart (*coeur*), and the words (in translation) "To a valiant heart nothing is impossible."

Just a few steps from the Palais Jacques-Coeur at tiny place Quatre Piliers, the old **Hôtel Angleterre** is perhaps the best inn in a city lacking outstanding hotels. Accommodations here are reasonable and recently renovated, and its location is the best for taking walks in the town. The Angleterre also boasts a pleasant, small dining room.

THE ENVIRONS OF BOURGES

Your plan may well be to see Bourges and then to barge on into Burgundy to the east, but that would mean denying yourself several fine detours in the immediate countryside.

The Cistercian Abbey of Noirlac

About half an hour's drive south of Bourges, Noirlac is the embodiment in pure, white, regional stone of the simple and austere regimens of the Cistercian movement. The stone can also be seen as a reflection of the soul of Saint Bernard, who wished to return his church—which he considered fat and fraught with excesses—to the leanness of earlier Christianity.

The founding Cistercian monks, under their leader, Robert de Clairvaux (a cousin of Saint Bernard's), suffered many privations during their first years (the order was founded in 1130). The 13th century brought success, but this would be supplanted by the Hundred Years War, the Wars of Religion, and the Revolution. The abbey was eventually sold to a manufacturer of porcelain.

Restoration began in the 1950s and proved enormously expensive. Today, however, the abbey stands again as one of the best built and most complete of its kind in the country. (Sénanque, near Gordes in Provence, is another top competitor in the rigorous Cistercian race.)

Noirlac is as perfect in its manner as a Gregorian chant.

Château de Meillant

North of Noirlac, on the other side a dense forest, Meillant is an important stop along the route Jacques-Coeur (see the Getting Around section at the end of the chapter) because of its Renaissance western façade, its face of a feudal fortress on the south, and its touches of Gothic and Flamboyant.

About a dozen of the 75 rooms in the château, richly decorated and furnished with Cordovan leather hangings, Louis XIV chairs, Bruges tapestries, and Turkish carpets, are open to the public.

Nohant

Upon the death of her father, young Aurore Dupin—one day to become George Sand—went to live with her grandmother in the château of Nohant, some 70 km (43 miles) southwest of Bourges, near the small town of La Châtre. The author of *Indiana* became George Sand with the publication of that first novel in 1832, and though she lived (passionately) in Paris, having left her husband and two children for several famous liaisons, she returned often to the calm and serenity of Nohant, where she died in 1876.

Despite her stormy romances and her many novels featuring the villages and folk of the Berry region, Sand was known in La Châtre as the Good Lady of Nohant, even serving the villagers from time to time as a local doctor.

The château has become a museum memorializing Sand and her famous guests, which included, at one time or another, Chopin, Liszt, Balzac, Delacroix, and Flaubert. The Good Lady (and better novelist) is buried in the family cemetery on the château grounds.

SANCERRE

Outsiders have no image of the tiny town (2,300 inhabitants) of Sancerre, which lies near the Loire about 46 km (28.5 miles) northeast of Bourges, other than that of a dry derivative of the sauvignon blanc grape. Sancerre is an

informal, everyday wine, to be drunk young and inexpen-
sively; while it is predominantly thought of as being
white, some reds and rosés also exist, from Pinot grapes.

The little village atop a beehive-shaped hill is a natural
place to stop for drivers eastward-bound from Bourges
into Burgundy. They usually park near the Esplanade de la
Porte César to inspect the view over the vineyards, and
perhaps they have lunch at the modest **Auberge Alphonse
Mellot** to try Sancerre on its home ground. The local goat
cheeses (try Crottins de Chavignol) and herb cheeses
made from cow's milk are delicious.

Annual fairs are held at Sancerre in honor of cheese
(the first week in May), wine (around Pentecost and the
last Sunday in August), and oysters (the end of October).

GETTING AROUND

The main road from Paris that proceeds through the Loire
Valley is Autoroute 10, which cuts around Orléans and
edges near Blois, heading for Tours. If you drive like the
French you can reach Blois, the heart of the Loire, in two
hours. Major route N 20 sweeps south from Paris via
Etampes to Orléans, then runs south of Vierzon for
Bourges. From Orléans, regional route N 152 leads to
Blois and Tours. As is almost always the case, however, the
best choices if you have time are the yellow local routes,
or even the wiggly white ones.

The Loire Valley is reached by train from Paris's Gare
d'Austerlitz, with about 24 daily trains to Tours, 10 or 12
to Bourges, and several to Angers. Inaugurated in the fall
of 1990, the new line of the TGV-Atlantique now whisks
travellers from Paris to Tours in about an hour and a half
at 320 m.p.h. Although rental cars are available at train
stations, it's better to book one in advance such as
through Kemwell's Fly/Drive program (in North America,
Tel: 800-678-0678) or Renault's short-term ownership
arrangement—both of which avoid the otherwise hefty
car rental tax.

The Relais & Châteaux group represents eight of the
major châteaux-hotels in the Loire (see Useful Facts).

Seven-day ballooning adventures are offered in the château country–Loire Valley region via the Bombard Society
in McLean, Virginia (Tel: 703-448-9407, 800-862-8537, or, in
France, 80-26-63-30) and Arc-en-Ciel in Beaune, France.
One- to three-day helicopter cruises with accommodations in châteaux are arranged by Hemphill/Harris Travel
Corp. of Encino, California, or Map Travel in Paris. There

are short flights out of Blois in July and August by both small plane and helicopter.

In Tours, A.R.T.E. Val-de-Loire-Centre supplies itineraries and makes arrangements for horseback tours, while hiking trips can be arranged along some 750 miles of the Loire by Fédération Française de la Randonnée Pédestre (National Committee for Long-Distance Footpaths) in Paris. Bicyclists flock to the Loire for its generally flat terrain and endless back roads; tours are planned by La Fédération Française de Cyclotourisme in Paris and by such high-ticket operators as Butterfield & Robinson; in North America, Tel: (800) 387-1147 or (416) 864-1354.

A list of captain-it-yourself boats is supplied by Syndicat National des Loueurs de Bateaux de Plaisance, Port de la Bourdonnais, 75007 Paris, or Blakes Holidays, Wroxham, Norwich, Norfolk NR12 8DH, England. More luxurious cruising, on the *Fleur de Lys* barge, can be arranged in the United States through Abercrombie & Kent; Tel: (800) 323-7308 or (708) 954-2944.

Out of Bourges, the enthusiast of castles and history may wish to drive the Jacques-Coeur tourist route, which shows off more than a dozen châteaux, manors, Noirlac abbey, and so on. A booklet in the *Routes de Beauté* series is available at the Palais Jacques-Coeur in Bourges, where the tourist office will also be happy to supply a map.

The Loire Valley is rapidly becoming a center for recreational golfers, with 29 courses, five of which opened in 1990. Several offer accommodation on the premises. Inquire at the Comité Régional du Tourisme, 9, rue St-Pierre-Lentin, 45041 Orléans; Tel: 38-54-95-42; Fax: 38-54-95-46.

ACCOMMODATIONS REFERENCE

▶ **Abbaye Royale de Fontevraud.** B.P. 14, 49590 **Fontevraud-l'Abbaye.** Tel: 41-51-73-16.

▶ **Angleterre.** 1, place Quatre Piliers, 18000 **Bourges.** Tel: 48-24-68-51; in U.S., (212) 477-1600 or (800) 366-1510.

▶ **Anjou.** 1, boulevard du Maréchal-Foch, 49100 **Angers.** Tel: 41-88-24-82; Telex: 720521; Fax: 41-87-22-21; in U.S., (212) 477-1600 or (800) 366-1510.

▶ **Jean Bardet.** 57, rue Groison, 37000 **Tours.** Tel: 47-41-41-11; Fax: 47-51-68-72; in U.S., (212) 477-1600 or (800) 366-1510.

▶ **Château d'Artigny.** 37250 **Montbazon** (2 km/1.3 miles southwest of town on D 17). Tel: 47-26-24-24; Fax: 47-65-92-79; in U.S., (212) 696-1323.

▶ **Château de Beaulieu.** 1, route de l'Epend, 37300

Joué-lès-Tours (5 km/3 miles southwest of Tours on D 7 and D 207). Tel: 47-53-20-26.

▶ **Château de Chissay.** Chissay-en-Touraine 41400 **Montrichard.** Tel: 54-32-32-01; Telex: 750393; Fax: 54-32-43-80; in U.S., (212) 477-1600 or (800) 366-1510.

▶ **Château de Danzay.** 37420 **Beaumont-en-Véron** (6 km/4 miles northwest of Chinon on D 749). Tel: 47-58-46-86; in U.S., (212) 477-1600 or (800) 366-1510.

▶ **Château de Marçay.** 37500 **Marçay** (7 km/4 miles southeast of town via D 116). Tel: 47-93-03-47; Fax: 47-93-45-33; in U.S., (212) 477-1600 or (800) 366-1510.

▶ **Château de Noizay.** 37210 **Noizay** (9 km/6 miles northwest of Amboise by D 78 and D 1). Tel: 47-52-11-01; Telex: 752715; Fax: 47-52-04-64; in U.S., (212) 477-1600 or (800) 366-1510.

▶ **Château de Pray.** 37400 **Amboise** (3 km/2 miles northeast of town via D 751). Tel: 47-57-23-67; in U.S., (212) 477-1600 or (800) 366-1510.

▶ **Château de Teildras.** Tiercé 49125 **Cheffes-sur-Sarthe.** Tel: 41-42-61-08; Telex: 722268; Fax: 41-42-17-01; in U.S., (212) 696-1323.

▶ **Château des Tertres.** 41150 **Onzain** (1.5 km/1 mile from town on D 58). Tel: 54-20-83-88.

▶ **Le Choiseul.** 36, quai Charles-Guinot, 37400 **Amboise.** Tel: 47-30-45-45; Fax: 47-30-46-10; in U.S., (212) 696-1323.

▶ **Domaine de Beauvois.** 37230 **Luynes** (4 km/2.5 miles northwest of town via D 49). Tel: 47-55-50-11; Telex: 750204; Fax: 47-55-59-62; in U.S., (212) 696-1323.

▶ **Domaine des Hauts de Loire.** 41150 **Onzain** (3 km/2 miles northwest of town). Tel: 54-20-72-57; Telex: 751547; Fax: 54-20-77-32.

▶ **Domaine de la Tortinière.** 37250 **Montbazon** (2 km/1.3 miles north of town via N 10 and D 287). Tel: 47-26-00-19; Telex: 752186; Fax: 47-65-95-70.

▶ **Escale du Port Arthur.** 205, rue de l'Eglise, 45160 **St-Hilaire-St-Mesmin** (7 km/4.5 miles southeast of Orléans via D 951). Tel: 38-76-30-36; Telex: 782320; Fax: 38-76-37-67.

▶ **La Giraudière.** 37420 **Beaumont-en-Véron** (6 km/4 miles northwest of Chinon on D 749). Tel: 47-58-40-36.

▶ **Le Grand Monarque.** Place de la République, 37190 **Azay-le-Rideau.** Tel: 47-45-40-08; Fax: 47-45-46-25.

▶ **Les Hautes Roches.** 86, quai de la Loire, Rochecorbon 37210 **Vouvray.** Tel: 47-52-88-88; Fax: 47-52-81-30; in U.S., (212) 477-1600 or (800) 366-1510.

▶ **Hostellerie du Château de Rochecotte.** St-Patrice

37130 **Langeais**. Tel: 47-96-90-62; Fax: 47-96-90-59; in U.S., (212) 477-1600 or (800) 366-1510.

▶ **Hostellerie Gargantua**. 73, rue Haute-St-Maurice, 37500 **Chinon**. Tel: 47-93-04-71.

▶ **Hostellerie Perce-Neige**. 37210 **Vernou-sur-Brenne** (3 km/2 miles east of Vouvray). Tel: 47-52-10-04.

▶ **Italia**. 19, rue Devilde, 37100 **Tours**. Tel: 47-54-43-01.

▶ **Moulin Fleuri**. Veigne 37250 **Montbazon** (5 km/3 miles west of town via D 287 and D 87). Tel: 47-26-01-12.

▶ **Le Prieuré**. Gennes 49350 **Chênehutte-les-Tuffeaux** (8 km/5 miles from Saumur via D 161 and D 751). Tel: 41-67-90-14; Fax: 41-67-92-24; in U.S., (212) 696-1323.

▶ **Le Rivage**. 635, rue de la Reine Blanche, 45160 **Olivet** (5 km/3 miles south of Orléans via avenue Loiret). Tel: 38-66-02-93; Fax: 38-56-31-11.

▶ **Sofitel**. 44, quai Barentin, 45000 **Orléans**. Tel: 38-62-17-39; Telex: 780073; Fax: 38-53-95-34.

▶ **Univers**. 5, boulevard Heurteloup, 37000 **Tours**. Tel: 47-05-37-12; Fax: 47-61-51-80; in U.S., (212) 477-1600 or (800) 366-1510.

BURGUNDY AND THE RHONE VALLEY

By Georgia I. Hesse

The traveller (as distinct from the geographer) can scarcely tell where Burgundy begins: with a first sight of Vézelay and its hilltop basilica of Ste-Madeleine, where Saint Bernard preached the Second Crusade, perhaps; or with the first sips of Montrachet slipping seductively down the throat (Alexandre Dumas said that princely elixir should be drunk on your knees with hat off); or even when you first stand before the enormous vessel known as the Treasure of Vix, in Châtillon-sur-Seine, and mentally stumble backward into dim memories of Vercingétorix and first-year Latin.

Burgundy is a bouquet of good things to eat, to drink, to touch and see and feel. It is very sensual country with nothing abstemious about it (except for the considerable world of the Cistercians).

When Charles le Téméraire (the Rash, or, as usually rendered, the Bold), last of the Grand Dukes of Burgundy, died in battle in 1477 before the walls of Nancy, his dukedom held sway over Holland, Luxembourg, Flanders, much of today's Belgium, Artois on the English Channel, Picardie, Lorraine, and Franche-Comté. In fact, his dukedom was larger than the kingdom of France, which it separated from the Germanic Roman Empire.

Burgundy has, of course, shrunk to a more comprehensible size: physically speaking, from about Sens in the north to Charlieu and Mâcon in the south, from the Loire in the west to the Saône river in the east, with Dijon as its principal city. After covering Dijon, this section will concentrate on the quadrant northwest of Dijon, then will move south to the Autun-Beaune area.

The Rhône Valley, for its part tied to Burgundy by gastronomy and travellers' traditions, reaches south from Mâcon and the Beaujolais country to Orange (which will be covered in the chapter on Provence), and from the Auvergne region in the west to the Jura mountain country east of Lyon; its center, for the visitor, is the city of Lyon.

MAJOR INTEREST IN BURGUNDY

Food and wine
Romanesque architecture

Dijon
Palais des Ducs
Musée Archéologique

Vézelay
Basilica of Ste-Madeleine

Auxerre
Cathedral of St-Etienne
Abbey of St-Germain

Excursion to village of Chablis
The châteaux of Tanlay and Ancy-le-Franc

Sens
The treasury at St-Etienne cathedral

Back roads south of Châtillon-sur-Seine
The Châtillon museum's Treasure of Vix
Abbaye de Fontenay
Château Bussy-Rabutin
Semur-en-Auxois

Autun
St-Lazare cathedral's tympanum sculptures
Musée Rolin

Beaune
Center of wine trade
Hôtel-Dieu

Tournus
Church of St-Philibert

Remains of the abbey at Cluny

MAJOR INTEREST IN THE RHÔNE VALLEY

Roman remains
Food

Lyon
Roman theater and Musée de la Civilisation Gallo-
   Romaine
Basilica of Notre-Dame-de-Fourvière
Walking tour of Old Lyon (especially *les traboules*
   passageways)
Museums: Beaux-Arts, Textiles, Decorative Arts

The walled city of Pérouges

Vienne
Temple d'Auguste et de Livie
St-Romain-en-Gal, Gallo-Roman city
Roman theater
Excursion to Mont Pilat and to Gouffre d'Enfer for
   scenic views

BURGUNDY

Deep in southern Burgundy near the town of Mâcon, an
enormous limestone escarpment, the Roche de Solutré,
announces the hamlet of Solutré and one of the most
intriguing archaeological sites in Burgundy—or all of
France, for that matter. During the Reindeer Age (15,000
to 12,000 B.C.) the Solutrian civilization of the same name
produced precision stone points and arrowheads, the
highest achievement of flint-working in the ancient Western world.

Digs that began in 1866 revealed the skeletons of at
least 100,000 horses in a bed two and a half acres large
and two to six and a half feet deep, the earliest evidence
of planned horse consumption in France. (Horse meat is
still eaten in France, but by law shops selling it must carry
a copper-gold horse's head over the door.)

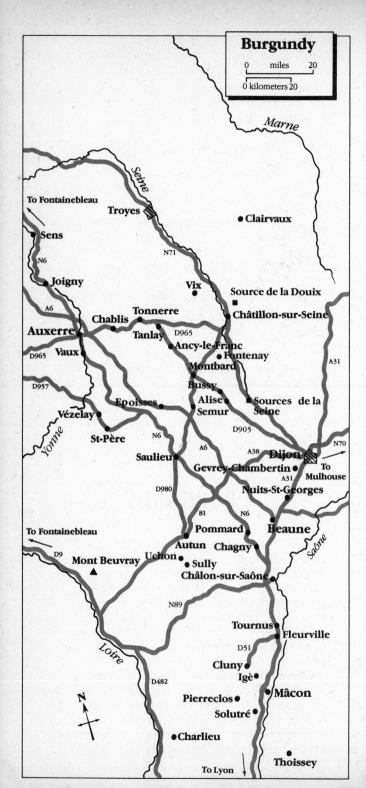

Less dramatically, later excavations have brought to light human remains from the older Aurignacian period and the following Neolithic period, along with tools, pottery, ceramics, and Bronze Age bodies. Some of the finds and their descriptions may be seen on the ground floor of the **Musée Municipal des Ursulines** in Mâcon. In the beautiful town of Châtillon-sur-Seine, on the northern borders of Burgundy, the local museum shelters the **Treasure of Vix** and other remarkable relics of prehistoric culture. These artifacts had been buried in a sepulcher with female bones (a warrior princess, perhaps) at nearby Vix in pre-Roman days and were discovered only in 1953, more than 2,500 years later.

The Celts

Before the Roman Empire, the Celts inhabited vast reaches of Europe stretching from Romania to Ireland, from the Rhine to the Pyrénées. Theirs was, and is, a fascinating civilization. As described by Oxford historian Barry Cunliffe in *The Celtic World,* the Celts "were barbarian in the classical sense of the word, energetic, quick-tempered, and 'war-mad'; but their craftsmen created a brilliant art style and by the first century B.C. a truly urban society had begun to develop in many areas. It was against these people that the Roman armies moved in the first centuries B.C. and A.D., leaving only a Celtic fringe in Scotland, Ireland, Wales, and Brittany to survive unconquered."

It was Gaius Julius Caesar who, in the seven years from 58 to 51 B.C., finally conquered the Celts of Gaul and who found a valiant opponent in Vercingétorix, leader of the Arverni tribe. "A man of boundless energy," Caesar wrote of his enemy, "he terrorized waverers with the rigors of an iron discipline."

Vercingétorix and an independent Celtic Gaul found their particular Waterloo on the battlefields of Burgundy at Alésia, today's Alise-Ste-Reine, in 52 B.C.

The House of Burgundy

Burgundy, the name on the land, is derived from the Burgundi, or Burgondiones, a people of Germanic origin who, as a result of wars against the Alemanni tribes, were forced in 411 to take refuge in Gaul under the leadership of their chieftan, Gundicar. The major towns of this first kingdom were Vienne, Lyon, Autun, Mâcon, Besançon, and Geneva. Except for the last two, those towns still come within the territories of Burgundy and the Rhône Valley.

The House of Burgundy as one thinks of it today, however, began in 1031 when Robert, son of the king of France, by heredity became the Capétian duke of Burgundy. For the next three centuries, Burgundy stood as a bastion of Christianity under the rules of the abbey of Cluny, followed by the monasteries of Cîteaux, Clairvaux, and some 350 others. The shining light of the whole movement was Saint Bernard (1091–1153), whose eloquence and genius dominated the 12th century. He alone was responsible for the establishment of 160 Cistercian abbeys.

The Romanesque Period

The nature of the feudal, monastic world was sedentary, even static. The barons of feudal times required workers to stay on the land, to produce, and to serve as soldiers in the seemingly endless petty wars between neighboring villages. Monasticism made an absolute virtue of not joining the world, of remaining isolated from it.

During the period known as Romanesque (roughly from the 11th to the 12th century), however, dramatic changes led to an increase in the mobility of the typical European. Feudal wars slackened, new lands were exploited, new villages built. Reclamation, drainage, and deforestation began in the early 11th century in Burgundy as well as in Normandy and Lombardy. With the advent of two major influences—the cult of relics and the Crusades—great numbers of people began to travel over roads and under conditions that today would be considered impassable and impossible.

All this energy and movement had as one of its manifestations the establishment of churches and abbeys. Architecture became to the Romanesque period what painting was to the Italian Renaissance.

Nowhere can a traveller interested in Romanesque art and architecture enjoy a bigger banquet than in Burgundy, where the regional committee of Burgundian tourism has counted no fewer than 100 *major* Romanesque churches. (Tourism offices in Dijon and other major towns can supply descriptive brochures in English.) The ornamental, often fantastic, sculptural detailing of these churches, especially in column capitals—which enraged the ascetically minded Saint Bernard—delights visitors today.

The historical Burgundy that is best known, however, is that of the proud and powerful Grand Dukes of the West, who ruled from 1364 to 1477: Philippe le Hardi (the Bold), Jean sans Peur (the Fearless), Philippe le Bon (the Good), and Charles le Téméraire (the Rash). Carl Rudolf Friml's musical *The Vagabond King* thus enshrined the worthy dynasty: "And bow down to Burgundy."

Beyond its historical importance Burgundy is, of course, known throughout the world for its food and wine, but because the cooking of the region is synonymous, in many minds, with French cuisine itself, it will not be discussed here. As for wines, there are many excellent publications on the subject (see the Bibliography), and a wine lover could not be properly served by a summary.

However, gastronomes should become acquainted with the creations of one or more of "Les Six"—the Big Six chefs of Burgundy: Michel Lorain, A la Côte St-Jacques, in Joigny; Marc Meneau, Espérance, in St-Père-sous-Vézelay; Bernard Loiseau, Côte d'Or, in Saulieu; Jacques Lameloise, Lameloise, in Chagny; Jean-Pierre Billoux, J. P. Billoux (Hôtel de la Cloche), in Dijon; and Georges Blanc, Georges Blanc, in Vonnas.

DIJON

The good Dijonnais—merchants, local leaders, university professors and students, wine growers and mustard makers—think of their city as a French, even a European, *plaque tournante,* or turntable, at the center of great commercial routes leading from Paris, the Mediterranean, across the Rhine from West Germany, and over the Alps from Switzerland and Italy.

It is true that motorways from all directions appear to lead to Dijon, that you can whisk here from Paris in an hour and 40 minutes aboard a TGV, that five international airports make for easy access to the region (though Dijon proper has only a small civil airport, with daily flights from both Paris-Orly and Paris-Charles-de-Gaulle).

It is also true that the Dijon Agglomération boasts properly bustling and traffic-tied industrial and commercial zones to the northeast and to the south of town, where emphasis falls less on Flemish sculpture and half-timbered houses than upon food-processing plants, automobile parts (Peugeot), and pharmaceutical research.

Yet here in the heart of things, at the site of the Roman

camp called Divio, a visitor can still summon up the days of the dukes, a period of economic and artistic dominance that for more than a hundred years inspired the envy of states across Europe, especially the kingdom of France.

Dijon is handsome, for one thing, which most metropolises are not. It centers on the hemispheric **place de la Libération** (the former place Royale), a pretty 17th-century layout by Versailles's architect, Jules Hardouin-Mansart.

It is difficult to imagine that after the death of Charles le Téméraire in 1477 the ducal palace was neglected, ignored, and all but abandoned for 200 years. Then, in the 17th century, Louis XIV reinstituted the ducal title for a short time, and Burgundy controlled a government within a government, a *pays d'états* (a kind of parliament of estates, consisting of clergy, nobility, and other citizens).

Dijon's grand days came in the 18th century when, according to the *Encyclopaedia Britannica*, "it became the seat of a bishopric, its streets were improved, its commerce developed, and an academy of science and letters [was] founded; while its literary salons were hardly less celebrated than those of Paris."

Dijon the Town

The former **Palais des Ducs et des Etats de Bourgogne**, a part of which today houses the Hôtel de Ville, rises just north of the place de la Libération, but only a portion of the palaces—the two towers (Tour de Bar and Tour Philippe-le-Bon), the guardroom (Salle des Gardes), and the kitchens—represents the original complex. These remnants are almost entirely enclosed within the current structures, built in the 17th and 18th centuries.

The east wing of the complex, near the Tour de Bar (named for its most illustrious prisoner, Good King René, duc de Bar and Lorraine and comte de Provence), houses the **Musée des Beaux-Arts**, among the richest and most unusual in France.

Taking precedence over the painting and sculpture galleries, the magnificent tombs of Philippe le Hardi and Jean sans Peur (buried along with his wife, Marguerite of Bavaria) in the Salle des Gardes are showstoppers, obsequies in stone, witnesses in great part to the genius of the Flemish sculptor Claus Sluter. There is nothing elsewhere like the alabaster "cloister" of Le Hardi's catafalque, around which parade 41 *pleurants* (mourners)—relatives,

friends, soldiers, clergymen—carved from life, heads covered in stony sorrow. Juan de la Huerta reproduced that
inspiration for the tomb of Jean and Marguerite.

The tombs so dominate the room that other masterworks might be missed: a scale model of Sluter's *Puits de
Moïse* (*Well of Moses*) from Dijon's Chartreuse (Charterhouse) de Champmol and the painted *Nativity* by Mel-
chior Broederlam, also from Champmol.

Banquets famous throughout the dukedom were prepared in the kitchens, which date from 1435. Six enormous chimneys surround a central, even larger one from
which smoky air soared several stories.

Sculpture is emphasized in the museum because of
Sluter and Dijon native François Rude (responsible for
Paris's Arc de Triomphe sculptures). Paintings are displayed according to schools: Italian, German-Swiss, Flemish, 19th-century French.

On rue Vaillant, the **Musée Rude** in the northern transept of the former church of St-Etienne, now the Chambre
de Commerce, remembers the local son with moldings of
all the sculptor's works that are not in Dijon, including an
exact replica of the *Marseillaise* bas-relief on the Arc de
Triomphe. (Rude and another native born nearby, Saint
Bernard, have given their names to squares. On place
François-Rude, the shop named **André Grillot** sells gifts
and gadgets for oenophiles.) Church-architecture enthusiasts will stop by nearby **St-Michel**, with its façade begun in
Flamboyant Gothic and completed in Renaissance style.

The gates of the ducal palace and its Cour d'Honneur
open on **rue de la Liberté**, a fashionable shopping street
where the Dijonnais go to keep themselves *en chic*. No
gallivanting gastronome can keep from popping in at
number 32, where the smart **Grey-Poupon** shop sells and
celebrates mustard, a regional resource since the days of
the great Gallo-Roman spice route. Considering the hand-
painted, museum-quality porcelain containers on display,
it's difficult to exit with a mere jar of familiar *moutarde de
Dijon*. On the same street, at number 16, the **Mulot et
Petitjean** store offers another traditional Dijonnais specialty: *pain d'épice* (spice bread) in several varieties.

Pré aux Clercs et Trois Faisans on place de la Libération serves informal meals including such down-to-earth
regional specialties as *coq-au-vin*.

Across rue des Forges (which has fine Renaissance
houses), north of the palace, the Gothic **church of Notre-
Dame** is best known for its **Jacquemart clock**, to which

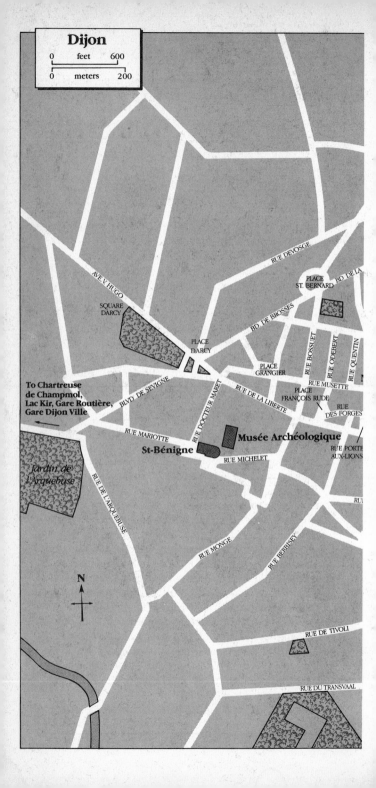

older Dijonnais remain devoted. Transported all the way from Courtrai (in Belgium) by bullock cart in 1382 on the order of Philippe le Hardi, the Jacquemart figure regularly striking the hours gained great sympathy and in 1610 was presented with a female companion. Over two centuries, a family was established with the addition of a Jacquelinet and a Jacquelinette, whose job is sounding the quarter-hours. (University students have been known to attempt outfitting these working worthies with Levi's and sombreros.)

Within Notre-Dame, the chief treasure is an 11th-century Black Virgin, one of the oldest wood sculptures in the country. Two tapestries honor deliverances from war: one from Tournai, Belgium, dedicated after the lifting of a 16th-century siege of Dijon by the Swiss; the other a Gobelins dedicated to the same siege as well as to the end of the German occupation in 1944. (Business people in the vicinity of Notre-Dame take their trade to a handy grill, **Le Central**, on place Grangier in the pleasant, unimposing **Central Urbis Hôtel**; a specialty: white turbot in dill cream.)

Off the rue des Bons-Enfants, east of place de la Libération, the **Musée Magnin,** occupying a handsome 17th-century town house, is decorated in elegant mid-19th-century fashion and displays the painting collections of Maurice Magnin, which were given to the nation in 1937. Italian and Flemish canvases hang here as well as French paintings, sketches, and drawings.

West of the palace in the direction of the railway station cluster attractions worth most of a day. The 13th- to 14th-century **cathedral of St-Bénigne** memorializes a missionary priest, apparently martyred in the second century, whose tomb was discovered near Dijon in the sixth century. It is Burgundian Gothic in style.

The crypt, the most interesting feature of St-Bénigne, is the work of an Italian abbot, Guillaume de Volpiano, whose work is also well known in Normandy. This structure is actually the remains of the late 10th- to early 11th-century Romanesque basilica that once occupied the site. The transept and choir boast 86 pillars. Some of those in the rotunda still bear their curious capitals; the best have features and forms of monsters.

A visit to the **Musée Archéologique**, adjacent to St-Bénigne, with its relics from the early Stone Age and Neolithic epochs, the Bronze Age, Gallo-Roman days, and

Merovingian times, is a must before making excursions to ancient sites in the Burgundian countryside. Many finds were uncovered at Alise-Ste-Reine and at sanctuaries near the source of the Seine.

The **Jardin de l'Arquebuse**, down rue Mariotte from St-Bénigne, is home to the **Musée d'Histoire Naturelle** in a former barracks of the *arquebusiers* and to a botanical garden. (The *arquebuse* was a gun of matchlock or wheel-lock mechanism much used by the Spanish, Italians, and French in the 15th and 16th centuries. Arquebuse is also the name of a fiery liqueur, which purists prefer to call a vulnerary, since its adherents modestly claim it cures anything. It is very difficult to find; inquire at La Cave du Clos—formerly La Cour aux Vins—on rue Jeannin.)

In 1383 Philippe le Hardi founded the charterhouse now known as the **Chartreuse de Champmol** (due west of the Jardin de l'Arquebuse) as a quasi-royal nécropolis and filled it with works of the best artists from around his vast lands. Today it is a psychiatric hospital, but visitors are admitted to see the two triumphs that remain: the *Puits de Moïse* (*Well of Moses*) and the chapel door Claus Sluter sculpted between 1395 and 1405.

Enthusiasts of period houses should walk several streets near Notre-Dame: Porte-aux-Lions, des Forges, de la Chouette, Verrerie, Chaudronnerie, Vannerie, and Amiral-Roussin. Friday is the day when the large, covered central market really hums, and the first two weeks of November bow to cuisine in the Foire Internationale Gastronomique. (Patricia Wells, the food writer, recommends **Simone Porcheret** in this neighborhood for buying cheeses and utensils to go with them.)

Throughout the year, other major happenings in town include L'Hiver Musical (winter musicale), first half of January; L'Été Musical and L'Estivade (summer musicales with animations in streets and gardens), June through August; and Les Fêtes de la Vigne (wine festival), first half of September.

Dijon's best inns are the **Hôtel de la Cloche**, off place Darcy (with superb two-star dining at **Jean-Pierre Billoux**; one specialty is terrine of young pigeon with garlic; reserve; Tel: 80-30-11-00), and **Chapeau Rouge**, at place Michelet, with a one-star kitchen; the warm soufflé of wild strawberries here is irresistible (reserve; Tel: 80-30-28-10). **La Toison d'Or** joins gastronomy to culture in a 15thto 16th-century town house with a private museum containing Medieval figures and vineyard tools (reserve; Tel: 80-30-73-52).

Dining on traditional Burgundian fare is recommended at warm, welcoming **La Chouette** on the street of the same name, which runs between Notre-Dame and the 17th-century Hôtel de Vogüé (La Chouette is renowned for veal kidneys in mustard; reserve; Tel: 80-30-18-10). (One of Dijon's most important parliamentary mansions, the Hôtel de Vogüé today is occupied by the city's architectural board; anyone interested in visiting it can do so by applying at the Office de Tourisme on place Darcy.)

The cuisine and stylish service of the **Parc de la Colombière** match its setting near the beautiful park of the same name (south of the city center), the once-royal domain of the princes of Condé. The hotel-restaurant offers 36 modest rooms. The park today is a favorite promenading area for the Dijonnais; a small portion of the Via Agrippa that led from Lyon to Trèves is visible.

On a sparkling spring or autumn afternoon, it's fine to make your way west of downtown to **Le Cygne** (reserve; Tel: 80-41-02-40) on Lac Kir. The lake was named for the late Canon Félix Kir, a local priest who doubled for many years as the Communist mayor of Dijon and, during World War II, languished for two months in a Gestapo cell as punishment for aiding in the escape of French prisoners. While you watch canoes, kayaks, and small boats at play, salute the mayor with his favorite drink, a *kir,* classically one-third Dijonnais *crème de cassis* (a black-currant liqueur) and two-thirds white Burgundian Aligoté. (The *kir* is popular throughout France today; a *kir royale* uses Champagne; the *kir communiste* is made with red wine—what else?—preferably a gamay or Beaujolais.)

VEZELAY

Tiny (fewer than 600 inhabitants) hilltop Vézelay, about 90 km (56 miles) west of Dijon (fastest route: A 38 to E 15-A 6 to Avallon, then west for 16 km/10 miles), is a place of pilgrimage. Its abbey was consecrated by Pope Jean VIII in 878, and it remained significant throughout the glory years of the 12th and 13th centuries.

It is mostly pilgrims in search of art and history who arrive now, climbing uphill in cars along a skinny one-way street, but their destination is the same: the **basilica of Ste-**

Madeleine, among the most impressive of all the Romanesque churches in Burgundy (it has been a basilica since 1920).

In the ninth century Girart de Roussillon, a Burgundian count, founded a settlement of nuns in the valley below, where St-Père-sous-Vézelay sits today. When that location was repeatedly attacked by Norman invaders, the decision was taken to reestablish the monastery atop a nearby, more defensible hill.

The relics of Sainte Madeleine (Mary Magdalen) and the miracles accredited to them lured so many pilgrims in the 11th century that the town's population swelled to 10,000 and the church was expanded. Then in 1120 a terrible fire broke out on the eve of July 22, the date of a traditional pilgrimage and the feast day of the saint. It destroyed the entire nave and more than a thousand of the faithful with it.

The story of Mary Magdalen is a fascinating one and had a profound impact upon the life and traditions of Medieval France. Early on, her cult became confounded with the story of the Three Marys, which holds that Magdalen, Mary the mother of James, and Mary the wife of Cléophas, driven out of Palestine, arrived miraculously west of Marseille near Arles (at the site now named for them, Stes-Maries-de-la-Mer, in La Camargue). They came in a boat equipped with neither sail nor oars. The company included Lazarus; his sister, Martha; and other people, who proceeded to evangelize Provence. This story is still believed by some Provençals.

Twenty-six years after the great fire, on March 31, 1146, Saint Bernard came to stand on Vézelay's "inspired hill" to preach the Second Crusade to a worshiping crowd that included France's Louis VII. At the time, Bernard, abbot of Clairvaux, was the man of most consequence in Christendom, and Vézelay (along with Autun, Orléans, Le Puy, and Arles) had become an origination point for the most important pilgrimage route, that to Santiago de Compostela, in Spain.

It was from Vézelay that France's Philippe Auguste and England's Richard the Lion-Hearted departed for the Third Crusade in 1190. In the next century, Saint Francis of Assisi founded the first brotherhood of Franciscans, the Frères Mineurs, in France here. In 1248, when the Seventh Crusade began, Saint Louis (Louis IX) made pilgrimages to Vézelay on several occasions.

In the late 13th century, however, with the discovery

of more relics of Sainte Madeleine in Provence, proud
Vézelay began to decline. Further difficulties were pre-
cipitated by the Wars of Religion, the ravages attributed
to the Huguenots, and the destruction wrought by the
Revolution.

Had Eugène-Emmanuel Viollet-le-Duc not been employed in 1840 to restore the whole to its ancient excellence, Vézelay now would attract no more curiosity than a
pile of rocks.

Today the basilica of Ste-Madeleine is under the gover-
nance of the Franciscans. The feast day, July 22, is marked
by a great religious celebration with special music, entertainment, and the like.

The pink-and-ocher Ste-Madeleine dominates a ter-
raced village of brown-roofed houses. The basilica's façade, which was almost entirely reconstituted in the 19th
century, is not universally applauded, but the interior
contains artworks acknowledged to be among the finest
in the Western world.

The central **Tympanum of Pentecost**, for example, depicts a gigantic Christ in Glory from whose hands the rays
of the Holy Ghost reach out to the 12 Apostles. To the
right and left of Christ and the Apostles, the people of the
world await the Word. These are wonderful, fantastical
figures, since the artists of the day knew little of the world
and thus imagined most of it: Some characters appear
with the heads of dogs, some with pendant-like ears,
others more monster than man.

The column capitals are even more entertaining and as
beautifully and imaginatively carved. Here, David defeats
a lion; there, Jacob wrestles with an angel. On the right,
the bad rich man dies in agony; on the left, Absalom is
decapitated.

Some of these capitals are so popular that medallion
copies are sold in souvenir shops around the square. Also
available near the basilica are handmade textiles and
jewelry.

Follow the narrow, crabbed streets of Vézelay to lunch
or spend the night at **La Poste et Lion d'Or**, a fairly
modest but most comfortable hideaway.

Today food lovers and aficionados make their pilgrimage to the hamlet of St-Père (some 350 inhabitants) at the
foot of Vézelay's hill to dine at the celebrated **l'Espérance**
(chef Marc Meneau has earned three Michelin stars for
his work; reserve well in advance; Tel: 86-33-20-45) and,
perhaps, to stay the night in one of its 21 rooms and

apartments. Elegance is the byword here, though nothing is fussy or pompous. Many experienced travellers rank l'Espérance among the two or three top country retreats in France and don't mind paying top dollar for the quality.

While in St-Père, take a look at **Notre-Dame**, begun in the 13th century and restored in the 19th century by Viollet-le-Duc; the **Musée Archéologique Régional** houses the finds from digs at nearby Fontaines Salées, where Gallo-Roman baths have been unearthed.

AUXERRE

Auxerre (locally pronounced O-sair) is one of the oldest towns in France, known at its beginning as Autricum to the Gauls, Autessiodurum to the Romans. It lies along the great trade route from Lyon to Boulogne, about halfway between Paris and Dijon, which is some 150 km (93 miles) to the south and east. By the end of the fourth century it was an important center, and even today it retains a wealth of art and business activity worthy of a much larger city. And, unlike some rural cities, Auxerre is growing younger; 60 to 65 percent of the population is less than 40 years of age.

Auxerre is known throughout France as the birthplace of the great Saint Germain, who was born in 378 to noble parents. He studied and practiced law in Rome and then returned to Gaul, married, and won a high official post. Though later sainted, Germain paid little heed in early life to religion. In 418 he was elected bishop of Auxerre by the clergy and the people, much against his will. He changed his life immediately, however, devoting himself to prayer and action in defense of the Church. When Saint Germain died in Ravenna, his body was returned to Auxerre and buried with pomp and circumstance under the abbey church that bears his name.

Saint Germain knew and supported Sainte Geneviève, now the patron saint of Paris. "Exemplified by these two," writes Katherine Scherman in *The Birth of France,* "the cultivation of the Gallo-Roman Christian merged with the tough vitality of the pagan Frank." Saint Germain is memorialized in Paris in the church of St-Germain-l'Auxerrois, behind the Louvre; he is often confused with another Saint Germain, a sixth-century bishop of Paris named Germanus, who lies in St-Germain-des-Prés.

The city's best face is that observed from across the busy river Yonne; from that vantage point the spires of St-Etienne, St-Germain, and St-Pierre-en-Vallée point skyward, symbols of age and importance.

Marie Noël (1883–1967), a popular poet, provides some insight into the collective psyche of her fellow citizens:

> The Auxerrois have in their veins both a drop
> of blood and a fantasy.
> It leads them to do good or to do bad,
> To the right or to the left,
> But always a little way off the beaten track.

There does seem to be a very pleasant capriciousness to the daily life of Auxerre, a sturdy and bourgeois business approach joined to a hat-in-the-air, youthful exuberance. Marie Noël herself, a wooden figure topped by a round black hat, neck swathed in gray scarf, contemplates the scene from her perch in front of the Hôtel de Ville.

The present **cathedral of St-Etienne** is the fifth structure built on the site of the original sanctuary, which was founded in 400 by Bishop Saint Amâtre and frequently altered over the years and centuries until it burned down in 1023. Some 500 years of architectural forays followed, and the result can be viewed today. The south tower never has been completed.

Among the remarkable achievements here are the 13th-century stained-glass windows and the 11th-century Romanesque crypt with its superb frescoes, including the unique portrayal of Christ Triumphant astride a white horse surrounded by angels, also on horseback. The treasury holds valuable manuscripts, books of hours, ivories, miniatures, and enamels.

What you first see of the **abbey of St-Germain**, north of St-Etienne up rue Cochois, is the Gothic 13th- to 15th-century church; nothing remains above ground of the sixth-century abbey. What you remember is the crypt, which essentially constitutes the sixth-century church erected in Saint Germain's honor by Clothilde, Christian wife of the Frankish king Clovis of the Merovingian dynasty. This crypt contains the oldest frescoes yet discovered in France, dating from 858 and depicting the martyrdom of Saint Etienne (Saint Stephen). Still in place, and still bearing weight, are beams of oak that are more than 1,100 years old. In this building a museum and cultural center make up one of the most valuable historical resources in the country.

In the center of town, the 15th-century **Tour de l'Horloge** (Clock Tower) is a graceful storybook structure in Flamboyant style built atop the Gallo-Roman wall and now the heart of the shopping area. One face of the clock features the movements of the sun and moon, while the other counts the hours.

Within the grounds of the psychiatric hospital, the six acres of **Clos de la Chaînette** with its few rows of grapes (producing white and rosé wines), are the last survivors of the great seventh-century vineyards of Auxerre. (These few acres lie just outside town to the northwest; take the rue des Migraines—named for a once-famous vineyard. We can only wonder what it produced!) At the beginning of the 19th century, Alexandre Dumas regarded the local production as among the greatest of French red wines, mentioning it in the same breath as Château Margaux and Romanée Conti. The phylloxera crisis of the 19th century and increasing urban pressures caused virtually all the other prestigious local vineyards to disappear, but some are being reborn several kilometers away in the environs of **Vaux**.

A revival of the arts of pottery, ceramics, and faïence so celebrated here during the 18th and 19th centuries is under way throughout the region of the Yonne today, and shops selling such crafts have sprung up everywhere, particularly in small towns. In Auxerre, François Brochet is re-creating the tradition of polychrome wood sculpture. New and attractive in form are the works of Pierre Merlier. Shops selling such goods are grouped around the Tour de l'Horloge.

The best restaurant in this area, **La Chamaille**, is located in an old farmhouse on the banks of the Yonne river in the village of Chevannes, 8 km (5 miles) southwest of Auxerre (reserve; Tel: 86-41-24-80). Also good are the **Jardin Gourmand** at 56, boulevard Vauban in Auxerre (reserve; Tel: 86-51-53-52) and **La Petite Auberge** in nearby Vaux (reserve; Tel: 86-53-80-08). The **Restaurant Maxime** in Auxerre, next to (but supposedly not part of) the Hôtel Le Maxime, is quite good and informal, and puts an emphasis on regional dishes and fresh fish from nearby rivers (reserve; Tel: 86-52-04-41). **Hôtel Le Maxime**, a 25-room inn right on the river, is the finest hotel in town and the best located for walking.

SENS

Travellers stop in Sens, about halfway between Fontainebleau and, to the southeast, Auxerre, chiefly to visit the **cathedral of St-Etienne**, which dates from 1140. The town itself, counting some 30,000 Sénonais, takes its name from one of the strongest Gallic tribes, the Senones. Its history is proud: The Romans made Sens the capital of one of the provinces of Lyonnaise. It was later the seat of an archbishopric when Paris had only a bishop, and when Pope Alexander III was in residence from 1163 to 1164 Sens effectively became the capital of Christianity.

It was at Sens that Abélard was condemned; Saint Louis married Marguerite de Provence in the cathedral. It was also in Sens (as well as in the abbey of Pontigny, nearer Auxerre) that Thomas à Becket lived six years in exile from England and Henry II.

The good Sénonais are likely to tell the visitor that their cathedral represents the birth of Gothic architecture in France—an opinion that is more enthusiastic than accurate. The choir of the cathedral of St-Denis in the Paris suburb of that name is universally acclaimed as the birthplace of Gothic; what *is* certain is that St-Etienne ranks among the first great Gothic edifices in France. Interestingly, the choir of St-Etienne became a model for the rebuilding of the eastern end of England's Canterbury Cathedral following its disastrous fire in 1174. The work was directed by one Guillaume de Sens (who fell from a scaffold in 1178 and was succeeded by a British William).

Note the early-Gothic Etienne on the central portal (wearing deacon's garb and carrying the Gospel) before entering the nave, where light streams through superb 12th-century to 17th-century stained-glass windows.

The cathedral has always been renowned for the value of its **treasury**, one of the most highly regarded in Europe (along with those of Ste-Foy, in Conques, and St-Maurice, in Switzerland). Other great collections are housed nearby in the **Palais Synodal** in the Dépôt Lapidaire. Since 1985 many works formerly dispersed throughout the city have been joined together in the **Musées de Sens**, a restoration of part of the cathedral complex.

The collection includes relics, antique textiles, liturgical ornaments, tapestries, mosaics, and silver, ivory, and enamel works; particular attention should, however, be paid to the **vestments of Thomas à Becket**. They appear

to have been fitted to a man extremely large and powerful for his time. Among other standouts are a 15th-century
Flemish tapestry, *Adoration of the Magi;* a gold and
bejeweled fibula (brooch) from Merovingian times; a
remarkably carved ivory reliquary, the *Sainte Chasse;* and
an eighth-century shroud depicting a gigantic Gilgamesh,
the hero of the ancient Babylonian epic.

Joigny

A fine headquarters for exploring all of northwest Burgundy is **A la Côte St-Jacques** in the town of Joigny, about
halfway between Sens and Auxerre on the river Yonne.
On a grassy terrace above the river, equipped with some
private balconies and an indoor pool with doors opening
to the terrace, it is a cultivated oasis. The 25 rooms and
four suites bespeak country elegance, and the kitchen,
under chef Michel Lorain, is one of the very best in
France. (The fish called *bar,* lightly smoked with cream of
caviar, is not to be passed over. Reservations are essential;
Tel: 86-62-09-70.)

The 17th-century **Château du Fey** in Joigny has been
opened as a cooking school (one-week classes) by Anne
Willan, whose La Varenne in Paris is one of the best
known such schools in Europe. (For information, write La
Varenne in Burgundy, P.O. Box 25574, Washington, DC
20007.)

CHABLIS AND EAST FROM AUXERRE

"I would give a fortune and all my titles to intoxicate
myself on a mixture of Chablis and oysters," Eugène
Deschamps once wrote. Or, he might have said, Chablis
and turbot... or *sole meunière*... or escargots... or
Saint Marcellin cheese.

Chablis, a few miles east of Auxerre, is one of the
most famous wine names in the world—and one of
the most misused. Outside France, in the United States, in
Australia, and in other wine-growing nations it is often
employed as an almost generic name for any white, but
frequently those of little distinction.

However, as winegrower, writer, and merchant Alexis
Lichine pointed out, "Used correctly, it refers to one of the

world's rarest great wines—to the steadily decreasing quantity of magnificent flinty, dry white wines which are made from grapes grown on hilly acres in and around the Burgundian town of Chablis." According to Edward Young, the distinctive taste of the wines results from the pocket of bituminous clay in which they grow, a soil found nowhere else except at Kimmeridge, Dorset, England.

At one time, Chablis boasted some charming old houses and was most picturesque during harvest. As Samuel Chamberlain remembers, "The doors of the wine cellars were open then, and you could hear the creaking of old oak presses and smell the haunting, fruity odor of newly pressed grapes.... Streets were animated with green-stained carts and pretty, full-hipped young grape-pickers."

Unfortunately, on a clear June night in 1940 some far-afield Italian flyers unloaded their bombs on the heart of the unsuspecting and unstrategic town. Fortunately, Chablis's real treasure grew in the chalky hills beyond.

Chablis today is a natural stop on a day's excursion out of Auxerre, and it is refreshing, since there's little to do here but sip Chablis (for maximum appreciation, you should request a *grand cru*—Les Bouguerots, Les Blanchots, Les Clos) and lunch or dine at Michel Vignaud's **Hostellerie des Clos** (reserve; Tel: 86-42-10-63). A conversion of an ancient *clos des hospices,* the *hostellerie* offers 26 quiet, comfortable bedrooms overlooking gardens to those in search of a real hideaway.

A festival of regional wines is held in Chablis the fourth Sunday in November.

Tonnerre

Tonnerre is little known to foreigners except to passengers aboard the luxury hotel-barges that cruise the canals of Burgundy. It is worth a stop, however, en route from Auxerre to the châteaux of Tanlay and Ancy-le-Franc (see below), largely because of the beautiful 13th-century **hôpital** that somehow survived ruinous fires in the 16th century.

Built at the order of Marguerite de Bourgogne, widow of Charles d'Anjou, the hospital is similar in style and purpose to the Hôtel-Dieu in Beaune. The chapel near the high altar contains a very moving *mise au tombeau,* a 15th-century form of Burgundian sculpture that is also called a *saint sépulcre* and, in English, an entombment. The one in Tonnerre, one at Notre-Dame in Semur-en-

Auxois, and another in the hospital in Dijon are the three most arresting examples of the form; the one in Tonnerre features a semi-recumbent Christ being laid upon his tomb by seven mourning figures.

Another reason to linger in Tonnerre is the outstanding restaurant and 15-room inn (including five suites) of the **Abbaye St-Michel**, which occupies a Benedictine abbey of the 10th century set in its own manicured park. (The unusual and delicious cream of cauliflower soup with shellfish is recommended.)

Tanlay and Ancy-le-Franc

In the 16th century Burgundian architecture began to change, having come under the influence of Renaissance arts imported from Italy. Unlike the Loire Valley, Burgundy had not seen a burgeoning of château-like country mansions until this period, to which Tanlay and Ancy-le-Franc (both to the east of Tonnerre) as well as Sully, near Autun, belong. **Tanlay** is in essence a comfortable palace, elegant yet unimposing, the kind of noble dwelling most commoners would be happy to call home. It was erected sometime around 1550 on the remains of a feudal fortress.

Several of the handsomely furnished rooms are open to visitors, and the most interesting of them is in the tower where Huguenot conspiracies were hatched during the Wars of Religion. The vault is covered with a most curious fresco from the Fontainebleau school, featuring—together—notable Catholics and Protestants.

Sébastien Serlio, an Italian architect brought to the region (as were so many other artists) by François I, designed **Ancy-le-Franc** for Antoine III de Clermont-Tonnerre in the mid-16th century. It is a harmony of four major structures linked by corner pavilions, the original model of pure Renaissance style in France. Among the 25 beautifully decorated rooms open to the public, the chapel, with its carved woodwork, is most notable.

ALONG THE UPPER SEINE

Châtillon-sur-Seine, farther east of Auxerre past Tonnerre and Tanlay, straddles the lazily flowing river, its beflowered bridges, pretty houses, winding streets, and coquettish air suggesting that nothing much ever has happened here.

That's not true, sadly. During World War II, the town center was badly mauled; in September 1914, General Joseph Joffre set up headquarters here so that his retreating French troops could counterattack the charging German army; and, just a hundred years before that, Napoléon chose the spot for a congress with the enemies allied against him during the famous Hundred Days.

Today, however, this town of some 8,000 inhabitants is mainly an excursion center, with facilities for horseback riding, tennis, hiking, fishing, and the like. Foreigners and French people in search of ancient history come to town, though, to visit one of the most interesting small museums in the country, the **Musée Municipal**. The handsome 16th-century Renaissance Maison Philandrier houses collections from protohistoric sites in the region: fifth-century ceramics from Mont-Lassois, a bronze alms basin from the chariot tomb at Ste-Colombe, votive sculptures from the sanctuary of Essarois, Gallo-Roman everyday tools and utensils from Vertillum (Vertault).

Most sensational are the finds from the tomb of Vix, discovered in 1953 at the foot of nearby Mont-Lassois. These consisted of the remains of a woman (most likely a Celtic princess) who died in the sixth century B.C. and was buried with goods probably intended to accompany her into the next world (a golden diadem, earrings, bejeweled bracelets), a huge ceremonial chariot, and—one of the most majestic finds of contemporary archaeology—the **Treasure of Vix**. This last is a giant vase five and a half feet high, weighing 460 pounds, and capable of holding 1,162 quarts of liquid (wine, perhaps). A masterpiece of archaic Greek bronze style, it is thought to have been created in about 500 B.C. It is richly decorated with a frieze featuring helmeted warriors and horse-drawn chariots, with Gorgon heads on the handles.

Châtillon offers one of the small, cozy, modestly priced inns that delight travellers who don't wish to make reservations well in advance, as required by more prestigious places. The **Côte d'Or** has ten rooms, a quiet, shady garden, and an agreeable kitchen.

Before departing Châtillon, stop near the **Source de la Douix** at the foot of a rocky hill where waters fountain forth from the limestone earth at a rate of up to 800 gallons a second to mingle, slightly farther along, with those of the Seine. The site is reminiscent of the Fontaine de Vaucluse in Provence but is much less tourist-ridden.

Fontenay

When Saint Bernard, then abbot of Clairvaux, came to the countryside near Montbard to seek a site for the foundation of a hermitage, he must have felt Nature had designed with him in mind. Set in a deep valley of intense green south of Châtillon, broken in autumn by outbursts of red and golden leaves, the **Abbaye de Fontenay** and its grounds are eminently suited to meditation, contemplation, and quiet pursuits.

Originally Fontenay was home to only 12 monks, but that number increased quickly, and the present abbey was constructed and waxed exceedingly prosperous from the 12th through the 15th centuries. Its buildings consisted of chapel, bakery, dovecote and kennel, church (with dormitories), cloister, infirmary, forge, and hostel.

Decline began in the 16th century, in part due to a system of appointing by royal favor abbots who were uninterested in the traditional roles of abbeys, though largely because of the devastating effects of the Wars of Religion. With the Revolution, Fontenay became a paper mill. It was resold in 1820 to Elie de Montgolfier (of the pioneering family of balloonists). In 1906 a Montgolfier son-in-law, Edouard Aynard, acquired the abbey, dismantled the factory, and began restoring it to its original appearance. The Aynard family currently lives at the abbey and maintains it as a historical monument. In 1981 UNESCO declared Fontenay a Universal Heritage site.

In the history of Cistercian architecture, Fontenay ranks as one of the most successful examples of form joined to monastic ideal (along with Noirlac, in Berry, and Sénanque, in Provence). What was desired, and here achieved, is a reduction of the unnecessary in a creation of admirable proportions—a severe but harmonious simplicity. Fontenay is as spare and elegant as a Gregorian chant.

Even on a summer's day the visitor shivers slightly in the communal dormitory and tries to imagine monks sleeping on straw mattresses in midwinter; the only heat allowed was in the copying room, where, near a great fireplace, the transcribing of manuscripts was carried out.

Georges Louis Leclerc, comte de Buffon and author of

the classic 44-volume *Natural History,* was born in nearby **Montbard** in 1707. His gardens and study, in what had been a stronghold of the dukes of Burgundy, are open to the public. An association was founded in 1978 to restore Buffon's 18th-century ironworks, and so far it has completed the employees' lodgings, the stable, the blast-furnace hall, the refinery, and the foundry. It's all quite fitting, since Montbard today is a metallurgical center specializing in steel tubing.

The Montbard Regional Fair is held during the first half of September.

Château Bussy-Rabutin

Marie de Rabutin-Chantal, Marquise de Sévigné, was not the only pithy writer in the family. Her cousin, Roger de Rabutin, comte de Bussy, had as pointed a pen and as developed a nose for naughty news. Unfortunately, Rabutin could not keep his wit to himself and was exiled by Louis XIV to his château in far-off Burgundy (far from Paris, that is, and therefore from civilization). His crime: having ridiculed, in a series of irresistibly amusing couplets, the king's affair with Marie Mancini.

In exile, Rabutin kept up a lively correspondence with his beautiful and talented cousin (whom he alternately adored and maligned) and wrote a chronicle titled "The Amorous History of the Gauls," satirizing the scandalous goings-on at court. As a result, he was imprisoned in the Bastille for more than a year and then exiled to the country again. Once challenged on his own purity of motives and behavior, Rabutin wrote, "Let me remind you, sir, that I condone only such scandals as I have myself occasioned."

The first castle at Bussy (Bussy is between Fontenay and Alise-Ste-Reine), constructed in the 13th century, had become a powerful fortress under the Rochefort family and passed into the hands of François de Rabutin in 1602. Roger, his grandson, devoted his years of country confinement to enlarging and beautifying his golden cage.

Of all the public and private rooms, several decorated by Rabutin himself in flights of original fancy, the most interesting may be the master bedroom, with furniture and woodworks of the day, highlighted by 26 portraits of women, among them Madame de Sévigné.

Bussy-Rabutin's masterpiece, however, may be the **Tour Dorée** (literally "gilded tower," though it makes up only one floor of the structure), which is entirely overwhelmed by paintings that feature mythological subjects as well as contemporary gallants accompanied by cutting, cynical couplets.

Alise-Ste-Reine

The heart of the Gallic empire beat its last in 52 B.C. near today's little town (fewer than 800 inhabitants) of Alise-Ste-Reine. A difficult village to find, it is southeast of Montbard/Fontenay near Les Laumes, northwest of Dijon.

Next to Alise was **Alésia**, a hilltop fortress chosen by Vercingétorix for what he planned to make the final rout of the Romans. Tactician though he was, he was no match for Caesar. As Katherine Scherman writes, "Caesar built siege works all around the base of the hill, and in a short time Vercingétorix's big army had exhausted the garrison supplies. In the fierce battle that finally ensued—in which Caesar himself took part, conspicuous to his own men and the enemy alike in the scarlet cloak he always wore in action—the Celtic troops were thoroughly routed and many of them simply ran away and went home."

The great Gaul surrendered himself and his horse to Caesar, who, though admitting his enemy's prowess, humiliated him by imprisoning him in Rome and then parading him through the streets. Vercingétorix was finally executed at the foot of the Roman Capitol.

Caesar was a creative conqueror; after all, he wanted a trouble-free Gaul. Celts of rank were awarded Roman citizenship, the Roman monetary system was established, and the Latin language was introduced. "He laid the groundwork for a Roman Europe," says Scherman, "that would fuse the continuing classical Greco-Roman tradition with the fresh Celtic-Teutonic ethos." In a deep sense, classical France was born in these Burgundian fields.

Today Vercingétorix in bronze bestrides a hill overlooking the village whence the vestiges of Gallo-Roman life come slowly to light: temple, theater, forum, streets, shops, wells, courtyards, even hypocausts (underground furnaces that heated water for the baths). Finds are displayed at the **Musée Alésia**, and archaeological excavations continue. (From mid-February to November 1 a ticket to the museum also allows entrance to the digs.)

On the Saturday and Sunday nearest to September 7, Alise celebrates Sainte Reine with a morning parade in appropriate costumes and an afternoon production of the

"Mystery of Sainte Reine." Local residents march with torches on the eve of the festival, one of the most attractive of the rural representations in Burgundy.

The Source of the Seine

On the N 71 south of Châtillon and just northwest of Dijon is **St-Seine-l'Abbaye**. Turn north from there in search of *les sources de la Seine,* not the easiest spot to find. (Inveterate church inspectors will stop at St-Seine itself, which marks in style the transition from Romanesque to Gothic, and is named not for the river but for a sixth-century Benedictine monk, Saint Seigne, who appears in one of the church frescoes in his black monk's robe.)

"Like the Jordan, the Ganges, the Rhine, the Seine is a holy river." So begins Anthony Glyn's *The Seine,* a book that since its publication in 1966 must certainly have inspired hundreds of readers to make their own pilgrimages to *les sources.* (In French *sources* means not only source, but also spring, fountain, or fountainhead.)

The name Seine derives from that of Sequana, a Roman goddess who was worshiped in the remote and wooded valley where the river rises. On the site, two temples succeeded the first clay-and-wattle hut, and in the center a spring gushed forth. Slightly downstream, a bathing pool almost 200 feet long lured the faithful from all over France to wash in the holy waters.

As do pilgrims to Lourdes today, the disabled and the merely curious came to cure themselves or to sell nostrums, votive offerings, and knickknacks. Archaeological digs here have unearthed thousands of items of tribute, today on show in Dijon's Musée Archéologique as well as several other museums in Burgundy.

For 300 years the goddess worked her miracles, but in the third century A.D. the temple was smashed and the site desecrated, possibly by invading Burgundians (the Burgondiones). What had been a hive of worshipers reverted to an empty, rather mournful valley.

You approach the source along a narrow road, and see nothing of civilization unless the small, rundown Café Sequana is open. Through a soggy meadow bordered by a fence, with signs announcing that the source is the property of the City of Paris, you eventually find it: an ugly, artificial grotto with a small, bubbling pool in its center and a fat water nymph reclining on a rock. From the pool, a trickle of water runs away through the cow pasture, on its way to Paris and the sea at Le Havre.

SEMUR

Just when you think Burgundy can come up with no more tempting little towns, you round a hill and there stands Semur-en-Auxois, an outsize storybook city of about 5,500 Sémurois situated on a pink granite outcrop above the valley of the river Armançon, west of Dijon near Fontenay and Alise-Ste-Reine.

Semur demands to be painted or at least photographed at once: a bridge that leaps the river toward a parade of picturesque old houses; round towers and ramparts (now a promenade); Medieval gates and the soaring spire of Notre-Dame; and a waterfall of gardens cascading over ancient stones.

In the 14th century Semur's ramparts supported 18 towers, and as each third of the town was encircled by its own wall, the whole was believed to be impregnable. The treasure was, and is, the **church of Notre-Dame**, founded in the 11th century, restored in the 13th and 14th; eventually it too enjoyed the tender care of Viollet-le-Duc. Within, the second chapel on the left shelters an **entombment** that ranks among the most beautiful created during the late Middle Ages; its monumentality is reminiscent of the work of Dijonnais sculptor Claus Sluter.

The **Musée Municipal et Bibliothèque**, in the former convent of the Jacobins (17th century), exhibits geological and paleontological finds as well as paintings and sculptures from the 13th to the 18th centuries. The library owns manuscripts and incunabula of great value, including a tenth-century illuminated manuscript, the Missal of Anne de Bretagne, and a work from the Gutenberg press.

Semur is a lively little place and stages several happenings during spring and summer: the Course des Chausses et des Desmoiselles (since 1369) in late May; the Fête de la Bague (since 1639, the oldest horse race in France) on May 31; the Course à la Timbale d'Argent, around June 1; and a two-week theater, music, and dance festival that begins in late July or early August. (A *course* is a race, of people or animals.)

Lovers of cheese will detour from the route to **Epoisses**, only 12 km (7.5 miles) west of Semur, perhaps not so much because of its château as for a taste of its renowned, buttery Epoisses cheese, produced originally by Cistercian monks. For tasting and buying for picnics, stop in at **Fromagerie Berthaut**; try Epoisses with the fiery liqueur marc de Bourgogne.

SAULIEU

There are aspects to Saulieu other than wining, dining, and sleeping, but to many visitors they are mere dividends. The essential attraction in this small, pleasant town (of just more than 3,000 Sédélociens) south of Semur is the restaurant **Côte d'Or**, with its **Résidence** (three rooms, seven suites, plus 12 simpler rooms in an older, separate building). Owner-chef Bernard Loiseau and his wife, Chantal, have joined contemporary style and comfort to old-fashioned calm, while the kitchen is renowned for the lightness and creativity of its dishes (reserve; Tel: 80-64-07-66).

Cheese lovers should stop by **Laiterie Overney** for some of the things good picnics are made of, such as a five-week cheese washed with local Chablis.

Saulieu's gastronomic reputation was already well established in the 17th century, when it became an important post stop on the route between Paris and Lyon. Rabelais wrote of the good living here (on which, of course, he was an authority), and Madame de Sévigné was made absolutely tipsy by the quality and quantity of food and drink.

In 177 Saint Andoche and two companions, Thyrse and Félix, were martyred at Saulieu, and a church was erected on the spot in 306, only to be destroyed before long by the Saracens. The present **basilica of St-Andoche** was begun in the 12th century and has endured several indignities during its long life, including fires that destroyed the choir and transept during the Hundred Years War and the mutilations of the Revolution.

The strong point of St-Andoche is the remarkable set of powerfully carved column capitals somewhat reminiscent of those in Autun, featuring grinning monsters, incredible foliage from an imaginary jungle, and biblical scenes such as the flight to Egypt, the hanging of Judas, the false prophet Balaam and his ass, and more.

Next to St-Andoche, the **Musée Régional** (sometimes called the Musée François-Pompon) exhibits a fine collection of Gallo-Roman steles; Medieval, Renaissance, and Classical sculptures; items of craftwork from the Morvan mountain region; and bronzes, terra-cottas, and the like by Pompon, a native of Saulieu who specialized in animal sculptures. He seemed to like polar bears and tigers in particular.

Today Saulieu supplies much of France with Christmas trees from the forests of the Morvan; they are also exported to the rest of Europe as well as to North Africa. The woods near the town serve for picnics, hiking, horseback riding, and trout fishing in stocked ponds.

Shops in nearby **Nontron-le-Beau** sell the pleasing handicrafts—pottery and ceramic figures—created by Jean-Louis Pasquet, a well-known regional artist.

AUTUN

Autun and Rome—today nothing of one would suggest the slightest inkling of the other. Pleasant, calm (indeed, half-asleep might be a better description) little Autun of about 16,000 citizens snoozes on its slope below the wooded hills of the Morvan (south of Saulieu and west of Beaune).

Autun owes its existence to the demise of Bibracte, a Gallic town at the summit of Mont Beuvray (an easy excursion about 17 km/11 miles west from Autun) and capital of the tribe called Eduens, where Vercingétorix held a council of war in 52 B.C. It was at Bibracte that he took command of the Gallic armies and organized his troops against Julius Caesar. After Vercingétorix was defeated at Alésia, Caesar wiped out Bibracte.

In the days of the Emperor Augustus (27 B.C. to A.D. 14), Autun was established as Augustodunum and matured into a flourishing city, an important stop on the trade and defensive routes from Lyon to Boulogne. Indeed, contemporary road maps show Autun as the hub of a six-spoked wheel.

During the late Roman Empire (180 to 395) the fame of Autun's schools was widespread, its diocese was one of the oldest in Gaul, and it was the premier suffragan of the mother church in Lyon. Over the centuries an impressive number of abbeys flowered in Autun, including that of St-Martin, founded in the sixth century by the Merovingian Queen Brunhild. It defended its independence even in the face of Cluny.

Brunhild's harsh life (her husband was murdered as a result of the wicked machinations of her sister-in-law, Frédégund) inevitably hardened the queen, who used to retreat from the troubles of her regency to the relative serenity of Autun. Historian Katherine Scherman tells that the quarrels of the two queens and the downfall of Brunhild's husband King Sigibert I are the stuff of the Medieval German epic *Niebelungenlied;* Autun is thought to have been the home of the Niebelungs, and Sigibert metamorphosed into Siegfried.

Vestiges of Roman days are: the **theater**, the largest in Gaul, with seats for 15,000 spectators; the **Porte St-André** to the northeast, one of two gates and 62 towers in the Gallo-Roman wall; **Porte d'Arroux** to the north; and the **Temple de Janus**, of which only two sections remain. Tradition says it was near Porte St-André that Saint Symphorien, one of the most revered martyrs of Roman Gaul, was beheaded as his mother shouted condolences to him from the wall.

After the decline of the Gallo-Roman world, Autun slept for a while, only to awake to new prosperity in the Middle Ages, from which dates its major monument, the **cathedral of St-Lazare**, which in its entirety is one of the most important examples of the Romanesque in Burgundy.

The tall stone spire that marks the cathedral dates from the 15th century, but the church itself is one of the major works of Cluniac art, constructed between 1120 and 1146 and consecrated by Pope Innocent II in 1130. Its artistic marvels are the sculptures (in local gray stone) on the tympanum of the central portal, **The Last Judgment**, and its column capitals in a stippled stone containing mica.

Probably it is best that Autun again declined during the Renaissance; otherwise "renovations" of these triumphs might have taken place, as happened elsewhere. The tympanum is a true sermon in stone, designed by the artist to be "read" by illiterates—and paid heed to. (Following Medieval habit, public works of art were usually anonymous, but the tympanum is signed: "Gislebertus hoc fecit.") An inscription carved in Latin advises, "Let this horror appall those bound by earthly sin." In the center, Christ sits in Byzantine majesty, a figure not yet capable of seeming human. All around him there is wicked and wonderful action: three children bound for Paradise hold on to an angel; a woman headed for Hell is being eaten by serpents; Saint Peter holds the hand of a nude soul; Saint Michael tries to weigh the good and bad honestly, even as Satan pulls the scale down in his direction.

A *son-et-lumière* performance is held at the cathedral on Fridays and Saturdays from mid-May through June, daily except Sundays and Mondays from July to late September.

The **Musée Rolin** occupies the 15th-century town house built for Nicolas Rolin, the founder of the Hôtel-Dieu in Beaune. Displayed are Gallo-Roman artifacts, some superb Roman statuary, a Temptation of Eve that is part of a Gislebertus relief, French and Flemish primitive paintings, a 15th-century Nativity by the so-called Master of Moulins, and items of regional archaeological interest.

Also be sure to visit the **Hôtel de Ville** for its rich collection of manuscripts and the **Musée Lapidaire** for Roman and Medieval antiquities.

The best hotel in town is the 29-room **Ursulines**, located south of the cathedral and not exceedingly expensive. The best place in town to eat is the **Hostellerie Vieux Moulin**, near the river (it also has 16 rooms); for a better dining experience, drive 43 km (27 miles) east to Chagny and the three-star restaurant **Lameloise**, which occupies an elegantly reworked Burgundian home with 20 rooms for overnight guests (dining reservations are important; Tel: 85-87-08-85). An unusual dish to try is *ravioli d'escargots de Bourgogne*.

A driving route of about 70 km (43 miles) called the **Signal d'Uchon** will include an exterior view of the lavish Château de Sully, northeast of Autun. To make the drive of 24 km (15 miles) to Uchon and its panoramic overlook, leave Autun by the little road to the south marked D 120, veer west on D 256, and follow clearly marked D 46 and D 228 to the village of Uchon (pop. 67). Wiggle south and uphill on D 275 for about a mile. There's a little hotel and a parking lot near the top; leave the car and follow the path for a few yards to the marker at 2,133 feet.

The hamlet of **Uchon** is most photogenic; note the oratory with a figure of the Virgin Mary atop its column, where pilgrims came in the 16th century to pray for the end of the Black Death.

The **Château de Sully** is on the northeast perimeter of the circular drive around Autun. Should you wish to go there directly, take D 973 east of Autun to a point just west of the hamlet of la Drée, where D 26 turns north for the 4.5-km (3-mile) run into Sully. The château, often called

the Fontainebleau of Burgundy, may remind you in its
Renaissance beauty of Ancy-le-Franc.

For complete details, ask at the Office de Tourisme in
Autun, at 3, avenue Charles-de-Gaulle near the Hôtel de
Ville.

BEAUNE

The oenophile approaches Beaune, south of Dijon and
east of Autun, reverentially, admiring the rich slopes of
hills and the names on the land: from Dijon, Gevrey-
Chambertin, Vougeot, Vosne-Romanée, Aloxe-Corton;
from Mâcon in the south, Chassagne-Montrachet,
Puligny-Montrachet, Meursault, Volnay, Pommard, and
more.

Beaune itself lives up to the nobility of the neighboring
vineyards. "This is one of the most soul-satisfying of
towns," wrote Samuel Chamberlain, "the pure essence of
rural France—civilized, bourgeois, unruffled. Its fat chimneys bespeak a well-fed race."

To the traveller, Beaune comes as a respite: It doesn't
bustle, it strolls; it need not shout, it chants; it is less chic
than comfortable. Beaune, after all, is scarcely an upstart;
it's a town of fewer than 22,000 Beaunois enjoying a
respected old age.

Beaune was a sanctuary for the Gauls, then the Romans,
and, finally, the Grand Dukes of Burgundy (before they
seized upon Dijon as their capital). Its 14th-century walls
and some towers remain, hemming in art and other
evidences of the good life.

The **Hôtel-Dieu**, also known as the Hospices de Beaune,
was founded in 1443 by Nicolas Rolin, the chancellor of
Burgundy under Philippe le Bel, as a charity hospital.
Rolin's intentions may not have been quite so splendid as
the architecture: Louis XI of France is said to have sniffed,
"It is indeed just that having made so many people poor,
Rolin should now construct a hospital to shelter them."

Whatever. The hospice catered to the souls as well as
the sores of the poor—and in style—for more than 500
years. The patients moved out in 1971 when it became a
museum; it has been renovated periodically and now
serves the aged.

The look of the place has scarcely changed since architect Jehan Wiscrère created its Flamboyant design, the
most striking elements of which are visible only after you

pass the sober, somewhat formidable façade and step into the courtyard. The multicolored tile roofs, the small towers from which Rapunzel might let down her long hair, the ranks of inviting dormer windows, the eccentric weather vanes—all conspire to put you in the mood of a storybook rather than sickness.

The Grand'Salle served as a ward as well as a church, designed so that patients could share the Mass without leaving their beds. (Beds were scarcely king-size, as the visitor will notice, and several of the sick were squeezed into each one, probably with infectious results.) Among the several other installations that can be seen, the most interesting are the kitchen and the pharmacy.

The *chef d'oeuvre,* however, is the immense **Last Judgment** by Flemish painter Rogier van der Weyden. On the covers of the panels, Rolin and his wife, Guigone, appear as they did in life, no warts or wrinkles overlooked. A display arrangement of van der Weyden's work—complete with a giant magnifying glass that moves back and forth at the push of a button, allowing visitors to inspect details—is quite inventive in its own right.

Chancellor Rolin willed his vineyards to the hospital, and today, the holdings slightly increased, income from the annual wine auction goes to preserve and implement its good works. The mid-November auction is the central event of Les Trois Glorieuses, a three-day festival of feasting watched over by the merry group known as the Confrérie des Chevaliers du Tastevin.

It is fitting that the **Musée du Vin de Bourgogne** is located in Beaune, within a former mansion of the dukes, a handsome wood-and-stone structure from the 15th and 16th centuries. The history of winemaking is represented by artworks, tools, costumes, and photographs.

The **collegiate church of Notre-Dame**, begun about 1120, is worth visiting particularly for its collection of tapestries in the choir behind the high altar. Titled "The Life of the Virgin," the collection appears to have one artistic foot in the Middle Ages and one in the Renaissance.

One way to get a pleasant view of the town is to take the walk of about a mile atop the ramparts. Ask at the Office de Tourisme (across from the Hôtel-Dieu) for details about where to mount the wall.

A pleasantly furnished hotel handily located on rue Maufoux, just a couple of curves away from place de la Halle, is **Le Cep**, with 49 rooms, the stylish **Bernard Morillon** restaurant (Tel: 80-24-12-06) next door, and

fairly high prices. Its competition is **La Poste**, on boulevard Clemenceau near the city ramparts, with 21 slightly
pricey rooms. Tops in taste among local restaurants—
reservations should be made in all—are: **Jacques Lainé**
(on the northern edge of town near the Bastion des
Filles in a lovely turn-of-the-century home; Tel: 80-24-76-
10); **Relais de Saulx** (not far from the Hôtel-Dieu; try the
cassolette d'escargots; Tel: 80-22-01-35); **Rôtisserie la
Paix** (outside the ramparts to the southeast on rue du
faubourg Madeleine; Tel: 80-22-33-33); and **Ermitage de
Corton** (about 5 km/3 miles north in Chorey-lès-Beaune,
with five beautiful rooms and five expensive suites; Tel:
80-22-05-28).

Some of the most delightful dining in the entire area is
at the **Hostellerie de Levernois** in the village of Levernois,
just 5 km (3 miles) southeast of Beaune, following rue du
faubourg Perpreuil and route de Verdun, continuing on
D 970 and D 111. The restaurant sits in its own pretty park
and has 12 guest rooms. Reserve for both restaurant and
rooms; Tel: 80-24-73-58.

Modestly priced with a friendly staff and no restaurant,
the **Belle Epoque** hotel sits on rue du faubourg Bretonnière, on the way out of town heading toward Autun.

Shopping in Beaune runs less toward fashion than to
food and kitchen and table accessories. A worthwhile stop
is **Beaune Choses**, where the tableware is almost as irresistible as the pun. **Parfumerie Ambre** is a reliable outlet for
those who've exhausted their supply of Azzaro or Hermès
or Lanvin. For hotter mustards than those from Dijon, stop
by **Fallow et Compagnie**, 31, rue du faubourg Bretonnière;
they will ship overseas. Beaune's market bustles on Saturdays right in front of the Hôtel-Dieu.

Only a few kilometers from Beaune, at the rest stop on
the A 6 motorway from Auxerre and Paris, the **Archéo-
drome** displays life-size representations of the important
stages of the settlement of Burgundy, from Paleolithic to
Gallo-Roman times.

TOURNUS

Thundering along A 6, traffic tends to bypass Tournus.
Perhaps that is why the little city (about 7,000 Tournu-
siens) south of Beaune seems antique and slumbering. It
deserves to slumber; it was a settlement of the Eduen
tribe long before the Romans built a camp in the area.

Around A.D. 180, Saint Valerien came to Tournus as an evangelist and was martyred on a hill overlooking the river Saône.

History ignored the settlement, it seems, until the ninth century, when monks from Ile de Noirmoutier, off the coast of Brittany, fled Norman invaders and arrived in this quiet spot to shelter the relics of their founder, Saint Philibert.

Your first stop in town should be the **church of St-Philibert**, reached by taking rue Albert-Thibaudet east off N 6 and passing between two round towers into the place de l'Abbaye. Begun in the late 10th or early 11th century and completed by the end of the 12th, this grand example of early Romanesque style is older than the better-known abbey at Cluny.

The thick-walled crypt and the narthex, with its short, powerful pillars, are the two oldest elements of the abbey, and their solidity, strength, and simplicity are impressive. The nave, with its alternating pink and white stones and unusual arrangement of transverse bays and very tall masonry pillars, soars with a lightness unusual in the Romanesque.

The traveller with an interest in prehistory will stop at the **Musée Greuze**, a short walk south of St-Philibert on rue A. Bessard, to inspect the archaeological collections rather than to spend time with the canvases of local painter Jean-Baptiste Greuze, which may seem overly sentimental to today's eyes.

Directly across the narrow street north of the church, the **Musée Perrin-de-Puycousin** occupies the 17th-century treasury building and features reconstructions of old Burgundian home interiors, complete with wax figures wearing traditional costumes, period furnishings, and a wine cellar.

A couple of good hotels, **De Greuze** and **Le Rempart**, make Tournus a pleasant stop for excursions into the countryside, particularly to Cluny. De Greuze offers 19 rooms and four suites just across the corner from the remarkable abbey, and is not related to the well-known Restaurant Greuze a couple of doors away, where chef Jean Ducloux commands as much respect as the better-known, aforementioned, "Les Six." The latter is renowned for its pike *quenelles* and *pâté en croûte;* it's fairly expensive; reserve; Tel: 85-51-13-52.

Le Rempart, right at the old wall across a little park south of De Greuze, has 31 rooms, six suites, and its own fine kitchen, starring a salad of roasted spiny lobster; reserve; Tel: 85-51-10-56.

CLUNY

Cluny nestles among woods and fields in the green valley of the meandering Grosne southwest of Tournus. (The best way to reach Cluny from Tournus is to follow N 6 south for about 14 km/9 miles to Fleurville, then take the turnoff via D 15 another 24 km/15 miles.) It is quiet; its Romanesque and Gothic houses breathe deeply; its battles are over. Today, out of the spotlight, it is a peaceful and small country town of fewer than 5,000 Clusinois.

In the Middle Ages, though, Cluny, "as dark as the hood of a monk's cloak," as poet Alphonse de Lamartine had it, dominated the religious, artistic, intellectual, and political life of Western Europe. Its struggle with the Cistercians and Saint Bernard split Christianity in ways still evidenced today.

Saint Benedict created the order that bears his name at Montecassino, in Italy, about 529, but its greatest monastery did not appear in the wilds of Burgundy for another 400 years.

The abbey at Cluny was founded on September 11, 910, by Guillaume le Pieux (the Pious), duke of Aquitaine. Less than a hundred years later it had achieved immense power and prestige: Some 1,500 brotherhoods across France and in England, Germany, Spain, Switzerland, and even Poland depended on Cluny. "Wherever the wind blows," went a saying of the time, "the abbot of Cluny owns."

The immense **abbey** was conceived by one of Cluny's abbots, Saint Hugues de Semur, who laid the first stone in 1088. Major construction was completed in only 20 years, but building went on until 1130. Cluny was the physical as well as spiritual pride of Christendom, remaining the largest church in the world for 500 years until it was exceeded (and then by only ten yards in length) by St. Peter's in Rome.

The Benedictine rule made liturgical prayer the primary occupation of monks, to be complemented by sacred reading, manual labor, practice of the arts, and *opus divinum* (praising God) through the splendor of churches and the beauty of liturgy and hymns.

The rule came to be recognized as the fundamental

monastic code of Western Europe. "Its flexibility enabled it to be adapted to the needs of society," writes David Hugh Farmer, "so that monasteries became centers of learning, agriculture, hospitality, and medicine in a way presumably unforeseen by Benedict himself."

Cluniac houses—the first at Barnstaple, the second at Lewes—were introduced to England by William the Conqueror; by the 13th century there were 40 dependencies in England.

"You are the light of the world," Pope Urban II said to Cluny abbot Saint Hugues in 1098. The greatness of Cluny sprang from the genius of its seven great abbots (Pontius is usually excepted) over 250 years. When Peter the Venerable died in about 1157, slow decline set in, perhaps the inevitable result of riches and international power.

The Cistercians

Saint Bernard, a Burgundian from Fontaines, near Dijon, was born to a noble family (his father, a knight, later died on crusade). Educated at Châtillon-sur-Seine, at age 22 he and some 30 companions joined the poverty-stricken monastery of Cîteaux, not far from Nuits-St-Georges and northeast of Beaune. Under Bernard, the Cistercian order was transformed and became the second great Romanesque religious movement.

After only a few years, Bernard was named abbot of the newly formed Clairvaux, some 40 miles southeast of Troyes and east of Sens. Here he found extreme poverty. Largely because of Bernard's intense moral suasion and his brilliant preaching (in Latin), Clairvaux grew steadily, founding houses even in England (the first in North Yorkshire in 1132). At Bernard's death, there were some 350 Cistercian abbeys, and 700 monks were in residence at Clairvaux.

Food writer Waverley Root saw the Cluny-Clairvaux struggles in terms of eating and drinking. "It is in harmony with the nature of the order," he wrote, "that it was the Benedictines who invented, and gave their name to, a rich, sweet, and unctuous liqueur. One would hardly have expected such a development from the Cistercians, whose regulations forbade them to eat meat, fish, eggs, milk dishes, or white bread, and to drink anything other than water.

"When the art of cooking emerged from the monasteries, it had to be Benedictine skills that were passed on to laymen, not Cistercian. The Cistercians had nothing to offer. Even if their ecclesiastical victory had been complete, they could hardly have expected, with their ascetic ideas, to have dominated the gastronomy of a country so fertile and naturally rich in food as Burgundy." (There is no suspense in wondering which order Root would have joined.)

When Bernard thundered, people listened. He assailed the Benedictine bishops who "can't go four leagues from home without dragging along 60 horses . . . Will the light shine only if it's in a silver or gold candelabra?"

In 1330 the abbey of Cluny bought land in Paris on which to build a residence for abbots attending a college near the Sorbonne; in the late 15th century it was enlarged by Jacques d'Amboise, Bishop of Clermont, with such comforts and ornamentation that even kings and queens slept there as guests. What remains of the luxurious residence constitutes today's **Musée de Cluny** in Paris, which houses the finest examples extant of architectural details, furnishings, and decorative arts of the ecclesiastical style of the period.

Serious decline set in for Cluny in the 14th century; the Wars of Religion in the 16th century almost struck a death blow, and the Revolution completed the job. The abbey was closed in 1790, and in 1798 the whole was sold to a merchant from Mâcon, who demolished the nave. By 1823 only the near ruins visible today were left of Cluny's Medieval magnificence.

Cluny Today

What remains of the abbey today are the two Baraban towers at the entrance to the narthex, part of the porch, bits of the south side aisle, a chapel on the south side of the lesser transept, an octagonal belfry known as l'Eau Bénite (Holy Water), and the south end of the larger transept. Even so, this last manages to transmit a sense of the strength, daring, and splendor of the immense abbey. (Hour-long guided tours from July to late September are an invaluable aid to understanding what Cluny really was.)

In the **Farinier**, once the flour or meal barn, remnants of the abbey are displayed, including some capitals from the choir—masterpieces of Romanesque sculpture. There are also various models of the abbey.

An ancient palace, the work of Abbot Jean III de Bourbon, has become the **Musée Ochier**, which houses the collections of the 19th-century Ochier family: some decorations taken from ancient houses, capitals and small columns, a few paintings and portraits, some furniture and objets d'art, a collection of ceramics, and some 4,000 books in the museum's library.

A walk around the streets and ramparts of Cluny will reveal several Romanesque houses, and a climb up the 120 steps of the Tour des Fromages is worthwhile for the view.

Across from the abbey's ruins, the **Hôtel Bourgogne** has an eminently satisfactory restaurant. However, only 11 km (7 miles) east via D 134, the **Château d'Igé**, a handsome retreat in the tiny village of Igé, offers six rooms and six suites in a fortified château built by the dukes of Mâcon in the 13th century.

Southeast of Cluny and 16 km (10 miles) south of Mâcon, in the village of Thoissey, the **Hôtel de Chapon Fin et Restaurant Paul Blanc** has been sought out by discriminating travellers for years. Perhaps it's the warm welcome of the Blanc-Maringue family that turns the trick, or the elegance of its 20 rooms, the relaxed setting, or the excellence of the kitchen. (Try the crayfish ravioli in herb butter, from June to December, or chicken fricassee with creamed morel mushrooms.) This is also a good place in which to introduce yourself to the Mâconnais wine named St-Véran.

A music festival, Les Grandes Heures, is held in Cluny in August.

THE RHONE VALLEY

Since the beginning of recorded history in Europe, the Rhône, its tributaries, and its valley have constituted a major highway system for invaders, traders, civilizers, and conquerors.

As long ago as 20,000 B.C. Paleolithic man left engravings on the rock walls of caves. Many sites bear witness to the occupations of Neolithic times (around 8000 B.C.), and by the time the Bronze Age arrived (2000 B.C.) the

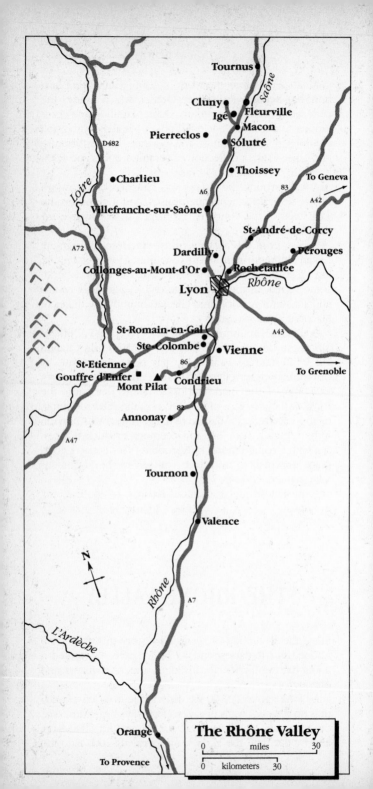

The Rhône Valley

Rhône had become a watery thoroughfare for the transportation of amber and tin.

In 121 B.C. Roman legions established camps on the left bank of the river at the site of today's Vienne. Lyon was established (as Lugdunum) in 43 B.C. and soon became the capital of the Gauls.

The Burgundian tribes likewise selected Vienne as their capital, in the fifth century, while in the Middle Ages various French kings attempted to seize control of the valley. In 1419 the first fairs held in Lyon were established by the future Charles VII, making the town one of the world's great commercial centers. The fairs lost much of their importance after Medieval times, but the one at Lyon was revived in 1916.

During World War II, Lyon was a headquarters of the Resistance; retreating German armies destroyed many of the river's bridges in 1944.

For the traveller's purposes, the valley of the Rhône stretches from Mâcon in the north to Orange in the south (for Orange, see the Provence chapter), from the regions of Auvergne and Causses in the west to the Alps in the east.

Most visitors to the Rhône Valley confine themselves to the cities along the river corridor—Lyon, Vienne, Valence—at the same time complaining about over-industrialization. Yet to the east and particularly to the west of A 7, the rough plateaus, the woods, and the glacier-sliced valleys are almost empty of inhabitants, certainly of travellers. Some fascinating drives may be made through this region, especially in the valley of the Ardèche, north of Orange.

LYON

It is not easy to evade Lyon. Autoroutes from the north (A 6), from the south (A 7), from the east (A 42) and southeast (A 43), and through-routes from all directions are sucked into the maw of the city like so many strands of spaghetti.

The third largest city in France, with a population of about half a million and its metropolitan area comprising one and a quarter million, Lyon has to be aggressive to attract the travellers who would otherwise decide to settle down for days in such smaller cities as Strasbourg or Nice.

Yet in some ways Lyon is just an overgrown village. Away from the high-rises and commercial centers that

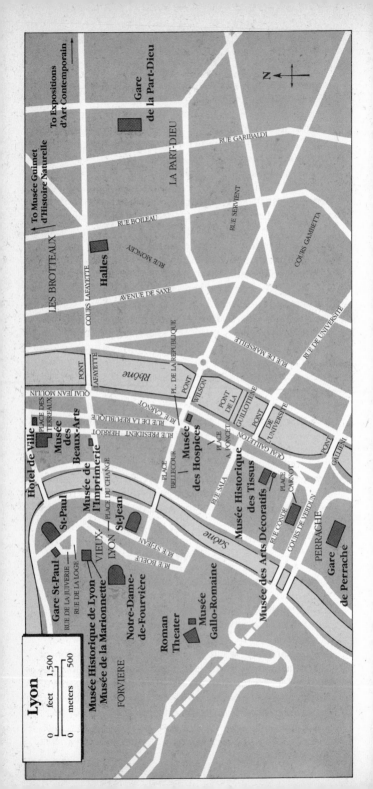

Lyon

feet 1,500
meters 500

To Expositions d'Art Contemporain →

To Musée Guimet d'Histoire Naturelle ←

Gare de la Part-Dieu

LA PART-DIEU

RUE GARIBALDI

RUE BOILEAU

LES BROTTEAUX

Halles

RUE MONCEY

RUE SERVIENT

COURS GAMBETTA

COURS LAFAYETTE

AVENUE DE SAXE

RUE DE MARSEILLE

RUE DE L'UNIVERSITÉ

Rhône

PONT LAFAYETTE

QUAI JEAN MOULIN

Hôtel de Ville

PLACE DES TERREAUX

Musée des Beaux-Arts

St-Paul

Gare St-Paul

RUE DE LA JUIVERIE
RUE DE LA LOGE

Musée de l'Imprimerie

PLACE DU CHANGE

St-Jean

VIEUX-LYON

RUE BOEUF

RUE STEFAN

Musée Historique de Lyon
Musée de la Marionnette

Notre-Dame-de-Fourvière

FORVIERE

Roman Theater

Musée Gallo-Romaine

RUE DE LA RÉPUBLIQUE

RUE PRÉSIDENT HERRIOT

PLACE BELLECOUR

RUE CARNOT

PL. DE LA RÉPUBLIQUE

PONT WILSON

Musée des Hospices

PLACE A PONCET

RUE SALA

Musée Historique des Tissus

RUE DE VERDUN

RUE CONDE

PLACE CARNOT

Musée des Arts Décoratifs

PONT DE LA GUILLOTIÈRE

QUAI GAILLETON

PONT DE L'UNIVERSITÉ

PONT GALLIÈNI

COURS DE VERDUN

PERRACHE

Gare de Perrache

Saône

N

have sprung up during the last two decades or so, the narrow lanes of Old Lyon give you the sense of Paris in the 1930s, the one familiar from Gertrude Stein, Hemingway, Joyce, and Ford Madox Ford.

To orient yourself to Lyon, imagine it as if you were looking down from a helicopter, with its peninsula cradled in the arms of the Saône river to the west and the Rhône to the east. Centered over the old railway station near the tip of the peninsula, you would look directly down at Perrache, in the second *arrondissement;* ahead is the smartest district, Bellecour, also in the second *arrondissement;* just north of that is Cordeliers/République and place de la République, where the first and second *arrondissements* meet; then there's Terreaux, a division of the first *arrondissement,* with place des Terreaux and the Hôtel de Ville. Far beyond is a meeting of the fourth and first *arrondissements* in Croix-Rousse, where the silk industry first flourished.

Off to the left of the chopper, you would spot Vieux-Lyon/Fourvière (fifth *arrondissement*), while to the right is Guillotière (seventh–third *arrondissements*), Part-Dieu (third *arrondissement,* the new railway station, shopping centers, etc.), and—on the eastern horizon—Gerland (seventh *arrondissement*) and the international airport at Satolas.

The Heritage of Lyon

As the story goes, two Celtic princes stopped one day at the dramatic meeting place of the Saône and Rhône rivers and deemed it a propitious spot for a city, so they began to dig. A cloud of ravens swept up and over them. Taking that as a sign from Providence, they dubbed their new town Lugdunum, hill of the ravens.

In 43 B.C. the Romans made Lugdunum their base for the conquest of Gaul. Agrippa built five great roads extending out from it, and Augustus later built aqueducts, temples, and a theater.

Tiberius Claudius Drusus was born in Lugdunum on August 1, 10 B.C., during Augustus's reign. Considered a booby as a child, he nonetheless became Claudius, Emperor of Rome, in A.D. 41, as which he conquered most of Britain and accomplished much else besides. After a fire in 59, Nero reworked and beautified the city, and succeeding emperors continued the job.

In 177 Marcus Aurelius ordered the slaughter of local

Christian leaders in the amphitheater, an act followed 20 years later by Septimius Severus's massacre of some 18,000 Christians, including Irenaeus, Bishop of Lyon. His shrine remained in the church of St-Irénée until it was destroyed by Calvinists in 1562.

Lyon always has been in the forefront of France's political life. In 1793 widespread resistance against the Convention resulted in a terrible reaction by Robespierre and, subsequently, the Terror. Hundreds of Lyonnais were murdered, beautiful old houses around place Bellecour were put to the torch, and the very name of the town was changed, to Commune Affranchie (Free Community).

The 15th century saw the installation of the great fairs that made Lyon a commercial hub, so that when silk manufacturing (until the 16th century a purely Italian craft) spread, Lyon jumped into the industrial world. New fabrics were invented: silks woofed with wool, watered silks, poplins, moirés, and so forth.

In the early 19th century J. M. Jacquard introduced a loom here by which a single worker could do the work of six in creating elaborate fabrics. Homes became factories for piece workers (*canuts*) to whom silk makers supplied fabrics. The center of this activity was today's Croix-Rousse district.

Lyon never has ceased to build upon its industrial inheritance; today's enterprises are grouped in contiguous suburbs. Lyon is also a center for scientific research, engineering, and communications, and it has an international airport at Satolas, a fairly new Métro system, and TGV traffic to and from Paris and the south.

The tradition of the literary salon may seem to have been confined to Paris, but it flourished in Lyon from time to time as well, most spectacularly at the end of the 15th century in the days and nights of Louise Labé, la Belle Cordière. (She married Ennemond Perrin, a rope maker, or *cordier*.) Accomplished in several languages, beautiful, a musician and poet, la Belle Cordière held open house for the intelligentsia of her day; she was a precursor of Madame de Sévigné.

By 1548 there were more than 400 printing studios in town, as well as a host of painters, sculptors, and ceramicists. Rabelais published his *Gargantua and Pantagruel* in Lyon, to be sold during the annual fairs.

The creator of the wooden puppet named Guignol and thus of all the Grand Guignol shows in France was

Laurent Mourguet, a Lyonnais weaver born in 1769. André-Marie Ampère, a locally famous physicist and absent-minded professor, gave his name to the basic unit of electrical current.

The Musée Claude Bernard in nearby St-Julien-en-Beaujolais honors the creator of experimental medicine. In 1896 Louis and Auguste Lumière debuted their first films here, and the world witnessed the birth of cinematography.

Fourvière, the Roman Hill

The view from the terrace of the 19th-century **basilica of Notre-Dame-de-Fourvière** is what the Romans saw in the second century—the joining arms of the Saône and the Rhône rivers and, off in the distance, the mountainous horizon that rises to become the Alps. In the foreground, however, those builders saw no metropolis, no industrial suburbs, no towers or hotels or railroad stations testifying to the importance of COURLY (Communauté Urbaine Lyon). Looking at that view, the Romans turned their backs upon the great structures of their own age: the **circus** outside the walls and, within, the theater, the smaller Odéon, and the capitol.

Today's traveller begins an exploration of Lyon atop Fourvière with visits to the handsome stone remains of the **Odéon** (designed for concerts and small conferences) and the **theater,** the oldest in France and about the size of those in Orange and Arles. (Today the theater serves as venue for performances of music and dramatic arts from about mid-June to mid-July.)

If you see nothing more in Lyon than Fourvière's **Musée de la Civilisation Gallo-Romaine**, adjoining the Roman theater, the trip will have been worthwhile. Opened in 1975, it is an unsurpassed repository of prehistoric, Gallic, and Roman art in France: Paleolithic and Neolithic tools, a chariot from the early Iron Age, a Gallic calendar engraved in bronze, magnificent mosaics, antique glass, pottery, and kitchen utensils.

Perhaps the most valuable find from modern digs in the city was that of the **Claudian Tables**, an inscription on bronze of a speech by Claudius delivered in A.D. 48 before the Roman Senate, in which the Lyon-born emperor urged that the chiefs of Gallic nations might succeed in their attempts to be elected as Roman magistrates.

Vieux (Renaissance) Lyon

The old town, comprising the quarters of St-Jean, St-Paul, and St-Georges, stretches along the Saône at the foot of Fourvière, preserving a wealth of at least 300 houses dating from the Renaissance. Along rue Juiverie, rue de la Loge, rue de Gadagne, and around the place du Change march these proud houses shoulder to shoulder, representing the end of the Gothic period, the Italian-inspired Renaissance, the French Renaissance, and pre-Neoclassic days. Normally, the *maisons* Laurençin, Thomassin, Mayet-de-Beauvoir, and Buillioud are closed to the public; the Gadagne houses the **Musée Historique** and the **Musée de la Marionnette**.

Also of interest in this area are the cathedral of St-Jean and the church of St-Paul. Begun in the 11th century, the **cathedral of St-Jean** is a Gothic mass rising upon a Romanesque base; it was the seat of the primate, or first bishop, of Gaul. The façade owes its fine decorations to the 14th century. Inside, the greatest treasure is the 12th-century choir, and some beautiful 13th-century stained glass has survived. On the north side of St-Jean, excavations of a much earlier church are under way. A beautiful lantern-tower and some handsomely sculpted animal figures distinguish the **church of St-Paul**.

In Old Lyon, as in the Croix-Rousse district, the *traboules* form a network of passages tunneling underneath and around the ancient houses, opening into tiny court-yards, leading to otherwise unseen Renaissance galleries, debouching suddenly into minuscule market squares. (*Traboule* derives from the Latin *trans ambulare,* to walk through.)

Places Bellecour and des Terreaux

Place Bellecour and the peninsula of which it is the center, between the Saône to the west and the Rhône to the east, is the heart of contemporary Lyon and one of the largest such squares in France, bordered on east and west by handsome, symmetrical Louis XVI houses. It sits atop a large parking garage, a handy place to leave your car. Place Bellecour is within walking distance of several hotels (in various price ranges), museums, and shopping streets. Smaller than Bellecour but also more animated, place des Terreaux was near the confluence of the rivers in Roman times. Today it's the confluence of sidewalk cafés; its fountain is the work of Bartholdi. Walks in the area of Terreaux reveal several curious *traboules,* the Musée des Beaux-Arts, pretty squares, and a collection of renowned restaurants.

Left Bank of the Rhône

The TGV and most other trains deposit travellers at the giant Gare de la Part-Dieu, which has become the center of an entirely new commercial area, with hotels to match. It boasts Le Grand Espace Shopping, with numerous movie houses, restaurants and bars, a bowling alley, a disco-thèque, and more than 200 stores. It's also a central depar-ture point for the local Métro. You could get lost in this totally modern complex and never find your way out. (Some trains still arrive at the Gare de Perrache on the peninsula; check your ticket at time of purchase.)

North of Part-Dieu, the 42-acre **Parc de la Tête d'Or** (named Golden Head because of a traditional story that a head of Christ worked in gold was found buried here) holds Europe's largest rose garden, La Roseraie, with more than five million blossoms in season. It's also a good place to limber up on the huge rowing lake and along jogging paths. There are outstanding zoological and botanical gardens here as well.

The Museums of Lyon

Few French cities outside Paris possess as large and satis-fying a collection of museums as does Lyon; the best known (justifiably) is the **Musée des Beaux-Arts**, located off place des Terreaux in the enormous Palais St-Pierre, and built in the 17th century as a Benedictine nunnery for gentle ladies. The 90 rooms are devoted to sculptures of various periods and paintings from all the great ages of European art. There are also some Oriental displays. The Musée Gallo-Romaine, described above, is the other mu-seum that should on no account be overlooked.

Of interest chiefly to enthusiasts of fabrics, the **Musée Historique des Tissus** contains the largest collection of textiles in the world, including a wing of 12 rooms devoted to Oriental rugs, fabrics, and tapestries. The French collec-tions are naturally the most important; overall, fabrics date from the fourth century to today. The museum is about halfway between place Bellecour and the Perrache station and adjoins the **Musée des Arts Décoratifs**. This latter museum is a step back into the 18th century; it is completely outfitted in furniture, objets d'art, faïence, tapestries, porcelain, tableware, and so forth. Especially noteworthy is the Italian Renaissance faïence collection.

In Vieux Lyon near the place du Change, the **Musée Historique de Lyon** shows off a remarkable collection of Romanesque sculptures, furnishings, faïence from Nevers, and descriptions of Lyon throughout the centuries. Part and almost parcel of this museum is the **Musée de la Marionnette**, with an exceptional puppet show of figures from as far away as Cambodia and Java but centered, quite naturally, on the Guignols.

If you are strongly inclined toward museum meandering and have time to spare, also consider the **Musée Guimet d'Histoire Naturelle** (all animals represented from mammoths to humans, with special emphasis on regional finds); the **Musée de l'Imprimerie et de la Banque**, which illustrates the importance of banking and printing through the ages; the **Musée de la Résistance et de la Déportation**, with evidences of the horrors of war and the Nazi death camps; the **Musée des Hospices Civils**, containing exhibitions of medical and hospital life from the 17th century on; the **Musée Africaine**; two venues for contemporary art—the **Musée St-Pierre d'Art Contemporain** and the **Espaces Lyonais d'Art Contemporain**; and, in the suburbs, the **Musée Français de l'Automobile**, with cars from 1890 to 1970, including some very prestigious vehicles.

Hotels in Lyon

Lyon's hotels are grouped in nine or ten areas in the city center and its immediate surroundings; most of the best are in Bellecour-Terreaux and Perrache.

Vieux Lyon
La Cour des Loges. Until 1987, no hotel in this great ambling shopping area could be recommended. Then this strikingly modern, almost futuristic, art-filled inn appeared within a cluster of four 14th-century to 17th-century Medieval and Renaissance houses. The combined effects are stunning and meld with surprising success. Ancient beamed ceilings have been preserved to look down on bathrooms with two-person tubs.

Rooms are opened by electronically coded keys and

offer color TVs and videocassette units; the wine cellar is nobly stocked; and there are thermal baths, a restaurant—**Tapas des Loges**—and a private garage. All this comes at a price, and it's worth paying.

Bellecour-Terreaux

Sofitel. That this is the best hotel in its area and one of the two tops in Lyon indicates that the city has always lacked hostelries of an old-fashioned quality to match its size. There is no Crillon here, no Bristol, no Ritz, no Plaza-Athenée. Still, the Sofitel has pretty much everything you need, a handy location, and a good restaurant, **Les Trois Dômes**.

   Grand Hôtel Concorde. Just back from the river, this 140-room hotel is second best in its neighborhood, with the pleasant **Le Fiorelle** grill and three roomy suites.

   Royal. A fine location on Bellecour adds to the attractiveness of this 90-room member of the Mapotel group; it also has a good grill.

Perrache

Bordeaux. A suitcase-carrying distance from the railway station, it offers willing service but has no restaurant.

   Pullman Perrache. It's right at the corner of the train station and has 122 comfortable rooms and two suites, plus a restaurant and bar.

La Part-Dieu

Pullman Part-Dieu. You couldn't call it cozy, but this is the place to witness futuristic France at work in the hotel industry. It's in a good location for those travelling by train and has two fine restaurants: **L'Arc-en-Ciel**, with a panoramic rooftop view, and **La Ripaille** grill. The hotel proper begins on the 32nd floor of a commercial building.

Lyon Airport/Satolas and Bron

Novotel. A handful of miles southeast of central Lyon, just off highway N 6, this 191-room hotel is handy for travellers using either the Aeroport Lyon-Bron or Lyon-Satolas; it also has an informal restaurant.

   Sofitel. On the third floor of Satolas Aérogare itself, this hotel maintains 120 rooms and, on the first floor, the restaurant **La Grande Corbeille** and the brasserie **Le Bouchon**.

Porte de Lyon

Novotel Lyon-Nord. Approaching from Paris or Dijon, you'll find this 107-room hotel with grill right near the junction of A 6 and N 6 (Limonest exit, about 10 km/6 miles) a handy stop if you want to avoid the swirl of city traffic.

Environs

Alain Chapel. This distinguished three-star restaurant in the village of Mionnay, 20 km (12.5 miles) northeast of Lyon, offers 13 rooms in an atmosphere of quiet and rural chic; it is a member of the Relais & Châteaux group (dining reservations essential; Tel: 78-91-82-02).

Dining in Lyon

The quality of cooking in Lyon has changed much over the last few decades—and yet, as the French would always have it, it remains the same.

As recently as 1970, Waverley Root wrote that "the cooking of Lyon fits the character of the city—it is hearty rather than graceful, and is apt to leave you with an overstuffed feeling . . . my personal experience has been never to have eaten a really good meal in Lyon."

Even so, and whatever it may mean (and in terms of tourism dollars, it means a lot), greater Lyon tots up one three-star, two two-stars, and ten one-stars (including Mère Brazier). The truth is, not all Lyonnais restaurants are shooting for the stars. As Patricia Wells puts it: "It's a place to roll up your sleeves, put on your walking shoes, turn your thoughts to no-frills eating, and enjoy." In order to enjoy some of the best restaurants in Lyon, you must first make reservations.

The room at the top is that of **Paul Bocuse** in the suburban village of Collonges-au-Mont-d'Or. Bocuse may be the best known (he is surely the most peripatetic) restaurateur in the world, and while it is possible to have a less than memorable meal *chez* Bocuse, it is not likely. Like a person shopping for a yacht, if you have to ask the price, you can't afford it. Just settle into the surprisingly unpretentious dining room and order something familiar—leg of lamb, say, or filet of sole, or chicken from Bresse—and realize how unfamiliar really fine, simple cooking can be. Tel: 78-22-01-40.

Virtually all experts agree that a meal should be taken at **Léon de Lyon** (at 1, rue Pleney, near the Musée des

Beaux-Arts) for several reasons, the most persuasive of which is its remarkable presentations of Lyonnais classics. In addition, the decor and ambience are warm, welcoming, and not intimidating; chef Jean-Paul Lacombe is a *maître cuisinier* of France. Tel: 78-28-11-33.

Another *maître cuisinier* is Gérard Nandron of **Nandron**, at 26, quai Jean Moulin. He infuses his traditional cooking with lightness; try the *quenelle de brochet Nantua*. Tel: 78-42-10-26.

Refined, friendly, classic, and yet up-to-date, **Orsi** (Pierre Orsi at the helm) lures the discerning to 3, place Kléber, in the Left Bank area of Brotteaux, in part, perhaps, to taste his pigeon of Bresse *en cocotte*. Tel: 78-89-57-68.

Philippe Chavent of **La Tour Rose**, in the heart of Vieux Lyon at 22, rue du Boeuf, is being bruited about as the most creative young chef in town; he serves *nouvelle* turns on classic cuisine in a handsome 17th-century town house. Tel: 78-37-25-90.

Nobody can consume *haute cuisine* at every sitting, and Lyon excels in bistros, *bouchons,* and cafés. Right now, try **La Meunière** (in the first *arrondissement* near the Musée des Arts Décoratifs), with a typically brusque boss with a heart of gold, Maurice Debosses, a former Bocuse maître d'; **Le Passage**, in a *traboule* north of the place des Terreaux; **Café des Fédérations** (rue Major-Martin, also in the Terreaux area), with sawdust on the floor, sausages dangling in midair—you get the picture; and **Brasserie Georges**, behind the Perrache railway station and about the size of Grand Central Station.

Shopping in Lyon

Fashions, Traditional

The chic street is **rue du Président–Edouard-Herriot**, which connects place Bellecour to place de Terreaux. Here are the shops of Descamps, Charles Jourdan, Alain Manoukian, and Georges Rech, among other ruiners of budgets. **Rue de la République**, in the same area, also is smart.

Fashions

The one-stop shopping center of **La Part-Dieu** provides a pick of some 220 stores, big and small, including Galeries Lafayette, Jelmoli, Darty, and England's imperishable Marks and Spencer. **Rue St-Jean**, the crowded pedestrian main street of Vieux Lyon, takes the cake and other items for trendy fashions. Stop on the place du Change at **L'Ateyer de Guignol** for a gift nobody else has: a traditional Guignol puppet handmade to resemble a friend or yourself (take along photographs).

Antiques

More than 150 galleries offering antiques and high-quality secondhand items are gathered in **Brocante Stalingrad** in the Villeurbanne district, the eastern, industrial part of greater Lyon. It's the third-largest European market for antiques. (*Brocante* is French for secondhand.)

Specialties and Silks

In the traditional cloth-making quarter of Croix-Rousse, **La Maison des Canuts** is a weavers' cooperative that operates a museum-cum–retail outlet. Old cut velvets, damask, and portraits woven in silk are on display, as are a Jacquard handloom and a demonstration of silk making. Before the Industrial Revolution, some 60,000 looms clattered away in Lyon's family workshops. This cooperative still creates and sells silks at very reasonable prices: ties, scarves, handkerchiefs, foulards, and more.

PEROUGES

Pérouges is one of the most evocative villages in all of Europe, an outcrop of the Middle Ages atop its hill and behind its ramparts only 39 km (24 miles) northeast—but centuries removed—from Lyon.

Pérouges owes its name to settlers who arrived from Perugia, Italy, before the Roman occupation. During the Middle Ages, the lords of the Dauphiné and Savoy squabbled over the small but rich (the chief industry was linen weaving) town, leading to the major event of its history, the siege of 1468.

On the exterior of the lower of the two city gates (**Porte d'en Bas**), an inscription in somewhat bastardized Latin reads: "Pérouges of the Pérougiens! Impregnable town! Those rogues from Dauphiné wanted to take it, but couldn't. However, they took away the gates, the hinges, and locks, and rolled off with them. The devil take them!"

During the 19th century, Pérouges's prosperity ebbed, and by 1910 only 90 souls remained to shelter in the shade of the great and gracious linden trees in the heart of the matter, the **place du Tilleul**. Owners of ancient houses began to hack them down, and proud Pérouges seemed about to plunge into the past tense.

Then to the rescue came artists and artisans from Lyon and elsewhere, supported in part by government *beaux-arts* funds. A committee for Old Pérouges lured weavers, potters, cabinet makers, and other artisans to build shops along the old streets. A few wealthy investors restored handsome merchants' homes with their beamed and sculpted ceilings, huge fireplaces, and immense rooms once covered with frescoes.

Today you can walk the narrow, sloping, Medieval streets of the town, with rain channels down the center, where once only people of a certain importance could pass under the jutting eaves of houses to keep themselves dry.

At **Ostellerie du Vieux Pérouges**, a cozy inn with 28 rooms and an excellent kitchen, it is possible to spend a night in the past here while enjoying the amenities of the present.

VIENNE

In Roman times it was "Vienne the beautiful"; in the high periods of Christianity, "Vienne the holy"; in the 19th century Frédéric Mistral wrote of it, "In an elbow of the Rhône, seated like an altar against the buttresses of the noble Dauphiné. . . ."

The fact is, it is the natural site, bathed in the luminous light above the river, that makes Vienne attractive. Aside from its Roman ruins, Vienne today is a rather nondescript, small-business town of about 29,000 inhabitants.

Since the halcyon days between the world wars, gourmets and gourmands have paraded in pilgrimage to Vienne, however—presidents of the République, food writers, and merchant princes all bound for the door of La Pyramide, that "gastronomic temple" once without peer in France, or anywhere else, for that matter.

Pyramide (named for a Roman marble that stood in the center of the fourth-century circus) was the inspired creation of Fernand Point, the now legendary super-chef who was considered the foremost restaurateur in the world when he died in 1956 at the age of 57. One of his three Michelin stars faded with him (as is Michelin's practice when a great, presumably irreplaceable, chef dies). Wonder of wonders: Maintained by Point's crew and his admirable wife, Marie-Louise ("Mado"), Pyramide quickly regained its third star, under the name Chez Point.

Madame Point died in July 1986, and the three-star rating was again reduced to two; and when Chez Point-Pyramide was razed in 1988, the stars disappeared altogether. Today two sites in Vienne bear the hallowed name. **La Pyramide** itself, back on the old site at 14, boulevard Fernand-Point, has regained one shiny star in its parklike setting. The inn has 20 fine rooms and four expensive suites. At 41, quai Riondet, on the east bank of the Rhône, **La Résidence de la Pyramide** offers 15 quite reasonable rooms and one suite; it sends its guests to its more prestigious relative for meals.

The **cathedral of St-Maurice** (honoring a soldier-saint supposedly martyred nearby in the third century) is notable chiefly for its portal sculptures, long nave, and marvelous capital carvings. Collectors of antiquities will take time also for the **church** and **cloister** of **St-André-le-Bas** and the former **church of St-Pierre**, which today houses a lapidary museum.

Roman Vienne

Half a century before Caesar conquered Gaul, Vienne was established as the capital of the tribal Allobroges; under the Romans, the city preceded Lyon as a metropolis and was the home of such magnificent monuments and residences that the poet Martial dubbed it "Vienne the Beautiful."

Among the relics of Roman Vienne, the **Temple d'Auguste et de Livie**, somewhat reminiscent of the Maison Carrée in Nîmes but smaller in size, is the grandest. Built during the reign of Augustus, it has undergone several permutations, serving as church, Jacobin headquarters during the Revolution, a Temple of Reason, a museum, and a library. It was restored to its original look in the 19th century.

The **Roman theater**, abandoned as long ago as the fourth century under Emperor Constantine, underwent archaeological work in 1922 and has been returned to excellent condition. It ranks among the largest theaters of Gaul and is only slightly smaller in diameter than the Theater of Marcellus in Rome. Productions are still staged here in summer.

Even more interesting to those who enjoy evidence of

daily life in past ages, the towns of **St-Romain-en-Gal** and **Ste-Colombe** have been unearthed across the river from Vienne.

St-Romain boasts superb mosaics (in the little museum), a marketplace, warehouses in which dyeing and tanning vessels remain, baths, and sewers. Ste-Colombe was the site of giant baths, palaces, and fine residences.

South of Vienne

From Condrieu, 40 km (25 miles) south of Lyon and south of Vienne, a remarkable route wiggles south and west along the Crêt de l'Oeillon (splendid views over the mountains and valleys of the Rhône country) to **Mont-Pilat** and **Gouffre d'Enfer** (*enfer* is hell—here an impressive dam site at the end of a rocky, narrow gorge involving a healthful hike), and then on to the hill hamlet of **Rochetaillée**, with its feudal château ruins.

The end of this particular road comes at St-Etienne, a large industrial town from which you may continue west or cut back to the Rhône route via Annonay and Tournon. Continuing south along the Rhône river from Vienne will bring you to Orange, the Rhône wine country, and Provence, all covered in a later chapter.

In Condrieu, you should plan to stop at **Le Beau Rivage et l'Hermitage du Rhône**, with 20 rooms and four suites overlooking the river. The lovely terrace restaurant is in fact right on the Rhône; reserve; Tel: 74-59-52-24.

GETTING AROUND

From Paris, Autoroute A 6 heads southeast to Beaune, with a cutoff via A 38 to Dijon, and continues via Chalon-sur-Saône and Mâcon to Lyon; A 7 continues to Provence. As usual, the back roads are slower and reveal more of the countryside.

Dijon has no international airport but is linked by daily flights to and from Paris-Charles-de-Gaulle and Paris-Orly. Lyon's Satolas Airport receives flights from Paris and other cities via Air Inter; from Avignon via Air Inter and Air Jet; from Limoges via Air Limousin; from various airports in southern France, Italy, and Spain via Air Littoral; from Brittany and Normandy via Brit Air; from Clermont-Ferrand and Angoulême via Compagnie Languedoc. The passenger capacity of Lyon/Satolas doubled in 1991. Air France has five weekly direct U.S.–Lyon flights.

The TGVs (high-speed trains) cover Burgundy, with

direct service from Paris to Dijon, Montbard, Beaune, and Chalon-sur-Saône. The train for Lyon also stops at Le Creusot and Mâcon-Loché stations. TGV trains from Besançon (in the Jura) and Lausanne, Switzerland, provide service to Dijon, while TGVs from Savoy and Geneva stop at Mâcon-Loché. This swift service is complemented by regular rail services from cities throughout Europe.

In September 1983 the futuristic railway station Lyon Part-Dieu opened to receive new TGV lines that now make the Paris–Lyon run in two hours. Regular Lille–Lyon service, bypassing Paris, runs a few times a day.

Several companies operate luxury **Burgundy canal cruise-barges,** including French Country Waterways, Inc., aboard three craft; contact them at P.O. Box 2195, Duxbury, MA 02331; Tel: (617) 934-2454 (in Mass.) or (800) 222-1236 (rest of U.S.); Abercrombie & Kent, 1520 Kensington Rd., Suite 212, Oak Brook, IL 60521; Tel: (708) 954-2944, or Sloane Square House, Holbein Place, London SW1 W8NS; Le Boat, Inc., P.O. Box E, Maywood, NJ 07607; Tel: (800) 922-0291, or (201) 342-1838; Floating Through Europe, 271 Madison Ave., New York, NY 10016; Quiztour, 19, rue d'Athènes, 75009 Paris; or contact Barge About France/Quiztour, B & D de Vogüé Travel Services, P.O. Box 1998, Visalia, CA 93279; Tel: (800) 444-1188. Also, Le Duc de Bourgogne, Port de Plaisance, 21000 Dijon; Aquarelle, Port de Plaisance, quai St-Martin, 89000 Auxerre; and Locaboat Plaisance, quai du Port-au-Bois, 89300 Joigny. Inquire at any regional tourist office for information on short-term boat rentals for four to 12 passengers.

Ballooning in Burgundy may be arranged through Buddy Bombard's Balloon Adventures, 6727 Curran St., McLean, VA 22101; Château Laborde, 21200 Meursanges-par-Beaune; and Air Escargot, Remigy, 71150 Chagny. In Canada, France Unlimited arranges Burgundy barge cruises and apartments in Paris; write them at 135 Isabella St., Suite 708, Toronto, Ontario M4Y 1P4; Tel: (416) 920-6329.

City tours, wine tours, gastronomic outings, and float and barge trips throughout the area may be booked through regional tourist offices. Several organizations arrange horseback and covered-wagon trips for a day, weekend, or longer, as well as hiking and bicycling trips. A major U.S. operator of bicycling excursions in Burgundy is Progressive Travels, Inc., 1932 First Ave., Suite 1100, Seattle, WA 98101; Tel: (800) 245-2229. In Canada, com-

fortable bicycling excursions are the province of Butterfield & Robinson, 70 Bond St., Toronto, Ontario M5B 1X3;
Tel: (800) 387-1147 (in U.S.), (800) 268-8415 (in Canada),
or (416) 864-1354.

Automobile tourists interested in vineyards, architecture, and markets may obtain brochures outlining routes
at regional tourism offices in major cities.

ACCOMMODATIONS REFERENCE

▶ **Abbaye St-Michel.** Rue St-Michel, 89700 **Tonnerre.**
Tel: 86-55-05-99; Telex: 801356; Fax: 86-55-00-10; in U.S.,
(713) 783-8033; Fax: (713) 783-0951; in Australia, (02)
957-4511; Fax: (02) 929-6326.

▶ **Alain Chapel.** 01390 **Mionnay.** Tel: 78-91-82-02; Telex:
305605; Fax: 78-91-82-37; in U.S., (713) 783-8033; Fax:
(713) 783-0951; in Australia, (02) 957-4511; Fax: (02)
929-6326.

▶ **Le Beau Rivage et l'Hermitage du Rhône.** 2, rue du
Beau Rivage, 69420 **Condrieu.** Tel: 74-59-52-24; Telex:
308946; Fax: 74-59-59-36; in U.S., (713) 783-8033; Fax:
(713) 783-0951; in Australia, (02) 957-4511; Fax: (02)
929-6326.

▶ **Belle Epoque.** 15, rue du faubourg Bretonnière,
21200 **Beaune.** Tel: 80-24-66-15; Fax: 80-24-17-49.

▶ **Bordeaux.** 1, rue du Bélier, 69002 **Lyon.** Tel: 78-37-
58-73; Telex: 330355; Fax: 78-37-48-02.

▶ **Central Urbis Hôtel.** 3, place Grangier, 21000 **Dijon.**
Tel: 80-30-44-00; Telex: 350606; Fax: 80-30-77-12.

▶ **Le Cep.** 27, rue Maufoux, 21200 **Beaune.** Tel: 80-22-
35-48; Telex: 351256; Fax: 80-22-76-80; in U.S., (212) 477-
1600 or (800) 366-1510.

▶ **Chapeau Rouge.** 5, rue Michelet, 21000 **Dijon.** Tel:
80-30-28-10; Telex: 350535; Fax: 80-30-33-89; in U.S. and
Canada, (800) 528-1234 or in U.K., (081) 541-0033; in
Australia, (02) 212-6444.

▶ **Chapon Fin et Restaurant Paul Blanc.** 01140 **Thoissey.** Tel: 74-04-04-74; Telex: 305728; in U.S., (713) 783-8033;
Fax: (713) 783-0951; in Australia, (02) 957-4511; Fax: (02)
929-6326.

▶ **Château d'Igé.** 71960 **Igé.** Tel: 85-33-33-99; Telex:
351915; Fax: 85-33-41-41; in U.S., (713) 783-8033; Fax:
(713) 783-0951; in Australia, (02) 957-4511; Fax: (02)
929-6326.

▶ **Côte d'Or.** Rue Ronot, 21400 **Châtillon-sur-Seine.** Tel:
80-91-13-29.

▶ **Côte d'Or et Résidence.** 2, rue Argentine, 21210

Saulieu. Tel: 80-64-07-66; Telex: 350778; Fax: 80-64-08-92; in U.S., (800) 372-1323, (212) 696-1323; Fax: (212) 213-2297.

▶ **A la Côte St-Jacques et la Résidence.** 14, faubourg de Paris, 89300 **Joigny.** Tel: 86-62-09-70; Telex: 801458; Fax: 86-91-49-70; in U.S., (800) 372-1323, (212) 696-1323; Fax: (212) 213-2297.

▶ **La Cour des Loges.** 6, rue du Boeuf, 69005 **Lyon.** Tel: 78-42-75-75; Telex: 330831; Fax: 72-40-93-61; in U.S., (800) 366-1510, (212) 477-1600.

▶ **Ermitage de Corton.** Route de Dijon, 21200 **Beaune Nord.** Tel: 80-22-05-28; Telex: 351189.

▶ **L'Espérance.** St-Père 89450 **Vézelay** (3 km/2 miles southeast of Vézelay). Tel: 86-33-20-45; Fax: 86-33-26-15; in U.S., (713) 783-8033; Fax: (713) 783-0951; in Australia, (02) 957-4511; Fax: (02) 929-6326.

▶ **Grand Hôtel Concorde.** 11, rue Grolée, 69002 **Lyon.** Tel: 72-40-45-45; Fax: 78-37-52-55; in U.S., (212) 838-6554 or (800) 333-1212.

▶ **Hôtel Bourgogne.** Place de l'Abbaye, 71250 **Cluny.** Tel: 85-59-00-58.

▶ **Hôtel de la Cloche.** 14, place Darcy, 21000 **Dijon.** Tel: 80-30-12-32; Telex: 350498; Fax: 80-30-04-15; in U.S., (212) 477-1600 or (800) 366-1510.

▶ **Hostellerie des Clos.** 89800 **Chablis.** Tel: 86-42-10-63; Telex: 351752; Fax: 86-42-17-11.

▶ **Hostellerie de Levernois.** 21200 **Levernois.** Tel: 80-24-73-58; Fax: 80-22-78-00.

▶ **Hôtel de Greuze.** 5, rue A. Thibaudet, 71700 **Tournus.** Tel: 85-40-77-77.

▶ **Hôtel Le Maxime.** 2, quai de la Marine, 89000 **Auxerre.** Tel: 86-52-14-19.

▶ **Hôtel de la Poste.** 1, boulevard Clemenceau, 21200 **Beaune.** Tel: 80-22-08-11; Telex: 350982; Fax: 80-24-19-71; in U.S., (212) 477-1600 or (800) 366-1510.

▶ **Hôtel Ursulines.** 14, rue Rivault, 71400 **Autun.** Tel: 85-52-68-00; Telex: 801297.

▶ **Hostellerie Vieux Moulin.** Porte Arroux D 980, 71400 **Autun.** Tel: 85-52-10-90.

▶ **Lameloise.** 36, place d'Armes, 71150 **Chagny.** Tel: 85-87-08-85; Telex: 801086; Fax: 85-87-03-57; in U.S., (713) 783-8033; Fax: (713) 783-0951; in Australia, (02) 957-4511; Fax: (02) 929-6326.

▶ **Novotel.** 260, rue Lionel Terray, 69500 **Bron.** Tel: 78-26-97-48; Telex: 340781; Fax: 78-26-45-12; in U.S. and

Canada, (800) 221-4542; in U.K., (071) 724-1000; in Australia, (02) 246-5955.

▶ **Novotel Lyon-Nord**. Autoroute A 6, Porte de Lyon, 69570 **Dardilly**. Tel: 78-35-13-41; Telex: 330962; Fax: 78-35-08-45; in U.S. and Canada, (800) 221-4542; in U.K., (071) 724-1000; in Australia, (02) 246-5955.

▶ **Ostellerie du Vieux Pérouges**. 01800 **Pérouges**. Tel: 74-61-00-88; in U.S., (212) 477-1600 or (800) 366-1510.

▶ **Parc de la Colombière**. 49, cours du Parc, 21000 **Dijon**. Tel: 80-65-18-41; Telex: 351482.

▶ **La Poste et Lion d'Or**. 89450 **Vézelay**. Tel: 86-33-21-23; Telex: 800949.

▶ **Pullman Part-Dieu**. 129, rue Servient, 69003 **Lyon**. Tel: 78-62-94-12; Telex: 380088; Fax: 78-60-41-77; in U.S., (212) 575-2228/29 or (800) 223-9862; in U.K., (01) 621-9247; in Canada, (800) 451-3356.

▶ **Pullman Perrache**. 12, cours de Verdun, 69002 **Lyon**. Tel: 78-37-58-11; Telex: 330500; Fax: 78-37-06-56; in U.S., (212) 575-2228/29 or (800) 223-9862; in Canada, (800) 451-3356; in U.K., (071) 621-9247.

▶ **La Pyramide**. 14, boulevard Fernand-Point, 38200 **Vienne**. Tel: 74-53-01-96; Fax: 74-85-69-73.

▶ **Le Rempart**. 2, avenue Gambetta, 71700 **Tournus**. Tel: 85-51-10-56; Telex: 351019; Fax: 85-40-77-22.

▶ **La Résidence de la Pyramide**. 41, quai Riondet, 38200 **Vienne**. Tel: 74-53-16-46.

▶ **Royal**. 20, place Bellecour, 69002 **Lyon**. Tel: 78-37-57-31; Telex: 310785; Fax: 78-37-01-36; in U.S. and Canada, (800) 528-1234; in U.K., (071) 541-0033; in Australia, (02) 212-6444.

▶ **Sofitel**. 20, quai Gailleton, 69002 **Lyon**. Tel: 78-42-72-50; Telex: 330225; Fax: 72-40-05-50; in U.S. and Canada, (800) 221-4542; in U.K., (071) 724-1000; in Australia, (02) 264-5955.

▶ **Sofitel**. 69125 **Lyon/Satolas Aéroport**. Tel: 72-22-71-61; Telex: 380480; Fax: 72-22-71-72; in U.S. and Canada, (800) 221-4542; in U.K., (071) 724-1000; in Australia, (02) 264-5955.

THE JURA

By Fred Halliday

Where do the smart Swiss go when they want to breathe cool mountain air and wander a hilltop gold and red with wildflowers, or sit down to lunch with a lover, a rich Comté cheese, and a view of Mont Blanc? Or when they want to save money? And where do these same canny Swiss go to buy a good bottle of kirsch from a garage sale, visit a major art museum overhanging a trout stream, watch the cows come home to the barn behind the hotel at *l'heure de l'apéritif,* and shop for one of France's zestiest wine treats at the co-op? Why, to the Jura, in France. In the Franche-Comté region of France, the Jura is bordered by Alsace and Lorraine to the north, Champagne and Burgundy to the north and west, the Savoy to the south, and Switzerland to the east.

Save money in France, you say? Yes, and it's high time to get over to this land of the Jura, with its old châteaux guarding great gorges, old hotels on gurgling rivers, and old-fashioned menus at old-fashioned prices.

In addition to these bucolic blessings, the Jura boasts a big, beautiful capital in the sun—Besançon. A center of architectural richness, Besançon is just two and a half hours by train from Paris.

But of all these assets, the Jura's most striking feature is its landscape, dotted with gorges, falls, cirques (deep, steep-walled stone canyons), and rivers. The land itself is a mountain plateau of pressure ridges, a foot table, really, of the Alps. Its features were cracked, crazed, and chiseled by mountain torrents, underground streams, and grinding glaciers that only recently—geologically speaking—retreated from the region. Covered with trees, the Jura gets its name from the Low Latin word *juria,* meaning forest; in its most spectacular folds, this region of France calls to mind a verdant Grand Canyon.

MAJOR INTEREST

Besançon
Grande-Rue
St-Jean cathedral
Roman ruins
Musée des Beaux-Arts

The Jura
Wild landscapes
Picturesque villages in the Doubs, Loue, and Lison valleys
Trout fishing
Charcuterie and cheese
Châteaux

BESANÇON

The door to all this fresh air opens in Besançon, the capital of Franche-Comté, some 400 km (250 miles) southeast of Paris and less than a quarter of that distance from the Swiss border. The morning train from Paris (7:14 A.M. from the Gare de Lyon) arrives in time for a fine stroll before lunch. Sunday is a good day to arrive, as it is in any French provincial capital, because Sunday is market day. Everybody from the surrounding countryside comes streaming into town with his or her wares to join in the yelling and selling down by the stalls where the river Doubs flows beneath the Pont Battant. Here are to be found some of the best food products of the Jura. And as Besançon is the most likely place to rent a car—all the major rental agencies are here—for the trip through the Jura, this is an outstanding opportunity to stock up with baskets of food for the road.

All varieties of the region's farm produce are sold at Besançon's market. Try the hams, and be sure to pick out a smoked variety. Thinly sliced, it's as good as prosciutto but more savory. Also try the cheeses: the Vacherin, a soft, orange-rinded cheese (the Mont-d'Or, Haut-Doubs is almost local); or the Gruyère de Comté, the king of Gruyère, soft and nutty and easily cut by the pocket knife that you will buy here. (Always buy Opinel when buying pocket knives in France.) There are wonderful fruits, too, apples and pears especially, and cherries, a specialty of

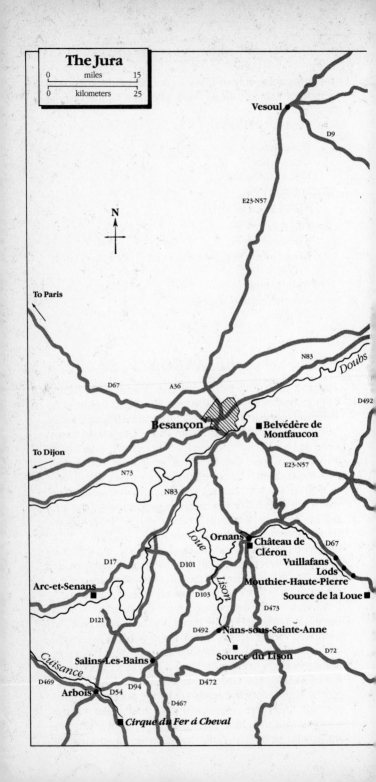

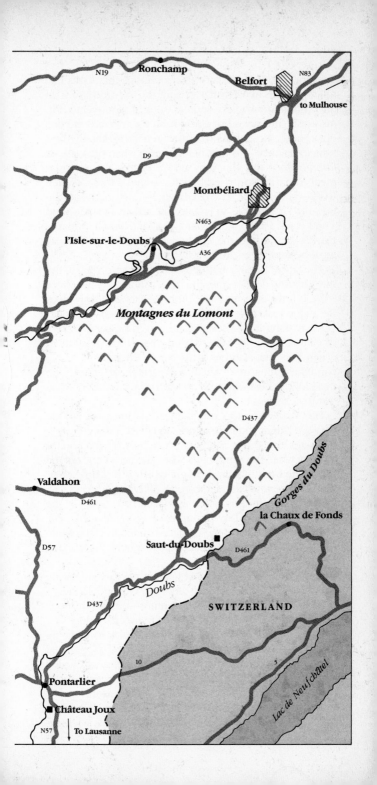

the Jura. The Jésus de Morteau, a sausage that looks like salami, comes in particularly handy during car trips, as do the *pastilles des Vosges,* candies tasting of pine-scented air. Also tasty, but not so practical for a car trip, are the live ducks and chickens. As with any French market, the best time to drink all this in is before lunch when the *mère de famille* does the shopping and prepares the noonday meal. You'd be surprised how fast some of these women work—speed is the style of Ginette Mathieu, author of the best-read cookbooks in France. The activity peaks around 11:30 A.M.; arrive much after that and you'll find the market struck and the city quiet, preparing its Sunday meal behind long rows of windows.

The city of Besançon itself was laid out according to the three cardinal principles on which Roman cities were founded: the site, the site, and the site. Not only does Besançon have a lariat loop of river (the Doubs) to encircle it, making it almost an island, but in practically every direction from its watery ring rise slope-shouldered green hills that stand as walls before the moat. And beyond these hills are mountains to part the sky and pen up the clouds, bestowing on Besançon a microclimate as fortunate as its site.

How and when to see it, then? In summer and fall the days are bright and never stuffy, and there's skiing nearby in winter. But spring is the best time for the Jura. Admire this city when the sun is high, when the pastel-hues of the limestone buildings are brought out by direct light, their Renaissance reliefs underscored with black shadows.

The place in Besançon to begin your tour is the **Grande-Rue**—but leave your car outside the old city walls. Inside, much of the going is banned to automobile traffic, preserving an authentic atmosphere for walking through antiquity.

Start at the **cathedral of St-Jean**, at the far end of the Grande-Rue. Its exterior may seem a patchwork of styles—most of it dates from the 18th century—but the inside is worth a look. On the wall next to the sacristy door is a painting of the Virgin with saints by Fra Bartolomeo, dating from 1512. The cathedral also possesses an astronomical clock, a 19th-century masterpiece composed of 30,000 parts and 70 different faces supplying 122 pieces of information, including time, temperature, and season.

No one leaves the cathedral and gets very far very quickly, thanks to the **square A. Castan**. ("My, what a delightful city this Besançon is," they cry from here. "Look, we just got going and we can't get anywhere.") The square A. Castan has almost as many faces as the cathedral's astronomical clock. Here is the **Porte Noire** (Black Gate), a Roman triumphal arch dating from the second century A.D. It was this relic that persuaded the Bisontins (out in the countryside the people are called Comtois) to start digging. What they unearthed on this site—Castan was the chief digger—was a Roman urban center huddled around today's square. Among the ruins is a spherical building that was first a theater and then a reservoir for the aqueduct that watered the city, which was growing furiously by Marcus Aurelius's time. The square also contains the remains of a temple and is prosaically framed by eight Corinthian columns.

To one side of the square, the charming restaurant **Le Castan** preserves that Roman ambience. Ask to eat in the cave downstairs, which is at the same underground level as the excavations. The food here is home-style and tasty, especially the goat. Ask for an Arbois wine, or better, a 1986 Pupillin rosé put up by Désiré Petit & Fils. At any rate, both are local Jura wines waiting to be discovered and will provide a foretaste of things to come.

Emboldened by lunch and no longer a stranger to Besançon, you're now prepared to poke your nose inside its many courtyards. Number 64, Grande-Rue is a private home with gateless portals well worth strolling through. Inside is the architectural rarity of a courtyard within a courtyard. The second of these, behind the first, deserves the longer look. Framed by old wooden stables, it illustrates the rather complete town house lifestyle of the mid-18th century.

Nearby, at number 140, is the birthplace of Victor Hugo, whom the Bisontins never forgave for calling their city "an old Spanish town." They, in turn, referred to Hugo as "a half-breed from Brittany and Lorraine," an epithet the writer never disputed. He sought, and found, his adventure elsewhere. At number 91 is a convenient hotel, the **Regina**. It's handsome, comfortable, and in keeping with the style of the block. A more modish choice would be the **Altéa Parc Micaud** across the river on avenue E. Droz, with its good restaurant, **Le Vesontio**.

Besançon is an outdoor town. Vest-pocket cafés are planted in open spaces, and the Grande-Rue is so wide and the buildings so uniformly low that there is never the sense of being hemmed in. At the place du 8-Septembre the Grande-Rue opens onto the main city square, where

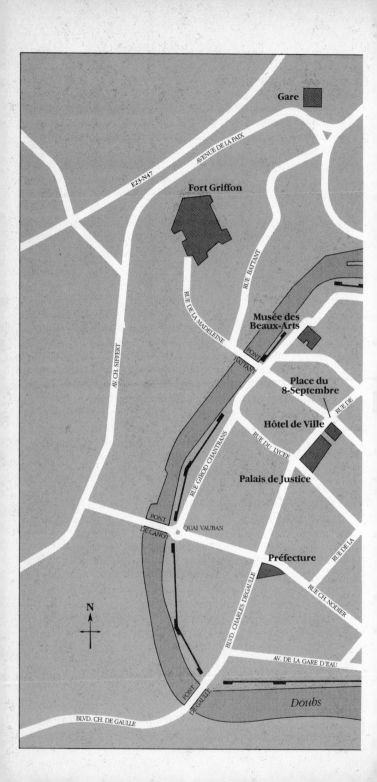

Gare

E23-N47

AVENUE DE LA PAIX

Fort Griffon

RUE DE LA MADELEINE

RUE BATTANT

AV. CH. SIFFERT

Musée des
Beaux-Arts

PONT
BATTANT

Place du
8-Septembre

RUE DE

Hôtel de Ville

RUE DU LYCÉE

Palais de Justice

RUE GIROD CHANTRANS

PONT
DE CANOT

QUAI VAUBAN

Préfecture

RUE DE LA

BLVD. CHARLES DEGAULLE

RUE CH. NODIER

N

AV. DE LA GARE D'EAU

PONT
DE GAULLE

Doubs

BLVD. CH. DE GAULLE

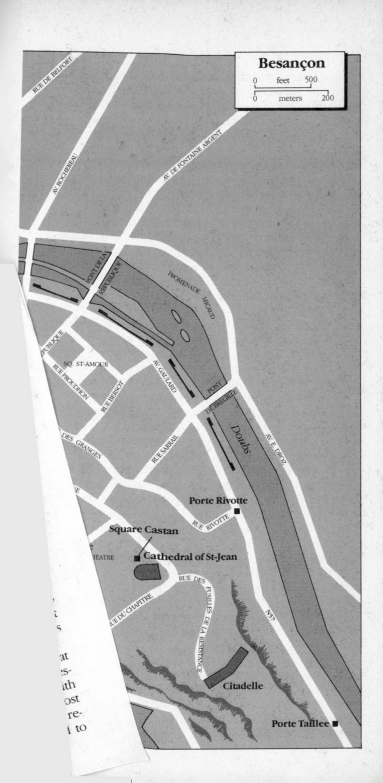

stand the separate elements of a superb architectural surprise. Here rise two impressive buildings: the 16th-century **Hôtel de Ville** and, right behind it, the 16th-century **Palais de Justice**. The façade of the latter is conspicuously Burgundian, a style imposed by the French crown and a gross injustice, considering that when the original structure was erected Franche-Comté had long been established as an independent state (*franche* meaning "franchise," or privilege, and *comté* meaning a fiefdom held by a count).

It was in 1635 that Cardinal Richelieu cast a covetous eye upon the Jura and sent an army to fetch it for the crown of France. It wasn't so easy. Though outgunned and outnumbered, the locals fought fiercely, and the struggle between the French and the Comtois was to last for more than 40 years. In its most desperate hours the battle was charged with all the classic elements of guerilla warfare. Besançon was a city, the cardinal was to learn, that was accustomed to combat. Along with the rest of the Jura it had been subdued by Julius Caesar, but not without nine years of strenuous effort. In the tenth century the Hungarian cavalry swept in, sacking and burning the city and displaying a taste for raw young flesh. The Bisontins called the Hungarians many things, but when they said it in French—*Hongrois*—they did not pronounce the "H." According to some sources, this is how the word "ogre" was coined.

So, with the horrors of war the Bisontins were painfully acquainted. That still didn't prepare them for what the cardinal had in mind. When the Bisontins turned back the French armies, Richelieu tried again, this time with Swiss mercenaries. These made bonfires of homes and then entombed fleeing partisans in the subterranean grottoes where they had sought shelter. Anyone suspected of hiding the family fortune had hot water, hot oil, or worse poured down his throat. But still the Comtois fought on, and the war lengthened over generations until, at last, the French gained the upper hand. They then erected the Besançon courthouse in an obviously French design to show the Comtois what brand of justice they could expe henceforth. Resistance ends when public works to futility are erected in its midst.

The Grande-Rue, also a survivor, is the same street t originally cleaved the old Roman town. It has seen proc sions of Romans, Huns, and Hungarians, and today, v pleasant cafés lining its length, it pushes on toward its happy perspective: the **Pont Battant**, along with the mains of a Roman bridge, part of the original roa

Rome. It is on this bridge, looking down the river Doubs—one of the unsung rivers of France—and on the 16th-century quai Vauban that the visitor often decides to stay in this city of the ruddy past and beguiling present.

Across the river and up the rue Battant is the cinema Styx, playing old classics like *A Streetcar Named Desire* in their original languages. Another old courtyard, at 37, rue Battant, of rose and blue *grès* (sandstone), warrants a look. Near the end of the rue Battant is a walkway to **Fort Griffon**. Here a long, paved incline, punctuated with flights of steps, leads up a steep hill, the town gradually falling away to surrounding vistas and gardens. All along the promenade are shops, small hotels, and, out on little setbacks, restaurants and cafés for the weary. Off the promenade Micaud, which runs alongside the river, is the delightful and reasonable barge-restaurant **Le Chaland** (Tel: 81-80-61-61). You'll have a lovely view of the town while you dine.

Now turn back across the Pont Battant; just to its left and down the little hill, hard by the Besançon market, is the **Musée des Beaux-Arts**, at place de la Révolution. The excellent collection here includes works by Fragonard, Boucher, Goya, Matisse, and Courbet; its old halls have been restored by students of Le Corbusier. A must to see.

Back across town on the rue Rivotte is the turreted stone gatehouse of the **Porte Rivotte**, the last of the old Comté gatehouses that guarded the city in the war with the French. And farther along the same street is the Porte Taillée, an opening the Romans chiseled in the rock to pass through their aqueduct. This rocky slope is the only overland route into Besançon, and here stands its fortress, the **Citadelle**. Inside its walls the citadelle houses three museums. One is a natural history collection of local and other fauna, skeletons, butterflies, shells, and such; the other two—the **Musée Populaire Comtois** and **Musée de la Resistance et de la Déportation**—are far more engrossing. The Comtois is devoted to that most interesting of species, people; here, specifically, the Comtois. The 15 halls start with pottery, weaving, and spinning and go on into an authentic Comtois house with its artifacts, as well as a puppet collection, a vintage 1820 "Théâtre Mécanique." There are farm tools and wine tools and a collection of handcrafted wrought-iron objects, including 16th-century weather vanes. The museum depicting the horrific chapter of history on the Holocaust and Resistance includes German posters announcing the advance of Nazism, as well as a collection of drawings and sculptures created by concentration camp inmates.

Three hundred feet atop the rock rise the walls, ramparts, and towers engineered by the French to protect what was so hard to win. It was on this very hill that Julius Caesar first gazed down and appreciated what a marvelous spot Besançon occupied in the world.

THE JURA
The River Doubs

If all this traipsing around hard pavement whets your appetite for a refreshing plunge into nature, the wonders of the Jura are ideal. One option is along the river Doubs from Besançon, following its sinuous and delectable curves along route N 83, past the nearby **Belvédère de Montfaucon** of the verdant views; past l'**Isle-sur-le-Doubs**, where the river splits in three and the lovely 12th-century **Château de Belvoir** overlooks the Sancey valley; past the curve at Montbéliard and its famous brown and white cows; and then down toward the **Saut-du-Doubs**, a waterfall with a drop of roughly 100 feet. It is, however, a long trip (200 km/125 miles), ending, some say, in isolation and souvenir stands. An alternative is to leave the Doubs at Montbéliard and continue north on A 36 to **Belfort**, just 98 km (60 miles) from Besançon. In its ancient fortress near the Franco-German border lurks the beast of the keep, the **Lion de Belfort**.

Seventy feet long and 35 feet high, in chunks of red rock, the lion crouches in the foundations of the town's citadel as if barring the gap in the hills through which traditionally came the invaders of France. In 1870 the German army advanced. Like the Celts, Romans, and barbarians before them, the Germans laid siege to the rock and fortress that stood in their way, but with a difference: The Germans had artillery. They fired 5,000 shells a day into the fortress; 400,000 shells fell in toto on the citadel, and still the garrison held. The defenders resisted until 21 days after the Franco-Prussian war had ended. This dramatic holdout in the Jura enabled France to wrest better terms of peace—and a shred of honor—from her otherwise total defeat.

And so, after the battle, a great sculptor came to the base of Belfort's citadel and erected this lion in tribute to those defenders who would not let their enemy pass. For all the region's wild hills and crags, it is perhaps these blocks of sculpted stone that best capture the rugged spirit of the Jura. It is significant that this should have been done by Auguste Bartholdi, the man who created the Statue of Liberty.

Belfort is not a stop on any culinary itinerary. That is to say there is no army of tasters come from hither and yon, and the scribbling of tasting notes is not heard in any of its restaurants. But Belfort is, after all, in France, so it does have a culinary extravaganza: an evening at the **Café de Paris** (within the old Hôtel de Paris, 1, avenue Wilson, opposite the train station; Tel: 84-21-58-10). What the café lacks in "gastronomic" stars it makes up for in atmosphere. Here is where Old France—the milliner, the tailor, the old generals and their spouses—comes to dine. It is one of those places in the provinces that fill up at night with local luminaries. Enter, and what's put on your plate matters little next to the all-encompassing swirl of flirtatiousness and gentility filling the room. Everybody knows everybody else, for they all live in the town and come to pass by one another's table and take part in the general Gallic uproar. No matter what else is around, this is the best show currently playing. But it is subject to end without further notice. The government could add another TV channel and—poof! So see it now—and order Champagne.

The River Loue

Meanwhile, there is another river at hand that is just as impressive and more manageable to undertake than the Doubs; it can be seen by travelling just 25 miles of its length. To boot, it is the most outstanding trout stream of France.

The river Loue carves an impressive itinerary. Its valley has everything: a canyon, falls, châteaux, the most picturesque villages in France, irresistible restaurants, magical accommodations, a museum overhanging the river, and a delightful road to lead you through it all.

One of the uncalculated bonuses in wandering the eastern Jura in general and the towns along the Loue—such as Mouthier, Lods, Vuillafans—in particular is that, couched safely against the wall of Switzerland, they are full of surprises. No military harm has passed this way for centuries; these towns and blessed streams have remained far above the roar of modern artillery. So, first rule: Get out of the car. These unscathed streets often bear unsuspected treasures—a stone statue at eye level, a bust of a saint, a piece of wrought-iron artwork. Also, there has been very little restoration here (not much was needed) in the Viollet-le-Duc sense—only upkeep, and now, with the arrival of Swiss and Parisians seeking country homes, gentrification. But the modern plumbing inside doesn't show on the outside, and walking through the towns of the Loue Valley is like walking through the time of Martin Guerre.

For a grand perspective of the overall area, begin your Loue Valley trek at the 11th-century **Châteaux de Joux**, perched high on a rock above the road to Lausanne, just 4 km (2.5 miles) from Pontarlier, and 62 km (38.5 miles) southeast of Besançon. There is a museum of antique arms and uniforms within, and outside are awe-inspiring views of the Doubs and the Alps foothills.

On to the source of the Loue.

Twenty kilometers (12 miles) northwest of Pontarlier, along route D 67, the river bubbles up from a grotto, swells, and goes churning off, carving a rock canyon, now breathtakingly deep. And the road goes off after the river, zigging around chasms and hopscotching towns nestled in valleys, huddled in coves, or sitting high in the notches between hilltops. These are the kinds of villages every traveller comes to France to find.

The first is **Mouthier**. Four miles from the source and on the curve of the Loue deep in its gorge, the village is built of buff stone, its houses roofed in tiles. It steps up from the river, looking like orange layers of puff pastry; on one side of the road Mouthier huddles around its church spire and square, its streets tightly knit. Then upward it goes again, a zigzag of road and farmhouses and cherry orchards, to the heights of a cliff-toothed mountain, old **Haute-Pierre**.

Mouthier is a good place to stop, for a good hotel awaits down on route D 67, **La Cascade**. La Cascade has the country simplicity that fits in so well here, but with sophisticated cuisine, magnificent views from the restaurant, and balconies offering views of the gorge from the bedrooms. Below, the river, swollen with water, twists by, all white and racing. The nights are cool, even in summer. With the balcony doors left open to the roar of the river and the warm perfume of woodfires from the many chimneys below, sleep comes easily.

By day there is the town, a microcosm of Jura villages,

and the countryside to see, while *biquettes*—what French goats are called when they stay in their own yards—munch around the slope of the gorge. In the two to three hours before lunch it might be wise to limber up your legs with a hike to the top of Haute-Pierre. The climb provides refreshing exercise, fresh air in big gulps, benches along the way to collapse on, wonderful views of the whole of Mouthier in its valley below, and a nice place to lunch up top. You will find a goat trail through the fields, but unless you're a goat, it works better for descending.

The way to Haute-Pierre moves upward through Mouthier past a pretty turn-of-the-century school, a village square, and an intact 15th-century church. Behind and to the left of the church, and marked by a little sign, is a path that follows a particular joy of the Jura—kirsch—to its source. Smelling this clear brandy (eau-de-vie) distilled from cherries is like having your nose in a barrel of the fruit itself. In fact, it takes 28 pounds of cherries to make a single bottle. Here it is made and sold out of their garage by two retired Parisians.

The path then continues past a *lavoir,* a chiseled stone tub brimming with clear running water. Rarely, however, will you see women on bended knee pounding their linen on a rock; nowadays you are more likely to find couples washing their Renaults. By the last house, a springer spaniel comes out, wagging its tail, and there the village-proper of Mouthier ends. A 4-km (2.5-mile) hike up the mountain brings you to Haute-Pierre's little farm settlement, where you'll be rewarded with a view of the valley and Mont Blanc glistening in its snows beyond, as well as an *épicerie* (French deli) where the omelettes are delicious, the ham is from local pigs, and the Beaujolais is about 60 francs a bottle.

About a mile after Mouthier comes Lods, the second pearl of the Loue. (It claims to be the first.) **Lods** (pronounced Lô) has received an official award designating it "the most beautiful village in France." Though out of their endless bureaucracy the French are always manufacturing certificates, Lods is a legitimate gem deserving of such recognition. The parking lot across the Loue provides not just a place for your car but also the best view of the village across the fast-moving stream. From here are visible the effects of centuries of erosion and human efforts to counteract it. On the other side of the river a walk through the town will take about an hour, and there is a restaurant-hotel, the **Truite d'Or**, a "Logis de France" well worth visiting for lunch or dinner. It enjoys a pretty setting between the river and the woods and offers hearty cooking and 13 unassuming rooms.

It might be advisable to take time here for a word or two on food and accommodations in the rural Jura. The **Logis de France** are strongly represented here. Chain-dodgers take note: Logis de France is not a chain but an association of rural, family-owned restaurant-hotels and inns. In the Jura, at least, these often seem to be the most charming buildings, occupying the most picturesque sites, and offering cuisine that is local, fresh, and very appealing.

Four and a half miles downstream from Lods is **Vuillafans**, a prosperous little town with prosperous houses, housewives who nod and look at the tourists (especially at women in slacks), a big church, and one of the prettiest bridges across this prettiest of rivers.

Ornans is the creative and commercial center of the Loue, but don't look for a big town. It's creative because it houses one of the most likable museums of France in the home of one of the leading painters of pre-Impressionist realism. And it's commercial because you can cash a check. Ornans, population 4,000, is also very picturesque. Here the river slows down and, having done so, widens. It almost forms a lake, which reflects elongated images of the Medieval buildings on both sides. **Gustave Courbet** was from Ornans, and it is his house that has been turned into the appealing museum mentioned above. Stairways lead through the rooms set up as galleries for Courbet's works, and a boutique sells reproductions, periodicals, and postcards. It is not the Picasso museum in Paris or the Rembrandt in Amsterdam, but the visitor comes away with a better idea of who the painter was than is offered by most other museums devoted to the work of a single artist. Just across the river from D 67, Courbet's house offers lovely views of the Loue from some of its windows. The museum is open to the public every day except Tuesdays during the Easter-to-October season, and at other times of the year on weekends and holidays.

Directly across the river from the Musée Courbet is the splendid **Hôtel de France**. This superb structure is an ideal headquarters for visiting the Loue and enjoying the ample charms of Ornans if you are willing to pay a fair price for the pleasure. And just outside of town, the charming eight-room restaurant-hotel **Moulin du Prieuré** fits hand-in-glove with the elegance of the Hôtel de

France. The seafood Napoléon is not to be missed. (Tel: 81-59-21-47.)

The street leaving town, the avenue Président-Wilson, passes a wine shop, an excellent place for picnic provisions and advice on the wines of the Jura. There are whites and reds, and the rosés take a mousse rather well. But for a real *connaissance* of the breed, it's best to hit the road to Arbois, the wine capital of the Jura, less than 40 km (25 miles) away.

The road, now D 103, continues to follow the river past more lovely *belvédères*—riverside places to picnic—to the most enviable of waterside habitations, the **Château de Cléron**. Seldom does the graceful reality of towers, turrets, and crenellations exist in such authentic chunks. The effect is complete; the castle occupies its own island park encircled by a moment of calm in the Loue. It does receive visitors, but only between July 9 and August 19, and then only after lunch, which puts it in the same time zone as Brigadoon.

Proceeding to D 101, there is a series of loops up and then back down (as D 17) through **Arc-et-Senans**, sort of an 18th-century theme park more interesting in concept than in reality.

Arbois

Arbois, 15 km (9 miles) south of Arc-et-Senans, is more of a wine village than a wine center. To the naked eye there looms nothing commercial—no storage vats, no truck parks, no eyesores. Arbois has a lovely curl of river, the Cuisance—what a remarkable name!—running through it. The town has old stone arcades buttressing its buildings and cul-de-sacs with views through to backyards.

Arbois was the home of Louis Pasteur, and his memory is still very much alive here. Anyone with a feeling for Pasteur's contributions to modern science must visit his home on the rue Courcelles. Here are the things of his life, his laboratory and instruments, just as he left them.

From this side of the river the **church of St-Just**, its bulbous dome characteristic of the Comté, can be glimpsed through the clotheslines. Also not to be missed for its arcades and wrought-iron work is the 18th-century place de la Liberté.

Try to arrive in Arbois before lunch, then be warned: The regional fondue is copious at **La Finette** (22, avenue

Pasteur; Tel: 84-66-06-78). Should you stay for dinner and the night, do so at **Le Paris** on rue de l'Hôtel de Ville. Among their specialties is *poularde au vin jaune et morilles,* and there is a good selection of regional wines for the tasting that have not taken the trouble you have to get here. Try the famous and seldom tasted (by outsiders) *vin jaune* itself. As the name implies, it is golden. It is also aged at least six years in oak casks topped only with fermenting yeast. This cap serves the double purpose of giving the wine its nutty flavor and keeping it from oxidizing. A neat trick, when it works, for then the wine has much the taste of sherry—a *fino*—from a mass that is heavier. It is this taste that locals crave, and when they get it they claim to feel it down to their toes, crying rapturously as their toes curl, "Ah, that's *jaune*." Very few outsiders know what they're talking about.

Just outside the town are the Arbois vineyards. These may not be the most formidable in the world, but thanks to the site they occupy on a ridge above a national forest, they are certainly among the prettiest. (On the way to the vineyards, stop at the **Fruitier d'Arbois**, a local co-op that is the best place to buy Arbois wines.) Seven kilometers (4 miles) south of Arbois via D 469 is the **Cirque du Fer à Cheval**, a magnificent forested box canyon that rises 655 feet above the springs.

From here there are lovely miles of road to travel before you sleep. One of the loveliest—D 54 to D 94—climbs up to **Salins-les-Bains**, an old thermal spa–cum-cosmopolitan village. There's a real salt-water spring bubbling up from the ground (the only one in the Jura) and shops that specialize in health and beauty products. The road (now route D 492) plunges back down to the lush **Lison river**, where trout, their shadows blue in the crystal eddies, are just waiting for a fly. Here at the gurgling source of the Lison are serendipitous hotels with beach umbrellas and foie gras at poolside, and hawks that glower at you from atop telephone poles.

Coming out at the other end, midships in the valley, you arrive in the village of **Nans-sous-Ste-Anne**, the prettiest of all. At the 11-room hotel **La Poste** the cows come home under the verandah at cocktail hour; the barn is in the back, the roosters in front, and the price is only 180 francs a day. In the village, not far from the hotel, is another *fruitier* (in the Jura, a shop that sells foodstuffs and wine). This time the bargain is local Comté cheese.

Across from the store is a billboard with directions to all manner of nature walks. The one up to the *belvédère*—here an overlook—starts across the Lison and leads through a pine forest, where you will find wildflowers basking in sunny pools and translucent snails with white heads that look like linguini. There is a great view of the valley from the *belvédère,* and the way down passes through pastures filled with red and gold flowers and brown cows. And all this way there is not another human being, not the sound of an automobile or the sight of anything to buy. All you need is a loaf of bread, cheese, and a good pair of shoes.

GETTING AROUND

The TGV from Paris direct to Besançon departs the Gare de Lyon at 7:14 A.M. and again at 12:25 P.M., weekdays, and takes about two-and-a-half hours. Two additional trains make the trip to Besançon, with a 12-minute stop in Dijon, departing the Gare de Lyon at 8:05 A.M. and 9:37 A.M. weekdays. On weekends the 7:14 A.M. train stops in Dijon and arrives in Besançon at 10:00 A.M., and there is a direct train at about noon as well as another later in the evening. You can then rent a car in Besançon; all the major rental agencies are here, and driving is the best way to see the Jura.

ACCOMMODATIONS REFERENCE

▶ **Altéa Parc Micaud.** Avenue E. Droz, 25000 **Besançon.** Tel: 81-80-14-44; Telex: 360268; Fax: 81-53-29-83.

▶ **La Cascade.** 25920 **Mouthier-Haute-Pierre.** Tel: 81-60-95-30.

▶ **Hôtel de France.** Rue P. Vernier, 25290 **Ornans.** Tel: 81-62-24-44.

▶ **Hôtel Régina.** 91, Grande-Rue, 25000 **Besançon.** Tel: 81-81-50-22.

▶ **Moulin du Prieuré.** Route de Bonnevaux-le-Prieuré (via routes D 67 and D 280), 25620 **Mamirolle.** Tel: 81-59-21-47; Fax: 81-62-12-03.

▶ **Le Paris.** Rue de l'Hôtel de Ville, 39600 **Arbois.** Tel: 84-66-05-67; Telex: 361033.

▶ **La Poste.** 25330 **Nans-sous-Ste-Anne.** Tel: 81-86-62-57.

▶ **Truite d'Or.** 25930 **Lods.** Tel: 81-60-95-48.

THE SAVOY AND THE FRENCH ALPS

By Jonathan Weber and Mimi Tompkins

Jonathan Weber spent three years working as a reporter and editor in Paris and Geneva and is now a business writer at the Los Angeles Times. *His work has appeared in the* International Herald Tribune, Paris Passion *magazine, and many other publications. Mimi Tompkins is a journalist who has been based in Paris for the last seven years. She writes about European culture, business, and politics for* U.S. News & World Report, *public radio networks,* Toronto's Globe & Mail, *and other publications.*

For the sports enthusiast or nature lover, there's no place in France quite like the French Alps. Foreign visitors and French natives alike flock to the Alps to take advantage of an extensive array of outdoor recreational activities or simply to contemplate mountain vistas, rushing streams, and wildflowers. But the region, proud of its independent history yet comfortable in its Frenchness, is more than an outdoor playground. It is a prosperous area rich in historical and cultural diversions and home to the lively small cities of Chambéry, Annecy, and Grenoble.

MAJOR INTEREST

Skiing (December to April)
Hiking (July and August)
Mont Blanc

National and regional natural parks
Cirque du Fer-à-Cheval
Notre-Dame-de-Toute-Grâce (the church at Plateau
  d'Assy)
Abbaye de Hautecombe
Vauban fortifications at Briançon

Chambéry
The old city

Annecy
The old city
Sights relating to Saint François de Sales
Sailing and swimming

Grenoble
The Bastille
Musée Dauphinois
Musée des Beaux-Arts

Life in the Alps has always had a seasonal quality. In pre-tourist times herds of cows and goats moved up to high Alpine meadows for the summer grazing and retreated to the valleys before the first autumn snowfalls. Nowadays the ebb and flow of vacationers marks the change of seasons here. Winter brings skiers to the two breeds of ski resorts: the mountain-village-turned-modern-recreational type (Megève, Chamonix, Morzine, Val-d'Isère) and the integrated vacation complex built from scratch in virgin snowfields (Tignes, Courchevel, La Plagne, Flaine, Avoriaz).

Summertime activities are more varied. The ski towns offer golf, tennis, and swimming, and so do the many lakeside villages and campgrounds. Hikers can take advantage of a well-organized network of trails and mountain shelters that allow the well-provisioned to stay in the wild for days or even weeks on end. Those who prefer more unusual sports can try rock-climbing, hang gliding, sailing, and spelunking. Or, those who think strenuous activities are for the birds can head for Annecy, Chambéry, and Grenoble to shop, visit museums and churches, or just sit in cafés.

The French Alps stretch from north to south along the Italian border, bounded by Lac Léman and Switzerland to the north (Geneva and Lausanne are on Lac Léman) and the Mediterranean foothills to the south. While the area is mountainous, not all its mountains were created equal.

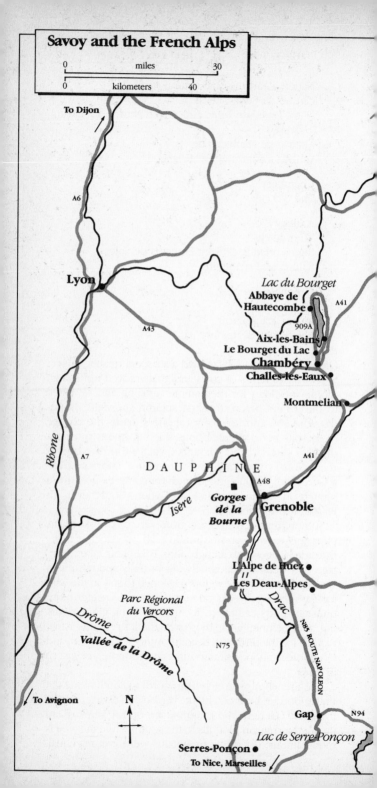

The rugged 10,000- to 14,000-foot-high peaks around Mont Blanc and Ecrins contrast sharply with the gentler mountains near Annecy and Lac Léman and the sunnier slopes south of Grenoble.

Water is everywhere here. The Isère, the Arve, the Durance, and the Arc rivers cut deep ravines through the mountains, making the region accessible to trains and cars. The lakes of Léman, Annecy, and Bourget are popular with weekend sailors and big enough for steamships. Water cascades down the spectacular falls at Cirque du Fer-à-Cheval and forms icy white glaciers on Mont Blanc; medicinal springs soothe the infirm at Aix-les-Bains and St-Gervais-les-Bains, and mineral water is bottled and sold at Evian-les-Bains.

A great deal of water also sits behind dams waiting to pass through hydroelectric power turbines. This "white oil" fueled a 19th-century industrial revolution in the Alps, as energy-intensive industries such as chemical manufacturing and metallurgy sought out cheap sources of electricity. While many of these businesses have since relocated or succumbed to deindustrialization, enough remain to create a discouragingly thick smog in some of the major river valleys. This is not a plastic vacation paradise. Rather, it is a prosperous and economically diverse area with a growing population. Local industries include the making of wine and cheese in the hills, aluminum and detergent in the valleys, and everything from microchips to church bells in the larger towns. For better or worse, this once-isolated region is now irrevocably integrated into modern France.

Moreover, the mountains look and feel lived-in, and the remote Alpine village, untouched by the modern world, is almost a thing of the past. All this is to say that those seeking a North American–style wilderness in the Alps are likely to be disappointed. What the Alpine towns lack in quaintness, however, they make up for with authenticity.

Historically, the French Alps were divided into two areas: the Savoy to the north and the Dauphiné to the south. The **Savoy**, which occupies the modern administrative departments of the Savoie and the Haute Savoie, was a proud and powerful independent kingdom. It didn't become part of France until 1859, making it the last region to join the nation. The **Dauphiné**, which includes the departments of Isère, Hautes Alpes, and Drôme, has belonged to France since 1349. While both areas are now firmly French, they retain a subtle kinship not only with one another but with their neighbor across the northern border in the mountains; the local cuisine, featuring fondue, dried meats, and a tableside barbecue called *braserade,* seems to be more Swiss than French.

THE SAVOY

The early history of the Savoy hardly hints at its later glory. Rome wrested the region from the Celtic Allobroges tribe—who had overrun it in the sixth century B.C.—in 121 B.C. and attached it to the province of Narbonne. It wasn't until the first century A.D. that Rome fully subjugated Savoy. Although settlements sprouted along the Roman road linking Milan and Vienna—notably at Aime and Annecy—no significant ruins from this period remain. As Christianity became institutionalized in the fifth century, a group of Burgundians migrated here and named the region Savoy, from the French *pays des sapins,* or "fir-tree country." The area thus became part of the kingdom of Burgundy, a powerful political entity in France.

The House of Savoy is the oldest sovereign family in Europe. It was founded at the beginning of the 11th century by Count Maurienne Humbert aux Blanches Mains (White Hands), who received title to the region in exchange for supporting Conrad le Salique's bid to be the Holy Roman emperor. His new kingdom held control of the Alpine passes to Italy and to the Germanic territories to the east and thus had great geopolitical importance. The later dukes of Savoy fully exploited their position as "porters of the Alps," and many kings were forced to pay humiliating tribute for the right to pass. The kingdom's golden era came in the 14th century when the three Amadeuses—all powerful rulers of the family—extended their domain to Nice, the Jura, Piemonte, and Geneva. At various times Savoy also controlled large chunks of what are now Italy and Switzerland as well as the Mediterranean island of Sardinia. Repeated French invasions—in 1536, in the 17th century (three times), in 1742, and again in 1792—failed to bring Savoy under the control of Paris. But when the Savoy, weary of war, finally joined France, it did so with some relief; an 1860 plebiscite showed 130,533 votes in favor of the union and just 235 against.

Chambéry

As the historic capital of the Savoy, Chambéry's fortunes rose and fell with those of the House of Savoy. Though it has lost its onetime prominence, the city remains a governmental center. The Château de Chambéry, seat of the dukes of Savoy, is now occupied by the prefecture and the regional council of Savoy. Today Chambéry, 90 km (56 miles) east of Lyon on A 43, remains a stately but animated town. Nearly all the interesting sites lie in the compact old city; the tourist office, located on the tree-lined boulevard de la Colonne, is exceptionally helpful in directing visitors. There are not many hotels in Chambéry, so it's a good idea to book ahead in summer. The very modern **Au Prince Eugène de Savoie** on the esplanade Curial is a practical choice for its central location and its proximity to the elegant **Roubatcheff** restaurant at the same address, serving several authentic Russian dishes as well as French nouvelle cuisine. **Les Princes**, on rue de Boigne, is a bit less expensive and also has a great location and a fine restaurant, which more than compensate for the small rooms and the hotel decor, a somewhat unsuccessful melange of modern styles. But it is clean and—thanks to double-glazed windows—quite quiet. If you prefer a country setting, try the **Château de Challes**, 6 km (4 miles) south of town in Challes-les-Eaux. Open all year, this clean and bright hostelry occupies a 15th-century château. Try to book one of the two rooms still with the original wood-inlay flooring and 11-foot ceilings. However, each of the 63 rooms in the hotel or the renovated *bergerie* (sheep pen) outside is attractive, and all overlook the courtyard and sculpted gardens in the hotel's private park.

The **Château de Chambéry**, actually a collection of buildings on a low, walled hilltop, dominates the town. Many of the original 14th-century structures burned down in the 18th century, and the massive building that now houses the prefecture was erected then. The church, the dungeon, and the treasure tower, however, retain their original Medieval lines. The grounds make for a pleasant walk, but to really see the place the guided tour is a necessity.

Chambéry's **old city** has numerous small architectural delights behind its archways and doorways and in its well-proportioned squares. On the festive rue Croix-d'Or, the ground floors of beautiful old houses have been converted to shops. The rue de Boigne, a street of grand façades and Italianate porticoes, is lined with pastry and candy shops that serve tea. The 15th- to 16th-century cathedral of St-François-de-Sales houses some interesting religious art, and the cathedral square is home to fine art galleries. At the intersection of the rue de Boigne and the boulevard de la Colonne stands the slightly bizarre elephant fountain, erected in 1838 in memory of Générale Comte de Boigne's trip to India. It has become, to the chagrin of many residents, one of the most popular monuments in town. At the edge of the old city is the new cultural center, **L'Espace André-Malraux**, designed by the prominent young Swiss architect Mario Botta and featuring a cinema, a concert hall, and meeting rooms. It is complemented nicely by the **Caserne Curial** next door, a huge, square army barracks that has been transformed into a tasteful shopping center that should please even the most ardent mall-hater. For a gift of Chambéry origin, try the local chocolate or the famous Opinel knives, available anywhere in town. Another alternative is a bottle of Vermouth. Chambéry has long been a center of Vermouth making, and the distilleries Dolin, on avenue de Grand Ariétaz, and Routin, on rue Emile Romanet, offer guided tours, but only on request (write or call in advance: Dolin, 73000 Chambéry, Tel: 79-69-59-09; Routin, 73000 Chambéry, Tel: 79-62-33-91).

For a nice excursion from Chambéry—and a good historical complement to the château—visit the **Abbaye de Hautecombe**, a beautiful lakeside monastery where the dukes of Savoy are buried. Take N 201 16 km (10 miles) north to Aix-les-Bains, a Victorian spa town that has lost much of its luster, and then either follow the *tour du lac* around Lac du Bourget or take the boat (summer only) from the main port to the abbey. There is a recorded tour of the church and tombs in French as well as in English. There is also a museum with displays on the life and history of the abbey. Hautecombe is still used as a burial place—Umberto II, the last king of Italy, was buried here in 1983—but the Benedictine monks fled the grounds just last year in the face of the tourist invasion. South of the abbey, perched in seclusion on a hillside above the lake, rises the **Ombremont**, a gorgeous 20-room, two-suite inn. With tranquil gardens and magnificent views from the dining terrace and most of the rooms, the Ombremont offers an excellent value in the luxury class. The restaurant is also first-rate.

Aix-les-Bains has been popular with tourists since the

Romans began coming here to take the cure in its thermal baths. The **Thermes Nationaux**, just east of the train station overlooking the town and the lake, are open all year. The modern facilities were built atop the old Roman baths, the ruins of which are still visible in the cellar. The ruins of the **Arc de Campanus** and the **Temple de Diane**, the most significant Roman monuments in the Savoy, are in the museum behind the tourist office across from the Thermes Nationaux. Aix also has a beautiful lakefront promenade, several fine parks, and many beautiful Victorian buildings. In fact, the beauty of the place inspired the poet Alphonse de Lamartine both to fall in love and to write some of his finest verse here. The **Musée du Docteur-Faure**, next to the Thermes, houses a fine collection of pre-Impressionist art.

Annecy

If Chambéry is the historic capital of the Savoy, Annecy, 49 km (30 miles) northeast of Chambéry on A 41, is its spiritual capital. It was the home of Saint François de Sales, the patron saint of arts and letters, and when Geneva succumbed to the Reformation in the 16th century, Annecy became a regional capital. Magnificently situated on Lac d'Annecy across from imposing peaks, Annecy today is a prosperous and growing city that has become an extremely popular vacation spot.

Its **old city** is almost too charming: 17th-century buildings painted in pastel oranges and reds line the trickling rivers and canals, and an excellent flea market takes over the streets and squares on the last Saturday of every month. Annecy bustles with touristy shops and restaurants, and it is necessary to be careful about what you buy and where you eat. The renovated **Auberge du Lyonnais**, at 9, rue de la République, has an excellent quai-side location in the heart of the old city and good, straightforward French food. If you're feeling more upscale, try the **Auberge de l'Eridan**, 7, avenue de Chavoires, on the lake just north of town. This award-winning restaurant is elegant in every respect, with a fine view of the water and food that ranks with the best anywhere. Reserve several weeks in advance, and be prepared to spend a fortune; Tel: 50-66-22-04.

Annecy's château, beautifully restored after hundreds of years of abandonment, sits on a small hill above the old city and provides an excellent view. Along the lakefront are the public gardens and the refreshingly large and informal (for France) Parc du Pâquier. The tourist office is in the Centre Bonlieu, a large modern building across from the park; it won't provide much help with local history, but it's a good place to find out about cultural events and hiking in the nearby mountains. It is possible to rent sailboats, motor boats, and pedal boats from June to September at Le Petit Port in Annecy-le-Vieux, and you can swim just about anywhere along the lake. There are also organized boat tours of the lake and a floating restaurant in an old steamboat.

Saint François de Sales is the undisputed local hero. Born to a prominent Savoyard family in 1567, he studied law in Paris but gave up a promising political career at age 26 to take the vows. Named head of the cathedral of St-Pierre, a large but unremarkable church in the center of the old city, Saint François led a bitter struggle against Calvinism in the region. His oratory was said to be "soft as honey" and was so persuasive that his fame spread throughout France. In 1606 he joined the renowned lawyer Antoine Favre in founding the Académie Florimontane, one of the earliest literary societies in Europe. It is still headquartered at 18, rue Ste-Claire, its original location.

In 1608, while living in the beautiful Lambert house at 15, rue Jean-Jacques Rousseau, Saint François wrote *Introduction to the Devoted Life,* a spiritual treatise that was the 17th-century equivalent of a best seller. He was also the sponsor of the first convent in the region devoted to the Virgin, and he was canonized in 1665 (at the church that bears his name just across from the *mairie*) 43 years after his death. His remains lie at the basilica of the Visitation, an agreeable 20th-century structure just south of the old city.

Those who like their historical figures a little more profane might want to pay homage to the writer and philosopher Jean-Jacques Rousseau, who fled to Annecy from his native Geneva in 1728. Madame Louise-Eléonore de Warens took the young refugee in, and they began an idyllic liaison. A bust of Rousseau stands on the site of the former de Warens house in the courtyard of the old episcopal palace.

The **Lac d'Annecy** is unequivocally beautiful; a drive around it makes a good afternoon excursion. The tranquil **St-Germain l'Hermitage**, where Saint François de Sales spent his last days, lies about 16 km (10 miles) from

Annecy on the east side of the lake, off Route D 42. There's a delightful little chapel here and a splendid view of the lake. Just above the church is a nice meadow for picnicking. If you're feeling less rustic, continue up the road to the Col de la Forclaz and have a lunch of traditional French cuisine on the terrace of **La Pricaz** while you watch hang gliders swoop off the ramp next to the restaurant. The drive back down toward the lower lake and Albertville is harrowing but pretty.

On the lake road, D 909A, just south of the turnoff for Route D 42, lies the charming port town of Talloires, where there are two excellent inns. The **Auberge du Père Bise** has 25 rooms and nine suites, lovely grounds, and one of the most prestigious restaurants in France, now run by the daughter of the original owner and still as good. It is essential to make reservations far in advance; Tel: 50-60-72-01. The **Abbaye** occupies a 17th-century abbey. The beauty of its antiques- and tapestry-filled rooms is equaled only by the stunning lakeside location and excellent dining room.

The Countryside

Evian-les-Bains, a dignified old spa town on Lac Léman, is most appealing to gamblers, connoisseurs of fine hotels— the prestigious but stuffy **Royal** offers a superb view from its hilltop park, as well as swimming, golf, and tennis—and those who intend to take the (cold) waters. But for anyone coming from Switzerland (by lake steamer, for example), it's also a good starting point for a summertime driving tour of the Haute Savoie. Begin on D 902 toward Morzine, which passes through the spectacular **Gorges du Pont du Diable** (Devil's Bridge); you can descend for a close look in summer.

From Morzine, Route D 354 meanders over the mountains toward Samoëns, past the ski trails of Les Gets, providing superb vistas and many good opportunities for walking. **Samoëns** is a perfectly tended village of fewer than 2,000 inhabitants. It is well worth a stop, if only for the **Jaysinia**, a remarkable botanic garden devoted to Alpine plants from around the globe. It was the gift of Marie-Louise Jay, a local shepherdess who married a peddler named Ernest Cognacq. Together they made good and founded the Parisian department store La Samaritaine.

From Samoëns it's just a 20-minute drive up to **Cirque du Fer-à-Cheval**, a flat valley floor surrounded by a near-perfect semicircle of towering cliff walls and angular peaks, the highest of which sit directly on the border with Switzerland. In spring and early summer, an incredible array of some 30 waterfalls spills down the mountains. Hiking opportunities range from a quick jaunt up to one of the falls to a 12-hour trek over the mountains to Chamonix. Bicycles are for rent next to the welcome center.

South of the road leading into the cirque is the Maison de la Réserve at **Sixt-Fer-à-Cheval**. It's open at least a few hours a day all year round and is a friendly place that offers helpful information on the flora and fauna of the nearby nature reserve. Sixt itself is a pleasant, low-key town and a good base for serious exploration of the area. Unfortunately, the only direct route from Sixt to Chamonix is on foot. By car, it's necessary to backtrack through Samoëns to Cluses and take the autoroute.

In the spa town of Plateau d'Assy, on the way to Chamonix about 20 minutes off the autoroute north of Le Fayet, is **Notre-Dame-de-Toute-Grâce**, a controversial and fascinating church. Begun in 1937 and consecrated in 1950, the church features the work of a remarkable array of prominent 20th-century artists. The huge mosaic on the front of the building is by Fernand Léger; the painting of Saint François de Sales is by Pierre Bonnard and that of Saint Dominique is by Henri Matisse; the spectacular tapestry over the altar is by Jean Lurçat; and the ceramic just to the right of the entrance is by Marc Chagall. There are sculptures by Jacques Lipchitz and Germaine Richier and wood carvings by the Savoyard artist Demaison. The overall effect is sacrilegious for some—in part because it is dedicated to the Virgin and her powers of comforting the afflicted (this is a spa town, remember)—but wonderful for lovers of modern art. Be sure to see the crypt, too (entrance in the back).

The Chamonix–Mont Blanc area southeast of Samoëns and due east of Annecy is a hiker's paradise, a fact not lost on Europe's hordes of hikers. The resulting overcrowding would almost make it a destination worth skipping were not **Mont Blanc** such a truly grand and powerful sight. You'll need a guide to climb the glacier-covered peak itself, but many easier walks yield great views of the massive mountain. If you want to save your strength, take a ski lift up one of the mountains and then walk from there. The tourist office, located near the church and the *mairie* in the old town square at Chamonix, has hiking information; Tel: 50-53-00-24.

The town of **Chamonix** today may make you wish you'd been there 30 years ago; its charms are somewhat swamped by new development and tourists. The town claims to be the world capital of mountaineering, and its guide school is renowned and exclusive; only recently has the school admitted members not born in Chamonix. The small mountaineering museum, with its display of primitive early equipment, shows just how brave the early climbers were. (See also Skiing, below.)

Chamonix has no shortage of restaurants; the best is **Albert I**er, at 119, impasse du Montenvers, with its pleasant dining room, flower-filled garden, and refined traditional cuisine. The address is also home to a friendly family hotel; ask for a room with a view of the mountains. Perched on a hillside just outside Chamonix is the beautiful **Auberge du Bois Prin**, an 11-room country inn that boasts tastefully decorated (and pricey) rooms and exceptional views; its fine restaurant is run by the proprietors of the Albert I er. Advance reservations are crucial in high season; Tel: 50-53-33-51.

From Chamonix take N 212 south through the resorts of St-Gervais-les-Bains and Megève and the lush, meandering canyons of the Gorges de l'Arly. A turn to the west at Ugine will take you back toward Annecy, while continuing south on N 212 will bring you to Albertville. This ugly industrial town has nothing to recommend it except its convenient location at a train and road intersection; this situation is what led organizers to choose Albertville as host of the 1992 Winter Olympic Games, although the town itself is not a sports center. Most of the Olympic events will be scattered throughout the numerous ski resorts within easy reach. Those looking for lodging in Albertville might try the **Million**, the nicest hotel in town, or **La Berjann**, a quiet, moderately priced hotel just outside of town. The elegant restaurant at the Million has made a name for itself as one of the region's finest, thanks to the refined classic cuisine prepared by chef Phillipe Million.

From Albertville, a detour up D 925 to the northeast leads through the charming **Beaufort** region, famous for the excellent cheese made there. (The cheese factory at Beaufort offers tours.) Beaufort is also a good spot to buy local handicrafts, such as wooden household items and pewter mugs and plates. The vacation boom has side-swiped this region (although the hydroelectric boom hit it full force), so it's a bit calmer than some of the neighboring areas.

The Isère valley south of Albertville, served by road and rail, is the access route to some of Europe's best ski stations, including Courchevel, Méribel, Val-Thorens, La Plagne, Les Arcs, Tignes, and Val-d'Isère. The town of Aime has a first-rate 11th-century Romanesque church and a pleasant roadside restaurant called **L'Atre**. At Bourg-St-Maurice, where the rail line terminates, you can head by car toward Italy over Col du Petit St-Bernard (where Hannibal is supposed to have made his fateful crossing of the Alps) or toward Val-d'Isère (for skiing, see below), the 8,900-foot-high Col de l'Iseran, and the **Parc National de la Vanoise**. The park, in the remotest part of the Savoy, has some 300 miles of hiking paths. You can enter the park from almost any of the towns along D 902 out of Val-d'Isère or from N 6 south of the park. The tourist offices at Modane, Val-d'Isère, and Bourg-St-Maurice are helpful, as is the Maison du Parc in Chambéry.

Skiing

Skiing in the French Alps is a serious business: The resorts are huge and well equipped, and though they tend to lack charm, they provide an endless variety of slopes. Unlike North American ski centers, they are usually not organized around a single base lodge. Instead, the newer stations have multiple clusters of apartments, shops, hotels, and concessions; ski lifts and restaurants are strewn far and wide across the massive, treeless expanses of snow. The modern stations were developed primarily as real-estate projects and have acres of cheap, small apartments owned by middle-class families. Most visitors rent these apartments when they come to the resorts for stays of more than a weekend; prices start at about 1,500 francs for a studio during a non-holiday week at a mid-size resort. Bookings for both apartments and hotels can be made easily through the tourist offices at the individual resorts.

Typical of the newer resorts are Courchevel, Méribel, and Val-Thorens, which are linked by ski lifts and together make up an area called **Les Trois Vallées**. **Courchevel** is for the ultra-chic; it boasts many luxury hotels, the fanciest being the new **Byblos des Neiges** (sister to the Byblos in St-Tropez) and the **Bellecôte**, with an "elegant rustic" decor. **Méribel** caters to families and attracts many British visitors; both resorts have skiing to suit every taste. A comfortable hotel in Méribel located beside the slopes is the **Grand**

Coeur. Mid-size and quiet, it also has a good restaurant serving hearty French cooking. **Val-Thorens** has extensive off-trail skiing possibilities and exceptional high-altitude runs, which allow for summer skiing. As in Courchevel and Méribel, there are numerous hotels in Val-Thorens from which to choose, but the best is the elegant chalet-style **Fitz Roy.** For all three resorts remember to pack appropriate après-ski attire; discos, piano bars, concert halls, and movie theaters make for an active nightlife.

La Plagne is another large, modern resort, especially good for beginning and intermediate skiers. Experts might be frustrated by the abundance of broad, gentle trails; only the spectacular runs from the Bellecôte glacier offer a real challenge. La Plagne also has limited summer skiing. Neighboring **Les Arcs**, accessible by cable car from Bourg-St-Maurice, has 73 ski lifts and attracts many international visitors.

Farther up the Isère valley, Val-d'Isère and Tignes are the best destinations for accomplished skiers. The hometown of Olympic skiing champion Jean-Claude Killy, **Val-d'Isère** is a real village that existed long before the skiing boom, and its facilities are second to none. You'll find a variety of hotels here in all price ranges. A good choice is the **Blizzard,** with comfortable rooms, pleasant service, and a nightclub just downstairs. The mountains above Val-d'Isère are very high and offer many harrowing expert runs and superb off-trail skiing. **Tignes**, which shares much of the same skiing domain, is a newer resort complex several miles away. Both are popular with a young, fast crowd, drawn in part by the hopping nightlife in Val-d'Isère.

Chamonix, a family resort in the summer, becomes younger and more hip during the ski season. The ski installations are spread across the valley and are not linked with one another, so it's necessary to choose your destination carefully according to your aptitude; Chamonix, therefore, is not ideal for a group including both expert and novice skiers. (For Chamonix see also The Countryside, above.) **Les Grands Montets** at Argentière, up the valley from Chamonix, is the best all-purpose ski center in the area, with a nice mix of expert, intermediate, and novice runs.

A special attraction in Chamonix for those who ski reasonably well is **La Vallée Blanche**, the glacier-covered canyon that tumbles down from Mont Blanc. There are serveral off-trail runs here that are recommended for advanced skiers only. The strenuous but magnificent descents begin with a 550-yard hike down from the ski lift at 12,466 feet and end near town 24 km (15 miles) and the better part of the day later. La Vallée Blanche is a glacier, not a ski slope, and thus cannot be negotiated without a guide. The Compagnie des Guides de Chamonix Mont Blanc (Maison de la Montagne, 190 place de l'Eglise, 74400 Chamonix; Tel: 50-53-00-88) offers trips for one to four people for about 750 francs; individuals and couples can also join group outings.

For a slightly different traditional skiing experience, try the domain called **Les Portes du Soleil**, on the Swiss border in the northeast corner of the Haute Savoie. It centers on **Avoriaz**, a modern resort done with more taste than some others, and includes a string of nine small ski centers, some in France and some in Switzerland. Except at Avoriaz itself, the lift installations are less comprehensive than elsewhere. Connections between the different ski areas are not always easy, but the smaller villages are pleasantly low-key. As its name indicates, the region is very sunny, but it is not especially high and is best for intermediate skiers.

In the southern Alps, the biggest ski centers are L'Alpe d'Huez and Les Deux-Alpes. **L'Alpe d'Huez**, one of the oldest ski centers in France and the site of Jean-Claude Killy's heroics in the 1968 Winter Olympics, has completed a 750 million-franc upgrade. It offers a fine array of long, uncrowded, high-altitude expert trails, as well as a good beginners' area. **Les Deux-Alpes**, also quite high, has summer skiing.

The ski season extends from December to April, but good snow is not assured outside of January, February, and March. Indeed, the lack of snow during most of the season over the past three years has dealt a blow to the economic health of the region, the most hard hit being the low-altitude resorts and those with exposure to the sun during most of the day. Certain of the smaller resorts have declared bankruptcy, but the larger resorts have managed to cope by offering summer sports activities such as horseback riding, hiking, and tennis, using a "fresh air" or "outdoor health" twist to their promotions. A dozen or so resorts at high altitudes in the northern Alps—whose turnover normally represents 50 percent of the skiing industry in France—have even increased business, profiting from the lack of snow elsewhere. Overall, however, the poor skiing conditions have managed to put a halt to what has been a booming industry in France up until now.

Snow or no snow, if at all possible avoid the Christmas holidays and mid-February, when French schools take their winter break. Weekend ski traffic can be horrendous, especially along the Isère valley. The only way to avoid it is to travel late at night.

The 1992 Winter Olympics (from February 8 to February 23) will take place at no fewer than ten venues throughout the Savoy, with still other sites for the Olympic Village and the press center—which explains the proud signs proclaiming "Ville Olympique" at every other bend in the road. Downhill skiing will take place at Val d'Isère, Les Meunières, and Méribel (which will also host hockey); speed skiing will be at Les Arcs, ski jumping at Courchevel, bobsledding at La Plagne, artistic and acrobatic skiing at Tignes, and cross-country skiing at Les Saisies. Only the opening and closing ceremonies and the skating events will be in Albertville.

THE DAUPHINÉ

Despite the extensive reach of the Savoyard empire, it never succeeded in absorbing the Dauphiné to the immediate south. The Dauphiné was an independent feudal kingdom from the early 11th century until 1349, when the mercurial King Humbert II, bankrupt after the Crusades, sold his domain to Philippe VI of France. This is not to say that the Dauphiné was a peaceful place. Fierce wars with the Italian kingdoms from 1494 to 1515 brought Pierre Terrail Bayard, the *chevalier sans peur et sans reproche* ("the knight without fear and without faults"), to prominence as lieutenant-general of the Dauphiné. Religious wars racked the region in the second half of the 16th century, when the indomitable general and politician François de Lesdiguières ruled as a virtual viceroy. Later the Dauphiné was in the vanguard of the French Revolution; some say the Revolution started with the "day of tiles" in 1788, when the Grenoble citizenry erected barricades and fought off royal troops with roof tiles in reaction to edicts from Louis XVI that threatened local sovereignty.

Grenoble

The history of the Dauphiné is inseparable from the history of Grenoble, a bustling and picturesque city at the junction of the Drac and Isère rivers, 55 km (34 miles) south of Chambéry on route A 41, and 104 km (65 miles) southeast of Lyon on A 48. The Romans built an important fortified settlement here called Gratianopolis in honor of the emperor Gratian; from that came the name Grenoble. Today Grenoble is a major regional capital with an important university, a budding high-tech industry, and a solid but unimposing tourist infrastructure. It is also a good example of intelligent urban planning, with a sparkling downtown shopping district served by a new tram line, and controlled urban expansion.

While significantly larger than Annecy or Chambéry, Grenoble is still small enough to be navigated easily. The city's most luxurious hotel is the modern **Park Hôtel**, on the place Paul Mistral near the Hôtel de Ville. Calm and comfortable, it looks out over the Grésivaudan Valley—so loved by Stendhal—and the Belledonne mountains. Grenoble is an excellent place to get a reasonably priced top-flight meal. At **L'Escalier**, 6, place de Lavalette, old stone walls combine with ultra-contemporary furniture and fixtures to stunning effect; the atmosphere is informal, the clientele young professionals, and the food excellent. Try tiny and friendly **A Ma Table**, at 92, cours Jean-Jaurès, for fish specialties (reserve; Tel: 76-96-77-04).

If you like to begin your sightseeing with a proper panorama, take the cable car from the riverbank north of the old town up to the **Bastille**, a set of early 19th-century fortifications perched on the big hill overlooking the city. On the Bastille you can scramble around the chaotic collection of archways, stairways, and tunnels that once defended Grenoble against invasion from the north, then stroll back down to the city (cable-car tickets are one-way or round trip, but the half-hour walk down is more scenic). If you go by foot, stop at the **Musée Dauphinois**, located in an old cloister. The museum has a fascinating multimedia exhibit on the evolution of village life in the region, but no English translations are available. However, non–French speakers can still enjoy the paintings that evoke the mystical spirits of the mountains.

At the bottom of the hill is a pizzeria-lined quay, and just across the photogenic bridge is the **old town**. The Flamboyant Gothic building near the river is the late 15th-century Palais de Justice, home of the original Dauphinois parliament. Across the place St-André to the right is the home of Lesdiguières, complete with a tower dating from the 14th century. The building now houses the **Musée Stendhal**, with objects and temporary exhibits honoring the novelist (born Marie-Henri Beyle), one of the city's most famous sons.

A piece of the old Roman wall is visible near the garish Maison de Tourisme. The 14th-century Tour de l'Ile on the quai Jongkind is another interesting site, part of Grenoble's early fortifications. The **Musée des Beaux-Arts**, or Musée de la Peinture et de la Sculpture, facing the botanical gardens near place de Verdun, has one of France's better collections of contemporary art, and its classical collections are among the best to be found in a provincial museum.

Outside Grenoble, mountains spread out in every direction. To the southwest lies the regional park of **Vercors**, which, unlike the national parks, is relatively crowded and not very wild. The park offers courses on the natural features of the area and instruction in rock-climbing, spelunking, and cross-country skiing. The landscape here is gentler and lusher than in the High Alps; the **Gorges de la Bourne**, with its steep, twisting crevasses, is among the more dramatic gorges in the region.

East of Grenoble is high-mountain country, with several major ski stations (L'Alpe d'Huez, Les Deux-Alpes; see Skiing, above) and the national park of **Ecrins**, another high-mountain wilderness park with abundant hiking opportunities. Due south of Grenoble, Route N 85 leads toward Gap, following the route Napoléon took when he made his famous return from Elba. However, the highly touted Route Napoléon is actually just a road with an occasional incongruous statue of the general sitting in a field. It's a pretty ride, though, and a good route south to the Mediterranean coast (and therefore crowded in summer).

From Gap, if you're not heading for the sea, take N 94 or the train northeast to Briançon, which, at an elevation of 4,300 feet, is the highest town in France. You'll pass Lac de Serre-Ponçon, which has an exceptionally lovely lakeside campground and a number of good picnic spots. **Briançon** is a spectacular, unsung little town set in a high mountain pass almost on the Italian border. Its strategic position explains the remarkable fortifications, a masterpiece of protection built by Louis XIV's famous engineer Vauban. The old town is surrounded by layered, jutting walls; and a string of nine forts lines ridges around the city. The defenses were put to their most serious test in 1815, when an Austro-Savoyard army, which had already seized most of the Dauphiné, laid siege to the town.

Briançon held out against an attacking army 20 times as strong for four months, until the treaty of Paris was signed. Since then it's been known as *"petit ville, grand renom"* ("little city, big reputation").

Founded as the Gallo-Roman settlement of Brigantium, Briançon has the feel of a place apart, and indeed its political history is unusual; it was long an autonomous semi-republic, called an *escarton,* which had purchased its right to self-government. Its pure air gave it a minor reputation as a spa; now Briançon is trying to build its tourist appeal with a new ski lift linking it to nearby ski resorts. If you're spending the night here, the modest but friendly hotel **Vauban** is a good choice. Modern yet warm, it backs onto a pleasant tree-filled garden and has its own restaurant, which serves straightforward French fare.

About 16 km (10 miles) northwest of Briançon on the N 91 in the resort town of Le Monêtier-les-Bains is the **Auberge du Choucas**, an 18th-century farmhouse that's been turned into a cozy, rustic retreat. This exceedingly welcoming inn has an excellent restaurant and is a good base for outdoor activities.

GETTING AROUND

Annecy, Chambéry, Grenoble, and Geneva are the gateways to the Alps. Frequent TGV service puts all four cities within three and a half hours of Paris by rail, and the highway connections are also good, if somewhat slower. It's not worth flying from Paris, but if you're starting from outside the country, Geneva, with its international airport, might be the best gateway. From Italy, the tunnels of Mont Blanc and Fréjus, as well as several seasonal mountain roads, provide auto access.

Despite occasional heavy traffic, the Alps are indisputably car country. Trains serve the major river valleys to Chamonix, Bourg-St-Maurice, and Briançon, and there are buses to the big resort towns, but unless you're headed for a single destination you'll be much better off driving yourself. The A 41 autoroute provides the basic north–south link west of the mountains, and from there the Routes Nationales—along with the smaller A 40 autoroute to Passy just before Chamonix—bring you into the high country along the river valleys. Extensive road work is now under way in preparation for the Olympics: The first part of the autoroute has opened, and work on the second half should be completed by early 1992. The N 90 from Albertville to Bourg-St-Maurice has been enlarged to four lanes as far as

Moûtiers, and another lane will be added to the final stretch by the end of 1991. New pieces of autoroute have replaced parts of the N 6 between Pont-Royal and the Tunnel de Fréjus, and all roads around Albertville are being improved. Secondary roads follow all manner of improbable routes through the mountains, where the going tends to be slow but scenic. Outside of July and August, check with the tourist office before planning an elaborate touring itinerary; any route that doesn't involve extensive backtracking will cross mountain passes that are not open all year round. Tire chains are a good idea in winter even if you're sticking to the main roads, and they're equally advisable in spring and fall if you're planning any high-altitude routes. A word of warning: Something about the mountain air makes people drive like fools on the narrow, winding roads; about all you can do is remain calm.

For information on the facilities, lodging, and transportation at all the French ski resorts, contact the **Association des Mairies des Stations Français des Sports d'Hiver**, 61, boulevard Haussmann, 75008 Paris; Tel: (01) 47-42-23-32; Fax: 42-66-15-94. They do not book accommodations, and not all representatives speak English. Their recording in French of daily ski conditions at major resorts can be heard by calling Tel: 42-66-64-28.

The summer tourist season is short—essentially limited to July and August—and crowded. Hikers can get detailed information on trails and refuges from the Maison de la Randonnée, 7, rue Voltaire, 38000 Grenoble (Tel: 76-51-76-00) and from the various tourist offices mentioned above. Travel in the spring and fall is a mixed bag; there aren't many tourists, but many places are closed and the weather is fickle.

ACCOMMODATIONS REFERENCE

▶ **Abbaye**. Chemin des Moines, 74290 **Talloires**. Tel: 50-60-77-33; Telex: 385307; Fax: 50-60-78-81; in U.S., (212) 696-1323.

▶ **Albert Ier**. 119, impasse du Montenvers, 74400 **Chamonix**. Tel: 50-53-05-09; Telex: 380779; Fax: 50-55-95-48; in U.S., (212) 477-1600 or (800) 366-1510.

▶ **Auberge du Bois Prin**. 169, Chemin de l'Hermine, Les Moussoux 74400 **Chamonix**. Tel: 50-53-33-51; Fax: 50-53-48-75; in U.S., (212) 696-1323.

▶ **Auberge du Choucas**. 17, rue de la Fruitière, 05220 **Le Monêtier-les-Bains**, Serre-Chevalier. Tel: 92-24-42-73; Fax: 92-24-51-60.

► **Auberge du Père Bise**. Route du Port, 74290 **Talloires**. Tel: 50-60-72-01; Fax: 50-60-73-05; in U.S., (212) 696-1323.

► **Bellecôte**. 73120 **Courchevel**. Tel: 79-08-10-19; Fax: 79-08-17-16.

► **La Berjann**. 33, route de Tours, 73200 **Albertville**. Tel: 79-32-47-88.

► **Byblos des Neiges**. Jardin Alpin, 73120 **Courchevel**. Tel: 79-08-12-12; Telex: 980580; Fax: 79-08-19-38; in U.S., (212) 477-1600 or (800) 366-1510.

► **Fitz Roy**. 73440 **Val-Thorens**. Tel: 79-00-04-78.

► **Grand Coeur**. 73550 **Méribel-les-Allues**. Tel: 79-08-60-03; Fax: 79-08-58-38.

► **Hôtel de Château de Challes**. 73190 **Challes-les-Eaux**. Tel: 79-72-86-71; Fax: 79-72-83-83; in U.S., (800) 528-1234 or (800) 334-7234.

► **Hotel le Blizzard**. 73150 **Val-d'Isère**. Tel: 79-06-02-07; Fax: 79-06-04-94.

► **Million**. 8, place de la Liberté, 73200 **Albertville**. Tel: 79-32-25-15; Fax: 79-32-25-36.

► **Ombremont**. N 504, 73370 **Le Bourget-du-Lac**. Tel: 79-25-00-23; Telex: 980832; Fax: 79-25-25-77; in U.S., (212) 696-1323.

► **Park Hôtel**. 10, place Paul-Mistral, 38000 **Grenoble**. Tel: 76-87-29-11; Telex: 320767; Fax: 76-46-49-88; in U.S., (212) 477-1600 or (800) 366-1510.

► **Au Prince Eugène de Savoie**. Esplanade Curial, 73000 **Chambéry**. Tel: 79-85-06-07; Fax: 79-85-61-01.

► **Les Princes**. 4, rue de Boigne, 73000 **Chambéry**. Tel: 79-33-45-36; Fax: 79-70-31-47.

► **Royal**. 74500 **Evian-les-Bains**. Tel: 50-75-14-00; Telex: 385759; Fax: 50-75-38-40; in U.S., (212) 838-3110 or (800) 223-6800.

► **Vauban**. 13, avenue Général-de-Gaulle, 05100 **Briançon**. Tel: 92-21-12-11.

PROVENCE AND THE COTE D'AZUR

By Stephen O'Shea with Georgia I. Hesse

For many people, Provence and the Riviera fuse into a glamorous, sun-splashed picture of the south of France and the good—or perhaps naughty—life. They think of the Fitzgeralds sipping Champagne from slippers, of White Russians imploring roulette wheels, and of lithe jet-setters peeling off to bronze themselves to perfection. All of these images are appropriate, thank God, but they are just a small fraction of what the smiling land of Provence has to offer. For every cosmopolitan treat on the Riviera there is a peaceful hilltop village in the hinterland, and for every sumptuous meal in a swank seaside restaurant there is a simple feast of olives, goat cheese, melons, and wine in a rural paradise.

The Riviera, or Côte d'Azur, comprises the southeastern coast of Provence, a region that stretches from the lower Rhône Valley to the Maritime Alps near the Italian border. A richly diverse land, Provence includes the towering mountains north of Nice and the gentle plains around Arles, the unearthly white cliffs near Marseille and the placid interior valleys east of Avignon. Although the cosmopolitan Côte d'Azur no longer resembles its rustic cousins, it has nonetheless not lost its roots. The traveller has only to step north of Cannes to find a village as sleepily Provençal as anything that sprang from the imagination of playwright Marcel Pagnol.

For our purposes it's best first to compare the two areas—greater Provence and its wayward, sophisticated Côte d'Azur—and then to treat them separately, for they are, as far as the traveller is concerned, two entirely different destinations. However, the real problem lies not in which one to choose but in how to leave the southeast of France once you've seen it. Long ago the richest of the Roman Empire's provinces—whence its name and its fascinating classical heritage—Provence remains an ideal place to colonize. Its superb climate and cultural treasures, along with the bounty of its land and the beauty of its nature, make the region one of those rare lands where the sensitive have two pleasant urges: to create or to do nothing at all. While you make up your mind, museums, galleries, festivals, historic cities, ageless villages, and delicious cuisine are all here to help you pass the time.

MAJOR INTEREST

Provence
Art
Roman and Greek ruins
Early Christian antiquities
Vineyards
Village life

Côte d'Azur
Seaside resorts
Perched villages
Gambling
Modern-art museums
Roman ruins

The similarities between Provence and the Côte d'Azur run deep. Even in the glitziest parts of the Riviera there are traces of Provence—a Latin flavor in both food and temperament, a Roman cultural heritage, and a certain laid-back lifestyle that typifies the Mediterranean. When you enter Provence–Côte d'Azur you know you have arrived in the Mediterranean: The intense sunlight, blue skies, dry climate, olive trees, chalky hills, and red-tiled roofs are unmistakable.

But Provence is more than just a Mediterranean land. Provençal is a style, a language, and a history—starting with the Roman Republic and Empire, developing into a kingdom ruled independently of France until the 15th century, and then becoming a special-statute state of the ancien régime—until the French Revolution created Provence as an administrative region.

If Provence, to the visitor, is the timeless producer of simple joys, the Côte d'Azur is the flashy starlet—and the two have their respective audiences among foreign (that is, non-Provençal) visitors. Resorts such as St-Tropez, Antibes, and Cannes appeal to the practitioners of France's great contribution to civilization, unabashed hedonism. With its spectacular vistas, of both the human and the natural varieties, the French Riviera has deservedly become one of the most popular playgrounds on the Mediterranean. A succession of 20th-century artists, a breed not insensitive to the pleasures of the flesh, was drawn to the cypress-covered hills overlooking the sea, bequeathing the region an impressive collection of galleries and museums. Sophisticates, cultural connoisseurs of every sort, and the plain old filthy rich made their homes here as well, their influence evident in the excellent jazz and arts festivals that punctuate the Riviera's long summer season. And even Monte-Carlo, its blueblood clientele diluted as exiled European aristocracies grow poorer with each passing generation, still seems the only place in the world where the phrase "Bond, James Bond" might conceivably be uttered in real life.

In Provence proper, however, you hear that the conspicuous worldliness of the *côte* is a trifle vulgar. Admittedly, this sentiment is most often expressed by the Parisian literati who flock southward for their summer-long cocktail parties amid the olive groves of the Alpilles and the Vaucluse, but it does hint at a fundamental difference between the two regions: At its best, the Côte d'Azur is richly sensual; Provence, on the other hand, is uncommonly sensuous. Only the truly oblivious traveller can fail to notice that the striking landscapes of Provence are for the lover of color and smells, the purple fields of lavender mixing with the gentle scent of lime on the outskirts of age-old villages. "This country," wrote one admirer of the plain near Arles, "seems to me as beautiful as Japan for clarity of atmosphere and gay color effects. Water forms patches of lovely emerald or rich blue in the landscape ... the pale orange of the sunsets makes the fields appear blue. The sun is a splendid yellow." The passing of a century has not made Vincent van Gogh's appraisal any less true.

Still, the modern era has not left the region untouched.

Along with the Côte d'Azur, the cities of Provence have become France's sun belt. Millions of northern French have migrated south to escape gray skies and city pressures. Some have been retirees, but a large part are among the most educated and highest-paid workers in France: doctors, lawyers, engineers, and administrators. Even these new Provençaux feel a kinship with those who have been here for generations—united by climate, the proximity of the sea, and the easygoing lifestyle.

In 1962, another wave of immigrants hit the region: *pieds-noirs,* French colonists returning to the mainland after Algeria achieved its independence. The *pieds-noirs* brought a new, large segment of political and social influence: Politically conservative, they share a common North African culture.

The *pieds-noirs* were followed by waves of ethnic Algerian, Moroccan, and Tunisian immigrant workers. Economic stagnation in France in the late 1970s and early 1980s and a slowness to assimilate foreigners have caused a backlash of prejudice against these non-French immigrants. As a result Provence and the Côte d'Azur have both shifted to the far right. (Until recently, Marseille, Avignon, and Arles had a left-leaning political tradition, while the wealthier Nice, Cannes, and Antibes were conservative strongholds.) Shifting political values aside, Provence and the Côte d'Azur officially form one of 23 regional governments in France. On a practical level, this means a strong regional network for tourism and cultural affairs.

The real binding factor in Provence is the language, Provençal being a regional variation of the old Occitan. Today the dialect itself is quickly disappearing, but its lasting effects can be heard here even in the accents of the young. Strong local differences within Provence can be heard as well. Because Provençal was never a written language, a great ancient oral tradition of tales, legends, and proverbs has been and continues to be passed down.

LA PROVENCE

To fly into Marseille-Marignan airport to visit Provence is somehow to miss the whole point. Provence should un-

fold itself gradually, slowly, deliberately. Provence is as much a state of mind as it is a geographic entity.

In nearly every corner of Provence, small, wondrous discoveries await those willing to find them. Even the most unlikely and unheard-of village can offer an archaeological treasure, a 12th-century church, a beautiful view, or a culinary delight.

So forget the plane. Instead, take the train from Paris or Lyon; Provence is best discovered from the north southward. Rent a car at Avignon or Marseille and cherish the ancient, ever-changing landscape. James Pope-Hennessy, one of the great observers of the region, wrote in his lyrical *Aspects of Provence:* " ... this rich countryside has been lived in and lived over for many centuries. Up in the hillside vineyards, down amongst the groves of twisted olive trees, you can smell antiquity." Even the cities conspire to bewitch the traveller, each competing to win admirers with its distinct charms: Roman Arles or papal Avignon, ragged Marseille or elegant Aix.

But it is the village that lies at the heart of Provençal charm. Many hamlets appear to be caught in a lazy trance, just like the inevitable clutch of men playing boules in the village square. "I'll come see you in the morning—at about dusk" may be the northern French wisecrack about the unhurried Provençal way of life, but it contains more than a trace of jealousy. Ford Madox Ford, another convert to the cult of Provence, knew the value of indolently sitting with a glass of wine as the sunlight plays on the plane trees and the walls of an ocher village. His poem about just such an afternoon is called "On Heaven."

Although he may have overstated his case, there can be no doubt that Provence, if not perfect, is at least a very magical place. Stories about imaginary beasts abound in its traditional folklore, the best-known being the child-gobbling Medieval monster, the Tarasque, still seen swimming in the Rhône near Tarascon. The countryside itself adds to the spell. The flower-filled fields of St-Rémy-de-Provence abruptly give way to the stark white peaks of the Alpilles midway between Avignon and Arles, the only pass through them flanked by eerie Roman ruins. An innocuous road south of Vaison-la-Romaine becomes a treacherous defile that opens out suddenly onto the sublime monastery of Sénanque. In the midst of the green orchards of a valley in the Vaucluse east of Avignon stands a gentle abutment that is violently red, its crowning village, Roussillon, a painter's palette of 17 different shades from scarlet to orange. Provence stimulates the imagination, even as it rewards the senses with a rosemary-filled breeze, the pungent cooking odor of garlicky *aïoli,* or the soothing sound from a centuries-old village dovecote. As the sun sets and Vincent's starry starry night embraces the countryside, the traveller immediately knows why in its long history the kingdom of Provence has been coveted by so many, so often and so ardently.

Although the Phoceans (Greeks from ancient Ionia on the west coast of Asia Minor) settled Marseille six centuries before Christ and were soon followed by other Greeks, the conquerors who were first to leave their mark on the land were the Romans. From 102 B.C., the year the consul Marius beat back the Teutons just north of what is now Aix-en-Provence, to the disintegration of the empire five centuries later, this swath of fertile land was one of Rome's wealthiest provinces. Its ancient amphitheaters, aqueducts, arenas, and bridges (the outstanding vestiges are in Arles, St-Rémy, Orange, and Vaison) attesting to its importance in classical times, the region was later swept by successive waves of Alemanni, Visigoths, Moors, and just about every other marauding people of the Dark Ages. When temporary political consolidation came in 972 under Count Guillaume, Provence then entered into centuries of checkerboard development: Part went to the Holy Roman Empire, Orange fell to the Duchy of Nassau, and the counts of Toulouse and Barcelona quarreled incessantly over their rival Provençal fiefdoms. While these Medieval princes deployed their armies amid the almond groves and laid siege to fortified villages, such rich cities as Aix became centers of art and poetry. In a great flowering of the Provençal language, 12th-century troubadours composed songs of courtly romance that were performed by itinerant singers—called *jongleurs*—in the castles of the region, most notably at the spectacular site of Les Baux-de-Provence. Such forgotten troubadour poets as Marcabru, Bernard de Ventadour, and Raimbaut d'Orange shaped a new ideal of love between a knight and his lady in what a French historian has aptly termed "the precocious spring of modern Western culture."

However short-lived that spring of the troubadours, politics and religion soon stepped in to add further complexity to the Provençal patchwork. The papal state centered at Avignon became the northern Vatican, as popes and antipopes held worldly court by the banks of the Rhône, thus encouraging the development of the arts and sciences. Even after the popes had returned to Rome, their Provençal holdings, known as the Comtat Venaissin, functioned as a refuge for those made unwelcome in the kingdom of France. Refugees poured into this corner of Provence, and the market towns of Carpentras and Cavaillon now possess those rarities of French religious architecture: ornate 18th-century synagogues.

When an expansionist Parisian monarchy finally laid hold of Provence in 1481 (the Comtat Venaissin fell to French revolutionaries in 1791), the same ills of absolutist centralism felt by other provinces of France befell this southern region. During the Renaissance and the Enlightenment, Provençal gradually disappeared as the common spoken language. In the 19th century, dramatic economic and social changes—railroads, industry, and tourism—further eroded what was once Provence's dreamy isolation from the bustle of Paris.

In reaction to the changes, a group led by the poet Frédéric Mistral founded a movement—called le Félibrige—advocating a return to the old traditions. The organization tried to revive a Provence of legend: a peaceful, rural community of peasant farmers, bourgeois, and fishermen held together by the Provençal language—and a great faith in the Roman Catholic Church.

Reality lay elsewhere, however. Since the last decades of the 19th century, Provence has developed into a modern and technologically oriented region whose past is nevertheless still stamped on nearly every corner of every town.

It is that living past, where tradition and the love of the good life still abide, that makes Provence so compelling. Although not without its harsh aspects—few things are so demoralizing as the insistent mistral wind that rushes down the Rhône for days on end—Provence is a gentle and beguiling region. To return to the enthusiastic anachronisms of Ford Madox Ford: "[In] a peasantry that has seen many of its sons ennobled because of poetic gifts . . . that has seen painting and sculpture held in high honor, there arose and continued the tradition that occupation with one art or the other is a proper thing for sound men."

MAJOR INTEREST IN PROVENCE

Avignon
Palais des Papes
Rhône wine country to the north

Orange
Roman theater and ruins

The Vaucluse
Vaison-la-Romaine
Abbey of Sénanque
Villages of Coulon valley

The Alpilles
Greco-Roman ruins at St-Rémy
Fortress at Les Baux-de-Provence
Montmajour Abbey

Arles
Van Gogh colors and landscapes
Roman amphitheater and theater
Church of St-Trophime

Aix-en-Provence
Cézanne interest

Marseille
Vieux Port
Bouillabaisse
Château d'If
Excursion to the *calanques*

Provençal Cuisine

Sun is one constant in Provence and on the Côte d'Azur.
The olive is the other.

In the south of France man has been eating the olive,
crushing it for oil, and making salad bowls from its wood
for a very long time. The trees along the Riviera are
thought to have been introduced by the Greeks more
than 2,500 years ago, and nobody knows how long the
Greeks had cultivated them before that. Quite simply, the
olive gave birth to the art of Provençal cookery. A local
saying confirms this: "A fish is an animal that is found
alive in water and dead in oil."

Garlic is nearly as pervasive as the olive, as is the
tomato. When any dish on a menu appears *à la provençale,* you can be certain it will be served with cooked
tomatoes seasoned with garlic.

Following are some of the Provençal dishes that entice
travellers to Provence and the Côte d'Azur:

Aïoli. This is simply garlic mayonnaise—*aïl* means garlic. Called "the butter of Provence," "the soul of the

South," and "cream of sun," this wonderful sauce makes an appearance, hot or cold, on vegetable and fish and lobster dishes. In addition to garlic, aïoli contains olive oil (of course), sometimes crushed garlic, egg yolks, ground pepper, and perhaps lemon juice.

Aubergine. The word means eggplant, specifically the small, dark-purple variety. It appears in many guises throughout the region, especially in Nice.

Bouillabaisse. Although everyone agrees this fish stew is the signature Provençal dish, no one agrees on what should be put in it, aside from olive oil, tomatoes, saffron, and fish. The question of what kind of fish is hotly debated, except that *rascasse* (a spiny, coarse fish) must be included; without it, *bouillabaisse* does not exist. Is lobster included, or is it not? Friendships have broken on the rocks of that decision. As the late food writer Waverley Root describes the two schools of thought: "One holds that a man who would put lobster in *bouillabaisse* would poison wells. The other is that a man who would leave it out would starve his children."

Bourride. This savory cream soup, made from bass, cod, and other fish, is particularly popular around Nice and is preferred by some to *bouillabaisse;* unlike the latter, it does not contain shellfish but sometimes uses *aïoli.*

Brandade. This is dried salt cod, usually worked with olive oil, garlic, potatoes, and spices into a kind of mousse. It's a peasant dish, served year-round, and traditionally during the "lean dinner" on Christmas Eve.

Daube. On menus it usually appears as *daube de boeuf à la provençale*—a heavy, slowly cooked, infinitely flavorful stew of marinated beef, Cognac, olive oil, onions, carrots, and spices, to which are added bacon, raw mushrooms, tomatoes, garlic, black olives, and bitter orange peel. Daube takes forever to make, and is worth every minute.

Estouffade. Seen mainly around the Camargue region, *estouffade* is another version of beef stew and sometimes includes lamb as well. Home cooks often make it a day in advance of serving; it freezes extremely well.

Loup or *loup de mer. Loup* is, literally, sea wolf. It's really sea bass, tastily served grilled with fennel or vine shoots. *Loup farci à la niçoise* implies the presence of tomatoes, olives, and mushrooms.

Pan bagnat. The name itself is not French, but Provençal. It means, simply, bathed bread; the bath is of olive oil.

Pan bagnat makes a wonderful midday sandwich, a picnic unto itself. A round bread is sliced in half, hollowed out, soaked in oil, and filled with any number of items in the French repertoire: tomato, green pepper, black olives, garlic, red wine vinegar, radishes, and often tuna. Then it's pressed down until squishy. *Pan bagnat* is often sold on the streets of the Riviera.

Pissaladière. In Italy they say *pissaladière* is an Italian gift to France. In Nice they say it's a French invention predating pizza. In any case, it's delicious and appears everywhere. Everyone has his own version, but basically a large, pie-shaped pastry shell is filled with minced onions, olive oil, crushed garlic, spices, puréed black olives, and topped with strips of anchovies. Sometimes tomato sauce is mixed in.

Pistou. Possibly related to the Genoese sauce *pesto,* *pistou* is actually the special seasoning added to a thick vegetable soup made by mashing together a Gruyère-type cheese, small-leaved basil, garlic, and olive oil. Sometimes in Nice this thick soup (also called *pistou*) includes white beans, tomatoes, and *courgettes* (zucchini).

Raïto. Traditionally, this sauce is served hot with grilled fish, but it's also superb with pasta. It involves many of the Provençal *spécialitiés:* sturdy red wine, garlic, tomatoes, black olives, and many spices.

Ratatouille. Eggplant (*aubergine*) is the essence of this vegetable stew steeped in olive oil: red or yellow peppers, zucchini, tomatoes, onions, garlic, spices, lemon juice, and white wine. It's served both hot and cold, as an accompaniment or a light, complete meal.

Salade niçoise. This is the ultimate salad, a summer feast. As in the case of *bouillabaisse,* some of its ingredients arouse debate. What it must have are tomatoes cut in quarters, cucumber, *fèves* (lima-like beans), artichokes, green peppers, onions, anchovies or *pissala* (anchovies ground into a paste), olives, olive oil, red wine vinegar, and spices. Nowadays, hard-boiled eggs are considered a just addition; purists still frown upon potatoes, but they often appear.

Socca. Made of chickpea flour, *socca* is usually found in pancake form, and is used as a dessert or sold in open-air markets wrapped in brown paper cones. It's also good as an appetizer taken with *apéritifs.*

Tapenade. The apogee of black olive paste, this spread is served on thin toasts, used as a dip for raw vegetables, or diluted with olive oil to serve as a sauce. It is made with capers, garlic, lemon juice, and chopped, fresh basil. Ground anchovies are always mixed with the olive paste.

Bon appétit!

—*Georgia I. Hesse*

AVIGNON

Avignon benefits from a strategic geographic location: on a major north–south water route—the Rhône river—halfway between Spain and Italy. This was partly what led the popes to Avignon in the 14th century. Unfortunately, the city's position also has a climatic disadvantage: the powerful, icy mistral wind that sweeps down the Rhône Valley, particularly in winter, blowing through Avignon's narrow streets and whipping around its large squares. It is said locally that the mistral can "blow the ears off a donkey." Because Avignon is at the northwestern corner of Provence, it is a good place to start a visit to the region, especially if you are arriving from the north.

The first-time visitor is always awestruck by the city's massive Medieval monuments: the imposing Palais des Papes (Popes' Palace), the wall that encircles the city, and the famous bridge where "*on y danse.*" Considering Avignon proper's relatively small size and population (91,000), the weight of history can seem heavy. Lawrence Durrell noted: "The past embalmed it, the present could not alter it." A Provençal proverb cautions: "He who leaves Avignon loses his good sense." Avignon leaves no one indifferent.

For centuries, the city has been a state within a state, a city of tolerance that has welcomed foreigners and political and religious refugees from around Europe in times when freedom and travel were at a premium. Even today, Avignon is among a group of "free" French cities: French law forbids certain released prisoners to live in or near the area of their convicted crime; they must take up residence in a free city—such as Avignon. Political refugees are also sent to live in one of these *villes libres*.

The Walled City

In front of the train station you come face to face with twin stone towers and the outside of the wall that stretches for two and a half miles around the city. Don't be fooled: Despite their Medieval appearance, the towers were con-

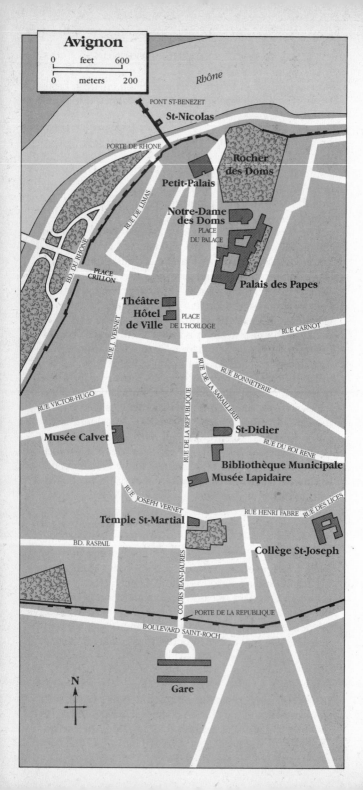

structed in 1863, and most of the wall and ramparts were heavily reconstructed at about the same time and again 30 years later. (The original wall went up between 1359 and 1370 under the direction of Pope Innocent VI.)

Once you are past the gate, the Medieval mirage momentarily vanishes as you confront the bustle of contemporary Avignon—cafés, restaurants, and shops—along the rue de la République. Still, amid the clamor of 20th-century commerce, reminders of a rich past are everywhere to be seen. Every few yards a monument or alluring building stands out. One example: the **Temple St-Martial**, a Benedictine monastery founded in 1378. Major sections of the monastery and its church were destroyed or rebuilt in the 19th century when the boulevard was constructed to join the train station with the Palais des Papes. Avignon's Office de Tourisme now occupies a corner of one of the old buildings.

Farther down the street is the **Musée Lapidaire**, built as a chapel for a Jesuit college in 1620. The building is hailed as one of the most beautiful examples of French Baroque architecture and houses a magnificent collection of antiquities.

Just past the museum and behind the rue de la République is the **church of St-Didier**. This fine example of Provençal Gothic style, constructed during the papal period in 1356, has not been significantly retouched. Next to the church on rue de la Saraillerie is the restaurant **Christian Etienne**. In a town that has more than its share of pretentious restaurants, Christian Etienne is a fine choice. Its owner and chef, Etienne, is a young, energetic Avignon native who learned his trade at the Ritz in Paris. He often comes to the tables to take orders and talk with customers. The fare is light and imaginative, with a Provençal flavor at relatively reasonable prices (Tel: 90-86-16-50). Slightly steeper in price, but universally recognized as one of the best of all Provençal restaurants, is **Hiély** (5, rue de la République; Tel: 90-86-17-07), a gastronomic shrine, especially during the summer theater festival. When not dining there, visiting thespians at Avignon's annual theater festival snooze the afternoons away in the old city's hotel **Europe**, an ornate 19th-century gem.

Nearby on rue Joseph Vernet, off rue de la République, is the **Musée Calvet**, which occupies an elegant 18th-century mansion and houses an impressive collection of paintings and archaeological treasures. Of particular interest is the extensive collection of French paintings from the 16th century to the present. The rue de la République ends at the large **place de l'Horloge**, a pedestrian zone and the center of near-round-the-clock activity during most of the tourist season and especially during the Festival d'Avignon theater extravaganza in July. The several unexceptional outdoor café-restaurants that line one side of the square are constantly packed, providing a captive audience for street performers. Avignon is, in fact, a major meeting place for itinerant musicians, especially in the warm months.

The square's two monumental buildings—the **Hôtel de Ville** and the **Théâtre**—were both heavily reconstructed in the last century. In July, during the Festival d'Avignon, a month-long carnival atmosphere animates this onetime Catholic capital (unlike the sober ambience at Aix's music festival): The town is invaded by thousands of theatergoers, actors, performers of all types, vagabonds, and tourists. The festival has two faces: the official, highly acclaimed Classic Performances at the Théâtre—Shakespeare, Molière, etc., all in French—and the "Festival Off," in which dozens of offbeat and less-established troupes put on performances ranging from one-person shows to traditional plays and experimental theater in various locations around town and in the outskirts (Villeneuve-lès-Avignon; Orange). Avignon has become a showcase for what is best in contemporary French—and European—theater; its only equal is the Edinburgh Festival.

The Palais des Papes

The main show in Avignon is nonetheless the Palais des Papes, just north of the place de l'Horloge. The heavily fortified palace is a reminder that Avignon was—from 1305 to 1378—the capital of Christianity. Contested antipopes stayed until 1417, when the schism between Rome and Avignon ended. To visit this magnificent building is to step back several centuries. Although the revolutionaries of the 1790s stripped the palace of its secular trappings, the immensity of its now-silent audience halls nevertheless evokes the tremendous power of the Medieval papacy. Several vistas from its north windows, looking out over the roofs of Avignon, seem unchanged since the 14th century. The palace is one of the most remarkable buildings in France.

Chance played a part in bringing popes to the city. For years, the popes in Rome consolidated their power over temporal leaders. The new papal position was clear: The pope was the vicar not just of Saint Peter but of Jesus Christ himself. The pope was heir to the spiritual kingdom, directly under God, and therefore was above individual monarchs and territorial rulers. The French kings did not agree and maintained that they were sovereign in matters concerning the Church in France. In 1303 King Philippe le Bel arrested the pope for interfering in the affairs of the French Church. This blow severely weakened the Roman Church.

Two years later Clement V, the former archbishop of Bordeaux, was elected pope. In 1309 he came to Avignon to prepare for a Church council to be held in Vienne, just up the Rhône. Grave security problems in Italy—war and rebellion against the papal state—made his return to Rome unwise.

The next elected pope, in 1316, was Jean XXII, the bishop of Avignon. He, too, decided to stay in his city, and he was installed as pope in the bishop's palace. His successor, Benoît XII, another Frenchman, also chose Avignon as his residence. He ordered the demolition of the bishop's palace and, in its place, the construction in 1336 of a *demeure* worthy of a pope.

Benoît XII was succeeded by Frenchman Clement VI, who not only more than doubled the palace's size but in 1348 purchased Avignon itself from Queen Jeanne of Naples, who was also the countess of Provence. From that moment until the French Revolution, Avignon was a papal state. Several other important buildings date from the early papal period: The **Petit Palais**, at the northern part of the square in front of the palace, was the residence for archbishops and bishops; during the past few years it has become a superb museum of Medieval and Renaissance painting and sculpture, featuring some 400 Italian canvases of the 13th to 16th centuries and regional Avignon paintings from the 14th and 15th centuries. The Italian paintings are special treasures. The **Livrée Ceccano** (now a municipal library), just south of St-Didier church, was built by Cardinal Ceccano, the archbishop of Naples, in 1330. Some of the original painted ceilings remain intact.

Avignon at Apogee

During the popes' residence, Avignon became one of the most important cities of the Western world. Nearly the entire papal administration, including the College of Cardinals, lived here. The city developed significant economic and cultural activities, in part because the Avignon popes were immensely rich from taxes levied on states and church *domaines*. However, Avignon's prestige long outlasted the Avignon popes (the last of them, Grégoire XI, abandoned the city in 1376). The return of the popes to Rome didn't end the story, it only made it more interesting.

After Grégoire's death an Italian pope was elected. Months later the French protested the election, claiming it had been influenced by a menacing Roman population. The French cardinals then elected a second pope (a so-called antipope), who took his seat at Avignon. The Church was now divided in two: England, the German Empire, Poland, Hungary, Bohemia, Flanders, and most of Italy were in favor of the Roman pope; Spain, France, Savoie, Scotland, Sicily, and Portugal were on Avignon's side.

The schism ended in 1417 with the election of a pope seated at Rome. Avignon was governed by Rome until it became French during the Revolution in 1791—a fact the Church didn't accept until six years later.

The Pont d'Avignon

Standing next to the palace is the 12th-century cathedral of Notre-Dame des Doms. Past the cathedral, steps rise to the **Rocher des Doms**, a rocky hill that offers a panoramic view of the valley, the neighboring town of Villeneuve-lès-Avignon, and especially the Pont St-Bénézet, a.k.a. the Pont d'Avignon. To visit the bridge, of which only a partial span and four of the original 22 arches remain, walk westward through the Porte du Rhône, just past the Petit Palais.

Legend has it that an angel appeared before a simple shepherd, Bénézet, and ordered him to build a bridge over the Rhône. Between 1177 and 1185 he built a wooden bridge, which was destroyed in 1226 and then reconstructed in stone. In spanning the river the bridge crossed the small Ile de la Barthelasse. Most of the dancing noted in the song "Sur le Pont d'Avignon" probably took place in taverns located on this island *under* the bridge's arches.

The bridge was also once a place for prayer. The **chapel of St-Nicolas** still stands on the second pillar and is open daily to paid visits. Built in the 13th century on Romanesque lines, the chapel was enlarged in 1513. Over the centuries the ravaging Rhône eroded St-Bénézet's arches, and repeated attempts to rebuild the fallen supports eventually failed. In 1715 the chapel was closed for purposes of worship.

France excells—and Provence excells especially—in the art of blending sophistication in service and cuisine with country comfort and informality. Two examples near Avignon are **Le Prieuré**, across the river in Villeneuve-les-Avignon (in an antique priory), and **Auberge de Noves**, 13 km (8 miles) to the southeast in an elegantly reworked manor house with a notable kitchen. Both are Relais & Châteaux members, and both are expensive, although not unduly so.

RHONE WINE COUNTRY

"The Rhône is a river of wine," writes Alexis Lichine, and he puts the geography nicely: "It drains vineyards on its broad delta plain, along the steep cliffs above Avignon, in the Cévennes and Jura mountains, and around the Lake of Geneva. Yet the only wines to bear the name are those which come from the central section—the Côtes du Rhône."

These *côtes* extend from Lyon in the north to Avignon in the south, a strip about 140 miles long.

In the company of the greatest Bordeaux and Burgundy wines, whose names are shouted aloud, those of the Rhône are whispered: Condrieu, Côte Rôtie, Château Grillet, Gigondas, Hermitage, Saint-Péray, Tavel, and Châteauneuf-du-Pape.

Yet the Rhônes have much to recommend them. They are eminently drinkable, for one thing; for another, usually they are reasonable in price.

The most famous of these is Châteauneuf-du-Pape, and the *pape* (pope) referred to is generally considered to be Pope John XXII, who from 1316 to 1333 built a new castle (*château neuf*) in the sloping hills about 17 km (11 miles) north of Avignon. The château was mostly ruined in 1552 during the Wars of Religion, and its remaining keep was wiped out during bombings on August 20, 1944. Only one evocative façade remains to hint at the majesty of the original.

Even among the worldly, extravagant Avignon popes, John XXII was notorious for high living and debauchery. He slept on an ermine-trimmed pillow shared, it was said, by a nearly endless parade of pretty *demoiselles*. Soon his reputation began to enhance that of his wines. As Frederick Wildman, Jr., reminds us in *A Wine Tour of France,* "He let it be known that his Châteauneuf-du-Pape was not only a glory to taste, but—and he stood as living proof—also a rejuvenator and aphrodisiac of remarkable potency. The fortunes of Châteauneuf-du-Pape were made."

Today **Châteauneuf,** off D 192 halfway between Orange and Avignon and home to about 2,000 inhabitants, most of them wine enthusiasts, is the most interesting village in the valley for the traveller who has time for only one stop.

A few sites in town are worth visiting—notably the **Château des Papes** for its splendid views over the valley—but the main attraction is wine: drinking it, fine dining to accompany it, visiting vineyards, spending a night in seductive surroundings.

The largest estate of Châteauneuf today is **Mont-Redon,** to the north of town on the Route d'Orange. Born as Mourredon in the 14th century, it has been a property of the Plantin family for three generations and is now the largest producer of little-known white Châteauneuf as well as the familiar reds and less highly bred bottles called simply Côtes-du-Rhône. Cellar visits are conducted on weekdays; the tasting and sales room is open daily.

A lighter, more "modern" Châteauneuf is produced by the **Château des Fines Roches** domaine, which also, handily, maintains a fine inn and outstanding restaurant in the highly picturesque 19th-century château. Just south of the village via D 17 and a marked private road winding through vineyards, Fines Roches is renowned for lamb dishes perfectly suited to its wines. The seven rooms are only moderately expensive; the winery itself is open for visitors daily between March and December.

A wine fair is held in autumn in Châteauneuf; the date depends on the harvest (usually mid- to late September). The restaurant **La Mule du Pape,** touted by discerning gourmets such as Samuel Chamberlain, serves elegant meals in the center of town on the place de la Fontaine, though time has slightly dimmed its luster.

Travellers who have time to familiarize themselves with other towns and other bottlings might consider (from north to south) **Tain-l'Hermitage** (17 km/11 miles north of Valence, across the Rhône from Tournon), **Gigondas** (see the Vaucluse section below; 17 km/11 miles east of Orange; only 650 inhabitants but two estates to visit), or **Tavel** (15 km/9 miles northwest of Avignon; there are four estates in its immediate vicinity).

Two small, modestly priced inns in attractive settings can be found near Gigondas: the 15-room **Les Florets** and the 46-room **Montmirail**, in the nearby hamlet of that name (see the Vaucluse section below). Tavel is known for the **Auberge de Tavel**, a restaurant-hotel with 12 modestly priced rooms and a swimming pool.

—Georgia I. Hesse

ORANGE

Orange, just 31 km (19 miles) north of Avignon by Route A 7 or N 7, shares with Nîmes and Arles important reminders of Roman Provence: a theater, a gymnasium, and a commemorative arch that lived on as evidence of the importance of Roman Arausio long after that city of some 85,000 was trampled by Alemannic and Visigothic invaders. Later, the battered monuments were used as rock quarries for the construction of homes and fortifications.

Orange is one of the most momentous sites in the history of Christianity: In 529 the Council of Orange, convened here, declared for Augustinian predeterminism and against all forms of Pelagian doctrines of free will. By the 13th century the original Celtic market town upon which the Romans built had become a holding of the German Duchy of Nassau, later joined to the Dutch House of Orange. Thus through the quirks of history this tranquil town lent its name to a king of England, an Irish political faction, and a state of South Africa.

From Celtic days to our own, Orange sat right on France's main north–south route, the commercial Roman road that became Route Nationale 7. Today, however, the town of some 27,000 people has been bypassed by A 7, the Autoroute du Soleil, and it is possible—though not recommended—to hurry by without hesitation.

The plane trees, the sleepy, shady squares, the sidewalk cafés where strollers sit, musing and unmoving, mark Orange as a southern, Provençal town. The works of long-gone Rome remain the major lure.

Orange's **Théâter Antique** usually is considered the best looking and best preserved classical theater in existence, having been constructed during the last decade of the first century B.C. under Emperor Augustus. It follows the Greek plan of a semicircle of tiers facing the orchestra and stage and was about the same size as that in Arles, with a marble and mosaic backdrop of niches, columns, statues, and other decorations. From the square behind the theater, the backdrop and its supporting wings were known to Louis XIV as the "finest wall in the kingdom."

Long ago, the stage lost all its accoutrements, but the acoustics remain unsullied, and classical plays are still performed on a regular basis, watched by the theater's imperial statue (all Roman theaters had one; only the one in Orange remains), a 10-foot-2-inch-tall Augustus, discovered, somewhat the worse for fall and burial, in the orchestra pit.

Near the theater, excavations proceed on an early **temple** and **gymnasium**—the latter is one of only three known in France. Off a courtyard, the gym boasted baths (of course), open and enclosed running tracks, and a dais for the awarding of prizes. Orange's **Arc de Triomphe**, in the triple-arched style, was completed about A.D. 26 and is the third largest, as well as the best preserved, in France.

In 1939 French art collector Count William de Belleroche (whose family had lived for two centuries in Britain) presented to the city some 400 works by one Sir Frank Brangwyn: prints, drawings, watercolors, engravings, all showing town and country activities in France and England and now on display in the **Musée Municipal**.

Orange is the source of some fragrant, long-lasting milled soaps in the French tradition, fine and useful gifts with scents of lavender, orange, and herbs.

The smartest place to stay in the immediate area of Orange is the **Château de Rochegude**, about 15 km (9 miles) north via D 976 and D 11. This converted castle—its keep dates from the 12th century—offers a spectacular view of the valley below. The 25 rooms range from expensive to very expensive; the four apartments are in the latter category. Its excellent restaurant specializes in lamb, flavored with the rosemary and thyme that is so assiduously cultivated in Provence.

In town, on the road leading to the A 7 expressway, the modern **Altéa** offers 99 rooms for moderately high prices; it has a good restaurant and pleasant dining terrace.

An accomplished but reasonably-priced restaurant, **Le Pigraillet** (on the road that enters the hillside Parc de la Colline St-Eutrope on the south), specializes in duck and local wines. **Le Forum** is an unpretentious and satisfying restaurant at 3, rue Mazeau, very near the Théâtre Antique.

Travellers who seek historical passages may make an excursion of about 100 km (62 miles) to the northeast, departing Orange on D 975, which links the Rhône Valley and the high Alps via a 4,210-foot-high pass, the Col de Perty, and is thought to follow the route used by Hannibal and his elephant train (and army of 60,000 men) in 218 B.C. Many attractive old villages lie along the way, **Mollans-sur-Ouvèze** and **St-Auban-sur-l'Ouvèze** among them.

—Georgia I. Hesse

THE VAUCLUSE

Although the name of the entire *département* (or French administrative district), the Vaucluse for most travellers conjures up the beautiful villages and gentle valleys that lie east of Avignon and are dominated by the towering Mont Ventoux and the tall ridge of the Lubéron. As the region spreads out over several hundred square miles and displays surprising changes of landscape, no one itinerary can be said to be the best. For our purposes we will work from north to south. Aside from a capacity to enjoy the simple things of life, you need a car—or the legs of a champion cyclist.

Vaison-la-Romaine

In contrast to imperial Orange on the plain, Vaison-la-Romaine—27 km (17 miles) northeast of Orange on the vineyard-splitting D 975—presents a glimpse of a prosperous Roman market town nestled in wooded hills. For those whose imagination can rise above the ruins, the ancient neighborhoods thus far excavated—the **Quartier de Puymin** and the **Quartier de la Villasse**—give an indication of how well wealthy Roman families lived in their spacious villas. As with many old Provençal towns, Vaison also possesses a fine amphitheater.

What adds further to the charm of the town is its extensive Medieval quarter. The Romans, safe in a secure civilization, built expansively on the flat land of the right bank of the Ouvèze river; their successors in Vaison were less sure of themselves and elected to build a fortified town on the steep hill of the left bank. Reached by a sturdy Roman bridge spanning the river, the upper town is a picturesque warren of sinuous streets that lead up to the ruins of a 12th-century castle. In a romantic setting with an arresting view of the surrounding hills, the small Medieval settlement contains the intimate hotel **Le Beffroi**, named for the centuries-old belfry perched on the main gate to the quarter. The hotel, a beautiful town house built in the 16th century, is tailor-made for people in love.

As the threat of invading armies gradually faded with the passing of time, the people of Vaison moved back across the river and built their town on top of the Roman ruins. Modern Vaison, a small 19th-century grid of wide streets, is now known for its excellent market held every Tuesday. To sit on the terrace of the otherwise unremarkable **Sporting Bar** and look out over the busy place du 11 Novembre, which itself overlooks the ruins of the Roman forum, is to realize the antiquity of Vaison's commercial tradition. Of course, it might be more practical to head into the bustle and admire the flowers and herbs on sale, or pick up some truffles and lavender-scented honey for a lazy feast later in the day.

Montmirail and Mont Ventoux

There is no shortage of picnic areas south of Vaison. As wine is the essential lubricant of any impromptu meal in the French countryside, it's advisable to take D 977 out of Vaison and head south to the nearby vineyards of **Gigondas** and **Vacqueyras**. Vintners there have long adapted themselves to foreign admirers—Pliny spoke warmly of the fruity Gigondas—and roadside tasting stands abound for the thirsty. To the east of these vineyards are the Dentelles de Montmirail, eroded, teeth-like crags that rise from an irregular terrain of unusual natural beauty. The village of **La Roque-Alric**, perched on a jagged rock, is particularly striking.

Malaucène—10 km (6 miles) south of Vaison on D 938—marks the point of departure for the ascent of Mont Ventoux, the mountain that can be seen from many parts of Provence. Famous for its wind-whipped summit, Mont Ventoux is also noted for its varied vegetation: European pines grow on its north face; cedars-of-Lebanon and cypresses climb its southern flank. If the sky is clear and— this is important—the mistral is not blowing, the mountain of the wind is well worth the tortuous 21-km (13-mile) drive up D 974 to the summit. Here, at a height of over 6,000 feet, all of Provence stretches out to the south and the Alps can be made out in the north. On exceptionally clear mornings, before the heat haze of the warm spring and summer days cuts down visibility, the taller peaks of the distant Pyrénées appear on the horizon to the southwest.

Plateau de Vaucluse

South of the grandeur of Ventoux and, in more ways than one, far more down to earth, stretches the uneven Plateau de Vaucluse. A collection of lovely villages and sleepy towns, this area, once part of the papal Comtat Venaissin, is rural France at its best. **Vénasque**, the hilltop village that gave its name to the Comtat, typifies Provençal indolence, its narrow streets an oasis of calm. Still, local craftsmen have set up shop in the village for souvenir hunters drawn to the site by the **church of Notre-Dame**, part of which dates as far back as the sixth century. A pleasant stop before visiting the region's other attractions, the garden of the **Auberge de la Fontaine** here is a cheerful place to eat a splendid, inexpensive meal.

From Vénasque, the traveller has hard choices to make about where next to go. Ten kilometers (6 miles) up D 4 is the town of **Carpentras**, its magnificent 18th-century synagogue awaiting inspection. The region's other major town, **Cavaillon** (32 km/20 miles south of Vénasque), houses a similar architectural treasure, although its fame in France resides solely in its production of delicious melons. Cavaillon's immediate neighbor, the **Fontaine de Vaucluse**, a bubbling spring that feeds the Sorgue river, is, if not overrated, then certainly over-visited. Still, Petrarch composed sonnets during his 16-year sojourn here in the 14th century, so the site, despite the large parking lots, is not totally prosaic.

Less crowded than the market towns and the Fontaine de Vaucluse are the winding D 4 and D 177, which lead from Vénasque to the narrow pocket of land occupied by the **abbey of Sénanque**. Fields of purple lavender defy the arid earth in the defile where the Cistercian monks first decided to settle in 1148. Austere and gracefully Romanesque, the abbey's church and cloisters have not been altered since their construction more than eight centuries ago. To those of a more worldly bent, the monkish guides will gladly sell the distilled specialty of the monastery, an aromatic drink that treads a fine line between elixir and mouthwash. In the buildings open to the public, the history and practices of the monks from Cîteaux (see the

Burgundy chapter) are admirably presented in explanatory notes hanging in each room.

Just a few kilometers farther south on D 177 stands the town of **Gordes**, one of the most photogenic in all of Provence. Spilling down a hillside, the tawny-colored houses that make up this Provençal acropolis overlook the Coulon Valley to the south. At the summit is a restored castle, one of its buildings a fine example of decorative Renaissance architecture; it now houses a museum given over to Hungarian artist **Victor Vasarely**. On the route de Sénanque are two outstanding, if pricey, restaurants: **Les Bories** (reserve; Tel: 90-72-00-51), with 18 moderately expensive, picturesque rooms, and the **Domaine de l'Enclos** (Tel: 90-72-08-22). The latter includes a deluxe nine-room, five-apartment hotel that, with its views of the valley, should inspire any well-heeled would-be painter. This luxury is a far cry from a neighboring attraction called the **Village des Bories**, a fascinating cluster of mortarless stone huts thought to have been used by peasants for storing implements and threshing grain. An architectural/archaeological wonder not to be missed.

Two other stops may keep you in Gordes country longer than you planned. The first is the **Bastide de Gordes**, an 18-room enchantment overlooking the Lubéron; it's expensive, as is its outstanding kitchen, which turns out a fine *nage de rouget* (red mullet) *façon barigoule*. Just down the hill in the hamlet of Joucas is the stunning **Mas des Herbes Blanches**, with 16 rooms done in inspired-rustic style, a heated pool, tennis courts, and regional dishes suited to the local wines; expensive, and worth it.

The Coulon Valley below Gordes is bounded on the south by the **Lubéron**, a lozenge-shaped mountain that separates rural Vaucluse from the plain leading to Aix. The area is studded with villages of arresting beauty, none more so than **Roussillon** (8 km/5 miles east of Gordes), a study in all the different hues of red. Startling hillsides of brilliant ocher can be seen in the immediate vicinity of Roussillon. True lovers of the color can take D 22 to **Rustrel**, where deserted ocher quarries make for a natural Day-Glo landscape. South of Roussillon the scenery changes once again: where D 108 crosses the Coulon river, the 2,000-year-old **Pont Julien** awaits amateur archaeologists. In the advance prominences of the Lubéron that overlook the site are the handsome villages of **Oppède-le-Vieux** and **Bonnieux**, the latter having the signal advantage of possessing a bread-making museum.

From the Medieval heights of Bonnieux the red slash of Roussillon's hillocks is clearly visible, as are the orchards around the main town of **Apt**. The observant should look out for an anachronism over the ageless landscape: To the northeast jet fighters frequently can be sighted heading back to their base in the Plateau d'Albion, home to France's nuclear strike force. Perhaps it would be more cheering to descend from Bonnieux and then climb to neighboring **Lacoste**, where you can sit in the village café and stare thoughtfully at a ruined castle—it was here that the Marquis de Sade spent much of his eventful youth.

THE ALPILLES

Midway between Avignon and Arles, a peculiar 25-km-(15.5-mile-) long range of jagged white hills points up into the blue skies. In some places a brilliant white, the Alpilles range divides the plain of the lower Rhône Valley: the fields to the north, around St-Rémy-de-Provence, are covered in flowers and orchards; those to the south, around Maussane-les-Alpilles, are a succession of almond and olive groves. With the exception of the arid Alpilles themselves, this region has known the hand of human beings, both as creators and destroyers, since the first millennium B.C. Roman and Greek ruins guard the approaches to the north (at St-Rémy), just as an abandoned Medieval citadel crowns the range to the south (at Les Baux). Nearby, a magnificent abbey (Montmajour) stands deserted atop a hillock, looking out over the Roman city of Arles and the Medieval fair towns of Beaucaire (see also the Languedoc–Roussillon chapter) and Tarascon. Add to this sense of history the Provençal climate and slow-moving pace of life, and you may choose to while away weeks beneath the cypresses and plane trees on the village squares.

St-Rémy and Salon

While the circular old town of St-Rémy-de-Provence has nothing to attract the tourist in search of the spectacular, this flowery Provençal center offers peace of mind— which may be why it, along with Salon-de-Provence, has recently proved so alluring to vacationing pundits from fast-talking Paris. Both towns lay claim to the Provençal seer, Nostradamus, who spent much of his time on earth

gazing starward and predicting what would happen when
he was gone. Born in St-Rémy, Nostradamus died—he is
supposed to have calculated that date, too—in Salon in
1566. The latter town, by far the busier of the two, lies 32
km (20 miles) southeast of St-Rémy along D 99 (a beautiful tree-lined road) and N 7. Not a pretty place, Salon
nonetheless possesses a much-remodeled tenth-century
castle that houses an outstanding military museum and, in
late July, plays host to an intimate jazz festival.

But it is in St-Rémy that the visitor might more profit-
ably linger. The **Château des Alpilles**, a 17-room hotel set
amid tall trees, offers a charming, if pricey, respite from
the ardors of sightseeing. St-Rémy also claims a number
of adequate regional restaurants, the most informal being
a turn-of-the-century affair called the **Bistrot des Alpilles**
at 15, boulevard Mirabeau (Tel: 90-92-09-17). Of particular interest to the gourmet is the **Croque Chou** (Tel: 90-
95-18-55), located 11 km (7 miles) northwest of St-Rémy
along the D 29 in the village of Verquières. As well as
choosing such habitual regional fare as lamb and rabbit,
the adventurous eater may decide to go for a peculiar
house specialty—octopus cooked in wine with its ink—
while admiring the 11th-century church across the way.

However mesmerizing these local culinary treats, the
true spell of St-Rémy is cast by the quiet monuments to the
south of the town. At **St-Paul-de-Mausole**, a Medieval monastery converted into an asylum during the last century, a
weary Vincent van Gogh spent all but the final months of
his last years in the calm cloister and gardens. It was here
that the penniless artist executed the paintings that now
fetch such astronomical prices at auction in London and
New York. The mausoleum so lugubriously included in the
monastery's name refers, in fact, to a non-Christian monument of considerable archaeological significance.

Just before D 5 disappears into the Alpilles, two odd
Roman constructions known as **Les Antiques** can be seen
to the right of the roadway: a triumphal arch celebrating
Julius Caesar's subjugation of Marseille in 49 B.C. and a tall
funerary monument commemorating the untimely deaths
of two of the Emperor Augustus's grandsons. Remarkably
well preserved, as well as evocative in their setting near the
strangely shaped hills, these monuments stand across the
road from the ruins of a Greco-Roman city, **Glanum**. Obviously a site of some importance to Greek settlers—rivaled
in the western Mediterranean only by Emporiae in Spanish
Catalonia and Marseille—the ruins of Glanum hug the

flank of the Alpilles in testament to the vanity of human pretensions to permanence. As James Pope-Hennessy warns of this peculiar spot: "The Plateau des Antiques and the ruins of Glanum are among several places in Provence that I should not recommend imaginative persons to visit alone by the light of the moon."

Les Baux-de-Provence

A towering rock plateau—a natural fortress—formed of twisted limestone weathered into haunting forms. Below, on either side, two valleys: On one side, a pastoral scene from the tales of Daudet, is the Vallée d'Entreconque; on the other, a tormented landscape, the Val d'Enfer (Valley of Hell) in the cracks of the Alpilles mountains. Atop the rock plateau are ruins of a feudal fortress carved out of stone and long since destroyed by successive wars waged against the castle's powerful and ambitious rulers: This is Les Baux.

Isolated in the countryside northeast of Arles, Les Baux still stimulates the imagination as it did seven hundred years ago when it welcomed troubadours and their ideal of courtly love. Today it is a lively touristic and artistic center of fewer than 500 permanent inhabitants whose main occupations are staffing the few galleries and shops in the upper town and running the celebrated restaurants in the valley below. It is also a meeting place for a segment of France's extreme right, the royalist parties, who hold an annual rally near the village.

While historians debate the exact origins of the name Les Baux—some say it means "high place" in Ligurian, others contend it's Provençal for "cave," and still others believe it's a derivative of Balthazar, one of the three Wise Men—there is no question that Les Baux gave us the word *bauxite,* for the mineral mined in the nearby Alpilles chain.

Because the village of Les Baux sits on such a small rock plateau—only 2,600 feet long and 650 feet wide—no cars are allowed on its streets. The village is split into two: the early-Medieval ghost town—*ville morte*—and the latter-day Provençal village, with its arts-and-crafts shops, restaurants, museums, and exceptional Renaissance mansions.

The village has a few moderately priced hotels and restaurants; in the summer hotel reservations are a must. While you can get a snack or a decent meal with a spectacular view or charming ambience almost anywhere in Les Baux, it would be a shame to come here and not try—budget willing—the **Oustaù de Baumanière** (reserve; Tel: 90-54-33-07). The food here runs to heavy dishes with rich sauces; the house specialty is local lamb cooked in a crust. Baumanière also has 25 elegantly rustic and comfortable rooms in a restored Provençal farmhouse and a swimming pool and tennis courts. Down the road is the less expensive but charmingly rustic **La Cabro d'Or**, with 22 rooms and a good restaurant, owned and run by Raymond Thuilier, who also owns Oustaù.

The story of Les Baux is one of a regional feudal power engaged in nearly incessant (and usually lost) wars and rebellions lasting several hundred years. The princes of Les Baux were often cruel and ambitious warmongers. Nevertheless, their court was considered highly refined and brilliant, especially during the 12th and 13th centuries, when it was home to the troubadours.

When Provence became French in 1481, Les Baux revolted against Louis XI and the castle was destroyed (not for the first or last time). The Renaissance brought better times for Les Baux; the castle was rebuilt and splendid mansions were constructed, including the Hôtel de Manville and the Hôtel de Brion—the latter now housing a museum of printing, with artifacts dating to the beginnings of printing in the West.

The renaissance of Les Baux didn't last long. The lords of Les Baux supported the wrong causes all too often: the Protestants, the duke of Orléans against King Louis XIII, and Aixois insurgents rebelling against Cardinal Richelieu. As a result, the king ordered a military occupation of Les Baux, and the castle and city ramparts were torn down for the last time. Les Baux became a ghost town as its 3,000 inhabitants moved to greener pastures.

The writings of Mistral (of the Félibrige movement; see also Arles) and Daudet helped Les Baux regain some of its past glory by rediscovering its historic importance and above all its touristic potential. Daudet's tales tell of a peaceful, pastoral village coping with economic hardships and displaying a fervent attachment to the Church and its traditions.

One of his stories describes a centuries-old Christmas ritual still performed today: the midnight Mass procession—the *fête des bergers* (shepherds' festival)—in the now significantly modified 12th-century church of St-Vincent.

Church authorities often forbade the fête because of

suspicions that it was rooted in paganism. The procession provides a good show for the several hundred people, mostly visitors, who cram into the small church on Christmas Eve. Provençal music—flute and tambourine—replaces traditional Christmas carols.

Just 4 km (2.5 miles) south of Les Baux, away from the constant stream of visitors, is the town of **Maussane-les-Alpilles**, a center of olive oil production. Although possessing neither a spectacular site nor a glorious past, Maussane has that one Provençal trait denied Les Baux: a large boule-playing square with a charming, reasonable restaurant, **La Pitchoune**, and a cranky café, the **Café de la Fontaine**, frequented by olive growers. To watch them at work you may visit the oil-pressing cooperative on the rue Chaloun and pop olives as you tour the facility.

Montmajour, Beaucaire, and Tarascon

Southwest of the Alpilles, almost on the outskirts of Arles, a ruined monastery stands on a small hill in the midst of waving wheat fields. Montmajour is now a ghostly collection of Romanesque buildings, rendered even more striking by the precarious state of disrepair of some of the upper floors. How the Benedictines who settled here in the tenth century eventually turned worldly and decadent makes a good counterpoint to the successful monastic community at Sénanque. When Louis XVI suppressed the wanton abbey in 1786, the fattened monks were not missed by a peasantry ready for revolution.

Aside from an immense barrel of a church and a well-restored cloister, Montmajour possesses only one other fully intact feature—a Medieval keep that rises more than 100 feet above the plain. Those willing to make the climb will see the red roofs of Arles to the south, the Alpilles to the northeast, and the towns of Beaucaire (see also Languedoc–Roussillon) and Tarascon to the northwest. These last-mentioned sites merit a brief visit before heading to the wonders of Arles, for both are Medieval towns that were famous for the great fairs they held for more than six centuries. The Rhône, though bridged here, separates the two towns, leading visitors in a hurry to ask themselves a soul-searching question: Do I like my castles in ruin or intact? If you opt for the former, the dream-like ruin of Beaucaire's castle on the right (western) bank is a beautiful place to clamber over stone walls and stare out over the Rhône. Tarascon, on the other bank, was preternaturally lucky in backing the right horse during France's dynastic squabbles, thereby saving its lovely castle from dismantlement by a wrathful Richelieu. A golden 15th-century gem, the **Château du Roi René**—Provence's beloved monarch—reflects its machiolated towers in the waters of the river and stuns visitors with its interior, which shows the transition from Flamboyant Gothic to early Renaissance styles. If you've ever seen French B-movies featuring knights parading for the edification of their ladies high up on the battlements, you will recognize Tarascon's castle immediately.

ARLES

Should you be on the southbound train from Avignon, which stays on the left bank of the Rhône as it goes through the countryside, the words of an artistic genius who took the same journey can guide you: "Before arriving at Tarascon I noticed a magnificent landscape of immense yellowish crags strangely entangled with the most imposing forms. The valleys were lined with small, round trees covered with olive-colored or gray-colored leaves." The train travels farther south, through "magnificent reddish land planted with vineyards," and eventually you, like Vincent van Gogh, will arrive in the lovely town of Arles.

Van Gogh, whose one-year (1888 to 1889) sojourn here marked a feverish burst of creativity during which the artist executed more than 200 canvases, may have been ridiculed, persecuted, and interned by intolerant town fathers, yet he immortalized what was already a city of considerable antiquity and charm. Although many of the buildings Van Gogh knew have disappeared (his "Maison Jaune" fell to Allied bombs in 1944) or have been curiously reconverted (the hospital in which he was placed in solitary confinement is now a Van Gogh center and souvenir mall), the light and colors of this city and its rural surroundings have not changed at all.

Not that Van Gogh is Arles's sole claim to fame. Arlésiennes, it will be remembered, have long been celebrated for their manes of dark hair flowing down over shawls of fiery red and deepest black. Almost as impres-

sive is the city's historical pedigree as capital of Roman
Gaul and center of Provençal folklore. Arles, in short, is a
city with a past.

To make sense of this compact cluster of sinuous
streets, magnificent churches and museums, and massive
Roman constructions, it's perhaps best first to sit square
in the middle of it all and have a drink. **Place du Forum**, a
narrow rectangle of shaded café terraces that face a statue
of Frédéric Mistral—Provence's turn-of-the-century cultural savior—*and* two forlorn Corinthian columns from a
long-vanished Roman temple, gives an idea, by its very
disorder, of the confusing welter of cultures that is Arles.
The temptation is to leave the café and go in three directions at once: To the north a few blocks is the tranquil
Rhône riverfront, to the east are the great Roman theaters,
and to the south await outstanding museums and Medieval churches grouped around the 18th-century place de
la République. For our purposes, we begin with the
Arlesians' most imposing ancestors, the Romans.

The Two Theaters

The amphitheater and the neighboring Roman theater
are witnesses to Arles's prestigious place in the Roman
world. The name Arles was derived from Arelate (City of
Swamps), a reference to the marshes that once surrounded the city (only the Camargue was left untouched
by industrious swamp-draining Arlesians). Despite the
inhospitable environment, the Romans developed Arles
as an important port and economic center.

The rise of the city dates from 49 B.C., after Julius
Caesar had ousted his rival Pompey in a civil war. Neighboring Marseille had the bad luck to have sided with the
loser. Consequently, Caesar rewarded his friends in Arles
with the lucrative trading connections to Rome that had
once been Marseille's source of wealth. A canal was built
to join Arles with the Mediterranean, and the city inherited the major portion of Marseille's territory, which extended along the coast to Nice.

During Arles's golden period (first through fourth centuries A.D.) the emperors endowed it with monuments
worthy of a major Roman city: a circus, a triumphal arch, a
12,000-seat theater, lavish baths, an aqueduct, temples,
and an amphitheater.

Les Arènes, once the haunt of gladiators and now the
home of bullfighters, is the largest Roman amphitheater in

Provence. Although its uppermost story is conspicuously absent, the massive structure, dating from the first century, is lucky to have survived at all. During the Middle Ages it was used as a military camp and it later became a city within a city, with some two hundred houses and two chapels built inside and outside its walls. The city cleared out the houses and their residents in 1825, and shortly afterward the amphitheater was restored to its original state.

Next to les Arènes are the ruins of the **Roman theater**, which was constructed before the amphitheater, in about A.D. 30, during the first years of the reign of Augustus. Several artifacts were found here, including the Venus of Arles, a beautiful classical bust that was given to Louis XIV. It is now on view at the Louvre.

Augustus and Caesar weren't the only prominent Roman rulers who supported Arles. Constantine (288 to 337) adopted Arles as one of his two capitals (Constantinople was the other). He brought his family, friends, dignitaries, and treasury here but stayed only for short periods. Constantine ordered new construction at Arles, embellishing the ramparts ordered by Caesar and Augustus and enlarging the city to include the right bank of the Rhône, Trinquetaille.

As a result of Constantine's patronage and Arles's status as capital of the Western Roman Empire, the city is also a treasure trove of ancient Christian art. But to find it, you must leave the great theaters and go west to the **place de la République**, where the pagan, patristic, and Medieval all share pride of place.

Environs of Place de la République

On the western side of the square stands a 17th-century church, which—until 1992—houses the **Musée d'Art Paien**. On display here is a monumental head of Augustus unearthed at the Roman theaters, as well as classical statuary, sarcophagi, columns, and friezes from the Arlesian region. Its rival, in the nearby rue Balze, is the **Musée Lapidaire Chrétien**, which is considered to have the richest collection of sarcophagi after the Vatican Museum. Most of these, dating from the fourth century, were transferred in excellent condition from the late empire burial grounds at Alyscamps (see below).

To understand what stands on the eastern side of place de la République, it is necessary to pass through several centuries of history first. After the Germanic tribes overran the Roman Empire, Arles fell into the hands of the Visigoths, then, in succession, the Burgunds, the Franks, the Saracens, and finally the Carolingian Franks—who were later to establish the Holy Roman Empire under Charlemagne. Charlemagne's descendants further divided the new empire with each succession. Arles was first integrated into the kingdom of Provence, then became the capital of the kingdom of Burgundy-Provence (from 934 to 1032). This development was the source of new prosperity for the city. Such was the enduring importance of Arles that Frederick Barbarossa of the Holy Roman Empire (then in effect German) was crowned emperor at the nearly completed **church of St-Trophime** in 1178. It is this imposing Romanesque complex that stands across the place de la République from the Roman museums.

St-Trophime is the most interesting of Arles's early-Christian buildings. It was a major stopping point along the Medieval Christian pilgrimage route to Santiago de Compostela in Spain. Built from the ruins of a fifth-century church, St-Trophime is an example of early Provençal Romanesque architecture, strongly influenced by Roman and Greek style. The church's cloisters (12th to 14th centuries) are of a rare beauty, and exhibit intricately sculptured cornices that recount the resurrection of Christ and the glorification of Arles's patron saints. Also beautiful is the main doorway to the church, which shows a profusion of apostles and saints on the tympanum, commonly held to be a masterpiece of Provençal Romanesque art.

But this historic neighborhood does not stop here. The subsequent development of Provençal culture—and its revival at the end of the 19th century—is well-represented at the **Museon Arlaten**, a few steps away from the square on the rue de la République. Founded by the leader of the Félibrige movement, Frédéric Mistral, with the money he received for winning the Nobel Prize for Literature, the museum traces the history of Arles from prehistoric times to the 20th century with an amazing collection of furniture, local dress, documents, and works of art.

Just south of the place de la République, the 20th century mercifully takes hold. Like every typical Provençal town, Arles has its main café-lined avenue, the boulevard des Lices. Here is the city's only four-star hotel, the reasonably priced **Jules César**, in a rebuilt 17th-century convent. The hotel's restaurant, **Lou Marquès**, which spe-

cializes in Arlesian cooking, provides a relaxed yet somehow fussy atmosphere.

Place du Forum to the Rhône

It should come as some solace to the history-weary that
most of the attractions of this neighborhood are of a
resolutely sybaritic nature. Overlooking the place du Forum are the balconies of a fine regional restaurant, **Le Vaccarès**. In the adjacent rue Sauvage, the hotel **D'Arlatan**, a
Medieval town house of the local nobility, offers a quiet
garden setting and rooms furnished in impeccable 18th-
century style. For those who care to venture farther north
toward the river—and toward gastronomic adventure—
L'Olivier (Tel: 90-49-64-88) offers such treats as snails and
smoked pork in puff pastry. New to the Arles restaurant
world, this establishment has been earning an enthusiastic welcome from picky Provençal food critics.

Just across the street from this newcomer stands one
of Arles's oldest museums, the **Musée Réattu**. Formerly a
priory of the Knights of Malta, the 15th-century structure
now houses works by Picasso and local artists, as well as
the city's permanent photographic collection—which
serves as a backdrop to the Rencontres Internationales
de la Photographie held every June in Arles. This city
being what it is, this very modern event takes place in
the shadow of the museum's next-door neighbor: the
ruins of baths built for the Emperor Constantine.

Before leaving Arles, those with a taste for the evocative
should visit the **Alyscamps**, the greatest necropolis in the
West during the first millennium. Located to the southwest of town, beyond the ramparts, this deserted burial
ground is now reduced to a single, shady lane lined with
antique sarcophagi and dotted with ancient chapels. It is
the best way to take your leave of such a historic city.

AIX-EN-PROVENCE

It doesn't take an art scholar to understand why Cézanne
was captivated by Aix (pronounced "X"). All it takes is
witnessing an afternoon sun casting a reddish hue on the
massive Montagne St-Victoire and reflecting off the city's
rose-colored tile roofs and well-groomed orange Baroque buildings.

Aix is a Baroque gem, where sitting on a café terrace and doing absolutely nothing is a worthy calling. Throughout most of its history, Aix has cultivated a noble air and an elitist front. Its reputation for providing the good life, especially among upper-middle-class Parisians, has been responsible for making it one of France's fastest-growing cities. Aix has mushroomed from 30,000 people before World War II to nearly 140,000 today. The growth, however, has taken place outside of what is referred to as Old Aix, which has remained virtually unchanged over the past two hundred years.

In the second and third centuries B.C., Aix was the capital of an important Celtic-Ligurian community. Its ruins can still be visited, at Entremont, just outside the city. In 123 B.C. the Greeks in Marseille called on their Roman allies for military help against the Celtic Ligurians. The Roman armies led by the proconsul Caius Sextius Calvinus defeated the Celts and founded a military outpost on land that contained underground springs. The camp was named Aquae Sextiae, which was eventually shortened to just Aix. Today the Hôtel des Thermes—with its thermal-water cure—stands next to the site of the old Roman baths. The town boasts dozens of fountains, but only one—in the middle of cours Sextius—gives forth mineral water. (A few years ago a scandal struck when it was discovered that the pure water of Aix was not so pure after all.)

Under the Roman Empire, Aix became an important city and was lavishly bestowed with temples and amphitheaters. However, successive calamities, including the Moorish invasions of the ninth century, caused the destruction of Aix's fabulous Roman buildings.

Another landmark—the court palace of Provence—fell victim to architectural snobbishness. When Provence became French in 1481, the old palace was used as the parliament building for the Provence region. By the early 18th century the practical need for more modern facilities and a mania for architectural symmetry led to the demolition of the palace.

Cours Mirabeau

The best example of this fashion for symmetry is the cours Mirabeau—a short tree-lined boulevard created in the late 17th century as a promenade based on a triple architectural harmony: the uniform height of the buildings and the length (1,452 feet) and width (145 feet) of the street. It is one of the most attractive streets in France.

Along one side of the cours stand a half-dozen majestic *hôtels particuliers* (city mansions) constructed during the 17th and early 18th centuries. Today the buildings house several street-level *pâtisseries* where you can buy Aix's gourmet specialty, *calissons* (a soft, almond paste candy, still handmade in the city's several *calisson* factories).

On the other side of the cours are less impressive Baroque buildings, notable only for the numerous large sidewalk cafés that front them. In the summertime trees on both sides of the cours form a green roof that shields the cafés from the Provençal sun. During most of the year the café terraces are filled with sippers who spend hours watching the parade of passersby. Buskers, clowns, and other sidewalk performers add spice. The cours remains the center of life in Aix, as it was three hundred years ago.

Recently the Aixois committed another architectural faux pas when they tore down the exquisite four-star Hôtel Roi-René to make room for a modern replacement. The loss of the Roi-René has made the **Augustins** even more appealing. On a side street off the cours—the rue de la Masse—this former convent is intimate, and each room has a charming Medieval air. Be sure to ask for one with a balcony (there are only two); they cost about 100 francs more but are worth it, looking out as they do over a small, quiet courtyard with a view of a 15th-century bell tower and a panorama of tiled rooftops.

At the bottom of the cours, in front of a statue of Good King René—the last great ruler of Provence—stands Aix's most famous café: **Les Deux Garçons**. During the First Empire the café was the meeting place of the "Golden Youth," and after that, under the Restoration, the "Romantic Youth." Later it became the favorite café of Cézanne, Emile Zola, and others. Now it is protected as a national landmark.

In recent years the cours has lost some of its spark. Just as one example, during Aix's music festival, which lasts nearly two months (late June to early August), heavily armed police patrol the street to stop any music played after 10:00 P.M.—which, not surprisingly, has soured the formerly festive atmosphere more than a bit. Still, a recent—and thoroughly unscientific—survey commissioned by a French magazine found that staid old Aix is the "sexiest city in France."

Despite this unexpected distinction, Aix's music festival

is still the city's big draw. It is really two different festivals: **Aix en Musique**, daily free classical and folk concerts in various locations around the city; and the **Festival d'Aix**— the opera festival—which features highly acclaimed performances under the stars in a newly renovated theater at the 17th-century archbishop's palace (on rue Gaston de Saporta, next to the cathedral). Tickets must be reserved months in advance and cost an average of 400 francs. Aix's festival has become a major stepping-stone for up-and-coming opera stars. The theater runs three different operas per festival and specializes in Mozart. For information, Tel: 42-23-37-81; for reservations, Tel: 42-23-11-20.

Festival time or not, for a break from the more touristy and higher-priced cours take a two-minute walk to the majestic place de l'Hôtel de Ville in the center of the old city, Vieil Aix. An almost enclosed courtyard, the *place* is dominated by the 17th-century city hall and the former Halles aux Grains, now a post office. Just behind it is the small daily produce market—one of the most outstanding in Provence. At the small market you can find a vast selection of Provençal specialties, including braids of garlic, fresh and dried herbs, fresh goat cheese, and melons.

Parallel to the cours, on the rue Espariat, is the 17th-century Hôtel Boyer d'Equilles, a natural history museum. The paleontological collection includes dinosaur eggs and ancient seashells.

Despite the fresh food available, Aix is not especially known for its restaurants. The city is filled with eating places, though, and while very few offer gastronomical treats, nearly all of them—except for some chain restaurants—are small, intimate, and charming, or else well situated with comfortable outside terraces. These places are scattered throughout the center of the old city, and you can't go wrong by just wandering around checking out menus and decor until the fancy hits. Try the relaxed and rustic **Comté d'Aix** on the rue de Couronne or the slightly pricier (and fishier) **Le Clam's** on the cours Sextius.

Aix Cathedral

Passing through the place de l'Hôtel de Ville en route to the cathedral, you must go through an arch in the ancient bell tower. The large white stones on the tower's bottom date from Roman times; the rest was built in the 11th century and rebuilt in the 16th.

The tower marks what most historians now believe to be the boundary of ancient Roman Aix. It was perhaps the guard tower of the military outpost, Aquae Sextiae. Beyond the tower and away from the cours begins what was once the main Roman street, now called the rue Gaston de Saporta. This is the hub of a part of Aix's student life: The political science building and the foreign student institute sit side by side facing the architecturally interesting **cathedral of St-Sauveur.**

The cathedral's mélange of styles clashes with the studied symmetry of the other structures of Aix. While many *hautain* Aixois took swipes at its lack of continuity ("Ugly and irregular," noted one university president in 1739), archaeologists find it a gold mine of information.

Its styles span 2,000 years of Western history, with traces of Roman, early Christian, Romanesque, Gothic, and Renaissance architecture. Recent digs proved that the cathedral was built on the site of a former Roman building, and Roman stones were used to build one wall of the 12th-century Romanesque section. Inside, there is a remarkable triptych of the Burning Bush by Nicolas Froment, King René's court painter. The painting remains shuttered most of the year and you must ask the keeper or guide to open it. The baptistery dates from the fourth and fifth centuries, and the bell tower from the early 15th century. Next to the cathedral, and accessible through the courtyard of the adjoining archbishop's palace, is a small Medieval **cloister**, well worth visiting for its sculptured cornices. In the place de l'Archevêché is the **Snack Bar Charlie et Maggie**; open during the summer until midnight or later, this is a great place to eat a quick and not too expensive meal outside.

Paul Cézanne in Aix

Paul Cézanne may be Aix's best-known native, but it's only recently that he has become the city's favorite son. While he lived here the eccentric Cézanne was at odds with the staid Aixois. Children mocked him and his fellow citizens shunned him. Until 1985 no Cézanne painting hung in the city. Today, the **Musée Granet**, to the south of the cours Mirabeau off the rue d'Italie, houses several major Cézannes.

Cézanne preferred working away from the city, mostly in the foothills of the imposing Montagne St-Victoire, which he painted more than 60 times. He also had a

workshop just outside Vieil Aix, past the cathedral, at what is now 9, avenue Paul Cézanne. American admirers have restored the workshop to the same state it was in at the time of Cézanne's death in 1906.

Excursions from Aix

The chalky white massif of Cézanne's beloved **Montagne St-Victoire**, which received its name in the 16th century as a reminder of the Roman victory over the Teutons in 102 B.C., dominates Aix and the surrounding countryside. At sunset it turns a brilliant red. The summit, with a 17th-century chapel and a panoramic view of the valley, can be reached in about three and a half hours on foot from the village of Cabassols.

Route D 17 east from Aix runs along the southern side of St-Victoire; along the route are several lovely villages, including **Le Tholonet** (with its 19th-century Château Noir), **St-Antonin**, and **Pourrières**.

Along the route on the northern side of the mountain, D 10, is the village of **Vauvenargues**, where Picasso lived until 1961. This is the Vauvenargues of the early 18th-century marquis de Vauvenargues, author of the famous (in France) *Maximes,* which had a strong influence on Stendhal. The castle of Vauvenargues, unfortunately, is not open to the public.

MARSEILLE

Marseille, a mere 30 km (19 miles) south of elegant, well-heeled Aix, strikes terror in the hearts of some travellers because of its reputation as a nest of gangsters. That's too bad, because this port town is so endowed with charm and beauty that limiting a visit here to changing trains at the Gare St-Charles would be a shame.

If nothing else, a quick morning boat ride from the Vieux Port to the **Château d'If** to see the castle made famous by Alexandre Dumas's *Count of Monte Cristo* is well worth the approximately two-hour detour. The trip across the harbor lets you view Marseille the right way, from the water, so you can feel a closer identification with the Marseillais, whose town has been linked to the sea for 26 centuries. The château was built as a fort by François I from 1524 to 1528, after Marseille had been held under siege by the armies of Spanish ruler Charles V. It was converted into a prison in 1634 and shut down in 1872 when the Third Republic was established.

Marseille has several prominent museums and monuments, including the **Musée des Beaux-Arts**, which contains one of France's richest painting collections, and the **Vieille Charité**, a 17th- to 18th-century hospital that has been converted into a vast cultural center housing a new archaeological museum. The city's most famous monument is no doubt the **cathedral of Notre-Dame de la Garde**, high on a hill above the city. Done in the Byzantine pastiche that afflicts Paris's Sacré-Coeur basilica, Marseille's cathedral nonetheless commands a breathtaking view of the entire city.

Marseille's tarnished reputation is, in fact, part of its attraction. Maverick, mysterious, violent, passionate, and Byzantine, Marseille is a teeming, sprawling, hilly port town of one million inhabitants, most of whom were—or are descended from—immigrants: Italians, Arabs, North African Jews, and Spaniards.

As a major trading and commercial center, Marseille was for centuries focused more toward the Far East and Africa than toward Europe, especially during the Renaissance. Today sections of the city—Porte d'Aix, for example—are much like the souk in Algiers.

Throughout its long history Marseille has been independent and often rebellious. Neither royalist nor conservative, Marseille has been fiercely democratic ever since it was founded as a republic in 600 B.C. by colonizing Greeks.

The story of France's national anthem, "La Marseillaise," is an example. During the Revolution fervent Marseillais revolutionaries marched to Paris, singing a military chant written in Strasbourg along the route as a battle cry. The song thereafter became synonymous with the Revolution—much to the chagrin of its composer, who was a royalist.

Ancient Marseille

The Marseillais have a well-founded reputation of being great tellers of tall tales, and they've got a whopper for the founding of their city by the Phoceans (Greeks from ancient Ionia on the west coast of Asia Minor) in 600 B.C. The Marseillais themselves are not the source of the legend; it comes from the third-century Latin historian Justin. As he described it, a Greek leader, Protis, went in search of Celtic-Ligurian king Segobia Nannus to ask permission to found a city on the coast of his territory. The day Protis arrived, King Nannus was preparing a wedding-day festival for his daughter. Custom was to choose the groom at the festival. The Greeks were invited. The king told his daughter to offer water to the man of her choice. She chose Protis. As a gift, the king granted Protis the land to found his port, which became known as Massilia.

For the Greeks, Marseille was the perfect site. French geographer Vidal de la Blanche noted: "With its small islands, acropolis, detached hills and cliffs, small river and deep port, Massilia is the classic type of a Greek city."

Developed as an independent but distinctly Greek republic, Marseille quickly emerged as a powerful mercantile and political center. Its control spread throughout the region, including Nice to the east and Agde to the west.

The city's fortunes changed in 49 B.C., when Julius Caesar's army crushed it for siding with Pompey during Rome's civil war. Marseille paid dearly for the blunder, losing its navy, port, and territories—all except Nice. The city then slipped into the shadows for centuries. You can witness much of this history in the Jardin des Vestiges (see below) and in the nearby **Musée d'Histoire de Marseille**, with a collection that includes a well-preserved third-century Roman ship.

The Vieux Port

The Vieux Port (Old Port) is a protected basin that cuts right into the center of Marseille. The new port, La Joliette, lies at the Marseille end of a 45-mile-long seaside complex that stretches west to the Port-St-Louis-du-Rhône. Now used by pleasure boaters, tour guides, and fishermen, the Vieux Port is lined with restaurants—most of which are unscrupulous tourist traps that serve bogus bouillabaisse at seemingly reasonable prices. The few honest establishments have banded together and created a bouillabaisse certificate that guarantees authentic traditional quality.

Real bouillabaisse is a Marseillais specialty and should not be missed. **Michel**, 6, rue des Catalans (Tel: 91-52-30-63), serves the best. The fish is bought fresh every morning from the Vieux Port market, and only the proper high-quality Mediterranean fish—such as *Saint-Pierre* and *rascasse*—is used. A real bouillabaisse is made with at least four different types of fish. The restaurant **Miramar**, at 12, quai du Port (Tel: 91-91-10-40), is less expensive and nearly as good. It has the advantage of being easy to find and affords a lovely view of the Vieux Port.

Just behind the Vieux Port is La Bourse de Commerce, a modern shopping complex that nevertheless is near two points of interest—the best hotel in Marseille, the Altéa, and the **Jardin des Vestiges**, an archaeological site with Greek, Roman, and early Christian ruins. (The walls of Marseille's original port have been uncovered here.)

What the **Altéa** lacks in intimacy it makes up for in convenience, comfort, and view. A seven-story modern hotel, its prices go up with the floors. Be sure to ask for a room with a view of the Vieux Port.

If you want a quieter hideaway in Marseille, a good choice would be **Le Petit Nice**, with its **Restaurant Passédat**, along the corniche John F. Kennedy, south of town along the coast. Less expensive but nevertheless charming is the **Concorde–Palm Beach**, with its seaside fish restaurant, **La Réserve**. Palm Beach is farther south on the corniche route. Also on the attractive corniche route is **Parc Borély** and its 18th-century château, which houses the **Musée d'Archéologie Méditerranéenne**—France's second-largest collection of Egyptian antiquities (after the Louvre).

Excursions from Marseille

Drive east on D 559 to be astonished. White, wafer-thin high-rises marking the outer reaches of Marseille are suddenly behind you, and a Mediterranean moorland stretches out in front of you. The barren limestone plateau of the **Marseilleveyre** looks like nothing else in Provence, until you take a cruise around the needle-like promontories and bleached islands, past deep coves called **calanques**, from the neighboring town of Cassis. Tucked in an inlet bordered by towering cliffs, **Cassis** has become Marseille's pleasure port, the masts in its marina always whistling in the pleasant Mediterranean breeze. Provençal yachters frequent **La Presqu'île**, the best of this charming little port's seafood restaurants; Tel: 42-01-03-77. Possessing few historic sites and a rarely open local museum, Cassis is a pleasant place to sit and admire the sea. Even the remarkable castle atop the hill to the east is inaccessible, although some guidebooks neglect to mention it altogether. This omission may have something to do with the castle's owners: the heirs to the Michelin fortune.

The scenery becomes truly awe-inspiring if the motorist takes the **corniche des Crêtes** (D 141) from Cassis to **La Ciotat**. Cliffs reaching almost 2,000 feet drop dizzyingly into the sea, their color changing from pale blue to bright white as dawn breaks over the Mediterranean. Standing on these wild heights, it is hard to imagine that a nearby city of more than one million people can be hidden from view.

From La Ciotat, a shipbuilding town, take the A 50 expressway in either direction, depending on your military ardor. A few minutes to the north, the unremarkable town of **Aubagne** houses the remarkable French Foreign Legion, the famous regiment that was repatriated at the end of the Franco-Algerian war in 1962. A museum recalls the exploits of Beau Geste and his fellows.

The other option is to go east on A 50 for a half-hour to **Toulon**, an unprepossessing city in a beautiful natural harbor that is the home port of the French navy. Here, predictably, a **Musée Maritime** awaits admiration, as do the **Musée d'Art et d'Archéologie** and the **Musée d'Histoire Naturelle**, both located in a modernized building on boulevard Maréchal Leclerc in the heart of the new town. The antiquities are well arranged and include Oriental as well as Western finds; the collection of paintings extends from the 13th century to the present. The works of modern art in this museum are just a foretaste of what lies east—the great galleries of the Côte d'Azur.

COTE D'AZUR

The contemporary impression of the French Riviera as a place for beautiful people dies hard. Each succeeding generation has had its own images of the chic and rich who have made the Côte d'Azur their partying ground. Today we dream of the dolce vita days of Bardot and swinging, topless St-Tropez, while 30 years ago people reminisced about F. Scott Fitzgerald's Antibes crowd. Fitzgerald himself wrote in *Tender Is the Night* about Rosemary Hoyt being driven along the Riviera: "The resplendent names—Cannes, Nice, Monte Carlo—began to glow through their torpid camouflage, whispering of old kings come here to dine or die, of rajahs tossing Buddha's eyes to English ballerinas, of Russian princes turning the weeks into Baltic twilights in the lost caviar days."

Today Arab sheikhs may have replaced Russian and English royalty, and the entire coast is crawling with thrill- and sun-seekers of all types and classes, but the jet and moneyed sets still come here.

The Riviera's natural setting proved attractive to paint- ers as well. Following in Van Gogh's brushstrokes, the Fauves centered in St-Tropez, Picasso settled in Antibes, Matisse moved to Nice, Chagall chose Vence, and count- less other artists have found their way to this sunny land.

Today art of the past (especially Impressionist) and of the present is as integral a part of the Riviera as sun, sea, garlic, and wine. More than 30 museums of various per- suasions stud the coast and hills between Menton and Hyères.

The Côte d'Azur is two distinctly different worlds: the coast and the *arrière-pays,* or back country. The latter includes the French Alps, less than an hour's drive north from Nice. The *arrière-pays* presents startlingly beautiful countryside (the rocky Vallée des Merveilles, the Gorges Rouges, and the Trois Corniches) and interesting vil- lages—the tiny, Medieval Colomars-les-Alpes, for exam- ple. These must be approached by car, and seeing them requires several days.

MAJOR INTEREST ON THE COTE D'AZUR

Iles d'Hyères
Nature and relative tranquillity

St-Tropez
Fishing-port charm with glitz
Musée de l'Annonciade

Cannes
Film festival
Hedonism

Antibes/Juan-les-Pins/Cap d'Antibes
Musée Picasso in Antibes
Swinging summer beach resort at Juan-les-Pins
More exclusive resorts at Cap d'Antibes

Biot
Musée National Fernand Léger

Vence/St-Paul-de-Vence
Matisse chapel

Fondation Maeght
La Colombe d'Or restaurant

Nice
Promenade des Anglais
Vieux Nice
Musée Chagall
Villa des Arènes: Matisse museum

Perched villages

Monaco
Monte-Carlo casino

Menton
Genteel Belle Epoque beauty
Musée des Beaux-Arts

The Late Rise of the Côte d'Azur

The name Côte d'Azur was coined in 1887 by Stephen Liégeard, politician and writer, who published a book on the Riviera entitled *La Côte d'Azur.* The new name was adopted almost immediately by the region and the rest of the French.

Liégeard described the area as a "coast of light, of warm breezes, and mysterious and balmy forests... from Genoa to Hyères, the route is short but delicious."

Perhaps the first visitor to discover the French Riviera was Hercules, who, according to legend, created the port of Villefranche-sur-Mer with his own hands. The first real tourist, in the modern sense, came in the 18th century: an Englishman, Tobias Smollett. What he saw wasn't exactly what's printed in today's vacation brochures. In his *Letters from Nice* he explained how he narrowly escaped from bandits in the Maures hills and almost drowned while crossing the then bridgeless river Var. He found the streets of Nice "full of excrement," the servants "repulsively dirty," and that "day and night, flies and fleas" swarm. The overall picture Smollett painted was a rosy one, however—he also told of the Riviera's natural beauty and lovely climate—and it attracted a great many English travellers to the city. Later, Russians and French followed.

The second half of the 19th century was the Riviera's Belle Epoque. "Princes and princes, everywhere princes!" remarked Guy de Maupassant in 1888. The railroad made it possible to travel from Vienna to Cannes in 31 hours in a luxurious Pullman sleeping car. By the end of the

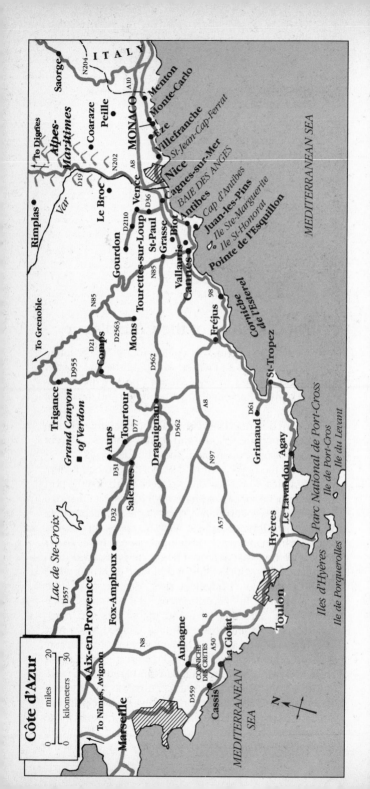

century a weekly St. Petersburg–Vienna–Cannes line carried the privileged to the azure coast. Casinos, splendid
villas, and grand hotels were built along the beaches;
Champagne, caviar, and money flowed.

The Era of the Summer Season

Yet it wasn't until the 1920s that the Riviera became a
summer, sea-bathing resort. Until then people came to
the coast to escape northern winters. By summertime
most of the Riviera set had either gone home or migrated
to Normandy and Brittany. A worldly Russian, Marie
Bashkirtseff, described the Riviera in summer as a deso-
late place: "It's deserted. I'm ready to cry, I'm suffering
so." Stepping into the sea for a dip was only for those with
a medical prescription, not yet a general fashion.

Summer tourism slowly came to the coast after World
War I, thanks to American soldiers. Antibes was the first
hot spot. John Dos Passos remarked that "rich British and
French would rather be dead than be seen here in the
summer. The place is too hot for them. But for us Americans, the temperatures seem perfect and the bathing
delicious. The sun cult is just beginning." Gertrude Stein,
Rudolph Valentino, Picasso, the Fitzgeralds, and Rex In-
gram were among the first summer tourists to come to
Antibes in the early 1920s. World War I also affected the
visitors from Europe: The October Revolution brought an
end to the Russian monarchy.

The major change in the Côte d'Azur took place after
1936, when the Socialist government, the Front Populaire, granted French workers the right to paid vacations
in July and August. For the first time a vacation on the
Riviera was possible for the masses. And the masses did
indeed come, as they still do.

ILES D'HYERES

The four islands of Hyères form an oasis of unspoiled
beauty just off the western end of the highly developed
Côte d'Azur, thanks to strict environmental-protection
controls. Of the four islands, only two are completely
open to visitors: Ile de Port-Cros and Ile de Porquerolles.
A major portion of the third, Ile du Levant, is reserved for
the French navy, and part of it harbors a large nudist
colony. The fourth, Ile de Bagaud, is an off-limits national

park reserve. Boats for Ile de Port-Cros and Ile de Porquerolles leave from Le Lavandou and Hyères. Le Lavandou is a bit off the beaten track, between Toulon and St-Tropez, but from there the crossing takes only 35 minutes. From Hyères, the boats leave less frequently and the trip takes one and a half hours.

For a quiet holiday amid some of the Mediterranean's most striking natural scenery, **Ile de Port-Cros** should top anyone's list. Motor vehicles are forbidden in the national park, and smoking, camping, and hunting are outlawed.

The island has one tiny village of 30 inhabitants, and few restaurants. Nevertheless, it does have a hotel, **Le Manoir**, which is situated in a hilltop park. It has only 26 rooms, so reservations must be made long in advance. (The hotel is closed from October 15 to Easter.) Several footpaths provide for a tranquil hike through the island's forests and hills. The path through the Vallée de la Solitude takes two and a half hours and leads to the southern coast. Along the way are some of the small forts rebuilt by Napoléon after the English and Spanish occupied the islands in 1793.

The most interesting of the forts is **Estissac** (open June through September). Built in the 17th century, the fort is on the path to the bay of Port-Man, a three-hour round-trip walk that leads to the northeast part of the island. Less hilly and less shaded than the Vallée de la Solitude path, this one ends in a magnificent horseshoe-shaped bay ringed by woods.

Tourism aside, the main activity of the island is the preservation of endangered Mediterranean marine species, including fish. Recently, monk seals from throughout the western Mediterranean were captured and brought to the island to protect them from extinction.

More developed than Port-Cros, **Ile de Porquerolles** nevertheless is car-free and has only a few hotels, including the secluded and moderately priced **Mas du Langoustier** and the more modest **Sainte-Anne**. The island has wide white-sand beaches, countless nature walks, and that rarity of the summertime Riviera—privacy.

ST-TROPEZ

St-Trop, as the hip call it, is indeed *trop*. Situated off the main highway, it requires a detour. This is both a blessing and a curse. These days it's more of a curse because it seems everybody wants to go to St-Tropez, and as a result the traffic snarls are intolerable on the small roads that lead in and out of this glitzy resort.

Those in the know, however, still go there, preferring the hidden St-Trop. They're the ones who have villas tucked away just outside the town. Or have their own swimming pools so they avoid the crowded beaches. Or know the spacious beaches—located mostly south of the city near the hamlet of Pampelonne: **Tahiti**, **Moorea**, and **Bora-Bora**.

These people include top writers—Françoise Sagan; movie directors—Claude Zidi; photographers—David Hamilton; actors and singers—Charles Aznavour and, of course, Brigitte Bardot, who recently threatened to move out because of people-pollution. The indignant mayor retorted by pointing out that before 1958—the year Bardot and her ilk descended on St-Tropez trailing paparazzi— the town never had any problem with crowds.

In spite of the congestion, St-Trop's old town center has kept much of its Provençal fishing-port charm. Some of the old-timers remain, and a few of them still even make a living fishing.

Artwork of universally high quality has been hung in the **Musée de l'Annonciade**, which occupies a former chapel right off the port. Signac, Derain, Maillol, Seurat, Vuillard, Vlaminck, Utrillo, Dufy, and the rest of that crowd are represented here.

No visit to St-Tropez would be complete without a trendy afternoon spent on the terrace of the **Sénéquier**, a café on quai Jean-Jaurès that overlooks the Vieux Port. It is local custom to bat one's eyelashes furiously when the skippers of the magnificent yachts moored in the marina saunter by on their way to pick up provisions of caviar and Champagne in the old town. If you fail to get an invitation aboard, consolation may be found at the excellent restaurant **Mas de Chastelas** south of town on the Route de Gassin. Local seafood is a specialty in the beautiful Tropezien garden setting. A tranquil hotel of the same name also stands on the site. Tan-exhibition in the guise of dancing might be called for back in town at the **Byblos** nightclub; conveniently, there is a deluxe— read expensive—hotel complex on the same spot.

CANNES

The coast road leading northeast from Agay to Cannes, called the **corniche de l'Esterel**, is a winding, spectacular succession of green maritime pines, red-clay cliffs, and, of course, deep-azure sea. This is convertible-sports-car country. Although the area lacks public beaches, the view from the **Pointe de l'Esquillon** includes Cannes's Golfe de la Napoule and, much farther on, Cap d'Antibes. The back country, the **Massif de l'Esterel**, makes for a beautiful outing among pine forests and red hills.

Cannes, a glamorous city of 72,000 residents, is a far cry from its early days as a resort, when Lord Brougham, an English traveller, was quarantined here in 1834 because of an outbreak of cholera in Provence. With its year-long round of conventions, Cannes offers visitors the sandy beaches west of town, a picturesque morning flower market in the Allées de la Liberté, and a harbor filled with yachts and sailboats. The old hillside quarter, **Le Suquet**, is a pretty Provençal citadel that contrasts with the quiet cosmopolitanism of the seaside hotels.

That relative stillness is shattered during the two middle weeks of May when the Cannes Film Festival is held. In the 1950s a small, exclusive affair—Grace Kelly met her prince here in 1955—the festival is now a gigantic media zoo: The city is awash in film billboards, starlets pose provocatively for paparazzi, and thousands of movie fans bask on the beaches or crowd the streets in the hope of glimpsing their screen idols.

The largest gathering of the world's cinema industry, its major players and deal-cutters—producers, directors, and actors—stay on the **Croisette**. The long coastal avenue begins at the Palais des Festivals (immediately dubbed "the bunker" on its opening in 1982) and ends at the Palm Beach casino. The Croisette has three palace hotels: the **Majestic**, the **Carlton Intercontinental**, and the **Martinez**. From five in the afternoon until two in the morning, the Majestic bar and poolside terrace are packed with festival-goers, journalists, and gawkers.

After the festival, the hotels empty out and Cannes quiets down. This is a good time to come. Although the three sumptuous Croisette hotels brim with romance and history, they are also very expensive. Seaside rooms are nearly double the rates of the others. Dining is good at all three hotels. The Carlton boasts two outstanding restaurants: beautiful **La Côte**, right off the lobby overlooking the boulevard de la Croisette, and **La Belle Otéro**, on the seventh floor. The winner at the Martinez is **La Palme d'Or**. At the moment, however, the top hotel-restaurant ranking in Cannes proper goes to the **Royal Gray** in the Hôtel Gray d'Albion on the rue des Etats-Unis.

Less splendid than its Croisette sisters is the **Splendid**, one of the best hotel bargains in Cannes. Just off the port, the Splendid is almost as comfortable as the other three but more homey and less fussy. It, too, has rooms facing the sea. To get away from the bustling center try the **Mont-fleury**, located on a hill overlooking the sea.

One of the pleasures of Cannes is lunching on the beach. A dozen beachside restaurants offer similar fare that is several steps up from—and many francs more than—typical snack food. Expect to pay 120 to 250 francs for any seaside meal. The Martinez serves an especially elaborate and impressive buffet.

In the evening **La Mère Besson**, behind the Croisette at 13, rue des Frères-Pardignac, serves traditional Provençal food. During the season, and especially during conventions or festivals, reservations are imperative (Tel: 93-39-59-24).

Excursions from Cannes

To get away from the crowds in Cannes, try hopping a boat at the Gare Maritime (next to the Palais) for a day trip to the **Iles de Lérins**. From April to September boats leave regularly, taking 15 minutes to get to Ile Ste-Marguerite and 30 minutes to the smaller and quieter Ile St-Honorat. Both islands have conserved their natural beauty, and motor vehicles are banned. Bring a picnic lunch.

In 410, Honorat, the son of a Roman consul, founded a monastery on **Ile St-Honorat**—one of the first in the Christian world. The island was chosen because of the Lérins's isolation and barren solitude. Nevertheless, the monastery's reputation spread quickly. Among its inhabitants were Saint Cassian, the founder of St-Victor in Marseille, and Saint Patrick of Ireland.

The original monastery was destroyed by the Moors in the eighth century but was rebuilt and fortified two hundred years later. The tenth-century tower still stands and is open to visitors.

After centuries of decline, the monastery was finally

shut, and the island sold, during the French Revolution. Monks returned in 1869, however, after the bishop of Fréjus purchased the island. A new monastery was built on the ruins of the old one and a group of Cistercian monks moved in. Cistercians still live here today. Although the island receives about 150,000 visitors a year, you can find quiet spots for a picnic and swim.

Ile Ste-Marguerite is larger and more touristic than Honorat, although its development has been tightly controlled by the government. The island has numerous nature trails lacing its 400 acres of forests, as well as the 17th-century Fort Royal, built with remains of Gallo-Roman monuments and construction materials. Originally a private castle, the fort has been converted into a sinister-looking prison.

Grasse, the famed heart of the perfume industry, is home to several fine museums well worth the 16-km (10-mile) drive north (via N 85) from Cannes. An elegant if small country house in a garden on the southwest edge of this hill town has become the **Villa Fragonard**. Fittingly enough, it's on the boulevard Jean-Honoré Fragonard, named for the 18th-century painter born in the village. Copies of panels painted for the countess du Barry (the originals are in New York City's Frick Collection) are displayed, as are original drawings, paintings, sketches, and etchings. (**Maison Fragonard** is among the most-visited *parfumeries* in this city of perfume-makers.)

An exceptionally interesting portrayal of the art and history of eastern Provence is shown in Grasse's **Musée d'Art et d'Histoire de Provence**, in a handsome 18th-century mansion just an amble from the Villa Fragonard off place du Cours. Collections range from prehistoric and Gallo-Roman remains to fine Moustiers china, rural tools, Louis XIV furniture, and paintings by local artists.

In 1988 the national **Musée International de la Parfumerie** opened a mere vial's throw away from the Provençal museum. As well as providing the standard—and at times impenetrable—technical explanations of perfume manufacture, this new museum differs from its privately run competitors by exhibiting an interesting collection of perfume bottles and advertisements on its third floor. The pride of this display is Marie Antoinette's *nécessaire,* an exquisitely crafted travelling makeup and perfume cabinet that the doomed queen last used during the royal family's unsuccessful flight from France during the Revolution.

ANTIBES, JUAN-LES-PINS, CAP D'ANTIBES

Antibes and its neighbors, Juan-les-Pins and Cap d'Antibes, contrast and complement each other. Antibes is one of the oldest ports on the Mediterranean; Juan-les-Pins was built in the late 19th century. While today these two towns are full of summer tourists, the Cap—the peninsula separating the two—remains one of the exclusive locations on the Riviera. About 30 km (19 miles) southwest of Nice, and only a stone's throw east of Cannes, the area is easily accessible by train, bus, or car.

Summertime, especially in July during the top-notch jazz festival, **Juan-les-Pins** swings, its nightclubs, cafés, and streets jammed with people late into the night. Jazz came to Juan-les-Pins with the first Americans, Jay Gould and F. Scott Fitzgerald. Over the years all the greats have passed through, including Louis Armstrong, Count Basie, Dizzy Gillespie, and Ray Charles. Most of the shows are held outdoors on a stage that borders the sea beaches.

A truly sybaritic seafood meal may be had at **La Terrasse** (Tel: 93-61-08-70) on the avenue Georges Gallice, although stingier gastronomes might prefer the tasty pigeon stew at the **Auberge de l'Esterel** on the rue des Iles. **Les Mimosas** is the least expensive of the beach resort's fine hotels and possesses an admirable swimming pool and park.

Juan-les-Pins's older cousin, **Antibes**, was founded in the fifth century B.C. by Greeks as Antipolis, meaning the city that faces. What it faced has always puzzled historians. Over the centuries, Antibes was a military stronghold, and ancient fortifications remain.

One of the city's most interesting attractions is the **Musée Picasso**, located in the Grimaldi castle, which was reconstructed in the 16th century. It shows off paintings, drawings, tapestries, sculptures, ceramics, and lithographs by the prolific Spaniard, who produced a surprising number of them during his six-month stint as curator of an antiquities museum, during which time he also used the rooms as a studio. (The antiquities Picasso oversaw are now in the **Musée d'Archéologie**, in the St-André Bastion, part of the city's old fortifications: 300,000 items illustrate 4,000 years of regional history.)

Not far from the Picasso museum, on the rue Clemenceau, is a typical Provençal market bordered by streets that contain several Medieval houses. In the winter of 1990 the **Musée Paynet** opened on place Nationale. It is devoted to the work of Raymond Paynet, who created the young lovers often seen on regional posters. He also illustrates books, paints theatrical backdrops, and works in animated films, as well as producing sculptures and porcelains—all charmingly naïve, in the happiest sense of the word. The place Nationale is a bustling square with outdoor cafés and two comfortable, small, moderately priced hotels, **Le Caméo** and the **Auberge Provençale**.

The most famous restaurant on the Riviera is **La Bonne Auberge**, located just outside of Antibes on N 7. While its classic Provençal cuisine remains highly rated (two Michelin stars), the restaurant is suffering from its international reputation and has lost its romantic touch. (Tel: 93-33-36-65.)

To get away from the crowds, head to **Cap d'Antibes**. For deep pockets, there's the **Hôtel du Cap d'Antibes**, with its superb view of the Mediterranean and its renowned restaurant, **Pavillon Eden Roc**. Most of the top Hollywood stars stay at the hotel during the Cannes Film Festival. With a car, cruise the Cap in search of an off-the-beaten-track beach. They still exist, but don't expect a deserted oasis. More likely the beach will be an extension of a seaside restaurant. For night owls, the depressingly named **Le Bureau** is bringing in the neighborhood's beautiful partiers.

Two nearby small towns—Biot and Vallauris—boast excellent museums that should not be missed. **Biot**, a pretty village of flower markets, ceramic shops, and glassworks, is known chiefly for the stark, light, altogether admirable **Musée National Fernand Léger**, created by the Cubist's widow in 1957, two years after his death. The more than 300 works on display include ceramics, stained glass, paintings, mosaics, and even tapestries. The museum is located southeast of the village, off Route D 4.

In **Vallauris**, a bustling little town just to the west of Antibes where Picasso came to create ceramics for several years after World War II, the centrally located château contains the **Musée Municipal**, with its exhibitions of ceramics from Etruscan times to our own, as well as the **Musée National la Guerre et la Paix**, a priory chapel decorated with an immense composition Picasso executed in 1952.

ST-PAUL-DE-VENCE

At one time St-Paul was the center for Europe's most vibrant artistic minds: Marc Chagall, Jacques Prévert, Georges Braque, Pablo Picasso, Yves Montand, Simone Signoret, André Malraux, and James Baldwin are but a few of those who have made this village perched on a hillside their home or meeting place in the fairly recent past. Time has taken its toll, and few of that generation are left. Nevertheless, the tradition continues, thanks in part to the Fondation Maeght.

One of the best modern art collections in France as well as one of the region's top visitor attractions, the **Fondation Maeght** was raised in the midst of a tangled pine forest in the early 1960s by Paris gallery owners and publishers Aimé and Marguerite Maeght. Even the architect was an artist, the Spaniard José Luis Sert. In such an environment, the works of Calder, Arp, Zadkine, Miró, Braque, Bonnard, Chagall, Léger, Kandinsky, Giacometti, and others seem peculiarly happy and at home. The foundation also has living quarters for artists and a vast art library.

St-Paul itself, with its 2,600 inhabitants, is invaded by tourists on spring holidays and during the peak summer season. Yet even at its busiest time, St-Paul is quieter than the beach resorts. March and late September are excellent times to visit here. The village has a Medieval fortress wall, a rebuilt Romanesque church, and narrow, hilly, winding alleys full of art galleries and craft shops. On the shaded terrace of the **Café de la Place**, visitors have ringside seats for the interminable games of boules (or pétanque) played by the locals—and occasionally by such resident celebrities as Yves Montand. The object of this Provençal obsession is to land your boule closest to the *cochonnet,* the small ball that is at the center of afternoon-consuming stratagems.

Surrounding St-Paul are forested parks where several hotels are located, among them the **Mas d'Artigny**. This outstanding Relais & Châteaux property, on a 16-acre park, has some reasonably priced rooms in off-season; most of them include large private balconies with views of the woods. Waking up to birds singing in the morning in this calm, pastoral setting is a far cry from the hubbub of the coast. For big spenders, 25 rooms have their own swimming pools (the hotel has a rather large pool for all guests as well)—an extravagance that can be very appealing for a honeymoon or other special occasion.

Many people pass through St-Paul just to have a meal at **La Colombe d'Or**—a pricey but delightful restaurant-hotel that has welcomed heads of state, artists, and actors to its rustic terraces and farmhouse interior.

Catherine Deneuve says that if she wants to be seen she goes to Maxim's in Paris; if she wants a quiet meal away from the crowds, she eats at La Colombe d'Or. During most of the year meals are served in its main dining room, which houses an impressive collection of paintings that artists—Modigliani, Bonnard, Dufy, Utrillo, Chagall, Picasso, Braque, Matisse, and Miró among them—presented to owner Paul Roux in their leaner days in return for his hospitality. In warm weather seating is available on the patio, which offers an unobstructed view of the valley below.

It's always best to reserve a table here no matter what the time of year; Tel: 93-32-80-02. The fare is traditional, and unexceptional, Provençal; the service is friendly and informal. The Colombe d'Or's hotel, with only 25 rooms, is usually booked solid at peak season. The cost of an overnight stay or a fine meal in such surroundings is a small price to pay for such an atmosphere; rooms are expensive, but the wall painting might be by Rouault. The hotel also has a heated swimming pool.

Vence

Vence, with 13,000 inhabitants, is much larger than St-Paul. You must pass through Vence to get to St-Paul, and it's well worth your time to stop, if only to see the Medieval walls and interesting cathedral. Rebuilt over the centuries, the cathedral is constructed in part with stones from the Carolingian period and has a late-19th-century Rococo façade.

A car-crowded resort in all seasons, Vence now enjoys serenity only in the **Chapelle du Rosaire**, which Matisse designed and decorated—down to the candles and vestments—between 1947 and 1951. Of it (and perhaps of his astonishing versatility), the artist wrote: "Despite its imperfections I think it is my masterpiece ... the result of a lifetime devoted to the search for truth." (The chapel is open only on Tuesday and Thursday mornings and afternoons.)

NICE

Nice is the grande dame of the Riviera. Its stately grid of Belle Epoque buildings faces a long pebble beach surmounted by the promenade des Anglais, the site of seaside constitutionals for generations of English aristocrats. This is not the place to look for picturesque Mediterranean squalor—even its old town, hard by a rocky citadel to the east, is as clean as any German tourist's fantasy. Inhabitants of the biggest city on the Côte d'Azur (population 340,000), the Niçois are the Parisians of the south, only here the rarely needed fur coats may be dyed purple, and the clothes and makeup of the *grandes bourgeoises* are usually far more colorful than those of their sisters in the north.

Yet Nice occasionally rouses itself from its genteel torpor, even in the off-season. In February an elaborate three-week carnival is held around the city's place Masséna. Although closing night (Mardi Gras) is uncharacteristically Dionysian with the burning of a huge carnival effigy, it is the series of Batailles des Fleurs (flower pageants) held Wednesdays and Saturdays that draw the Niçois to their pre-Lenten blow-out. Elaborate floats covered in blooms wend their way through town showering onlookers with every conceivable type of flower. In July, when the admirable Niçois weather goes from mild to hot, a month-long jazz festival takes place in the city's Cimiez district.

Like most cities on the coast, Nice is an ancient town, founded by the Marseillais in 350 B.C. It was first Roman, then part of Provence until 1388, when it was taken over by the Savoies of Switzerland and northern Italy. Nice didn't become French until 1861, a tardiness long ago compensated for by the droves of retired French who have made this city their home. Sophisticated and comfortable, Nice is nonetheless discreetly Mediterranean in its conduct of municipal business. Graham Greene, longtime resident of nearby Antibes, felt moved in the 1970s to write a controversial pamphlet, entitled "J'Accuse!", decrying the questionable practices of Nice's ruling elite.

But this whispered disrepute only adds to the grande dame's charm. Even if its older hotels seem a trifle musty and its new hillside suburbs a mite slipshod, the city core—the promenade des Anglais, Vieux Nice, Cimiez, and the floral esplanades leading to the Acropolis convention center—retains an understated attraction. The crowds at the Nice–Côte d'Azur airport, the second busiest in France, immediately tip off the observant traveller as to how well-heeled and well-groomed the city is. The spanking new botanical garden, the Parc Floral, across the street from the airport, reinforces first impressions. Whereas other gardens on the Riviera just offer you the opportunity of admiring the flora, in Nice the entire place is dotted with interactive video monitors. Nothing is too good for Nice—as long as it's discreet.

The Promenade des Anglais

The promenade, a long and bustling avenue that borders the bay, is lined with dozens of large hotels, posh apartment buildings, and museums. On avenue des Baumettes, not far off the promenade, the **Musée des Beaux-Arts Jules Chéret** devotes itself to 17th- and 18th-century European paintings, a collection of sculptures by Jean-Baptiste Carpeaux, 19th- and 20th-century landscapists, many posters and studies by founder Chéret, and several Impressionist works. On rue de France in a little park just off the promenade, the **Musée Masséna** (named for a local boy made Napoleonic general) illustrates the history, folklore, town planning, home decoration, and paintings of Nice and its region and houses some paintings from Italian, Spanish, and Flemish schools.

For a pleasant and affordable lunch with a clear view of the bay, go up to the seventh-story poolside restaurant in the modern and high-priced **Beach Régency Hotel**. If you stay there, the higher the room the better—if you value peace and quiet. Seaside rooms are usually more costly, but the scenery is worth it. This large, unpretentious hotel is a favorite with North American business people, but its location at the far western end of the promenade makes it inconvenient for visiting the city.

The promenade begins at the other end of Nice, in the east by the Jardin Albert I, and runs westward for what seems to be forever. At number 1 is the modern, comfortable **Méridien**. The promenade's older and grander hotels were built at the turn of the century, the grandest of all, with its Empire and Napoléon III decor, being the **Négresco**. Constructed in 1912 by a Hungarian immigrant, Henri Négresco, the hotel is now a national monument.

Before starting the hotel, Négresco was director of the city casino's restaurant—one of the *hauts lieux* frequented by the richest people in the world, including the Rockefellers and the Singers. Négresco built his hotel to attract this upper-crust clientele. Unfortunately, World War I was declared a year later, and the hotel was turned into a hospital. Négresco died a ruined man shortly after the war. The hotel survived, however, and flourished with the coming of Americans and the surprising discovery that summer on the Riviera can be even more fun than winter. Today you never know who you might bump into at the Négresco, from Elton John to heads of state.

The hotel's restaurant, the formal and expensive **Chantecler** (Tel: 93-88-39-51), is considered one of France's finest. Chef Jacques Maximin left the Chantecler to start his own restaurant, but not to worry: Dominique Le Stanc has stepped in to fill the bill with fine Provençal cuisine. The desserts continue to rank among the most brilliant in France, the service is efficient—and the prices, incredibly, have come down.

Reopened in 1990 after five years of renovation, that *hôtel du grand standing,* the **Beau Rivage**, is once again welcoming selective travellers to its quiet and comfort just off the promenade des Anglais (where it becomes the quai des Etats-Unis; entrance on rue St-François-de-Paul). It's ambling distance from place Masséna, the Jardin Albert I, and even Old Nice, and, though expensive, its rooms start at half the rate of the Négresco's. Don't miss its beachside restaurant, bar, and swimming-tanning area.

A sister to the Beau Rivage, the unremittingly modern **Elysée Palace**, at the opposite (western) end of the promenade des Anglais, made its debut in 1988, complete with rooftop pool, a sauna and gym, business club and conference facilities, and a very popular piano bar. Rates are comparable to those of the Beau Rivage.

In a category slightly below that of the above hotels, but still stylish, welcoming, and with an indoor-outdoor restaurant right on the promenade des Anglais, the **Westminster Concorde** is a super buy in its bracket (moderately expensive).

Vieux Nice and Cimiez

East of the promenade and away from the beach is the old center of town. Vieux Nice is full of animation—smacking of Italian influence—and has many small, inexpensive restaurants and pizzerias. Its main attraction is the **cours Saleya**, a colorful marketplace where the best of local fish catches, flowers, and the green-sprout salad known as *mesclun* are sold to throngs of Niçois and tourists. Delivery boys arrive occasionally with hot *socca,* a battered chickpea crêpe that is as satisfying as the old town itself. In its narrow Italianate streets, Baroque churches vie with hanging laundry and designer snooker parlors for the attention of the visitor. Totally unlike the formal grid to the west, Vieux Nice is manageably small, as are the *additions* in its many restaurants. The century-old **Au Chapon Fin**, on rue Moulin, is a perennial favorite with locals.

The oldest part of Nice is today a sophisticated residential area. **Cimiez** sits on a hill where the Romans settled a camp in the first century B.C. At its height, in the third century A.D., Cimiez had 20,000 residents and was the capital of a small eastern province of Gaul called Alpes Maritimae—today's Alpes-Maritimes *département.*

During the third century the Romans built thermal baths and arenas in Cimiez. The Roman **amphitheater** still stands but is in bad shape. Nice's jazz festival, which takes place in July in and around the amphitheater, is a relaxed affair, one ticket providing entry to concerts throughout the day. The event coincides with the older and more renowned Antibes festival.

Travellers intrigued by art as well as archaeology discover a double-barreled attraction in the **Villa des Arènes** in Cimiez. When Henri Matisse died in a nearby house in 1954, his widow donated a great number of works to Nice, specifying the 17th-century villa as the spot where they should be displayed. The rich collection includes paintings, drawings, sketches, models, bronze sculptures, and the artist's personal effects. The fascinating archaeological museum on the villa's ground floor contains exhibits from excavations in the neighborhood. Nearby is a newly opened modern art museum, the **Musée d'Art Moderne et Contemporain**, which has been conceived on a scale befitting Nice's grand ambitions in contemporary art.

In 1971 the **Musée National Message Biblique Marc Chagall** opened, also in Cimiez, to house the artist's gifts to France: 17 canvases of biblical inspiration, 300 graphic works, five sculptures, a tapestry, three stained-glass windows, and a huge mosaic. The lively, glowing, amusing fantasies are well served by the light and airy museum.

Other parts of the city are dotted with museums that deserve a visit, especially the amusing **Musée International d'Art Naïf** on the avenue du Val Marie in far western Nice. The Anatole Jakovsky bequest of some 600 canvases (about half on display at any one time) features amateur art from many countries, especially that of Jakovsky and other Yugoslavs. Childish, primitive, and illusory, the works are simultaneously well crafted, harmonious, and ingenious.

Nice museums devoted to subjects other than art include the **Musée d'Histoire Naturelle**, near place Garibaldi in Old Nice; the **Musée Maritime**, on the grounds of the Nice Château; the **Musée Terra Amata**, a fascinating and unique exhibition of a prehistoric habitat on the very site of its discovery, on boulevard Carnot east of the port; and the **Musée Vieux-Logis**, a priory outfitted with artworks and items from daily life of the 14th to 17th centuries, in St-Barthélemy on the northern edge of town.

Outskirts of Nice

Just east of Nice, on the beautiful wooded peninsula of **St-Jean-Cap-Ferrat**, is the **Villa Ephrussi de Rothschild**, the only villa here that is open to the public. The baroness's art collections and those of her wealthy father and husband (the combined collections are often called the Musée d'Ile de France) are complemented by the villa and its furnishings: Savonnerie carpets, Beauvais and Aubusson tapestries, Chinese vases, and the like. The gardens and their ornamentation also are magnificent.

In one of the most splendid settings on the entire Riviera, the **Grand Hôtel du Cap-Ferrat** sits in its own great park atop the ocean cliffs. Its cuisine is renowned, its swimming pool and ajoining Club Dauphin something Hollywood might have dreamed up for Esther Williams and a bevy of beauties, and breakfast on the terrace is the stuff of romances. It's also dizzyingly expensive.

On the way to St-Jean you might stop in at the **Chapelle St-Pierre** in **Villefranche**, right by the little port, once a fisherman's sanctuary; it was painted from top to bottom, inside and out, by Jean Cocteau in 1957. Cocteau also decorated **St. Peter's Chapel**, right in the heart of the port, with line frescoes of the life of Saint Peter.

To the west of Nice, just beyond the airport, stands the resort of **Cagnes-sur-Mer**. In 1902, Jean Renoir bought a property in Cagnes named Les Collettes, built a house, and lived in it with his wife for the last 12 years of his life. Now the **Musée Renoir**, the house remains as it was, containing a few artworks, furniture, and, in the studio, the artist's wheelchair (he suffered from rheumatoid arthritis in his final years and painted with brushes strapped to his hand); the delightful garden will be familiar to you from many of his paintings.

Haut-de-Cagnes, the now-fashionable older part of Cagnes, clusters around the reworked 14th-century Grimaldi castle, today the **Château-Musée**. Like the castle's current appearance, the collections are nothing if not eclectic, the two most interesting constituting a museum of the olive tree and a museum of modern Mediterranean art.

The 12-room **Hôtel Le Cagnard** is a rustic retreat in Haut-de-Cagnes, with a fine kitchen and a compelling view. The definition of coziness, it is only moderately expensive.

THE PERCHED VILLAGES

Like aeries, like tree houses, like nature's mysterious "hanging" rocks, the more than 60 "perched" villages of the Côte d'Azur sit on hilltops above the Riviera or cling precariously to the flanks of mountains, digging their toes into the rock.

Villages perchés, the French call them, haunts and hideaways, peasant dwelling places from the past that range from the now-chic Eze, overhanging Monte-Carlo, to Saorge, clinging catlike to a spur of the Alpes-Maritimes, to Gourdon, crouching around its 13th-century fortress and battling the ghosts of Saracens.

Most of the villages cluster in the high reaches north of Nice, this way or that, in an area extending roughly from the Grand Canyon of the Verdon in the west to very near the Italian border in the east—east or west of the roads marked N 204, D 19, or N 202. Others may be reached by driving north from Cannes or Fréjus or Toulon, east from Manosque or south from Digne: What's essential is a large-scale map of the region.

For centuries, the country people built their rampart-sheltered retreats in this way, hiding out from Alemannic and other invaders, from Muslim pirates and other mercenaries of the Middle Ages, and from lawless raiders of the Renaissance. Some of the towns, nearly deserted, seem to grow out of the hillside stones, their arcaded streets as tangled and intriguing as fairy tales.

They tend to have wonderful names, too: Rimplas and Le Broc, Fox-Amphoux and Tourtour.

Tourtour

As of this writing, 384 people live in Tourtour, which ambles through its small square in the shade of two 17th-century elms. An occasional visitor may be cited for parking violations by the policeman, who wants someone to chat with.

The main occupation in Tourtour would seem to be eating, since the comely little hamlet boasts not one but two remarkable restaurants: **Chênes Verts**, slightly west of town on route Villecroze (best to reserve; Tel: 94-70-55-06), and the dining room of **La Bastide**, route Draguignan, a 25-room inn of imposing size and shape that looks down upon its swimming pool and out to an uninterrupted horizon. (Most of its rooms are expensive, but then such privileged isolation always is these days.)

It is also possible to spend a night or so in comfort at substantially less cost at the **Auberge St-Pierre** (just east of town on D 51, 17 rooms, its own park, quiet) or the **Petite Auberge** (just south on D 77, 11 rooms, cozy, beautiful view). Tourtour is 10 km (6 miles) from Aups and 11 km (7 miles) from Salernes; it is best to drive west of Grasse to Draguignan on D 562, about 55 km (35 miles), continue on a wiggle named D 557, then arc north on D 77.

From the metropolis of Tourtour it's a hop and a skipped stone to **Trigance**, which almost isn't there at all (122 inhabitants), at the entrance to the wild Gorges du Verdon. (The most direct route is via N 85 from Cannes through Grasse to Le Logis du Pin, then a left hook to Comps on D 21 and a short swivel north on D 955.) What you do here is hide out at the eight-room **Château de Trigance** pretending to be a Medieval person of privilege and paying a very reasonable rate for that experience.

Northward then west on D 955 and D 952 respectively brings you to one of the most spectacular natural sights in France: the **Grand Canyon of the Verdon**. A day-long drive around this deep, narrow gash in the landscape is breathtaking—at some points the drop to the canyon is more than 2,000 feet. Trigance is the ideal starting and finishing point for the circuit.

The Central Area

Driving from west to east, the collector of perched villages may be content just to see them as relics, as rural phenomena in a countryscape stuffed with cities. On the other hand, a few sport sites of interest beyond their own sinuous streets: In **Grimaud**, 10 km (6 miles) from St-Tropez, the 11th-century Romanesque basilica and the one-star restaurant **Les Santons**; in **Mons**, 40 km (25 miles) west of Grasse, the church with five 17th-century altarpieces, and the fountain-splashed squares; in **Tourette-sur-Loup**, just west of Vence, the church's artistic treasures and the many craft shops; in **Peille**, 25 km (16 miles) northeast of Nice, the church and gorgeous old covered passageways; in **Coaraze**, not far from Peille, the cemetery, the artisans' shops, and the chapel of Our Lady of Sorrow.

Tourette-sur-Loup, Bar-sur-Loup, Gourdon, and other towns to the northwest of Nice are easily reached from the clean, modest **Du Rédier**, in Colomars. A member of Logis de France (Country Hotels & Inns of France), it has 26 moderately-priced rooms, a flower-filled garden, and a swimming pool.

Near Peille, the irresistibly picturesque hilltop village of Peillon boasts the pretty, comfortable **Auberge de la Madone**. Its 19 rooms are only 20 km (12 miles) from Nice, but seem to exist in another century; the inn is moderately priced.

Northeast of Nice

Saorge, northeast of Nice on N 204, via a road that climbs up gorges through the Roya Valley, ranks among the most photogenic of the perched towns, its houses backed against the steep slopes as if afraid of falling forward into the river. The streets are stairways, the views sensational.

Most stylish, most celebrated, easiest to reach of the perched villages (but worth the while despite all that) is **Eze**, which looks down upon Nice, Monte-Carlo, and the blue Mediterranean. To walk in the steps of Friedrich Nietzsche, take the mule path named after him down toward the lower corniche; Nietzsche dreamed up *Thus Spake Zarathustra* while walking this same path.

More than two thousand lucky cliff-hangers live atop this rocky spike and somehow, in cars, negotiate its skinny streets. Visitors put themselves up at the **Château Eza** (six very expensive rooms, three apartments) or at the older, more traditional **Château de la Chèvre d'Or** (five rooms, three apartments, just as expensive), both with smashing settings and superb dining rooms. These are definitely places for leading the oysters-Champagne–wild strawberries life.

—*Georgia I. Hesse*

MONACO

Monaco, situated on a 450-acre rock extending into the sea east of Nice and Eze, is crammed with towering high-rises, one-armed bandits, armed policemen, and a pampered population that pays no taxes and serves no one but their illustrious prince, Rainier III, the 26th head of the Grimaldi family, Monaco's founders. Popular legend has it that in 1297 François Grimaldi and his men, disguised as monks, took the rock by force. The Grimaldi family has served as its lords ever since.

Make no mistake, the Monégasques revere their sovereign prince, who runs this postage-stamp principality like a father. His rebellious daughter Her Royal Highness Princess Stephanie aside, Rainier III has been successful in keeping his kingdom in check. Monaco is the closest thing to a crimeless, clean, fiscally sound paradise on earth. Before rushing out to apply for citizenship, though, remember that of Monaco's 27,000 inhabitants, only 4,500 are full-fledged citizens. The rest, alas, are mere mortals—rich, maybe, but tax-paying.

Not everyone is welcomed in this quasi-police state. It's not unheard of for officers to stop questionable-appearing travellers and inform them not to linger in Monaco. Rainier is after image, and shabby people have no role to play in his film script—except, of course, for the thousands of immigrant workers who stay out of sight in Monaco's small food-processing factories.

Monaco's high elevation by the sea creates a micro-climate that results in extremely mild winter temperatures. The tiny principality consists of Monaco (the old town), La Condamine (its bustling port), Monte-Carlo (casinos and shops), and Fontvielle (small industry). The city of Monaco houses the royal family, the administration, and the famed Musée Océanographique.

The prince's palace offers 35-minute guided tours from June to October but is closed to the public the rest of the year. Every day come rain or even snow, the colorful changing of the palace guard takes place at 11:55 A.M. The oldest part of the palace was built in the 13th century as a fortress and rebuilt in Italian Renaissance style in the 15th and 16th centuries.

Prince Albert I, a sea explorer and inventor of underwater photographic techniques, created the **Musée Océanographique** in 1899. It took ten years to build the monumental white-stone building on a promontory that hangs over the sea. Nearby are the Jardin St-Martin and Monaco's cathedral.

Included in the museum's collection are 10,000 species of shellfish, a zoological exhibition of rare marine animals, and an immense aquarium stocked with Mediterranean and tropical fish. The aquarium is one of the largest and oldest in the world.

Monte-Carlo Casino

Monte-Carlo is the shining crown in the amazing success story of this fairyland. Today its name is so well known around the world, and its image so strong, that no one can mistake Monte-Carlo for anything other than what it is—a high-rolling, high-class gambling mecca that tries hard to be platinum to Las Vegas's tinsel.

This wasn't always the case. More than a hundred years ago Monaco was a poor, isolated rock run by a comic-opera prince, Floristan I. The artistically inclined prince painted while his principality headed for bankruptcy. He had already lost his major source of income—agricultural products from the fields of Menton and Roquebrune, two areas annexed to France in 1848. But Floristan I preferred painting his aquarelles to running Monaco, so he abdicated the throne to his son, Charles III.

Almost out of desperation, the new prince approved construction of a gambling house in the small village of Monte-Carlo, to be run by two Frenchmen—Aubert and Langlois—who had had their gambling license pulled by Napoléon III and had chosen Monaco because it wasn't under Napoléon's jurisdiction. The two men told Charles III that casinos would attract rich tourists from the Côte d'Azur.

The first Monte-Carlo gambling house was a disaster. Not only was the casino uncomfortably small and horribly decorated, but getting to Monaco from Nice was virtually impossible. Finally François Blanc, a banker, tried his hand. Blanc had already succeeded in Hamburg, but in

1862 Bismarck had come to power and outlawed gambling. Blanc packed his bags and headed for Monaco.

He explained to the now-weary Prince Charles III that "Monte-Carlo's vocation is written in its history... the Phoceans founded Monaco, and it's incontestable that Greeks are the greatest gamblers in the world." Blanc spared no expense in putting up his casino. To do the job he called in architect Charles Garnier, who later added to his fame by building the Paris Opéra. Garnier's casino was pompous and grandiose.

To overcome the transportation problem, Blanc arranged for an extension of the main railroad to Monaco. The train cut travelling time from Nice to Monaco from four hours to 15 minutes, and Monte-Carlo was finally on the map.

To welcome the new gamblers, Blanc built the **Hôtel de Paris**, one of the world's most glamorous hostelries. Today its two restaurants, the **Grille** and the astronomically priced **Louis XV**, are among the best in Monte-Carlo.

To finance the Monte-Carlo Casino, the hotel, and the original restaurant, Blanc and Charles III formed the new Société des Bains de Mer. Within a few years, the casino and Monaco were awash in European royalty and, subsequently, in millions of francs. So great was the casino's income that Charles III decided to exonerate the Monégasques from paying taxes.

The ornate **Monte-Carlo Casino**, the first of the principality's two gaming establishments, sits elegantly on a hillside terrace overlooking the sea. It is open to all well-dressed visitors over the age of 21. No entry fee is required for the main rooms, which have a few blackjack tables, dozens of fruit machines, and a beautifully appointed café. A taste of glamor, however, costs money— about 50 francs to enter the posh gaming rooms (jacket and tie mandatory). Even if you're not going to gamble, a visit to these Belle Epoque rooms is worth the admission, for both the hushed elegance and the sleek clientele. Private rooms are available and are usually reserved for gamblers who have moored their ocean liner–sized yachts in Condamine harbor.

Decline and Rebirth

Monte-Carlo's reputation suffered greatly over the years. By the time Rainier III took power, 95 percent of Monaco's economy was reliant on the sagging and aging gambling industry. Rainier decided to transform the rock into a fiscal paradise with a broader economic base, including business and light industry. The turning point in Monaco's modern-day fortunes was Rainier's marriage in 1956 to American actress Grace Kelly, who created a powerful public relations machine for the principality.

Rainier also threw open Monaco's doors to real-estate speculators, who some observers contend have turned this country-club country into a high-rise horror. He introduced American-style gambling and brought in the sprawling 636-room **Loews Hotel**—the antithesis of the Paris or Monaco's other splendid Belle Epoque hotel, the **Hermitage**. Loews, the most "American" and modern of the major hotels, has its own casino and cabaret. The seven-story hotel is built over the water, and its seaside rooms are the only reason to book into this otherwise characterless place. In fact, these seaside rooms are among the best accommodations on the Riviera, as they give the impression that you are on an ocean cruise.

MENTON

"Cannes is for living, Monte-Carlo for playing, and Menton for dying," goes the old wheeze. Indeed, it's true that Menton always has appealed to the elderly, largely because the steep mountains behind it wall out the miserable mistral and create milder winters than elsewhere along the Riviera.

Menton is the last stop along the Côte d'Azur before Italy, France's last Riviera hurrah. Once Geoffrey Bocca (in *Bikini Beach*) wrote of it, "At various times . . . Menton has belonged to France, Italy, and Monaco, and it has been a separate republic. But none of this has ever succeeded in making it interesting."

Today Menton *is* interesting, possibly because more than any city on this tourist-trammeled coast it retains a gentility, an understated and upper-crust classiness, a Belle Epoque beauty.

Menton, in its quieter corners, still speaks of the late 19th and early 20th centuries, when Katherine Mansfield joined Blasco Ibáñez on local celebrity lists. European aristocracy mingled with *les artistes* (successful ones, that is) on the broad terraces of the promenade du Soleil, still the chosen spot for strolling.

Today the visitor comes to town to see the Jean Cocteau, the Palais Carnolès, and the municipal museums, to attend the chamber music festival on the Italianate parvis St-Michel in August, to admire the fine Baroque church of St-Michel, to celebrate the lemon festival on Shrove Tuesday (Menton's lemons are for lemon connoisseurs), and to photograph and quietly enjoy the Jardin Biovès in the heart of town, the tropical gardens near the Villa Val Rahmeh, and the Jardin des Colombières edging the smart Garavan residential area.

The **Musée des Beaux-Arts**, also called the Musée du Palais Carnolès, occupies the former summer residence of Monaco's Grimaldi Prince Anthony I on avenue de la Madonne. It was later a casino, then the home of Dr. Edward P. Aldiss, an American. A museum since 1977, it displays the works of various French and Italian old masters as well as contemporary works, including one by Graham Sutherland.

Right on the quai Napoléon in Menton's 17th-century bastion, the **Musée Jean Cocteau** features the writer's fantasies in art: ceramics, paintings, gray-white tesserae (pebble paintings). A ticket to this museum also allows entrance to the **Salle des Mariages** in the old Hôtel de Ville, a room decorated by Cocteau in pseudo-Greek-temple style.

Menton's **Musée Municipal** is a repository of ancient arts and archaeological artifacts.

Menton is outfitted with hotels in all categories except, for some reason, the grandest. Because of its location right on the promenade du Soleil, the **Princess et Richmond** frequently gets the nod; although it has no restaurant, it has 43 rooms and reasonable prices by Riviera standards. **Chambord**, which enjoys a somewhat quieter location near the Jardin Biovès, also has no dining room and ranks in the same price category.

For dining, the choice is clear: **Chez Mireille-l'Ermitage** (Tel: 93-35-77-23) on the promenade du Soleil near the casino, where in clement weather meals are served on a sunny terrace.

Two very different Riviera experiences within a few miles of Menton illustrate the varied nature of this historic coast. Just 3 km (2 miles) east and up on the Grande Corniche near Roquebrune-Cap-Martin, the smart **Vista Palace** perches atop cliffs that rise steeply from the sea. It's a smashing 42-room inn with a restaurant—Vistaero—worth a detour even from Nice (especially for a twilight drink and dinner). As you would expect, it's expensive.

Make a short side-trip to the village of **La Turbie**, with its surprising Roman highway marker, La Trophée des Alpes.

On the other hand, simplicity, unspoiled rusticity, and a pretty mountain-valley setting can all be found in the village of Sospel. For lunch and a seemingly remote place to stay overnight, try the modestly-priced ten-room **Etrangers** right in town, or perhaps the even more reasonable 10-room **Auberge Provençale** on a bluff just beyond town.

—*Georgia I. Hesse*

GETTING AROUND

The gateway to the south of France is Nice. It is about seven hours from Paris via the TGV, and its international airport services flights from Paris as well as from New York, London, and other major cities around the world. From Nice you can make easy train and bus connections to Cannes, Monaco, Avignon, Aix-en-Provence, Marseille, and all other major towns and cities in the region. Larger cities, among them Marseille, Arles, and Avignon, are directly serviced by train from Paris. (If you are beginning a tour of Provence and the Côte d'Azur from the north, you can take the TGV directly from Paris to Avignon.) Even the smaller villages—such as Les Baux and St-Paul-de-Vence—are usually connected to larger towns by frequent bus service.

Autoroute A 8 and other major roads connect towns throughout the south. The most scenic road, though, is the old, winding corniche that follows the Riviera all the way from St-Tropez to Menton.

Personalized art trips to museums and—equally enjoyable—to the homes and/or studios of the Nice-Riviera school of contemporary artists are arranged by P.A.T., the creation of Canadian Pat Hyduk, at 2, allée des Ormes, Les Hauts de Vaugrenier, 06270 Villeneuve-Loubet (9 km/5 miles west of Cagnes); Tel: 93-20-37-60.

In addition, P.A.T. operates Riviera on Request, which arranges for personalized antiques-hunting and shopping excursions, gastronomic events, wine tours, and yacht charters. Contact: Unitravel Riviera, 119 bis, boulevard Carnot, 06110 Le Cannet (next to Cannes); Tel: 93-68-25-50.

An affiliate in the United States is Langcom International, 250 S. Beverly Dr., Beverly Hills, CA 90212; Tel: (213) 273-7833.

ACCOMMODATIONS REFERENCE

▶ **Altéa**. Rue Neuve St-Martin, 13001 **Marseille**. Tel: 91-39-20-00; Fax: 91-56-24-57; in U.S., (212) 719-9363 or (800) 223-9862.

▶ **Altéa**. Route de Caderousse, 84100 **Orange**. Tel: 90-34-24-10; Telex: 431550; Fax: 90-34-85-48.

▶ **D'Arlatan**. 26, rue Sauvage, 13200 **Arles**. Tel: 90-93-56-66; Telex: 441203; Fax: 90-49-68-45; in U.S., (212) 477-1600 or (800) 366-1510.

▶ **Auberge de l'Esterel**. 21, rue des Iles, 06160 **Juan-les-Pins**. Tel: 93-61-08-67.

▶ **Auberge de la Fontaine**. Vénasque 84210 **Pernes-les-Fontaines**. Tel: 90-66-02-96; Fax: 90-66-13-14.

▶ **Auberge de la Madone**. 06440 **Peillon**. Tel: 93-79-91-17.

▶ **Auberge de Noves**. 13550 **Noves** (2 km northwest via D 28). Tel: 90-94-19-21; Fax: 90-94-47-76; in U.S., (713) 783-8033, (212) 696-1323, or (800) 372-1323.

▶ **Auberge Provençale**. 61, place Nationale, 06600 **Antibes**. Tel: 93-34-13-24.

▶ **Auberge Provençale**. 06380 **Sospel** (1.5 km south via route col de Castillon). Tel: 93-04-12-31.

▶ **Auberge St-Pierre**. Tourtour 83690 **Salernes**. Tel: 94-70-57-17.

▶ **Auberge de Tavel**. 30126 **Tavel**. Tel: 66-50-03-41.

▶ **Augustins**. 3, rue de la Masse, 13100 **Aix-en-Provence**. Tel: 42-27-28-59; Telex: 441052; Fax: 22-26-74-87.

▶ **Bastide de Gordes**. 84220 **Gordes** Tel: 90-72-12-12; Fax: 90-72-05-20.

▶ **La Bastide de Tourtour**. Route de Draguignan, Tourtour 83690 **Salernes**. Tel: 94-70-57-30; Telex: 970827; Fax: 94-70-54-90.

▶ **Beach Régency**. 223, promenade des Anglais, 06200 **Nice**. Tel: 93-37-17-17; Fax: 93-71-21-71; in U.S., (617) 581-0844 or (800) 223-6764.

▶ **Beau Rivage**. 24 rue St-François-de-Paule, 06000 **Nice**. Tel: 93-80-80-70; Fax: 93-80-55-77.

▶ **Le Beffroi**. Haute Ville, 84110 **Vaison-la-Romaine**. Tel: 90-36-04-71; Telex: 306022; Fax: 90-36-24-78.

▶ **Les Bories**. 84220 **Gordes**. Tel: 90-72-00-51.

▶ **Byblos**. Avenue Paul-Signac, 83990 **St-Tropez**. Tel: 94-97-00-04; Telex: 470235; Fax: 94-97-40-52.

▶ **La Cabro d'Or**. Les Baux-de-Provence 13520 **Maussane-les-Alpilles**. Tel: 90-54-33-21; Telex: 401810; in U.S., (212) 696-1323 or (800) 372-1323.

▶ **Le Caméo.** Place Nationale, 06600 **Antibes**. Tel: 93-34-24-17.

▶ **Carlton Intercontinental.** 58, boulevard de la Croisette, 06400 **Cannes**. Tel: 93-68-91-68; Telex: 470720; Fax: 93-38-20-90; in U.S., (402) 498-4300 or (800) 448-8355.

▶ **Chambord.** 6, avenue Boyer, 06500 **Menton**. Tel: 93-35-94-19.

▶ **Château des Alpilles.** 13210 **St-Rémy-de-Provence**. Tel: 90-92-03-33; Telex: 431487; Fax: 90-92-45-17.

▶ **Château de la Chèvre d'Or.** Rue Barri, 06360 **Eze-Village**. Tel: 93-41-12-12; Telex: 970839; Fax: 93-41-06-72; in U.S., (212) 696-1323 or (800) 372-1323.

▶ **Château Eza.** 06360 **Eze-Village**. Tel: 93-41-12-24; Telex: 470382; Fax: 93-41-16-64; in U.S., (212) 477-1600 or (800) 366-1510.

▶ **Château des Fines Roches.** 84230 **Châteauneuf-du-Pape**. Tel: 90-83-70-23 Fax: 90-83-78-42.

▶ **Château de Rochegude.** 26790 **Rochegude**. Tel: 75-04-81-88; Telex: 345661 Fax: 75-04-89-97.

▶ **Château de Trigance.** Trigance 83840 **Comps-sur-Artuby**. Tel: 94-76-91-18; Fax: 94-47-58-99.

▶ **La Colombe d'Or.** Place de Gaulle, 06570 **St-Paul-de-Vence**. Tel: 93-32-80-02; Telex: 970607; Fax: 93-32-77-78; in U.S., (212) 477-1600 or (800) 366-1510.

▶ **Concorde—Palm Beach.** 2, promenade de la Plage, 13008 **Marseille**. Tel: 91-76-20-00; Telex: 401894; Fax: 91-77-37-83; in U.S., (800) THE-OMNI.

▶ **Domaine de l'Enclos.** Route de Sénanque, 84220 **Gordes**. Tel: 90-72-08-22; Telex: 432119.

▶ **Elysée Palace.** 59 promenade des Anglais, 06000 **Nice**. Tel: 93-86-06-06; Fax: 93-44-50-40.

▶ **Etrangers.** Boulevard de Verdun, 06380 **Sospel**. Tel: 93-04-00-09; Fax: 93-04-12-31.

▶ **Europe.** 12, place Crillon, 84000 **Avignon**. Tel: 90-82-66-92; Telex: 431965; Fax: 90-85-43-66.

▶ **Les Florets.** Gigondas 84190 **Beaumes-de-Venise**. Tel: 90-65-85-01.

▶ **Grand Hôtel du Cap-Ferrat.** Boulevard Général de Gaulle, 06230 **St-Jean-Cap-Ferrat**. Tel: 93-76-00-21; Fax: 93-01-62-49.

▶ **Gray d'Albion.** 38 rue des Serbes, 06400 **Cannes**. Tel: 93-68-54-54; Fax: 93-99-26-10.

▶ **Hermitage.** Square Beaumarchais, **Monte-Carlo** 98000 Monaco. Tel: 93-50-67-31; Telex: 479432; Fax: 93-50-47-12.

▶ **Hôtel Le Cagnard.** Rue Pontis-Long, 06800 **Cagnes-sur-Mer** (au Haut-de-Cagnes). Tel: 93-20-73-21; Telex: 46-

22-23; in U.S., (713) 783-8033, (212) 696-1323, or (800) 372-1323.

▶ **Hôtel du Cap d'Antibes.** Boulevard Kennedy, 06600 **Antibes.** Tel: 93-61-39-01; Telex: 470763; Fax: 93-67-76-04.

▶ **Hôtel de Paris.** Place du Casino, **Monte-Carlo** 98000 Monaco. Tel: 93-50-80-80; Telex: 469925; Fax: 93-25-59-17.

▶ **Juana et Restaurant La Terrasse.** Avenue Georges-Gallice, 06160 **Juan-les-Pins.** Tel: 93-61-08-70; Telex: 470778.

▶ **Jules César.** 7, boulevard des Lices, 13200 **Arles.** Tel: 90-93-43-20; Telex: 400239; Fax: 90-93-33-47; in U.S., (212) 696-1323 or (800) 372-1323.

▶ **Loews Hotel.** Avenue des Spélugues, **Monte-Carlo** 98000 **Monaco.** Tel: 93-50-65-00; Telex: 479435; Fax: 93-30-01-57.

▶ **Majestic.** 6, boulevard de la Croisette, 06400 **Cannes.** Tel: 93-68-91-00; Telex: 470787; Fax: 93-38-97-90. in U.S., (407) 679-8338 or (800) 223-5652.

▶ **Le Manoir.** 83145 Ile de Port-Cros. Tel: 94-05-90-52.

▶ **Martinez.** 73, boulevard de la Croisette, 06400 **Cannes.** Tel: 93-94-30-30; Telex: 470708; Fax: 93-39-67-82; in U.S., (212) 838-3110 or (800) 223-6800.

▶ **Mas d'Artigny.** Chemin des Salettes, 06570 **St-Paul-de-Vence.** Tel: 93-32-84-54; Telex: 470601; Fax: 93-32-95-36; in U.S., (212) 696-1323 or (800) 372-1323.

▶ **Mas de Chastelas.** Route de Gassin, 83990 **St-Tropez.** Tel: 94-56-09-11; Telex: 462393; Fax: 94-56-11-56.

▶ **Mas des Herbes Blanches.** 84220 **Joucas.** Tel: 90-05-79-79; Fax: 90-05-71-96.

▶ **Mas du Langoustier.** 83400 **Ile de Porquerolles.** Tel: 94-58-30-09; Fax: 94-58-36-02.

▶ **Méridien.** 1, promenade des Anglais, 06000 **Nice.** Tel: 93-82-25-25; Telex: 470361; Fax: 93-16-08-90.

▶ **Les Mimosas.** Rue Pauline, 06160 **Juan-les-Pins.** Tel: 93-61-04-16.

▶ **Montfleury.** 25, avenue Beauséjour, 06400 **Cannes.** Tel: 93-68-91-50; Fax: 93-38-37-08; in U.S., (800) 221-4542.

▶ **Montmirail.** Montmirail 84190 **Beaumes-de-Venise.** Tel: 90-65-84-01; Fax: 90-65-81-50.

▶ **Négresco.** 37, promenade des Anglais, 06000 **Nice.** Tel: 93-88-39-51; Fax: 93-88-35-68; in U.S., (407) 679-8338 or (800) 223-5652.

▶ **Oustaù de Baumanière.** Les Baux-de-Provence 13520 **Maussane-les-Alpilles.** Tel: 90-54-33-07; Telex: 420203; Fax: 90-54-40-46. in U.S., (212) 696-1323 or (800) 372-1323.

► **Petite Auberge.** 83690 **Tourtour.** Tel: 94-70-57-16; Telex: 470673; Fax: 94-70-54-42.

► **Le Petit Nice.** Anse de Maldormé, 13007 **Marseille.** Tel: 91-59-25-92; Telex: 401565; Fax: 91-59-28-08.

► **Le Prieuré.** Place du Chapître, 30400 **Villeneuve-lès-Avignon.** Tel: 90-25-18-20; Fax: 90-25-45-39; in U.S., Tel: (713) 783-8033, (212) 696-1323, or (800) 372-1323.

► **Princess et Richmond.** 617, promenade du Soleil, 06500 **Menton.** Tel: 93-35-80-20; Fax 93-57-40-20.

► **Du Rédier.** 06670 **Colomars.** Tel: 93-37-94-37.

► **Sainte-Anne.** 83400 **Ile de Porquerolles.** Tel: 94-58-30-04.

► **Splendid.** 4, rue Felix-Faure, 06400 **Cannes.** Tel: 93-99-53-11; Telex: 470990; Fax: 93-99-55-02.

► **Vista Palace.** Grand Corniche, 06190 **Roquebrune-Cap-Martin** (4 km west via D 2564). Tel: 93-35-01-50; Fax: 93-35-18-94.

► **Westminster Concorde.** 27 promenade des Anglais, 06000 **Nice.** Tel: 93-88-29-44; Fax: 93-82-45-35.

LANGUEDOC–ROUSSILLON

By Fred Halliday

Languedoc–Roussillon is an enormous sausage in the south end of France, situated along the Mediterranean between the Rhône and Spain. Its insides often appear as mysterious as the ways to them seem inaccessible. Yet it is a region as rich in history as any in France. Its fables are as dashing, its traditions as romantic, its panoramas as sweeping, its cuisine as savory. It has great seacoast towns (filled with youthful populations), old Roman ruins less ruined than any in Rome, vast deserts, and mountain forests popping with mushrooms.

The best way to take all this in is the way to bite into any sausage—from either end. We have chosen to begin in the east with the great fortress city of Beaucaire, on the banks of the Rhône; from there we travel westward (with a dip south into the Camargue and Aigues-Mortes) to Nîmes, with its unrivaled Roman ruins; and then on to the youthful, dynamic city of Montpellier. From these southern "cities of the sun" we travel northwest up into the heart of the Cévennes forest, passing through such gems as St-Guilhem-le-Désert, a lovely village tucked in a gorge; the Cirque de Navacelles, a sort of natural amphitheater carved from chalk; Le Vigan, a virtually unspoiled (i.e., untouristed) hamlet in the heart of the Cévennes; and finally, up and over to the breathtaking Gorges du Tarn, one of the great natural wonders of France. From the highlands we take the highway (N 9–E 11) southeast back to the coast and travel the old Roman road through such towns as Sète, Béziers, and Narbonne—and along one of

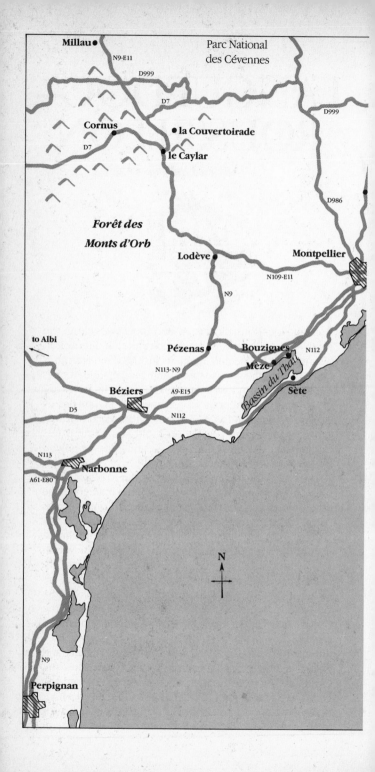

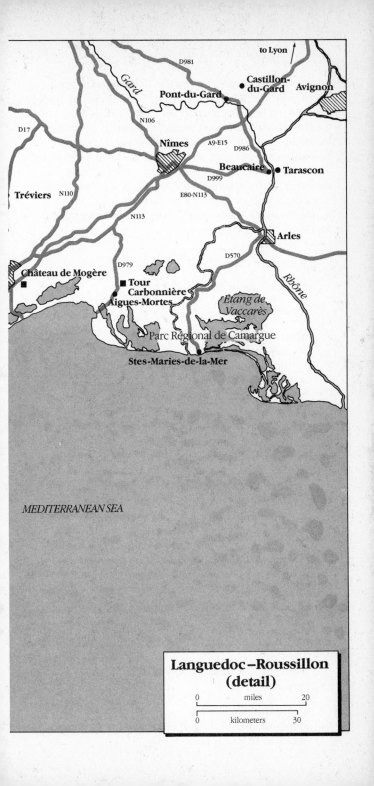

to Lyon

D981

Castillon-du-Gard

Avignon

Gard

Pont-du-Gard

N106

D17

Nîmes

A9-E15

D986

Tréviers

N110

Beaucaire

Tarascon

D999

E80-N113

N113

Arles

Château de Mogère

D979

D570

Rhône

Tour Carbonnière

Aigues-Mortes

Étang de Vaccarès

Parc Régional de Camargue

Stes-Maries-de-la-Mer

MEDITERRANEAN SEA

Languedoc–Roussillon
(detail)

0   miles   20

0   kilometers   30

the most exquisite beaches on the Mediterranean. Finally we explore Perpignan and Collioure, lovely and fascinating for their blend of Spanish and French influences, and the abbey of St-Martin-du-Canigou, perched atop the highest mountain in this part of the Pyrénées. (Languedoc–Roussillon is a vast area, and we have not tried to cover it all in this chapter. We suggest, for example, that Carcassonne and Castelnaudary—technically in the provinces of Languedoc–Roussillon—be combined with a trip to Toulouse; for them see the chapter on Toulouse and the South.)

MAJOR INTEREST

Medieval Beaucaire

Aigues-Mortes

Nîmes
Maison Carrée
Jardin de la Fontaine
Roman arena
Side trip to Pont-du-Gard

Montpellier
Place de la Comédie
The old town

St-Guilhem-le-Désert's ninth-century abbey

Prehistoric ruins at Prieuré de St-Michel-de-Grandmont

Cirque de Navacelles

The Cévennes Forest
Le Vigan
Mushrooming
Great natural beauty

Gorges du Tarn

The Coast
Towns of Sète, Béziers, and Narbonne
Exquisite beaches

The Spanish Frontier
Perpignan and Collioure: Franco-Hispanic culture
Abbey of St-Martin-du-Canigou

The Cuisine, Gîtes, and Geography

Cuisine always follows geography, and in Languedoc–Roussillon there is a lot of geography to follow. Behind its ribbon of coastline is high plateau (between 600 and 1,000 feet), for the most part of chalky composition and supporting, in the main, stunted oak forests. Here rabbit, chicken, and, lately, lamb—much of it shipped to Italy—are added to the supply of fish from the Mediterranean coast.

Most of the meat is eaten grilled. The lamb, often served as ribs, is simply roasted over coals. Duck is usually *maigret de canard,* or chest meat, cut in thin strips that look like sliced steak, served very rare and never done in herbs.

Beyond the plateau is the high country, with great pine forests and green pastures. The big trucks that roll through here at night are loaded with timber and beef cattle, again, much of it destined for Italy. The steak in the high country is always marinated *aux fines herbes*—fresh parsley, *ciboulette* (chives), and tarragon—so thickly that it's green before it's grilled. And nearly always after a rain, there are pungent *cèpes, girolles,* and *trompettes-des-morts* to be had, wild, savory mushrooms that have nothing in common with the tame old *champignons de Paris.*

All throughout the two back-country strips, both facing the sea as if they were long amphitheater rows, there is often found—usually near a château or its park, or via a roadside sign before a village—accommodations and dining simply labelled "Gîte," with an arrow. This sign can lead to a mouth-watering and money-saving experience for those who want to get out into the country, get to know the people, and eat what they eat—and are willing to roll a little with the social punches.

At a gîte you are invited to dine and stay at a farmer's home. You are invited to pay, too, but in Languedoc–Roussillon it's never very much. You eat at a family-style table, but this is not a bed-and-breakfast. The dining room is huge, like a hall; the walls are decorated with animal heads and maybe jars of goose confit; and the tables are rough-hewn and long, seating as many as 10 to 20 each. The food passed around is home-grown, and you eat as a very large family. There is noise and clatter, boarding-house reaching, and the breaking of bread and chicken with the hands. Movie buffs might feel as if they're eating with Ma and Pa Kettle in *l'Oeuf et Moi,* but only until the platter comes 'round; the food can be remarkably good.

When it comes to what is called *cuisine du terroir* (local food), remember that the farmer has the edge over restaurants advertising it as such. Wherever you go farmers eat the best, because they know what they're eating. This is an outstanding opportunity to taste what freshness is. The lamb or rabbit they pluck hot off the coals at the gîte has the taste of the sun, salty soil, and herbs of the land. It is like tasting barbecue in the U.S. Ozarks, country food cooked at the source.

So for those who would take a gastronomic trip through France, for once, get away from the little guidebooks and the star trails, and leave home without your credit cards. Get down to a gîte in Languedoc–Roussillon. Two gîte locations:

- At **Valleraugue**, in the heart of the Cévennes (see below), is **Les Salles**, an old, renovated gîte just 3 km (2 miles) from the village. Mont Aigoual, river fishing, forest walks, and tennis are nearby.
- At **Aumont-Aubrac**, **Les Crozes** is a lovely stone house on producing farmland; a joy to lovers of canoeing because of nearby rivers and a lake, and walks along the Gorges du Tarn (see below).

Individual accommodations in these gîtes, however, can range from cozy to catastrophic, so it's never advisable to reserve sight unseen. Instead, stick your nose in, and if you like what you find, make a deal.

THE CITIES OF THE SUN
Beaucaire

Beaucaire is a great fortress city along a great river, the Rhône. A bridge spans the river here, connecting the region to Tarascon in Provence and affording impressive views. From high above, the city looms as the sort of fortress frequently seen in the romantic mind's eye but rarely visited. Its crenellations, ramparts, chimney pots, and castle parts form a massive barrier atop the rock that serves as a pedestal. Beaucaire is a failed Gibraltar, a fortress that was built to defend against Saracens and pirates and armies of marauding dukes and kings but that kept none of them out; bit by bit Beaucaire absorbed them all, becoming a city of invaders and brigands, a pirates' nest.

For those travelling the south of France today who are tired of seeing the likes of themselves coming around every corner or occupying every seat in every café, Beaucaire is a welcome find. Its Medieval streets, like narrow, cracking fissures, unwind into a world that is undiscovered and remarkably uncrowded. There is no long street, no main drag. But wherever there are people is the potential for remarkable tableaux framed by arches, under arcades, or at the end of a street. You have only to wait; sooner or later someone steps into the light—a boy chewing a baguette; a flower girl; an old, old man with a floppy beret and a cane. Not a city of wide, striking vistas—except from its citadel—Beaucaire is a place for visually striking street scenes. Happily, there are no trinket or camera shops to spoil these captivating views. So cameras should come loaded; there's plenty to shoot.

At one end of the place Neuve, under plane trees and arcades, is the late-17th-century **Hôtel de Ville**, a remarkable Renaissance eccentric with an exposed center stairway. The confined area of the nearby place de la République harbors more plane trees, and vaulted arcades that support 17th-century apartments, some for rent. The plane trees are all healthy here, filling the open spaces with a soft, rustling green; venturing from the green squares you seem to plunge into darkness that is relieved by a pool of light striking the end of a narrow, dark street. Perhaps the close spaces contribute to the sense that there's something unknown just around the corner. Beaucaire has a persistently dreamlike quality. It's not a reconstruction or a restoration of something Medieval preserved for the sake of antiquarians. It *is* Medieval.

The whole city is ringed by a wall of many centuries' worth of diverse architectural components, a graffiti-like patchwork of gaps plugged with buildings, backs of chapels, scraps of Roman columns—impromptu swatches incorporated as the wall was built around them. In other words, Beaucaire has yet to be taken apart and its pieces sent to museums in other places. Its museums are its streets; its best portraits, the faces of its people. The arbiters of where everyone should go and where everything should happen have yet to descend on Beaucaire.

Just outside the wall of the city is a place to stay that is as dreamlike as Beaucaire itself: **Les Doctrinaires** (quai du Général de Gaulle), a 17th-century stone *collège* on the side of a tree-shaded canal, with a pretty outside dining area. Rooms are moderately priced. Inside the wall is an interesting arabesque hotel, **La Cauquière**, on rue de l'Hôtel de Ville. It has 12 rooms and a restaurant around a lush interior garden. Prices for rooms and meals are very reasonable. Pensions and garage space are available.

There are two main roads out of Beaucaire that lead deeper into Languedoc–Roussillon: the high road and the low road. The high road, D 986, goes up through the mountains toward Pont du Gard, for which see below, at the end of the Nîmes section. Lined by big pine trees, it is, alas, frequently encumbered by slow-moving trucks. The low road, D 999 (or the Autoroute A 9–E 15), takes you west toward Nîmes and then south into the Camargue.

Aigues-Mortes and the Camargue

The Camargue, with its summertime caravans of gypsies and Germans, is an overcrowded Rhône delta destination with very few flamingos, uninspiring beaches (the kind with kiddie rides and midget Ferris wheels), a few wild ponies, fewer wild bulls, and perhaps the most unattractive wine of France. *Vin de sable* must be so called because it is planted in and tastes like wet sand. The roads are narrow, the traffic tedious in summer, the shoreline mudflat- and marsh-ridden, and fellow tourists, whom you meet while lining up for ferry (*bac*) rides, not the kind you're likely to have a cocktail with.

Les Stes-Maries-de-la-Mer, too, is low on attractions, pleasant beaches, and restaurants. The one Camargue bright spot is Aigues-Mortes, a drop of water on an otherwise pleasure-parched landscape. In *Impressions of a Voyage,* Alexandre Dumas *fils* remarked, "We noticed Aigues-Mortes, or rather we noticed its walls, because not one house or building is higher than its ramparts. The Gothic city appears like a jewel carefully wrapped in a case of stone."

Dumas's description still holds nearly a hundred years later. **Aigues-Mortes**, which is just about 45 km (28 miles) south of both Arles and Nîmes, is one of the few cities in France—along with Carcassonne—whose walls are intact. The small town, with a population of only 4,000, makes a good base from which to visit the surrounding Camargue—should you wish to do so. It has two excellent hotels and several top restaurants; it is best to avoid it during the busy July-to-August season, however.

Aigues-Mortes was created by the French king Louis IX—Saint Louis—out of a sandy desert bordered by estuaries and swamps—hence the name, which means "dead waters." Aigues-Mortes's history and fame thus belong to Medieval royal France. In fact, for nearly a hundred years Aigues-Mortes enjoyed its status as the kingdom's only Mediterranean port. Saint Louis encouraged neighboring inhabitants to move to his newly created but highly inhospitable town by offering them generous tax breaks. Thousands moved in, and the port was used by traders from throughout the northern Mediterranean coast: Catalonia, Genoa, and Provence. At its height, its population was 15,000.

After Saint Louis chose Aigues-Mortes as his Mediterranean port, he used it twice to embark on crusades to the "Orient," once in 1248 to Egypt and the second time, in 1270, to Tunis. The king died on the latter trip, and historians believe the cause of death was malaria he contracted in the swampy and mosquito-infested area surrounding Aigues-Mortes.

Most of the ramparts and walls were built by Saint Louis's sons and successors, Philippe III and Philippe IV. Although Aigues-Mortes was heavily fortified, its greatest defensive asset was the swamps, which rendered the city unapproachable by all but one road. To guard that road the king built the **Tour Carbonnière**. The fortress tower still stands, virtually untouched, just out of town on D 46 off D 58. (D 979 from Aigues-Mortes leads into D 58.)

A visit to the **ramparts** begins at the castle and the massive **Tour de Constance**. The tower—originally isolated by a ditch—was the centerpiece of Aigues-Mortes's defenses and contained the city's arsenal.

Next to the tower, in the place Anatole France through the main entrance into the city, is the **Hostellerie des Remparts**, a cozy hotel in a converted two-story 18th-century guardhouse with a view of the tower.

The main square of this small town is named after its founder—Saint Louis. Several restaurants, café terraces, and the Office de Tourisme are located on it. Unusual for such a small place, Aigues-Mortes has two fine restaurants, one of which—**Minos**—is also on the place St-Louis. The Minos has a vine-covered terrace overlooking a

statue of the king, friendly service, and specializes in fish
and a local Camargue meat dish in sauce, *gardiane*. And
just off the square on the rue Amiral-Courbet is a rustic
hotel, the **St-Louis**. Its enclosed private terrace can be a
welcome retreat during the crowded season.

Aigues-Mortes's second major restaurant is of national
renown: **La Camargue**, at 19, rue de la République. In fact,
many visit the town just to eat in this converted, centuries-
old, rustic Camarguais house and listen to gypsy and
flamenco music. Reservations are necessary for dining on
the terrace in July and August (Tel: 66-53-86-88), and the
restaurant is closed in January. Plaques mark the booths
where dignitaries, former president Georges Pompidou
among them, have eaten. The specialties are regional—
tellines, shellfish, *boeuf gardiane* in a black-olive sauce.
The restaurant is pricey, but worth it.

Nîmes

Nîmes is an old Roman city amid a trayful of French
apéritifs. Anyone who has not sat in its midst in the last
decade will be astonished by the growth of apartments and
vacation condominiums and their supporting shopping
malls and widened roads. No matter. In Nîmes all roads
lead to ancient Rome, which means to the **Maison Carrée**
(Square House), the ancient, columned building considered by many to be the finest example of Roman temple
architecture in the world. The house is not actually square,
but rather rectangular. (The Romans considered a building square if its angles were symmetrical.) Modeled in the
Greek style on its highly visible perch during the reign of
Caesar Augustus (first century B.C.), the Maison Carrée was
erected as a temple to the grandsons of Emperor Augustus.
Thus it remained for 400 years, until Visigoths overran
Nîmes and used it as a stable for their horses. Later it was a
church, then a monastery. Given the turbulence of the
2,000-year history surrounding the temple, the fact that it
has survived is a miracle in itself. It was probably spared
from destruction by the grace of its own beauty. Consider
that it almost wound up being whisked away to Louis XIV's
great garden of vanity, Versailles. Another admirer of the
Maison Carrée was Thomas Jefferson, then the U.S. minister to France, who recommended the temple as the inspiration for the capitol building in Virginia.

The role the temple plays today is as a museum for the
antiquities found around Nîmes, which seems fair enough.

A satisfying way to appreciate this graceful structure is to retire to one of the sidewalk cafés in the museum's shadow at cocktail time, wait for the yellow light to play on the marble as it has been for 20 centuries, and lift a glass to perfection and to Louis XIV, who, at the last moment, decided the temple was too beautiful to rape even for himself and left it where it was.

Not a five-minute stroll northwest from the Maison Carrée, and deliciously scented with jasmine, laurel, and eucalyptus, is the magical **Jardin de la Fontaine**. Here, finally, is the life for which all those migrants from the north have filled the proliferating condos: the gardens of the south, lush with tropical flora in brilliant, exotic colors and the gurgling sound of falling water.

In the other direction from the Maison Carrée, down boulevard Victor-Hugo at the aptly named place des Arènes, is the **Roman arena** (nearly identical to the one in Arles; see Provence and the Côte d'Azur), which was probably constructed around A.D. 70. Today matadors rather than gladiators spill blood in the ancient arena, which holds 21,000 people.

To see how the Roman Empire really worked and how it got all this water from the mountains to subtropical Nîmes, a trip 23 km (14 miles) northeast to the **Pont-du-Gard** is a must. There are tour buses to this major monument of Roman engineering, a triple-tiered aqueduct almost a quarter-mile long, built in a series of connecting arches over the green gorge of the river Gard. Here was the last and most impressive leap in a water system 37 miles long that gathered in the mountains and descended to Nîmes. But this is not merely a 2,000-year-old monument to look upon: It is one you can crawl through. The intrepid traveller may walk, stooped forward, within the aqueduct's cylindrical water channel section by section as if walking through a tunnel. Here and there breaks in the pipe admit shafts of sunlight that are almost adequate to see by. It is mainly by groping, though, that you inch forward. Finally a section of the pipe is missing, but never fear, the structure underneath remains and you emerge into sunlight. Beneath your feet is the casing for the conduit, two other tiers of aqueduct, and the gorge of the river Gard 150 feet below. It is a lesson in ancient engineering unmatched in any classroom. There were no pumps in the Roman system; the waters travelled through the countryside down to Nîmes by gravity feed alone.

Just 4 km (2.5 miles) north of Pont-du-Gard via D 19 and D 228, in the town of Castillon-du-Gard, is the atmospheric, delicious little hotel **Le Vieux Castillon**. It consists of a group of joined and restored Medieval houses perched on a rock at the edge of the village, with a lovely terrace, patio, swimming pool, and a charming dining room.

All through the south of France roads lead to the works of Rome—except when they go to Montpellier.

Montpellier

Montpellier has no Roman ruins. It is a comparatively young city, having been founded as late as the so-called Dark Ages, but it vies with Toulouse in claiming to be the leading metropolis of the south. And as long as France's population continues to shift southward, Montpellier will be in the running to become the country's number-one city in the next century.

For a glimpse of what France is likely to become, and for what it is in its own right, Montpellier is worth a long look.

First, it is a southern city. In France that usually means a city with Spanish roots, accents, and ways. Not surprisingly, Montpellier has closer ties to Barcelona—just 230 miles away and a frequent vacation destination—than to Paris. Second, Montpellier is a city blessed with ten months of sun each year and three major universities that attract a huge student population numbering some 50,000. Add to this the many recent graduates who, because of the sun and the nearby seashore, mountains, and skiing, are loath to leave. This youthful population not only lends an idyllic ambience to Montpellier's streets and cafés but also has an important economic impact. Nothing is expensive, and in Montpellier the best things in life are free.

Among the most amusing pastimes is "doing the dalles." The *dalles* (pronounced *dahl*) is a promenade, a strolling place of public prominence. Almost every old Roman town along the route between Italy and Spain had a dalles, which was a leftover from slave-trading days. (Although Montpellier has no Roman history, it has not been slow to adopt certain Latin tendencies.) Around sundown, or slave-market time, the locals, garbed in togas, would go to the dalles to strut or sit or just walk around, to catch an eye or an ear, catch a wink or throw one. With the passage of time cool drinks came to be served; then came chairs, next tables. From these first steps emerged—*voilà*—café society, with all its nosiness and noisiness.

Montpellier is the best place to practice this ancient art, for it has a huge dalles, a great elevated boardwalk in the center of town that stretches for blocks and blocks. It is called the **place de la Comédie**, named for the opera theater located at one end of the boardwalk. The comedy going on outside the building beats anything going on inside. The *place* is *the* place in this university town for strolling, for having lunch or dinner, or for buying a mimosa bouquet from a flower girl. The happily soundproof **Sofitel** Montpellier—at the foot of the place de la Comédie, looking down on the dalles—is the place to stay in town.

The old town, dating from the 13th to 19th centuries, is behind the dalles, radiating from the rue du Bras-de-Fer. This is French Renaissance chic—wide steps, ancient buildings replete with boutiques, randomly spaced terra-cotta urns of flowers, doll shops, and *épiceries* and alfresco bistros. But remember, this is Montpellier, where purchasing power is at the student level, so nothing is expensive. Boutiques that would elsewhere house Vuitton, for example, here offer Lancel. Charming shops that would elsewhere have Cardin or Saint-Laurent are here stocked with bargains instead of name brands. As free as the air is the **Jardin des Plantes** (Botanical Gardens), a fine floral walk that changes with the seasons. Locals claim it's the oldest in France (1593), but the Romans were creating them to go with their fountains in Provence more than a millennium earlier.

For those who want to eat like sophisticates but at prices that won't remind them of the Rothschilds, the riverside **La Réserve Rimbaud** (820, avenue St-Maur; Tel: 67-72-52-53) is worth dropping into. It's a place filled with music and opera; that is, musicians from the opera come here and play while they wait. Students come from the School of Music and Art and mostly wait tables. Everybody sings, and the result is a delight.

For wandering souls who thirst for the grape, **l'Hôtel Montpellieraine des Vins de Languedoc**, a restaurant and tasting bar with more than 80 wines for sale on the rue Jacques-Coeur, just a couple of blocks from the place de la Comédie, will satisfy even the biggest craving to explore the enormous range of regional wines. The Minervois and Corbières wines are well known, but the St-Pons is superior. Vineyards come right up to the roads just out of town.

The Château de la Mogère and its vineyards sit right on Montpellier's autoroute only 3 km (2 miles) from downtown at the north exit. It offers an excellent opportunity to see an elegant château inside and out, roam typical Languedoc vineyards, take a tour of the *caves,* and have a wine-tasting experience and a gift thrown in. Greater vine concentrations can be found at **Tréviers** (on D 17 via D 112 about 20 km/12.5 miles to the north), where the official *route des vins de coteaux du Languedoc* begins. But roadside vineyards there are aplenty all through Languedoc–Roussillon, which produces the greatest volume of wine in the country.

TO THE CEVENNES

Route N 109–E 11 from Montpellier is the way to go. It leads west and then north to a region of natural beauty and down-to-earth people. Some say the Cévennes forest is the last truly wild spot left in France.

The Cévennes is a sort of French version of the U.S. Ozarks, covered with forests rising from smokey mists up and down hillsides separated by rivers. On each ridge is a community, a land unto itself, where people make moonshine and the government lets them. It's where burned-out doctors and their spouses come from Paris to live in stone houses that catch water in cisterns. Here they paint, tend gardens, and sell wares on Sundays in towns inhabited by perhaps no more than 200 people. As Montpellier is emblematic of the future, the Cévennes is a story of people returning to the land.

On the way to the forest, however, there are bright jewels to collect. The first, via D 27 off N 109, is **St-Guilhem-le-Désert**, a village tucked in the narrow Verdus gorge and steeped in the history of many centuries past. A château supported only by a wall hangs from a rock, and below, in the arms of the escarpment, is a Benedictine abbey founded in the ninth century, that of Saint Guilhem. So popular did the abbey become as a pilgrimage site that its great prosperity permitted a new cloister to be built in 1206. Parts of this 13th-century structure—columns and pilasters—were eventually pried away by the Metropolitan Museum of Art in New York for a building overlooking the Hudson called The Cloisters. Today concerts are held amid the remains on gentle summer evenings. Afterward in the square a man sells truffles to exiting concert-goers, so

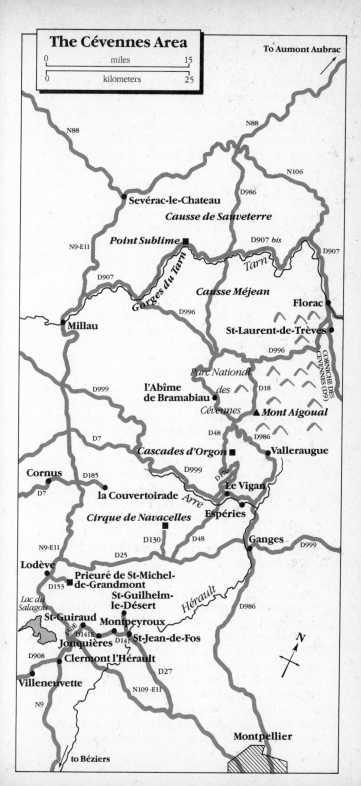

remember to bring a jar packed with rice to carry them home in. Inside the church are relics of the saint, his bones asleep in the crypt, and pages of illuminated manuscript.

Outside, the summertime air feels as if someone left the bakery door open. There is the château to climb to, horses to rent, houses in the street that date back to Roman Gaul, and boating and bathing in the **Hérault** river. The stream is cool and clear—not icy, but not to linger in, either.

You may well decide to stay in this rugged, sun-baked landscape long enough for a meal, and maybe overnight at a good country hotel. Both options are near at hand. To find them, first follow the Hérault south from St-Guilhem for just 4.5 km (3 miles) to the little town of **St-Jean-de-Fos**. This is a cheerful place where the major pastimes are café-sitting in the main square and plunging into the river. From here, a narrow road, D 141, will take you through vineyards and the little wine towns of Montpeyroux and Jonquières, each with a *cave* selling local wines. In Jonquières, a tiny slip of a road, D 141 E, squeezes between two houses and cuts across the vineyards to the hilltop hamlet of **St-Guiraud**. Follow it, for here, in a big old rustic house on the town square, is **Le Mimosa**, to many tastes the best restaurant in Languedoc. The local bounty that enters the kitchen door here—oysters from the Bassin de Thau, quail from the surrounding vineyards, vegetables from villagers' gardens—comes to the table in elegant but simple creations that attract local landowners and business executives who drive out here on weekends from Montpellier. The wine list includes the best the region has to offer and excellent labels from all over France. (Reservations are usually necessary; ask for a table on the terrace; Tel: 67-96-67-96.)

For lodging: Leave St-Guiraud on D 130 E for the few minutes' drive to N 9; take that south 5 km (3 miles) to the prosperous market town of Clermont-l'Hérault, and from there follow D 908 west about 5 km (3 miles) to **Villeneuvette**. French kings and Napoléon kept this one-industry town busy making uniforms for their conquering armies. Then the machine age took business away to the factories of the north, and Villeneuvette stood empty behind its gates for almost a century. Recently a couple of dozen pioneers have resettled its centuries-old buildings. Among the settlers are some enterprising hoteliers who have opened a simple, very comfortable hostelry,

La Source. Rooms are scattered throughout the village in vine-covered cottages; meals are served under a grape arbor. Even the French government has cooperated in making this a stage-setting idyll by damming a nearby river to form the huge **Lac du Salagou**.

Now follow N 9 north and turn off onto D 153 near Lodève—a nice café town—for the perched and lovely **Prieuré de St-Michel-de Grandmont**. The Middle Ages in Languedoc–Roussillon were incredibly turbulent times; of the 171 monasteries that flourished in that era, this is the only one that still survives. Grandmont has always been a place of worship. In prehistoric times, long before Christianity arrived, people came here to celebrate religious rites. The stone dwellings at this site are crude temples and are classified as being among the oldest buildings in the world.

The road into the Cévennes leads to other enchantments. One possible route is via D 25 and D 130, which leads to the bottom of the **Cirque de Navacelles**, a circular depression in chalk forming a sort of natural amphitheater that could have been a sandbox for dinosaurs. It somewhat resembles the White Cliffs of Dover with the English Channel drained away. Not a place to stay.

As you work your way northward, a giant step across limestone takes you through a land of bedrock to a plateau where the rainfall is regular and vegetation intense. You've entered the woods, where the air feels as if it's from an open cinema door. This is the **Cévennes National Park**, 53 miles in length, lightly sprinkled with hamlets and towns. Among the prettiest is Le Vigan, in the heart of the Cévennes, where the cultural heritage of these hamlets is sifted and their futures considered, not in town halls but out by the fountains. Men in berets sit under plane trees, lounging over Ricards (the local, anise-based drink) and vowing once again as they watch the procession of tourists drive into town that they will never let Le Vigan be changed.

Le Vigan

A surprising number of travellers never leave Le Vigan. This is where our Parisian doctor and spouse come to sit in a sidewalk café and look at the world, and where students who have gone to live in the nearby hills— students no more—come on Sundays. To a young man and woman they say they cannot understand why anyone would want to live in Paris, London, or New York and go to the movies. In the evenings they go home to their gardens and do the repairs for the week. (Home may be a tenth-century ruin in a hill town of 12 where the lights go out at nine.) Everybody here seems tan and healthy; the medicine is socialized, the food organic, and the bright lights of Montpellier's place de la Comédie only a few hours away.

These newcomers have brought money into Le Vigan. The doctors and other professionals have savings, which go farther in Languedoc–Roussillon than they would in, say, Provence. And the students are responsible for a rash of reasonable, accessible restaurants. The Cévennes is seeing its old ruins restored and furnished with local antiques and turned into dwellings and bistros. By the turn of the century there won't be a ruin left.

For a walk through the history of the Cévennes—before the cottage industry became the cottages themselves—a visit to Le Vigan's **Musée Cévenol** provides an informative look at the silkworm-growing and chestnut-gathering industries.

Spanning the river Arre, the old Roman bridge seems patently authentic; art critics call it "superb." At any rate, it looks exactly as if the fifth Roman legion just marched across it under the command of Robert Taylor. This seems a good place to sit and wait for the troops to return; should they not, there are other places to sit and wait.

One possibility is **Des Voyageurs** at 12, place du Quai, which is practically under the bridge—a pleasant place to have a Ricard (only North Americans drink wine) and wait for your lamb grilled in wild thyme. Des Voyageurs is a good place to nibble at the edges of the Cévennes, and it has a menu for under 85 francs. It is also a hotel, offering rooms with pension or without. Another option is a gîte such as **Les Salles** (described earlier) in Valleraugue, about 20 km (12.5 miles) north via D 999 and D 986.

Just a handful of kilometers east of town via D 999 are velvety green hills where orchard trees proliferate like wildflowers, stepping down to meadows and across lawns crossed with streams. The most delicious fruits here are the apples. In the rural village of **Espéries** (take D 326 off D 999), have a tart made with *reinettes,* neither large nor perfectly round but perfumed and delicious.

Back in Le Vigan, the Cévennes National Park Information Center will help you break trail with maps and brochures before you plunge deeper into the woods.

Into the Forest

As you enter the Cévennes on D 48 there is a sudden closing in of green. The forest, however, is not dark or threatening but broad-leaved and pierced with shafts of light that create golden-green pools on the floor of the forest. This sunlight not only is pleasing for the color it reveals, but it also opens up the possibilities for one of France's favorite sports: mushrooming. Anyone can play; you don't have to be French. It's both a spectator and a participant sport that can be enjoyed while walking the roadside or riding along in a car, and is perhaps the ideal game for the whole family or a family of friends. Here's how to play. Long forest stretches make the Cévennes, along with the neighboring Hérault, possibly the best mushrooming area of France. Mushrooms show up as bright white smudges against the dark forest background. Peripheral vision will do: It is the brief flash or glimmer in the green that catches the eye. (Around some of the curves and bends it is better if the driver drops out of the game and watches the road.) Thirty to 40 miles an hour is a good speed, though some people—professionals, admittedly— have effectively mushroomed at speeds of up to 60. As the car whizzes along the two-lane road you concentrate on the rapid play of sunlight and shadow over the fallen leaves on the forest floor. Perhaps concentration isn't the right term; French-rules mushrooming is always played with an air of gaiety and open-spiritedness, as if everyone cared only about having a good time and nobody cared about winning. Hah!

With the sighting of the first mushroom all this changes. The cry "*Cham-pi-gnon!*" is raised by the first to spot the fungus in question and is delivered in a mocking, smart-alecky tone, as if any poor soul who hasn't seen the whitened smudge is as blind as Tiresias. Sightings can be made from starboard to port along narrow roads, so there's little advantage to squeezing right or left in the car.

When the car is stopped, reversed, and returned to the site, the mushrooms are picked and deposited in a kerchief (preferably Hermès), the receptacle deemed de rigueur according to French rules. The sighter then receives the total number of mushrooms as points. Drivers are changed after each picking; the player with the most points wins. It's almost better to be looking not directly at the forest but obliquely away so as to catch only the highlights, so singing in the car is good. It is also wise to know a little something about mushrooms.

In the Cévennes, as well as the Hérault, number one in the hierarchy of mushrooms is the *cèpe*. (If luck is not with you while motoring, cèpes can be found in places like St-Pons or Le Vigan in baskets outside grocery stores.) As very few grocers spend their time hunting them, harvesting wild cèpes (they cannot be cultivated) is an important part of the sub-economy of a region filled with sub-economies. French tourists and natives, and even mushroom-mongers from the north, pay such a fair franc to add this pungent staple to their tables that whole Cévennes families have grown up on little else but this furtive fungus. Tourists who peel an eye for the cèpe have turned their trouble to quick profits at the region's little grocery stores. But first you must recognize the target.

There are two kinds of cèpes, the true and the false, and as luck would have it they are difficult to tell apart. Both look like cartoons of mushrooms; the false cèpe is a little longer in the stem. Both have a head large enough to shelter a gnome: It can be as big as two fists. Breaking apart their cream- to buff-colored skin, however, reveals the unmistakable difference between the two species. If the meat is white it's a true cèpe. But if it's blue, it's the Snow White—so called, supposedly, because "if you eat it you'll see the Seven Dwarfs." A hallucinogen, then, but hardly fatal. Still, no payoff at the grocery at Le Vigan. Throw it away. (Incidentally, the winner buys lunch for the others with his or her earnings.) Another mushroom to stay away from while picking in the Cévennes and Hérault is sometimes mistaken for the stringy, yellow *girolle*. Brown and yellow, it is called the Satanic. When cut it spouts yellow blood; don't add it to your *salade*. If you're in *any* doubt about what kind of mushroom you have—edible or dangerous—*don't eat it*.

All these amusements should tickle even the stoic on the way to the wonders of the Cévennes, among them the **Cascades d'Orgon**, a tangle of waters cascading through a panorama of forests, just east of D 48. Farther north along the same basic route (now D 18)—and these attractions are all connected—is **Mont Aigoual**, the highest peak in the Cévennes and the source of rivers that run to both the Atlantic and the Mediterranean. Here there is skiing in the winter, hiking in the summer, and spectacular views of the valley below year-round. Back westward via D 18 on D 986 is **l'Abîme du Brama-biau**, where the ground opens up beneath a village that hangs above the bottomless crevasse, looking like a set for the remake of *San Francisco*. Farther north via D 986 then northeast via D 996 is **St-Laurent-de-Trèves**, where time quite literally stands still, frozen, as it were, in its tracks—dinosaur tracks. A dinosaur paused around 100 million years ago on the limestone hill, looked down where one day a village would be, and left a lasting impression.

St-Laurent-de-Trèves is on one of the most spectacular roads in France, the **corniche des Cévennes**. No matter what direction you are heading from St-Laurent, take time out to drive this high road (the D 9), which follows the tops of the Cévennes for 50 km (30 miles) or so southeast to St-Jean-du-Gard. From the St-Laurent end of this magnificent route, follow D 907 (via D 983) up through Florac.

As you continue north and west the road becomes 907 *bis* and plunges through the spectacular **Gorges du Tarn**, where 15 miles of river turns on itself, looking as if it came out of a firehose, and where, in moments of calm, vine-covered banks slope down to placid, pool-like waters. The Tarn river is one of the great natural wonders of France. Perhaps its point of greatest wonder is—surprise!—**Point Sublime**. From this single ridge above the Cirque des Baumes can be seen stunning contrasts between desert and forest, rock and green gorge that typify a transitional landscape.

Take time out on your drive south to the coast on N 9 for an excursion, only about 10 km (6 miles) round trip, to **la Couvertoirade**. (The turnoff, onto D 185, is 36 km/22 miles south of Millau.) The Knights Templar built this fortress-town in the 12th and 13th centuries as they crossed Languedoc en route to and from the Crusades. In feel, their walled, stone village on the isolated *causse* is much like Carcassonne. But it is much smaller, less touristic, and, unlike that more famous city, has never been reconstructed or in any other way altered over the centuries. A good place to stay in the area is **La Musardière**, a 12-room find in its own park in Millau.

THE COAST
The Roman Road

Down on the coast, Route N 112 leads to three major stops: Sète, Béziers, and Narbonne. **Sète** is a very colorful, thoroughly Mediterranean delight. This picture-postcard port has a large Italian population, an active fishing fleet, and a noisy pier jammed with crowds, cafés, restaurants, and boat slips. The restaurants range from marvelous to indifferent. One way to ensure a wonderful experience is to turn to the person pushing you toward a table and calmly and carefully ask for *cigales de la mer,* delectable, locust-like crustaceans. If those shown to you are fresh, stay; if not, walk out. At the foot of the pier, follow the line of net menders to the Italian section, an area as interesting as the esplanade along the sea or a hike to the heights of Mont St-Clair, from which Sète gets its name. If you visit in summer, around midday have a picnic along the sandy spit—the **Plage de la Corniche**—between the sea and the Bassin de Thau, a sound teeming with savory oysters and clouds of flamingos. But swim off the sea side, where nine miles of natural sand—very rare on France's southern coast—along N 112 constitute possibly the best beach on the Mediterranean.

For good eating, though, you need to be on the other side of the Bassin de Thau in **Bouzigues** and **Mèze**, the little fishing villages along Route N 113. In both, roadside stands sell coquillage fresh from the oyster beds. Heaping platters of the same are served on the lovely terrace of the **Motel Côte Bleue** in Bouzigues. This establishment's comfortable rooms are often booked months in advance by seafood fanciers who vacation here to feast on the basin's succulent oysters and mussels.

After Sète, as you continue southwest along N 112, a host of marinas leads to **Béziers**. Up on its hill the town looks like a mini Marseille. Founded by Romans, Béziers still boasts the remains of its ancient thoroughfare, the **Via Domitia**, named for Domitius, Rome's master road builder. (The longest stretch still extant consists of an unbroken 200 yards of original Roman pavement, complete with milestones, which can be trod near Lunel.) In Béziers itself the riveting **Musée Lapidaire** counts two of these man-sized milestones among its treasures.

Leave the Roman road long enough to explore Langue-

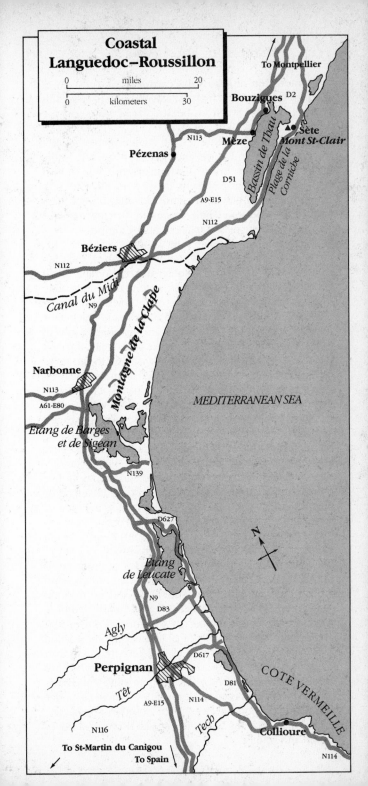

Coastal
Languedoc–Roussillon

| 0 | miles | 20 |

| 0 | kilometers | 30 |

To Montpellier

Bouzigues

D2

Sète

Mont St-Clair

Mèze

N113

Pézenas

Bassin de Thau

D51

A9-E15

Plage de la Corniche

N112

Béziers

N112

Canal du Midi

N9

Montagne de la Clape

Narbonne

N113

A61-E80

MEDITERRANEAN SEA

Étang de Bages
et de Sigean

N139

N

D627

Étang
de Leucate

N9

D83

Agly

D627

COTE VERMEILLE

Perpignan

D617

D81

Têt

A9-E15

N114

Tech

N116

To St-Martin du Canigou
To Spain

Collioure

N114

doc's more recent history in **Pézenas**, the favorite city of the 17th-century French playwright Molière. To reach this ancient, sleepy town from Béziers, backtrack across the fertile plain for 23 km (14 miles) on N 9. The Estates of Languedoc was for centuries the administrative body of much of southern France, and Pézenas was home to the Estates' governors from 1456 until France was unified under a central government in Paris in the late 17th century. The nobility left behind their magnificent mansions and a beautiful little stone city that has resisted almost all change over the intervening centuries.

The ancien régime also built many estates in a wide circle around Pézenas, and one of them is now the **Château Hôtel de Rieutort**. This quiet and comfortable small hotel is just a short drive from town on D 32 and is quite inexpensive, given the grandeur of the surroundings.

Farther southwest down Domitius's road, which after Béziers becomes N 113, is the ancient Roman city of Narbo, today's **Narbonne**. The trail leads right through the doors of the **Archaeological Museum** (in the archbishop's palace), where the oldest Roman milestone from Gaul can be found inscribed with the name of the master engineer himself, Domitius. (Inscribed as well are the name of the reigning emperor, his titles, and his lineage.) Also in the museum are Roman frescoes, still vibrant with color, and marble sculptures taken from local churches and digs.

Narbonne began as a regional Roman administrative center and evolved into a rich city-state, à la Venice or Genoa, as well as a powerful banking center. In doing so it resisted all efforts on the part of the French crown to integrate it with the rest of the kingdom. In fact, during the Crusades, Narbonne sided with the Arabs.

Narbonne today remains a crossroads of the western Mediterranean, a mosaic of cultures—Latin, Arabic, and French—imprinted on a multitude of edifices, magnificently preserved in promenades and courtly ambles, which bear witness to the city's history of power and opulence. Boats wend the canal (formed by the Robine river, which divides the city) as in Venice, but here they are always in the sun. Narbonne is a city of surprises, of cul-de-sacs and ancient walls opening onto courtyards filled with columns and gardens, of flower markets under plane trees, open-air cafés, and closed-in streets festooned with lanterns and dripping with flowers—a riot of colors and smells.

Ironically, Narbonne, though meridional in its soul, is the most Gothic city in the Mediterranean basin. Its **cathedral of St-Just** is one of the great northern-style Gothic glories of France, attesting to the triumph of the fleur-de-lis of the north over the bay laurel of the south. The attached **Hôtel de Ville**, formerly the archbishop's palace, houses a sumptuous museum of random collections. The tapestries, paintings, manuscripts, and goldwork, together with the treasures of the cathedral, make for a wealthy parade of everything that ever became of old Narbo—and the end of the road Domitius built.

Perpignan

Perpignan: Where Dalí and Picasso came, where the liberal Iberian came went when Spain was fascist, and where Spain came before there was a Louis. Where women who look like ivory carvings look right through you; where old men sit with their guitars in front of a bank and play the most bewitching airs; and the place Dalí called "the center of the world," because he was in it. Here flowering trees line wide esplanades in the center of town, and there is lawn space to lounge on. Perpignan has a Spanish palace, that of the kings of Majorca; a Spanish cathedral, the cathedral of St-Jean; a Spanish gate, Le Castillet; and a delightful pedestrian ramble of streets emanating from the place de la Loge and containing secluded hotels on hideaway squares, open-air markets, and good shopping.

The best place to get an overview of all this and begin a tour of the city is at the 14th-century **Castillet**, the gateway fortress that still flies the Catalonian flag. It offers more than panoramic views of Perpignan from its tower, however; inside, the **Musée des Arts et Traditions Populaires du Roussillon** (within the Casa Pairal) provides an intimate, room-by-room walk through the popular tastes and folk crafts of Catalonian Roussillon. Rare is the museum that so captures the essence of its people. Here is the art of the homespun: The dolls, dresses, and hats all speak with a tender eloquence. The heart of the people is visible in the table linens, woodcarvings, and pottery as well as in the tools of their industry—wrought iron and objects connected with the making of wine.

Close by Le Castillet looms the **cathedral of St-Jean**, built between 1324 and 1509. This is no French Gothic work but an Iberian one, made of stones from the Pyrénées polished by churning mountain rivers. Inside, the immense nave is flanked by shadowy side chapels whose frescoes and altars are temporarily illuminated at the touch of a button.

Outside, there is are great advantages to getting lost in the streets, but there are landmarks to help you navigate. Across the cathedral square and down delightful twists and turns is the 14th-century **Loge de Mer**. Refurbished in the 16th century in Spanish Renaissance style, it was an early stock exchange. Down the pedestrians-only rue de Loge stands Maillol's statue of Venus, whose longing gaze rests on the **Hôtel de Ville**. Behind the grillwork and public arches dwells another statue by Maillol, this one depicting in blazing bronze the siren La Méditerranée.

From here the streets run outward, lined with shops rich in chocolate thanks to the chocolate factory in nearby Cantalou. Other things to look out for are all sorts of leather items, particularly shoes, and hooded red and black figurines of the mystical procession of la Sanch. This procession occurs during Holy Week, which is celebrated on Good Friday as enthusiastically here as it is in Spain. It's been going on since 1416 under the auspices of the Confrérie de la Sanch (Brotherhood of the Blood), and winds through the streets from the church of St-Jacques to the cathedral, led by a red-robed Penitent wearing the hood of persons condemned to death, followed by Penitents in black who carry wax and wooden figures representing the personages of the Passion.

Finally, like a star smashed into the earth, there is the six-point **Citadelle**. Inside the massive walls is the curious **Palace of the Kings of Majorca**, who once ruled Catalonia from here. The construction, dating from the 13th century, utilizes the same indigenous riverbank rock found in the cathedral. Nature provided this building material ready-made in the form of smooth, rounded stones (*galets*) polished and washed down from the Pyrénées by the Têt river.

A couple of good restaurants in Perpignan are **Le Chapon Fin**, in the Park Hotel on boulevard Jean Bourrat (Tel: 68-35-14-14), which serves some of the finest regional food in the Catalan region; and **La Casa Sansa**, at 2, rue des Fabriques d'en Nadal (Tel: 68-34-21-84), with true Catalan specialties including Catalan codfish, hot *bolas* (meatballs), and *parillada* (mixed fish grill). There's also *meli mato* (honey-and–cream cheese dessert). Inexpensive.

In Perpignan you are already in the lap of the eastern Pyrénées. The highest of these is Canigou. Spectacularly perched atop Canigou at the edge of a cliff is the **abbey of St-Martin-du-Canigou**, an 11th-century Cluniac abbey. Within view of the monastery is a glacier field. A few hours' reflection under snowcapped peaks will do you a world of good before you reenter the world of traffic and baggage.

And still that is not it for Languedoc–Roussillon. Twenty-seven km (17 miles) south of Perpignan on the **Côte Vermeille**—the Vermilion Coast, which runs from just south of Peripignan to the Spanish border—there is one last town, one very small and precious place to visit.

Collioure

Collioure is the perfect French hamlet by the sea. It runs down to a peninsula hemmed in by green hills around a blue gulf. On the very end of the peninsula is an ancient lighthouse much loved by some of the world's greatest painters. They were all here at one time or another—Picasso, Dalí, Matisse, and all that crowd. What they left were impressions that townsfolk and visitors still can admire.

Facing the sea on the crescent-shaped *croisette* is a tile-floored hotel and café, **Les Templiers**, which has an accommodating bar, tables, and wicker chairs. The men start coming in the early afternoon to play cards, drink Banyuls, and eat *friture*. (Only the tourists sit in the sun.) The *friture* here—little fish deep-fried to a crisp—is better than in most places; the Banyuls—a sweet apéritif tasting like a cross between *fino* Sherry and Port—is as good as it is anywhere. But there is another reason to come here. This is probably the best undeclared art gallery in France. The walls are filled with the bright strokes of Picasso, Dalí, and Matisse; so numerous and so jammed together are the paintings that there is no room for labels. It was to this café that these great masters came, as did everyone else, to play cards and speak Catalan. They liked the place so much that it became a hangout, and they gladly gave some of their pictures in return for the hospitality. For its part, the café always kept faith and has continued to keep the paintings on the walls long after selling them could have brought great profits.

The Templiers's rooms are pleasant and sunny, done in the southern style. Some look out toward the **Castle of the Knights Templar**, across the canal. On Sundays, women—mothers and daughters—parade two by two down the promenade in front of the café looking for prospective sons-in-law and husbands to come forward.

There was no Latin word for yes, so they borrowed one here from the French. But when they batted their eyelashes and nodded and softly cooed *"oui,"* it rolled off their tongues like a brick and what came out was *"oc."* The French laughed, and named this whole vast and wonderful place after the language that first distinguished it, the *langue d'Oc.* Languedoc.

GETTING AROUND

Languedoc–Roussillon is approximately eight hours by car from Paris via the Autoroute du Soleil; take the Montpellier spur. There are direct flights between Paris and Nîmes and Montpellier, and between London and Perpignan. By train, the TGV runs express as far as Lyon and thereafter makes limited stops. While the train is much slower and often as expensive as air travel, if you are resourceful you can find very good deals by travelling at the right times. Check with SNCF for an explanation of their red (full-fare), white (less-expensive), and blue (cheapest) categories. All schedules are rather tenuous and subject to sudden change. Cars, a necessity in Languedoc–Roussillon, are available at major rental agencies in Montpellier, Perpignan, and Nîmes, and should be reserved in advance.

For a Spanish connection, Montpellier is easily reached in just a few hours from Barcelona, making a Spain/south of France vacation extremely feasible.

ACCOMMODATIONS REFERENCE

▶ **La Cauquière**. 5, rue de l'Hôtel de Ville, 30300 **Beaucaire**. Tel: 66-59-30-10.

▶ **Château Hôtel de Rieutort**. Saint-Pargoire 34230 **Pézenas**. Tel: 67-25-00-61.

▶ **Les Doctrinaires**. Quai du Général de Gaulle at 32, rue Nationale, 30300 **Beaucaire**. Tel: 66-59-41-32; Telex: 480706.

▶ **Hostellerie des Remparts**. 6, place Anatole France, B.P. 25, 30220 **Aigues-Mortes**. Tel: 66-53-82-77; Fax: 66-53-73-77.

▶ **Hôtel Restaurant la Source**. 34800 **Villeneuvette**. Tel: 67-96-05-07; Fax: 67-96-31-16.

▶ **Motel Côte Bleue**. Bouzigues 34140 **Mèze**. Tel: 67-78-31-42.

▶ **La Musardière**. 34, avénue République, 12100 **Millau**. Tel: 65-60-20-63.

▶ **St-Louis**. 10, rue de l'Amiral-Courbet, 30220 **Aigues-Mortes**. Tel: 66-53-72-68; Telex: 485465; Fax: 66-21-27-16.

▶ **Sofitel**. 34000 **Montpellier**. Tel: 67-58-45-45; Telex: 480140; Fax: 67-58-77-50.

▶ **Les Templiers**. 12, quai de l'Amirauté, 66190 **Collioure**. Tel: 68-82-05-58.

▶ **Le Vieux Castillon**. Castillon-du-Gard 30210 **Remoulins**. Tel: 66-37-00-77; Telex: 490946; Fax: 66-37-28-17.

▶ **Des Voyageurs**. 12, place du Quai, 30120 **Le Vigan**. Tel: 67-81-00-34.

TOULOUSE AND THE SOUTH

By Stephen Brewer

Stephen Brewer, a New Yorker, has edited several guide-books in this series. He retreats to the south of France regularly, frequently on assignment for magazines and newspapers.

The Midi, or, in translation of the old French, Midday: This legendary part of France takes its name from the noonday sun that shines upon its fields and vineyards year-round. To the French, the Midi is, simply, the South—where it is sunnier and warmer than it is in the rest of France, where the food is simple and delicious, where the wine flows freely, where life is easy and the lavender grows in wild abandon.

When Parisians or other northerners announce they are off to the Midi, they will most likely board a south-bound train for the Gare Matabiau in Toulouse; this old city, once the most important in all the south, and the countryside around it is where you are most likely to find the spirit of the Midi as it once was. These southwestern lands, which adjoin Languedoc–Roussillon, lie far to the west of Provence and the Côte d'Azur, those more sophisticated places that most non-French travellers are more likely to think of as the south of France (Toulouse is a full 400 km/250 miles west of Marseille). You will not find here the worldly attractions of Biarritz, on the Atlantic

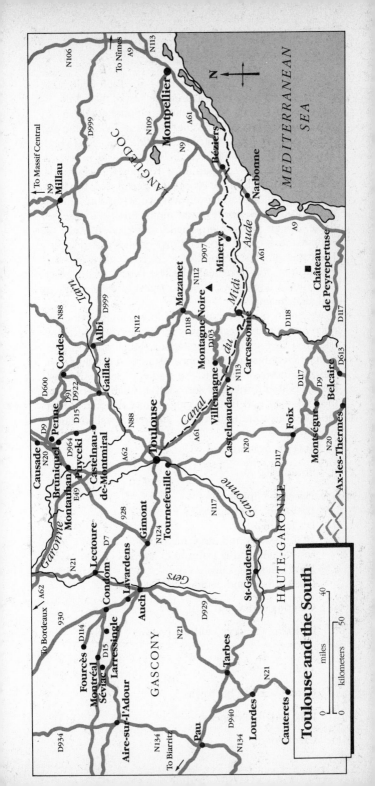

Toulouse and the South

some 300 km (180 miles) west, nor is the Toulousain Midi as heavily travelled as the Dordogne, just to the north.

The fields and vineyards around Toulouse are the most bountiful in France. A traveller here can follow narrow roads across rolling countryside and find a meal and a bed in rustic villages that have scarcely changed at all in several centuries. In the southernmost reaches the vineyards climb the foothills of the Pyrénées. From most of this sun-drenched region—even from the town of Lectoure, almost a hundred miles north of the mountains—you can see these craggy peaks, perpetually snowcapped. And, of course, much of the appeal of this region is gastronomic. Even the simplest restaurant is likely to serve its own variation of *foie gras* (literally "fat liver") and a good cassoulet, followed by *pruneaux fourrés* (stuffed plums) and an Armagnac.

We begin our coverage in Toulouse, a city that is at once ancient and aggressively modern. From there we take you in four directions: west to Auch and on into romantic countryside that once comprised the duchy of Gascony; north and east to the Medieval city of Albi and the unspoiled towns that surround it; south to Foix and the Pyrénées; and finally, southeast to Carcassonne, the most famous (and touristic) of all French walled cities.

MAJOR INTEREST

Toulouse

Place du Capitole
Basilique St-Sernin
Les Jacobins
Hôtel Bernuy and other mansions
La Daurade and la Dalbade quarters
Musée des Augustins
Place Wilson and commercial Toulouse

Gascony and Auch

Lectoure, Condom, and the *bastides* (fortified
    towns)

Albi

Cordes and the hill towns

Foix and the Pyrénées

Carcassonne

TOULOUSE

Chances are you will pass through Toulouse on your way to almost any of these other places. The speedy Autoroute des Deux Mers skirts its suburbs; its international airport, Blagnac, accommodates nonstop flights from New York, London, and many large cities on the Continent; and between 7:00 and 9:00 each morning four overnight express trains arrive from Paris. Unfortunately, all too often visitors rush through these points of entry for places that are smaller and more immediately appealing.

Granted, with its sprawling modern suburbs, traffic jams, and the somber brick façades of its older sections, Toulouse is a city that reveals its charms only slowly. "A flat, torturous town," is how Henry James described Toulouse on a stopover here in 1882. By the time of his visit, Toulousains already numbered 150,000, twice as many as a hundred years before. The city expanded even more rapidly in the 1920s, when local factories began to turn out the first passenger aircraft and the aviator Antoine de Saint-Exupéry commenced his historic transatlantic flights from its new airfield. Since then Toulouse's many immigrants, mostly from Spain and northern Africa, have found work in the city's industrial parks; its factories turn out Concordes and Airbuses, automobile parts and electronics.

It would be very easy to miss Toulouse's greatest treasure, one of the largest unspoiled historic quarters in Europe. The oldest parts of Toulouse cluster along the east banks of the Garonne river, which here makes a turn toward the west on its way from the Atlantic.

Place du Capitole

Old Toulouse can be explored only on foot. It is, as Wraxall wrote in 1775, "composed of streets so crooked, so narrow and winding . . . it requires a clue to conduct a stranger through them." The obvious starting point is the place du Capitole, a vast sea of paving stones that is named for the *capitulari* (magistrates) who ably governed Toulouse through several turbulent centuries. Europe's first step toward democracy occurred here in 1152 when Raymond V, Count of Toulouse, gave this elected body of 24 legislators full power to administer the law and mete out justice.

Even this enormous *place,* a handsome assemblage of brick and stone, has not escaped critics of Toulouse's distinctive brick architecture. Stendhal wrote of the *place*'s enormous **Hôtel de Ville**: "the ugliest building you could imagine, but the rest of the town is so shabby that this huge structure is quite a pleasant sight." It is the heaviness of Toulousain red brick—the best building material the local soil yields—that many visitors find so unattractive. Toulousains, on the other hand, call their city the Ville Rose (the Pink City) because of the gentle hue the brick takes on in the strong sunlight.

The buildings that surround the place du Capitole house some of Toulouse's smartest cafés. The **Brasserie le Bibert**, a sparkling, mirror-filled place, is popular with well-dressed patrons who come to eat oysters and drink Sauterne at its sidewalk tables. The **Grand Hôtel de l'Opéra**, practically next door, is named for the theater that occupies a wing of the Hôtel de Ville. In the hotel's restaurant, **Les Jardins de l'Opéra**, chef Dominique Toulousy prepares elaborate meals accompanied by wines from the largest cellar in Toulouse. The adjoining **Grand Café de l'Opéra** is no less fashionable, but its fare is considerably lighter. Upstairs, the guestrooms are luxuriously appointed and very large. (Accommodations in Toulouse are relatively inexpensive—not much more than 600 francs a night for the best room at the Opéra— and most of the better hotels offer a 25 percent discount on Friday, Saturday, and Sunday nights.)

Before you venture down any of the narrow streets leading off the *place,* walk to the little park in back of the Hôtel de Ville. Here, in a restored 16th-century tower called the **Donjon du Capitole**, the Syndicat d'Initiative provides maps and English-language pamphlets. You can also make a reservation here for the tours that the Association Toulousain d'Histoire d'Art conducts daily, in French; each covers a particular neighborhood or building.

St-Sernin

Your first excursion off the *place* should be down the rue du Taur, a narrow street that leaves the northwest corner of the square and several blocks later ends at the Basilique St-Sernin.

The "street of the Bull" is named for the animal to

whose tail the Roman legions tied Saturnin, patron saint and first priest of Toulouse, in A.D. 250. The beast dragged Sernin, as the martyr is known in French, to his death through the streets of the encampment. It finally stopped halfway down this narrow street, and the 13th-century **Eglise Notre-Dame du Taur** was built on the spot.

Sernin is entombed at the end of the rue du Taur, beneath the tower of the **Basilique St-Sernin**. For centuries this five-tiered octagonal tower drew pilgrims across the Toulousain plain on their way to Santiago de Compostela, 200 miles away on the other side of the Pyrénées in Spain. St-Sernin's 12th-century builders constructed an extraordinarily long nave to accommodate these travellers, who worshiped, slept, and set up temporary marketplaces beneath the high barrel-vaulted ceiling. Henry James wrote that this impressively austere place—the largest Romanesque structure in France—"alone was worth the journey to Toulouse."

Local lore has it that the **Hôtel du Barry**, a handsome house next to the basilica, now occupied by the Lycée St-Sernin, was once the home of Madame du Barry. It is unlikely that Louis XV's worldly mistress, a shopgirl turned courtesan, ever set foot in Toulouse, though the house did probably once belong to her brother-in-law. Closer to the truth is the city's claim to have educated France's greatest essayist, Michel Eyquem de Montaigne. Though he pursued most of his studies at the Collège de Guyenne in Bordeaux, for a while at least Montaigne attended what is now the **Université de Toulouse**. Count Raymond VII founded this great center of learning in 1299, and for years it was second in reputation only to the Sorbonne. The unremarkable buildings of the present-day institution stretch to the west of the place St-Sernin, and its 17,000 students crowd the cafés in almost every part of old Toulouse.

The **Musée St-Raymond**, devoted to the city's Roman past, occupies a 16th-century building directly across the place St-Sernin from the front of the basilica. Toulouse has few structures to bear witness to its founders, who pitched a settlement on the banks of the Garonne in the second century B.C. and maintained a relatively peaceful presence until their withdrawal in the middle of the fifth century A.D. But over the centuries the land beneath the city has yielded a wealth of coins and other artifacts. In one particularly fruitful dig, archaeologists dredging the bottom of the

Garonne in the early 1970s found 46,000 Roman coins and other paraphernalia. Many of these are now in the Musée St-Raymond's rather disorganized collections.

Les Jacobins

The other great religious presence in Toulouse is the **Eglise des Jacobins**, with another distinctive tower that you can see from St-Sernin. As with most places in Toulouse, it is not easy for a first-time visitor to find: Retrace your steps up the rue du Taur, cross the place du Capitole to its southwest corner, follow the rue Gambetta several blocks to the rue Lakanal, and turn right (north).

The Dominicans put up this imposing, fortress-like church and cloisters in the late 13th century. Their purpose was to restore a Catholic presence after the Albigensian heresy (this bloody religious war is discussed later in our coverage of Albi, the little city for which it is named). For centuries to come, from the pulpit in this stark, narrow nave the priests labored to impose the will of Rome upon freethinking Toulousains, relentlessly and, apparently, effectively. Catholic Toulouse turned on its heretical neighbors repeatedly over the next several centuries—but never so violently as in the bloody days of May 1562, when Catholics murdered a thousand Protestants and exiled the survivors.

One of the most poignant stories in the city's religious history is that of the boy Marc Antoine Calas. In 1762 he was found hanging from a beam in front of his house in the rue des Filatires, not far from Les Jacobins. He had recently broken away from his Protestant family and converted to Catholicism. A mob formed, accused his father of the murder, and broke him on the wheel. The man's widow fled to Switzerland. There she met Voltaire and told him her horrible tale. After years of effort, the philosopher rallied the support of the crown and convinced the tribunal of Toulouse to clear the besmirched name of the family.

Napoléon's troops commandeered Les Jacobins as a garrison and stabled their horses in the nave. Only in the past 20 years has Toulouse restored the vast church, housing here one of the city's most prized treasures: a gilded reliquary enshrining the head of Thomas Aquinas. For centuries the skull had been kept in full view of the faithful in a glass case in St-Sernin.

The Bookshop, just down the rue Lakanal from the

church's entrance, at number 17, is one of the few places in Toulouse to find English-language literature. This is surprising in light of the fact that Toulouse counts the British among its most noted citizens of the past. Laurence Sterne, wracked with consumption, made a futile journey here for his health in 1767. He spent a year in a rented house, working on *Tristram Shandy*. Adam Smith came to Toulouse in 1764 with his pupil, the duke of Buccleuch. The Scot spent most of his time here holed up in a room writing *The Wealth of Nations*.

Hôtel de Bernuy

The Hôtel de Bernuy, at the other end of the rue Lakanal at its intersection with the rue Gambetta, is just one of the hundreds of mansions that wealthy Toulousains built in the 16th century. By then Toulouse was providing most of Europe with *pastel,* a blue-colored dye. This commodity was much in demand as Europe's increasingly fashion-conscious aristocracy and a growing merchant class were enjoying the luxury of dressing in finery and lavishly furnishing their homes. These prosperous times for Toulouse would soon end when the Spanish began to import indigo from the Far East and the Americas. Until then, though, newly wealthy merchants outdid one another building handsome mansions on twisting lanes in this neighborhood, known as La Daurade, near the Garonne.

Bernuy was the most prosperous Toulousain merchant of his day. A story of rather doubtful authenticity has it that he alone raised the funds to ransom François I when the Spanish took the French king prisoner after the Battle of Pavia. (This is unlikely, as the king quickly handed his two young sons over to the Spanish in his stead. The boys were not released until the Treaty of Madrid was signed two years later.) The hotel now houses a school, and visitors can venture into the columned, ornamented courtyard.

La Daurade

Toulousains like to come to this part of the city to walk along the old quais above the slow-moving Garonne. (A series of delightful murals in the Hôtel de Ville on the place du Capitole depict Toulousains' 19th-century ancestors enjoying a Sunday afternoon the same way.) The quarter takes its curious name from the Provençal word *duratta* (gold). Its origins lie behind the heavy doors of the melancholy **Basilique Notre-Dame de la Daurade**, at the end of rue Gambetta. A few golden mosaics here are all that remains of the Roman temple upon whose ruins the church was built in the 18th century.

It is not easy to find food and drink in this part of Toulouse, but there are two very nice exceptions. **Au Chat Dingue**, just around the corner from the church at 40 *bis,* rue Peyrollières, is an old-fashioned place with an excellent and reasonably priced menu. It's best to make reservations for dinner; Tel: 61-21-23-11. The most popular restaurant along the river is the always busy **Brasserie des Beaux-Arts**, just down from the church at 1, quai de la Daurade (at the corner of rue de Metz). Apronned waiters hurry to and from the canopied sidewalk, where they dish up a vast array of shellfish from ice-filled bins. Windowside tables afford a view of the Pont Neuf (completed in 1659 and the only bridge to withstand the floods of 1875) and, across the river, the 17th-century hospital, the domed Hôtel-Dieu St-Jacques. Upstairs from the brasserie, the **Hôtel des Beaux-Arts** has recently renovated its 12 reasonably priced rooms with taste and an eye to comfort.

Hôtel d'Assézat

The finest house in Toulouse is the Hôtel d'Assézat, a few blocks from the river along the busy rue de Metz. Having made his fortune in pastel, Pierre d'Assézat commissioned Nicolas Bachelier, a native son and the city's most prominent architect of the period, to build a mansion for him. Assézat never saw his house completed. A Protestant, he was driven from Toulouse in 1557 and died penniless and homeless several years later.

His mansion now houses Europe's oldest literary society. Until the 15th century, Toulouse and the rest of the south spoke *langue d'Oc,* while the north spoke *langue d'Oïl* (both mean "language of yes"). *Oïl* has since evolved into *oui,* and the Langue d'Oïl into modern French.

Langue d'Oc was the lingua franca of the troubadours, poet-musicians whose aristocratic ranks included many of the counts of Toulouse. To preserve their dying language, in 1323 seven Toulousain troubadours founded the Compagnie du Gai Savoir (Company of Gay Learning), which has since become the Académie des Jeux

Floraux (Academy of the Floral Games). Every year on May 3, Toulousains gather in the hotel's courtyard to watch the academy's *jeux,* a spirited poetry reading.

La Dalbade

Bachelier also built many of the mansions along the rue de la Dalbade, a lovely street that begins at the rue de Metz as the rue des Couteliers and runs south, changing its name in front of the Eglise Notre-Dame de la Dalbade. The opulent Hôtel de Clary, at number 25, is better known as the **Hôtel de Pierre** (House of Stone). Jean de Bagis had Bachelier cover his house with stone, an extravagance in Toulouse that signified his wealth and success.

Return to the place du Capitole by retracing your steps to the rue de Metz and following that two blocks west to the place Esquirol (the construction here is for Toulouse's new Metro; the first leg of this extensive system will open next year). From the place Esquirol, the place du Capitole is about five blocks away up the **rue St-Rome**, a pedestrian precinct whose old half-timbered houses have been converted to shops.

Musée des Augustins

Before you turn up the rue St-Rome, it is well worth your while to walk two more blocks up the rue de Metz to Toulouse's favorite museum, the Musée des Augustins.

By the late 19th century the Canal du Midi and new rail connections with Bordeaux promised a bright and prosperous future for Toulouse, and the city began to rebuild to accommodate it. The sacrifice of the city's architectural past was enormous, however: Down came the ramparts to make room for the rue de Metz and other Parisian-type boulevards; the cloisters of St-Sernin and Notre-Dame de la Daurade were destroyed to make room for new buildings. Columns, capitals, and many other victims of the onslaught were brought to this old convent, where they are still on display and, judging by the crowds that fill these rubble-filled galleries, much admired.

Place Wilson

Toulousains often end a day of shopping or an evening on the town at one of the many cafés on the place Wilson, about three blocks west of place du Capitole via rue Lafayette. The most popular are the busy **La Frégate**, at number 16, and **Restaurant La Bohème**, just off the *place* at 3, rue Lafayette. The best-known restaurant here, and, many would argue, the finest in Toulouse, is the family-run **Restaurant Vanel**, just to the west of place Wilson at 22, rue Maurice-Fontvieille. The Vanels have been serving pigeon, pig's-feet stew, sweetbreads, and other hearty fare for two generations, and have earned two Michelin stars for their efforts. Reservations are essential; Tel: 61-21-51-82. Seafood and seasonal game, innovatively prepared, are the specialties at **Restaurant Darroze**, nearby at 19, rue Castellane. Again, it is wise to reserve; Tel: 61-62-34-70.

The food is remarkably good and the service almost too attentive at the **Hôtel et le Restaurant d'Occitanie**, 5, rue Labéda. This hotel school sends its graduates to some of the finest establishments in France. As part of their studies, students prepare and serve a five-course dinner at a prix fixe of about 100 francs. Reservations are a must; Tel: 61-21-15-92. Guest rooms are extravagantly large and nicely appointed, and even suites are moderately priced. The slick **Hotel Altéa Wilson** next door is popular with business travellers.

As in many large cities, the area around Toulouse's train station is no place to stay. But there are three comfortable, reasonably priced hotels on the rue Raymond IV, only a ten-minute walk from both the Gare Matabiau and place Wilson: the **Hôtel Raymond IV**, at number 16; the **Hôtel Le Président**, at number 43–45; and the nicest, **la Caravelle Hôtel**, at number 62.

Shopping on the busy streets that surround the *place* is of the fairly ordinary Daniel Hechter and Rodier variety. Given the bounty of the farmland surrounding Toulouse, though, it is not too surprising that the most appealing items to be had are those in any number of food shops and in the city's four public food markets. **Germain**, near the *place* at 6, rue de Rémusat, sells foie gras, cassoulet, crystalized violet roots (a delicious sweet), and other regional specialties in tins and from behind a delicatessen-like counter. The **Marchés des Carmes** is only a ten-minute walk south of place Wilson along rue d'Alsace-Lorraine. The stalls in this marketplace are stocked with all the makings for a meal, ordinary or exotic, which you can enjoy alfresco in the **Jardins des Plantes**. This trim, palm-shaded patch of greenery is just a few steps down the rue Ozenne from the market.

Toulouse is surrounded by delightful open countryside and some of the nicest old villages in France. Whether you leave town by car or on one of the many trains that make frequent runs to Albi, Auch, Foix, and other regional centers, you will be in open countryside just 15 minutes after you leave central Toulouse.

GASCONY

The old lands of Gascony run right up to Toulouse's western suburbs. The region is known for its food (especially its rich dishes made from every organ and appendage of ducks, geese, and pigs), its Armagnacs, and for the Gascons themselves. It is no coincidence that the French verb *gasconner* means to exaggerate.

Auch

By train, or by car travelling west along the N 124 out of Toulouse, the first you will see of the town of Auch is its late 15th- to 16th-century **Cathédrale Ste-Marie**, rising high above the green countryside and surrounded by steep lanes known as *pousterles*. Auch, about 80 km (50 miles) from Toulouse, is a busy little place, the préfecture of the Gers, one of the nine *départements* into which the historic lands of Gascony have been divided.

The newer town stretches along the tree-lined banks of the river Gers, and from here the **Escalier Monumental** climbs to the old Haute Ville (High Town). Halfway up this broad expanse of 370 steps is a statute of D'Artagnan, trusted friend of the three musketeers and the most famous Gascon of all. He was born near Auch in the village of Lupiac sometime around 1620, and was christened Charles de Batz. But upon joining the French royal guards he adopted the nobler sounding D'Artagnan, his mother's family name. By the time D'Artagnan was killed in 1673 in a battle of the Thirty Years' War he had been made a captain-lieutenant of the king's musketeers. His career was important and colorful enough to warrant a little biography, *Les Memoirs de Monsieur d'Artagnan;* it was this book that provided Alexandre Dumas with background when he wrote *Les Trois Mousquetaires* in the 1840s.

Your first encounter with a living Gascon may well be inside the cathedral. For a small fee you can enter the choir stalls—along with the stained glass, these are the most notable furnishings in this barnlike place—and obtain the service of a guide. Your lack of French will not deter your host from a loud and very animated description of the 1,500 intricately carved figures that crawl over and above the 132 stalls.

Most visitors come to Auch for one reason: to eat. André Daguin does well for these travellers at the **Hôtel de France**, just across the place de la Libération from the cathedral (Tel: 62-05-00-44). Daguin has a habit of walking from table to table and, in perfect English, reassuring his American and British guests that most Gascons eat such fat- and cholesterol-rich food every day and live to be very old. You will enjoy your meal here, and if you'd like to continue testing Daguin's recipe for a long life, many of his culinary secrets are revealed in a cookbook, *Foie gras, Maigret and other Good Foods from Gascony* (published in English). It is for sale, along with many of the ingredients you will need, in a shop on the premises. The accommodations here cost more than you would expect in a provincial town. But with its sunken tubs placed directly next to enormous beds, upholstered walls, and marble baths, the Hôtel de France is not a simple country inn. More modest accommodations are to be had at the **Relais de Gascogne**, at the foot of the Haute Ville on the avenue de la Marne.

Auch's "second" restaurant is **Claude Lafitte**, in an old house at 38, rue Dessoles. (This busy shopping street, closed to traffic, leads downhill from the place de la Libération.) Like almost anywhere else in this region, your meal here will begin with a *floc de Gascogne* (Armagnac and fresh grape juice) or a *pousse Rapière* (an orange liqueur mixed with Armagnac). These potent aperitifs will sufficiently lessen your inhibitions about eating the duck hearts, stuffed goose neck, and other sumptuous and exotic fare to follow. Reserve; Tel: 62-05-04-18.

AROUND AUCH

It would be a shame to come to Auch and not venture any farther into Gascony. The Syndicat d'Initiative, directly in front of the cathedral in a half-timbered house, will provide you with literature on the many bastides that surround Auch. For centuries these fortified towns housed a populace who worked in the fields by day and returned to the shelter of the stone walls by night.

A particularly pleasurable trip takes you north from Auch toward Lectoure and Condom, both in the heart of Armagnac country. Leave Auch to the west along the N 124. After 6 km (4 miles) there will be a turnoff to the north on a little departmental road, D 930. (This and many other roads around Auch are marked "Circuit des Bastides"; you can follow them aimlessly with no fear of becoming lost, for you will never be more than an hour or so from Auch.) Follow D 930 through rolling golden fields for another 11 km (7 miles), where you will come to a turnoff, D 103, for the little bastide of **Lavardens**. From this tiny collection of buildings, huddled together on a grassy hill in the shadow of a château, you can complete the 50 km (30 miles) to Lectoure on any number of roads. All are scenic, passing tiny villages, each with its covered market, and properous farms where barnyards are filled with geese; the most direct route is the D 148 to the D 123.

Lectoure

Lectoure, situated along the crest of a hill, is an agreeable place to spend several days. The sights here won't occupy much more than a morning: the 13th-century church; the promenade du Bastion, from where you can see all the way to the Pyrénées in good weather; the museum in the Hôtel de Ville, where 34 Celtic sacrificial altars from the second century, remnants of the town's first inhabitants, are on display. But Lectoure is an excellent touring base. The **Hôtel de Bastard**, a sunlight-filled mansion once owned by a family of the same name, could not be more pleasant; its swimming pool and elegant dining room are both welcome after a hot day on the road.

Condom and Environs

One of your trips out of Lectoure should take you 20 km (12 miles) west along D 7 to Condom. The residents of this busy, appealing bastide will already have heard any caustic remarks you might make about the name of their town. None other than Vladimir Nabokov once wrote, "There's many a mile between Condom in Gascogne and Pussey in Savoie."

Condom has nothing do to with the manufacture of this

eponymous product, but it is quite famous for the distilling, distribution, and consumption of Armagnac, the regional brandy that is aged in oak barrels.

You will have your choice of the finest Armagnacs (the best are those marked Hors d'âge, Napoléon, XO, and Vieille Réserve, indicating they have been aged for more than five years) at **La Table des Cordeliers**, a much-lauded temple of gastronomy that occupies a 14th-century chapel on the rue des Cordeliers. Diners here, in fact, often cleanse their palates with Armagnac between, perhaps, a course of langoustine and one of confit de canard. The 21 rooms in the adjoining *logis,* in a garden surrounding a swimming pool, are pleasant. You must call in advance for a table; Tel: 62-68-28-36.

If you set out in almost any direction from Condom you will come upon other beautiful little bastide towns. After driving in a northwesterly direction from Condom on the D 114 for 13 km (8 miles) you come to **Fourcès**, an utterly charming town whose half-timbered houses form a perfect circle around a tree-filled *place.* If utterly charming isn't enough, to spend time in the most romantic village imaginable you need drive only 5 km (3 miles) or so west from Condom along D 15 to **Larressingle**, where ivy and roses creep up the walls of a ruined castle and church.

The aura of ancient romance also hangs in the air at **Séviac**. This ruined Roman villa is on the southern outskirts of **Montréal**, yet another old hill town, 15 km (9 miles) west of Condom on D 15. Farmers unearthed mosaics at Séviac in 1868, but it wasn't until 1911 that a Docteur Lammilongue, a Gascon practicing medicine in Paris, returned home and began to excavate in earnest, unearthing baths, a heating system, oval-shaped rooms, and other remnants of the fourth-century villa. None of the findings, though, is quite as compelling as the remains of a man and a woman buried in a single grave. Now the *amants des Séviac* lie in a glass-topped coffin for all to see. How they died, or who they were, remains a mystery.

ALBI

If you request a *vin du pays* in Toulouse, you will probably be served a hearty red or sharp white from a Gaillac vineyard. There are at least 75 producers in the sun-drenched Gaillac region, which stretches from Toulouse northeast toward Albi. Route N 88 cuts right through the vineyards, and will deliver you to Albi, only 76 km (45 miles) from Toulouse, in a little over an hour.

The very name of this pretty little city is associated with the bloodiest religious revolt in Western history, the Albigensian Heresy. The followers of this movement rejected the Church of Rome in favor of Catharism. Between the mid-12th and 13th centuries, the religion engulfed most of the southwest and spread as far north as England. Cathari believed in two gods: The good god ruled the spiritual world and the evil god ruled the physical world. A good Cathar (known as a *parfait,* a perfect one) was celibate, ate no food that resulted from sexual union, and did not believe in the Mass, marriage, the organized church, any form of government, and certainly not in the payment of tithes or taxes.

It is easy to understand how the Cathari rankled both the Church in Rome and the Crown in Paris. Pope Innocent III dispatched Domingo de Gúzman to the region. This Spaniard, eventually canonized as Saint Dominic, and his followers (the forebears of the Dominican order) wandered the Toulousain Midi preaching the will of Rome. But it was sheer physical might that finally subdued the Cathari. Lords from the north could reap all the benefits of a crusade—plunder, land, and pardon for their sins—without travelling to far-off lands. The bloodshed these crusaders wrought was horrible: 20,000 men, women, and children were butchered in Béziers; at Minerve, 190 Cathari set themselves afire rather than surrender to Simon de Montfort, the papal emissary. Rare is the town in the southwest that does not have some such tale of massacre in its past.

It was in the best interest of the archbishops of Albi to build a church and residence where they would be safe from their heretical parishioners and that would also intimidate the see into submission. This explains why the **Cathédrale Ste-Cécile** has 29 defense towers and battlement walls. The cathedral rises almost directly from the southern banks of the river Tarn, and it is here that most travellers begin a tour of Albi.

One end of the cathedral's nave is covered with a fresco of the Last Judgment, a very good one that has been curiously ruined. In later renovations to the church, a large opening was cut through the center of the fresco to afford entrance to a chapel; the upper portion has been cut away to accommodate the organ's pipes. All that remain are hundreds of screaming, writhing, doomed figures, with no sign of Christ to provide redemption. The treasure here is the massive choir, which is surrounded by a carved limestone screen. As the story goes, 15th-century Albigensians were shocked when these carvings and those above the choir stalls were unveiled: The cherubs and devils bore a striking resemblance to the city's more prominent citizens.

Musée Toulouse-Lautrec

Henri de Toulouse-Lautrec was born into an aristocratic Albigensian family in 1864. It has been said that the warm tones of the brick, the profusion of wisteria, and the cobalt blue of the Midi sky greatly influenced the painter's use of color.

An enormous collection of Lautrec's work now hangs in the Musée Toulouse-Lautrec, in the **Palais de la Berbie**, the former archbishop's palace next to the cathedral. The rambling brick house where the painter was born, the **Hôtel du Brosc**, is nearby, at 14, rue Toulouse-Lautrec. His parents, the Comte et Comtesse de Toulouse-Lautrec, were first cousins. They were prosperous and civilized, and Henri enjoyed a privileged and, until he was crippled in a fall when he was 14, very active childhood. He left Albi for Paris to paint when he was barely 20, and there led a life so debauched that he was dead at 36. A branch of the family still lives in the house, and opens parts of it to the public.

Albi's other famous son is the great Socialist reformer Jean Jaurès, who was assassinated in 1914. Born in nearby Castres, he taught in Albi for many years and created one of France's first worker-owned factories here, the Verrerie Ouvrière (Workers' Glassworks).

Staying in Albi

You would be hard pressed to find a place better than Albi to spend a few days relaxing. You can wander here at leisure through the magnificent gardens behind the Palais de la Berbie, built along the old ramparts; in the lovely little **cloisters of the church of St-Salvi**; and along crooked streets that are closed to all but pedestrian traffic. There are two especially nice hotels in town, both owned and run by the same family. **La Réserve**

Fonvialane, a member of the Relais & Châteaux group, is just beyond the northern outskirts of the city in a large garden on the banks of the Tarn. The **Hostellerie du Grand St-Antoine** is in town, off the animated place Jean-Jaurès; it has a very good restaurant where it is best to reserve a table; Tel: 63-54-04-04. The **Hôtel Modern Pujol et Restaurant Michel André**, a little farther out on the avenue Colonel-Teyssier, is another good place to dine, and its modern rooms are comfortable.

CORDES

From Albi you will want to continue on to Cordes, just 25 km (15 miles) northwest on D 600. Cordes is built atop a very high hill, and as you approach it from the valley below it is not unusual to see the city floating above the clouds. This inaccessible location afforded the Cathari who founded Cordes in 1222 an almost impregnable defense. Indeed, it is said that troops sent to rout the heretics never even attempted to scale the summit. Legend also has it that three inquisitors who managed to infiltrate Cordes were thrown down its 300-foot-deep well, at the very top of the city near the **place de la Halle**.

Today Cordes is besieged by tourists. Fortunately, most are day trippers who arrive around noon and leave well before sunset. So if you overnight here, as you should, you will have many quiet hours in which to climb up and down stepped streets that afford dizzying views or to count the mythological creatures that crawl across the façade of the **Maison du Grand Veneur** (Master Huntsman's House). It is well worth the trip to Cordes to dine and then retire upstairs to sleep amidst the Medieval grandeur of the **Hôtel-Restaurant le Grand Ecuyer** (formerly the residence of the Master Horseman). The same management runs the **Hostellerie du Vieux Cordes**, more modest but also very nice. Unlike that of the Grand Ecuyer, its restaurant has not earned a Michelin star, but that should not keep you from enjoying a meal in its palatial dining room.

If you are travelling by car, you can venture into the countryside that looks so inviting from on high in Cordes. Much of the land around here is given over to the dense **Forêt de Grésigne**. The surrounding hill towns are not as architecturally endowed as those in Tuscany, but they are certainly reminiscent of them. One circular route, well under a hundred miles all told, takes you west from Cordes via routes D 19 and D 9 to **Penne** and **Bruniquel**, both situated high above the river Aveyron, then south and east along D 964 to **Puycelci** and **Castelnau-de-Montmiral**, and back to Cordes on the D 15 and D 91. Services, restaurants included, are difficult to find in these remote towns, so if you set out for an afternoon, plan to be back at your hotel before the dining room closes.

Another worthwhile outing from Cordes takes you 25 km (15 miles) north on D 922 to **Najac**. You can enjoy a pleasant lunch here at **L'Oustal del Barry**, and afterwards explore this little stone town that huddles beneath its *fortresse royal,* built by the brother of Saint Louis in 1253. That the houses here are built of stone and their roofs of slate is a sign that you are leaving the tile-roofed Midi. Charming as Najac is, with sunset it is time to head back south.

FOIX

It seems very odd to board a train for sunny Toulouse and find yourself sharing a compartment with skiers. Actually, Toulouse is less than two hours away from some of the best ski slopes in Europe. And Foix, in the foothills of the Pyrénées, is only 80 km (50 miles) south of Toulouse along the N 20.

The great marvel of Foix is its location, hedged in on one side by the river Ariège, on another by the river Arget, and on yet another by a craggy hillock topped by the legendary **Château de Foix**.

For centuries, the counts of Foix controlled the trade routes over the Pyrénées from their virtually unassailable château. From behind its thick walls they were also able to repel the advances of Simon de Montfort, sent by Rome to quell the town's heretical leanings toward Catharism. The château now houses a museum, its eclectic contents including a rather dull collection of fossils and *pyrénéen* folk costumes.

The largest structure on the narrow lanes below the château is the **Eglise St-Volusien**, steeped in a remarkable local legend. Volusien was a sixth-century bishop of Tours who was killed by the Visigoths. Foix requested the body and it was brought it here on an ox-drawn cart. When the cortège came to the Ariège, the waters parted, or so the story goes. Roger Bernard, count of Foix, erected the church in the 15th century to provide a suitable resting place for the popular saint's remains.

Many visitors to Foix remain loyal to the dowdy **Hostellerie Barbacane**, probably because the old hotel affords such dramatic views of the château. The **Hôtel Audoye-Lons**, among the half-timbered houses of the *vieille ville,* is much more appealing. Its big old-fashioned guest rooms and glass-roofed dining room are directly over the Ariège.

AROUND FOIX

From Foix it is only 40 km (25 miles) southeast via N 20 to the pleasant mountain spa of Ax-les-Thermes (for which see below), and from there only 60 km (36 miles) on to Andorra. It would be a shame, though, to speed up the highway and miss the offerings of this mountainous countryside.

A much-frequented attraction near Foix is **Labouiche**, said to be the longest underground river in the world. Visitors descend 250 feet to the river at a point near the village of Vernajoul, about 3 km (2 miles) northwest of Foix on D 1. There they board boats and sail a mile and a half along this eerie waterway.

Montségur

From Foix, D 117 takes you east some 30 km (18 miles) to what is perhaps the most famous Cathar citadel, mountain-top Montségur (en route you will pass another ruined stonghold of this sect, **Roquefixade**). In 1242 a party of 60 Cathari set out from Montségur for the town of Avignonet, near Carcassonne, where they killed the papal tribunal responsible for burning their fellow believers at the stake. Rome retaliated: A year later 6,000 soldiers arrived at the foot of the mountain and laid siege. Montségur, with its vast holding tanks for water and large reserves of food, lasted through a summer and a winter. But, come spring, the soldiers hired Gascon mercenaries to show them secret paths up the cliffside. The attackers surrounded the citadel with catapults. Montségur surrendered, and its 215 inhabitants were burned at the stake.

Visitors can climb up to the ruined stonghold, a trip of at least an hour on precipitous paths. In the village below, a hearty meal and a good bed awaits at the simple but comfortable **Hôtel Costes**.

About 20 km (12 miles) south of Foix, the N 20 comes to a turnoff for the **Grottes de Niaux**. The drawings here, 12,000 to 16,000 years old, are comparable to those at Lascaux in the Dordogne. Unlike those more famous caves, though, these at Niaux can be visited. Another cave in the same vicinity, the **Grotte de Lombrive** (off the N 20 just south of the turnoff for the Grottes de Niaux), is the largest in Europe, and also of historical interest. In the 13th century, several hundred Cathari took refuge here. Royal troops, discovering their whereabouts, sealed the mouth of the cave, and the heretics starved to death.

Ax-les-Thermes

Ax-les-Thermes, in the shadow of craggy pyrénéen peaks, is a cheerful town with 80 natural hot springs. The French come here to soak their rheumatic joints in the sulphurous waters and to breathe the clean mountain air. You can test the waters in the large public tub right in the middle of the town square, the place du Breilh. Regulars bring a newspaper and a pastry, take off their shoes and socks, and soak their feet here for the better part of the morning.

Among the many hotels in Ax, a nice choice is the new **Hôtel-Restaurant La Lauzeraie**, reached by its own footbridge across the Ariège. As for skiing, the Office de Tourisme Haute-Ariège, on the avenue Delcassé in the center of town, can provide you with reports of snow conditions at **Ax Bonascre**, a resort with 19 runs just 5 km (3 miles) south.

A very pleasant excursion from Ax takes you through a bucolic Alpine-looking valley on D 613 to **Belcaire**, 21 km (13 miles) to the north. Its simple **Hôtel du Bayle** (Tel: 68-20-31-05) serves a large and delicious lunch and dinner. If you are continuing on from these parts to Spain, a repast here would certainly be a suitable last meal on French soil.

SOUTH TO CARCASSONNE

Many travellers to the southwest skip Toulouse altogether and head directly to Carcassonne, 92 km (57 miles) southeast of Toulouse along either the Autoroute des Deux Mers or the N 113.

It is easy to understand why Carcassonne is so appealing, of course. This stronghold is one of the largest, best preserved Medieval cities in Europe. Therein, too, lies a problem. Quite simply, the place is overrun with visitors. Within the walls there are some 130 souvenir shops and so many cafés that tables and chairs line almost every square and street. If you are planning a trip down from Toulouse, know in advance that you will be contending with crowds.

Castelnaudary

En route to Carcassonne you may well want to stop for a meal in Castelnaudary, about 60 km (37 miles) from Toulouse. The French Foreign Legion maintains a garrison here, and the legionnaires, walking through the old quarter in their kepis, lend an exotic air to this hot and not particularly attractive little backwater. The Canal du Midi opens into a large basin here as well, and bargers and pleasure boaters stop for provisions, further giving the landlocked town the air of a Mediterranean port.

The real reason to visit Castelnaudary is to eat, because this is the home of cassoulet. (Toulousains claim that they invented cassoulet, which is made in a squat clay pot called a *cassolo,* but most experts give the credit to Castelnaudary.) This blend of beans, pork fat, preserved meats, and sausage is not for the delicate appetite. But when prepared well it is astonishingly tasty, all the more so when accompanied by a light regional wine, such as a Corbières. When Chauriens, as locals are called, wish to dine out on cassoulet, they often go to the **Grand Hôtel Fourcade**, at 14, rue des Carmes. There are 14 comfortable guestrooms upstairs as well.

From Castelnaudary, Carcassonne is only 40 km (25 miles) farther. Staying in the latter (more on hotels in Carcassonne later) can be quite unpleasant, given the crowds and the attendant noise. A very nice alternative would be to book a room about 15 km (9 miles) to the northeast of Castelnaudary at the **Castel de Villemagne**, a beautiful old château in the little hamlet of Villemagne. The proprietress, Madam Maksud de Vezian, grew up in this comfortable old house near the forested Montagne Noire, and she puts up her guests in seven antiques-filled rooms at a fraction of the cost of most château hotels.

From here you can dip into Carcassonne on the N 113 and return in time for a home-cooked meal and an Armagnac in the garden.

CARCASSONNE

Carcassonne is actually two cities separated by the river Aude: the newer Ville Basse (Lower City), a busy agricultural center that is of little interest to travellers, and the Cité, the Medieval stronghold surrounded by double walls that stretch for more than a mile.

The most dramatic views of the Cité are those from afar, and the best view to be had is from a rest stop about a mile due east of the Cité, between the exits for Carcassonne Nord and Carcassonne Sud on the Autoroute des Deux Mers (it is clearly marked as an overlook). As picture perfect as the Cité looks, much of it has been restored, and much of that clumsily. The 19th-century architect who did the dirty deed is Viollet-le-Duc, who had political connections and is responsible for so many "restorations" across France that a phrase has actually come into the French language to sit forever in judgment of his efforts: "Violé par Viollet ("raped by Viollet").

The Cité's Walls

The original fortress was built by the Romans during the third and fourth centuries. Geographic considerations— the river Aude, the hilltop view, the site's location between Toulouse and the Mediterranean—made Carcassonne an important military garrison. Sections of the original Roman wall may still be seen to the left of Pont Levis (the Roman portion comprises the sections in which the stores are packed more tightly than they are in the others), and several Gallo-Roman relics are on display at the **Musée Lapidaire** in the Château Comtal.

The Visigoths swept into the region in the fifth century and dealt a death blow to Roman control. Carcassonne then became a Visigoth stronghold, and it wasn't until the Arab invasions in the eighth century that the Visigoths forfeited their control. It took nearly a hundred years and all the soldiers of Charlemagne to dislodge the Moors from Carcassonne and the rest of the Narbonne region.

Legend has it that Carcassonne owes its name to a Moorish woman, Dame Carcas. In the ninth century the

Moors invaded and occupied the fortress. Responding to the invasion, Charlemagne laid siege to the city and captured the Moorish king Balaak. When the Moor refused to convert to Christianity, the French killed him.

Balaak's wife, Dame Carcas, resolutely continued to hold the fortress and kept the Christians outside the walls. The siege lasted five years, during which time nearly all of the Dame's soldiers died of hunger and thirst. Even so, to trick Charlemagne into believing that she had provisions to burn, Carcas showered her last five gallons of water over the walls. She then gathered the last of the remaining wheat and fed it to the last sow, which she also heaved over the walls. The poor beast burst open upon hitting the ground, revealing all of the wheat. Convinced he was defeated, Charlemagne about-faced his army and began a retreat. Wanting an audience with the emperor, Carcas began to sound the bells of the fortress. "Carcas is ringing," the soldiers shouted, or in French, *"Carcas sonne,"* which is how the town got its name.

Carcas met with the emperor and was converted to Christianity. Charlemagne was so taken by the woman's courage, it is said, that he asked her to stay and be the master of the city. He wed her to one of his noblemen, Trencavel, which was then the custom when a great lord wanted to keep a woman for himself without marrying her. Carcas and Trencavel founded the dynasty of the viscounts of Carcassonne.

The Cathar Crusades

By 1209 Carcassonne was a well-protected, prosperous city, visited by troubadours and enlivened by tournaments, hunts, and festivals. Most of the festive activities took place in the space between the two encircling walls—the *lices.*

Then began the crusade against the Cathars. Although Raymond-Roger de Trencavel, Carcassonne's lord at the time, was a Catholic, he was a strong believer in protecting the right to freely worship—an opinion that was not shared by many of his fellow lords. Called to Montpellier to an assembly of knights who asked him to chase all heretics from his city, Trencavel replied: "I offer a city, a roof, a shelter, a loaf of bread, and my sword to all those banned who will soon wander throughout Provence, without a city, or a roof, or asylum, or bread." Trencavel's speech led to his downfall. Carcassonne was attacked by

20,000 men; Trencavel was captured, imprisoned, and soon died in one of the towers of his own fortress.

In the 13th century, the very Catholic king of France, Louis IX, a.k.a. Saint Louis, ordered the construction of the Cité's outer wall to guarantee the fortress's defensive invulnerability. His son, Philippe III, put the finishing touches on the fortress. Carcassonne became an impregnable stone wonder and a military model for the rest of Europe, earning in the process the title "Maiden of Languedoc." It is no coincidence that no one ever attacked the Cité again.

Looking at the towers, you can see how the defense of the Cité was carried out. Archers were situated on four floors of the major towers behind narrow-slitted openings just big enough to shoot an arrow through but not large enough for enemy arrows to penetrate. Wooden platforms atop the towers were equipped with ramps from which heavy iron balls were rolled and dropped on the hapless invaders below.

Inside the Gates

Two gates give entrance to the Cité, the Porte d'Aude and Porte Narbonnaise. There is surprisingly little to see or do inside, aside from walking through old streets that are still home to 1,000 residents and, as best you can, soaking up the history of the place. In addition to its walls, Carcassonne really boasts only two buildings of architectural interest, and one of these, the **Château Comtal** (the Count's Castle), circa 1125, has been altered horribly over the years. Not so the **Eglise St-Nazaire**, a very fine church with remarkable stained glass from the 14th to the 16th centuries.

Few of Carcassonne's restaurants distinguish themselves, and you are best off with a simple meal at any number of cafés or crêperies. As for lodgings, the **Hôtel Cité**, just across the *place* from St-Nazaire, is a good choice, with a large garden and antique furnishings. The **Hôtel Donjon**, on the other side of the Cité on rue Comte-Roger, is simpler and less costly. But after a day in the Cité, you may well want to retire to a quieter retreat elsewhere in the region, such as at the Castel de Villemagne mentioned above.

If crowds don't bother you, July is a good time to visit. For all hotels in and near the Cité, reserve well in advance, especially for the Bastille Day (July 14th) celebration. The Bastille Day fireworks at the Cité rival the Parisian event. In addition, the outdoor amphitheater on the southern rampart is the scene of various concerts and plays throughout the month-long Festival de la Cité.

GETTING AROUND

It is a sign of just how cosmopolitan Toulouse is becoming that Air France now flies there nonstop from New York City (Kennedy International Airport) once a week. On days when the New York–Toulouse flight does not operate, Air France will fly you from its North American gateways to Paris and book you through to Toulouse on one of several daily Air Inter flights. Dan-Air and British Airways fly to Toulouse from London.

Travellers also have their choice of a dozen trains that leave for Toulouse at all hours of the day from Paris (from the Gare d'Austerlitz). Four trains make the seven- to eight-hour journey at night and are equipped with sleeping cars and couchettes. Though Toulouse is France's technology capital, it is not yet serviced by the TGV.

For those travelling by car, the Autoroute des Deux Mers (A 61) connects Toulouse to Bordeaux (near the Atlantic, 240 km/150 miles northwest) and to Narbonne (near the Mediterranean, 150 km/90 miles southeast). At Bordeaux you may connect with the A 10, which runs north then east toward Paris; at Narbonne, with the A 9, which runs southwest toward the Spanish border and Barcelona, and north then east toward the Côte d'Azur and Italy. Many French drivers boast they make the Paris–Toulouse run, a journey of some 700 km (420 miles), in a little over five hours—a claim that should convince you to take the train.

Toulouse is at the very center of the region covered in this chapter, and even the most remote towns and villages are no more than an hour or two away by train or car. From the Gare Matabiau, a very complete rail network connects Toulouse, Agen, Albi, Auch, Bordeaux, Carcassonne, Castres, Foix, Montauban, Rodez, and most other towns of any size within a radius of 100 miles or so. Hertz, Avis and other major rental-car firms have offices at either Blagnac airport or in central Toulouse.

Driving in this region is what motoring once was: leisurely excursions along well maintained, less travelled roads, with stops at village restaurants and hotels. Using departmental roads (marked by the letter "D" followed by a number) almost exclusively, you could make a very scenic "back roads" circuit of the entire region, driving, for instance, from Foix to Auch, from Auch to Albi, and from Albi to Carcassonne.

A few notes of specific concern: If you take the train from Toulouse to Cordes, you will disembark in the countryside and find yourself, surrounded by geese, a good 4 km (2.5 miles) from town. Any number of local car services post their numbers at the little station; alternatively, the walk, with Cordes floating in the distance, is pleasant. During the summer months an open-air *petit train* takes visitors from Cordes's Ville Basse to the Haute Ville above. From Castelnaudary, Blue Line Midi (whose motto is "Green France in a Blue Boat") makes tours along the Canal du Midi. Contact: Blue Line, 11400 Castelnaudary; Tel: 68-23-17-51.

ACCOMMODATIONS REFERENCE

▶ **La Caravelle Hôtel.** 62, rue Raymond-IV, 31000 **Toulouse.** Tel: 61-62-70-65.

▶ **Castel de Villemagne.** 11310 **Villemagne.** Tel: 68-94-22-95.

▶ **Grand Hôtel Fourcade.** 14, rue des Carmes, 11400 **Castelnaudary.** Tel: 68-23-02-08.

▶ **Grand Hôtel de l'Opéra.** 1, place du Capitole, 31000 **Toulouse.** Tel: 61-21-82-66; Telex: 521998 FESPI; Fax: 61-23-41-04.

▶ **Hostellerie Barbacane.** 1, avenue Lerida, 09000 **Foix.** Tel: 61-65-50-44.

▶ **Hostellerie du Grand St-Antoine.** 17, rue St-Antoine, 81000 **Albi.** Tel: 63-54-04-04; Telex: 520850 MAPALBI.

▶ **Hostellerie du Vieux Cordes.** Rue Saint-Michel, 81170 **Cordes.** Tel: 63-56-00-12.

▶ **Hôtel Altéa Wilson.** 7, rue Labéda, 31000 **Toulouse.** Tel: 61-21-21-75; Telex: 530550; Fax: 61-22-77-64.

▶ **Hôtel Audoye-Lons.** 6, place G-Duthil, 09000 **Foix.** Tel: 61-65-52-44.

▶ **Hôtel de Bastard.** Rue Lagrange, 32700 **Lectoure.** Tel: 62-68-82-44.

▶ **Hôtel des Beaux-Arts.** 1, place du Pont-Neuf, 31000 **Toulouse.** Tel: 61-23-40-50; Telex: HBA 523 451 F; Fax: 61-22-02-27.

▶ **Hôtel Cité.** Place de l'Eglise, 11000 **Carcassonne.** Tel: 68-25-03-34; Telex: 500829.

▶ **Hôtel Costes. Montségur** 09300 Lavelanet. Tel: 61-01-10-24.

► **Hôtel Donjon**. 2, rue Comte-Roger, 11000 **Carcassonne**. Tel: 68-71-08-80; Telex: 505012; Fax: 68-25-06-60.

► **Hôtel de France**. Place de la Libération, 32003 **Auch**. Tel: 62-05-00-44; Telex: 520474; Fax: 62-05-88-44.

► **Hôtel-Restaurant le Grand Ecuyer**. Rue Voltaire, 81170 **Cordes**. Tel: 63-56-01-03.

► **Hôtel-Restaurant La Lauzeraie**. Avenue Delcassé, 09110 **Ax-les-Thermes**. Tel: 61-64-20-70.

► **Hôtel et le Restaurant d'Occitanie**. 5, rue Labéda, 31000 **Toulouse**. Tel: 61-21-15-92.

► **Hôtel Le Président**. 43–45, rue Raymond-IV, 31000 **Toulouse**. Tel: 61-63-46-46; Fax: 61-62-86-60.

► **Hotel Raymond IV**, 16, rue Raymond-IV, 31000 **Toulouse**. Tel: 61-62-89-41; Fax: 61-62-38-01.

► **Logis des Cordeliers**. Rue des Cordeliers, 32100 **Condom**. Tel: 62-28-03-68.

► **Modern' Pujol et Restaurant Michel André**. 22, avenue Colonel-Teyssier, 81000 **Albi**. Tel: 63-54-02-92.

► **Relais de Gascogne**. 5, avenue de la Marne, 32003 **Auch**. Tel: 62-05-26-81.

► **La Réserve Fonvialane**. Route de Cordes, 81000 **Albi**. Tel: 63-60-79-79; Fax: 63-47-10-47.

BORDELAIS, COGNAC, AND THE DORDOGNE

By Georgia I. Hesse

A vineyard-rich slice of limestone plain called the Bordelais edges the wide Gironde river, which flows into the Atlantic, its waters joined by those of the tributaries Garonne and Dordogne.

The Bordelais, the heart of the old province of Guyenne (sometimes Guienne), covers almost all the modern department of the Gironde. It is also the linchpin of ancient Aquitaine.

Aquitaine, the many-rivered "land of waters," is a region still clear in the mind of every Frenchman, though it no longer exists as an entity on most maps. In Julius Caesar's day it was *Aquitania,* that part of Gaul lying between the Pyrénées on the south and the Garonne river (flowing by Bordeaux) on the north. (The name "Basque" is, through many linguistic permutations, related to Aquitania.) A Roman province, then a Frankish duchy, it became the possession of the English kings when Eleanor of Aquitaine died in 1204, and as such it was the principal arena of the Hundred Years War.

The Cognac region in the Charente lies north of Bordeaux and the rivers.

The Dordogne, one of France's longest rivers, rises in the plateau known as the Massif Central; for most of its life tumultuous, it has recently been tamed by dams, artificial lakes, and hydroelectric stations. Still, it remains a capricious river in places (especially along the 38-mile run from Sarlat to St-Cyprien), slicing through the history and prehistory of humankind.

For some reason, the regions of Bordeaux, the Bordelais, Cognac, and the valley of the Dordogne remain among the lesser-roamed major regions of France, despite being home to some of the world's greatest wines, most fascinating human antiquities, and most magical landscapes. The best times to visit these areas—as for many parts of France—are May and June or September and October.

MAJOR INTEREST

The Bordelais

Bordeaux
Grand-Théâtre
Musée des Beaux-Arts
Musée d'Aquitaine
Cathedral of St-André
Musée des Arts Décoratifs
Walk from esplanade des Quinconces along
 Garonne river to place de la Bourse
La Vinothèque

Wine châteaux and tastings
St-Emilion

Cognac
The town of Cognac
Saintes, Roman and Medieval sites
Royan, seaside resort and casinos

The Dordogne
Prehistoric sights, especially caves
Drive along the Cingle de Trémolat
Les Eyzies-de-Tayac area of prehistoric sites
Sarlat-la-Canéda, old town for strolling
Domme, La Roque-Gageac, and Beynac-et-Cazenac,
 scenic villages
Monpazier
Rocamadour, scenic Medieval religious site
Pech-Merle prehistoric cave site

In the 12th century, Eleanor of Aquitaine was the most

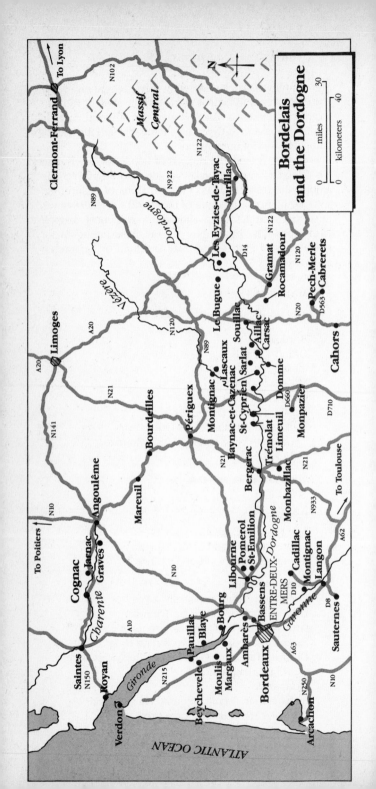

Bordelais and the Dordogne

ATLANTIC OCEAN

To Lyon

To Poitiers

To Toulouse

Massif Central

Dordogne

Vézère

Charente

Gironde

Garonne

ENTRE-DEUX-MERS

Clermont-Ferrand
Limoges
Angoulême
Cognac
Jarnac
Saintes
Royan
Verdon
Beychevelle
Moulis
Margaux
Pauillac
Blaye
Bourg
Ambarès
Bassens
Bordeaux
Libourne
Pomerol
St-Émilion
Graves
Cadillac
Montignac
Langon
Sauternes
Arcachon
Mareuil
Bourdeilles
Périgueux
Montignac
Baynac-et-Cazenac
Lascaux
Sarlat
St-Cyprien
Le Bugue
Les Eyzies-de-Tayac
Aurillac
Souillac
Aillac
Carsac
Gramat
Rocamadour
Pech-Merle
Cabrerets
Cahors
Domme
Monpazier
Trémolat
Limeuil
Bergerac
Monbazillac
Mérignac

N
N102
N122
N922
N120
N89
N21
N20
N141
N10
N150
N215
N250
A10
A20
A62
A63
D10
D8
D14
D660
D710
D563
N933

miles 0 — 30
kilometers 0 — 40

powerful person here. Her lands, inherited in 1137 upon the death of her father, the duke, stretched north from the Pyrénées to the Loire and east from the Atlantic to central Auvergne, constituting a region at least as large as the kingdom of France itself.

Realizing that, Louis VI (called Louis the Fat), who was rather ill, seized the prize for his son, Louis the Young. The Capétian prince married Eleanor in 1137, the year he became Louis VII, gaining not only a wife but also a dowry comprising Guyenne, Périgord, Limousin, Poitou, Angoumois, Saintonge, Gascony, Auvergne, and Toulouse.

After 15 years of misunderstandings, manipulations, and machinations, Louis VII arranged the pronouncement of divorce from his wife by the Council of Beaugency. Two months later, Eleanor (with her lands) married Henri Plantagenêt, who himself held Anjou, Maine, Touraine, and Normandy.

The marriage of Eleanor and Henri was disastrous for France and the house of Capet, and the situation only worsened when, two years later, Henri was crowned Henry II of England (as a descendant of William the Conqueror). The French-English struggles that ensued were to last almost 300 years, culminating in the Hundred Years War. Everywhere in the Bordelais and the valley of the Dordogne, evidences of this epic antagonism are at hand.

As Desmond Seward writes in *The Hundred Years War*: "The protagonists are among the most colorful in English and French history: Edward III, the Black Prince, and the even more formidable Henry V; the splendid but inept John II who died a prisoner in London; the sickly, limping intellectual Charles V, who very nearly overcame the English; and the enigmatic Charles VII (Joan of Arc's Dauphin), who at last drove them out. The supporting English cast included such men as Sir John Chandos, John of Gaunt, the Duke of Bedford and Old Talbot, as well as Sir John Fastolf—the original of Shakespeare's Falstaff. On the French side were figures like the Constable du Guesclin, the Bastard of Orléans, and the 'witch-saint from Domremy.' "

THE BORDELAIS

BORDEAUX

Henry James wrote, "Bordeaux is... dedicated to the worship of Bacchus in the most discreet form."

Food writer Patricia Wells mentions no gods: "I find Bordeaux a rather stuffy, characterless town—too snooty *bourgeois* for those of us who are not part of the clan. . . ."

"Take Versailles," Victor Hugo opined, "add Antwerp to it, and you have Bordeaux."

Bordeaux means business, and has since the days of the Romans, who introduced the vine into the region. During the 14th century and the Hundred Years War the wine trade never slowed, and in the 18th century the keys to Bordeaux's port were the heaviest in the kingdom. Only the Revolution of 1789, followed by the Napoleonic Wars and some miserable harvests, succeeded in defoliating the success of the vineyards. Not until after World War II did the sun of success and sales shine fully on Bordeaux again.

Today, despite its distance of 60 miles from the sea, Bordeaux, including Verdon, Bassens, Ambès, Blaye, and Pauillac on the Gironde estuary, is France's major industrial port.

Whether you arrive by train, plane, ship, or car, it is the business of business that you notice here first: the warehouses and cargo sheds that march along both banks of the Garonne, the new university city on the outskirts, several industrial zones, the still-burgeoning fair-sports-convention-hotel-exposition conglomeration known as Le Lac (The Lake), and Mériadeck, a new commercial quarter. (Much of the current economic expansion of Bordeaux has resulted from the efforts of Jacques Chaban-Delmas in his positions as mayor, president of the regional council, and occasional candidate for the French presidency.)

Every day in summer, boat tours on the river show off Bordeaux's bustling port and industrial areas, but most travellers head first for the old city center.

Classic Bordeaux

The center of things civilized is **place de la Comédie**, site of the Roman forum and a Gallo-Roman temple torn down by Louis XIV and replaced by today's magnificent Grand-Théâtre. Wide avenues and tree-lined esplanades radiate from the *place:* cours de l'Intendance, the best street for smart, idle strolling; cours Georges Clemenceau, a flagstone-paved shopping street that links place Gambetta to place Tourny; and the allées de Tourny, along which chic boutiques edge fashionable sidewalk cafés. Any amble here should cure the delusion that Bordeaux is aloof and indifferent. It is simply itself, with a refreshing absence of the usual rivalry with Paris. Keep your eyes open for the **Brasserie de Noailles** along Tourny; it speaks of the 1930s and is a super place to relax with a seafood snack and a few glasses of dry, snappy Entre-deux-Mers.

First things first: settling in. Now that the cozy old Grand Hôtel is gone, the best choice within walking distance of many attractions is the **Hôtel Burdigala**, not far from place Gambetta, the Musée des Beaux-Arts, and other attractions. Its 71 rooms are fairly expensive, as is the restaurant. A worthwhile hotel for active types is **Sofitel Aquitania** in Bordeaux-Lac, with its own swimming pool, convention facilities, and 212 modern rooms. The restaurant, **Le Flore**, is closed Saturdays, **Le Pub** on Sundays.

Before you start exploring, make three stops on cours du 30-Juillet, which runs the short distance from place de la Comédie to the esplanade des Quinconces. Here are the Office de Tourisme (with maps, details of special events), the Maison du Vin de Bordeaux (for tastings, vineyard touring information, and reservations), and **La Vinothèque** (a wine store the size of a warehouse).

A walk from the esplanade des Quinconces to the place de la Bourse, past classical façades and wine-merchants' town houses, reveals one of the most elegant waterfronts in Europe. The gentle curve of the river here gave Bordeaux its old nickname, Port of the Moon. Place de la Bourse itself shows off harmonious 18th-century architecture.

Back on place de la Comédie, the **Grand-Théâtre** is one of the handsomest in France, inside and out, an echo of Greece in 18th-century stone. Performances the year round (and especially during the prestigious music festival in May) are staged under its magnificent Bohemian

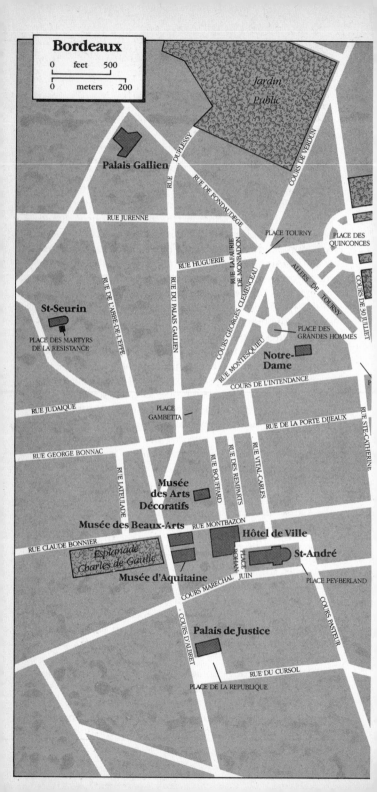

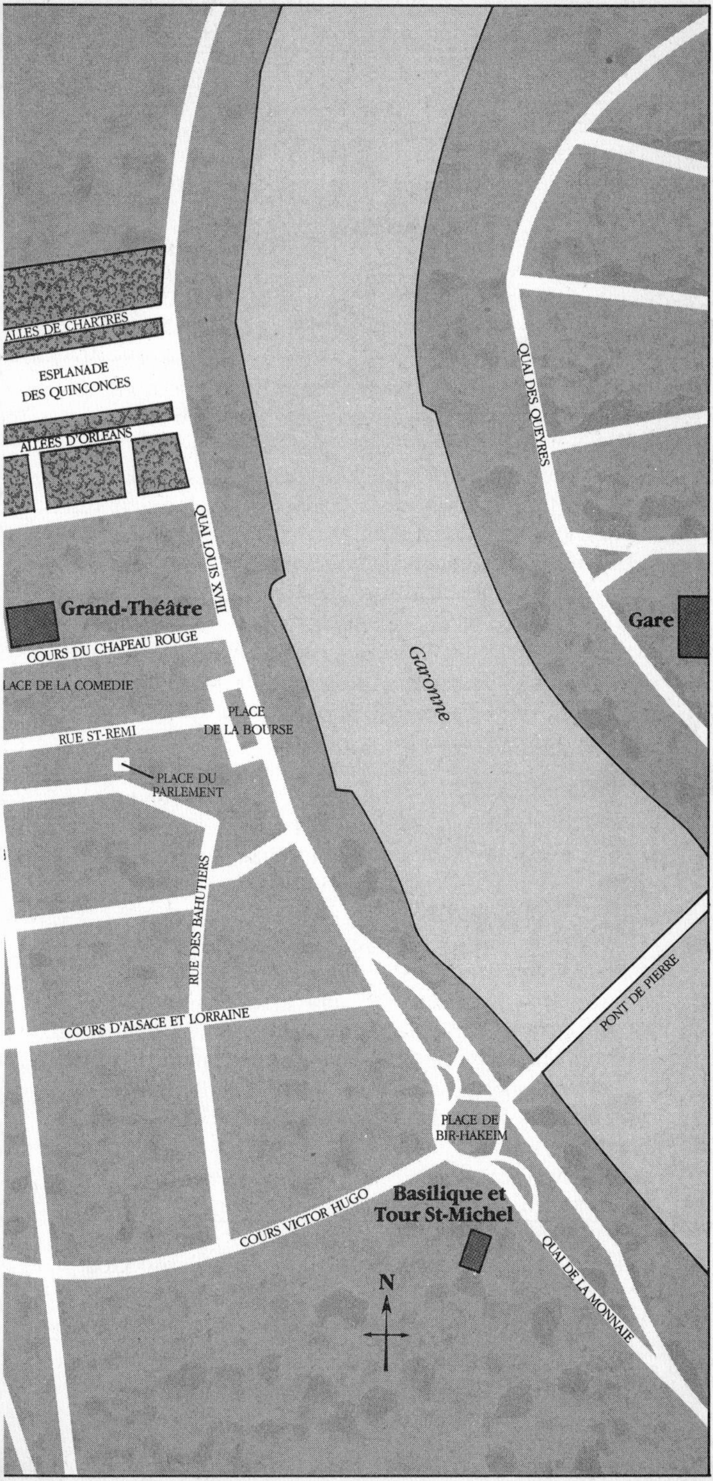

ALLES DE CHARTRES

ESPLANADE
DES QUINCONCES

ALLES D'ORLEANS

Grand-Théâtre

COURS DU CHAPEAU ROUGE

PLACE DE LA COMEDIE

RUE ST-REMI

PLACE
DE LA BOURSE

PLACE DU
PARLEMENT

QUAI LOUIS XVIII

Garonne

QUAI DES QUEYRES

Gare

RUE DES BAHUTIERS

COURS D'ALSACE ET LORRAINE

PONT DE PIERRE

PLACE DE
BIR-HAKEIM

COURS VICTOR HUGO

**Basilique et
Tour St-Michel**

QUAI DE LA MONNAIE

N

crystal chandelier. Guided tours of the theater are given on Saturdays only, throughout the year.

Many of Bordeaux's major sights cluster around the Hôtel de Ville, near place Pey-Berland, which occupies the 18th-century **Palais des Rohan**, built for the archbishop and prince of the noted and sometimes notorious Rohan family. Those who have time to see everything in town may want to tour the building on Wednesday afternoons, but others will be content to admire the gardens behind and then view the works of art installed in the two galleries of the **Musée des Beaux-Arts**. The Beaux-Arts' collections of paintings and sculptures range from the 15th century to the 20th and are arranged by national schools. The museum is particularly rich in Dutch art, and also includes works by three men born in Bordeaux: Odilon Redon, André Lhote, and Albert Marquet.

The **Musée d'Aquitaine**, at the corner of cours Victor-Hugo and cours Pasteur, displays a treasure trove of prehistoric and ancient relics, tools, and artworks, ranging from the Paleolithic period to the Renaissance. Among the most famous (and, today, humorous) items is the fat little *Vénus de Laussel,* sculpted some 20,000 years before the birth of Christ.

Almost facing the Rohan Palace, the **cathedral of St-André** was built in the 11th century and has endured several reincarnations. Its most important elements are the Porte Royale, with its extraordinary 13th-century sculptures, and the curious belfry, the Tour Pey-Berland, isolated on the grounds.

The nearby **Musée des Arts Décoratifs**, at 39, rue Bouffard, owns handsome furniture groupings as well as glassware, enamels, silverwork, and ceramics from around the Continent. Of particular interest are the *pots-Jaqueline,* rustic, traditional pieces from Lille that are reminiscent of English Toby jugs. Also on place Pey-Berland, the Musée Jean-Moulin is devoted to World War II and the Resistance movement.

Within walking distance of the Musée des Beaux-Arts and just north of the esplanade Charles de Gaulle on rue Robert-Lateulade, the **Pullman-Mériadeck** is the most modern and highly ranked hotel in town, well respected for its restaurant.

Not far from the public gardens to the north, the **Palais Gallien** recalls Rome in its third-century amphitheater remains. At **St-Seurin**, off the place des Martyrs de la

Résistance, there is a paleo-Christian site with a necropolis, sarcophagi, and amphorae.

Travellers who enjoy the tranquillity of a country inn at
night after a busy day of sightseeing in the city might want
to try **La Réserve**, just southwest of town near Pessac on
the route to Arcachon. The 19 rooms have a garden
setting, there is an excellent restaurant on the premises,
the good vines of Médoc grow all around, and the atmosphere is calm and welcoming. The cellar stores bottles
that cost more than the rooms.

The Office de Tourisme keeps a list of rural celebrations in the Bordeaux region—an oyster festival among
them. Foreign guests will be wined and dined to within a
centimeter of collapse.

Dining in Bordeaux

Surprisingly, in the recent past Bordeaux suffered a dearth
of fine restaurants. Today the situation is sunnier. Among
the tops for cuisine and atmosphere, or both, are: **Le
Chapon Fin**, still in its original location at 5, rue Montesquieu and serving the traditional stews, soups, and roasts
of the region (reserve; Tel: 56-79-10-10); and **Christian
Clément–Dubern**, on the elegant allées de Tourny, named
for the young chef who took over the restaurant and
installed creative cuisine. There is lighter and less expensive cuisine upstairs at **Le Petit Dubern**. **La Chamade**, at 20,
rue Piliers-de-Tutelle, offers elegant service and cuisine in
an 18th-century cellar (reserve; Tel: 56-48-13-74). Francis
Garcia, formerly of the Chapon Fin, now works at **Le
Bistrot du Clavel (Gare)**, near the St-Jean railway station,
where regulars include members of the local soccer team.
Some say **Chez Philippe**, on place du Parlement, serves the
best seafood in town.

Also: **Jean Ramet**, contemporary, fresh decor, just off
Tourny (reserve; Tel: 56-44-12-51); **Le Rouzic**, chef Michel Gautier's masterworks at 34, cours du Chapeau-
Rouge near the Grand-Théâtre (reserve; Tel: 56-44-39-
11); **Bolchoï**, for folkloric food and drinks on the first
floor of the same building; and **Tupina**, behind the quai
de la Monnaie. Chef J. P. Xiradakis—a Gascon despite his
Greek-sounding name—is president of the association
for the preservation of southwestern culinary traditions;
this is a casual and colorful bistro.

The highest ranking in the region usually goes to **Le**

Saint-James, southeast of town in suburban Bouliac, where chef Jean-Marie Amat prepares whatever's fresh from the market; the shady terrace and views of Bordeaux add to the enjoyment of the whole (reserve; Tel: 56-20-52-19).

Shopping in Bordeaux

As far as couture in Bordeaux is concerned, you could be shopping in Paris. This is especially true along the cours de l'Intendance and rue Ste-Catherine (they meet at place de la Comédie). For shopping with a difference, consider everything for your favorite wine enthusiast from **Humbert** on the cours Victor-Hugo; cheeses from **Jean d'Alos** on rue Montesquieu off l'Intendance; wines and wine-associated eccentricities plus a museum and tastings at **Hôtel des Vins** on allées de Tourney; and books, many from Great Britain, on everything at **Librairie Mollat**, on rue Vital-Carles.

Sip while shopping at the **Salon de Thé/Pour La Maison**, not far from the Palais des Rohan on rue des Remparts: Antiques, gifts, tableware, embroideries, and decorative light fixtures can be considered while consuming a *café filtre*.

Antiques are best found in the area of Notre-Dame, the St-Michel quarter (centered around the old Basilica and Tower of St-Michel, south of the Pont de Pierre), and around place Gambetta; flea markets change locations daily—ask at the Office de Tourisme. The best of a handful of covered markets is at **place des Grands-Hommes** (have a little something here at the Belle Epoque **Bar des Grands-Hommes**).

Le Golf in the Area

When thinking of Bordeaux, Pomerol not putters, and châteaux not clubs, readily come to mind. Nonetheless, the region of the Aquitaine is rapidly expanding its golf courses. Three outstanding public courses in the Gironde are **Golf d'Arcachon**, about 65 km (40 miles) from Bordeaux; **Bordeaux-Lac**, in Bordeaux's new sporting-exhibition area; and **Golf Country Club de l'Ardilouse**, at Lacanau-Océan, 60 km (37 miles) west of Bordeaux. All are open year-round. In addition, as elsewhere in France, private clubs may allow members of top overseas clubs to play their courses and use club facilities. Inquire at the Office de Tourisme. At

Bordeaux-Lac, sports-minded types may also swim, ice skate, shoot clay pigeons, boat, and play squash.

WINES AND VINES

To many oenophiles worldwide, the Bordeaux region is unchallenged as the greatest winescape on the globe. Here, after all, vines first imported from Greece have grown happily since the beginning of the Christian era. North of Bordeaux blush the noble "red princes" of **Médoc** (the big four are Château Lafite, Château Latour, Château Margaux, and Mouton-Rothschild; others are St-Estèphe, Pauillac, and St-Julien). These are wines that age with grace: "All the angles grow round in the bottle," say the Médociens.

Here, also, mature great whites: the sumptuous **Sauternes**, south of Bordeaux, and the dry and nifty **Graves** between Sauternes and the city. Across the Garonne and the Dordogne to the east, the rewarding reds of **St-Emilion**, **Pomerol**, and **Fronsac** are at home, with Château Pétrus shining the most brilliantly among the Pomerols.

Then there are the crisp whites of **Entre-deux-Mers**, in the triangle where the two rivers meet to become the Gironde, and the **Côtes de Blaye** on the east bank of the Gironde. These are the delicious everyday wines the French term great "ordinaires." Other *appellations* are prestigious in their own right: **Côte de Bourg**, just south of Blaye, and **Pécharmant**, to name but two.

The prettiest time to wander these winelands is in autumn—it is also the hectic harvest time, when visitors are not greeted with glee and frequently are not greeted at all. Except when picking and crushing are in progress, though, it is possible to visit most of the above properties; plan an itinerary with the assistance of wine authorities in Bordeaux. (In general, great Bordeaux châteaux are more chary of welcoming outsiders than are those in other regions of France.)

A few châteaux, such as **Beychevelle** and **Lafite**, operate guided tours on a regular basis. (Beychevelle owes its name to *baisse-voile,* or "lowered sail," a salute demanded by the 17th-century owner, the Duc d'Éperon, who demanded respect and a toll.) To visit others, write or call ahead for an appointment (it's easiest to deal with the agencies in Bordeaux). Not to be missed (reservations required) is the museum in the *caves* of the **Château**

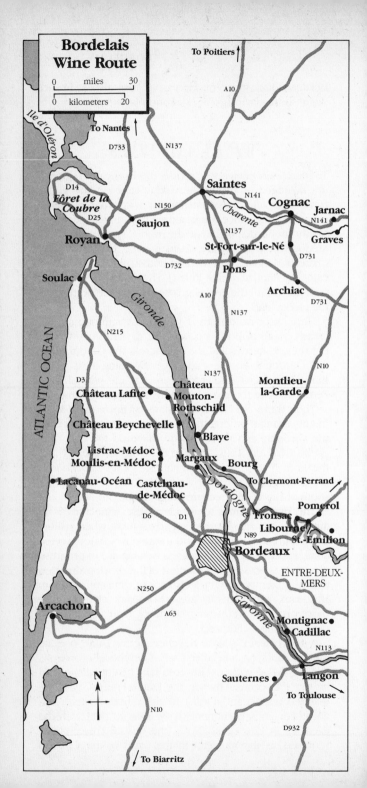

Bordelais
Wine Route

miles 0 — 30
kilometers 0 — 20

To Poitiers

A10

To Nantes

Île d'Oléron

D733

N137

D14

Fôret de la
Coubre

Saintes

N141

Cognac

Jarnac

N150

N141

D25

Saujon

Charente

Graves

Royan

N137

St-Fort-sur-le-Né

D731

Soulac

D732

Pons

Archiac

Gironde

A10

D731

N215

N137

N10

ATLANTIC OCEAN

D3

N137

Montlieu-
la-Garde

Château Lafite

Château
Mouton-
Rothschild

Château Beychevelle

Blaye

Listrac-Médoc

Margaux

Moulis-en-Médoc

Bourg

To Clermont-Ferrand

Lacanau-Océan

Castelnau-
de-Médoc

Dordogne

Pomerol

D6

D1

Fronsac

Libourne

St.-Emilion

N89

Bordeaux

ENTRE-DEUX-
MERS

N250

Arcachon

A63

Garonne

Montignac

Cadillac

N113

N

Sauternes

Langon

To Toulouse

N10

D932

To Biarritz

Mouton-Rothschild: Artworks from various historical periods that have to do with wine and grapes, magnificent tapestries and glassware, and so forth are on display. The estate is about 2 km (just over a mile) north of Pauillac (itself 48 km/30 miles north of Bordeaux); Tel: 56-59-22-22.

In general it's easiest to visit estates and wineries that display the signs *Vente au détail* (loosely translated as "individual sales") or *Dégustation* (tastings). In some villages and at some estates, the reception center even sells light meals to be accompanied by wine purchased on the spot.

As in the case of St-Emilion (see the next section), a few wine villages are worth visiting in themselves: **Blaye**, with a citadel constructed by Louis XIV's great military architect, Sébastien le Prestre de Vauban (a good hotel-restaurant there is **La Citadelle**); and **Cadillac**, where part of the ramparts remain—while there you should visit the Château Fayau.

An uncommonly good headquarters for tours of the Médoc is the **Relais de Margaux** in the village of Margaux, about 25 km (15.5 miles) northwest of Bordeaux, where 26 splendid rooms and five suites and a pampering staff are complemented by a most able chef. Châteaux visits can be arranged. The luxurious Relais has a splendid wine cellar and is expensive—but worth it.

St-Emilion

Of all the wine towns in the Bordeaux region, St-Emilion (about 40 km/25 miles east of Bordeaux near Libourne) is the most alluring and enticing. Sitting atop its little lime-stone hill overlooking the Dordogne, it seduces even non-oenophiles. The very best time to visit is during the annual Jurade, a ritual dating from Medieval times in which several councilmen dressed in scarlet ermine-edged robes parade through town to a hilltop ruin known as **La Tour du Roi** (The King's Tower). From there, they pronounce in stentorian chant the result of the year's harvest, echoed by the townsfolk in the square below, who cheer "Hallelujah!" in increasingly excited tones. The Jurade is held in late September or early October, depending upon the harvest. ("And what would you say if one year the wine was no good?" a *jurat* was asked. "We should pronounce it 'insufficiently fine,'" he answered solemnly.)

Two figures step out of history in St-Emilion: the

fourth-century Gallo-Roman poet and proconsul Ausonius and the eighth-century Breton monk Emilion. The first is remembered in the classic wines produced by the nearby Château Ausone (they may have been served to the Roman emperor), while the latter gave his name to the town. Today the peace of the golden-stoned village of 3,000 inhabitants belies its bloody history of battles between English and French during the Hundred Years War; between Catholics and Huguenots during the Wars of Religion; and between the radical Jacobins and the moderate Girondists in 1792. (The Girondists were so named because their most persuasive members came from Bordeaux—in the Gironde.)

St-Emilion sits on two levels. About the only place for drivers to park is on the upper, near the **Eglise Collégiale**, from which the whole village may easily be explored on foot. The interior of the church is rather disappointing, but its cloister is worth a quick look. From the church a cobbled street winds through the porte de la Cadène and down to the lower level, the center of town. The **place du Marché**, the former marketplace (the lively Sunday-morning market is actually on place Bouqueyre), is somnolent most of the time, with the buying and selling (of wines, mostly) proceeding languidly, if at all. (The best wine shop in town is **Le Cellier des Gourmets** on rue Guadet.)

St-Emilion's major treasure, the **Eglise Monolithe**, is entered from the square; a sign on the door tells which shop is keeping the key. The rare subterranean church, the largest and most important of its kind in France, was hewn from the rock walls of several adjoining caves by Benedictine monks at the beginning of the 12th century. Stripped of decorations, treasures, and even the bones of the buried monks during the Revolution, it is today a massive, cold, forbidding, almost mystical space. (The hack marks still show in its bays and vaults, and on its pillars.) The tower of this marvel reaches aboveground clear to the upper level of the town (on the place du Clocher, where cars are parked) like "a finger of God [rising] from a sea of vines," as wine writer Ernst Hornickel put it.

At the end of the square, the 13th-century **chapel of the Trinity** stands on top of a grotto known as **L'Hermitage St-Emilion**, which was supposedly the cave in which the hermit lived, sleeping on a bed cut out of the rock and drinking from a spring that still bubbles, as if the saint were to return by evening. Next to the chapel, the **catacombs** are another poignant underground curiosity.

The **Hostellerie de Plaisance** on place du Clocher is a pleasant, informal, 12-room inn with a kitchen that serves regional fare and boasts an impressive list of St-Emilion wines. For rural, family-style dining, **Logis de la Cadène** is the best in town, although **Chez Germaine**, across the street from the inn, also is recommended. On the main street, rue Guadet, the **Galerie Jean Guyot** offers excellent buys in regional pottery.

Between St-Emilion and Pomerol, the Château Cheval Blanc produces what experts consider the most highly bred of the St-Emilion wines. It is open only by appointment on weekdays, as is the equally renowned Château Figeac.

COGNAC

"The Charente is a rolling patch of French countryside just north of Bordeaux where the actinic quality of the sunlight is extraordinary, and where the majority of rural postmen have liver trouble." So Samuel Chamberlain prefaces his study of the world-famous brandy from Cognac, a small city-port on the Charente river about 120 km (74 miles) north of Bordeaux, where the great château builder François I was born in 1494.

Cognac the Brandy

Wines have been grown in the Charente region since the Romans planted vines there in A.D. 300; together with salt, the Roman wines were a major export to England, the Netherlands, and Scandinavia. However, the white table wines have never been very good, and even today they tend toward tartness, meanness, and cloudiness, so that the postman who stops to take an occasional glass on his rounds will not only make the mail tardy but will give himself a *crise de foi*.

More than three centuries ago, however, it was discovered that the same spirits, when distilled, metamorphose into an elixir permitting no competition for excellence from anything except Armagnac. Besides, the government had begun to exact a heavy tax on wine exports that did not extend to distilled, or "concentrated," wines.

It was the English and the Dutch who in the 17th century began to import this *vin brûlé,* or "burnt wine" (from the distillation process), which in Dutch is *brande-wijn* and was long ago Anglicized as *brandy.*

The production of Cognac is complicated; travellers who wish to make a short study of it will find more than enough information in the Office de Tourisme in the town of Cognac. Suffice it to say that the name Cognac may be put on the label only if the grapes have been grown in an area comprising about 150,000 acres outside the town. Aging is all-important, as is the use of Limousin oak for the casks.

The seven grades of Cognac come from territories spreading out from the towns of Cognac and Jarnac in concentric circles: Closest in is *Grande* or *Fine Grande Champagne* (nothing to do with the region of the bubbly), followed by *Petite Champagne, Borderies,* the rings of *Fins Bois, Bons Bois,* and *Bois Ordinaires.* Finally, on the coast and islands of Oléron and Ré, there is *Bois à Terroir.*

According to wine connoisseur Alexis Lichine, the star device on labels began about a hundred years ago when the first three-star Cognac was designated for the Australian market. (Today 50 percent of Cognacs sold are of the highest quality.) Younger and less worthwhile spirits have no stars and, as Lichine puts it, "are best drunk with soda." The third type is designated V.S.O.P. (for Very Superior Old Pale). For export, some firms add such names as Réserve, Extra, X.O., and Cordon Bleu to the label.

Because Cognacs don't age after bottling, a Cognac made in 1814 but bottled in 1815 would now be only a year old, or younger than one produced in 1983 and bottled today. While V.S.O.P.s are at least five years old and sometimes ten, increasingly high costs of production for older ones means that one day they will be priced out of the market. A sweet liqueur made in the Cognac region, Pineau des Charentes, may be drunk as an apéritif.

Cognac the Town

It is possible to make an excursion (or a pilgrimage) to Cognac from Bordeaux in one long day, but a more satisfactory itinerary is to combine the visit there with ones to Saintes and Royan.

Your first stop in Cognac should be at the Office de Tourisme right near the heart of things—on place Jean-Monnet—in order to discover which *chais* (wine sheds or storage places) are open to the public on what days: **Otard** (in the former château where François was born), **Polignac**, **Martell**, **Hennessy**, and others. The office can provide information about *son-et-lumière* performances in nearby châteaus and can also arrange visits to the respected glass factory of **St-Gobain**.

On place Jean-Monnet, a **Cognathèque** provides information about Cognacs and sells an enormous selection of them at reasonable prices. Also available for purchase are the deep-blue glasses used by professional tasters. The **Musée du Cognac**, in the Dupuy d'Angeac town house (set in the kind of unmanicured park the French term *accidenté*), joins archaeology to art to the eau-de-vie industry in a fascinating manner. Fossils, ceramics, tools for viticulture, paintings—all meet in this entirely engaging museum.

The making of Cognac leaves its mark everywhere in the town (about 21,000 Cognaçais), even on many buildings near distilleries, which have assumed a curious brown shade imparted by a fungus that lives on the vapors of the distillation process. Aside from visits to the *chais* and museum, your primary pastime in Cognac will be walking along Grande-Rue, with its pretty 15th-century half-timbered houses, and the more aristocratic rue Saulnier, where town houses of the 16th and 17th centuries stand proudly. Right at the edge of the old quarter, the **church of St-Léger** boasts a beautiful rose window in Flamboyant style.

The best answer for both dining and staying the night in Cognac's neighborhood is **Moulin de Cierzac**, about 15 km (9 miles) south near St-Fort-sur-le-Né. The Moulin is a peaceful 17th-century country house that offers ten rooms and a marvelous collection of Cognacs. In the dining room, from October to April, order oyster *cassolette à la Fine Champagne*. An informal atmosphere prevails here, and the Moulin is a good value per franc (for reservations, Tel: 45-83-01-32).

Fairs are staged in Cognac throughout the year. As is so often the case elsewhere, the liveliest market days here are Saturday and Sunday.

SAINTES

Hurtling by on A 10 from Tours and Poitiers to Bordeaux, you will have no sense at all of Saintes, an ancient and attractive town of about 27,000 Saintais, or Santons, that today is sliced in two by the Charente. In Roman days the town was a major trading city called Mediolanum Santonum, and mainly was confined to the river's left bank.

In Medieval times, under Plantagenêt domination, the town watched year in and year out as thousands of pilgrims passed through the Arc de Germanicus and crossed the bridge, bound for the shrine of Santiago de Compostela in Spain. Today a regional center of industry, agricultural markets, and crafts, Saintes well deserves at least one day of exploration.

Arriving from the east and Cognac or the coast and Royan, you will want to slow down along the bustling main street, a meeting of avenue Gambetta and cours National et Lemercier, perhaps to search for a seat at one of the sidewalk cafés shadowed by plane trees (the **Brasserie Louis** on Gambetta, for example). From this perspective, Saintes seems pleasant enough—animated, well-supplied with shops, but relatively anonymous.

In its old town, however, and in what were once suburbs on the right bank, Saintes boasts witnesses to every age since that of the Romans.

As usual, traipsing begins best in the old town, which surrounds the cathedral of St-Pierre and place du Marché. The cathedral, built atop a Roman structure, owes its appearance mainly to the 15th century and is of only passing interest. Up rue St-Michel and a jog to the left on rue Victor Hugo, the **Musée des Beaux-Arts** is housed in the classic, 17th-century Hôtel Présdial in the center of an attractive pedestrian district. Beautifully restored in the modern manner (i.e., the exhibitions can be seen clearly), the Présdial's six rooms house Saintonge ceramics from the 11th century to today, as well as paintings from the 15th through 19th centuries. (The best restaurant in this part of town is that in the hotel **Commerce Mancini**, nearby on rue des Messageries.)

An amble past the flowery place de Nivelle, the center of municipal goings-on, leads to the **Musée Dupuy-Mestreau**, an example of the regional collections in which France excels. The *hôtel* itself abounds in handsome woodwork, fireplaces, and ceilings, and the displays include items of maritime importance, stamps, peasant headdresses and costumes, weapons, and reconstituted rooms in regional style. From here, it's a pleasant walk back along the quai de Verdun, with its handsome 17th- and 18th-century mansions sporting gardens and wrought-iron balconies.

Farther out, on what was once the western rim of the city, the **church of St-Eutrope** ranks among the most important in western France. Its prize remains the lower, half-buried church that Pope Urban II consecrated in 1096. The body of the saint rests here in its sarcophagus, secure in surroundings of sturdy, fat Roman pillars, some of their capitals decorated with unlikely looking vegetables.

Beyond, an amphitheater almost the size of that in Nîmes once held 20,000 spectators; today grass grows over the tiers. Built in the first century, it is among the oldest remaining from the Roman world, and it is a moving setting for the musical performances staged here on many summer nights.

The **Arc de Germanicus** has been standing on the right bank of the river, the Gambetta side, since 1842, when the Roman bridge on which it originally stood had to be demolished. (Prosper Mérimée, author of the *Carmen* on which Bizet's opera was based and an inspector of historical monuments, insisted it be saved.) The wonder of this arch, built of local limestone in the year A.D. 19, is that its inscriptions, by one Caius Julius Rufius, may still be read in dedication to Germanicus, Emperor Tiberius, and his son Drusus.

Nearby, the **Archaeological Museum** and its park show off remains of walls, churches, and houses from Roman days; archaeologically inclined visitors may sometimes arrange to see the digs still going on in the immediate region. In the center of town on the right bank is the Benedictine **Abbaye aux Dames**, which dates from 1047. Not far from the railway station, a stud farm (*haras*) houses about 60 horses of varying breeds. It is open to visitors on many late afternoons throughout the year.

As in Cognac, there is a scarcity of outstanding inns in central Saintes. The best is out past the amphitheater on the way to Royan: the **Relais du Bois St-Georges** stands in a large park where quiet and good living are bywords, families and dogs are welcome, and pretensions are checked at the door.

ROYAN

Travellers from places other than France will thoroughly enjoy or completely deplore Royan, west of Cognac and Saintes, depending upon their views of what is or is not typically French.

Almost nothing remains of the old port of Royan on the northern lip of the mouth of the Gironde. During the battles to liberate the region in the autumn of 1944, German troops holed up here and in other nearby pockets, only to be bombed by Allied forces in April 1945, less than a month before the armistice of May 8.

Today Royan is nicknamed "Queen of the *Côte de Beauté*," and it is the largest and most modern sea resort between La Baule to the north in Brittany and Biarritz to the south on the Spanish border. There are those who wax nostalgic about old Royan, the Royan of elegant cliffside chalets, of breezy Victorian hostelries with wide corridors and intimidating façades and concierges, of palatial casinos in Renaissance or Baroque dress. It is said that some sense of the olden days may be glimpsed in the smart suburb of Pontaillac, although most visitors stop there not because of nostalgia but to play at the Sporting-Casino.

Today expressions such as *resto en vogue* (trendy restaurant) are more suggestive of Royan than *aristocratique* or *traditionnel.* Indeed, the top tourist attraction in town is a triumph of reinforced concrete dating from 1958, the **church of Notre-Dame.** Seen from the front, the soaring belfry (almost 215 feet high) suggests the giant prow of a ship sailing into town from the Atlantic.

The heart of the modern town curves around the Grande Conche, a large bay flanked on the north by a fine sandy beach and a seafront promenade backed by shops, banks, and apartment houses. Across the bay, the port is filled with resting trawlers, sardine-fishing boats, and pleasure craft, right at the foot of the **Grand Casino.** (In European fashion, the visitor to the casinos is expected to be properly dressed, quiet, and serious, and to respect an atmosphere utterly unlike that in Reno, Las Vegas, or Atlantic City.)

The resort setting may best be admired by driving northwest of town on the coastal road in the direction of the **Forêt de la Coubre.** Rounding the various *conches* (bays, coves) on cliffs above or down by sandy dunes where sea pines bow, you will begin to appreciate the natural beauty that brings inland souls to this place. The best day along **la Grande Côte** between Royan and the lighthouse in the Forêt de la Coubre is a cold, windy one when waves batter the shore and spray drenches the windshield.

Looking out at the beach, the **Family Golf Hôtel** is the best one in town, though it's quite modest and has no restaurant. Better is the **Résidence de Rohan**, just a couple of miles north along the coast; a 41-room inn occupying a handsomely furnished 19th-century home, it's comfortable but far from ostentatious (no dining room).

For dining, **Le Squale** (at 102, avenue des Semis, right in the heart of things back of the seafront) and **Le Chalet** (at 6, boulevard La Grandière, in the southeast part of town near the main city park) stand out. They are both solid, middle-ground restaurants offering such dishes as salmon in a parsley cream sauce, grilled sole, and oysters. You might also try **Trois Marmites**, right in town at 37, avenue Regazzoni.

THE DORDOGNE

The green, serene valley of the Dordogne is inexplicably spooky. One tends to drive carefully, as if expecting the mysterious, prehistoric Cro-Magnon man, who 40,000 years ago called this valley home, to materialize in the rear-view mirror.

Perhaps it is the autumnal light-and-shadow haze that hangs above the countryside almost all year long—a drapery as delicate as a Japanese screen. Maybe it's the flickering forms of willows and poplars that reflect themselves in the clear waters of the Dordogne and its tributary, the Vézère.

The Dordogne ranks among the longest rivers in France, taking both its source and its name from the meeting place of the Dore with the Dogne near the town of Clermont-Ferrand and the Puy de Sancy—at 6,184 feet the highest peak in the Massif Central. From its headwaters, the river used to skip swiftly over its volcanic bed and slice through narrow ravines, but it has been slowed by dams and artificial lakes constructed to turn the turbines of huge

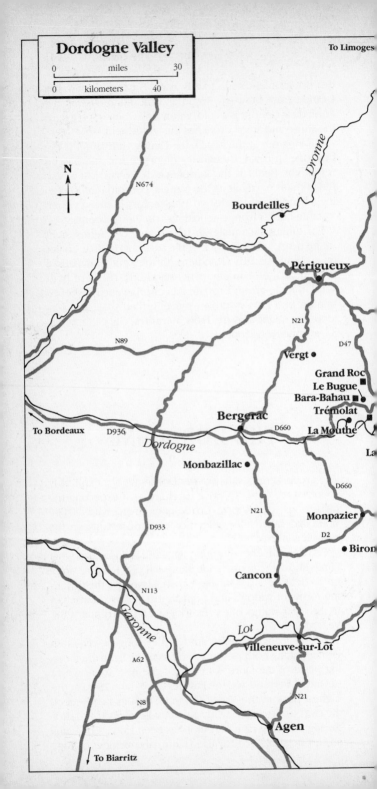

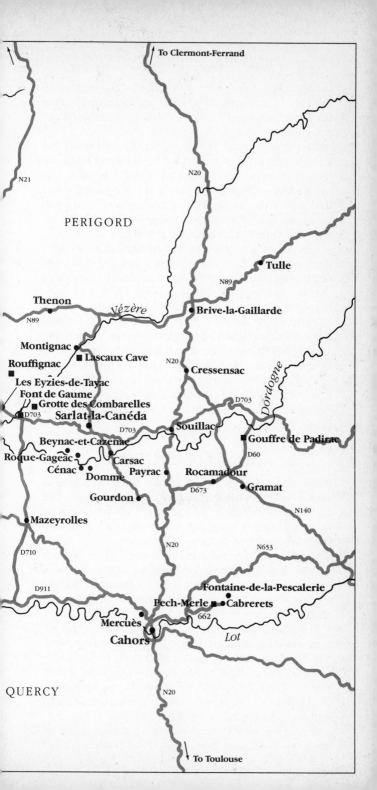

power plants. Those who wish to follow the river along (and about and around) its length will start upstream at Bort-les-Orgues and continue down to Libourne, about 500 km (310 miles) to the west.

On the other hand, the Dordogne of lore, legend, and archaeological interest can best be explored by beginning at Bergerac, east of Bordeaux and St-Emilion, and proceeding with measured pace east toward Souillac and the Gouffre de Padirac, making detours north and south en route. The river roams through the regions of Périgord and Quercy, rich in underground caverns.

It is not nature, however, but the mark of humankind that dominates in so many places along the Dordogne and throughout this region. No other place on earth is so rich in evidences of early man, who left behind many outstanding examples of his Paleolithic art and tools. The most intriguing and most advanced of these early peoples were the Cro-Magnons, a tall (about 5 feet, 11 inches in average height) and erect race that recorded elements of its existence on the cave walls of the Dordogne-Vézère.

In addition to the traces of these prehistoric civilizations, enticing Medieval villages and evidences of the struggles of the Hundred Years War lure the traveller here today.

The Art of Early Man

Prehistoric artworks in France have been unearthed at sites from the Charente river to northern Spain. The earliest of these, line drawings of animals on cave walls and sculptures in stone, horn, or bone (among the best known is the **Vénus de Laussel**, now in Bordeaux's Musée d'Aquitaine), were succeeded by simple wall decorations such as those made with outspread hands placed upon a rock wall and outlined in black or red. Examples of these are best seen in the caves at Bara-Bahau, Font-de-Gaume, and Pech-Merle.

The Magdalenian people, who flourished in this region, made beautiful carvings in bone and reindeer horn. With this culture, cave painting reached its acme: Horses rear their heads from bodies shot full of arrows; a deer slumps under the weight of his own horns; a multicolored bison steps from one to three dimensions, his hump formed of the natural curve of the rock face.

Among the most exceptional cave paintings yet found are those in **Lascaux cave**, a few miles northeast of Les

Eyzies near Montignac. These works, dating from about 14,000 to 13,500 B.C., were discovered in 1940 by young boys in search of a dog that had fallen into a hole. The cave, dubbed "the Sistine Chapel of Périgord," was opened to an amazed public in 1948. Alas, despite all precautions, the green sickness (moss and algae) and the white (calcite deposits) proliferated as a result of carbon dioxide and humidity. To preserve the paintings, Lascaux was closed in 1963.

In 1983, after ten years of labor, **Lascaux II**, a brilliant facsimile in a cement shell, opened near the original cave. Here you can see archaeological finds from the site as well as ingeniously reproduced paintings, achieved by using the same methods as those employed by the original Paleolithic artists.

Le Thot Center of Prehistory, south of Montignac, is an excellent one-stop introduction to the animals, environment, cave paintings, and civilizations of the Paleolithic era, employing films, audiovisuals, still photographs, casts, and models. Here, too, you will find a list of recommended sites. The adjoining park is home to animals represented in the paintings, such as the extremely rare Przewalski's horse.

Many of the prehistoric sites mentioned here are covered in more detail in the following sections.

BERGERAC TO LES EYZIES

There is no compelling reason for the traveller to visit Bergerac, although from an economic standpoint it is the most important town along the Dordogne. If you arrive at noon, however, there *is* an excellent excuse for stopping: the restaurant known as **Le Cyrano**, in honor of the local 17th-century duelist and writer who won fame only posthumously in the writing of Edmond Rostand. Le Cyrano, at 2, boulevard Montaigne, offers the regional wines of Bergerac (fruity red, dry or sweet white) to accompany fine local dishes. Restaurants in the Dordogne are committed to serving well the finest dishes of the Périgord and Quercy cuisines: truffles, foie gras of geese and ducks in various persuasions, confits (preserved goose, duck, and pork dishes), truffle or cèpe omelettes, garlic soup, sautéed potatoes from Sarlat, Limousin beef with *sauce Périgeaux, Chabichou,* and Pouligny-St-Pierre cheeses.

After lunch you might visit the **Musée du Tabac**, unique

in France, dedicated to the history, influence on society, and growth of the "American weed."

Wine enthusiasts will certainly want to make a detour south (about 17 km/10.5 miles round-trip) to **Monbazillac**, from the vineyards of which comes the heavy, sweet dessert wine that has made the term "noble rot" a synonym for perfection throughout the centuries. The vineyard's elegant 16th-century château is open as a museum of Calvinism, but photographing its exterior may be satisfaction enough for non-Calvinists. The wine may be tasted; buying is also encouraged at the shop near the castle gate.

From Bergerac, D 660 (which becomes D 703) runs east toward **Lanquais château**, an architectural mishmash rising from the ruins of a fortress battered by the English during the Hundred Years War. Students of Louis XIII furniture will admire the interiors.

Near the pleasant village of **Trémolat**, the road climbs a coil of white cliffs from which there's a splendid view of the **Cingle de Trémolat** (*cingle* means "meander" in French). Below, the Dordogne bends in remarkable S-curves through fields that look like green or golden chessboards. If twilight is approaching, wait for the sun to set over the ordered landscape. A fine overnight retreat, **Le Vieux Logis**, awaits in Trémolat. The accent at Logis, a handsome old country mansion set in pleasant gardens, is on dignified quiet and comfort; only well-behaved dogs are allowed, for example.

Past Limeuil, where the Dordogne meets the Vézère, drivers bound for Les Eyzies will cruise through the town of Le Bugue and into prehistory. (If you're in Le Bugue at lunchtime, try the river terrace of **l'Albuca** in the unassuming, always-busy Hôtel Royal-Vézère.)

LES EYZIES

High, ocher cliffs rise from the narrow green valley that shelters the village (about 800 people) of Les Eyzies-de-Tayac, east of Trémolat on the Vézère. Prehistoric people lived here during the Ice Age, occupying caves for tens of thousands of years and leaving behind a legacy of tools, weapons, pottery, and—particularly provocative—the marvelous works of art that are their cave paintings. (In ancient times, the bed of the Vézère lay some 90 feet above today's level, and the caves were more accessible than they are today.) Les Eyzies is a natural base for investigations of the prehistory evident in the surrounding area. (Another suggestion is Sarlat-la-Canéda, of which more later.) Although it is a small town, Les Eyzies sports two outstanding inns: **Le Centenaire**, with 26 rooms, and **Cro-Magnon**, with 24. Both kitchens are acclaimed, but the Cro-Magnon's gardened grounds and large outdoor pool give it the edge, and it's slightly less costly. (Reservations for meals suggested at both; for Le Centenaire, Tel: 53-06-97-18; Cro-Magnon: 53-06-97-06.) Besides, local tradition has it that Cro-Magnon remains were found at what is today the latter's men's room. Both are popular and centers of local activity, with English-speaking visitors gathering at dinnertime to tell tales of what they've seen. From Easter through September, a lively Monday market fills Les Eyzies's main street.

Les Eyzies's **Musée National de Préhistoire** occupies the castle of the barons of Beynac, and from modest beginnings it has grown to rank among the best of its kind in France. Discoveries in the region are described and outlined, while many original objects and reproductions of paintings are displayed. A visit to this museum is required as an introduction to the sites themselves. Nearby, an amusing statue of Cro-Magnon man, as envisioned by sculptor Paul Dardé in 1930, stares out from beneath an overhanging rock.

Around Les Eyzies

Just outside the village, where the mouth of the St-Cyprien valley opens, the grotto of **Font-de-Gaume** (just east of town off D 47) makes believers of those who would doubt the creative talents of Paleolithic people. The wall paintings at the grotto form a veritable catalog of creatures of the hunt: bison, mammoths, horses, reindeer, and more. A well-fed horse outlined in black relief thrusts its front legs against a bend in the wall, while another wall helps form the hump of a multicolored buffalo.

Stalactites, stalagmites, and more eccentric formations fill the cave of **Grand Roc** (to the northwest on D 47), many of them younger than the paintings within. At the **Grotte de Rouffignac** (just north of Les Eyzies on a spur off D 32), an electric railway passes through two and a half miles of underground galleries, their walls alive with engravings, drawings, and paintings.

The prehistory museum in Les Eyzies provides a list of recommended sites in the immediate neighborhood. It includes **La Mouthe** (just a croissant's toss south of town; the first cave to be discovered), the **Grotte des Combarelles** (a short detour east of town on D 47; portrayals of nearly 300 animals), and **Bara-Bahau**, a short spurt west of Le Bugue (very early flintwork engravings).

MONPAZIER

Not all of the Hundred Years War was devoted to destruction. Constant struggles between the French and English forces necessitated the construction of fortified towns, mostly along disputed frontiers. These *bastides* (*bastide* derives from the old-French verb *bastir,* to build) are among the most interesting examples of military architecture in France.

Sitting a straight shot south of Les Eyzies to Mazeyrolles and then a bit to the west, Monpazier is among the two or three best-preserved bastides still functioning, 700 years after being built, as towns.

French and English bastides once faced each other wall to wall near the rivers Garonne, Lot, and Dordogne. They were all new towns, and whether French or English they adhered to an identical plan. Unlike old villages with their narrow and crooked streets, the new towns conformed to a checkerboard or rectangular design of straight streets that cut across alleys, and small spaces that acted as drains, firebreaks, or latrines. At the center of each town, a *cornière* (plaza-like square) was surrounded by roofed arcades. Nearby stood a church, commonly fortified.

Life in the new towns was fairly good for the defending citizenry: Houses could be bought and sold, offspring were free to marry at will, and town affairs were conducted by locally elected consuls, though under the watchful eye of the king's bailiff.

Monpazier was an English bastide, founded on January 7, 1284, by Edward I, and later joined by Beaumont, Molières, and Roquepine. Attackers and defenders often changed roles in those confusing days, and Monpazier was assaulted by both sides with some regularity, depending upon which forces were in power at the time. In 1594 and 1637, Monpazier also served as a center for some of the fiercest peasant revolts in the region.

Remarkably, Monpazier retains its grid pattern, its fortified church (restored in the 16th century), and its roomy
square flanked by covered galleries. The sturdy old
houses still stand, and the measuring standards for judging weights hang in place in the covered market. Shops
selling souvenirs, fruits and vegetables, and arts and crafts
snuggle into the arcades, shading themselves from the
summer sun, and it seems as though the whole place has
been hibernating since the 13th century.

If rich historically, the immediate area is poor in a
gastronomical sense. Make use of simple cafés or retrace
your steps, perhaps to Bergerac.

SARLAT

It is easy not to stop in Sarlat-la-Canéda, east of Les Eyzies,
if you careen past on the "modern" rue de la République
(1837). The "traverse," as it is called by the locals, cuts
unheedingly right through the old quarter and is lined by
rather nondescript houses. Off to each side, however, the
old stone buildings with their slate roofs still march
around circuitous streets that are now safeguarded as
historic monuments.

Sarlat's most famous son is Etienne de la Boétie, magis-
trate of the Bordeaux parliament in the 16th century, but
better known internationally as a prolific political writer
and close friend of Montaigne. His house, with its handsome gables, mullioned windows, and medallions—an
exuberance in Renaissance style—still stands right across
from the cathedral. From this *place* (the cathedral may be
skipped) runs a tangle of arches and alleyways recently
and tastefully restored to their original beauty.

The marketplace in front of the **Hôtel de Ville** bustles
and bubbles during the Wednesday and, particularly, Saturday markets. Sarlat is sought out for products of the
Dordogne and Périgord: unbeatable walnut oils, foie gras,
black truffles, *chabichou* cheese, canned *confits d'oie,*
dried mushrooms, a walnut-flavored liqueur named Eau
de Noix, and a wonderful chocolate treat called *éphémères,*
from Confolens. Patricia Wells suggests that picnickers
pick up a loaf of *pain de seigle* (rye bread) or *pain suri*
(sourdough) from the **B. Pauliac** bakery.

In summer, productions of Molière, Shakespeare, and
the like go on stage during the Sarlat theater festival. At
any time, Sarlat is for strolling; you might stay overnight at

La Couleuvrine, an old house wedged into the city wall (unpretentious and popular with younger travellers who like to be in the heart of things) or the **Hostellerie Meysset**, on a hill above town in a wooded setting (calmer, ideal for slower-moving travellers).

THE DORDOGNE NEAR SARLAT

South of Sarlat the Dordogne meanders at the foot of golden rock walls crowned by beetling castles and perilously perched villages. There are several attractions clustered in this area.

The **Château de Montfort**, just beyond the village of Carsac, sits on its rock outcropping above a wide bend in the Dordogne, its towers and turrets threatening at any moment to teeter over the precipice. Today privately owned, the château has survived a history of sieges, battles, and reconstructions, having been burned to the ground in 1214 by Simon de Montfort in one of his anti-Albigensian crusades. To call its style a mélange is to understate.

Domme

From near Cénac, the road climbs up a crag to Domme, a village of fewer than a thousand people whose ancestors were embroiled in the struggles of the Reformation. At a mere suggestion, any one of them will tell the tale of Huguenot Captain Geoffroi de Vivans, who with daring (say Protestants) or trickery (say Catholics) took the town in the middle of the night in 1588.

From Domme's Belvédère de la Barre you can look over the rich, crop-checkered valley where the Dordogne eases slowly between its poplar-lined banks. The **Château de Beynac**, across the river in Beynac (see below), and the great cliff of La Roque-Gageac thrust their silhouettes against the sky. The caves (the entrance is near the covered market) that sheltered the townspeople during the Hundred Years War and the Wars of Religion are rich in stalactites, stalagmites, and bones of Ice Age bison and rhinoceri; the trek through the caves leads to the pretty Promenade des Falaises (Cliff Walk) and then to the Promenade des Remparts.

Those who can't bear to leave Domme quite yet may lunch at the very fine **Esplanade** and even, if departure still seems premature, stay over in one of the inn's modest but clean and adequate rooms.

La Roque-Gageac

It seems unlikely that La Roque-Gageac should exist at all: Perhaps it and its fewer than 500 Gageacs are figments of an inspired imagination. The flat faces of old stone houses are reflected in the river, while behind them narrow alleyways scale the cliff face and lead to the humble 12th-century church. The castle at the west end of the village is a 19th-century imitation of a 15th-century style; still, it appears very authentic in this setting.

La Roque is best seen and photographed from the west: If you arrive from the east, make sure to see the western approach before leaving.

Beynac

Beynac-et-Cazenac, and especially the views from its formidable château, stay in the traveller's mind long after leaving. Somehow, a fierce past lies lightly on this pastel, impressionistic countryside.

The Capets and Plantagenêts were rivals here, and Richard the Lion-Hearted employed the thuggish Mercadier to pillage the countryside on his royal behalf. He seized Beynac in 1189, but the indefatigable Montfort wiped it out in 1214. A great part of today's château dates from the 13th century; the well-restored hall of state is notable, and there's a smashing view from the battlements. It's a setting worthy of a Cecil B. De Mille epic.

There is not much to do here except gaze into the distance and imagine the forces of Richard the Lion-Hearted attacking. That done, it's time to eat a little something on the terrace of the small inn called **Bonnet**.

In the Middle Ages Beynac was, with Biron (castle also worth seeing), Bourdeilles (outstanding furnishings in its castle), and Mareuil (castle less interesting, rebuilt since 1965), one of the four grand baronies of Périgord.

Directly south across the sinuous river from Beynac, there is a museum of the Middle Ages in **Castelnaud**, one of Europe's finest fortified castles. Its most popular attraction is a reconstructed wooden catapult that in its heyday could hurl a 99-pound stone ball 600 feet with impressive accuracy. Tours are self-guided; several films are projected. This new view of the Old World should not be missed.

ROCAMADOUR

Narrow roads from Les Eyzies, Sarlat, Beynac, or any number of other little towns skitter eastward to Rocamadour, east of N 20 and south of the Dordogne, a gathering place for pilgrims in the past and a required stop for tourists today.

Although the site is one of the most stunning in all Europe, Rocamadour is sometimes skipped over by travellers who scorn it as over-commercialized. Yet in a sense the town has always been the same, with streets full of buyers and sellers, often dealing in religious trinkets.

It's important to approach from l'Hospitalet and to look down and out from the small terrace of the hamlet. Below, the river Alzou wanders through the wide gorge, while houses and shops climb its banks, nearly standing on each other's shoulders as they cling to the steep cliff face, rising to the château on the summit.

Nobody knows who Saint Amadour was, though it is generally acknowledged that he was a pious hermit. The current theory is that he was Zaccheus, who came here with his wife, Saint Veronica (she who wiped the face of Christ on the route to Calvary), and after her death lived on, alone, on the cliff. He first was called *roc amator* ("one who knows and loves the rock"), hence the name Rocamadour. It is said that miracles began to occur as soon as the saint's bones were buried near the altar in the tiny **chapel of the Virgin**.

The resultant pilgrimages attracted thousands of the faithful, some of whom made this a stop en route to Santiago de Compostela. French kings, Saint Louis among them, came here, as did England's Henry II, Saint Bernard, Blanche of Castille, and thousands upon thousands of unremembered believers. Repentant sinners were a major source of revenue, paying severe penances in coin and then climbing the 216 steps (the *Via Sancta*) on bleeding knees to chapels atop the summit, known as the Ecclesiastical City.

Life was rarely peaceful in Rocamadour: In 1183, Henri Court-Mantel, rebelling against his father, Henri Plantagenêt, sacked the oratory in search of riches, only to die soon after in Martel, claiming to regret his actions.

Legend has it that during the Wars of Religion, pillaging Protestants dug up the body of Saint Amadour and tossed it into a fire, in which it refused to burn. The abbey finally fell to revolutionaries in 1789. Today the wealth and the splendor have vanished, but Rocamadour lives on, a fascinating witness to history and religious hysteria.

The entrance to the town is through the 13th-century Figuier Gate, where you will find yourself in a swirl of souvenir shops lining rue Roland le Preux. It's off-putting but must be braved. The street passes through Porte Salmon and becomes rue de la Couronnerie, growing somewhat less cute and more intriguing along the way.

The point of Rocamadour, however, is the **Ecclesiastical City**, reached either by elevator or by the self-same 216 steps, past shops and hotels situated on terraces along the way. The cluster of buildings at the top (most of them were restored during the 19th century) includes the fort, the seven churches on place St-Amadour, the Basilique St-Sauveur, the Chapelle Miraculeuse, and the Chapelle St-Michel.

Major treasures include the **Black Virgin and Child**, a wood sculpture above the altar in the Chapelle Miraculeuse; the chapel bell that rings on its own when a miracle is about to occur; and the **iron sword** on the wall of Chapelle Notre-Dame that tradition holds to be Durandal, the weapon of Roland.

On the open space in front of the church, a small but rewarding museum is devoted to sacred art. The main street offers a waxworks museum, Roland-le-Preux.

The delicious regional goat cheese, *chabichou,* should be available at cafés in town. The best is produced by the Ferme Jean Lacoste between Rocamadour and Gramat.

Rocamadour is another good center for exploration of the local countryside. In town, **Beau Site et Notre Dame** is the choice inn, a 50-room hostelry of agreeable nature and decoration that's always full. Four kilometers (2.5 miles) away, on the road leading southeast to Gramat, the unassuming **Auberge de la Garenne** is one of those warm, welcoming inns in which the French countryside excels, a calm retreat after a day's exploration.

Near Gramat, the **Château de Roumégouse** offers 12 rooms and three suites to travellers looking for elegance in their home away from the madding crowd. Also near Gramat, the rather new **Parc de Vision** (Safari Park), 94 acres of regional plants and trees, is home to various wild

European animals, including some beasts such as wild oxen and bison descended from prehistoric species.

While in Rocamadour and vicinity, be sure to sample the fine plum brandy from the Ségala distillery: *eau-de-vie du Vieux Pigeonnier.*

Gouffre de Padirac

If there is time to view only one *gouffre* (chasm) on a trip to France, it should be the Gouffre de Padirac, only a few minutes' drive northeast of Rocamadour. Elevators make the descent into a vast and mysterious—and definitely touristy—underground world of galleries and rivers created by rainwater percolating through porous limestone. After a visit to Padirac, on foot and flat-bottomed boat, the legend ascribing it to a face-off between Satan and Saint Martin will seem more probable to you.

Pech-Merle

About 40 km (25 miles) south of Rocamadour via Gramat and Labastide-Murat, to the east of N 20 and near the wide spot of Cabrerets, the cave of Pech-Merle is one of the most exciting of the painted caverns, since Lascaux can no longer be seen. It's entered through a chamber used by prehistoric people 20,000 years ago. Bison and mammoth parade in a frieze, human footprints of 200 centuries past are perfectly petrified, and two horses suffer the stenciled hands of would-be attackers. The **Musée Amédée-Lemozi** at the site is devoted to the prehistory of Pech-Merle and other nearby sites.

Two remarkable hostelries may keep the wanderer in Pech-Merle and the surrounding region: **La Pescalerie** in Fontaine-de-la-Pescalerie, 2 km (about a mile) northeast of Cabrerets, a gracious 17th-century country house where fine regional meals are served family-style (reserve; Tel: 65-31-22-55); and the more lordly and extremely fashionable but no less inviting **Château de Mercuès**, a 12th-century castle of the bishops of Cahors, in Mercuès 9 km (5.5 miles) northwest of Cahors.

CAHORS

The perfumed air of the Midi moves ever so slightly in the sleepy streets of Cahors and stirs the plane trees along boulevard Gambetta, which is lined with sidewalk cafés and seductive shops. (Among regional items for sale, the most interesting are the ceramics in brilliant and beautiful shades of gold, green, and a wine red.)

The boulevard, the main artery of Cahors, celebrates the favorite local son, Léon-Michel Gambetta, the 19th-century barrister and activist who floated over the German lines in a balloon, became war minister and prime minister, and gave his name to squares and streets all over France.

Cahors sits above a loop in the river Lot south of Rocamadour and serves as an excursion center for the valleys of the Lot and Célé, with their pretty perched villages, fortress churches, troglodyte caves, and châteaux. In town, look for the **Pont Valentré**, still a commanding example of Medieval military-bridge design, and the admirable tympanum and cloisters of the **Cathédrale St-Etienne**.

Saturday is the best market day in Cahors, as elsewhere in the region, though there is action on Wednesdays also. The Cahors wines, rich, powerful, and little known outside France, may best be tasted at **La Taverne**. The wines nobly complement the café's renowned dishes, which feature precious truffles.

GETTING AROUND

Bordeaux usually serves as the starting point for travellers to the region who arrive by air (13 daily one-hour flights from Paris Orly-Ouest or Roissy) or rail (at least ten trains arrive daily from Paris's Austerlitz station).

Driving is recommended here, as it is everywhere in France when you want to seek out remote valleys, small hotels, and little-known villages. Either pick up a rental car in Bordeaux or drive from Paris via the Loire Valley and Poitiers.

Pleasure boats may be rented in many ports, including Arcachon, Pauillac, Royan, Verdon, and Bordeaux.

In Bordeaux, a guided boat tour shows off the quais of the old city; departures are from quai Louis-XVIII, near the Quinconces.

Bus tours of from four to eight days are sometimes available through the Office de Tourisme in Bordeaux.

ACCOMMODATIONS REFERENCE

▶ **Auberge de la Garenne.** Rocamadour 46500 **Gramat.** Tel: 65-33-65-88.

▶ **Beau Site et Notre Dame.** 46500 **Rocamadour.** Tel: 65-33-63-08; Telex: 520421; in U.S., Canada, or Mexico, (800) 528-1234; in U.K., (081) 541-0033.

▶ **Le Centenaire.** 24620 **Les Eyzies-de-Tayac.** Tel: 53-06-97-18; Telex: 541921; Fax: 53-06-92-41; in U.S., (212) 696-1323 (reservations), (800) 372-1323, or (713) 783-8033; in Australia, (02) 957-4511.

▶ **Château de Mercuès.** 46090 **Cahors.** Tel: 65-20-00-01; Telex: 521307; Fax: 65-20-05-72; in U.S., (713) 783-8033; in Australia, (02) 957-4511.

▶ **Château de Roumégouse.** 46500 **Gramat.** Tel: 65-33-63-81; Telex: 532592; Fax: 65-33-71-18; in U.S., (212) 696-1323 (reservations), (800) 372-1323, or (713) 783-8033; in Australia, (02) 957-4511.

▶ **La Citadelle.** Place d'Armes, 33390 **Blaye.** Tel: 57-42-17-10.

▶ **La Couleuvrine.** 1, place Bouquerie, 24200 **Sarlat-la-Canéda.** Tel: 53-59-27-80.

▶ **Cro-Magnon.** 24620 **Les Eyzies-de-Tayac.** Tel: 53-06-97-06; Telex: 570637.

▶ **Esplanade.** 24250 **Domme.** Tel: 53-28-31-41.

▶ **Family Golf Hôtel.** 28, boulevard F. Garnier, 17200 **Royan.** Tel: 46-05-14-66.

▶ **Hostellerie Meysset.** 24200 **Sarlat-la-Canéda** (3 km/2 miles northeast, toward les Eyzies). Tel: 53-59-08-29.

▶ **Hostellerie de Plaisance.** Place du Clocher, 33330 **St-Emilion.** Tel: 57-24-72-32.

▶ **Hôtel Burdigala.** 115, rue Georges Bonnac, 33000 **Bordeaux.** Tel: 56-90-16-16; Fax: 56-93-15-06.

▶ **Moulin de Cierzac.** 17520 **Cierzac.** Tel: 45-83-01-32.

▶ **La Pescalerie.** 46330 **Cabrerets.** Tel: 65-31-22-55; Fax: 65-31-23-11; in U.S., (212) 696-1323 (reservations), (800) 372-1323, or (713) 783-8033; in Australia, (02) 957-4511.

▶ **Pullman-Mériadeck.** 5, rue Robert-Lateulade, 33000 **Bordeaux.** Tel: 56-56-43-43; Telex: 540565; Fax: 56-96-50-59; in U.S., (212) 757-6500 or (800) 223-9862; in Canada, (800) 638-9699.

▶ **Relais du Bois St-Georges.** Rue Royan, 17100 **Saintes.** Tel: 46-93-50-99; Telex: 790488; Fax: 46-93-50-99.

▶ **Relais de Margaux.** 33460 **Margaux.** Tel: 56-88-38-30; Fax: 56-88-31-73; in U.S., (212) 696-1323 or (800) 372-1323.

▶ **La Réserve.** Avenue Bourgailh, 33600 **Pessac.** Tel: 56-07-13-28; Telex: 560585; Fax: 56-07-13-28; in U.S., (212) 696-1323 or (800) 372-1323.

▶ **Résidence de Rohan.** 17640 **Vaux-sur-Mer** (3.5 km/

1.5 miles northwest of Royan). Tel: 46-39-00-75; Fax: 46-38-29-99.

▶ **Sofitel Aquitania**. Bordeaux le Lac 33300. **Bordeaux**. Tel: 56-50-83-80; Telex: 570557; Fax: 56-39-73-75; in U.S. and Canada, (800) 221-4542; in U.K., (071) 724-1000; in Australia, (02) 264-5955.

▶ **Le Vieux Logis**. 24510 **Trémolat**. Tel: 53-22-80-06; Telex: 541025; Fax: 53-22-84-89; in U.S., (212) 696-1323 or (800) 372-1323.

BIARRITZ AND THE PYRENEES

By Fred Halliday

Biarritz, that old Hemingway haven of *The Sun Also Rises,* sits pleased as punch on the Gascony sea—pleased with her wide sandy beaches and green rolling breakers, her promenades and wedding-cake hotels, her ballrooms, swimming pools, casinos, crowds of high rollers in Rolls-Royces, and her matchless Café de Paris, *the* Café de Paris, apart from which there is no other.

Biarritz is all the more impressive considering that not too long ago—up to the mid-19th century—it was only a sleepy fishing village where there was nothing more exciting to do than watch the Basques mending their nets or going down to the sea in their eel boats.

Then Biarritz was discovered by nobility on the lam. A Spanish countess who was on the outs with the Spanish royalty and who couldn't be seen in San Sebastián in Spain—then the "in" resort—wanted to be as close to the action as possible. *Voilà,* she, with her daughter, settled on Biarritz, a mere 30 miles up the coast. Napoléon III later married the daughter, who became the Empress Eugénie. Napoléon built a palace for his bride so she wouldn't be lonely, and her royal friends came running. Could the bourgeoisie of Europe do any less? The stampede was on. Biarritz was on its way to becoming a major international resort. The Basques were beaten back a little bit, the eel boats moved farther south. But Biarritz is still Basque France and her original heritage is still a presence.

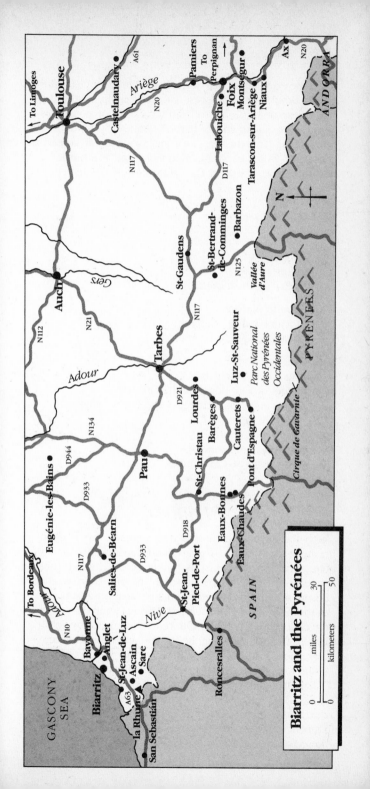

Biarritz and the Pyrénées

At the doorstep of Biarritz to the east is Bayonne (of the ham). South along the coast is the appealing little resort of St-Jean-de-Luz, and still farther along, of course, is pretty San Sebastián, its harbor defined by mountains sticking up from the sea, like a small-scale Rio de Janeiro. Eastward from the coast, mountains and the music of Bizet beckon: Biarritz is the gateway to the Golden Hills, the Pyrénées.

MAJOR INTEREST

Biarritz
Café de Paris
Victorian casino
Chez Pantchoa: outstanding foie gras

Around Biarritz
St-Jean-Baptiste church in St-Jean-de-Luz
Musée Basque in Bayonne

The Pyrénées
The Basque highlands
Waters of Pau, Béarn, and Lourdes
Skiing and spas in Barèges and Luz-St-Sauveur
Pont d'Espagne
Cirque de Gavarnie
Aspé and Aure valleys
St-Bertrand-de-Comminges

BIARRITZ

With the advent of the twentieth century—not a good century for nobility—royalty disappeared from Biarritz, but its residue remains, its buildings, beach, and cafés cheerfully taken up by upwardly mobile tourists and Basques returning to reclaim their place in the sun. Because there is only one heir per Basque family, the rest of the children leave. In the 19th century, crowded by nobility, 90,000 Basques emigrated to the Americas. This century, their fortunes made abroad, many have returned home to open restaurants and buy fishing boats.

It is frequently in Biarritz that the traveller first confronts Basque culture and learns that Basque is both a race and a language, neither having anything to do with French. The question then reasonably follows: Who are these Basques, and how did they get here?

Nobody really knows. The theories that have been advanced so far come from sentimental antiquarians or are the imprecise guesswork of stipend-seeking scholars. Still, the light of history has penetrated somewhat the mystery of the Basques.

Dawn picks them up 1,600 years ago in the eastern Pyrénées, the peace there having been shattered by the fall of Rome. The neighborhood filled up with Visigoths and the Basques pulled out. They moved westward and formed a new kingdom called Vasconie. Vasconie was divided into two parts, the (western) Pyrénées and the plains. The plains Vascons assimilated with the indigenous Aquitanians and became Gascons. The rest of their history gallops away toward d'Artagnan.

The Pyrénées "kingdom" still exists, however, in its mountain passes plunging down to the sea. The region overlaps both France and Spain, and, while it is not politically autonomous, it is neither French nor Spanish, but Basque. The Basques cling to their orphan language, "the mainstay of our race," and play *their* music, sing *their* chants, dance *their* fandangos, play jai alai, *their* game, in their frontons, and exercise *their* traditions—all of which keeps Biarritz from becoming just another haunted sand castle down by the sea.

But the royal Biarritz still simmers in its architecture. The **Hôtel Palais**, the villa Napoléon III lavished on his Eugénie, is a lush and lovely wedding cake—white, of course—as unblemished now as when the Spanish temptress had its windows afire with candles at night and its ballroom aswirl with guests. It is a pleasure and a dream to see it reborn today, ablaze in the night at the end of its Atlantic promenade, the sea crashing behind it, alive with music—even if its "guests" pay for the privilege of staying in the gilded rooms.

From the hotel the promenade leads to a 15- to 20-minute stroll along the Atlantic past some of the most interesting spots in Biarritz, with glimpses of the ocean in between, all the way to the beach on the Basque side, the **Plage de la Côte des Basques**.

Midway down the promenade a statue of the Virgin sits on a rock, the **Rocher de la Vierge**, the sea crashing all around her. The wind here seems always to be freshening. A short walk farther on is the Victorian **Casino Bellevue**, a Rococo extravaganza that at night attracts what looks to be the cast of a Fellini film, drawn here by the click of the ball and the shuffle of cards.

On the place Bellevue, down a flight of stairs, is one of the main reasons for coming to Biarritz: the **Café de Paris** (Tel: 59-24-19-53). Unpack something smashing and go at night. This gorgeous room is done in high-fashion blacks and greens. The menu is *nouvelle,* so the dishes vary. Try the tasting menu—*menu de dégustation*—and bow to owner Pierre Laporte's whim. Bearing in mind that the sense of well-being and invincibility that comes with splendid eating is sometimes false, afterward make your way to the casino and try a turn at fortune's wheel or baccarat, and then promenade back to the hotel.

For another serious eating experience, this time regional (Basque), try **Chez Pantchoa** (Chez François in French). Down by the railroad station at 10, boulevard de Marcel-Dassault (Tel: 59-23-15-83), it's a *charcuterie* as well as a restaurant, and very Basque in flavor. A waiter wanders around with three pounds of flesh on a plank: It's foie gras. And none of those dopey little tins for Chez François. It's foie gras as you've never seen it before (if you haven't been here before, that is). It's the whole foie, in the shape of a very large fish, not cooked at all, only marinated. Here in Basque country, on the fringe of les Landes, the geese and poultry play in the woods for use in foie gras *cru* (*cru* meaning raw), the king of all Basque delicacies.

The waiter points with the knife, or you push the tip for him, and he slices off a piece and slides it onto your plate. You yourself don't need a knife; the liver cuts with a fork. To compare it to ambrosia is to do the gods a favor. The deed done, from this moment on you will do anything to get fresh foie gras for the rest of your life.

Another menu delight from the region is fish cheeks. For many they are the sweetest part of the fish, the oyster of meat just under the eye. The Basques catch sea bass just for these morsels; they use the rest of the fish for soup. Containing a hundred jowls or so, a bowl of cheeks with sauce is served up like shimmering pasta—and it looks delicious. (Don't worry, they throw away the eyes.) This is a very popular dish in the fishermen's cafés to the south and across the Spanish border in San Sebastián. For a complete range of Basque tastes, try **Bakéa** (Basque for peace and quiet) in Biriatou, 32 km (20 miles) south of Biarritz on the Spanish frontier (Tel: 59-20-76-36).

Around Biarritz

Like Biarritz, **St-Jean-de-Luz** to the south is a Basque fishing village with a royal past and a Spanish association. No less a person than Louis XIV was married here, to the Infanta of Spain. The largest and best known of all Basque churches, **St-Jean-Baptiste** (13th- to 15th-century), is also here. The early role of the church in Basque life indicates that they were converted long before the arrival of the Visigoths. Basque church architecture is as singular as the language; especially noteworthy in St-Jean-Baptiste is the striking use of oak and wrought iron.

For a close-up view of a Basque town as it was 500 years ago, stroll the rue de la République, possibly the most authentic street of painted Basque wooden homes in France. For regional seafood specialties try the **Tavern Basque** at 5, rue de la République. If your taste runs to *royale,* however, there is the restaurant at the **Grand Hôtel** (43, boulevard Thiers; Tel: 59-26-35-36). (Somewhere around here you're bound to come across *piperade basquaise* on the menu—scrambled eggs blended with a variety of ingredients. Give it a try.)

For frontons, fandango, and other pieces in the Basque puzzle, it's on to **Bayonne**, just east of Biarritz. In fact Bayonne is close enough to Biarritz to be considered a suburb. Buses leave from Biarritz's railroad station, and most taxis will make the trip from your hotel. For a good walk, get out in front of Bayonne's Hôtel de Ville and explore the side streets around the square; here and there are little places for *tapas.*

If you are curious about the origins of the Basques and their culture you'll want to visit the **Musée Basque**, one of the best museums on local ethnicity in France, located in a typical Basque house on rue Marengo. Aside from being the official capital of the Basque country (on the French side of the border, anyway), Bayonne also has the afore-mentioned ham, famous throughout the world, and is the unofficial capital of espadrilles—the canvas shoes that have made their rope-soled mark on half the beaches of the world. If you want to see jai alai, this is the French fronton capital, too.

Then turn from the sea and set your sights on the most underrated mountains in Europe.

THE PYRENEES
The Peaks of the Basques

Here are the twists in the road, the long descents from breathtaking mountaintops, and the green pastures made famous in the opera *Carmen*. It is impossible to take in all the Basque highland; instead we will try to do justice to some of its more remarkable landscapes.

Going southward from Bayonne by the autoroute (A 63) for about 16 km (10 miles), exit for Ascain onto route D 4. **Ascain** is the perfect vacation village in the Basque Pyrénées, excellent for a stay of a few days—many an hour can be spent ambling its streets or exploring the environs—or just to pass through. It has a village square fronted by wooden homes painted in their traditional russet brown, round green hills surrounding it, and a marvelous Basque church with three tiers of wooden galleries embracing the bell tower. Ascain also has a couple of nice hotels: **La Rhûne**, with a park and swimming pool, and the **Basque**, with patio dining.

Follow D 4 out of Ascain through its gentle valley to the **St-Ignace pass** (about 5 km/3 miles), then drive onward and upward to the mountain of **la Rhune** (rhune in Basque means good pasture). La Rhune is on the Spanish border and affords a sweeping panorama over the Atlantic ocean to the west, the Landes forest and the Basque Pyrénées to the north and east, and Spain. The word "Spain" in southern French patois means pine tree; a look to the south will tell you why.

Nearly 7 km (4 miles) farther on D 4 is **Sare**. The people here still wear folkloric Basque costumes—flaring white pants and blouses with a broad sash around the middle. The surrounding countryside abounds in meadows, green pastures blanketed with white sheep, and prehistoric caves to explore.

As you follow the Nive river downstream along D 918, the Basque country starts to recede at St-Jean-Pied-de-Port, from which a road goes over the mountains through a pass to the Spanish town of Roncesvalles (Roncevaux in French). It was here that Roland blew his horn to summon Charlemagne—and, as the 12th-century *Chanson de Roland* has it, to save France.

The northerly route from Bayonne along N 117 leaves Basque country and leads to Pau and spa country.

Spa Country

The road to **Pau** (118 km/73 miles southeast of Biarritz) is travelled by the well-heeled. Driving its white line is like crashing a parade of the chariots of affluence. In Rollses and Mercedes they ride, most bearing the *plaque* 75 (Paris). They come with enlarged livers and prostates, aching kidneys, balloon bottoms, and cellulite, seeking a cure.

And if we are to believe what we read in the slick spa brochures—all claims unendorsed by any medical association, by the way—the miracle cure has been found. It's water. You have only to sit in spa waters or drink them. It's all quite specific: There's a water for cirrhosis, another for obesity (there are many for obesity), and others for respiratory problems.

People have been coming to take the waters around Pau (the spas are principally in the surrounding hill communities) from the time when water was not just the only medicine—it was the only hope. The Romans came; the plague-ridden of the Middle Ages came; the Empress Eugénie came.

Considering these last hopes it is only fitting that the restaurant **Les Prés d'Eugénie**, the home of *cuisine minceur* (haute diet cuisine), is found at **Eugénie-lès-Bains** 53 km (32 miles) north of Pau. Basically you pay a few hundred francs a plate and walk away starving because who can afford to eat at these prices? Fans claim it's elegant, but it doesn't seem as if they're losing except around the wallet. (Tel: 58-51-19-01.)

The spas of the **Béarn** are the most luxurious thermal stations, found in some of the most remarkable spa real estate, hugged by mountains and splendidly isolated. **Les Eaux-Bonnes**, **Les Eaux-Chaudes**, and **St-Christau** are south of Pau, while lovely **Salies-de-Béarn** is to the northwest. Take their waters for menopause (they help you get over it) and for sterility (they're against it). These places are so beautiful, however, and their calm so tranquilizing, the only wonder would be if they did no good at all. Write or call for the suitable brochure: Salies-de-Béarn: Office de Tourisme, 1, boulevard Saint-Guily, 64270 Salies-de-Béarn, Tel: 59-38-00-33; Les Eaux-Bonnes: Office de Tourisme, 64440 Les Eaux-Bonnes Laruns, Tel: 59-05-33-08; Les Eaux-Chaudes: Les Eaux-Chaudes, 64440 Laruns, Tel: 59-

05-31-55; St-Christau: Etablissement Thermal, 64660 St-Christau, Tel: 59-34-40-04.

On the other end of the spa spectrum, **Lourdes** (only 40 km/25 miles southeast of Pau) is a town for the poor, who come by tour bus from Spain and Italy as well as France. They also have their *maladies:* a club foot, blindness, a tumor. That the rich and the poor should each enjoy their own kind of waters is of no consequence. Pilgrims to Lourdes mount imposing steps to a tabernacle and come away with a prayer for a cure. The miraculous power of Lourdes—officially recognized by the Catholic Church—began with the appearance of the Blessed Virgin at a local grotto. Now the city of Lourdes has more hotel rooms than any other city in France except Paris.

The High Pyrénées

At 7,700 feet in the High Pyrénées, south of Lourdes via D 921 and D 918, **Barèges** offers a station for skiing and glassed-in thermal baths (in all seasons) all in one. The winter view from nearby **Pic du Midi de Bigorre** is spectacular. The largest ski area in the Pyrénées, Barèges has 69 ski trails and 52 lifts and tows. The town itself offers charming shuttered homes, ten hotels, steep side streets deep in snow, cafés, restaurants, and an après-ski unlike the ski factories of the Alps. Barèges also offers a package: ski and spa for one week for one low price, 400 francs, and in high season. There is also a restaurant-hotel of high reputation, **Le Richelieu**. It has 34 rooms at up to 230 francs and meals between 70 and 130 francs. (Tel: 62-92-68-11.) Meanwhile, l'Hôtel Central is across from the railroad station and offers rooms at reasonable rates. For information on hotels, ski runs, spa, and saunas, contact the tourist office at 65120 Barèges; Tel: 62-92-68-19.

Nearby **Luz-St-Sauveur** offers spas and skiing of comparable quality at comparable rates. Their tourist office is at place du 8 Mai, 65120 Luz-St-Sauveur; Tel: 62-92-81-60.

If you follow D 920 where it breaks from D 921 to its end you will come to the town of **Pont d'Espagne** in the heart of the **Parc National des Pyrénées**. At Pont d'Espagne and its glacier lake you'll find wide snowcapped vistas and waterfalls that tumble into verdant glades. Then go on to the **Cirque de Gavarnie**—a natural amphitheater set in a circle (*cirque*) of mountains with seven waterfalls plunging into a catch-basin plateau. There are hiking trails throughout the area, a rock-climbing school, teams of guides, expeditions on horseback or on foot, fishing in rapids or lakes, and abundant flora and fauna to spy on. To unlock this natural treasure trove in the south of France, contact the Maison du Parc National, Gedre Gavarne, Office de Tourisme, place du 8 Mai, 65120 Luz-St-Sauveur; Tel: 62-92-81-60. Sixty more miles of national park stretch along the **Aspé** and **Aure valleys** and offer a good chance to see wildlife such as bears, badgers, foxes, and eagles.

All the green glades might instill in the traveller a yearning for a village retreat, maybe one with a monastery and, even better, a good restaurant. There is just such a place nearby, to the east via N 117, with lodgings: St-Bertrand.

St-Bertrand-de-Comminges

St-Bertrand-de-Comminges is the perfect little town away from it all. Off the beaten track but comfortable, it is also adorable—and inexpensive, too. In fact, it has everything to recommend it for a mid-Pyrénées stay. It's on a hill. It has a 12th-century church with attached cloister whose carvings are in surprisingly good condition. The church's carved wooden choir is intact, superbly crafted and meticulously maintained. Down the hill on the plain is another charming church, as well as Roman ruins, antique grottoes with prehistoric cave paintings (rudimentary animals), and even prehistoric handprints (blown-ash technique). Whenever a group large enough gathers, a university student will lead a tour of the caves. Should you miss this, however, a youngster from the concession—which seems to be family-run—will be perfectly willing to take you on a more leisurely tour.

As for hotels in St-Bertrand, you will like the **Comminges**, not fancy, but cute. The little family restaurant just off the main square, **Chez Simone**, is open daily for lunch. It welcomes customers on a drop-in basis (Tel: 61-88-30-70), and there's a hotel next door. Meanwhile, nearby Barbazan has the **Hostellerie de l'Aristou**, a very nice old house with a good dining room. Should you wish to get away from it all, yet remain *en chic,* reserve at the 17-room, two-apartment **Hostellerie des 7 Molles**. It's just a skip southeast of Barbazan on D 9, and offers swimming, tennis, and golf privileges.

From St-Bertrand-de-Comminges, the route east to Foix on N 117 (see the Toulouse and the South chapter) runs through **St-Gaudens**. The impulsive bather should know that throughout this entire spa region there are special rates available for a single day or even an afternoon. Taking advantage of such rates, you could bathe your way across France.

GETTING AROUND

The Pyrénées are well serviced by flights from Paris to airports in Biarritz, Lourdes, Pau, Perpignan, and Toulouse (see the chapter on Toulouse and the South). Rail and bus service to almost all towns is excellent. However, the best way to explore the region is by car (you will find outlets of major rental agencies in Toulouse). Route N 117 cuts across the region from Bayonne to Toulouse, providing access to the roads that crisscross the Pyrénées. Hiking trails in the region are superb; for information, contact the Fédération Française de la Randonnée Pédestre, 9, avenue Georges V, 75008 Paris.

ACCOMMODATIONS REFERENCE

▶ **Basque.** 64310 **Ascain.** Tel: 59-54-00-12; Fax: 59-51-05-61 (specify Hotel Basque).

▶ **Comminges.** Barbazan 31510 **St-Bertrand-de-Comminges.** Tel: 61-88-31-43.

▶ **Hostellerie de l'Aristou.** Route Sauveterre, 31510 **Barbazan.** Tel: 61-88-30-67.

▶ **Hostellerie des 7 Molles.** 31510 **Sauveterre-de-Comminges.** Tel: 61-88-30-87; Fax: 61-88-36-42; in U.S., (713) 783-8033, (212) 696-1323, or (800) 372-1323.

▶ **L'Hôtel Central.** 65120 **Barèges.** Tel: 62-92-68-05.

▶ **Hôtel Palais.** 1, avenue Impératrice, 64200 **Biarritz.** Tel: 59-24-09-40; Telex: 570000; Fax: 59-24-36-84.

▶ **La Rhûne.** 64310 **Ascain.** Tel: 59-54-00-04; Telex: 570792.

▶ **Le Richelieu.** 65120 **Barèges.** Tel: 62-92-68-11.

CHRONOLOGY OF THE HISTORY OF FRANCE

Prehistory

France is one of the most rewarding countries in Europe for travellers in search of prehistoric art and architecture *in situ*. Naturally, delicate and portable pieces such as the plump, lumpy Venus figures repose comfortably in museums. Still, astonishing wall paintings and engravings remain in caves once occupied by Paleolithic hunters, chiefly in the Dordogne Valley and the central Pyrénées. The Carnac and Locmariaquer districts of Brittany also boast dozens of archaeological sites: standing stone alignments, megalithic tombs, passage graves, tumuli.

Prehistoric cultures in France are impressively old by any standards. English archaeologist Jacquetta Hawkes reports (in the *Atlas of Ancient Archeology*): "Le Vallonet cave, near Menton, is the oldest inhabited site in Europe, perhaps a million years old, and the other sea caves on this coast (the Côte d'Azur), the Grimaldi caves and the Observatory, near Monaco, and Lazaret, in the suburbs of Nice, contain early occupations representative of Neanderthal man and his predecessors."

Following these ancient, Acheulean, cultures, the main ones evidenced in France are the Mousterian (60,000–39,000 B.C.), Châtelperron (33,000 B.C.), Aurignacian (30,000 B.C.), Gravettian (24,000 B.C.), Solutréan (17,000 B.C.), and Magdalenian (15,000 B.C.).

- **15,000–10,000 B.C.:** Cave art in sites around Les Eyzies in the Dordogne: Lascaux, Font-de-Gaume, Cap Blanc, La Mouthe, Les Combarelles, and many cave shelters (*abri*).
- **3,800–2,000 B.C.:** Tombs and stone alignments (avenues of upright stones, *menhirs*, some 14 to 20 feet high), tumuli (earth-covered mound tombs), megaliths. The Menac alignment, near to and northeast of Brittany's Carnac on D 196, boasts more than a thousand standing stones.

- **3,500 B.C.:** Megalithic tombs in southern France, particularly the Grotte des Fées near Arles.
- **600–50 B.C.:** The *oppidum* (hilltop fort) of Vix, in Burgundy near Châtillon-sur-Seine.

Other prehistoric cultures are represented by pottery (Impressed Ware, about 5,000 B.C.), Chassey pottery (3,500 B.C., southern France), and open-air huts and farming settlements in the north of France.

The Celtic Period

Beginning about 1,000 B.C., the Celts, an Indo-European race, arrive in waves from the east, bringing decorative La Tène art (the Basse-Yutz flagon, the Janus head from Roquepertuse); hilltop strongholds (*oppida*); a warrior aristocracy; and many divinities as well as the Druids. Eventually they are driven out by the Romans, though they keep a toehold in Brittany.

The Coming of the Greeks

- **About 600 B.C.:** Founding of the trading colony of Marseille (Massilia) by the Phoceans of Ionia on the coast of Asia Minor.

The Romans and Gallo-Romans

- **121 B.C.:** Romans establish Gallia Narbonensis (present-day Narbonne in Provence).
- **58–51 B.C.:** Caesar conquers Gaul.
- **52 B.C.:** Vercingétorix battles Caesar, loses.
- **A.D.162:** Arrival of the first Alemannic hordes.
- **c. 250:** Christianity comes to the Gallo-Romans.
- **c. 355:** Invasions of Gaul by Franks, Alemanni, Saxons.
- **373–397:** Saint Martin is bishop of Tours.
- **418–507:** The Visigoths rule the south, out of Toulouse.
- **443:** The Burgundians establish themselves in the Rhône Valley.
- **451:** Attila and his Huns are defeated by the Romans and their allies in the battle of the Catalaunian Fields near Troyes.
- **481:** Merovingian Clovis I crowned king of the Franks.
- **c. 496:** Clovis is crowned at Reims and the Franks become Christian.
- **c. 511:** Gaul is divided into three parts: Austrasia, Neustria, Burgundy.

- **c. 630**: The first Benedictine monasteries are built.
- **732**: Charles Martel (the Hammer), son of Pépin of Herstal, defeats the Moors at the battle of Poitiers.
- **751**: Pépin the Short (le Bref), father of Charlemagne, is proclaimed king.
- **788**: Death of Roland, in the Pyrénées, when Charlemagne's army, returning from Spain, is ambushed. He is immortalized in the Medieval epic the *Chanson de Roland*.
- **800**: Charlemagne is crowned emperor in Rome.
- **843**: The Frankish empire is partitioned by the Treaty of Verdun.

The Romanesque Era

- **910**: Foundation of the abbey of Cluny in Burgundy.
- **From c. 950**: Expansion is the theme, with clearing of lands, growth of population, broadening of trade with fairs, movement of peoples on pilgrimages, building of new towns. Romanesque art is exemplified in Vézelay, Autun, Conques, and Sénanque, among other towns. Old French moves away from Latin in this time; monks at Jumièges add vocalizations to traditional Gregorian chants.
- **987**: Hugues Capet ("Little Cloak") is crowned king of the Franks, creating the Capétian dynasty (direct line to 1328, collateral until 1848).
- **1066**: William the Conqueror (Guillaume le Conquérant), duke of Normandy, conquers England.
- **1095–1099**: First Crusade, led by Raymond IV, count of Toulouse, and Godfrey of Bouillon (now Belgium). The Crusades continue periodically until 1250.
- **1115**: Saint Bernard founds Cistercian abbey of Clairvaux.
- **1122**: Birth of Eleanor of Aquitaine, queen consort of Louis VII of France, then of Henry II of England, mother of many children, including English kings Richard the Lion-Hearted and (Bad King) John. She dies in 1204.
- **c. 1132**: Cathedrals begun at Vézelay and Autun.
- **1137**: Start of construction of cathedral of St-Denis, first monumental Gothic structure.
- **1137–1180**: Major conflicts between Louis VII and English king Henry II.
- **c. 1140**: Development of Catharism, one of the Albigensian heresies.

- **1147–1149**: Disastrous Second Crusade, preached by Saint Bernard at Vézelay.
- **1150–1167**: Universities founded at Paris and Oxford.
- **1163**: Cornerstone of Notre-Dame de Paris laid.
- **1189–1192**: Third Crusade, led by France's Philippe Auguste, England's Richard the Lion-Hearted, and Holy Roman Emperor Frederick I.

In Gothic Times

- **c. 1200–1300**: Medieval France in full flower; trade and population expansion continue. Gothic art gives birth to cathedrals at Amiens, Beauvais, Chartres, Reims; stained glass brings light to those at Bourges, Laon, Notre-Dame, etc. Polyphonic music is heard at Notre-Dame.
- **1202–1204**: Fourth Crusade; Constantinople seized.
- **1208**: Beginning of the Albigensian Crusade.
- **1210–1294**: Construction of Reims's cathedral of Notre-Dame.
- **1226**: Accession of Louis IX, king and crusader; reigns 44 years; canonized as Saint Louis, 1297.
- **1233**: Start of the Papal Inquisition.
- **1246–1248**: Construction of Sainte Chapelle, one of the finest examples of Gothic architecture, on Ile de la Cité, Paris.
- **1253**: Foundation of the Sorbonne, which will become the nucleus of the University of Paris, by Robert de Sorbon.
- **1270**: Gothic cathedrals begun in Toulouse, Narbonne.

Late Gothic

- **1300–1400+**: Decoration and ornamentation come to architecture in Radiant Gothic (cathedrals of Strasbourg, Metz) and Flamboyant Gothic (flowing, flame-like forms), mostly in Normandy and Picardie.
- **1309–1378**: The "Babylonian captivity" of the popes in Avignon.
- **1328**: Accession of Philippe VI, first of the House of Valois.
- **1333**: Edward III of England claims the French crown.
- **1337–1453**: The Hundred Years War; it begins with dynastic squabbles between France and England.

- **1348–1351:** The Black Death kills as many as half the inhabitants of Europe.
- **1349:** The heir to the throne inherits the Dauphiné region; each kingly heir is afterward known as the Dauphin.
- **1356:** Edward, the Black Prince, son of England's Edward III, captures King John II (the Good) in the battle of Poitiers.
- **c. 1360:** The portrait of Burgundian Duke Jean le Bon (now in the Louvre) marks the debut of French portraiture.
- **1378–1417:** The Great Schism; rival popes in Rome and Avignon.
- **1407:** War breaks out between the Burgundians and the Armagnacs.
- **1415:** The battle of Azincourt (Agincourt in English) in northern France, won by Henry V of England.
- **1429:** Joan of Arc raises the English siege of Orléans and accompanies Charles VII to Reims and his coronation.
- **1431:** Joan of Arc is burned at the stake in Rouen on May 30; she is canonized in 1920.

The Renaissance

- **c. 1450:** Somewhere about here the Renaissance begins, moving out of the so-called Dark Ages with burgeoning trade, improving economy, renewed interest in building and the arts. The influence of Italy is a dramatic force in architecture (François I imports Italian artisans of every stripe), and Italian Mannerism influences painting and music, while the 16th century is a triumph for French sculpture.
- **1451:** Financier and minister Jacques Coeur is arrested and accused of having poisoned Agnès Sorel, Charles VII's mistress; he will die fighting the Turks in 1456.
- **1453:** The Hundred Years War comes to a shaky end as England loses all its possessions in France except Calais.
- **1455–1485:** War of the Roses in England between Houses of Lancaster and York, involving Henry IV's queen, Margaret of Anjou, daughter of René-le-Bon.
- **1469–1470:** Foundation of France's first printing house.
- **1477:** Charles le Téméraire, duke of Burgundy, dies; Burgundy and Picardie pass to the crown,

other lands go to Emperor Maximilian I, and the France–Hapsburg quarrels begin.

- **1484**: Meeting of the Estates-General in Tours; town representatives join clergy and nobility as the Third Estate.
- **1515**: Accession of François I of Angoulême, who reigns for 32 years, fights four major wars, and becomes the greatest master builder and art patron in French history with the help of Cellini, Leonardo, et al.
- **1517**: Martin Luther posts his 95 theses on the door of the castle church in Wittenberg.
- **1524**: Italian Giovanni da Verrazano, sailing under the French flag, explores the New England coast and becomes the first European to enter New York Harbor.
- **1534–1542**: Jacques Cartier departs St-Malo and ventures up the St. Lawrence in what is now Canada, giving France claims to the region.
- **1547**: Henri II, husband of Catherine de Médicis, lover of Diane de Poitiers, ascends to the throne.
- **1547–1559**: Henri II persecutes the Huguenots.
- **1561**: Persecution of Huguenots stopped, briefly, by Edict of Orléans.
- **1562–1598**: Wars of Religion—Catholics led by the Guise family, Protestants by the Bourbons.
- **1572**: Saint Bartholomew's Day Massacre (of Protestants), August 24, on orders of Catherine de Médicis.
- **1589**: Henri of Navarre becomes Henri IV, first of the House of Bourbon; becomes a Catholic in 1593 and claims "Paris is worth a Mass."
- **1598**: The Edict of Nantes grants freedom (conditional) to the Huguenots.
- **1609**: Samuel de Champlain establishes a French colony in Quebec.

Louis XIII

- **1610**: Henri IV is assassinated, succeeded by Louis XIII with his great ministers, Cardinals Richelieu and Mazarin.
- **c. 1630–1700**: Art styles in France reflect serenity, i.e., Poussin; classical values in literature are expressed by Racine's tragedies; Montaigne creates the essay (from 1571).
- **1635**: The Académie Française is founded to promote education and the arts. France involves itself

in the Thirty Years War on the side of Denmark and Sweden against Germany.

Louis XIV and the Classic Century

- **1643**: Louis XIV becomes king, and will reign for 72 years.
- **1648–1653**: *La Fronde* is a series of outbreaks caused by the efforts of Parlement to limit royal authority; eventually, Parlement will be joined by the nobility and the people of Paris.
- **1661–1715**: Louis XIV's Sun King period sees a flowering of Baroque art and architecture (Versailles, with Le Vau, Le Nôtre, Le Brun, others); painting (Georges de la Tour, Claude Le Lorrain, others); literature (Corneille, Racine, La Fontaine, Molière, La Rochefoucauld, others); music (Lully, Couperin); and philosophy, science, and mathematics (Pascal and many others).
- **1685**: Revocation of the Edict of Nantes; half a million Huguenots leave France.
- **1700–1800**: The French Enlightenment is born in the works of Montesquieu, Voltaire, Rousseau, Diderot. In art, Rococo emerges with Watteau, Neoclassicism with David.
- **1701–1714**: War of the Spanish Succession; the duke of Anjou and grandson of Louis XIV becomes Spanish King Felipe V over other claimants from around Europe.

Louis XV and the Enlightenment

- **c. 1715**: The economy booms, inspiring increasingly sophisticated salons and receptions, the construction of more châteaux, and a passion for knowledge.
- **1715**: Death of Louis XIV, succeeded by Louis XV, who loses Canada to the English and enjoys such favorites as Madame de Pompadour and Madame du Barry.
- **1751**: First volume of Denis Diderot's *Encyclopédie* is published.
- **1768**: France buys Corsica from Genoa.
- **1769**: Napoléon Bonaparte (Buonaparte) is born in Ajaccio, Corsica.
- **1774**: Louis XVI ascends to the throne.
- **1777**: Marie-Joseph-Paul-Yves-Roch-Gilbert du Motier, marquis de Lafayette, arrives in America, is made a major-general by the Continental Congress,

and serves in many battles. (In 1789, Lafayette will create the modern French flag.)

- **1783**: First manned free-balloon flight by brothers Joseph-Michel and Jacques-Etienne Montgolfier, over Paris.

The Revolution

- **1789**: Outbreak of the French Revolution; Louis XVI and Marie-Antoinette beheaded in 1793. This is followed by the Continent-wide French Revolutionary Wars until 1802.
- **1792**: France is declared a republic, but the wars, uprisings, and massacres go on.
- **1794**: Maximilien Marie Isidore Robespierre, chief architect of the Terror, dies on the guillotine.
- **1796–1804**: Napoléon's successes against the Austrians, Milan, Genoa, Mamelukes of Egypt, etc.

The 19th Century

- **1800–40**: Romanticism replaces Neoclassicism and Rococo; Théodore Rousseau leads the Barbizon school of painting; Victor Hugo expresses in his novels the new desire for freedom; Eugène Delacroix in paint the appeal of exotic locales.
- **1803–1815**: Napoleonic Wars against European powers.
- **1804**: Napoléon is crowned Emperor of the French, and civil law is codified in the *Code Napoléon*.
- **1805**: Napoléon crowns himself King of Italy; Viscount Horatio Nelson defeats combined French and Spanish forces at Battle of Trafalgar; Napoléon triumphs over Russians and Austrians at Austerlitz.
- **1812**: Napoléon's disastrous Russian campaign.
- **1814**: Continent-wide Wars of Liberation against Napoléon.
- **1814**: Napoléon abdicates, receives the island of Elba as a principality; the Bourbon dynasty is restored with Louis XVIII as king.
- **1815**: The 100 Days: During the Congress of Vienna, Napoléon lands at Cannes and marches to Paris. Louis XVIII flees and Napoléon rules until beaten by the British and Prussians in the battle of Waterloo; exiled to the British island of St. Helena, where he dies in 1821.
- **1815–1816**: The White Terror—Royalist uprisings, persecutions of Jacobins and Bonapartists.

- **1824**: Charles X, brother of Louis XVIII, ascends to the throne.
- **1825**: Louis Braille invents script for the blind.
- **1830**: The July Revolution forces abdication of Charles X; he is succeeded by Louis-Philippe and the House of Orléans.
- **1840–1880**: The official Beaux-Arts school of Paris sets an international style for public buildings and sculpture with such examples as the Paris Opéra and Bartholdi's Statue of Liberty. Realist painting is influenced by Daguerre and photography. Balzac provides a realistic look at social classes.
- **1848**: The February Revolution brings about the abdication of Louis-Philippe and installation of Louis Napoléon Bonaparte (nephew of Napoléon I) as president of the Second Republic.
- **1852**: The president becomes Napoléon III, Emperor of the French, to begin the Second Empire.
- **1854–1870**: France takes part in the Crimean War, takes Nice and Savoy from Austria, extends her possessions in Southeast Asia, aids in the construction of the Suez Canal, and sees the collapse of the Mexican Empire established for Archduke Maximilian of Austria.
- **1870–1871**: Franco-Prussian War—Napoléon III is defeated at Sedan, taken prisoner; the Third Republic is proclaimed, with Louis-Adolphe Thiers as president.
- **1874**: First exhibition of the Impressionists opens April 15; canvases by Cézanne, Degas, Monet, Berthe Morisot, Pissarro, Renoir, Sisley, 21 others; the school is named for Monet's *Impression, Sunrise*.
- **1879–1896**: France expands into parts of Central Africa, Tunis, Indochina, and Madagascar.
- **1880–1900**: *Fin-de-Siècle* period in art and literature—Flaubert, Zola, Verlaine, Rimbaud; Cézanne, Gauguin.
- **1889**: Paris International Exhibition stars the Eiffel Tower.
- **1890**: Birth of Charles de Gaulle.
- **1895**: The brothers Louis-Jean and Auguste Lumière patent first device for making and projecting films.
- **1894–1906**: The Dreyfus Affair, a case revolving around supposed treason, brings the left wing to

power, raises issues of anti-Semitism, and helps split church and state (Alfred Dreyfus exonerated in 1906).

The 20th Century

- **1900–1909**: France is the center of experimentation in the arts; Fauvism (Matisse a leader, 1905), Cubism (Picasso et al.); Diaghilev in Paris alters classical ballet; new sounds of music (Debussy, Satie, Stravinsky).
- **1909**: Louis Blériot is the first man to fly an airplane across the Channel.
- **1913**: Igor Stravinsky's *Le Sacre du Printemps* (*The Rites of Spring*) debuts on May 29 and, some say, the modern age is born.
- **1914**: World War I is occasioned by the murder of Archduke Francis Ferdinand, heir to the Austro-Hungarian throne, at Sarajevo, Yugoslavia, June 28.
- **1916**: Beginning of Dada movement in arts (Arp, Tzara).
- **1918**: Allied counter-offensive begins; Franco-German armistice at Compiègne, November.
- **1919**: Treaty of Versailles returns Alsace and Lorraine to France, gives her mandate over other lands; France becomes a founding member of the League of Nations.
- **1925**: Exhibition of Surrealists, now in their heyday: Breton, De Chirico, Dalí, Tanguy, Ernst, Magritte; in literature, Eluard, Cocteau, heirs of Baudelaire, Rimbaud, and, eventually, Freud.
- **1929**: Beginning of worldwide Depression.
- **1936**: Germany occupies the demilitarized Rhineland; no action from France or England.
- **1939**: World War II; after a series of unanswered German takeovers, culminating in an attack on Poland, France declares war on Germany, September 3.
- **1940**: German army occupies Paris, June 14; Vichy government headed by Henri Philippe Pétain; Third Republic ends; Charles de Gaulle forms a government in exile in England; resistance is formed.
- **1942–1943**: Existentialism in literature and philosophy; publication of Albert Camus's *The Stranger* and Jean-Paul Sartre's *Being and Nothingness*.
- **1944**: Allies land in Normandy, June 6, and in the

south of France, August 15, to liberate France; Charles de Gaulle forms a provisional government.

- **1945:** Germany capitulates.
- **1946:** De Gaulle resigns, succeeded by Félix Gouin and Georges Bidault.
- **1948:** The United States's Marshall Plan for the recovery of Europe begins.
- **1954–1956:** France loses Equatorial Africa, Indochina, Morocco, Tunisia, and West Africa to independence movements and wars.
- **1957:** European Common Market comes into being with France as a founding member.
- **1959:** Having dealt with the Algerian question as prime minister under René Coty, De Gaulle becomes president of the Fifth Republic.
- **1962:** Algeria is granted independence.
- **1969:** De Gaulle retires from the presidency, succeeded by Georges Pompidou.
- **1970:** De Gaulle dies and is buried near his home at Colombey-les-Deux-Eglises.
- **1974:** Valéry Giscard d'Estaing is elected third president of the Fifth Republic.
- **1981:** François Mitterrand is elected president of France.
- **1986:** Jacques Chirac, mayor of Paris, is elected France's premier by a center-right coalition, instituting the continuing period of *cohabitation* with Socialist President Mitterrand.

  The Musée d'Orsay, the Museum of Art of the 19th century, opens in the renovated Orsay train station on the Left Bank.
- **1987:** Klaus Barbie tried in Lyon for war crimes and is sentenced to life imprisonment.
- **1988:** President François Mitterrand is elected president of France for a second seven-year term.
- **1989:** Year-long celebrations are staged around the country in celebration of the bicentenary of the French Revolution.

  The Grand Louvre reopens after completion of the controversial I. M. Pei glass pyramid in the central courtyard and the first phase of the excavations of the 12th-century castle in the Cour Carrée.

  The Grande Arche de la Défense is completed, both among the government's *Grands Projets* of the decade.
- **1990:** In April the Opéra de la Bastille opens with Hector Berlioz's *Les Troyens*.

—Georgia I. Hesse

INDEX

636